D1738233

# Fundamentals of Private Pensions

Pension Research Council

## Other publications of the
## PENSION RESEARCH COUNCIL

# Fundamentals of Private Pensions

**Dan M. McGill, Ph.D.**
Wharton School of the
University of Pennsylvania

**Donald S. Grubbs, Jr., J.D., F.S.A.**
Grubbs and Company, Inc.

*1989  Sixth Edition*
Published for the
Pension Research Council
Wharton School of the
University of Pennsylvania

by

Homewood, Illinois 60430

*To Elaine and Melanie*
DAN M. MCGILL

*To Daisy and our family*
DONALD S. GRUBBS, JR.

**Acquisitions editor:** Lawrence E. Alexander
**Project editor:** Paula M. Buschman
**Production manager:** Carma W. Fazio
**Compositor:** Carlisle Communications, Ltd.
**Typeface:** 11/13 Times Roman
**Printer:** Arcata Graphics/Halliday

Library of Congress Cataloging-in-Publication Data

McGill, Dan Mays.
    Fundamentals of private pensions / Dan M. McGill, Donald S. Grubbs, Jr.—6th ed.
    p. cm.
    Includes bibliographical references and index.
    ISBN 0-256-06041-X : $31.00
    1. Old age pensions—United States.  I. Grubbs, Donald S.
II. Wharton School. Pension Research Council.  III. Title.
HD7105.35.U6M34  1989
658.3'253'0973—dc19        88–10341

*Printed in the United States of America*

1 2 3 4 5 6 7 8 9 0 H 5 4 3 2 1 0 9 8

## PURPOSE OF THE COUNCIL

THE PENSION RESEARCH COUNCIL was formed in 1952 to undertake academic research into those institutional arrangements designed to provide financial resources for a secure and dignified old age. It seeks to broaden public understanding of these complex arrangements through basic research into their social, economic, legal, actuarial, and financial foundations. While generally geared to the long view of the pension institution, projects undertaken by the Council are always relevant to real life concerns and frequently focus on issues under current debate. The Council does not speak with one voice and espouses no particular point of view. The members do share a general desire to encourage and strengthen private-sector approaches to old-age economic security, while recognizing the essential role of Social Security and other income-maintenance programs in the public sector.

# PREFACE

THE FIRST EDITION of this book appeared 34 years ago, in 1955. It reflected the state of the pension art at that time—or, at least, the author's perception of the prevailing state. The book contained 209 pages of text compressed into five long chapters.

During the intervening years, the private pension institution has expanded enormously in scope, diversity, and complexity. The successive editions of this book have mirrored the changes in the field, especially the increasing diversity and complexity. The second edition, which appeared 10 years after the first, contained 325 pages of text organized into nine chapters. The third edition, published 10 years after the second and reflecting the statutory provisions of the then recently enacted Employee Retirement Income Security Act (ERISA), encompassed 467 pages of text spread over 20 chapters. The fourth edition, published only four years after the previous edition, took up 601 pages in 24 chapters. The fifth edition, five years later, required 705 pages.

This edition bears little resemblance to the original. At the time of its publication, the original edition was thought to be a comprehensive and authoritative exposition of existing theory and practice. It won the coveted Elizur Wright Award of the American Risk and Insurance Association as the outstanding original contribution to the literature in the year of its publication. Yet by today's standards, the book was embarrassingly elementary and naive, particularly the portions dealing with the actuarial and financial aspects of pensions.

Each revision was a major undertaking, reflecting interim developments and refinement of concepts and terminology. The preface to the second edition stated as an apologia for the revision that "Plan provisions have been refined, new types of funding instruments have been developed, investment policies have been expanded, new tax rulings have been issued, and more meaningful terminology has evolved." Among the new developments that found their way into the second edition were variable annuities, cost-of-living plans, the investment year method of allocating investment income, separate accounts funding, and split funding.

A third edition was necessitated by the enactment of ERISA, even though it would have been justified by other forces and events. The third edition was more than a revision; it represented a recasting and rewriting of most of the materials in the second edition. No more than 20 percent of the material in the second edition survived in its original form. More emphasis was placed on the rationale for various practices in plan design and financing, including the advantages and disadvantages of the various approaches. The requirements and standards of ERISA were dealt with in context throughout the book. Reliance had to be placed on the statute itself and its legislative history since no regulations or interpretive rulings had been issued before the book went to press.

The major thrust of the fourth edition, brought out only four years after its predecessor, was to update the book in the light of the manifold regulations, rulings, and interpretations issued by the IRS, Department of Labor, and Pension Benefit Guaranty Corporation in explanation of ERISA. The section of the third edition dealing with actuarial considerations was completely rewritten and expanded, with new terminology and a new framework for the analysis of actuarial cost methods. New chapters on profit sharing plans, thrift plans, and the federal tax treatment of qualified asset accumulation plans were added. Thought-provoking questions and problems were prepared for each chapter, a feature designed to make the book a more effective educational tool. Finally, new developments, such as guaranteed income contracts (GICs) of life insurers were recognized, and refinements of various sorts were introduced.

   In recognition of the mushrooming volume of pension plan assets
and the responsibilities associated with their investment, the fifth
edition added three new chapters on investment policy and operations. There was also a new chapter on accounting for pension
plan costs and liabilities, a subject of growing importance and controversy. Individual account plans of various sorts were given expanded treatment, necessitating the addition of a new chapter on
IRAs and voluntary employee contributions. The material on plan
benefits insurance was thoroughly rewritten, incorporating the
changes introduced by the Multiemployer Pension Plan Amendment Act. A section on stochastic modeling was added to the chapter on forecasting plan costs, liabilities, and cash flow. The material
was again updated to reflect changes in applicable law and business
practices. Citations to statutes, regulations, rulings, and judicial
decisions were introduced throughout the book.

   Like the previous revisions, this edition contains much new material. Repeated rounds of federal legislation since the last edition
have touched almost every aspect of pensions, requiring substantial
changes throughout the text. These include the Deficit Reduction
Act of 1984, the Retirement Equity Act of 1984, the Single-Employer Pension Plan Amendments Act of 1986, the Tax Reform Act
of 1986 and the Omnibus Budget Reconciliation Act of 1987. Court
decisions, together with new regulations and guidelines from the
regulatory agencies, required extensive changes. The chapter on
accounting was completely rewritten to reflect *Statements of Financial Accounting Standards No. 87* and *No. 88* of the Financial
Accounting Standards Board. Changes in the types of contracts
used by insurance companies and changes in other areas required
revisions.

   As the content of this book applies to both women and men—
employees, retirees, annuitants, etc.—the authors intend that the
use of *he, him,* and *his* applies to all persons.

   The first five editions were under the sole authorship of Dan M.
McGill. This edition is under the co-authorship of Dan M. McGill
and Donald S. Grubbs, Jr., who was a collaborator in prior editions.

   Numerous other persons reviewed portions of the book and of-
fered helpful suggestions. The material on investments was read
by George W. Cowles, Senior Vice President of Bankers Trust
Company, and James E. Aguilar, Assistant Director of Pension
Underwriting of the Principal Financial Group. Edward Thomas
Veal, Senior Manager of Touche Ross, reviewed the chapters on

plan benefits insurance. Larry B. Wiltse, F.S.A., Consulting Actuary with Buck Consultants, Inc., reviewed the accounting chapter. Others who provided significant help in reviewing portions of the text were Vincent Amoroso, F.S.A., Senior Manager of Peat Marwick Mitchell & Company; Matthew G. Deckinger, Associate Actuary of the Wyatt Company; Howard Golden, Esq., Partner of Kwasha Lipton; David R. Kass, F.S.A., of David R. Kass & Company; and Jennifer Pilkington, Assistant Actuary of Buck Consultants, Inc.

Our gratitude for help rendered in connection with previous editions carries over to this edition. Robert J. Myers, F.S.A., former Chief Actuary of the Social Security Administration, and Dr. Howard E. Winklevoss, an independent consultant, deserve special recognition for their past help.

We would like to record our very special intellectual debt to a small group of eminent pension actuaries who over the years shared their insight and knowledge and in so doing contributed enormously to the understanding of the private pension institution: Preston C. Bassett; Dorrance Bronson (deceased); Joseph B. Crimmins; John K. Dyer, Jr. (deceased); Frank L. Griffin, Jr.; Meyer Melnikoff; Ray M. Peterson (deceased); and Charles L. Trowbridge.

Needless to say, the authors take full responsibility for the book and any errors that may remain after all the scrutiny to which the manuscript was exposed.

Finally, we want to recognize with profound appreciation Judith M. Russo, Dawson T. Grubbs, Daniel G. Grubbs, and Joseph D. Marsden of Grubbs and Company, Inc., for their arduous and exemplary efforts in connection with the sixth edition, including word processing, proofreading and indexing. We also pay tribute to the unstinted and capable services of Milly A. Brill, the senior author's secretary and administrative assistant for 32 years but now retired, in seeing the first five editions through publication. Without her help there might not have been a sixth edition!

We invite all of our readers to assist us with the next edition by calling our attention to any errors, omissions, or other shortcomings in the book.

**Dan M. McGill**
**Donald S. Grubbs, Jr.**

# CONTENTS

# LIST OF TABLES

# LIST OF FIGURES

# Introduction | Part One

# 1 | Underlying Forces

THE PRIVATE PENSION MOVEMENT in the United States is rooted in one of the most significant economic, social, and political developments of the 20th century—the progressive increase in the number and proportion of the population in the aged category (age 65 and over). This development has given rise to a multitude of problems, the most pressing of which, unquestionably, is that of providing a measure of economic security to the aged. Some conception of the magnitude of the problem can be grasped from the following brief account of the demographic, social, and economic influences at work.

## Economic Basis of the Old-Age Problem

### Population Trends

During the last 60 or so years the growth in the number and proportion of the aged population in the United States has been phenomenal. During that period the general population of the United States has doubled, while the number of persons age 65 and over has quintupled. In 1920, there were roughly 4.9 million persons age 65 and over, whereas 65 years later the number had grown to 28.9

million. The aged population is increasing at the rate of about 600,000 per year. It is estimated that by the year 2030, aged persons will number 67.5 million.[1] In relative terms, only 4.6 percent of the population in 1920 was 65 and over, whereas in 1985, 11.7 percent of the population fell in that category. It is estimated that from 18.2 to 25.6 percent of the population will be 65 and over by the year 2030; the wide range of the estimate results from the possibility that the total population may grow at different rates because of varying birthrate assumptions.

This spectacular increase in the past in the absolute and relative number of old persons in the United States reflects the combined influence of a decline in the birthrate, an increase in life expectancy, and the curtailment of immigration. The long-run decrease in the birthrate was reversed during World War II, and the birthrate remained at a relatively high level for a number of years thereafter. But between 1960 and 1975 the rate fell sharply, and since then has remained somewhat below the replacement level (i.e., producing zero population growth eventually). Population experts are reluctant to predict precisely the future course of fertility. The tremendous extension in life expectancy recorded during the last 50 years as a result of advances in medical science, particularly in the control of infectious diseases and the reduction of infant mortality, improvements in public health services, and a rise in general living standards, will probably not be duplicated during the next half-century. However, as medical science devotes more and more study to the diseases of old age, further gains in life expectancy are possible. On the other hand, either continued deterioration of the physical environment or a nuclear holocaust could reduce life expectancy. Immigration, which once contributed large numbers of young people to the U.S. population, has been a less important factor for the last several decades and is not expected to assume a more important role in the future.

### Employment Opportunities for the Aged

The increase in the proportion of old people has been accompanied by a decline in the employment of the aged. In 1890, the aged

---

[1]1986 *Annual Report* of the Board of Trustees of the Federal OASDI Trust Funds (Intermediate assumptions) p. 82.

constituted 3.9 percent of the total population and 4.3 percent of the total labor force. By 1985, the percentage of the population age 65 and over had tripled, but the percentage of the total labor force age 65 had declined to 2.5 percent.[2] In 1890, 38.7 percent of all persons age 65 and over were in the labor force, while in 1985 only 10.8 percent were in that category. This decline has taken place chiefly among aged males. In 1890, 68.3 percent of such males were in the labor force, but by 1985 the percentage had shrunk to 15.8 percent. The rate of female participation in the labor force age 65 and over decreased slightly during that period, from 7.6 percent to 7.3 percent.

Many factors have contributed to the decline in labor force participation by the aged, but one of the most significant, without question, has been the transition from an agrarian and essentially rural economy to an industrial and predominantly urbanized economy. Whereas persons in agricultural employment can continue working, at least on a part-time basis, to advanced ages, industrial employees, because of the physical demands of their jobs or employer personnel policy, are more likely to retire at a relatively early age. In recent years the hard core of long duration unemployment at the younger ages and the generalized effect of automation have placed increasing stress on early retirement. Other factors which have influenced the trend include the improvement in longevity, extension of social insurance and pension programs, and the widespread acceptance of age 65 as the normal retirement age. Recent legislation prohibiting mandatory retirement by employers because of age,[3] however, may tend to increase the average retirement age.

## Capacity to Save for Old Age

The implications of the foregoing are broadened by the lessened capacity of individuals to save for their own old-age maintenance.

---

[2]*Historical Statistics of the United States, Colonial Times to 1957* (Washington, DC: U.S. Bureau of the Census, 1960), p. 71, and *Statistical Abstract of the United States 1987*, Table 640.

[3]Age Discrimination in Employment Act of 1967 (ADEA) as amended by the Age Discrimination in Employment Amendments of 1986 P.L. 99–592.

Several developments within the last half-century have magnified the difficulties of accumulating an old-age estate. Frequently overlooked in this connection are the technological changes that have taken place during such period. A greatly improved and expanded industrial plant is pouring forth a vastly increasing quantity of consumer goods, of infinite variety, exerting relentless pressure on all classes of individuals to spend all or the greater portion of their income. High-pressure advertising and liberal extension of installment credit have conspired to tie up the worker's income even before it is earned. As a result, systematic provision for old age has become a secondary consideration in the budget calculations of the majority of families.[4]

A second factor that has complicated the accumulation of an estate is the general rise in personal and corporate income taxes during the last 40 years, somewhat alleviated by the tax cuts of 1981. The enormous fiscal needs of the federal government, traceable in large part to war and the threat of war, have led to the imposition of personal taxes which render it difficult for even those persons in the higher income brackets to make adequate provision for their old-age needs. High corporate taxes have added to the problem.

A third factor has been the corrosive influence of inflation. This phenomenon requires no documentation but does inspire the comment that inflation impairs the ability of fixed-income persons to save a portion of their income and undermines the purchasing power of funds which have already been accumulated by any group of income recipients.

### Changed Concept of Filial Responsibility

In earlier days it was not a matter of particular concern if persons reached old age without adequate means of support. Elderly members of a family resided with, and were supported by, younger members of the family. In many cases, the elderly persons were able to perform some tasks around the household or farm, thus lightening the burden on the younger people. With increasing ur-

---

[4]It may be argued that this development reflects a weakened propensity to save for old age, rather than a lessened capacity.

banization of society, changes in housing conditions, greater geographical mobility, and many other economic and social developments, the traditional approach to old-age care and support has been weakened. As a result society is looking increasingly to government and employers for old-age support.

## Public Pension Programs

The limitations of the individual approach to old-age financial security have led to the establishment of various governmental programs of old-age income maintenance. The most comprehensive and significant undertaking of this sort is the federal Old-Age, Survivors, and Disability Insurance system. This program has such a profound impact on private pension plans that careful consideration should be given to its structure and underlying philosophy.

### Federal Old-Age, Survivors, and Disability Insurance

**Coverage.**  Federal Old-Age, Survivors, and Disability Insurance (hereafter designated as OASDI) is the national program of social insurance created by the Social Security Act of 1935, covering the long-term risks, and, as such, is the foundation of all other programs of old-age income maintenance.[5] Unlike many national programs of old-age social insurance, including those of Canada and Great Britain, OASDI is not based on the principle of universal coverage of the entire population. Rather, coverage is conditioned on attachment to the labor market. The broad objective of the program is to cover all gainfully employed persons, including the self-employed. With certain exceptions, coverage for all eligible persons is compulsory and immediate. In other words, OASDI is a device by which gainfully employed persons are forced by statute to assume some responsibility for the old-age maintenance of persons who have retired.

The Medicare program, enacted in 1965, is closely associated with OASDI. One part, Hospital Insurance, generally covers the same employed persons as OASDI; it provides hospital and related

---

[5]For a comprehensive text on social security see Robert J. Myers, *Social Security*, 3rd *Ed.* (Homewood, Ill.: Richard D. Irwin, 1985).

benefits for insured persons who are over age 65 or disabled for at least two and one-half years (actually 29 to 30 months), and certain of their dependents, with financing by payroll taxes. The other part, Supplementary Medical Insurance, covers all persons over age 65 and all disabled persons covered by Hospital Insurance, on an individual voluntary basis; it provides benefits for physician and related medical services, with financing by individual premium payments and contributions from the federal government.

As to the technique of coverage, the program operates through exclusion rather than by inclusion. That is, all gainfully employed persons are covered except those specifically excluded. The original legislation, however, excluded some important groups, 4 out of every 10 gainfully employed persons being ineligible for coverage.

The exclusion of such a formidable proportion of employed persons introduced serious inequities into the program and, what was even more important, tended to frustrate the basic objective of the program. Therefore, by amendments in 1950, 1954, 1956, and 1983, the coverage was extended to many of the previously excluded groups. The concepts of elective coverage (for employees of state and local governments) and qualifying conditions as to regularity of employment (for domestics, farm laborers, and casuals) were introduced. Today 9 out of every 10 gainfully employed persons are covered under the system. The principal exclusions are railroad workers (who have their own plan which is coordinated with OASDI), federal employees hired before 1984 under any federal retirement system, those employees of state and local governments who are not covered by election, irregularly employed farm and domestic workers, and very low-income self-employed persons.

**Benefits.** *A. Eligibility for Retirement Benefits.* Benefits under the OASDI program are paid as a matter of statutory entitlement and are not generally conditioned on a showing of need. This characteristic of the program avoids the administrative complications of a needs or income test (except for the retirement test and proof of dependency for some categories of beneficiaries) and thus protects the privacy of the individual and preserves his self-respect. Equally important, it encourages the individual to accumulate savings to supplement the benefits of the OASDI program and any other retirement plan of which he might be a member. Before the 1983 amendments, the statutory retirement age at which unreduced benefits became payable was age 65. The statutory retirement age is still age 65 for those born before 1938 (who reach age 65 before 2003) and is graduated upward to age 67 for those born in 1960 and later. Retirement benefits are payable upon actual retirement at or after age 62 (benefits are permanently reduced for retirement before statutory retirement age) and the satisfaction of a service requirement. An individual is entitled to retirement benefits only if he has been credited with quarters of coverage[6] equal to one fourth of the calendar quarters that have elapsed since December 31, 1950 (or the year in which the individual became 21, if later), up to age 62 (which requirement will be at most 40 quarters of coverage), subject to a minimum of 6 quarters of coverage. An individual who has met such service requirements is said to be "fully insured." It might be said that the benefits vest[7] after 10 years of service (a shorter period for those over age 22 on January 1, 1951), with their amount being subject to diminution through periods of noncoverage.

As stated above, benefits are conditioned on actual retirement, the test of which has been substantial withdrawal from covered employment. Under the 1939 act, an otherwise eligible claimant was disqualified for benefits for any month in which he earned wages in covered employment of $15 or more. This earnings limit has been increased and moderated from time to time. The earnings limit has been eliminated for persons age 70 and over and partial payment of benefits was made possible when earnings somewhat exceeded the limit. In 1988, the law provides for reduction of $1 in benefits for each $2 of annual earnings in excess of $8,400 for those age 65 and older and $6,120 for those under age 65. In the year an individual first becomes entitled to benefits, however, benefits are not withheld for any month in which the beneficiary's remuneration as an employee is one twelfth the annual limit or less, and in which he renders no substantial services in self-employment. On the other hand, all earnings, not just covered earnings, are taken into account. The foregoing exempt amounts will be automatically adjusted in future years for changes in the general level of wages in the country.

---

[6]In 1988, an employee earns one quarter of coverage for each $470 of earnings in the calendar year (maximum of four quarters per year). The $470 will increase automatically in future years in proportion to average wages.

[7]Some persons question whether the concept of vesting can properly be applied to a noncontractual benefit.

Incorporated in the law in the first instance in considerable part as a device for forcing older workers out of a depressed labor market, the earnings limitation has been retained primarily to hold down the cost of the OASDI program. Complete elimination of the earnings limitation today would increase current outlays under the program substantially. It is difficult to justify benefit payments to persons who have not actually retired, particularly in view of the burdensome level which the cost of the program will eventually reach. Furthermore, an earnings limitation is necessary to preserve the basic character of the old-age element of the program, which undertakes to provide benefits only to those workers who are no longer connected in a substantial way with the labor force.

Those who oppose an earnings test argue that it discourages persons from continuing as active, productive members of the labor force, thus depriving society of the goods and services that they might otherwise have produced; that it encourages dishonesty; and that it induces individuals to enter the underground of the economy, with an accompanying loss of tax dollars.

**B. Nature of Benefits.** The OASDI program provides retirement, disability, and survivorship benefits, all of which are based on the insured's "primary insurance amount" (PIA), whose derivation is described below. The insured's retirement benefit, a life income, is designated the "old-age insurance benefit" and is identical with the primary insurance amount if he retires at the statutory retirement age (age 65 for those born before 1938). If he delays retirement past that age, his benefit is increased for each year of deferral up to age 70. If retirement takes place at any time between the ages of 62 and his statutory retirement age, his benefit is permanently reduced. For those born before 1938, the reduction is 20 percent at age 62 and is proportionate for retirement at any intervening age, being 10 percent at age 63½, for example. For those born later, the reduction at age 62 will range from 20 to 30 percent.

The wife of a retired worker is entitled to a benefit equal to 50 percent of the primary insurance amount if she is at the statutory retirement age or older or, irrespective of her age, if she has under her care a dependent and unmarried child of the insured under age 18 (or a child who has been disabled since age 18); if the wife has no such child, she may claim permanently reduced wife's benefits at any time between age 62 and her statutory retirement age. The percentage reduction is slightly larger than the percentage used in the determination of early benefits for retired workers. Further-more, each such child is entitled to a benefit equal to one half of the primary insurance amount. The husband of a retired worker is entitled to benefits determined like a wife's benefit, provided the husband is age 62 or older. The wife's or husband's benefit is paid only if it is larger than the benefit payable in respect of the spouse's own covered earnings and is subject to the earnings test. A spouse's benefit is currently payable in respect of about 15 percent of all retired workers. The combined family benefits may not exceed prescribed amounts, which generally are about one and three-fourths times the primary insurance amount.

Social Security provides survivorship benefits and includes a special category of insured status to facilitate the payment of such benefits to orphan children and their mothers. Such survivorship benefits are available if the deceased was "currently insured," a status which can be attained with 6 quarters of coverage, all of which, however, must have been earned within the 13 quarters preceding the date of death, including the quarter in which death occurs. The same survivor benefits are available if the deceased was "fully insured" without being "currently insured." In addition to a lump-sum benefit equal to $255, income benefits are payable to widows and widowers age 60 and over (age 50 and over if dis-abled), mothers of any age who have dependent children of the deceased under their care, dependent children under age 18 (or disabled since before age 22) or children age 18 through 21 if in school, and dependent parents age 62 and over.[8]

Social Security provides monthly benefits for permanently and totally disabled workers under age 65 after a five-month waiting period. Dependents' benefits are payable to the same categories of dependents as for retired workers. The benefit for the disabled worker is the primary insurance amount. To be eligible, the worker must be both fully insured and have 20 quarters of coverage during the last 10 years (fewer quarters required if disabled before age 31).

*C. Level of Benefits.* All benefits payable under the OASDI program are based on the insured's covered earnings. Benefits for individuals attaining age 65 before 1982 (and for many retiring in

---

[8]Mothers whose only children are age 18 through 21 and in school are not eligible for survivor benefits.

later years, under a grandfather provision) are based on the "average monthly wage" (AMW). Benefits for individuals attaining age 65 later, unless the grandfather clause is applicable, are based on the "average indexed monthly earnings" (AIME). Understanding the old method is useful, not only because it still applies to some persons but because it assists in understanding the new method of benefit computation.

The average monthly wage is a technical concept and is based on the insured's covered wages. The average monthly wage is computed for the $n$ years after 1950 in which earnings were highest. Here, $n$ equals the number of years after 1955 (or attainment of age 26, if later) and before the year the individual attains age 62. For those born in 1929 and later, $n$ will equal 35 years for retirement cases. For death and disability cases, the year of such event is considered to be the year of attainment of age 62, and the minimum value is two years. In addition, those years during which an insured individual is unable to earn income because of a condition of total disability (or any years of blindness irrespective of the person's income) are to be omitted from the determination of $n$ years in the calculation of the average monthly wage. A benefit formula is applied to the average monthly wage to determine the primary insurance amount, the monthly old-age benefit, payable at age 65 to the covered worker.

Starting for those attaining age 65 in 1982 (except for grandfather provisions), or dying or becoming disabled before age 65 in 1982, the primary insurance amount is based upon "average indexed monthly earnings" instead of "average monthly wage." The average indexed monthly earnings is calculated in exactly the same manner as the average monthly wage, except that the worker's earnings in each year before the year of attainment of age 60 (or the second year before death or disability prior to age 62) are indexed to reflect the increase in average nationwide wages during the intervening years. A different formula is used to determine the primary insurance amount based upon the average indexed monthly earnings than was used under prior law for the average monthly wage. The resulting "replacement ratios"—the ratio of the primary insurance amount for the initial month of retirement (as of the beginning of the year) to the annual covered earnings for the year just prior to retirement—will remain fairly stable under the amended law, and will be about 23 percent lower than the replacement ratios under the prior law for those retiring at age 65 in 1981. The replacement ratios for workers retiring at age 65 in the future are estimated as 42 percent for the average worker, 54 percent for one whose earnings were only half of those of the average worker, and 27 percent for workers whose earnings always equal the taxable earnings base. The survivorship benefits payable to a widow and two or more children run about 70 percent of the covered annual earnings for the case of the average worker, about 90 percent for the low-earnings worker, and 50 percent for the maximum-earnings worker.

The benefits are automatically adjusted each year by changes in the cost of living, as measured by the consumer price index.

**Financing.** To the present, the cost of the OASDI program, including both benefit and administrative expenditures, has been borne almost entirely by the covered workers[9] and employers. Almost all funds have been derived from a payroll tax levied in equal proportions on employers and employees and from a tax on covered earnings of the self-employed.

The rate of contribution in 1988 is 6.06 percent each for wage earners and their employers (plus 1.45 percent for Hospital Insurance). The ultimate rate, scheduled for 1990 and thereafter, is 6.20 percent each for OASDI, plus 1.45 percent for Hospital Insurance. For self-employed persons the rate equals the sum of the employer and employee tax rates (twice the employee rate). Beginning in 1990 self-employed individuals will be allowed an income tax deduction for half of their social security taxes, comparable to the deduction allowed to employers. For 1988 and 1989 the social security tax rates for self-employed individuals are reduced by 2 percent as a tax credit. The tax is levied on earnings up to a taxable wage base, $45,000 in 1988. This base increases automatically for changes in the general level of nationwide wages.

The present system of financing is a modified pay-as-you-go basis. The expenditures of the program are approximately equal to the income from contributions and interest earnings. The excess contributions over the years have led to the accumulation (in the OASI and DI Trust Funds) of $40 billion at the end of 1985, a sum

---

[9]The term *workers* includes self-employed individuals.

sufficient to pay benefits for about three months (in the absence of new contributions). Thus, without future income from contributions, this fund would not be capable of meeting the obligations of the program to those persons who have already begun to draw benefits, not to mention the accrued liabilities for those persons who are still working. Indeed, as of the end of 1983, the present value of the benefits to be paid to those persons already on the OASDI benefit rolls was estimated to be about $1.8 trillion.

## Federal Staff Retirement Plans

Entirely distinct from the national old-age insurance program, several staff retirement plans have been established under the aegis of the federal government. Designed, with one notable exception, to provide old-age benefits to various categories of federal employees, these plans bear a close resemblance to private pension plans. Employees hired before 1984 covered under these plans are not concurrently covered under OASDI, although coordination with OASDI has been achieved with respect to the Railroad Retirement System.

Largest of the federal plans and, in fact, the largest single employer pension plan in existence, is the Civil Service Retirement System established in 1920, which provides retirement, survivorship, and disability benefits to career employees of the federal government hired before 1984. The new Federal Employees Retirement System covers federal civilian employees hired in 1984 and later, as well as those who were hired earlier and who elect to transfer to the new system. Participation in these systems is compulsory for all eligible employees. As of September 30, 1984, about 1.4 million persons were drawing retirement and disability benefits from the system and another 500,000 were receiving survivorship benefits.[10] Federal civilian employees hired after 1983 were included in the OASDI program, as well as about 2.2 million members of the armed forces (who also have a separate noncontributory pension plan, which is primarily of value to career personnel).

In addition to the Civil Service Retirement System and the Federal Employees Retirement System, other retirement plans cover federal civilian employees. Some of the more important plans cover

---

[10]*Statistical Abstract of the United States 1987*, Table 581.

·members of the foreign service, employees of the Federal Reserve banks, employees of the Tennessee Valley Authority, and members of the federal judiciary. Most of these plans provide more liberal benefits than those of the Civil Service Retirement System.

On the periphery of federal staff plans is the Railroad Retirement System. This program is unique in the American pension field in that it is operated for a group of private employees but is administered by the federal government. It was established by the Railroad Retirement Act of 1937 (and enlarged by the Railroad Unemployment Insurance Act), partially in an attempt to restore financial stability to the various individual railroad plans which were threatened with insolvency after years of difficulties. Protection is provided against the four major hazards to economic security—old age, disability, death, and unemployment—and benefits are administered by the federal government.

### State and Local Retirement Systems

A heterogeneous assortment of public pension plans has been established at the state and local levels. These plans differ widely in their details, but in most jurisdictions separate plans exist for policemen, firemen, and teachers, all other employees, if covered at all, being lumped together into a general retirement system. Because of the hazardous nature of their work, policemen and firemen were the earliest groups of public employees to obtain retirement benefits, and, up to the present, plans for such employees have contained more liberal provisions than those for other public employees. As a rule, police and firemen plans provide for low employee contributions, retirement at an early age after relatively brief service (typically 20 years), liberal survivors' benefits, disability benefits, and retirement benefits based on compensation for the highest grade held. Teacher retirement systems are less liberal than the policemen and firemen funds, but even so, they usually accord more generous treatment than the plans maintained for all other employees.

### Other Public Pension Programs

Public pension programs financed entirely from general revenues represent another broad source of old-age benefits and deserve brief mention. The best known of these programs, Supplemental Secu-

rity Income (SSI), is broadly designed to complement the old-age
insurance scheme which is now termed OASDI. SSI applies to those
indigent persons age 65 or over who could not qualify for OASDI
benefits, or who could qualify but for one reason or another would
not receive adequate benefits, and to needy disabled and blind
persons. SSI is entirely financed and administered by the federal
government and is, in essence, a "guaranteed income" plan. The
SSI payment level at the beginning of 1985 was $325 per month for
single persons and $488 per month for married couples; from these
amounts is deducted other income (with certain disregards). The
payment level is automatically adjusted in the same manner as is
done for OASDI benefits. During 1985, $8.8 billion was paid under
this program; in December 1985, over 4 million aged, blind, and
disabled persons received payments under the program.[11] Some
states provide additional supplementary payments which amounted
to $2.3 billion in 1985.

Veterans' compensation for service-connected and nonservice-
connected disabilities provided through the Veterans Administration is another important source of old-age income. Payments to
disabled veterans and their survivors amounted to $14 billion in
1985.

## The Private Pension Movement

### Rationale

Industrial pensions appeared on the American scene during the last
quarter of the 19th century, but only within the last 50 years have
they assumed any significance in the old-age financial picture. In
the beginning, private pension benefits were universally regarded
as gratuities from a grateful employer in recognition of long and
faithful service. The payments were usually discretionary, the employer assuming no legal obligation to provide benefits. In fact,
most plans stated in specific terms that no employee rights were
being created thereunder and reserved to the employer the right to
deny benefits to any employee and to reduce or terminate benefits
which had already commenced. A few plans promised to continue

[11]Total number of persons under SSI in any particular year far exceeds the number in
any month of the year because of turnover.

benefit payments to retired employees but made no commitment to active employees. These plans exemplified the gratuity theory of pensions.

As the years went by, certain groups, anxious to encourage and strengthen the pension movement, sought to place on the employer a moral obligation to provide pensions to superannuated employees. As early as 1912, one student of the old-age problem wrote: ''From the standpoint of the whole system of social economy, no employer has a right to engage men in any occupation that exhausts the individual's industrial life in 10, 20, or 40 years, and then leaves the remnant floating on society at large as a derelict at sea.''[12] This point of view was frequently expressed during the next few decades, being the subject of widespread debate in the early 1920s. It was adopted by the United Mine Workers and used by that organization in its 1946 campaign to establish a welfare fund. The union's position was expressed by its president, John L. Lewis, as follows:

> The United Mine Workers of America has assumed the position over the years that the cost of caring for the human equity in the coal industry is inherently as valid as the cost of replacement of mining machinery, or the cost of paying taxes, or the cost of paying interest indebtedness, or any other factor incident to the production of a ton of coal for consumers' bins . . . [the agreement establishing the Welfare Fund] recognized in principle the fact that the industry owed an obligation to those employees, and the coal miners could no longer be used up, crippled beyond repair and turned out to live or die subject to the charity of the community or the minimum contributions of the state.[13]

The concept received its most influential endorsement in the report of the fact-finding board in the 1949 steel industry labor dispute. The board wrote, in part, as follows:

> As hereinafter amplified, we think that all industry, in the absence of adequate government programs, owes an obligation to workers to provide for maintenance of the human body in the form of medical

---

[12]Lee Welling Squier, *Old Age Dependency in the United States* (New York: Macmillan, 1912), p. 272.

[13]United Mine Workers of America Welfare and Retirement Fund, *Pensions for Coal Miners* (undated), p. 4.

and similar benefits and full depreciation in the form of old-age retirement—in the same way as it does now for plant and machinery.[14]

And again:

> . . . the steel companies have, with some exceptions, overlooked the fact that the machines and plant on which the industry has prospered, and on which it must depend in the future, are not all made of metal or brick and mortar. They are also made of flesh and blood. And the human machines, like the inanimate machines, have a definite rate of depreciation.[15]

The human depreciation concept has been criticized on various grounds. It has been pointed out, for example, that aging is not a result of employment but of physiological processes. In the minds of some, this would limit the employer's responsibility to the *increase* in the rate of aging attributable to the employee's occupation. Furthermore, the concept seems to place the obligation of providing retirement benefits entirely on the last employer. Only the terminal employer is accused of casting away the worn-out human machine, leaving it "floating on society at large as a derelict at sea." The same disapprobation does not attach to an employer who discharges an employee in his middle years without providing paid-up pension benefits. Finally, it is agreed that the cost of replacing a human machine is not comparable to that of replacing a physical machine. A human machine can be replaced only with the cost of training a replacement, whereas the purchase price of a new unit must be accumulated to replace a worn-out physical machine.

On the other side of the picture, it can be said that the concept does not question the physiological basis of aging, but simply asserts that the cost of maintaining a human machine both during and after his active working life should be a cost of production, analogous, for example, to the economic cost of industrial injuries and disease. The concept is normative; its validity is not negated by the fact that an employer may, as a practical matter, be able to discharge a long-service employee without making any provision for his old-age maintenance needs. Depreciation allowances are

---

[14]Steel Industry Board, *Report to the President of the United States on the Labor Dispute in the Basic Steel Industry,* September 10, 1949, p. 55.

[15]Ibid., p. 64.

made for physical equipment even though it is not actually replaced. Second, the increased interest in vesting is evidence of a growing realization or conviction that any employer who utilizes the services of an employee for an extended time has an obligation to make some contribution toward the individual's retirement needs. In fact, it might be argued that the human depreciation concept is the philosophical basis (along with the deferred wage theory) of the case for vesting. Finally, it may well be that social pressures will eventually compel all but the smallest employers to provide old-age support for their employees. In such event, the replacement of a superannuated employee would call for the accumulation of a capital sum, and the annual charges against the employer's revenue that would be associated with the funding of the pension obligation would be analogous to charges for depreciation or obsolescence.

The human depreciation concept has been supplanted—or supplemented—in some quarters by the theory that pensions are essentially deferred wages. The latter concept holds that an employee group has the prerogative of choosing between an immediate wage increase and a pension plan, and, having chosen the latter, is entitled to regard the benefits as deferred wages. Like the human depreciation concept, this point of view found early expression:

> Theoretically, the simplest way of dealing with labor would be the payment of a money wage, requiring the employee to provide for the hazards of employment and his old age. While here and there an employee does this, by and large the mass of employees do not.
>
> In order to get a full understanding of old-age and service pensions, they should be considered a part of the real wages of a workman. There is a tendency to speak of these pensions as being *paid* by the company, or, in cases where the employee contributes a portion, as being *paid* partly by the employer and partly by the employee. In a certain sense, of course, this may be correct, but it leads to confusion. A pension system considered as part of the real wages of an employee is really paid by the employee, not perhaps in money, but in the foregoing of an increase in wages which he might obtain except for the establishment of a pension system.[16]

From the standpoint of an individual participant, this concept has validity only if the funds paid into a pension plan in lieu of a

[16]Albert deRhoode, "Pensions as Wages," *The American Economic Review* 3 (June 1913), p. 287.

personal wage increase are administered in such a manner as to ensure their ultimate payment to him or his beneficiary in one form or the other. This implies full and immediate vesting of employer contributions on behalf of current participants, a practice rarely encountered among industrial pension plans. From the standpoint of an entire body of employees, such as those represented by a labor union, the concept is valid if, in the aggregate, the employer contributions to a pension plan are precisely equivalent to the foregone cash wages and are held in such fashion as to assure their use for the exclusive benefit of the employees as a group. With the tendency for the parties to a collective bargaining agreement to express the employer's pension commitment in terms of wage equivalency, such as $x$ cents per hour, and given the safeguards surrounding a formal, IRS approved pension plan, these conditions would seem to be fulfilled, at least when the benefits are collectively bargained. In the absence of collective bargaining, the relationship between pension contributions and foregone immediate wages would, at best, be only approximate. Nevertheless, "deferred wages" is gaining increasing acceptance as a label for the collective benefits associated with a pension plan.

The tenuous relationship between wages foregone and pension benefits received in the case of individual participants has caused some to look for another explanation of pensions. It has given rise to the view that an old-age retirement benefit represents a differential wage payment, similar in nature to a shift differential or other payment in recognition of the unusual or special character of the service. In the case of a pension, the differential payment goes only to those who remain in the service of the employer for a long time (possibly to retirement) and is made in recognition of the special contributions, not reflected in wage payments, of a long-service employee to the firm. These contributions include the preservation of the folklore of the industry, fostering of loyalty to the firm and its traditions, and the transmission of technical skills from older to younger generations of workers.

Still another view of pensions is that they are a device, instituted and nourished by business firms, to meet the social problem of old-age economic dependency. Persons holding this view see a duty on the part of the business community in a private enterprise society to provide the mechanism through which gainfully employed individuals, by direct contributions or foregone wages, can make provision for their own old-age needs. This obligation can be discharged only through the establishment and operation of plans which measure up to minimum standards of benefit adequacy, benefit security, and financial solvency. Advocates of this view assert that only if the business community meets this challenge can social insurance schemes be confined to their proper bounds.

Persuasive as some of these theories are, it is doubtful that the private pension movement can be explained in terms of any one social or economic philosophy. Its rationale lies in broad and conflicting forces that do not lend themselves to definitive characterization. One might conclude that the only tenable explanation of the development is business expediency. Yet this expression is so pervasive that it furnishes only the vaguest of clues as to the specific forces that motivate employers to adopt pension plans. It might be helpful, therefore, to examine some of the significant factors and developments that have made it seem expedient to an employer to establish a pension plan.

### Forces Influencing the Growth of Private Pension Plans

**Productivity of the Employee Group.** Unquestionably, one of the most compelling employer motives in adopting a pension plan is the desire to increase the productivity of his employees. This motive is usually mixed with others, including a sincere desire to provide financial security to retired or superannuated employees. Nevertheless, unless the employer believes that the cost of the pension plan can be substantially offset by savings in other phases of company operations, including production costs, he may not be overly receptive to the idea of pensions.

On balance there is little doubt that the efficiency of the labor force is enhanced through the establishment of a pension plan. American industrial development has reached the stage where most concerns of any size now, or soon will, face the problem of dealing with large numbers of employees near or beyond normal retirement age. This problem may be handled in one of three ways. The first possible approach is for the employer to discharge his employees without retirement benefits as they lose their productivity through diminished energy, impaired manual dexterity, and lessened mental agility. With federal OASDI benefits available at subsistence levels, at least, such action would not be as callous as it might otherwise be. Nevertheless, in the present state of social consciousness, most employers shun such an approach, not only for humanitarian reasons but because of the risk of public censure and the constraints imposed by age discrimination laws. A second possibility is for the employer to retain his superannuated employees on the payroll at full or reduced pay but in a capacity commensurate with their diminished ability and vitality. This policy is usually disruptive of employee morale and may prove to be uneconomical in other respects. The third approach, and in the great majority of cases the only one offering a satisfactory solution, is for the employer to establish a formal pension plan. This generally results in the retirement of overage employees from the payroll in an orderly fashion, without adverse employee and public reaction, enabling the employer to replace them with younger, presumably more efficient, workers. The inevitable result is a more productive work force.

The installation of a pension plan is thought to boost production in other ways. It is agreed, for example, that the morale of the employee group will be elevated through the elimination of the workers' anxiety over their old-age security, not to mention the favorable attitude engendered by such tangible evidence of the employer's concern for the welfare of his employees. While a pension plan is definitely a positive morale factor, one may wonder whether its influence among the rank-and-file employees, particularly those distant from retirement, is not overshadowed by more immediate considerations, such as wages, hospitalization benefits, and working conditions. But if the presence of a pension plan is not a strong morale builder for some employee groups, the absence of one may be a negative factor.

It is also argued that the establishment of a pension plan will reduce turnover and hence the cost of training replacements. This argument is difficult to evaluate, since it is impossible to isolate the influence of a pension plan from the other factors that have a bearing on turnover. It is of some relevance to point out that the highest rate of turnover occurs among employees who, because of their youth or short service, may not be eligible for membership in the plan, or even if active participants, may be only slightly influenced in their choice of employment by the promise of a retirement benefit many years in the future. Moreover, it should be remembered that any reduction in turnover will be reflected in higher pension costs, since a higher percentage of employees will qualify for severance or retirement benefits.

A pension plan is a particularly effective instrument of personnel policy with respect to supervisory employees. Supervisory personnel represents a more stable and permanent group of employees, to whom the promise of a pension appears less illusory than to the hourly workers. They tend, therefore, to be more responsive to the stimulus of a pension plan and to carry out their responsibilities more effectively. Furthermore, since the responsibilities of the supervisory personnel are, by definition, on a higher level than those of the ordinary employee, it is especially important that a means exists whereby the executives and other supervisors can be encouraged to retire at an appropriate time after they have passed the peak of effectiveness. Related to this is the importance of keeping open the channels of promotion. In a large organization, one retirement can precipitate a chain of promotions—all to the betterment of employee morale and efficiency. Finally, a pension plan unquestionably enables an employer to attract and hold better qualified executives than would otherwise be possible. This is particularly true of those firms which normally draw their executives from external rather than internal sources.

**Tax Inducements.** Related to the foregoing, in the sense that both are cost-reducing factors, are the tax inducements offered by the federal government. The Revenue Act of 1942 is frequently—and erroneously—cited as the genesis of the favorable tax treatment of private pension plans, but the real beginning of such policy is found in much earlier legislation.

The provisions of the 1942 act, as subsequently amended, were reenacted in the Internal Revenue Code of 1954 and the Internal Revenue Code of 1986, which with the refinements and extensions added over the years, still provide the statutory base for the tax treatment of private pension plans.

If a plan meets the requirements of the Code and implementing regulations it is said to be "qualified."[17] A qualified status carries with it certain tax advantages and in most circumstances is highly prized and earnestly sought. The first tax advantage associated with

---

[17]I.R.C. §401(a).

a qualified status is that employer contributions to the plan are deductible, within specified limits, as ordinary and necessary business expenses for federal income tax purposes.[18] A second advantage is that employer contributions to the plan are not includible in the taxable income of the participants until actually received by them.[19] A third advantage is that investment earnings on the plan assets, including realized capital gains, are not subject to income taxation until disbursed in the form of benefits.[20] A fourth advantage is that certain distributions from qualified plans receive favorable income tax treatment. The distributions of a participant's entire individual account balance within one taxable year, upon the participant's death, disability, or separation from service or after age 59½, is classified as a lump-sum distribution,[21] subject to reduced taxation. Taxation of certain distributions may be deferred by rolling over the proceeds into another qualified plan, an individual retirement account, or an individual retirement annuity (see rollovers).[22]

**Pressure from Organized Labor.**    A third broad factor influencing the adoption of pension plans has been the attitude of organized labor. Until the late 1940s or early 1950s organized labor was, in the main, either indifferent to the pension movement or openly antagonistic to it. Many of the older and well-established craft unions viewed employer-sponsored pensions as a paternalistic device to wean the allegiance of the workers away from the unions to the employer. They also harbored a fear that pensions would be used to hold down wages. Over the years, however, these attitudes changed to such an extent that in 1949, when another round of wage increases seemed difficult to justify, a large segment of organized labor demanded pensions in lieu of wages. The way was paved for such a switch when a federal court ruled that pensions are a bargainable issue.

This case arose out of a union grievance filed with the National Labor Relations Board in 1946, alleging that the unilateral action

---

[18]I.R.C. §404.

[19]Treas. Reg. 1.402(a)–1(a).

[20]I.R.C. §501(a).

[21]I.R.C. §402(e)(4)(A).

[22]I.R.C. §402(a)(5). See Chapter 29 for a fuller description of the tax treatment of qualified pension plans and their benefit distributions.

of the Inland Steel Company in enforcing a policy of compulsory retirement at age 65 constituted a breach of the provision of the general labor contract relating to separation from service. The grievance stemmed from the refusal of the company to negotiate the matter with the union on the grounds that compulsory retirement was an essential part of the company's pension plan and that pension plans did not fall within the scope of collective bargaining. The union did not contend that the provisions of a pension plan were of themselves subject to collective bargaining, but argued that the company could not take unilateral action with respect to any provision of a pension agreement that was also a part of the general labor contract and, hence, conceded to be within the scope of mandatory collective bargaining.

In 1948, the National Labor Relations Board ruled in effect that the Labor-Management Relations Act of 1947 imposes a duty on employers to bargain with representatives of their employees on the subject of pensions. This decision was based on the dual premise that the term *wages* as defined in the statute includes any emolument of value, such as pension or insurance benefits, and that the detailed provisions of pension plans come within the purview of "conditions of employment" and therefore constitute an appropriate subject for collective bargaining.[23]

Upon appeal by the company, the Court of Appeals for the Seventh Circuit approved the view of the National Labor Relations Board that the terms of a pension plan are subject to mandatory collective bargaining on the ground that they constitute "conditions of employment," but expressed some reservation with respect to the wage analogy:

> We are convinced that the language employed by Congress, considered in connection with the purpose of the Act, so clearly includes a retirement and pension plan as to leave little, if any, reason for construction. While, as the Company has demonstrated, a reasonable argument can be made that the benefits flowing from such a plan are not "wages," we think the better and more logical argument is on the other side, and certainly there is, in our opinion, no sound basis for an argument that such a plan is not clearly included in the phrase, "other conditions of employment."[24]

---

[23]*Inland Steel Company* v. *United Steelworkers of America* (CIO), 77 NLRB 4 (1948).

[24]*Inland Steel Company* v. *National Labor Relations Board,* 170 F.2d 247, 251 (1949). Certiorari denied by the Supreme Court, 336 U.S. 960 (1949).

The Inland Steel decision established a legal framework within which no employer during the term of an applicable labor agreement can install, alter, or terminate a pension plan for organized workers without the assent of the labor bargaining unit. This obligation rests on the employer whether or not the plan was installed prior to certification of the bargaining unit and whether or not the plan be compulsory or voluntary, contributory or noncontributory.

Since 1949, organized labor has been a vigorous and potent force in the expansion of the private pension movement. Union demands for pensions have brought old-age economic protection to millions of workers. While there are differences of opinion among the international bodies about the emphasis and reliance which should be placed on private pensions—some would concentrate their energies on liberalization of the federal old-age social insurance program—it may be said as a generalization that the support of the private pension institution is a "vital trade union aim and function."

**Social Pressure.** A final factor that has encouraged the spread of pension plans is the social and political atmosphere that has prevailed during the last 60 years. During that period the American people have become security conscious. The economic upheaval of the early 1930s swept away the life savings of millions and engendered a feeling of insecurity that shook the very foundations of the country. Prominent among the proposals for economic reform were those that envisioned social action in the area of old-age income maintenance. The federal OASDI program was the outgrowth of these proposals.

Since the federal program was deliberately designed to provide only a "floor of protection," the way was left clear for supplemental benefits to be provided through private measures. In view of the general liability—or unwillingness, as some would have it—of the individual to accumulate through his or her own efforts the additional resources required, society has come to expect the employer to bear a share of the burden. The employer may successfully shift his share of the costs to the consumer, but a great deal of social pressure is exerted on the employer to provide the mechanism through which additional funds can be accumulated. If the employer chooses not to install a formal pension plan, he may find that social pressure forces him to take care of his superannuated employees in some other manner. In anticipation of such a development, em-

ployers have turned to formal pension programs as the most eco-
nomical and satisfactory method of meeting the problem.

## Approaches to Providing Retirement Benefits

There are two basic approaches to achieving the management, labor, and social objectives that permeate and sustain the private
pension movement. One approach is to establish and maintain a
pension plan that promises a determinable set of benefits at retirement. The typical plan of this type provides that a unit of benefit,
a flat dollar monthly benefit or a specified percentage of compensation, will accrue for each year of creditable service. The unit of
benefit is set at a level that, with a normal working career and in
combination with Social Security and personal savings, will provide
the retired individual an income sufficient to maintain a comfortable
standard of living. The plan sponsor, typically the employer, undertakes to provide the funds, through periodic contributions and
investment earnings on the plan assets, that are needed to pay the
promised benefits as they become payable. The future cost of the
plan is unknown, being determined by the rate of mortality, withdrawals from the covered group, pattern of compensation, age of
retirement, investment earnings, and other factors. The participants may be required to bear a portion of the cost of the plan
through payroll deduction. Quite logically, this type of plan is identified in pension literature as a *defined benefit* plan. It is characterized by definitely *determinable* benefits, by given assumptions
as to years of service and level of compensation, and by *indeter-
minable* future costs.

The other approach is to specify the basis on which contributions
will be made to the plan, with no contractual commitment as to
the level of benefits that will be provided. Individual accounts are
maintained for the participants, the accounts being credited with
their allocable share of employer (and employee) contributions and
investment earnings. The retirement benefit of a given participant
depends upon the balance in the individual's account at date of
retirement. Contributions to the plan, generally expressed as a
percentage of compensation, are set at a level designed to produce
a satisfactory level of retirement income for a long-service employee. In contrast to the defined benefit approach, the employer's
future cost, as a percentage of covered payroll, is known in ad-

vance; but the amount of retirement benefit is not determinable in advance, being strongly influenced by investment results. Thus, it may be said that the future cost of the plan is *predictable* but the benefits are *unpredictable*. This approach to retirement planning is known as a *defined contribution plan,* also referred to as an *individual account plan.*

The practical consequences of these two approaches to retirement planning to plan sponsors, plan participants, and society are far-reaching and will be explored in detail throughout the remainder of the text.

---

## Questions

1. It has been said that the coverage of the OASDI program of the United States is determined by *exclusion,* rather than by *inclusion.* What does this mean, and what is the advantage of such an approach if a high proportion of coverage is the goal of the program?

2. Distinguish between a "currently insured" and "fully insured" status under the OASDI program. Why was the currently insured status created? Are there any benefits under the program for which a fully insured status does not satisfy the service requirement?

3. Which is the more fundamental concept under the OASDI program, the "primary insurance amount" or the "old-age insurance benefit"? Under what circumstances would these two sums be identical in amount?

4. To what extent have benefits and wages under the OASDI program been indexed? Explain.

5. The OASDI is financed on a modified pay-as-you-go basis. In your opinion, is this an appropriate approach to financing a national social insurance program? Why?

6. In your opinion, does an employer have a moral obligation to provide a pension to employees who reach retirement age while in his employment? In resolving this question, do you make a distinction between the long-service and short-service employee?

7. Explain the human depreciation concept and indicate whether, in your judgment, it provides a philosophical basis for an employer-sponsored pension plan.

8.  A pension has been variously characterized as a *gratuity,* a *deferred wage,* or a *differential wage.* In your view, which of these characterizations has the most validity?

9.  Which of the various theories of pension entitlement is most supportive of the vesting concept (i.e., nonforfeitability of accrued benefits)?

10. What are the motivating forces behind employers' decisions to install a pension plan? What situations make each of these particularly strong?

11. What constraints does a collective bargaining agreement impose upon an employer with respect to the establishment, amendment, or termination of a pension plan?

12. Why are plan sponsors so anxious to "qualify" their pension plans?

13. Should a participant in a pension plan have an interest in whether or not the plan is "qualified" under the requirements of the Internal Revenue Code and implementing regulations, or is this a matter of concern only to the plan sponsor (the employer)? Explain.

# 2 | Functions Associated with Private Pension Plans

THE MODERN PENSION PLAN is a complex mechanism. It creates obligations that may not be discharged for more than a half-century and involves costs that can be estimated only within a wide range of probability. It leads to the accumulation of vast sums of money, some contributed by employees, which must be managed and invested with a high sense of responsibility. Its development, installation, and administration call for various forms of technical, professional, and administrative skills. It relies upon the services of a number of different agencies, some specialized in character and others offering a wide range of services. Some of the services utilized by a pension plan are offered by more than one type of agency, and informed judgment must be exercised in the choice of agency to perform a specific function. The most basic decision, perhaps, concerns the management and investment of the funds accumulated under the plan, and the decision is complicated by the sharp differences in the philosophy and modus operandi of the competing funding agencies.

This chapter attempts to provide an appreciation of the scope of the pension undertaking and a brief glimpse into the activities of the various servicing agencies. Later sections of the book present a detailed analysis of the role of the principal types of funding agencies—life insurers, banks, and other money managers.

## Selling the Plan

For the last four decades the social and economic environment in the United States has been conducive to the establishment of private pension plans. There has been a quickening of management's sense of responsibility to persons who, through long years of service, have contributed to the growth and development of the firm. This moral consciousness has unquestionably been heightened—and nurtured—by the existence of the federal old-age social insurance program. A long period of unparalleled prosperity has made it economically feasible for employers to indulge their sense of social responsibility, and the federal government has aided and abetted by providing favorable tax treatment of private plans which meet certain requirements, primarily designed to assure fair and equitable treatment of the employee group. Moreover, organized labor has developed an avid interest in all kinds of employee benefit plans and the liberalization of old plans. These and a host of other forces, including the desire to attract and hold executive talent, have fashioned a ready-made market for private pension plans.

The receptivity of employers, especially those in the large- and medium-sized categories, to the notion of a pension plan has not deemphasized the sales function in this sector of the economy. To the contrary, it has triggered a fiercely competitive struggle among organizations and individuals catering to the pension market. The chief protagonists are the principal funding agencies—banks, insurance companies, and other money managers—but the sales battle is sometimes waged to a great extent by the coterie of agents, brokers, consultants, actuaries, accountants, lawyers, and others who sometimes ally themselves with one of the funding agencies.

From a procedural standpoint, the sales function connected with the inauguration of a *new* plan consists of two phases: arousal of interest on the part of the prospect, and motivating the prospect to accept the proposal presented by the sales representative.

At times the initial interest in a pension plan comes from the employer or a union. Sometimes, it originates with the employer's accountant or legal counsel recommending a plan, often for tax reasons. But frequently the funding agencies or service providers initiate the idea, making an attempt to arouse the employer's interest by reference to one or more of the advantages associated with a formal pension plan, some of which are not primarily identified with the interests of the rank-and-file employee. Allusion to the consequences of *not* installing a pension plan may also be persuasive. If the prospect is a union, attention is usually called to the need for supplementing federal OASDI benefits or the advantages of substituting deferred benefits for immediate wage increases.

The funding agency or service provider—insurance company representative, bank representative, pension consultant, or broker—may offer a complete plan, frequently standardized, designed to meet the general objectives of the prospect. On the other hand, the service provider may simply offer the services of actuaries, accountants, and other technicians in developing a plan that would be adapted to the special circumstances and needs of the prospect. In either case, the employer must provide the funding agency or service provider with the information needed to develop a proposal for a plan. If a defined benefit pension plan is to be considered, this must include the employee data—age, sex, compensation, and period of service—needed to develop cost estimates.

If the proposal is developed by a life insurance company, its development and the preparation of cost data will be carried out at no expense to the prospect. If the proposal, or an alternative one, is not accepted, the cost involved in its preparation and submission is charged to the general operating expenses of the insurance company, to be recovered, if possible, out of the premium income[1] from cases successfully placed. If the proposal is accepted and the plan is installed, the insurance company will recover its costs out of the gross premiums paid in under the plan,[2] and any agent or broker who made the initial contact will be compensated for his efforts—or influence—in the form of the commissions payable under the insurance or annuity contract.[3] Since an insurance

---

[1]The term *premium* is properly used in the legal sense only in connection with life insurance contracts. The consideration for group annuity contracts is referred to as "purchase payment," "stipulated payment," and in various other ways.

[2]Many companies treat proposal and similar costs on cases successfully placed in the same manner as those incurred on cases not sold.

[3]The agent or broker who made the initial contact does not invariably receive the commissions payable under the contract. The employer may designate another agent or broker, licensed in the state in which the contract was negotiated, to receive some or all of the commissions.

company representative will be inclined to espouse the type of contract or contracts offered by his company, the proposals emanating from that source tend to be less flexible than those prepared by operatives offering a wider range of choices.

Organizations not representing a particular life insurance company, many of which have represented on their staff all of the professional skills needed to develop and implement a complete pension proposal, generally charge the employer a specific fee for developing such a proposal. The fee varies with the amount of work involved and in large cases may run into five figures. If the recommendations of the organization lead to the establishment of an insured plan and commissions are payable to the organization, the fee may be reduced by the amount of the commissions. Many pension consulting firms, however, will not accept commissions under an insured plan, on the theory, presumably, that their recommendations might otherwise be influenced by the size of the prospective commissions. For larger plans, the insurer is usually willing to pay only negligible commissions or none at all, directly reducing their charges to the employer. The charging of an independent development fee, in addition to providing the consulting firm with a more dependable source of income, should, but may not, lead to broader consideration of the various available approaches and recommendations based upon more objective analyses of the factors involved.

## Development of Terms of the Plan

Once the decision to establish some sort of pension plan is made, the employer or other plan sponsor must give detailed consideration to the terms of the plan.[4] To be specific, the employer, in consultation with the collective bargaining unit, if any, must decide who will be covered under the plan, what kind of benefits will be provided, how generous the benefits or contributions will be, the conditions under which the benefits will be paid, and how the benefits will be financed. These are substantive matters, which will be dealt with at length in later chapters. The present brief section is concerned only with the process by which decisions as to the substantive matters are reached.

---

[4]Throughout this chapter and the remainder of the book, the use of the term *employer* should be construed to include "employers" when the plan under consideration involves more than one employer.

The coverage and benefit provisions of a particular pension plan are dictated in a broad sense by the amount of contributions that can be put into the plan. This tends to be true whether the plan is established through collective bargaining or the unilateral action of the employer, unless the employer has agreed to join an existing or imminent industry plan with respect to which the terms have already been set. In the latter event, the terms of the plan will dictate the amount of money which the employer must set aside for pension purposes. In most plans being established today, the benefits will have to be provided out of the contributions that can be set aside by the employer. Under most types of plans, employees are asked to contribute to the plan only if their financial participation is necessary to provide reasonably adequate benefits, or if the employer feels that employee sharing of the cost is essential to the preservation of the self-respect of the employees or to the fostering of a sense of appreciation for the plan. Two types of plans which always include employee contributions, however, are thrift plans and salary reduction cash or deferred arrangements (401(k) plans).

Once the employer has determined within approximate limits how much he is willing to contribute to the pension plan each year, a number of tentative plans, with cost estimates, will usually be drawn up to indicate the various combinations of coverage and benefits that can be provided within the limits of the available contributions. If these tentative or experimental plans indicate that adequate contributions or benefits cannot be provided to all classes of employees, a decision must be made whether some—though admittedly inadequate—contributions or benefits should be made available to all classes of employees or more liberal contributions or benefits should be provided to limited classes of employees. The process of reconciling the employer's objectives and desires with the potentialities of the available contributions will also involve a judgment as to the types of benefits which should be made available and the conditions under which they should be granted. The employer's deliberations may extend to a comparative analysis of the plans of other companies in the same industry or geographical area to arrive at a set of benefits that would be competitive and yet within acceptable cost limits. The results of such a study may convince the employer that more contributions must somehow be channeled into the proposed plan.

The broad policy decisions involved in the formulation of the terms of a pension plan do not require technical or professional skills and presumably could be made by the employer without the counsel or assistance of experienced pension consultants. Nevertheless, these decisions can be made in a rational manner only in the light of valid cost calculations, which fall within the purview of the actuary. The professional pension consultant can also be helpful at this stage by providing advice on current practices and the impact, both as to cost and employee relations, of various possible plan provisions. As a matter of fact, pension consultants normally do participate in this phase of pension planning.

## Choice of Funding Agency

Prior to, concurrent with, or subsequent to the development of the terms of the pension plan, the employer decides whether the plan benefits will be provided through an insurance company contract or through a trust fund. Ideally, this decision should follow and be subservient to the formulation of the substantive features of the pension plan, but in practice the choice of funding agency is frequently the first conclusive step in the adoption of a pension plan and exerts a strong influence on the terms of the plan. In any event, the type of funding arrangement to be used will affect the manner in which benefits are to be paid and determines the nature of the documents needed to implement the plan. Hence, if the funding agency has not been selected by the time the substantive provisions have been formulated, such action must be taken before any steps can be taken to implement the plan.

When firm decisions have been reached as to the terms of the plan and the funding agency, and estimates of future costs have been prepared, the board of directors of the company (and possibly the stockholders) is asked to give approval of the plan and authority to proceed with the additional steps needed to bring the plan into actual operation.

## Installation of the Plan

### Preparation and Execution of Formal Legal Documents

Once the broad outline of the proposed pension plan has been approved by the company's board of directors, the substantive and procedural details must be set forth in a formal document. Among the matters that will be dealt with in the document are: (1) persons eligible to participate in the plan, including any prerequisites that must be met; (2) types and level of contributions or benefits to be provided; (3) form and manner in which benefits will be provided; (4) method of determining employer contributions and employee contributions, if any; (5) rights of participants on termination of employment; (6) protection of employer's interest, including the right to alter or terminate the plan and the right to discontinue contributions; and (7) rights of participants on termination of plan.

Under a trust fund plan, a trust agreement will designate the trustee or trustees and describe the powers and obligations of the trustee. Under an insured plan, the group or individual annuity or insurance contracts similarly describe the obligations of the insurance company. Some plans using a trust, fund the plan partly or entirely through insurance or annuity contracts issued to the trust, in which case there are both a trust agreement and one or more insurance or annuity contracts.

The trust agreement setting forth the powers and obligations of the trustee is usually separate from the plan document, which describes the plan's benefit provisions. But sometimes the details of the plan are incorporated in the trust agreement, and a document setting forth only the features of the "plan" is not separately executed. The combination plan and trust agreement is usually drafted by the employer's legal counsel, with the assistance of the insurance company or pension consultant and sometimes the trustee. If the benefits are to be provided through a group annuity contract, the plan, again, will often not be promulgated as a separate and distinct document but will be embodied in the master group contract entered into between the insurance company and the employer. Under deposit administration and immediate participation guarantee group annuity arrangements, the plan is usually promulgated as a separate document and is not embodied in the group contract.[5] The contract will usually be written on a form that has been approved by the insurance department of the state in which the insurer is located, and, depending on the requirements of the various states, may also have been approved by the insurance department of the state where issued.[6] The contract will be prepared by the insurance

---

[5]The employer has greater flexibility with respect to changes in funding agency when the plan is divorced from the agreement between the employer and the funding agency.

[6]Contracts for out-of-state plans may be only *filed* with the insurance department of the state in which the insurer is domiciled.

company and reviewed by the employer. If the contributions are to be accumulated in a trust fund and disbursed by the trustee, there are usually two formal documents: the plan, which defines eligibility for coverage, describes the benefit structure, and so forth; and the agreement between the employer and the trustee, which is chiefly concerned with the duties, responsibilities, and rights of the trustee, primarily with reference to the investment of the funds turned over to the trustee.

Frequently, the pension consultant or insurance company assists the employer's legal counsel in drafting the plan document. Alternatively, the employer may merely adopt a standardized plan document, called a master plan or prototype plan, which has been developed by a bank or insurance company and previously approved by the Internal Revenue Service.

When the plan document is separate from the trust agreement, specimen or suggested forms may be provided by the trustee for use by the employer, consultant, or legal counsel. In such case the trust agreements are not subject to review and approval by any public agency.

If the plan is intended to be qualified, the formal legal documents are prepared with due regard to the qualification requirements of the Internal Revenue Code.

When in final form and acceptable to all parties, the formal legal documents are approved by the firm's board of directors and executed.

## Securing Approval of the Internal Revenue Service

Qualification of the plan, including deductibility of employer contributions, is such a vital feature of a pension plan that the employer generally seeks a ruling from the Internal Revenue Service on the acceptability of the proposed plan and related trust, if any, before placing the plan in actual operation or taking any irrevocable actions in connection with such plan. The request for an advance ruling is submitted to the appropriate key district office of the Internal Revenue Service, and the ruling is issued in the form of a so-called determination letter.

The request for approval may be submitted directly by the employer or an officer representing the employer, or through an attorney, certified public accountant, or pension consultant acting under a power of attorney. For a plan being established by joint agreement between a union and one or more employers, and to be administered by a joint board, the filing is made by the board or an attorney acting for the board. The form[7] requesting approval must be supported by copies of the plan, the trust indenture, if any, and insurance contracts, if any; and data designed to reveal any discrimination in favor of highly compensated employees. This information may be assembled by the insurance company, a consulting actuary or other pension consultant involved.

If the key district office of the IRS finds the plan and related trust indenture, or insurance contracts, to be acceptable in all respects, it will issue a favorable determination letter. In the event that the revenue officials find the plan or related documents unsatisfactory in some respect, they generally give the employer and his advisers an opportunity to discuss in conference the objectionable or questionable features. If the employer can overcome the objections of the revenue authorities or, failing that, will agree to the necessary modifications, a favorable ruling will then be issued. Should the key district revenue officials and the employer fail to reach agreement on the controversial features of the plan, either may request a review of the case by an appeals office of the Internal Revenue Service.[8] If the appeals office supports the key district revenue officials, the employer's only recourse is to the courts. Occasionally, an employer who is convinced that his proposed plan meets all the requirements for qualification will put the plan in operation in the face of an adverse determination letter in the thought that should the contributions to the plan be disallowed upon audit of his income tax return, he would resort to the courts at that time.

It should be noted that advance approval of a pension plan by the Internal Revenue Service does not relieve the employer of the burden of justifying the amount of the deductions claimed in each tax return for contributions to the plan. Moreover, it does not relieve the employer of the responsibility of clearing with the IRS any future changes or modifications in the plan that might affect its qualified status. Nor does it assure the employer that the IRS

---

[7]Form 5300 for a defined benefit plan, Form 5301 for defined contribution plan, Form 5303 for a collectively bargained plan, Form 5307 for an employer that adopts a master or prototype plan, or Form 5309 for an employee stock ownership plan.

[8]Rev. Proc. 80–30.

upon audit will not find that the plan is not qualified, perhaps because it discriminates in practice.

## Announcement of the Plan to Employees

The Employee Retirement Income Security Act of 1974 (ERISA) stipulates that the employer must provide each participant with a summary plan description written in plain, understandable language and must furnish, upon the participant's request, a copy of the complete plan and other related documents.[9] The simplified summary plan description is usually provided in the form of a plan booklet, which is made available to every plan participant at the time he becomes a member of the plan or whenever the booklet is revised. The booklet may be plain and brief or quite elaborate and detailed. It is not unusual for it to contain illustrations, both to enhance its readability and to portray an attractive picture of the benefits awaiting the employee who remains with the company until retirement or until vesting requirements are met. Some of the more definitive booklets reproduce, in an appendix or annex, the complete text of the plan and related documents.

A pension plan must be communicated to all employees eligible to become members of the plan before the request for approval is submitted to the Internal Revenue Service.[10] There are guidelines concerning what must be included in this presubmission communication. If the request for approval is submitted, this will satisfy the requirement. In other cases, employers post or distribute only very brief announcements with rather limited information about the plan.

## Enrollment of Employees and Establishment of Records

Whether participation in the plan is voluntary or automatic, certain information must be assembled concerning each participant to determine his benefit rights and to calculate the costs and liabilities under the plan. Hence, an individual record is prepared for each participant, showing such information as sex, date of birth, date

---

[9]ERISA §§102, 104(b).
[10]Treas. Reg. 1.401–1(a); Rev. Rul. 71–90.

of employment, present earnings, and beneficiaries (if applicable). If the plan is to be insured by the purchase of individual contracts from an insurer, an application for the coverage will be required of each eligible member of the plan, even though the employer is to bear the entire cost. An individual employee application or acceptance form is also required under *contributory* plans if participation is voluntary. Otherwise, if the plan is to be noncontributory, coverage is automatic, and consent of the employee to participation is not necessary. Sometimes, however, the employees are asked to sign an application for membership in the plan which, in effect, constitutes an agreement to the terms of the plan. Such an agreement is based upon the presumption that the employee has either read or had explained to him the terms of the plan and accepts them as binding on himself in his relationship to the plan.

If the employees are to pay any part of the cost of the plan, participation ordinarily is voluntary and some selling effort may be necessary to obtain a sufficient number of adherents to place the plan in operation.[11] An eligible employee must indicate his willingness to participate by signing an application for membership in the plan which, in addition to binding the employee to the terms of the plan, constitutes an authorization to the employer to deduct from the employee's regular pay his appropriate contribution to the plan.

In preparation for routine administration of the plan, forms must be prepared and records and other procedures set up in the interest of accuracy, promptness, and economy. Such records verify the members' status and rights, and the procedures facilitate the authorization and payment of benefits. An administrative manual may also be prepared, reproducing the various forms and describing the different procedures that will be used in recording additions to membership, terminations of membership, application for retirement, calculation of benefits, and other such actions.

Upon payment of an initial contribution or premium, the plan is presumably fully established and ready for normal operations.

## Operating the Plan

The detailed procedures involved in the operation of a pension plan are influenced considerably by the funding agency used, the size

---

[11]Participation in the plan may be a condition of employment for future employees.

of the plan, the facilities available, and the temperament of the personnel responsible for administration of the plan. A number of functions, however, are common to all plans, irrespective of funding agency, size, or other characteristics. These functions will be described briefly in the following pages.

## Maintenance of Basic Records

The most routine—and yet extremely vital—function associated with the operation of a pension plan is the maintenance of the basic records necessary to establish the rights of the participants[12] and to support the deductions claimed by the employer in his income tax returns. The most basic record has already been alluded to— the one for each participant showing sex, date of birth, date of employment, and earnings. If the plan is contributory, the record for each employee must reflect his cumulative contributions, since they will have a bearing on the sums payable to the employee or his dependents in the event of his death or withdrawal from the plan before retirement. If the plan calls for a unit of benefit for each year of service, the benefits must be recorded as earned in order that the proper amount of benefits will be payable at retirement. If the benefits are purchased in the form of paid-up deferred annuities as they accrue, the amounts of annuities purchased must be recorded. All of the information concerning each participant is not necessarily kept on one form or by the same department.

The cost data needed by the employer to support his income tax deductions can be derived from the basic records maintained for the individual participants.

## Certification and Payment of Benefits

Closely allied to, and in fact flowing out of, the record-keeping function is the certification of benefit entitlement. There may be a number of circumstances under which benefits of some sort become available and some agency must have the responsibility of determining whether all of the conditions for entitlement have been met and, if so, what the amount of the payment should be. For example, when a participant makes application for retirement benefits, some

---

[12]ERISA §209(a).

administrative agency must: (1) verify that the employee has reached the minimum age for retirement, (2) ascertain whether the employee participated in the plan for the prescribed time, and (3) determine the form and compute the amount of benefits, if any, to which the applicant is entitled.

While responsibility for the mechanical or clerical aspect of benefit certification is usually vested in the same administrative agency that maintains the basic records of the plan, the actual or formal approval of a claim for benefits must come from the person or persons charged with overall responsibility for administration of the plan. In small and medium-sized companies, this responsibility may be placed on a single individual, such as the comptroller or treasurer. In some cases, the chief executive of the company may personally supervise the administration of the plan. In the larger companies, however, responsibility for administration of the plan is usually placed on a committee, variously designated as the pension committee, retirement committee, or retirement board. This arrangement is invariably used in multiemployer plans and is highly favored in collectively bargained single employer plans.

Usually the plan document designates a plan administrator,[13] who is responsible under ERISA for satisfying the reporting and disclosure requirements for the plan. If no plan administrator is designated by the terms of the plan, the employer or other plan sponsor is deemed to be the plan administrator. The plan administrator is typically an individual but may be a board or committee. If the employer itself is officially designated plan administrator, the function will actually be delegated to an individual, board, or committee.

The plan administrator usually has jurisdiction over all phases of a plan's operation, but its authority in the sensitive area of benefit certification is of especial significance to participating employees. He interprets the provisions of the plan relating to benefit eligibility and amounts and adjudicates all claims for benefits, whether routine or controversial. If he reaches a negative decision, he must furnish the claimant a written explanation as to why his application for benefits was rejected and must also give him an opportunity for a hearing.[14] His decision in a particular case is final and conclusive,

[13]ERISA §3(16)(A).
[14]ERISA §503.

unless resort is had to the courts or to arbitration,[15] in which event the complainant would have to prove that the decision represented an abuse of discretion or was plainly contrary to law or to the specific terms of the plan.

Under most plans, the actual disbursement of benefits is handled by the insurance company or trustee, as the case may be, but, except as noted above, the authorization to commence benefit payments must come from the governing board.

## Determination and Disposition of Contributions

Sums of money must be set aside periodically if a pension plan is to fulfill the expectations of the participants or, for that matter, to retain its qualified status. For defined contribution plans the timing and size of employer contributions may be specified in the plan document or collective bargaining agreement or may be entirely at the discretion of the employer. For defined benefit plans the employer contributions are designed to be sufficient to fund the promised benefits; these contributions are subject to minimum and maximum limits under law and may also be subject to provisions of the plan document or collective bargaining agreement. Where not otherwise specified, some contribution to the plan is usually made during each tax year, but the timing and size of the contribution need not follow a regular pattern. If the participants are contributing to the plan through weekly or monthly payroll deductions, the employer normally remits their contributions at least once a month.

The bases on which the amount of the periodic contributions is determined may depend upon the type of funding agency utilized. If the benefits are to be provided solely through a group deferred annuity contract or through individual life insurance or annuity contracts, the contributions take the form of premiums (or, in the case of annuity contracts, "purchase payments"), the size of which is a function of the benefit formula and the rate schedule in effect at the time each set of benefits is purchased. In other words, within the framework of a given set of benefits, an employer's contribution

---

[15]See Benjamin Aaron, *Legal Status of Employee Benefit Rights under Private Pension Plans* (Homewood, Ill.: Richard D. Irwin, 1961), pp. 15–16, 43–45.

for any particular time interval is determined by the price charged by the insurance company for desired benefits. The contributions are paid to the insurance company, either directly or through the intermediacy of a trustee.

If the benefits of the plan are not to be funded in the above manner, the contributions must be deposited with a trustee or in an unallocated account of an insurance company. If the plan was negotiated between labor and management, the amount of the periodic contributions may be fixed by the terms of the labor contract as a given number of cents per hour or as a specified percentage of pay. If the level of contributions is not fixed by the plan document or agreement between the employer and the union, the amount to be set aside each year, or at some time interval, will normally be determined by the employer. For defined benefit plans this will be based on the advice or recommendation of an actuary.[16]

### Asset Management

One of the most critical functions associated with a pension plan is the investment of its assets. This function may be performed by the plan sponsor (through an investment committee), a bank or trust company, a life insurance company, an investment company (mutual fund), or an investment adviser. Title to the assets must be vested in a trustee (if they are not managed by a life insurance company), but the investment decisions may be made by someone other than the trustee.

The investment of plan assets is discussed in later chapters.

### Periodic Reports

The plan administrator must file an annual report[17] with the Internal Revenue Service and must provide a summary annual report to the plan participants. Some of the information for the annual reports to the regulatory agencies and plan participants comes from the records of the plan administrator, but most of it comes from

---

[16]The funding of defined contribution plans and defined benefit plans is discussed in detail in later chapters.

[17]Form 5500, 5000-C, 5500-EZ, or 5500-R. The Internal Revenue Service provides a copy to the Department of Labor.

other organizations that provide services to the plan. The trustee or investment manager supplies information concerning investment transactions, investment income, asset values, and the distribution of plan assets by broad categories. For defined benefit plans, actuarial information will be provided by the plan's actuary. The authenticity of the information in the official annual report may be certified by an independent accountant, and for defined benefit plans the plan actuary must make certain certifications as to the actuarial assumptions and methods used in determining plan costs and liabilities. Needless to say, compliance with the official reporting requirements is time-consuming and costly. However, the reports serve essential regulatory and communication functions.

### *Communication with Employees*

Progressive employers maintain a continuous program of information concerning their pension plan in an effort to sustain employee interest in, and appreciation of, the plan. Emphasis is placed on the benefits and advantages of the plan and on the responsibilities of the employees toward the plan. Communication media used include the company magazine, posters and displays, movies, letters from the top executive, the summary plan description, individual interviews and group meetings, individual benefit statements, and the summary annual report.

---

## Questions

1.  To what extent is the choice of funding agency and funding instrument (contractual arrangement) for a particular pension plan influenced by the person or organization that persuades the employer to install the plan?

2.  Is there any danger that the advice offered to a business firm considering the installation of a pension plan will be influenced by the manner in which the adviser (or consultant) is compensated for his advice? Explain.

3.  What role may an actuary play in the development and installation of a pension plan? What is the role that he is uniquely qualified to perform?

4.  Is it feasible to develop the terms of a pension plan independently of the choice of funding agency or funding instrument? Explain.

5.  Explain the relationship, if any, between the pension plan (as represented by the plan document), the trust agreement or insurance company contract, a relevant collective bargaining agreement, and the plan booklet or summary plan description.

6.  What is the purpose of a so-called determination letter sought from the Internal Revenue Service by an employer in the process of establishing a pension plan?

7.  Once the Internal Revenue Service issues a favorable determination letter to the sponsor of a pension plan, does it exercise any further jurisdiction over the plan? Explain.

8.  In a typical large single employer pension plan, what office or agency of the employing firm determines the benefit entitlement of a retiring employee and ascertains the amount of benefit to be paid? Are the procedures any different if the benefits have been purchased from a life insurance company? What remedies does the retiring plan member have if he disagrees with a decision of the administering agency concerning his benefit rights?

9.  In what specific respects has ERISA complicated the record-keeping function of a pension plan?

10. What functions associated with a pension plan are normally performed "in house" (that is, by the employer) and what are those normally performed by outside or external agencies?

# 3 | Regulatory Environment

Despite the fact that pension plans in the private sector of the economy were holding out the promise of retirement and other benefits to almost half of the nonagricultural work force in that sector and had accumulated an estimated $175 billion of assets to meet benefit promises, they were subject to only peripheral regulation prior to 1974. The prime statutory source of regulation was the Internal Revenue Code, which had only limited regulatory objectives. There was the largely ineffectual Federal Welfare and Pension Plans Disclosure Act that was enacted in 1958 and substantially amended in 1962. The Labor-Management Relations Act of 1947 (better known as the Taft-Hartley Act) imposed certain restrictions on collectively bargained multiemployer pension plans, the principal one being that they be jointly administered by labor and management trustees. Plans funded through life insurance companies had the benefit of general insurance regulatory laws, especially those relating to solvency and investments. The assets of plans funded through banks and trust companies had the protection afforded through general trust law, applicable investment statutes, and the supervision of federal and state banking authorities. Theoretically the fiduciary responsibility laws of the various states applied to persons and institutions managing the assets of pension plans, but the reach of the laws and the scope of the remedies were considered by most legal experts to be inadequate for pension plans, especially those operating across state boundaries. Thus, there was no single law or body of law designed to regulate the totality of the private pension institution. This situation was altered with the enactment of the Employee Retirement Income Security Act of 1974, better known by its acronym ERISA.

This chapter describes briefly the nature of pension plan regulation prior to ERISA; the political and legislative process by which ERISA came into being; the major features of ERISA; the general conditions that a pension plan must meet to receive favorable tax treatment; procedures available for the enforcement of benefit rights; reporting requirements; and the fiduciary standards that are now applicable to persons and institutions who control pension plans and manage their assets.

## Nature of Regulation Prior to 1974

This section is concerned only with the Internal Revenue Code and the Federal Welfare and Pension Plans Disclosure Act, the only two statutes that had general applicability to private pension plans.[1]

### *Internal Revenue Code*

The Internal Revenue Code contained certain provisions specifically directed toward pension plans as early as 1921, but it was not until 1942 that Congress attempted through the instrumentality of the Code to lay down general guidelines for the design and operation of private pension plans (along with profit sharing and stock bonus plans). The primary purposes of the 1942 amendments to the Code were (1) to prevent discrimination in favor of shareholders, officers, supervisors, and highly compensated individuals with respect to the coverage, benefits, and financing of private pension plans and (2) to protect the federal revenues against excessive and unjustified tax deductions. Responsibility for enforcement of the Code provisions was placed on the Internal Revenue Service.

---

[1]For a more comprehensive discussion of federal regulation of private pension plans prior to ERISA, see Edwin W. Patterson, *Legal Protection of Private Expectations* (Homewood, Ill.: Richard D. Irwin, 1960), pp. 85–112.

Over the next 12 years, the IRS promulgated a voluminous body of regulations and rulings designed to implement the dual objectives of the 1942 amendments. These had a material impact on plan design and some impact on plan financing. The Code was extensively revised in 1954, but few changes of any substance were made in the provisions pertaining to pension plans. Certainly, it did not change the philosophy, rationale, or thrust of pension plan regulation.

At no time prior to 1974 did the Code impose any obligation on the IRS to be concerned about the actuarial soundness of private pension plans—their ability to meet their benefit obligations. The IRS did issue a ruling that, if contributions to a pension plan were suspended, the plan could lose its qualified status if the unfunded liability at that time (or at any time thereafter) exceeded the initial unfunded liability or if the benefits to be paid or made available were adversely affected. To prevent the unfunded accrued liability from exceeding the initial unfunded liability, contributions to the plan had to be at least equal to the normal cost of the plan, plus interest on the initial unfunded liability, plus actuarial losses or less actuarial gains. This rule was widely (but erroneously) interpreted as requiring that plans maintain this level of funding throughout their existence. The IRS did nothing to disabuse plan administrators of this notion, and, as a result, the ruling undoubtedly brought about a minimum level of funding. The IRS also issued a ruling establishing a minimum level of funding for a plan established under a collective bargaining agreement (that expired within a stated period) in order for the plan to meet the requirement that it be intended as a permanent arrangement. However, the IRS had no authority to require a level of funding that would ensure the payment of all accrued benefits in the event of plan termination and because of its emphasis on the prevention of *over*funding it may well be that, on balance, the IRS had an adverse effect on the financial soundness of pension plans.

Nor did the Code provide much protection for the pension rights of individual participants. Except as required to prevent discrimination in favor of officers et al., there were no requirements relating to the preservation of the accrued benefits of participants terminating employment prior to early or normal retirement, the reporting of information to the participants on the status of their benefit accruals, or the enforcement of individual benefit rights. With a few exceptions, such as the prohibition against certain trans-

actions among parties at interest, and the general mandate that the
plan be operated for the exclusive benefit of the participants and
their beneficiaries, the Code articulated no standards of fiduciary
conduct for those responsible for the administration of the plan
and for the management of its assets. There was little or no protection of plan assets against incompetent or dishonest administrators, apart from the remedies in general trust law and the criminal
code.

### Federal Welfare and Pension Plans Disclosure Act

Congress sought to provide somewhat greater protection for the
rights of individual participants and protection against mismanage-
ment of plan assets through the enactment in 1958 of the Federal
Welfare and Pension Plans Disclosure Act. As its name suggests,
the act was designed to provide plan participants and their beneficiaries with enough information about the nature and operations
of their plan to permit them to detect any malpractices or wrong-
doing and to seek relief for themselves and the plan under existing
state and federal laws.

To carry out the purposes of the act, the administrator of any
plan covering more than 25 employees was required to file a description of the plan, and copies of all pertinent documents, with
the Secretary of Labor within 90 days after establishment and thereafter to render annual reports on the operation of the plan to the
secretary. The plan administrator was also required to make available to plan participants and their beneficiaries, upon their request,
a copy of the plan and the annual reports. The basic purpose of
the act was to protect the plan assets against fraudulent or criminal
behavior of the plan administrator and other parties at interest.
This purpose was to be accomplished through action against the
malfeasors brought by the plan participants under existing state
and federal laws, based upon evidence revealed through the annual
reports. While the act set forth the type of information to be included in the annual reports, the Secretary of Labor was not authorized to prescribe the forms on which the information was to
be submitted. Nor was he given any authority or responsibility to
enforce the act.

The act was amended in 1962 to give the Secretary of Labor
authority to prescribe forms, interpret the provisions of the act,

enforce compliance, and conduct investigations when he had reasonable cause to believe that such investigations would disclose violations of the act. Embezzlement, false reporting, bribery, and kickbacks in connection with welfare and pension plans were made criminal offenses, with the Justice Department being given responsibility, in cooperation with the Labor Department, of bringing appropriate legal action. Thus, the burden of protecting the plan assets against maladministration or outright fraud was shifted from the plan participants to government agencies. However, the thrust of the law continued to be protection of plan assets, rather than preservation of the rights of individual participants to those assets.

## Employee Retirement Income Security Act

### Gestation of ERISA

ERISA underwent a long period of gestation. Its origins can be traced to a suggestion in the long-since forgotten Report of the Commission on Money and Credit[2] that the relationship between the assets of a pension plan and the affairs of the sponsoring firm and the interests of the plan participants should be defined. The report also called for the periodic reporting of investments of pension plans and the establishment of "an appropriate regulatory body." These recommendations led President Kennedy in his 1962 Economic Report to comment on the savings and capital formation function of private pension plans and to call for a "review of rules governing the investment policies of these funds [plans] and the effects on equity and the efficiency of the tax privileges accorded them."

In March 1962, President Kennedy followed through by appointing a cabinet-level committee, later to be known as the President's Committee on Corporate Pension Funds, and charging it with the task of conducting a "review of the implications of the growing retirement and welfare funds for the financial structure of the economy, as well as a review of the role and character of the private pension and other retirement systems in the economic security

---

[2]*Money and Credit,* Report of the Commission on Money and Credit (Englewood Cliffs, N.J.: Prentice-Hall, 1961), p. 176.

system of the nation, and . . . [to consider] . . . how they may contribute more effectively to efficient manpower utilization and mobility.''

The committee developed a *provisional* report, which was submitted to President Kennedy in November 1962. In January 1963, President Kennedy referred the report to his 15-member Advisory Committee on Labor-Management Policy, which made its report to President Johnson in December 1963.[3] The President's Committee on Corporate Pension Funds, after reviewing the recommendations of the Advisory Committee, subsequently submitted a final report to President Johnson in early 1964.[4]

President Johnson held the report for almost a year, reputedly because of concern over its recommendations, before releasing it to the public in January 1965. The report concluded that there is a strong *public* interest in *private* pension plans because (1) they represent a major element in the economic security of millions of American workers and their families; (2) they are a significant, growing source of economic and financial power; (3) they affect the mobility of the American labor force; and (4) they are subsidized by the general body of taxpayers by virtue of the special tax treatment accorded them.[5] It made a number of recommendations designed to protect the public interest, as viewed by the committee, the principal ones proposing a mandatory minimum vesting standard, a mandatory minimum funding standard, a program of pension plan benefits insurance (called pension reinsurance in the report), and a mechanism for pension portability.

Following release of the Report of the President's Committee on Corporate Pension Funds, an Interagency Task Force was appointed to consider public reaction to the report and to develop

---

[3]The senior author of this text served as technical consultant to the Advisory Committee on Labor-Management Policy for the purpose of its review of the provisional report.

[4]*Public Policy and Private Pension Programs,* a Report to the President on Private Employee Retirement Plans by the President's Committee on Corporate Pension Funds and Other Private Retirement and Welfare Programs.

[5]Many tax experts have taken issue with the committee's conclusion that the private pension movement is subsidized by special tax concessions. They argue that private pension plans are taxed in accordance with the general principles of tax law. One of the most persuasive treatises on this theme is Raymond Goetz, *Tax Treatment of Pension Plans: Preferential or Normal* (Washington, D.C.: American Enterprise Institute for Public Policy Research, 1969).

legislation that would implement the recommendations of the report. The deliberations of that body resulted in a bill that was introduced into both houses of Congress in 1968 but did not get beyond hearings. It was rejected by the Nixon administration, which set about to develop its own proposal that was to feature tax incentives for individual retirement arrangements and employee contributions to employer-sponsored plans but was not unveiled until 1971. In the meantime, the House and Senate Labor Subcommittees, controlled by Democrats, were preparing their own proposals, and many Congressmen and Senators, recognizing the growing political appeal of "pension reform," introduced bills under their personal sponsorship.

The labor committees of the House and Senate reported their bills out in 1972. Over the next several months, the Senate Finance Committee and the House Ways and Means Committee began to assert jurisdiction over the legislation in their respective chambers, since the labor committee bills and a host of others with similar features were largely directed at plans that achieved their legitimacy by compliance with the Internal Revenue Code. Moreover, the administration bill contained some proposals for change in the tax treatment of pension plans. This jurisdiction dispute delayed consideration of pension legislation on the floor of the two houses for more than a year. The Senate Finance Committee did not develop and report out its bill until August of 1973. The House Ways and Means Committee did not report out its bill until February 1974.

During the final stages of the legislative process, the bills of the four committees were similar in substance (but diverse as to detail), except that only the bills from the tax-writing committees contained the administration's proposals for tax incentives for individual plans. The principal difference—and one that was highly charged with emotion—was the choice of a federal agency to administer the new body of law. The two labor committee bills called for administration of the law by the Labor Department; the tax committee bills gave the Treasury Department exclusive jurisdiction over all provisions affecting the tax qualification of pension plans. The matter was resolved in the Senate by splitting the agency jurisdiction. In the House, the compromise took the form of enacting both committee bills—with all their conflicts on language, substance, and enforcement (i.e., jurisdiction)—as separate titles in a single act.

The Senate adopted its version of pension reform in September 1973; the House did not act until March 1974. A conference committee with representatives and staff from the four legislative committees struggled for the next five months to iron out the differences and inconsistencies in the two bills. The final compromise version was enacted by both houses of Congress in August 1974 and signed into law by President Ford on Labor Day, September 2, almost 10 years after the Report of the President's Committee on Corporate Pension Funds was released and more than 7 years after the introduction of the first pension reform bill.[6]

### Structure and Summary of ERISA

The Employee Retirement Income Security Act of 1974 is a massive and exceedingly complex piece of legislation. It is massive because of the scope of the matters covered and the specificity with which the draftsman articulated the Congressional mandate. It is complex, partly because of the technical nature of the subject matter and partly because of the numerous compromises that had to be built into it to satisfy the four legislative committees that worked on the legislation and their staffs.

The major compromise—and one that added length and complexity to the document—was that which bestowed jurisdiction over private pension plans on both the Department of Labor and the Treasury Department. In some areas the jurisdiction is exclusive but in others it is joint and overlapping. Because of the overlapping jurisdiction, the act legislates with respect to certain important matters in two difference sections ("Titles") of the statute and not always in the same language.

One major section (Title I) of the act is concerned with the protection of employee benefit rights. The principal matters dealt with in this section are (1) reporting and disclosure, (2) participation and vesting, (3) funding, and (4) fiduciary responsibility. The provisions dealing with reporting, disclosure, and fiduciary responsibility replace and strengthen those heretofore contained in the

[6]This timetable overlooks the pension "reinsurance" bill introduced in 1964 by Senator Vance Hartke of Indiana and reintroduced with refinements and embellishments in several successive sessions of Congress. See Appendix A of Dan M. McGill, *Guaranty Fund for Private Pension Obligations* (Homewood, Ill.: Richard D. Irwin, 1970).

Federal Welfare and Pension Plans Disclosure Act, which was formally repealed. The Department of Labor has primary jurisdiction over reporting, disclosure, and fiduciary matters, while the Treasury Department has primary jurisdiction over participation, vesting, and funding. However, the Department of Labor is entitled to intervene in any matters or proceedings that materially affect the rights of the participants, even when the matters come under the formal jurisdiction of the Treasury Department and, under prescribed circumstances, can enforce the participation, vesting, funding, reporting, and disclosure requirements through civil procedures, and criminal proceedings. The Treasury Department enforces compliance with the participation, vesting, and funding requirements through tax disqualification and a new excise tax. The provisions of Title I apply to all pension plans, whether qualified or not, established or maintained by employers engaged in interstate commerce or by employee organizations representing employees engaged in interstate commerce, except governmental plans, church plans, unfunded excess benefit plans (as defined in the law), and plans maintained outside the United States primarily for the benefit of persons substantially all of whom are nonresident aliens. These provisions supersede and preempt all state laws applicable to the covered employee benefit plans, except the state laws that regulate insurance, banking, or securities. However, the law explicitly provides that a pension plan is not to be construed as engaging in the insurance or banking business for purposes of this exception.

Title IV of the act established a program of pension plan benefits insurance whose purpose is to ensure ultimate fulfillment of the vested rights of participants. The program is administered through the nonprofit Pension Benefit Guaranty Corporation (PBGC) located in the Department of Labor, with the Secretary of Labor as chairman of the board. The other board members are the Secretary of the Treasury and the Secretary of Commerce. There is an advisory committee of seven persons, appointed by the president, representing management, labor, and the public. This section of the act applies to all qualified defined benefit pension plans, with specified exceptions.

The other major section of the act (Title II) is primarily concerned with tax matters and, in form, is an amendment to the Internal Revenue Code of 1954. Thus, it pertains primarily to qualified plans. It contains the same requirements with respect to participation, vesting, and funding that are found in Title I, but in the context of conditions that must be satisfied for qualification of a plan. As amended by ERISA, the Code provides for minimum standards of funding of general applicability, enforceable through an excise tax, thus, for the first time, placing responsibility on the IRS for enforcing the actuarial soundness of plans falling under its jurisdiction.

Title III of the act directed the Secretaries of Labor and the Treasury to establish a Joint Board for the Enrollment of Actuaries to set the standards and qualifications for persons performing actuarial services for pension plans under the act. The actuarial reports required under the law must be signed by persons, called "enrolled" actuaries, who have met these standards. The actuary must certify annually that the actuarial assumptions and methods used to determine the costs and funding requirements of the plan are, in the aggregate, reasonable and reflect the actuary's best estimate of anticipated experience under the plan.

The IRS is responsible for developing regulations for the participation, vesting, and funding provisions of ERISA, except for certain matters specifically delegated to the Secretary of Labor under the act; but in doing so, it must consult and coordinate with the Secretary of Labor. By the same token, the Secretary of Labor must consult with the Secretary of the Treasury when developing regulations for matters coming under its jurisdiction.

The term *pension plan* has entirely different meanings in Title I and Title II. In Title II and in the Internal Revenue Code, pension plan refers to one of three types of qualified asset accumulation plans, namely, pension plans, profit sharing plans, and stock bonus plans. In Title I, however, pension plan includes all three types of qualified plans plus unqualified plans that provide retirement income or result in deferral of income.[7]

Title II also contains tax provisions not directly related to participation, vesting, or funding. Two of these were designed to expand the coverage of private pension arrangements. One liberalized the plans for self-employed individuals (generally referred to as Keogh or HR 10 plans). The second permitted individuals not covered by a qualified or governmental plan or a tax-deferred annuity to establish their own individual retirement savings plans with de-

[7]ERISA §3(2); I.R.C. §401(a).

ferral of tax on the contributions and investment earnings. This type of plan can be funded through an individual retirement account (IRA) administered by a trustee or custodian or an individual retirement annuity (IRA). Other provisions changed the tax treatment of lump-sum distributions and imposed certain limits on tax-deferred annuities issued under Section 403(b) of the Code. All of these provisions are under the jurisdiction of the Treasury Department (with delegation to the IRS).

Statutes enacted since ERISA have made important changes in the laws affecting pension plans. These include the Tax Reform Act of 1976, the Social Security Amendments of 1977, the Revenue Act of 1978, the 1978 Amendments to the Age Discrimination in Employment Act, the Multiemployer Pension Plans Amendment Act of 1980, the Economic Recovery Tax Act of 1981, the Tax Equity and Fiscal Responsibility Act of 1982, the 1983 Social Security Amendments, the Deficit Reduction Act of 1984, the Retirement Equity Act of 1984, the Single-Employer Pension Plan Amendments Act of 1986, the Tax Reform Act of 1986, and the Omnibus Budget Reconciliation Act of 1987.

The Tax Reform Act of 1986 touches almost every aspect of employee benefits and does so in enormous detail. It necessitated amendment of virtually every existing qualified pension, profit-sharing, and stock bonus plan. One objective of the changes affecting pension plans was to raise taxes to offset the revenue loss resulting from lower tax rates and other aspects of tax reform. Changes that increase revenues included both increased taxes on distributions and reductions in the maximum limits on contributions and benefits under plans. Other changes were designed to assure that benefits would be broadly available by strengthening the requirements concerning coverage, vesting, and integration of pensions with Social Security. Other changes were designed to stop actual or perceived abuse.

The legal requirements pertaining to participation, vesting, and funding are discussed in detail in later chapters as an integral part of the general treatment of those topics. The remaining portions of this chapter are devoted to a discussion of several other basic conditions that must be met by a pension plan under the law in effect today to achieve and retain a qualified status; the information that must be made available to participants and beneficiaries, whether the plan is qualified or not; procedures available for the enforcement of benefit rights; reporting requirements; and the fiduciary framework within which all plans must operate. Pension plan benefits insurance, minimum funding requirements, the tax treatment of plans, and other legal requirements are discussed elsewhere in the text.

## Basic Requirements for Qualification of a Pension Plan

The basic requirements for qualification are found in the Internal Revenue Code of 1986, as amended, and as elucidated by a series of regulations and rulings. Meeting these requirements is of crucial importance to the employer, since otherwise he could not take an income tax deduction for his contributions (unless they are vested in the accounts of individual participants), and the investment earnings on the plan assets, a significant source of cost saving, would not be exempt from current taxation. The participants also have a strong stake in the tax status of the plan. By and large, these requirements are designed to ensure that the plan is operated for the exclusive benefit of a broad classification of employees.

### Written Document

The first and most elemental requirement for every qualified (or nonqualified) plan is that its terms be set forth in a written document.[8] The fundamental purpose of this requirement is to ensure that the plan is a formal arrangement, communicated as such to all employees affected, and distinguishable from the informal and unenforceable arrangements that characterized the early years of the private pension movement in this country. On a more operational level, the plan needs to be in writing so the participants may examine the document and determine their rights and obligations thereunder. As a part of the disclosure requirements of ERISA, the plan administrator must make copies of the plan and related documents available to the employees, as well as a summary of the essential features and provisions.[9]

---

[8]ERISA §402(a)(1); Treas. Reg. §1.401–1(a)(2).
[9]ERISA §101(a).

## Permanency

Although not specified in any statute, IRS regulations require that the plan be established with the intent that it be a permanent and continuing arrangement.[10] A plan that is abandoned without a valid business reason within a few years after it is set up will be deemed not to have been a bona fide program for the exclusive benefit of employees in general from its inception. In that event, employer income tax deductions for contributions to the plan will be disallowed for all open tax years. To prevent discrimination in the event of early termination, all plans must include a limitation on the benefits of the 25 most highly paid employees should the plan be terminated within the first 10 years.[11]

## Segregation of Plan Assets

The assets of both qualified and nonqualified plans must be legally separated from those of the employer or other sponsoring organization. This is to comply with ERISA's fiduciary requirements, as well as with the Internal Revenue Code's mandate that the plan be operated for the exclusive benefit of the participants and their beneficiaries.

This segregation of plan assets can be accomplished by having them held in trust under a suitably drawn trust instrument[12] or held by a life insurance company under one or more of the various contracts that they make available for this purpose.[13] If a trust is used, the trustee may be an individual (or more likely, a group of individuals) or an institution with trust powers. A trust may be used for convenience or control even when the funding agency (the organization that holds and manages the assets) is a life insurance company. In that event, the insurance or annuity contracts serving as the funding receptacles are treated as trust assets. While not required, a trust or custodial account serves a useful purpose if the plan is funded through individual life insurance or annuity contracts.

---

[10]Treas. Reg. 1.401–1(b)(2). Courts have rejected this IRS view that a permanence requirement exists. *Lincoln Electric Co. Employees' Profit-Sharing Trust* (CA–6, 1951 rev'g and rem'g TC) 51-2 USTC §9371, 190F 2d 326.

[11]Treas. Reg. 1.401–4(c).

[12]ERISA §403(a); I.R.C. §401(a), (f).

[13]ERISA §403(b); I.R.C. §§403(a), 404(a)(2), 401(g).

## Coverage

The plan must benefit employees in general and not just a limited number of favored employees, and each plan is required to cover a minimum number of participants.[14] The coverage requirements, being a fundamental element of plan design, are discussed in detail in a later chapter.

## Nondiscrimination in Contributions or Benefits

Not only may a qualified pension plan not discriminate in favor of highly compensated employees about coverage, it may not do so with respect to contributions or benefits.[15] This sounds like a simple concept, easily enforceable, but in practice, a determination as to whether a particular arrangement will discriminate in favor of the proscribed group may be difficult and complex. In general, if the benefit structure is deemed to be equitable, it does not matter that the dollar contributions on behalf of the various participants are not equal. By the same token, if the contribution formula is equitable—when the employer's obligation is stated in terms of contributions—it is immaterial that the benefits will vary among the participants.

Variations in contributions or benefits are permissible as long as the plan, viewed as a whole and with all its attendant circumstances, does not favor employees who are highly compensated. It is of special significance that contributions or benefits based on remuneration excluded from the OASDI taxable wage base may differ from contributions or benefits related to that base, as long as the resulting differences in contributions or benefits do not exceed specified limits.[16] These limits are described in Chapter 10.

In the attempt to enforce this concept, statutes regulations and rulings have had a vital influence on plan design. Among the plan provisions that have been affected by governmental requirements in this area are those relating to the benefit formula; the salary base to be used for benefit determination; vesting; normal, early, and delayed retirement; annuity options; employee contribution rates;

---

[14]I.R.C. §§410(b), 401(a)(26).

[15]I.R.C. §401(a)(4).

[16]I.R.C. §401(a)(5), (1).

plan termination; and the whole complex subject of integration with Social Security (discussed in Chapter 10).

## Participation and Vesting Requirements

As noted above, the Internal Revenue Code and implementing regulations have long contained provisions relating to participation (stated in terms of coverage) and the crediting of benefits. These provisions had a limited and specific purpose: to prevent discrimination in favor of certain described classes of individuals. ERISA and the Tax Reform Act of 1986 enlarged these requirements by making them more rigorous and more general in application.[17] ERISA's participation and vesting requirements, which are discussed in later chapters of the book, are not primarily directed at discrimination and, through Title I (the labor portion of the act), even apply to plans that do not seek tax qualification. They are intended to foster the accrual and preservation of benefits with respect to all classes of actual and potential plan participants.

## Definitely Determinable Benefits

Under the Internal Revenue Code, a pension plan must provide definitely determinable benefits. This is a technical requirement designed to distinguish a pension plan from a profit sharing plan, which is subject to many of the same qualification requirements as a pension plan but is treated differently for some tax purposes. A plan that provides retirement benefits to employees and their beneficiaries will be deemed a pension plan if either the benefits payable to the employees or the contributions required of the employer can be definitely determined.[18] Benefits under a defined benefit plan are not definitely determinable if funds arising from forfeitures on termination of service, or other reason, may be used to provide increased benefits for the remaining participants, instead of being used as soon as possible to reduce the amount of contributions by the employer. (In a defined contribution plan, forfeitures from terminations *may* be allocated among the remaining participants.)

---

[17]ERISA §§202, 203, 204; I.R.C. §§410(a), 411.
[18]I.R.C. §401(a)(8), Treas. Reg. 1.401–1(b)(1)(i).

Benefits that vary with the increase or decrease in the market value
of the assets from which such benefits are payable or that vary
with the fluctuation of a specified and generally recognized cost-
of-living index, are consistent with the requirement for a pension
plan to provide definitely determinable benefits.

## Communication and Enforcement of Benefit Rights

### Communication of Benefit Rights to Plan Participants and Their Beneficiaries

The Internal Revenue Service has long required that a qualified
plan be reduced to writing and be communicated by appropriate
means to the plan participants and their beneficiaries.[19] The labor
portion of ERISA, applicable to all pension and welfare plans, with
some exceptions, whether qualified or not, contains much more
detailed requirements for informing plan participants of their rights
and status under the plan. Willful failure of the plan administrator
to comply with these provisions subjects him to both criminal and
civil sanctions.[20]

Since the plan document is usually complex and written in legal
jargon, the plan administrator is required to furnish to each participant and beneficiary a summary plan description (SPD) written
in a manner "calculated to be understood by the average plan
participant or beneficiary."[21] Detailed regulations specify the content of summary plan descriptions.[22] The summary must include,
*inter alia,* the name and address of the plan administrator, names
and addresses of persons responsible for the management of the
plan assets, important plan provisions, description of benefits, the
circumstances that may result in disqualification or ineligibility, and
the procedures to be followed in presenting claims for benefits
under the plan. Summary plan descriptions are to be furnished to
the participants within 120 days after the plan is established or, if

[19]Treas. Reg. 1.401–1(a)(2).
[20]ERISA §501.
[21]ERISA §§101(a)(1), 102(a).
[22]29 CFR 2520.102–1, 2, 3, 4.

later, within 90 days after an individual becomes a participant.[23] Updated plan descriptions are to be provided to participants every five years whenever there have been plan amendments in the interim.[24] In any case, a plan description, old or revised, is to be provided every 10 years. In addition, participants are to receive a summary of material modifications in a plan within 210 days after the end of the plan year in which the change or changes occur. A copy of the summary plan description and of any summary of material modifications must be filed with the Department of Labor.[25]

The plan administrator is also required to make available to the participants at his principal office (and at such other places as may be prescribed by regulations) the entire plan document and any collective bargaining agreement, trust agreement, insurance contract, or other instrument associated with the plan.[26] Upon written request, the administrator must furnish such documents, the plan description, and the latest annual report directly to a participant; but a reasonable charge may be made to cover the cost of complying with such a request.[27]

The administrator is required to furnish each participant within seven months after the close of the plan year a copy of the summary annual report (SAR), containing certain financial information about the plan.[28]

Upon termination of employment, upon a one-year break in service, or upon the request of a plan participant or beneficiary, the plan administrator must provide, on the basis of the latest information available, the total benefits that have accrued in respect of the participant, as well as those that have vested or become nonforfeitable.[29] No more than one request per year may be made by a participant or beneficiary for this information. Once a year, the employer submits to the Secretary of the Treasury a list of employees who terminated during the year with vested benefits, along with the amount of benefits, and the secretary sends a copy of this

---

[23]ERISA §104(b)(1)(A).
[24]ERISA §104(b)(1)(B).
[25]ERISA §104(a)(1).
[26]ERISA §104(b)(2).
[27]ERISA §104(b)(4).
[28]ERISA §104(b)(3); 29 CFR 2520.104b–10.
[29]ERISA §§105, 209; I.R.C. §6057(e).

list to the Social Security Administration.[30] The latter will provide this information to the participant or his beneficiary upon request and automatically when application is made for Social Security old-age benefits.

## Enforcement of Benefit Rights

If a benefit claim of a plan participant or beneficiary is denied, the plan administrator must inform the claimant in writing of the denial of the claim, setting forth the specific reasons for disapproval in a manner calculated to be understood by the claimant.[31] In addition, the plan administrator is required to afford a reasonable opportunity to any participant or beneficiary whose claim for benefits has been denied for a full and fair review of the decision by the plan administrator. If still dissatisfied with the administrator's decision, the claimant may bring suit in a federal district court for enforcement of his claim, or under certain circumstances in a state court of competent jurisdiction.[32] If the claimant brings the action in a federal court, he must provide a copy of the complaint to the Secretary of Labor and the Secretary of Treasury by certified mail. At their discretion, either secretary or both may intervene in the suit.[33]

It is unlawful for the plan administrator or other person to discharge, fine, suspend, expel, discipline, or discriminate against a plan participant or beneficiary for exercising any right under the law or the plan or coercively to interfere through the use of fraud, force, violence, or intimidation with the exercise of any right under the plan or applicable law.[34] Any person who willfully uses fraud, force, or violence, or threatens to restrain, coerce, or intimidate any participant or beneficiary for the purpose of interfering with his rights is subject to criminal penalties,[35] in addition to the civil enforcement actions available to prevent any interference.

---

[30]I.R.C. §6057; IRS Form 5500 Schedule SSA.
[31]ERISA §503; 29 CFR 2560.503–1.
[32]ERISA §502(a)(1).
[33]ERISA §502(h).
[34]ERISA §510.
[35]ERISA §511.

## Reporting Requirements

ERISA requires certain reports that must be submitted to government agencies on behalf of all plans. Annual reports are required, as well as reports upon certain events. Certain plans are exempted from the various reporting requirements.

For the annual report,[36] plans with 100 or more participants must complete Form 5500, while smaller plans complete the simpler Form 5500-C or Form 5500-R (or Form 5500-EZ in the case of certain plans with only one participant). The appropriate form must be filed with IRS within seven months after the end of the plan year unless an extension is obtained. IRS provides a copy of the report to the Department of Labor and provides certain information from the reports to the Pension Benefit Guaranty Corporation.

Form 5500 (and the shorter Form 5500-C) includes identifying information, statistics on participants, a balance sheet, a statement of income and expense, and other information about the operation of the plan. The form must disclose compensation paid from the plan to persons who rendered services to the plan. Plans with fewer than 100 participants generally may file a shorter Form 5500-R in two out of every three years.[37] If the plan had any prohibited transactions involving a party-in-interest, a detailed schedule must be attached. For plans with 100 or more participants, a detailed schedule of all assets must be attached, as well as schedules of any loans or leases in default, and a schedule of all transactions exceeding 3 percent of plan assets.

The financial statements and schedules required for the annual report must be examined by an independent qualified public accountant retained by the plan on behalf of all its participants. The accountant must give an opinion on whether the financial statement and supporting schedules are presented fairly in conformity with generally accepted accounting principles applied on a basis consistent with the preceding year. Such an opinion has to be based upon an examination carried out in accordance with generally accepted auditing standards. For purposes of ERISA, a qualified public accountant includes a certified public accountant, a licensed

---

[36]ERISA §103; I.R.C. Sec. 6058(a).

[37]Form instructions specify when use of Form 5500-R is permitted.

public accountant, and any person certified by the Secretary of Labor as a qualified public accountant in accordance with regulations published by him for a person who practices in a state that has no certification or licensing procedures for accountants. Plans with less than 100 participants are not required to have an audited financial statement.

If plan benefits are provided by an insurance company, Schedule A must be attached to the annual report. Schedule A reports the premiums paid, benefits paid, the number of persons covered, charges for administrative expenses, commissions paid to licensed agents or brokers, dividends credited, and other information. Insurance companies must transmit and certify the required information to the plan administrator within 120 days after the close of the plan year.

If the plan is subject to the funding requirements of ERISA, it must retain an enrolled actuary on behalf of all its participants.[38] The actuary must prepare an annual actuarial statement, Schedule B, which is attached to Form 5500, 5500-C, 5500-R, or 5500-EZ.[39] Schedule B includes an exhibit of the "funding standard account," which shows whether the funding requirements have been satisfied. It also includes additional information from the most recent actuarial valuation. The actuary must attach a statement of actuarial assumptions and methods used and certain other information. He must certify that the actuarial assumptions used to compute plan costs and liabilities are in the aggregate reasonably related to the experience of the plan and to reasonable expectations and represent his best estimate of anticipated experience under the plan. In making his certification, the actuary may rely upon the correctness of any accounting matter about which any qualified public accountant has expressed an opinion, if he so states his reliance. By the same token, an accountant may rely on the correctness of any actuarial matter certified by any enrolled actuary if the accountant indicates his reliance on such certification.[40]

In event of a merger, consolidation, or transfer of assets or liabilities involving a qualified plan, the plan administrator must file

---

[38]ERISA §103 (a) (4).
[39]ERISA §103 (d); I.R.C. §6059.
[40]ERISA §103 (a) (3) (B), (4) (D).

Form 5310 with IRS at least 30 days before the event. In the case of a defined benefit plan, an actuarial statement must be attached indicating that ERISA's rules concerning such events have been satisfied.[41]

Upon plan termination, the plan sponsor will ordinarily submit the same Form 5310 to request a determination concerning the qualification of the plan at that juncture. In addition, for a single employer plan subject to plan benefits insurance, the plan administrator of a defined benefit plan must provide advance notification of a plan termination to PBGC and to participants, as described in Chapter 24.

For plans covered by plan benefits insurance, Form PBGC-1 must be filed with PBGC within seven months after the beginning of the plan year to transmit the annual premium payment.

When a plan is established or amended, the plan sponsor will ordinarily request a determination of the plan's qualified status by submitting appropriate forms and information to IRS.

## Fiduciary Responsibility

ERISA imposes fiduciary responsibilities on any person who exercises any discretionary authority or control over the management of a pension plan, its administration, or its assets; or renders investment advice for a fee or other form of compensation.[42] Under this definition, directors and certain officers of the plan sponsor, members of a plan's investment committee, and persons who select these individuals are regarded to be fiduciaries. A fiduciary status attaches to these persons by virtue of their having authority and responsibility with respect to the matters in question, apart from their formal title. Investment advisers are by definition fiduciaries, and other consultants or advisers may be construed to be fiduciaries because of the special expertise (and hence authority) that they bring to the management or administration of the plan or its assets. In practice, the determination of who is a fiduciary under the plan turns to a great extent on the facts and circumstances of the case. While every person who has any official connection with a pension

---

[41]I.R.C. §6058 (b).
[42]ERISA §3 (21).

plan may incur some fiduciary obligation, not all persons who become fiduciaries have obligations extending to every phase of the management and administration of the plan. The obligations are governed by the nature of the duties involved.

## Named Fiduciaries

In order that the participants may know who is responsible for operating the plan, the plan document must provide for one or more "named fiduciaries" who jointly or severally shall have authority to control and manage the operation and administration of the plan.[43] Such persons may be identified by name or position in the plan document or be designated by a procedure that is set out in the document. For example, the plan may provide that the employer's board of directors is to select the person or persons to manage the plan. Under a collectively bargained multiemployer plan, the named fiduciaries would normally be the joint board of trustees selected in accordance with the procedure described in the plan document. The named fiduciaries may serve in more than one fiduciary capacity under the plan. For example, it is not unusual for a named fiduciary to serve also as administrator and trustee of the plan.[44]

## Management of Plan Assets

The management of the plan assets is an especially critical fiduciary function. Unless the plan is funded through a life insurance company or is a type (Keogh plan or individual retirement account) that is authorized to use a custodial account without a trustee, the assets must be held in trust by individual or corporate trustees.[45] The trustees may be appointed in the plan document, in the trust agreement, or by action of the named fiduciary or fiduciaries. However, to emphasize the importance of this responsibility the trustees must accept appointment before they can act in that capacity.

The trustees may be given exclusive control over the investment of the plan assets subject to applicable law, in which event they

---

[43]ERISA §402 (a) (2).
[44]ERISA §402 (c) (1).
[45]ERISA §403 (a).

are fully accountable for the results of their stewardship. However, the plan may provide that the trustees will be subject to the direction of the named fiduciaries.[46] This is generally accomplished by placing investment responsibilities in an investment committee appointed under the terms of the plan. (For example, the plan may specify that the investment committee is to consist of the president, financial vice president, and comptroller of the employer firm.) Since investment decisions are basic to plan operations, members of such an investment committee must be named fiduciaries. If the plan so provides, the trustee must follow the directions of the investment committee unless it is clear on their face that the actions to be taken under those directions would be prohibited by the fiduciary responsibility rules of ERISA or would be contrary to the terms of the trust or the plan. If the trustee properly follows the instructions of the investment committee, it is not legally responsible for any losses that may arise from compliance with the instructions.

Instead of directing that investment decisions be made by the plan trustee or an investment committee, the plan document may authorize a named fiduciary with respect to the control or management of plan assets to appoint a qualified investment manager (or managers) to manage all or part of the plan assets.[47] However, he must exercise prudence in selecting the investment manager and in continuing its use. In this case, the plan trustee would no longer have any responsibility for managing the assets controlled by the qualified investment manager and would not be liable for the acts or omissions of the investment manager.[48] Also, as long as the named fiduciary had chosen and retained the investment manager prudently, the named fiduciary would not be liable for the acts and omissions of the manager.[49] Investment responsibilities can be legally delegated only to an investment adviser registered under the Investment Advisers Act of 1940, a bank (as defined in that act), or an insurance company qualified under the laws of two or more states to provide investment management services.[50] To be quali-

[46]Ibid.
[47]ERISA §402 (c) (3).
[48]ERISA §405 (d).
[49]ERISA §405 (c).
[50]ERISA §3 (38).

fied, the investment manager must acknowledge in writing that it is a fiduciary under the plan.

The named fiduciary may allocate plan assets to several investment managers: to diversify investments, to obtain a wider range of investment philosophy and judgment, to encourage competition in investment performance among the various managers, or for any business reasons. In that event, each investment manager is responsible for the management of the assets entrusted to it and is not a co-fiduciary with the persons or institutions managing the other trusts.[51]

The trustee may hire agents to perform ministerial acts but is expected to exercise prudence in the selection and retention of such agents.

A trust is not required for plan assets that consist of insurance or annuity contracts issued by a legally licensed life insurance company.[52] Nevertheless, the person who holds the contracts is a fiduciary and must observe the ERISA rules of fiduciary conduct with respect to the contracts. For example, he must prudently take and maintain exclusive control over the contracts and must use prudent care and skill in preserving the property. To the extent that the law treats assets held by a life insurance company as "plan assets," the insurance company is treated as fiduciary with respect to the plan and must meet the ERISA fiduciary standards.

### Nondiversion of Assets

It is illegal for a plan fiduciary to divert any of the plan assets or income to any other purpose than the payment of benefits to plan participants and their beneficiaries and defraying reasonable expenses of administering the plan.[53] The trust agreement or other relevant documents must contain a specific statement to the effect that no funds can be diverted until all claims against the plan have been discharged. This prohibition is an integral part of the overall regulatory goal of having the plan set up for the exclusive benefit of a broad class of employees, with the employer making non-

---

[51]ERISA §405 (b) (3).
[52]ERISA §403 (b) (1).
[53]ERISA §§403 (c) (1), 404 (a) (1), 4044 (d); I.R.C. §401 (a) (2).

withdrawable contributions to the plan and the assets being managed in the interest of, and in a manner protective of the rights of, the plan participants and their beneficiaries.

The law intends that the employer contributions generally be irrevocable transfers of assets to the plan, not to be recaptured through plan termination after the favored participants have been provided for. There are certain circumstances, however, under which the employer is permitted to recover all or some portion of a contribution that he has made to his pension plan. The first involves a contribution to a newly established or amended plan on the presumption and *on the condition* that the plan be adjudged by the IRS as a tax-qualified plan. If, in fact, an adverse ruling is made by IRS, the employer may recover his contribution if the plan so provides and if claim for recovery is made within one year after denial of qualification.[54]

The second circumstance is similar, involving a contribution made on the condition that it be currently deductible for income tax purposes, a condition that is satisfied only if the plan continues to be qualified and the contribution does not exceed the amount that can be deducted currently under the limitations of the Code. If all or a portion of the deduction is disallowed, the employer may recover that portion of his contribution that was disallowed, provided the plan calls for such recovery and claim is made within one year after disallowance of the deduction.[55]

The employer may also recover a contribution based on a mistake of fact, such as an arithmetical error in the calculation of the amount that was required to be made to the plan or could be deducted in the current year. The claims for recovery must be filed within one year after the contribution was made.[56]

Finally, if a plan terminates in an acceptable manner and all benefits and other obligations are fully discharged, the employer may recover any assets that remain, if the plan document so provides.[57] This recovery is permitted only if the surplus arose out of an "erroneous actuarial computation," meaning that the costs to

---

[54]ERISA §403 (c) (2) (B).
[55]ERISA §403 (c)(2)(C).
[56]ERISA §403(c)(2)(A).
[57]ERISA §4044(d); Treas. Reg. 1.401-2(b).

provide the benefits accrued upon plan termination were less than the plan assets. Immediate recovery of the plan surplus is possible only if the administrator purchases from a life insurer single-sum paid-up annuities for all participants and beneficiaries or, alternatively, makes a lump-sum cash distribution to such persons.

The law also contains provisions designed to prevent the diversion of assets through unwise or improper management. As general guidelines: the cost of acquired assets must not exceed fair market value at the time of purchase; a rate of return on invested assets commensurate with the prevailing rate must be sought; sufficient liquidity must be maintained to meet the cash flow needs of the plan; and the other general standards that would govern the actions of a prudent investor must be observed.[58] In addition, there is an outright ban against a number of specific prohibited transactions, all of which would involve a measure of self-dealing.[59] An important exception to both the diversity and self-dealing rules is that which permits the plan to invest up to 10 percent, and in some cases 100 percent, of its assets in the securities or real property of the employer.[60]

## Delegation of Other Fiduciary Duties than the Management of Plan Assets

The law also permits the named fiduciaries to allocate and delegate fiduciary duties that do not involve the management of plan assets.[61] Upon proper allocation or delegation, the named fiduciaries are not liable for the acts or omissions of the persons to whom duties have been allocated or delegated. However, the plan must specifically authorize such allocation or delegation and must provide a procedure for it. For example, the plan may provide that delegation may occur only with respect to specified duties, such as the maintenance of participant records or the disbursement of benefits, and only on the approval of the plan sponsor or on the approval of the joint board of trustees of a so-called Taft-Hartley plan. Also, in implementing the procedures of the plan, the named fiduciaries

[58]ERISA §3(18), 404(a).
[59]ERISA §406; I.R.C. 4975(c).
[60]ERISA §§404(a)(2), 407, 408(e).
[61]ERISA §405(c).

must act prudently and in the interests of the participants and their beneficiaries. This requires prudence not only in the initial selection of the person or organization to whom duties have been delegated but in surveillance of the manner in which the duties are performed. Depending upon the circumstances, the surveillance requirement may be satisfied by a formal periodic review (by all the named fiduciaries who participated in the delegation or by a specially designated review committee), or it may be met through day-to-day contact and evaluation, or in other appropriate ways.

Named fiduciaries may also allocate responsibilities among themselves, just as the plan trustees may. Having made a proper allocation of duties among themselves, the co-fiduciaries are not responsible for the acts or omissions of each other so long as they are not a party to the breach or do not imprudently contribute to the breach.

### Basic Fiduciary Rules

Each fiduciary of a pension plan, regardless of his specific duties and responsibilities, must act "with the care, skill, prudence, and diligence under the circumstances then prevailing that a prudent man acting in a like capacity and familiar with such matters would use in the conduct of an enterprise of a like character and with like aims."[62] This is an adaptation and enlargement of a classic judicial prudent man rule that was enunciated as a standard for a trustee in managing the assets of a personal trust or an institutional endowment.[63] Because of its original purpose, it has been applied mainly to investment decisions. In contrast, the ERISA statutory standard of prudence is an attempt to apply the concept to all the actions of a fiduciary, whether or not they involve the management of plan assets. Thus far, the investment function continues to be the focus of the standard and to be the target of most regulatory and judicial pronouncements on the subject. It will be many years before the full scope and effect of the new standard will be known.

Another important manifestation of congressional concern over fiduciary behavior is a general prohibition in ERISA against busi-

[62]ERISA §404(a)(1) (B).
[63]*Harvard College* v. *Amory* (Mass. S. Jud. Ct. 1830) 9 Pickering 446.

ness and investment transactions between the plan and parties-in-interest, as defined in the law. This approach was adopted in lieu of a requirement that all transactions between the plan and parties-in-interest be conducted at "arm's length," an approach suggested by many groups at the time ERISA was being developed and still espoused by some as a more efficient way of dealing with this sensitive area.

The law lists certain transactions that are to be exempt from the general prohibitions and authorizes administrative exemptions for other transactions that are in accord with established business practices and provide adequate safeguards to the plan and its participants.[64] Under these exemptions, a life insurance company may purchase insurance and annuity contracts from itself on behalf of the participants in its own pension plan, and a bank may use its own investment facilities for its pension plan. Moreover, a bank or insurance company is specifically authorized to purchase, on behalf of a pension plan of which it is a fiduciary, investment units in a pooled account that it operates. Other exemptions permit a plan to provide for nondiscriminatory loans to its participants at a reasonable interest rate and with proper security, and to purchase services from party-in-interest under certain conditions.

Under the labor provisions of ERISA, a fiduciary who breaches the fiduciary requirements of the act is personally liable to the plan for any losses to the plan resulting from the breach.[65] Such a fiduciary must also turn over to the plan any profits that he may have made through the improper use of any plan asset. Other relief, including removal of the fiduciary, may be ordered by a court under appropriate civil actions. The fiduciary is not permitted to eliminate or reduce his liability for breach of fiduciary responsibilities through exculpatory provisions in the trust agreement or other document.[66] However, a plan may purchase insurance for itself and for its fiduciaries to cover their liability or losses from their imprudent behavior if the insurance contract provides for recourse by the insurer against the fiduciaries for breach of fiduciary responsibility. A fiduciary may purchase insurance to cover his own liability, and

---

[64]ERISA §408, I.R.C. §4975(c)(2).

[65]ERISA §409.

[66]ERISA §410.

an employer or union may purchase liability insurance for plan fiduciaries, and these policies need not provide for recourse.

The tax provisions of ERISA provide for civil penalties for "disqualified persons" (roughly equivalent to parties-in-interest under the labor provisions) who engage in prohibited transactions.[67] The penalty takes the form of an excise tax patterned after the tax on self-dealing enacted in the Tax Reform Act of 1969 with respect to private foundations. The tax is levied in two stages. The first-level tax, levied on the disqualified person, is at the rate of 5 percent of the amount involved for each taxable year (or part of a year) in the period that begins with the date when the prohibited transaction occurs and ends on the earlier of the date of collection or the date of mailing of a deficiency notice for the first-level tax. The first-level tax is imposed automatically without regard to whether the violation was inadvertent. The second-level tax is at the rate of 100 percent of the amount involved and is imposed on the fiduciary if the transaction is not corrected within a limited period.

A fiduciary is not subject to the penalties of both the labor provisions and the tax provisions for the same transaction.[68] If he performs the improper act in his capacity as a fiduciary, he is subject to the sanctions of the labor provisions. If he engages in a prohibited transaction as a party-in-interest (or disqualified person), even though he may be a fiduciary, he is subject to the excise tax.

There is a general requirement that every fiduciary of a pension plan be bonded for an amount not less than 10 percent of the funds handled, subject to a minimum of $1,000 and a maximum of $500,000 or such other amount as may be prescribed by the Secretary of Labor.[69] Banks and insurance companies meeting certain tests are exempt from this requirement. The Secretary of Labor is expected to develop regulations that will provide procedures for exempting plans where other bonding arrangements of the employer, employee organization, investment manager, or other fiduciaries (or the overall financial condition of the plan or the fiduciaries) meet specified standards deemed adequate to protect the interests of participants and their beneficiaries.

[67]I.R.C. §4975.
[68]ERISA §3003; I.R.C. §4975(h).
[69]ERISA §412.

## Questions

1. What were the objectives of pension plan regulation prior to the enactment of ERISA in 1974? To what extent have these objectives been altered or expanded by ERISA?

2. What was the underlying premise of the Federal Welfare and Pension Plans Disclosure Act as originally enacted? What fundamental change in thrust was brought about by the 1962 amendments to the act?

3. What were the objectives of the changes in pension law enacted under the Tax Reform Act of 1986?

4. Do you believe that the "favorable" tax treatment accorded a qualified pension plan and its participants is a justifiable and sufficient basis for federal regulation of private plans? What other rationale might be advanced for federal regulation?

5. What is the underlying purpose, or central objective, of the basic requirements for qualification of a pension plan, taken as a whole?

6. In what specific ways or by what specific provisions or requirements did ERISA attempt to provide greater certainty or assurance that an eligible claimant under a private pension plan will receive the benefits to which he or she is entitled? What does the act do to promote a fuller understanding by the plan participants of their rights under the plan?

7. What are the principal categories of pension plans that are not subject to the provisions of ERISA?

8. Why did the drafters of ERISA conclude that a new, federal standard of fiducial conduct was necessary to protect the interests of plan participants and their beneficiaries?

9. What is meant by the term "plan administrator"? Is the plan administrator different from the "named fiduciary"?

10. In what respects does the federal "prudent man" standard enunciated in ERISA differ from the classic common-law prudent man rule set forth in *Harvard College* v. *Amory*?

11. Who is a fiduciary in a pension plan under the concepts set forth in ERISA? Does the "named fiduciary" under a pension plan have heavier responsibilities than other fiduciaries in the plan?

12. Since 1938 the Internal Revenue Code has contained a prohibition against diversion of pension plan assets. This general provision was reaffirmed and clarified in ERISA. Under the present rules, are there any circumstances under which an employer can legally recover contributions that it has made to a qualified pension plan? Explain.

13.  Is there a distinction under ERISA between the trustee or trustees of a pension plan and the entity that manages the assets of the plan?

14.  May the plan administrator, named fiduciary, or plan trustees shed their fiduciary responsibilities for the investment of plan assets by transferring the investment function to a professional asset manager or several asset managers?

15.  Is it permissible under ERISA for the trustees and other fiduciaries of a pension plan to carry insurance against liabilities imposed upon them for their imprudent behavior? Explain.

# Plan Design | Part Two

# 4 | Coverage and Participation

A PARTICIPANT OR MEMBER of a plan is an individual who is specifically included under the plan. This includes retired employees and terminated employees who are entitled to future benefits under the plan, as well as active employees. *Participation* usually refers to the inclusion of *individuals* in the plan as participants.

*Coverage* refers to participation in the aggregate. Sometimes coverage is used to refer to the class of employees that are eligible, such as a plan that covers salaried employees. At other times, coverage is used to refer to a group the members of which are actually current participants in the plan, excluding, for example, employees who have not yet satisfied a minimum age or service requirement.

Most plans have a minimum age or service requirement, or both, before an employee may become a participant. In addition, in some plans participation can begin only on the first day of a year, quarter, or month.

The significance of the date participation begins varies from plan to plan. Under a plan that requires employee contributions, participation signals the commencement of the employee's obligation to make contributions to the plan. Under a defined contribution plan or a defined benefit plan using an allocated funding instrument (defined later), participation refers to the change in status of an employee that requires the employer to make contributions on the employee's behalf and credit them to his account. It may signify a status under which the employee is eligible for death or disability benefits, if the plan includes these benefits, although many plans defer eligibility for these until a later date. It may refer to the time when the employee begins to accrue benefit credits for service thereafter, but many plans accrue benefits for service both before and after the date participation begins. Some plans measure the *years of participation* to determine when an employee becomes eligible to receive normal retirement or other benefits, but other plans use the *entire period of service* for this purpose. Under some defined benefit plans with no employee contributions, the date that participation begins has no effect whatsoever upon the benefit entitlement of the individual participant; his eligibility for benefits and amount of benefits would be unchanged if the plan should be amended to increase or decrease the period before employees become participants.

Whether an individual is a participant may have several consequences for the employer or other plan sponsor and for the plan as a whole. It may mark the time when the plan administrator begins to keep records for the employee in question. It determines whether the individual must receive the disclosures that are required to be made to all participants. For defined benefit plans, a premium is payable to the Pension Benefit Guarantee Corporation (PBGC) for each participant, and participation usually marks the point at which the employee is first recognized in actuarial cost calculations that guide the employer's contributions to the plan. And in the aggregate, participation has a material effect on whether the plan satisfies the Internal Revenue Code's coverage requirements, discussed below.

## Coverage

### Multiple Employer Plans versus Single Employer Plans

Pension plans may be classified in various ways but in the scope of their coverage they fall into two broad categories: multiple employer and single employer.

In the broadest sense, a multiple employer plan is one which covers the employees of more than one employer. Generally, however, the term is more narrowly defined to embrace only those plans where the employing firms are not financially related. The more narrow definition excludes plans of a parent corporation which cover the employees of affiliated or subsidiary corporations and the multiplant plans of one employer. Furthermore, the term is properly reserved for those arrangements under which contributions, usually at uniform rates, are payable into one common fund, and benefits on a uniform scale are payable to eligible claimants from pooled assets of the fund. Thus, the multiple employer concept does not encompass arrangements under which two or more employers pool their pension contributions solely for purposes of investment, with separate accounts being maintained for each employer.

A special form of multiple employer plan has been given a statutory definition and the distinctive name of "multiemployer plan." ERISA defines a multiemployer plan as a multiple employer plan maintained pursuant to a collective bargaining agreement, to which more than one employer is required to contribute.[1] The multiemployer plan is often found in industries characterized by skilled craftsmen, numerous small employers, intense competition, and a high rate of business failure. It offers the overriding advantage of making pensions available to employees who, because of their employment relationship or the business environment in which they earn their livelihood, would not have access to this form of economic security. This type of plan standardizes pension costs for competing employers, stabilizes the experience of the pension fund, affords the economies of large-scale operations, and provides for transferability of pension credits among the participating firms.[2] The negotiated multiple employer plan may be national, regional, or local in scope. For reasons peculiar to the unions involved, few plans are truly industrywide. Plans of the following labor organizations, which account for a large portion of the employees covered under multiemployer plans, are virtually industrywide in operation: Amalgamated Clothing and Textile Workers of America, International Brotherhood of Electrical Workers, International Ladies'

---

[1]ERISA §3(37); I.R.C. §414(f). A different definition applied in prior years.

[2]There are, of course, certain disadvantages and problems associated with multiple employer plans, which are not relevant to this discussion. These plans are dealt with in a comprehensive manner in Daniel F. McGinn, *Joint Trust Pension Plans* (Homewood, Ill.: Richard D. Irwin, 1978), a Pension Research Council publication.

Garment Workers, International Typographical Union, United Brotherhood of Carpenters and Joiners, Laborers Union, and the United Mine Workers. Regional plans tend to cover several states, the plan of the Western Conference of Teamsters being an example. Plans covering the employees represented by a collective bargaining unit in one locality are numerous.

There are approximately 2,500 multiemployer plans covering 9 million participants. About 3 percent of these plans have over 20,000 participants each and account for more than half of all participants in multiemployer plans.[3] The overwhelming majority of these plans, 85 percent in fact, are of the defined benefit type.

Most nonnegotiated multiple employer pension plans cover employees of religious, charitable, and educational institutions. In the business field, several state banking associations have developed plans for their member banks.

Despite the imposing significance of multiple employer plans, plans which cover the employees of only one employer dominate the pension scene, both in number of plans and the aggregate number of employees covered. This type of plan needs no elaboration at this point other than to state that it may come into being as a result of collective bargaining or through the unilateral action of the employer. These plans range in coverage from a few employees to several hundred thousand.

## Coverage Requirements

As a part of the general thrust of the Internal Revenue Code to encourage broad coverage and prevent discrimination in favor of highly compensated employees, a qualified pension plan must satisfy certain coverage requirements. This is true whether the plan is multiple employer or single employer in scope or whether negotiated or unilateral in origin.

The Tax Reform Act of 1986 significantly changed these coverage requirements, making them more stringent. The new requirements, described below, generally apply for plan years beginning in 1989 and later.[4]

---

[3]U.S. Department of Labor, "Estimates of Participant and Financial Characteristics for Private Pension Plans," 1983.

[4]The prior requirements were contained in I.R.C. §410(b)(1).

**Highly Compensated Employees.** The definition of "highly compensated employee" is central to the new coverage requirements, as well as to other key requirements under the Tax Reform Act.

Prior to the Tax Reform Act the Code used different definitions of "highly compensated" for different purposes. For most purposes it depended on the "facts and circumstances," very subjective criteria.

A new uniform definition of "highly compensated employee" applies for almost all purposes under the Code.[5] The prior law proscription against discrimination in favor of the "prohibited group" of officers, shareholders, and highly compensated employees has been changed to apply only to highly compensated employees.[6]

A *highly compensated employee* is an employee who during the current year or the preceding year:

1. Was a 5 percent owner;
2. Received more than $75,000 in compensation;
3. Received more than $50,000 in compensation and was in the "top-paid group"; or
4. Received more than $45,000 in compensation and was an officer.

The $75,000 and $50,000 amounts are to be indexed to inflation, beginning in 1988, while the $45,000 amount is to be indexed to inflation beginning in some much later year.

For this purpose the "top-paid group" includes the top-paid 20 percent of employees of the employer, including all businesses in a controlled group with the employer and all businesses under common control. The top-paid group does not include nonresident aliens. For a plan not maintained under a collective bargaining agreement, collective bargaining employees are excluded from the top-paid group. In addition the top-paid group excludes employees who:

1. Have less than 6 months of service;
2. Normally work less than 17½ hours per week;

---

[5]I.R.C. §414(q).
[6]I.R.C. §401(a)(4).

3.  Normally work 6 months or less per year; or
4.  Are under age 21.

Shorter periods than the above (or none at all) may be used, if used consistently for all purposes.

An employee is a highly compensated employee if he meets the definition for either the current year or the prior year. But with respect to the current year, employees who are not 5 percent owners may be disregarded if they are not among the 100 highest paid employees. Any former employee, however, is treated as a highly compensated employee if he was a highly compensated employee when he separated from service or at any time after age 55.

The number of officers that need to be taken into account does not exceed the greater of 3 employees or 10 percent of all employees, but in no case more than 50 officers. If no officer earns over $45,000, the highest paid officer must still be included in the top-paid group.

In the case of 5 percent owners and the 10 highest paid employees, the compensation of certain family members is combined with that of the highly compensated employee as though they were a single individual.

For purposes of identifying highly compensated employees, compensation must include salary deferrals under any 401(k) plan, tax-sheltered annuity, simplified employee plan, or cafeteria plan.

**Nondiscrimination Tests.**   Prior to the Tax Reform Act there were two alternative methods of demonstrating that a plan's coverage was nondiscriminatory: the percentage test, and the nondiscriminatory classification rule. The Act substantially changed the requirements for demonstrating that coverage is nondiscriminatory.[7] The new rules are generally more difficult to satisfy.

The coverage of a plan must satisfy one of three alternative rules. Each of the rules involves the figure of 70 percent, but each uses the percentage in a distinctive way. The three alternative tests are called the *percentage* test, the *ratio* test and the *average benefits percentage* test.

In satisfying any of the tests an employer may treat two or more plans as a single plan if they provide comparable benefits, i.e.,

---

[7]I.R.C. §410(b).

benefits which are not discriminatory.[8] If an employer has only highly compensated employees, its plans are presumed to satisfy the coverage requirements.

**A.   Percentage Test.**   A plan passes the percentage test if it covers at least 70 percent of all nonhighly compensated employees of the employer. This is the simplest of the three tests.

**B.   Ratio Test.**   A plan meets the ratio test if the proportion of all nonhighly compensated employees of the employer who are covered under the plan is at least 70 percent of the proportion of highly compensated employees of the employer who are covered. An example of a plan that satisfies this rule is the following.

| | Number of Employees | | Percent Covered |
| --- | --- | --- | --- |
| | Total | Covered | |
| Highly compensated employees | 200 | 100 | 50 |
| Nonhighly compensated employees | 1,000 | 350 | 35 |
| Total employees | 1,200 | | |
| Ratio of percentages (35% divided by 50%) | | | 70 |

**C.   Average Benefits Percentage Test.**   A plan satisfies the average benefits percentage test only if *both* of the following requirements are satisfied:

**1.**   The plan covers a nondiscriminatory classification of employees (the "classification test"), *and*

**2.**   The average benefits percentage (the ratio of employer-provided benefits or contributions to the participant's compensation) for nonhighly compensated employees is at least 70 percent of the average benefits percentage of highly compensated employees.

The classification test is the subjective standard that the IRS has been using for many years. It is based on the facts and circumstances of each case, and is expected to be administered generally as in the past. A plan that passed the test in the past would ordinarily be expected to pass it in the future if its circumstances have not changed, but this is not guaranteed. However, in administering this test the IRS is to use the new definition of highly compensated employees, which could cause a plan to fail. IRS is to publish an

---

[8]The IRS was directed to revise the rules of Rev. Rul. 81–202, which it has used to determine whether plans are comparable.

objective safe harbor to facilitate compliance with the classification test.

The average benefits percentages do not relate to participants in any particular plan of the employer. Rather the intent is to reveal whether there is nondiscriminatory coverage with respect to the benefits of all employees of the employer (or of a line of business if the line of business exception applies). Thus, the average benefit percentages are based upon all employees of the employer (or of the line of business as discussed later), other than the employees specifically excluded, such as nonresident aliens and short service employees.

To calculate the average benefit percentage one must first calculate the benefit percentage of every employee of the employer (or of the line of business, if applicable), other than the specifically excluded employees mentioned above. The benefit percentage is the employer-provided contribution or benefit of an employee under all qualified plans of the employer, expressed as a percentage of compensation. The benefit percentage of every employee must be expressed in terms of either benefits or contributions. Thus, if an employer maintains both a defined benefit plan and a defined contribution plan, either benefits must be converted into a comparable level of contributions or contributions must be converted into a comparable level of benefits so that there can be a common measure. The IRS is to publish guidelines for making this conversion.

A simple example of a defined contribution plan with four participants which satisfies the 70 percent rule of the average benefits percentage test is as follows:

| Employee Highly compensated | Compensation | Contributions | Percent |
|---|---|---|---|
| A | $100,000 | $25,000 | 25 |
| B | 100,000 | 15,000 | 15 |
| Average | | | 20 |
| Nonhighly compensated | | | |
| C | 20,000 | 2,000 | 10 |
| D | 10,000 | 1,800 | 18 |
| Average | | | 14 |
| Ratio of average percentages (14% divided by 20%) | | | 70 |

**Exclusion of Certain Employees from the Tests.**  In making any of the above tests, nonresident aliens with no earned income from U.S. sources are to be excluded. For a plan not maintained under a collective bargaining agreement, collective bargaining employees are excluded from consideration. Employees not meeting the plan's age and service requirements are also excluded.

**Line of Business Exception.**  All three of the above tests involve consideration of all employees of the employer, including companies under common control, except for employees specifically excluded by the Code. But if the employer is treated as operating separate lines of business, it may apply the tests separately with respect to each separate line of business.

To be treated as operating separate lines of business an employer must operate the separate lines of business for bona fide business reasons.[9] This exception is not available unless the line of business covers at least 50 employees (not counting certain young, short service, part-time, etc., employees). In addition, the line of business must either satisfy forthcoming IRS guidelines, receive a determination letter regarding its separate line of business status, or satisfy a safe harbor rule.

The safe harbor rule is satisfied if the "highly compensated employee percentage" (the percentage of employees who are highly compensated) of the line of business is not more than twice the highly compensated percentage of all employees and if either (a) the highly compensated employee percentage of the line of business is not less than half that of all employees or (b) at least 10 percent of all highly compensated employees of the employer perform services solely for the line of business.

The IRS will provide guidelines regarding allocation of headquarters personnel among lines of business and the treatment of employees serving more than one line of business or none.

**Affiliated Service Groups.**  To prevent employers from bypassing the nondiscrimination rules by certain forms of organizational structure, Congress enacted rules regarding affiliated service

---

[9]I.R.C. §414(r).

groups.[10] An affiliated service group is a group of two or more organizations that have certain common ownership, where one of the organizations regularly performs services for another of them or they jointly regularly perform services for third parties. If an affiliated service group exists, all employees of its member organizations will be treated as if they were employed by a single employer for purposes of the coverage requirements and certain other requirements of the Code.

**Leased Employees.** A leased employee is an employee of one employer who performs services for another employer. The most common use is the engagement of a temporary employee to fill a short-term vacancy caused by the absence of a regular employee. Some employers have used leased employees on a longer term basis for a variety of legitimate reasons. Some employers have used leased employees to avoid the expense of pension plans related to regular employees.

To stop abuse, the Code requires that leased employees who provide full-time services for the same recipient for at least one year be treated as employees of the recipient for purposes of the coverage requirements and certain other requirements.[11] An exception is made if the leasing organization provides pension benefits for the leased employee that meet certain requirements.

## Minimum Number of Participants

Every plan must cover at least 50 participants, or 40 percent of all employees if less.[12] Employees who are eligible to make contributions under the plan or to have contributions made for them are considered to be covered even if they choose not to participate. For this requirement comparable plans may not be aggregated; each plan must satisfy the requirement separately.

In making the 40 percent test, the employer is to exclude the same groups as in other coverage tests, i.e., nonresident aliens, employees not satisfying the minimum age and service require-

---

[10]I.R.C. §414(m).
[11]I.R.C. §414(n).
[12]I.R.C. §401(a)(26).

ments, etc. However, the line of business exception does not apply to the 40 percent test.

A collectively bargained plan covering only bargaining employees may exclude nonbargaining employees in making the 40 percent test. Multiemployer plans are generally exempt from the minimum participation requirement.

Regulations may provide that any plan containing different benefit structures for different participants or two or more separate trusts must be considered to be two or more plans for the purposes of the minimum participation requirement.

### Summary of Coverage Requirements

In summary, the coverage requirements are as follows:

A.  Nondiscriminatory coverage requirements
   1.  Percentage test, or
   2.  Ratio test, or
   3.  Average benefits percentage test
       *a.*  Nondiscriminatory classification *and*
       *b.*  Average benefits percentage 70 percent
B.  Minimum number of participants (50 participants or 40 percent).

## Participation

### Eligibility for Participation

The plan document defines the broad classes of employees who are eligible to participate in the plan, as well as the specific conditions that must be met before participation becomes effective. Not all plans are designed to cover every employee on the payroll of the firm as of any given time. Some employees may never become eligible for participation in a particular plan, since the plan was not designed to cover that classification of workers. For example, seasonal and part-time employees (i.e., those working fewer than 1,000 hours per year) may be excluded from eligibility. Furthermore, separate plans may be operated for different groups of employees. There may be one plan for workers represented by a collective bargaining unit and another for the employees, both management and clerical, not covered by a collective bargaining agreement. There may be several bargaining units, each with its own plan. There may be a separate plan for each plant of a multiplant firm, and there will almost always be separate plans for foreign subsidiaries or nonresident alien employees. Such eligibility requirements are allowed if the coverage tests described above are satisfied.

### Age and Service Requirements

Within a particular plan, the members of a potentially eligible classification of employees may have to satisfy a service or age requirement, or both. The purpose of a service requirement is often administrative. There tends to be a high rate of turnover among recently hired employees, especially those at the younger ages, and it is an unnecessary administrative expense to bring such persons into the pension plan, with the attendant records, only to have them withdraw a short time later.

A minimum age stipulation has much the same purpose as a service requirement, with which it may be found in combination, namely to exclude high-turnover employees. When the plan is contributory, a minimum age requirement serves the additional function of excluding those employees who, because of their youth, have developed little interest in pensions and would object to making contributions for that purpose.

The service requirement cannot exceed one year, unless the plan provides for full and immediate vesting, in which case it may require two years of service.[13]

The minimum age cannot be higher than 21, except as noted below.[14] Thus, the general rule now is that an employee must not be denied membership in the plan because of age or service whenever he reaches age 21 and has a minimum of one year of service. A plan may require both conditions. It may require that the employee be at least 21 years of age and have at least one year of service. If he is hired at age 18, for example, he may be required to wait three years for plan membership. If he is hired at age 20

---

[13]ERISA §202(a)(1); I.R.C. §410(a)(1). Three years eligibility is permitted for plan years beginning before 1989.

[14]Ibid.

or beyond, the maximum service requirement is one year. As an exception to the general rule, any plan maintained exclusively for employees of a governmental or tax-exempt educational organization which provides full and immediate vesting for all participants may have a participation requirement of age 26 and one year of service.[15] An employee who has satisfied the minimum age and service requirements must be permitted to commence his participation in the plan at the beginning of the next plan year or, if earlier, within six months after satisfaction of the requirements.[16] All of these are minimum standards and do not preclude more liberal provisions.

It must be emphasized that these age and service requirements pertain to the time when the employee will begin to accrue benefits toward his retirement. They relate strictly to benefit accruals. They have nothing to say about what service must be recognized for purposes of determining a participant's place on the vesting schedule, a subject discussed in a later chapter. The law does not require retroactive recognition of preparticipation service for purposes of benefit accruals, but it does for the determination of the participant's vesting status. Some plans, most of them subject to collective bargaining, have nevertheless provided for retroactive recognition for benefit purposes of some or all service prior to date of membership in the plan.

Many plans have imposed a *maximum* age limitation, as well as a *minimum* age requirement. Such a limitation serves to exclude from plan membership any individual hired at or above the stipulated age. The purpose of the limitation is to hold down the cost of the pension plan—under a defined benefit plan the cost of each unit of retirement benefit increases with each increment in age of the employee—and to confine the employer's pension obligations to those employees who had rendered a substantial amount of service prior to retirement. For plan years beginning after 1987 plans may no longer contain maximum age limits.[17]

Some noncontributory plans do not contain any age or service requirements for membership eligibility. This is particularly true of collectively bargained plans that provide uniform benefits for each

---

[15]ERISA §202(a)(1)(B)(ii), I.R.C. §410(a)(1)(B)(ii).
[16]ERISA §202(a)(4), I.R.C. §410(a)(4).
[17]ERISA § 202(a)(2), I.R.C. §410(a)(2).

year of service. Where no eligibility requirements are stipulated, an employee who comes within the scope of the plan is automatically covered from the first day of employment.

**Year of Service.**   A pension plan may use the term *year of service* for three distinct purposes that are subject to ERISA's requirements:[18] (1) to determine eligibility for participation, (2) to determine benefit entitlement through satisfaction of the vesting requirements, and (3) to determine the amount of accrued benefits at any point in time.

ERISA and subsequent regulations provide for two alternative approaches to measuring a year of service for any of the three purposes set out above: the "hours of service"[19] approach and the "elapsed time"[20] approach.

Under the hours of service approach, a "year of service" for eligibility and vesting purposes is a 12-month period during which the employee works at least 1,000 hours or is credited with 1,000 hours, whether worked or not. For purposes of benefit accrual, the plan may require more than 1,000 hours of service for a full year of service, but pro rata credit must be given for 1,000 or more hours of service in a 12-month period. The 12-month periods used to determine whether the various requirements have been met are called "computation periods." The *eligibility computation period* determines whether an employee has fulfilled the service requirements for formal admission to plan membership. The *vesting computation period* defines the participant's place on the vesting schedule and, in most cases, establishes whether or not a break in service has occurred. The *accrual computation period* determines whether a participant accrues full, partial, or no retirement benefits during a certain time period.

For purposes of the minimum participation requirements, the 12-month eligibility computation period is measured from the date when the employee first enters the service of the employer. Thus,

---

[18]Years of service may also be used to determine eligibility for normal retirement, early retirement, disability, and other benefits, but this use is not regulated by ERISA.

[19]ERISA §§202(a)(3), 203(b)(2). I.R.C. §410(a)(3). 29 CFR 2530.200b, 2530.203-2, 2530.204–1, 2. Treas. Reg. 1.410(a)–5, 1.411(a)–6.

[20]Treas. Reg. 1.410(a)–7. The elapsed time method is not specifically described in the statutes.

the employee has fulfilled the 1,000-hour requirement if he has had 1,000 hours of work by the first anniversary of his employment.

If the employee does not complete 1,000 hours of service by the first anniversary of his employment but is still employed, he must start over toward meeting the requirement. For this purpose, the plan can provide, on a uniform and consistent basis, that the relevant 12-month period is either (*a*) the year between his first and second anniversary dates, or (*b*) the first plan year that began after the individual was first employed.[21]

An essential element of this approach is, of course, the definition of "hour of service."[22] The generic definition of an hour of service is *an hour for which an employee is paid or is entitled to payment (including back pay)* for the performance of duties or on account of a time period during which no duties are performed. Thus, hours of service during a given computation period include not only hours actually worked but hours for which the employee is paid, such as holidays, vacation, sick leave, and jury duty. When a plan administrator must determine hours of service for periods prior to the time ERISA applies to the plan (generally 1976), he is permitted to limit his search to reasonably accessible records. If records are not available or accessible, reasonable estimates may be used.

The regulations permit a plan to measure hours of service in terms of certain "equivalencies" to the basic definition.[23] These equivalencies may be expressed in terms of *working time, periods of employment,* or *earnings.* If a plan counts only actual working time, including overtime, it must credit a year of service for 870 hours. The difference between 1,000 and 870 is presumed to represent the hours in the computation period during which no duties are performed but for which payment is made. If only regular-time hours of work are recognized, excluding overtime, a year of service must be credited for only 750 hours.

Rather than determining actual hours of regular or overtime work, a plan may credit 10 hours of service for each working day, 45 hours for each week, 95 hours for each semimonthly period, or 190 hours for each month. These equivalencies make allowance for the

[21] 29 CFR 2530.202-2.
[22] 29 CFR 2530.200b-2.
[23] 29 CFR 2530.200b-3.

compensable time periods during which no duties are performed. This is the periods-of-employment basis of crediting hours. If a plan sponsor chooses this basis, he must credit the full number of hours for the period specified if the individual is employed at least one hour during the period. In other words, if the plan stipulates that hours of service are to be credited on the basis of *months of employment,* 190 hours would have to be credited for a minimum of one hour of employment during the month in question.

If an employee is paid on the basis of an hourly rate, his hours of service may be determined by dividing his earnings during the computation period by either (1) his hourly rates of pay in effect from time to time during the period, (2) his lowest hourly rate of pay during the year, or (3) the lowest rate of pay for an employee in a similar job. A plan using this basis of measurement must credit 1,000 hours of service for each 870 hours computed to give equivalent recognition to compensable periods during which no duties are performed. A similar approach may be used for employees who are *not* paid on an hourly basis if 1,000 hours of service are credited for each 750 hours determined under the method.

Entirely apart from and as an exception to the foregoing rules, a maritime employee who has 125 days of employment during an eligibility or vesting computation period is credited with a year of service.[24]

The other major approach, the *elapsed time method,* ignores hours of service altogether.[25] Under this approach, the plan gives credit for an individual's total period of employment, irrespective of the actual number of hours worked or compensated. The period of employment begins on the first day an employee performs an hour of service and ends on his *severance from service date.* If employment is terminated, the severance from service date is the last day worked; but if the employee is absent because of layoff, leave, or disability, the severance from service date is one year after the day on which the last service is performed. If an employee returns from layoff, leave, or other temporary absence within one year from the last day worked, he must be treated for all purposes as though he had worked throughout the entire period of absence.

---

[24]ERISA §§202(a)(3)(D), 203(b)(2)(D); I.R.C. §§410(a)(3)(D), 411(a)(5)(D); 29 CFR 2530.200b–6,7,8.

[25]Treas. Reg. 1.410(a)–7.

However, if an employee returns to work within one year after a quit, discharge, or retirement, the intervening period must be taken into account for eligibility and vesting purposes but not for benefit accruals.

For purposes of participation and vesting, the *days* of elapsed time in different calendar or plan years must be aggregated to determine whether the service requirements are met. For example, a one-year service requirement for participation would be satisfied with 200 days of elapsed time in employment in each of two successive plan years. For this purpose, a year of elapsed time in employment is 365 days. For purposes of benefit accrual, elapsed time may be measured in terms of years, months, or days, depending upon plan provisions.

In seasonal industries where the customary period of employment is less than 1,000 hours, the term *year of service* is to be defined in regulations.

A plan may use different methods of measuring years of service for purposes of eligibility for participation, fulfillment of vesting requirements, and computation of the amount of accrued benefits. It may also use different computation periods for different purposes. In addition, it may prescribe different methods for different groups of employees, so long as the methods are reasonable and do not result in any prohibited discrimination. For example, it could use the elapsed time method for full-time employees and some version of the 1,000-hour method for part-time employees. Or it might use the 1,000-hour method for employees whose regular workweek is less than the standard workweek for their job classification and use the elapsed time method for employees who work the standard week.

**Break in Service.** ERISA contains very specific rules with respect to breaks in service for purposes of participation, vesting, and benefit accruals. For *participation* purposes, a one-year break in service occurs in any calendar year, plan year, or other consecutive 12-month computation period (the same computation period as used to measure the years of service) in which the employee has 500 or fewer hours of service.[26] If the plan uses 870 hours or

---

[26]ERISA §202(b), I.R.C. §410(a)(5), 29 CFR 2530.200b–4, Treas. Reg. 1.410(a)–5.

750 hours to determine years of service, the hours for breaks in service are reduced proportionately. For plans using elapsed time, a 12-month period of severance following a severance from service date is treated as a break in service.[27]

For purposes of determining whether there has been a break in service, certain periods of absence for maternity and paternity must be treated as though the individual was actively at work.[28] However the period so credited need not exceed 501 hours for plans using the hours method or one year for plans using the elapsed time method.

The general rule is that all service with the employer, pre-break and post-break, is to be taken into account for purposes of determining whether the participant has met the participation requirements. However, if a participant has a one-year break in service, the plan may require a one-year waiting period before reentry, at which point the participant's prebreak and postbreak service are to be aggregated, and the employee is to be given full credit for the waiting period service.

A plan that is permitted to use a two-year service requirement (because it provides full and immediate vesting) may stipulate that an employee who has a one-year break in service before completing the two-year probationary period must start over toward satisfying that requirement after the break in service.[29]

### Participation in Contributory Plans

If the objectives of the pension plan are to be achieved, maximum participation by eligible employees is imperative. Employees reaching retirement age without entitlement to benefits can be a source of embarrassment to the employer, even though the employee voluntarily chose not to participate in the plan. This problem is minimized in a noncontributory plan, since all employees who meet the eligibility requirements are automatically included in the membership of the plan.

When employee contributions are included, however, participation in the plan is usually made optional, especially for employees

---

[27]Treas. Reg. 1.410(a)–7(a)(3).
[28]ERISA §202(b)(5), I.R.C. §410(a)(5), Treas. Reg. 1.410(a)–7T(a).
[29]I.R.C. §410(a)(5)(B).

already in service at the inception of the plan. Some plans make participation a condition of employment for new employees, thus ensuring ultimate coverage of all eligible employees. Most plans stipulate that an employee, having once chosen to participate, must continue participation throughout his employment. This provision prevents an employee from terminating his membership in the plan just to draw down his accumulated contributions. Some plans permit an employee to discontinue contributions while still in service but prohibit withdrawal of accumulated contributions prior to termination of service. Some plans permit an employee to terminate his coverage while still in the service of the firm but forbid subsequent reentry into the plan. Increased participation among younger employees is sometimes obtained by making membership in the pension plan a condition for coverage under other employee benefit plans, such as group life and group health insurance, which at their age might have more appeal to them.

## Questions

1. From the standpoint of an individual employee, what is the difference, if any, between being *covered* by a pension plan and being a *participant* in the plan?
2. Identify the various categories of participants in a pension plan.
3. Who is a "highly compensated employee"?
4. Contrast the percentage test and the nondiscriminatory classification test as approaches to satisfying the nondiscriminatory coverage requirements of the Internal Revenue Service and implementing regulations.
5. Why might a plan which satisfies the nondiscriminatory coverage requirements fail to satisfy the minimum participation requirement? What purpose does the minimum participation requirement serve?
6. Indicate the various classifications of employees that may be excluded from the nondiscriminatory coverage tests.
7. To what extent, if any, may an employee's age be taken into account in determining eligibility for participation in a pension plan?
8. Identify the various purposes for which a pension plan may use and define the term "year of service."

9.  Describe the various definitions of an "hour of service" permitted under Department of Labor regulations.
10. In what essential respects does the "elapsed time" method of measuring service differ from the "hour of service" approach?
11. What is the significance of the "severance from service date" under the elapsed time method of measuring service? Is that date for a particular individual the same, regardless of the circumstances surrounding his termination of service? Explain.
12. Must length of service under a pension plan be measured in the same way for purposes of participation, vesting, and benefit accrual? Explain.
13. What constitutes a break in service for participation purposes?
14. Describe the approaches that have been used by employers to encourage and enforce participation in a contributory pension plan.

# 5 | Retirement Benefits

AN UNDERLYING PURPOSE of a pension plan is to enable the employer to remove his superannuated employees from the payroll in a manner that is morally and socially acceptable. In practical terms, this means that a life income in some amount must be made available to an employee who has reached the end of his economically productive life. The plan may provide benefits in the event that the employee dies or becomes permanently and totally disabled before retirement, but such benefits are collateral and subservient to the fundamental objective of providing an income after retirement.

## Amount and Determination of Benefits

### Retirement Income Objective

If a pension plan is to fulfill its basic function, it must provide an income which, supplemented by OASDI benefits and other resources, will be adequate to maintain the retired worker and his dependents on a standard of living reasonably consistent with what he enjoyed during the years immediately preceding retirement. Otherwise, some employees may want to continue on the active payroll beyond the point at which they are still functioning efficiently, and the pension plan will fail of its purpose.

In most cases, the personal savings of the retiring employee will not be substantial enough to provide a meaningful supplement to the pension and Social Security benefits payable to the individual. Thus, realistically the income objective should be stated in terms of the combined benefits of the pension plan and the Social Security program. Specifically, the spendable income (Social Security and pension benefits less income taxes) of the retired employee should be compared with his spendable wages (gross wages less income taxes, Social Security taxes, contribution to the pension plan, and expenses associated with his employment) immediately prior to retirement. Because of differences in the individual's tax bracket before and after retirement, and the elimination of Social Security tax payments, pension plan contributions (if any), and work-related expenses, the retired individual can enjoy the same standard of living on a combined income considerably less than his gross pay at the time of retirement, especially if his lessened requirements are taken into account. In the usual circumstances, the retired individual will have completed the education of his children, liquidated the mortgage on his home, and fulfilled (or abandoned) any savings program that he might have undertaken. Moreover, his lifestyle will have changed over the years and, with the possible exception of medical expenses and travel outlays, he can enjoy a standard of living appropriate to his circumstances with a smaller outlay of real dollars than when he was younger and working. The higher the individual's gross earnings, the smaller the proportion that needs to be continued into retirement because of his greater tax savings in retirement (for example, Social Security benefits are partially tax exempt) and the smaller proportion of his income that he has to spend (as compared to saving).

When all these factors are taken into account, it can be demonstrated that a total retirement income of 60 to 75 percent of an individual's gross earnings at time of retirement will enable him to enjoy a standard of living that is reasonably commensurate with what he enjoyed during the latter stages of his employment. The highest percentage applies to the lowest-income employees, the target percentage grading downward as the income level of the employee goes up. For a particular pension plan, the income target or objective must be stated in terms of some preconceived period of service, and the suggested range of 60 to 75 percent of final earnings is considered appropriate only for employees with fairly long service, such as 30 to 35 years. The target for employees with shorter periods of service would be scaled down proportionately.

Since the Social Security benefit formula is slanted in favor of the low-income employee, the percentage of an individual's gross earnings that will be replaced or continued through Social Security benefits declines as his income rises. Thus, even if the pension plan were to provide benefits that constitute a level or constant percentage of compensation for any given period of service, the employees retiring under the plan would receive combined plan and Social Security benefits that would represent a varying percentage of compensation, declining as the compensation base increases. Hence, it is feasible and realistic to articulate a combined benefit objective that embodies a range of income continuation, recognizing the varying circumstances of the plan participants.

In formulating income objectives in terms of combined pension and Social Security benefits, a pension plan sponsor must decide what Social Security benefits to take into account: only the old-age benefit (primary insurance amount) payable to the retired worker, or the benefits payable to the wife (or spouse) as well.[1] In the past, most married women were not employed outside the home, but an increasing proportion of married women are now employed and receive Social Security and private pensions based on their own employment. Thus, income objectives need to be considered separately for three groups: single, married with both working, and married with one working. For the latter group, an assumption must be made as to the age of the wife at the time her Social Security benefits commence. The logical options would be age 65, in which event she would be entitled to a benefit equal to one half that of the retired worker, or age 62, the youngest age at which she can qualify for benefits, in which event she would receive only 37½ percent of the worker's old-age benefit. The latter assumption is generally thought to be more logical, in view of the fact that most wives are at least three years younger than their husbands. If a male worker retires at age 65 and his wife is more than three years younger than he (a common occurrence), no wife's benefit will be payable until she reaches age 62.

To include the spouse's anticipated Social Security benefit in the target formulation is to discriminate against the employee without

---

[1]Currently a spouse's benefit is paid to only 14 percent of all retired workers under OASI.

a spouse. It clearly projects too much income from Social Security and cuts back on the benefits to be provided under the plan. This would argue for exclusion of the spouse's Social Security benefits in designing the benefit formula of the pension plan. On the other hand, to ignore the spouse's benefit can lead to a situation where the combined pension and Social Security benefit for the worker and his spouse would exceed the employee's earnings while he was working. This would usually happen only with respect to the employees at the lower end of the earnings spectrum and, more likely than not, when the plan's benefits are not formally integrated with the Social Security program. However, there are some integrated plans under which the combined plan and Social Security benefits for lower-income employees substantially exceed their earnings at the time of retirement, sometimes by as much as 20 or 25 percent. This makes no sense unless it is assumed that the employees were receiving substandard wages when they were working and were subsisting on an unacceptably low standard of living.

Once a defensible retirement income objective has been established, provision should in theory be made for protection of the income against loss of purchasing power. There are various ways to approach this problem, most of which will be discussed in a subsequent chapter, but the surest and most direct way is to provide for automatic adjustment of the benefits of retired employees to reflect changes in the cost of living. This approach is used by the Social Security System, the federal Civil Service Retirement System, the Uniformed Services Retirement system, the retirement systems of more than half of the states, and some municipal retirement systems. Few plans of business firms have benefits linked to changes in the cost of living (through the use of the consumer price index, for example) but pressures in that direction are building up, especially from organized labor. Many plans have followed the practice of periodically adjusting the benefits of retired employees on an ad hoc, noncontractual basis, using changes in the consumer price index as a guide, but with the increases being less than the full amount of the CPI change. Because of the cost involved and the uncertainty over the magnitude of future price inflation, the business community generally has preferred to retain the flexibility associated with ad hoc adjustment, rather than binding themselves contractually to adjust benefits in conformity with CPI changes. The fact that the Social Security component of the total benefit package is formally linked to the CPI provides some protection against inflation and helps to ameliorate the problem faced by the private plan sponsor.

## Manner in Which the Plan's Undertaking Is Expressed

The obligation assumed by an employer in establishing a pension plan may take one of two forms: (1) an undertaking to provide benefits in accordance with a specific schedule, or (2) an undertaking to make contributions on a specified basis. The first approach is referred to as a *defined benefit* plan, and the second is designated a *defined contribution* plan. Under either approach, the employees may contribute toward the cost of the plan.

**Defined Benefit Plan.** A defined benefit plan[2] is one in which the benefits are established in advance by a formula, and employer contributions are treated as the variable factor. Plans of this type may be broadly classified as plans where the amount of monthly pension after retirement is fixed, and as plans where the amount varies after retirement. The latter plans are discussed in a subsequent chapter dealing with variable annuities and other devices for protecting pension benefits against loss of purchasing power. This chapter is devoted solely to plans that provide fixed-dollar benefits, which are the dominant type. The *cash balance plan,* a type of defined benefit plan that in some ways resembles a defined contribution plan, is separately discussed later in this chapter.

*A. Benefit Formulas.* Benefit formulas of defined benefit plans vary greatly as to details, but on basic characteristics they may be classified into two categories: (1) unit benefit and (2) flat benefit.

*1. Unit Benefit.* The distinctive feature of the unit benefit formula is that an explicit unit of benefit is credited for each year of recognized service with the employer. The unit of benefit may be expressed as a percentage of compensation—the usual procedure under a plan for salaried employees—or as a specific dollar amount.

When the benefit unit is expressed in terms of compensation, the plan must clearly indicate the items of compensation that will be treated as part of the earnings base. Such items as overtime

---

[2]ERISA §3(35), I.R.C. §414(j).

pay, holiday pay, sick pay, bonuses, and commissions must be specifically excluded or included. The definition of compensation used must satisfy requirements established by the Tax Reform Act.[3] It is always permissible to define compensation as compensation received which is currently includible in gross income for tax purposes, i.e., earnings included on Form W-2. It is also permissible to increase such taxable compensation by any elective salary deferrals under a 401(k) plan, tax-sheltered annuity (403(b)), simplified employee plan (SEP), or cafeteria plan (125); and unless such salary deferrals are included in the definition of compensation, participants who elect to make salary deferrals will have their compensation as defined under the pension plan effectively reduced, thus reducing their pension benefits. Regulations also allow the use of other definitions, such as basic or regular compensation (excluding special compensation and overtime) in situations where this does not tend to discriminate in favor of highly compensated employees.

For plan years beginning after 1988 no qualified plan may take account of compensation in excess of $200,000.[4] This amount is to be adjusted for inflation.

After compensation has been defined, it must be decided whether to credit the benefit earned each year in terms of the compensation for that year or to credit all benefits in terms of the average compensation for a few years close to retirement. When the unit of benefit credited during any particular year of employment is based upon the employee's compensation during that year, the benefit formula is characterized as a *career average* formula. This term is derived from the fact that, except as noted later, the pensioner's retirement benefit, in effect, is based upon his average earnings during the entire period of his recognized, or credited, service. However, if recognition is given to service prior to establishment of the plan, as is customary, benefit credits for such periods are usually based on compensation at the inception of the plan to avoid the necessity of tracing past wage histories. In that event, a lower percentage of compensation may be credited, as compared to future service, in recognition of the fact that the level of compensation is likely to be higher at the inception of the plan than it was during

---

[3]I.R.C. §414(q).
[4]I.R.C. §401(a)(17).

the years when the past service credits were accruing. Under a contributory plan, the lower past service benefits may also be a recognition that no employee contributions were made in past years. The percentage used for past service credits is often 75 percent of that applicable to future service credits. The career average concept is also distorted by the fact that, from time to time, the accumulated benefit credits of a plan may be increased in value by applying the appropriate percentages to compensation at date of liberalization, rather than to the wage levels prevailing during the period the credits were earned. Despite the periodic updating of the compensation base for accumulated benefit credits, the career average formula retains its basic facility of fixing, as of any given time, the dollar amount of benefit credits accrued to that date.

In contrast to the career average formula is the so-called final average type of formula. In its pure form, *final average* formula provides for the accrual of benefits on the basis of the participant's average compensation during a specified period, such as 3, 5, or 10 years, immediately preceding retirement. A modification of this formula provides for the use of a specified period of consecutive years of highest average compensation, whether or not the period fell immediately before retirement. Under a final average formula, the amount of annual benefit earned with each year of credited service is not known until the participant reaches retirement,[5] creating uncertainties about the magnitude of the employer's undertaking. The principal appeal of this approach is that it automatically provides benefits appropriately related to the participant's compensation during the years close to retirement.

Once the earnings base is defined, the percentage to be credited for each year of service must be selected. With a unit benefit formula, the percentage usually falls within the range of 1 to 2 percent, with 1½ percent being fairly common. Under a career average plan, if in a particular year a covered employee earns $12,000, for example, and the benefit formula calls for an annual benefit of 1½ percent of compensation, the employee is credited with an annual benefit at retirement of $180 for this year of service. If his compensation remains unchanged, he will be credited with another

---

[5]Most of these plans provide that in the event of an employee's withdrawal from covered employment prior to retirement, any vested benefits will be based on the average salary for the years preceding the date of termination of service.

benefit unit of $180 the following year. The annual benefit payable at retirement is the sum of the units of benefit credited for each of the years of employment.[6] Under a final average pay plan, his benefit for all years might be based, for example, on his average pay during his last five years of employment.

The percentage of compensation reflected in the benefit formula may vary with the level of earnings, with several earnings classifications sometimes being employed. Because Social Security provides benefits which are a larger percentage of compensation for lower-paid workers than for those who are higher paid, it is quite common to apply a lower percentage to earnings up to some stated level called the "integration level" than to those earnings in excess of that integration level, in which case the plan is said to be integrated with Social Security, a subject treated in Chapter 10. There may be a distinction between past and future service, with lower percentages being applicable to the past service.

The type of formula that provides a stated amount of benefit—unrelated to compensation—for each year of service is popular among negotiated plans where the range of hourly wage rates is relatively narrow. With continual increases in prices and wages and greater emphasis in the collective bargaining process on pension benefits, the stipulated monthly benefit in many industries is now $15 or more for each year of credited service.

The basic appeal of the specified dollar benefit is its simplicity. The concept is easily grasped by the parties to the collective bargaining process, and the benefits are easily communicated to the plan participants. For a time the approach seemed to offer employers a way of freezing pension benefits for service already rendered, in contrast to the escalating effect of the final average salary approach. The freeze was to be accomplished by limiting increases in the unit benefit to years of service rendered after the change. However, continuing inflation has made it desirable to give retroactive recognition to benefit increases, thus nullifying the contemplated advantage to the employer. In other words, the benefit amount negotiated in a new labor contract is often applied to all years of credited service, including those rendered prior to the change. But under multiemployer plans, employers often strongly resist any

---

[6]The annual benefit is payable in monthly installments, the monthly benefit being one twelfth the annual benefit.

increase in the benefits for prior years to avoid increases in potential withdrawal liability (discussed later). As a further safeguard against the erosive effect of inflation, some unions have sought and obtained a minimum benefit expressed in terms of final salary. In periods of rapidly escalating wages, a minimum benefit of this type can become the basic benefit.

Virtually all plans that relate benefits to years of service recognize service performed prior to establishment of the plan in order to provide adequate benefits to persons nearing retirement. Many plans, however, place some limitation on the amount of past service that will be recognized. Various forms of limitation are used, the most common being the exclusion of (1) all service performed before a specified age, (2) the first year or few years of service, or (3) all service over a maximum number of years, such as 10, 15, or 25, or before a specified date. The first two types of exclusion are often set equal to the age and service requirements to be eligible for participation in the plan, thus treating old employees the same as new employees. The primary purpose of the type (3) exclusion is to limit the cost of past service benefits, an accrued liability which is almost invariably borne by the employer. This type of exclusion is becoming less common, especially among collectively bargained plans.

*2. Flat Benefit Plans.* The second broad category of benefit formulas—flat benefit plans—is based upon the philosophy that, beyond a minimum period of service, retirement benefits should not be related to the years of service.

This type of formula may provide a benefit at retirement equal to a specified percentage of compensation, without regard to years of service. The compensation base is normally the average earnings during a specified period before retirement, but the career average may be used. A wide range of percentages is in use, the benefit typically being 30, 40, or 50 percent of compensation. The percentage applicable to that portion of compensation below the integration level may be lower than that applied to the portion in excess of the integration level. The same percentage applies to all employees who satisfy a minimum period of service, such as 15 or 20 years. Past service may be credited against the minimum requirement. Employees who fail to satisfy the minimum period of service have their benefits reduced proportionately. As is true of the "final average" type of unit benefit formula, the benefit payable to a particular employee cannot be definitely ascertained until he reaches retirement.

The distinction between unit benefit plans and flat benefit plans may be only cosmetic. A flat benefit plan of 60 percent of pay reduced one thirtieth for each year less than 30 is identical to a unit benefit plan of 2 percent of pay per year of service with a maximum of 30 years credit, if the same definition of pay is used for both.

Another type of flat benefit formula ignores differences in both compensation and length of service, and provides a flat dollar benefit to all employees who satisfy a minimum period of credited service. This type of formula was typical of the early negotiated plans but is less common today.

**B. Definition of Year of Service.** Implicit in all of the foregoing formulas is the concept of a "year of service." There is no restriction on the manner in which a plan measures years of service for purposes of calculating the amount of accrued benefit at normal retirement age. However, there are restrictions on how years are measured to determine the amount of accrued benefit that is vested upon termination before normal retirement age. These restrictions are described in the chapter on withdrawal benefits. In practice, most plans choose to use the same method for measuring years for determining the accrued benefit upon normal retirement as they use for withdrawal benefits.

**C. Pattern of Benefit Accruals.** A pension plan need not provide the same amount of benefit accrual for each year of service. Depending upon the employer's conception of the equities involved or the personnel policy to be served, the plan may provide one scale of benefits for the first portion of total service, such as the first 10, 15, or 20 years, and a *higher* or *lower* scale for service thereafter. If the employer wants to encourage and reward long service, he may provide a higher scale of benefits for the later years of service than for the earlier years. This practice is sometimes referred to as "back loading." A mild form of back loading is contained in the federal Civil Service Retirement System, which provides for an annual benefit accrual of 1.5 percent for the first 5 years of service, 1.75 percent for the next 5 years, and 2 percent for all service beyond the first 10 years, the percentage in each case being applied to the participant's average salary for the three consecutive years of highest compensation.

On the other hand, if the employer wishes to encourage early retirement or at least discourage excessively long service, he may reduce the rate of benefit accrual after some period of service, such as 30 years, or eliminate further accruals altogether. That is, the plan may place a limit on the number of years of service that will be recognized for benefit purposes. This approach is sometimes used to favor executives who are near retirement when the plan is set up. The practice of providing more liberal benefits for the early years of service is known as "front loading."

Prior to ERISA, the employer had complete discretion as to the pattern of benefit accruals that he would build into his plan, so long as the plan in operation did not favor officers, shareholders, and highly compensated employees. Concerned lest employers attempt to undermine the new mandatory vesting standards through back loading the benefit formula, Congress removed that latitude and incorporated three alternative tests that serve to set limits on the extent of back loading that will be permitted in computing vested benefits under defined benefit plans.[7] Since these tests have their primary impact on the benefit accruals of terminated vested participants, they are described in the chapter on withdrawal benefits.

***D. Minimum Benefits.*** Many plans provide a floor of protection through inclusion of a minimum benefit provision that operates independently of the normal benefit formula. It is very common for unit benefit plans that base benefits on compensation to stipulate that the annual benefit accrual will not be less than a specified amount. For example, a plan that provides an annual benefit accrual (payable in monthly installments) of 1.5 percent of current compensation might stipulate that the annual benefit for any year of service is not to be less than $120. This is tantamount to saying that the minimum annual wage or salary for benefit purposes is $8,000 (1.5% of $8,000 = $120). There may be a minimum benefit for each year of service or a minimum for the total benefit. The minimum may be restricted to participants having a minimum period of service.

Some plans whose normal benefits are based on career average compensation make provision for a minimum benefit that is expressed as a percentage of final compensation or a percentage of

---

[7]ERISA §204(b), I.R.C. §411(b).

compensation as of some specified date. This type of provision is designed to update the career average salary base to a level that bears a reasonable relationship to the participant's earnings during the years immediately preceding retirement. Whereas the dollar benefit minimum is general and applies to all participants, the percentage of compensation minimum is specific to the individual participant. The latter is generally conditioned on a minimum period of service, such as 20 or 25 years, with reduced minimum benefits being payable for shorter periods of service.

**Defined Contribution Plan.**  A defined contribution plan or individual account plan is a plan that provides an individual account for each participant and bases his benefits solely upon the amount contributed to the participant's account and any expense, investment return, and forfeitures allocated to such participant's account.[8]

A defined contribution plan defines the amount of contribution to be added to each participant's account. Some plans do this directly by defining the amount the employer will contribute on behalf of each employee (e.g., 10 percent of pay). Other plans do not define the amount of contribution to be made, leaving that completely to the employer's discretion; but these plans define how whatever contributions are made will be allocated among the accounts of participants (e.g., in proportion to compensation).

The individual accounts must receive, at least annually, their share of the total investment return, including investment income received and realized and unrealized appreciation of market values.[9] Some plans allocate investment return quarterly, monthly, or even daily. Most types of assets are subject to fluctuation in market values, although some, such as bank savings accounts and certain annuity contracts, are maintained on a book value basis and, hence, suffer no diminution in value. If market values can decline, individual account balances can decrease as well as increase.

Ordinarily, the total plan assets are completely allocated to individual accounts. The sum of all of the account balances on any valuation date usually equals the total market value of the plan assets. If a participant terminates employment before he is vested,

[8]ERISA §3(34), I.R.C. §414(i).
[9]Rev. Rul. 80–155.

his account balance is forfeited and is applied either to reduce future employer contributions or to increase the accounts of other participants.

When a participant becomes eligible to receive a benefit, his benefit equals the amount that can be provided by his account balance. It may be paid in the form of a lump-sum distribution, a series of installments, or an annuity for the lifetime of the participant or the joint lifetimes of the participant and his beneficiary.

The principal types of defined contribution plans are generally classified as follows:

A.   Qualified plans under Code Section 401(a).
    1.   Money purchase pension plans.
        *a.*   Traditional money purchase plans.
        *b.*   Target benefit plans.
        *c.*   Thrift plans (other than profit sharing plans).
    2.   Profit sharing plans.
        *a.*   Traditional plans.
        *b.*   Thrift plans.
        *c.*   Cash or deferred arrangements (401(k)).
    3.   Stock bonus plans.
        *a.*   Traditional plans.
        *b.*   Employee stock ownership plans.
    4.   Voluntary employee contributions under qualified plans.
B.   Tax-deferred annuities under Code Section 403(b).
C.   Deferred compensation plans for state and local governments and tax-exempt organizations under Code Section 457.
D.   Individual retirement savings (including simplified employee plans) under Code Section 408.
    1.   Individual retirement accounts (IRAs).
    2.   Individual retirement annuities (IRAs).
E.   Nonqualified plans.

Plans of these many types are frequently established with two objectives: provision of retirement income and deferral of current taxable income. Sometimes one is the primary objective and sometimes the other is. Traditional money purchase plans and target benefit plans are frequently designed with a primary objective of providing retirement income, and they are discussed in the remainder of this chapter. The other types of plans, while often established to meet retirement income needs, are more frequently adopted primarily to defer taxable income; these types are discussed in later chapters.

*A. Money Purchase Pension Plan.* The essence of the defined contribution plan is that the employer does not—in form, at least—undertake to provide retirement benefits in accordance with any predetermined scale. By the terms of the plan, the employer—and the employees, if the plan is contributory—is committed to contribute to the plan pursuant to a fixed formula, but the benefits are treated as the variable factor. The scale of contributions will normally be set in the light of an anticipated level of benefits, but the undertaking is stated in terms of contributions rather than benefits.

Where the undertaking is to set aside periodic contributions according to a predetermined, or agreed upon, formula, the plan is referred to as a money purchase pension plan. Contributions are generally expressed as a percentage of covered payroll, the rate sometimes varying with the employee's age of entry into the plan. The plans are often contributory, the employer and employee sometimes contributing at the same rate, such as 5 percent of the employee's current salary. In some public employee retirement systems, the employee contributes a specified percentage of his salary and the employer contributes at a rate sufficient to provide a retirement benefit equal to that provided by the employee's contributions, but with no benefits being paid from the employer's contributions in the event of the employee's death before retirement. Under such an arrangement, the employer contributes at a lower rate than the employee, the differential depending upon the participant's sex and age of entry into the plan. The prevailing practice, however, is for the employer to contribute at a higher rate than the employee. Both the employer and the employee may contribute at a lower rate on that portion of the employee's salary subject to Social Security taxation than on the portion in excess of the taxable wage base.

Because the money purchase plan is a pension plan, the contributions must be definitely determinable.[10] This means that contributions may not be related to the employer's profits. However, forfeitures that result from the termination of employment of non-

---

[10]Treas. Reg. 1.401–1(b)(1)(i).

vested participants may be allocated to the accounts for the remaining participants.[11]

**B. Target Benefit Plan.** A target benefit plan has some characteristics of a defined benefit plan but is actually a defined contribution plan. Like a defined benefit plan it has a benefit formula that is used to determine a "target benefit." When the plan is established, the projected target benefit at normal retirement age is determined for each participant, assuming he continues employment with no change in compensation. The level annual contribution needed to fund each participant's target benefit is then computed, this amount being contributed for each participant and allocated to his individual account.

After a contribution in respect of a particular participant is made, the plan operates like any other defined contribution plan. At retirement, the individual's account may be paid in a lump sum or may be applied to the purchase of an annuity. If any annuity is purchased, it may be more or less than the original target benefit, depending upon whether the actual investment earnings of the fund and the annuity purchase rates used are more or less favorable than those assumed in the actuarial factors used to determine the contributions.

In any year subsequent to the establishment of the plan, a participant may receive an increase in compensation, increasing his projected target benefit. A calculation is then made of the level annual contribution required from his then-attained age to his normal retirement age to fund the increase in the target benefit. The employer contributes this increase in the required annual contribution plus the annual amount previously determined.

The target benefit plan has most of the simplicity of operation of a traditional money purchase plan. No actuarial valuations or actuarial reports are required. The contributions are determined by multiplying the target benefit by a factor in the plan that varies by age. To the extent that the experience follows fairly closely the assumptions used to develop the factors originally, the benefits may approximate those provided under a defined benefit plan with a benefit formula based on compensation and years of service.

---

[11] I.R.C. §401(a)(8).

Like other defined contribution plans, the target benefit plan is not subject to ERISA's plan benefits insurance program. However, it is subject to ERISA's maximum limits on contributions, discussed below, which may limit the contributions that could otherwise be made for older participants. If the target benefit is determined under a benefit formula that would be nondiscriminatory under a defined benefit plan, the target benefit plan is deemed nondiscriminatory, regardless of what benefits the plan actually pays as the result of its investment performance.[12] But this rule only applies if the plan uses an interest rate assumption of 5 percent to 6 percent for purposes of determining its contributions. In effect, all target benefit plans are forced to use the 5 percent to 6 percent range.

The Tax Reform Act appeared to inadvertently eliminate the possibility of a target benefit plan under which the benefit formula is integrated with Social Security. At the time of this writing, however, it appears that integration of a target benefit plan will be permitted if the benefit formula for the target benefit satisfies the requirements for integrated defined benefit plans.

**C. Negotiated Contribution Plan.**   There is another type of pension plan under which contributions are defined, with characteristics quite distinct from the traditional money purchase plan. It generally stems from collective bargaining and commonly covers the employees of a number of firms. The periodic contributions are determined by reference to rates of compensation, hours of work, or some productivity factor, and are accumulated in a pooled fund out of which defined benefits, not related to individual account or equities, are eventually paid. The fund, supported solely by employer contributions, is virtually always administered by a board of trustees on which the participating employers and unions are equally represented and are sometimes called Taft-Hartley plans. Most are also multiemployer plans (see Chapter 25).

At the time such a plan is set up, the trustees, with actuarial guidance, must establish a scale of benefits that can presumably be supported by the prospective flow of contributions. The benefit scale will usually be structured according to one of the patterns described above for defined benefit plans, a stated monthly benefit for each year of credited service currently being favored.

---

[12]Rev. Rul. 76–464.

Occasionally, a collective bargaining agreement will call for both a prescribed scale of benefits and a fixed rate of employer contributions. This is an actuarial anomaly, since only by sheer coincidence could these two functions remain in balance over any time period. The anomaly is resolved through periodic adjustments of either the benefit scale or the contribution rate, or both, or through varying the assumption as to the length of the period over which the initial past service liability is to be funded.

Such plans are defined benefit plans for purposes of ERISA.[13]

**Cash Balance Plan.** A cash balance plan is one that bears a strong resemblance to a defined contribution pension plan of the money purchase genre but is really a defined benefit plan. However, instead of benefits that accrue in accordance with a specified formula, the cash balance plan provides that the plan sponsor will establish and maintain an account for each participant and credit it annually with a specified percentage of the employee's compensation. The percentage may vary with the participant's length of service if this does not discriminate in favor of highly compensated employees. Each account is credited with interest at a rate specified in the plan or at a rate determined with reference to some index, such as the yield on one-year Treasury bills. The amounts to be credited to the participants' accounts may be determined with an objective of producing a normal retirement benefit equal to some targeted earnings replacement ratio.

Upon retirement a participant may elect to receive his benefit in the form of an annuity or (with spousal consent) a lump-sum distribution. If the employee elects a lump-sum distribution, the amount of the distribution is precisely equal to the account balance. If the employee, instead, elects to receive the benefit in the form of an annuity, the amount of monthly pension equals the amount that is actuarially equivalent to the account balance, based upon factors or actuarial assumptions specified in the plan.

Similarly, upon termination of employment before retirement, a vested participant may elect to receive his benefit in the form of a deferred annuity or (with spousal consent) a lump-sum distribution. If the employee is 100 percent vested upon termination of employ-

---

[13]*Connolly* v. *PBGC* (CA–9 rev'§ DC Cal) 581 F2d 729 cert. denied.

ment, the amount of lump-sum distribution that would be available is, again, exactly equal to the account balance. If the employee, instead, elects to receive the benefit in the form of an annuity, the amount of deferred monthly pension equals the amount that is actuarially equivalent to the account balance.

The accounts maintained for the individual participants are merely a bookkeeping device to keep track of the credited sums, the account balances at all times representing the accrued benefits. The account balances do not reflect actual employer contributions and actual investment earnings, as they do under a conventional money purchase pension plan. The credits to the accounts are "notional" contributions and investment earnings are not necessarily backed by assets of equal magnitude. That is why some call the individual accounts under the cash balance plan "phantom" accounts or "funny money" accounts.

The contribution that the plan sponsor makes to the plan in a particular year may be more or less than the aggregate sum credited to the accounts in that year. Using conventional actuarial assumptions and techniques, the plan actuary estimates the account balances that will accumulate with respect to the participants under the plan at date of valuation and determines the annual contributions, at some assumed rate of investment earnings, needed to "fund" the account balances when they are converted into a lump-sum or annuity payments. The investment earnings on the accumulated plan assets may be intended to be, and probably will be, greater than the "notional" interest credited to the participant accounts.

If the plan is terminated, the plan assets may be more or less than the sum of the individual account balances at that point. If the assets are insufficient to meet the benefit obligations under the plan, the Pension Benefit Guaranty Corporation will assume the unfunded benefits on the same terms as those applicable to traditional defined benefit plans. Some benefits may not be paid.

Proponents of the cash balance plan believe that it combines the best features of defined contribution and defined benefit plans. They point to several specific characteristics that, in their mind, should make the plan more appealing to employees than a conventional defined benefit plan. The bases on which benefits are credited are easily understood. Account balances, which are reported quarterly, appear to have more substance than the promise of a future benefit, especially for younger and mid-age employees with many years to work before claiming a benefit. While not an unmixed blessing, the account balance of an employee who leaves the employment of the plan sponsor is usually available in a lump sum, to the extent vested. Finally, the plans are generally structured to favor younger, short-service employees, typically the most numerous group, at the expense of the older, long-service employees.

The cash balance plan is not appropriate for all situations and has its own potential disadvantages, especially discrimination against long-service employees (unless adjustments are made for them). To date, relatively few employers have chosen to install it.

## Limitation on Benefits and Contributions

Before the 1974 legislation, it was not customary for plans to impose an upper limit on the benefits that will be payable other than that implicit in a flat benefit formula. Employers who provide benefits related to compensation have felt, by and large, that the relative economic status that prevailed among their active employees could properly be carried over into retirement. There were no laws that imposed limits on benefits[14] other than the general prohibition against discrimination in favor of certain groups and a specific limitation on the benefits that could be paid to the 25 highest-paid employees (at plan inception) in the event of plan termination within a few years after establishment.[15] This state of affairs was changed by ERISA, which added Section 415 to the Internal Revenue Code to impose a limit on the benefits that can be provided under a defined benefit plan and a limit on the contributions that can be made under a defined contribution plan. These limits were further reduced by the Tax Equity and Fiscal Responsibility Act of 1982 (TEFRA) and by the Tax Reform Act of 1986.

**Defined Benefit Plan.** Under the Code, as amended, the largest annual benefit that can be paid under a defined benefit plan in the

---

[14]There is a general requirement that compensation, including benefits, must be reasonable to be deductible as a corporate expense. In addition, there are limits upon the amount of deductible contributions for the plan as a whole. Deductions are discussed in a later chapter.

[15]Treas. Reg. 1.401–4(c).

form of a straight-life annuity is an amount equal to the lesser of
(*a*) $90,000 or (*b*) 100 percent of the participant's average compen-
sation during the three consecutive calendar years of highest compensation.[16] The $90,000 limit is adjusted annually after 1987 to
reflect changes in the cost of living, pursuant to regulations of the
Secretary of the Treasury.[17] These limits need not be scaled down
for preretirement ancillary benefits (such as medical, death, or disability benefits), but are subject to actuarial adjustment if the benefit
is payable in any form other than a straight-life annuity or a joint
and survivor annuity on the lives of the participant and his spouse.
There is an adjustment for the joint and survivor annuity if the
benefit payable to the survivor is greater than the benefit payable
during the joint lives of the annuitants. Upward adjustments are
permitted to reflect any employee contributions to the plan, including rollover contributions from another qualified plan or from
an individual retirement account.[18] An annual benefit of $10,000
may be provided, notwithstanding the salary limitation or the required adjustment for postretirement ancillary benefits, if the participant has not also been covered by a defined contribution plan
of the employer.[19]

The $90,000 limit is reduced for retirement before the Social
Security retirement age and is increased for retirement at any later
age.[20] For this purpose "Social Security retirement age" is deemed
to be age 65 for those born before 1938, age 66 for those born in
the period 1938 through 1954, and age 67 for those born later.[21] The
adjustment is made using Social Security early retirement reduction
factors for ages between 62 and the Social Security retirement age,
and using actuarial equivalent factors at other ages. For participants
born after 1954, the result is a limit at age 65 of $78,000 and at age
55 of approximately $35,000.

---

[16]I.R.C. §415(b).

[17]I.R.C. §415(d). The adjustments are to be based on the same procedures as are used
to adjust benefits under Social Security and will automatically change if the Social Security
basis changes.

[18]Rollover contributions are tax-free transfers of assets from another qualified plan or
individual retirement account. To be tax free, the assets must be transferred within 60 days
of the original distribution and other rules must be observed. Individual retirement accounts
are discussed in a later chapter.

[19]I.R.C. §415(b)(4).

[20]I.R.C. §415(b)(2).

[21]I.R.C. §415(b)(8).

The $90,000 limit is reduced proportionately for participants with less than 10 years of participation in the plan, while the $10,000 limit and the 100 percent limit are reduced proportionately for participants with less than 10 years of service.[22]

**Defined Contribution Plan.** There are corresponding limitations on the amounts that may be set aside for a participant in a defined contribution pension plan.[23] The annual addition (as defined) to a participant's account is limited to the lesser of $30,000 or 25 percent of the participant's compensation from the employer. This limit is applicable to the total additions to an employee's account during a year that are attributable to employer contributions, to employee contributions, and to forfeitures. The $30,000 will be adjusted to equal one fourth of the dollar limit for defined benefit plans after that limit, $90,000 in 1987, exceeds $120,000.[24]

**Two or More Plans.** If an employer operates two or more plans of the same type (i.e., defined contribution or defined benefit) and an employee participates in more than one, the aggregate contributions or benefits, as the case may be, must be within the limitations set forth above, as if only one plan were involved.[25]

If one plan is of the defined benefit type and another is of the defined contribution type, each plan is subject to the limitations appropriate to its type and, in addition, the two must be combined for the purpose of determining whether they satisfy an overall limitation.[26] The benefits and contributions of the combined plans cannot be more than 140 percent of the limitations applicable to one plan if the percentage of compensation limits apply, or more than 125 percent if the dollar limits apply.[27] For example, assuming the

---

[22]I.R.C. §415(b)(5).

[23]I.R.C. §415(c). Special rules apply to tax-deferred annuities for certain nonprofit organizations.

[24]I.R.C. §415(c).

[25]I.R.C. §415(f).

[26]I.R.C. §415(e).

[27]To accomplish this, §415(e) defines a *defined benefit plan fraction* and a *defined contribution plan fraction* to be determined for each year. The numerator of the defined benefit plan fraction is the projected annual benefit, assuming the participant keeps working at his present rate of pay until his normal retirement age. The denominator is the lesser of 1.25 times the dollar limit applicable to the year ($90,000, or adjusted amount after 1987) or 1.4 times the participant's average compensation for his high three years. For the defined contribution plan fraction, the numerator is the sum for the current year and all prior years

dollar limits do not apply, if the defined benefit plan provides benefits of 80 percent of the limit for a defined benefit plan, the defined contribution plan may provide 60 percent (140% − 80%) of the limitation for a defined contribution plan. If the combined benefits and contributions exceed the overall limitation, one or more of the plans is disqualified. The order in which the plans are to be disqualified is determined under regulations, subject to the stricture that no terminated plan may be disqualified until all other plans of the employer have been disqualified.[28]

## Top-Heavy Plan

Additional requirements apply to contributions and benefits under top-heavy plans.[29] A *top-heavy plan* is a plan under which the value of accrued benefits for *key employees* and their beneficiaries exceeds 60 percent of the value of accrued benefits for all employees and their beneficiaries.[30] Key employees include certain officers and owners.[31] Most small plans are top-heavy. Whether a plan is top-heavy is determined each plan year.

If a plan is top-heavy, it is subject to adjustments in the maximum limits on contributions and benefits, a maximum limit on recognizable compensation, more rapid vesting (described in Chapter 7), and, for non-key employees, minimum benefits or contributions.

A top-heavy plan must provide at least minimum benefits or contributions for all participants who are not key employees.[32] As a practical matter, when the requirement applies, most plans will

---

of the allocations to the participant's account that are subject to the limits under Section 415. The denominator is the sum for the current year and each prior year of the participant's service with the employer (regardless of whether the plan was in existence during those years) of the lesser of 1.25 times the dollar limit applicable to the year ($30,000 for 1983 and later, other amounts for prior years) or 1.4 times 25 percent of pay for each such year. The sum of the defined benefit plan fraction and the defined contribution plan fraction may not exceed 1.0 in any year. Special transition rules modify these calculations.

[28]Treas. Reg. 1.415-9.

[29]I.R.C. §416.

[30]I.R.C. §416(g). Certain plans are aggregated.

[31]I.R.C. §416(i). Key employees include all officers up to a total of 50 employees (or, if lesser, the greater of 3 employees or 10 percent of the employees). Key employees also include any owners who are among (*i*) the 10 employees owning the largest interests in the employer, (*ii*) 5 percent owners, and (*iii*) 1 percent owners whose compensation exceeds $150,000.

[32]I.R.C. §416(c).

probably apply it to all employees. Under a top-heavy defined benefit plan, the minimum accrued benefit must equal 20 percent of average compensation or, if less, 2 percent of average compensation multiplied by the employee's years of service, excluding plan years when the plan was not top-heavy and excluding all plan years beginning before 1984. Average compensation is generally for the five highest consecutive years, with certain years excluded. Under a defined contribution plan, the minimum required contribution is 3 percent of the employee's compensation or, if less, the highest percentage at which contributions are made for any key employee.

A top-heavy plan may not take account of compensation in excess of $200,000 in determining benefits or contributions.[33] Beginning in 1989 this requirement also applies to plans which are not top-heavy. This $200,000 will be subject to cost-of-living adjustments after 1989 in the same manner as the dollar limits under Section 415.

Under top-heavy plans, if there is both a defined benefit plan and a defined contribution plan, the 125 percent limit for the dollar limit on contributions and benefits under the combined plans is reduced to 100 percent.[34] However, this reduction does not apply to top-heavy plans where the value of accrued benefits for key employees does not exceed 90 percent of such value for all employees and where certain additional benefits or contributions are provided for non-key employees.

## Advantages and Disadvantages of Plan Approaches

Each of the various types of plans described in this chapter has advantages and disadvantages.

The basic appeal of the traditional money purchase approach is its simplicity. It is easy for the employees to understand and for the employer to administer. It is essentially an arrangement under which funds can be accumulated on behalf of active employees, without actuarial complexities, and used to provide retirement benefits within a wide range of ages, as permitted by the plan. There is no need to designate a normal retirement age, the significance of which is discussed later.

---

[33]I.R.C. §416(d).
[34]I.R.C. §416(h).

Under money purchase and target benefit plans, the accumulation of contributions in the participant's own individual account has strong psychological appeal and reinforces his feeling of security. Sums in an individual account, whether fully vested or not, have more reality to the participant than the accrual of pension credits toward a distant and uncertain retirement.

Defined contribution plans (both traditional money purchase plans and target benefit plans) do not ordinarily require actuarial computations. This creates an expense saving, compared to defined benefit plans. When a defined contribution plan provides benefits in the form of an annuity payable for life, an annuity is usually purchased from a life insurance company, which performs the needed actuarial functions. A minority of defined contribution plans provide for payment of life annuities directly without the purchase of an annuity contract; in these cases, actuarial calculations are required.

Another advantage of defined contribution plans from the standpoint of the employer is that his pension cost for all service rendered to date is fully funded. Unlike defined benefit plans, a defined contribution plan has no unfunded liability. A closely related advantage is that the defined contribution plan is not subject to plan benefits insurance (discussed later). The employer pays no premiums to the Pension Benefit Guaranty Corporation (PBGC) and is not exposed to a contingent liability if the plan should terminate. From the employee's viewpoint, there are no unfunded accrued benefits to be lost if the plan terminates.

A traditional money purchase plan has the further advantage that the future cost is fixed as a percentage of pay, subject only to reductions for forfeitures. Target benefit plans have higher costs for older participants, which may cause the cost of the plan to increase as a percentage of total pay as older employees receive pay increases and related increases in the target benefit to be funded. Future costs for defined benefit plans are even less predictable, since the employer's costs will depend upon future investment experience and other factors, and may differ markedly from the actuary's initial estimate.

Defined benefit plans offer more flexibility in meeting costs than a money purchase plan or target benefit plan. In a money purchase plan or a target benefit plan, each year the employer must contribute the exact amount required to be credited to employee accounts, less any forfeitures. In a defined benefit plan, the existence of an unfunded liability creates flexibility in funding, depending upon the rate at which the employer chooses to fund the unfunded liability. The employer who has been funding the unfunded liability more rapidly than required has a credit balance[35] that can be used to reduce or entirely eliminate the required contribution for a particular year.

Defined benefit plans and target benefit plans can provide benefits for years of past service before the plan was established. A traditional money purchase plan cannot. For this reason some employers have established defined contribution plans for future service and defined benefit plans for past service benefits.

The Internal Revenue Service requires that all qualified pension plans (defined benefit, money purchase, and target benefit), make benefits available in the form of an annuity, either an annuity payable for life or an annuity for a period of years.[36] A plan may also provide a benefit in the form of a lump sum, but no plan is required to do so. In practice, the availability of lump sums is less common among defined benefit plans than among money purchase plans. But where lump sums are available, the defined contribution plan in effect encourages the retiring participant to take his account balance in a lump sum rather than in the form of a life income. The periodic reporting to the participant of his account balance increases his awareness of the monies in the account and seems to dispose him to cash out the balance at retirement.

Under a defined benefit plan the investment risk is borne by the employer, while under a defined contribution plan the investment risk is borne by participants. If investment experience is favorable, it is clearly an advantage to the party that enjoys it, and may be considered a disadvantage by the party that does not share it. If investment experience is unfavorable, exactly the opposite is true. Under defined contribution plans, there may be participant dissatisfaction with the plan if the investment results are poor.

Many defined benefit plans provide annual benefit statements to all employees showing the amount of retirement income payable at normal retirement age, both the accrued benefit based upon service to date and the projected benefit based upon projected

---

[35]Funding requirements are described in Chapter 17.
[36]Treas. Reg. 1.401-1(b)(1)(i).

service. The defined contribution approach does not lend itself to simple calculation or expression of projected retirement income. The benefits will be whatever the accumulated account balance will provide. Benefit projections are sometimes prepared, but they generally rest on the assumption that current compensation and some assumed rate of investment earnings will prevail to a specified retirement age, with no change in annuity purchase rates or the corresponding actuarial assumptions of a trust fund plan. It should be noted, however, that uncertainty also surrounds the projection of benefits under a defined benefit plan because of the unpredictability of future salaries.

This greater unpredictability of benefits under defined contribution plans is not only a problem of communication through benefit statements; it is also a problem of achieving benefit objectives. A defined benefit plan with a final average pay formula can come close to meeting objectives for retirement income amounts; but a defined contribution plan—even a target benefit plan—may miss its mark. A defined contribution plan may prove more effective for younger workers than for older workers, or vice versa.

The negotiated contribution plan under collective bargaining has some characteristics of a defined benefit plan and some characteristics of a defined contribution plan. It shares some of the advantages and disadvantages of each type.

This discussion of advantages and disadvantages has been limited to defined benefit plans, traditional money purchase pension plans, and target benefit plans. Other types of plans that may be used to meet retirement needs, such as profit sharing plans, will be considered in later chapters.

---

## Questions

1. What is the basis for the statement that a total retirement income of 60 to 75 percent of an individual's gross earnings at time of retirement will enable him to enjoy a standard of living reasonably commensurate with what he enjoyed during the latter stages of his active service?

2. The percentage of an individual's gross earnings at point of retirement that is needed to sustain his preretirement standard of living

has been termed the *standard of living equivalency,* or SLE. Discuss the arguments for and against taking the following factors into account in computing an individual's SLE:

    *a.* His contribution to the pension plan in which he is participating.

    *b.* His individual savings.

    *c.* His personal earnings from other sources than wages or salary from the plan sponsor.

3. To what extent, if any, should the spouse's Social Security benefit be taken into account in setting the target replacement ratio for the employee?

4. Contrast the "career average" and "final average" types of benefit formula.

5. Explain the chief *disadvantages* of the career average and final average approaches to defining benefit entitlement.

6. Once an employee has satisfied the membership or participation requirements of a pension plan, must all future years of service with the employer be recognized for benefit accrual purposes? Explain.

7. What constraints does ERISA impose on the definition of a "year of service" for purposes of benefit accrual?

8. Identify the principal applications or uses of the money purchase approach in today's pension environment.

9. Why might it be argued that the employer sponsor has a greater fiduciary responsibility under a money purchase pension plan than under a defined benefit plan?

10. Describe the maximum limitations on benefits and contributions under qualified defined benefit and money purchase pension plans. What limit is applicable if an employee participates in both types of plans concurrently?

11. What factors tend to moderate the severity of the maximum benefit limitation imposed on defined benefit plans?

12.   *a.* What is a top-heavy plan?

    *b.* Describe the special requirements that must be met by a top-heavy plan to qualify for favorable tax treatment.

13. Evaluate the relative advantages and disadvantages of money purchase pension plans, as compared to defined benefit plans.

14. Identify the basic characteristics of a typical negotiated multiemployer pension plan.

15. Explain the nature and purpose of a target benefit pension plan. Would you classify this type of plan as a defined benefit or defined contribution pension plan? Justify your answer.

# 6 | Retirement Benefits (continued)

## Time of Payment

A SECOND BROAD ASPECT of retirement benefits relates to the conditions under which the benefits become payable. Under the great majority of plans, a participant is entitled to receive the full amount of his accrued benefits upon his retirement on or after attainment of a specified age, referred to as the normal retirement age. This is a contractual right and can be exercised without the consent of the employer. In some plans, however, the age requirement is supplemented by a minimum service requirement, such as five years. The plan may provide full or reduced benefits upon retirement prior to the normal retirement age. The Age Discrimination in Employment Act (ADEA) generally prohibits mandatory retirement at any age.[1]

The discussion of this chapter relates primarily to defined benefit plans. Considerations regarding the time and manner of payment of benefits are frequently different for defined contribution plans and are discussed in Chapters 26 to 28.

---

[1]ADEA §12(a),(c).

## Normal Retirement Age

The normal retirement age has traditionally been considered to be the earliest age at which eligible participants are permitted to retire with full benefits. However, ERISA defines normal retirement age simply as the normal retirement age specified in the plan, but not later than attainment of age 65 and completion of 10 years of participation.[2] For plan years beginning after 1987 the 10-years requirement is reduced to five years for any employee who becomes a participant within five years of the normal retirement age.

The definition of normal retirement age is one of three essential components in the definition of a benefit accrual, the components being the *dollar amount* of the benefit, the *age of the participant* at which the benefit is payable in full, and the *annuity form* under which the benefit is payable. The latter component refers to whether the benefit is expressed in terms of a single life annuity, a joint and survivor annuity, or a single life annuity with a refund feature. No benefit definition is complete without all three of these components. The dollar amount of prospective retirement benefits to be paid to two participants of the same age and sex under two separate pension plans may be identical, but the actuarial value of the accrued benefits (and, hence, their cost) will be quite different if they do not become payable at the same age and under the same annuity form.

Thus, the normal retirement age should be viewed more as an element in the definition of the retirement benefit than as a statement of when the participants are expected to retire. In actuality, the participants may retire over a wide range of ages, with appropriate adjustments in their benefits. Most plans permit retirement before the normal retirement age, usually subject to specified age and service restrictions, and most permit deferment of retirement beyond the normal retirement age.

Many retirement plans have linked retirement age to 5 or 10 years of service or participation, but some have a much longer period if the minimum age is under 65. For example, the normal retirement age may be the earlier of age 65 with 5 years of service, 60 with 20 years of service or 55 with 30 years of service. Discontinuities in benefit entitlement may be avoided by providing benefits

---

[2]ERISA §3(24), I.R.C. §411(a)(8).

unreduced by the employee's age whenever his age and service equal a specified number, such as 90. A provision of this sort is referred to as the "Rule of 90," although the concept may also be applied in establishing eligibility for vested benefits. Under the Rule of 90, such combinations as age 60 and 30 years of service would entitle the participant to full benefits for his credited years of service. The rule may, of course, be stated in terms of other numbers, such as 85 or 95. Some plans with a nominal normal retirement age permit retirement before that age, subject to minimum service requirements, with full benefits for the years of accrued service. Under some collectively bargained plans, participants are permitted to retire with full accrued benefits after a specified amount of service, such as 30 years, irrespective of age. Some plans have alternative criteria for normal retirement age, such as the earlier of age 65 or the completion of 30 years of service. Under all the foregoing arrangements, it would have to be said that there are *multiple* normal retirement ages, dependent upon the related service requirement and the participant's age of entry into the plan.

In addition to its actuarial function, the normal retirement age serves as an instrument of personnel policy. In most companies it does indicate the age at which the great majority of employees would be expected to retire—or certainly the age by which most employees would have retired. Some plans previously specified an age, usually 70, at which retirement was to be mandatory but mandatory retirement generally is no longer permitted.[3]

In practice, many employees elect to retire at the normal retirement age, the earliest age at which they can receive unreduced benefits. From the standpoint of the personnel policy of an individual employer, the normal retirement age should be the age beyond which the service of his employees would be uneconomical. This point, of course, is not easy to determine. In theory, multiple retirement ages should be adopted in many cases, since a retirement age that would be suitable for one class of employees might be completely inappropriate for another group. In the airlines industry, for example, flight personnel should—and do—have a lower retirement age than nonflight employees. Jobs which require physical

---

[3]An exception applies where age is a bona fide occupational qualification reasonably necessary to the normal operation of the particular business. Special rules apply to law enforcement officers and firefighters. ADEA §4(f),(i). *Western Airlines, Inc.* v. *Criswell*, 472 U.S. 400(1985).

strength and endurance may call for a lower retirement age than those which emphasize mental agility. Within particular job classifications, moreover, there are differences in individual employees which, ideally, should be recognized. Nevertheless, the practice, subject to certain exceptions, is to have a normal retirement age that is applicable to all employees, with provisions for adjustments to particular situations through optional retirement arrangements, which are discussed below. Since ADEA generally does not allow an employer to discharge an employee on the basis of age, any discharge of an older employee may require evaluating the mental and physical fitness of the individual for continued employment.

Under ERISA, the normal retirement age for vesting purposes cannot be later than age 65 or, if later, the 10th anniversary of the participant's entry into the plan (5th anniversary for those hired after age 60). Age 65 is designated as the normal retirement age for all employees in the large majority of plans. At one time, some plans stipulated a lower retirement age for female employees, but that is now forbidden under the rules of the Equal Employment Opportunity Commission. An exception to the normal retirement age is sometimes made for employees who are beyond a specified age at the time the pension plan is established. This applies to employees over 55 or 60 on the effective date, for whom the normal retirement age may be set in terms of completion of 5 or 10 years of participation or attainment of age 70, whichever occurs first. This approach is primarily used for plans funded through individual insurance or annuity contracts. The purpose of this staggered retirement is primarily to spread the cost of the benefits, composed principally of past service credits, over a longer period than would otherwise be available. Other reasons for staggered retirement at the inception of the plan are to permit high-age, low-service employees to accumulate larger pensions and to cushion the personnel impact.

### Early Retirement

It is customary to provide that an employee may retire earlier than the normal retirement age, subject to the attainment of a specified age, typically 55, and possibly the fulfillment of a minimum period of service, such as 10, 15, or 20 years. Employer consent for early retirement may be required, in which event the value of the early retirement benefit must not exceed the value of the employee's vested benefit at that time. Plans that require employer consent tend to rely on the age requirement alone, while those that permit early retirement at the option of the employee are inclined to impose both an age and service requirement. Proposed IRS regulations would no longer allow a plan to require employer consent for early retirement.[4]

Some plans permit early retirement only in the event of total and permanent disability, which is discussed in Chapter 8. In such plans, age and service requirements are also imposed. Some of the plans provide a special disability benefit, while others pay only the same percentage of the regular accrued benefit that would normally be paid on early retirement.

The calculation of the early retirement benefit involves two steps. The first is to determine the amount of benefit that would be payable at normal retirement age on the basis of the participant's service and compensation to date of *early* retirement. This determination is made in the same manner as the computation of the vested benefit, described in Chapter 7. The second step is to multiply the *accrued* benefit payable at normal retirement age by an early retirement factor reflecting the fact that benefit payments begin earlier than was contemplated and, therefore, extend over a longer time; the assets supporting the benefits earn less investment income before payments commence; and there will be no gains to the plan from participants' dying before benefit payments commence (the benefit of survivorship).

When the accrued retirement benefits are reduced by a scale of percentages that reflect the foregoing factors, they are said to be "actuarially reduced" or "actuarially equivalent." The expression "full actuarial reduction" is frequently applied to the process that gives full recognition to the longer payout period and loss of investment earnings (and benefit of survivorship) to distinguish it from the results obtained by applying a higher scale of percentages to the accrued benefits.

The reduction in the accrued benefits for early retirement depends upon the mortality and interest assumptions that underlie the calculation of the actuarial value of the normal retirement benefits. The greater the assumed rates of mortality and the higher the interest rate assumption, the greater will be the reduction for each

---

[4]Prop. Reg. §1.401–4, Q–3.

year of early retirement. The percentage reduction in the accrued benefits for each year of early retirement slopes downward. When the actuarial value of the normal retirement benefits is computed on the basis of the UP–1984 Table and a 6 percent interest assumption, the percentage reduction in the accrued normal retirement benefits is about 10 percent per year, expressed as a percentage of the benefit for the next higher age. For example, the benefit payable at age 64 is about 90 percent of that payable at age 65; that payable at age 63 is about 90 percent of that payable at age 64; and so on. This relatively uniform progression continues down to at least age 55.[5]

The proportion of the accrued normal retirement benefit that would be payable in connection with early retirement at ages 55 through 64, under the mortality and interest assumptions set forth above, are shown in Table 1. It must be emphasized that the percentages are applied to the benefit credits accrued to the date of early retirement and not to the benefits that would have been payable at age 65 had the employee continued working to that age. No distinction is allowed between male and female employees because of the difference in their life expectancy.[6] Since retirement at age

**TABLE 1**
**Proportion of Accrued Normal Retirement Income Available in Event of Early Retirement at Various Ages under a Plan with Normal Retirement Age 65***

| Age at Retirement | Benefit Percentage |
|---|---|
| 64 | 89.6% |
| 63 | 80.5 |
| 62 | 72.5 |
| 61 | 65.5 |
| 60 | 59.3 |
| 59 | 53.8 |
| 58 | 48.9 |
| 57 | 44.5 |
| 56 | 40.6 |
| 55 | 37.1 |

*These percentages apply to the benefits earned to the date of early retirement and not to the benefits that would have been payable had the employee continued working to age 65.

[5]It is interesting to note that the Social Security Administration reduces the normal old-age insurance benefit by a uniform 6⅔ percent for each of the first three years prior to the Social Security retirement age, and 5 percent for each additional year between the Social Security retirement age and age 62.

[6]*Arizona Governing Committee* v. *Norris,* 463 U.S. 1073 (1983). *Long* v. *State of Florida,* Nos. 86–3282 and 86–3410, December 19, 1986, 11th Cir.

55 results in a benefit of less than half the normal accrued benefit under any scale that purports to reflect actuarial reductions, most plans do not permit retirement more than 10 years prior to the normal retirement age.

Some plans, especially those subject to collective bargaining, provide for a stipulated percentage discount for each month by which actual retirement precedes the normal retirement date. These monthly factors may approximate the annual factors that are geared to a full actuarial reduction, or they may be clearly designed to produce a smaller reduction than what would be called for if full weight were being given to actuarial considerations. There is great interest among employee groups generally in more liberal early retirement benefits or, conversely, in early retirement discounts that are smaller than the full actuarial reduction. More and more plans are using an arbitrary scale of early retirement discounts unrelated to the actuarial scale and frequently the same for each month or year by which actual retirement precedes normal retirement. Typical discounts are one half of 1 percent per month (6 percent per year) or 1/180 per month (6.666 percent per year). Some plans use a uniform scale of discounts, such as 1/180 per month, down to a specified age, such as 60, and a smaller scale, such as 1/360 per month, thereafter down to the youngest age at which early retirement is permitted.[7] The arbitrary scale, particularly the one half of 1 percent reduction per month, is easier to explain to participants than the full actuarial reduction. The scale may provide for full accrued benefits for retirement not earlier than a specified age, such as 62,[8] and then percentage discounts of different patterns for early retirement factors when they are not based on the full actuarial reduction. Liberal factors are frequently designed to encourage early retirement, being coordinated with the overall personnel policy of the employer. More often, they are granted in response to collective bargaining demands. The general practice of using early retirement factors more favorable than the actuarially equivalent ones is referred to as "subsidized early retirement."

---

[7]This scale is included in Rev. Rul. 71–466 as a permissible basis for adjusting allowable integration limits, described in Chapter 10.

[8]This, of course, is tantamount to reducing the normal retirement age for individuals going directly from active service to retirement to the lowest age at which no early retirement factor is applied.

Special provision may be made for employees who retire early because of poor health. These arrangements are described in the discussion of disability benefits.

## Deferred Retirement

As was indicated earlier, under ADEA and many state laws, employers must generally allow continuation of employment beyond the normal retirement date, which is usually the end of the month in which the employee reaches the normal retirement age. Employees may want to continue in service beyond the normal retirement date to earn additional benefit credits, to enlarge the salary base to which the benefit formula will apply, to spread the liquidation of the accumulated assets over a shorter period of years (and thus increase the amount of the periodic payments), or to enjoy the continuation of their salary. There may also be nonfinancial reasons for wanting to continue on the job.

When an employee delays his retirement beyond the normal retirement date, his retirement benefits are usually withheld until the actual date of retirement. Three alternative methods have been commonly used to determine the amount of monthly benefit payable upon deferred retirement. Under one method the amount of monthly pension is frozen at the normal retirement age and the amount paid upon actual later retirement is precisely the same dollar benefit that the participant would have been entitled to had he retired on the normal date. Under the second approach the amount just described is increased to be the actuarial equivalent of the amount that would have been payable at the normal retirement date.

Under the third approach the amount of monthly benefit is computed as if the employee's actual retirement date were his normal retirement date. The critical feature of this approach is that benefits continue to accrue in the normal manner for service beyond normal retirement, any changes in the compensation base being recognized in the benefit formula. The result is that if two employees, one age 45 and the other age 50, for example, are hired at the same time and both work for 20 years at equal salary rates, retiring at age 65 and 70, respectively, they will receive equal monthly payments under this method. Other methods generally produce unequal benefits. The benefits determined under this third approach are sometimes greater and sometimes smaller than the normal retirement benefits adjusted to their actuarial equivalence.

For plan years beginning after 1987 benefits credited upon deferred retirement generally may not be less than those determined under the third approach described above.[9] For plans not already using this continuing accrual approach, the simplest method of compliance is to adopt it. An alternative is to specify that benefits will be the greater of those determined by the continuing accrual approach and some other method, such as the actuarial increase approach. One permissible approach that has been used by a few plans is to provide both continuing accrual for the additional service and an actuarial increase of all accrued benefits for the period of deferral.

For calendar years after 1988 all participants generally are required to begin receiving their pensions no later than April 1 following the year they attain age 70½, regardless of whether they have actually retired.[10] When coupled with the requirement to continue accruing benefits, the result is curious. An employee who continues working past age 70½ must begin receiving his pension and also must continue accruing benefits. Presumably the amount of pension being paid in this case must be increased periodically to reflect the continuing accruals.

## Manner of Payment

Implicit in most pension plans is the payment of a retirement benefit that continues throughout the remaining lifetime of the retired employee.[11] The plan may provide various collateral benefits, but underlying the whole scheme must be the promise of a life income to the participant upon his retirement. If this promise is underwritten or guaranteed by a life insurance company, the life income will be provided in the form of an annuity contract of some type. If the plan is funded through a trust, the benefits may be provided through an annuity contract purchased from an insurance company, probably at the time of the employee's retirement, or they may be paid directly from the trust fund. A series of annual or monthly

---

[9]ADEA §4(i); ERISA §204(b)(1); I.R.C. §411(b)(1).

[10]I.R.C. §401(a)(9)(C).

[11]The Internal Revenue Service requires a qualified pension plan to make benefits available in the form of an annuity, either a life annuity or an annuity for a period of years. Treas. Reg. 1.401–1(a)(1)(i).

payments is referred to as an "annuity" or "annuity benefit," whether or not it is insured by a life insurance company.

## Types of Annuities

Several forms of annuities are available for the disbursement of pension benefits. Classified broadly, life annuities may be of the single life or joint life variety, and within that classification they may be either of the pure or refund type. As indicated by its title, a single life annuity is one which is based on only one life. The pure form of single life annuity, usually referred to as "straight-life annuity," provides periodic, usually monthly, income payments that continue as long as the annuitant lives and terminate upon his death. The annuity is considered fully liquidated upon the death of the annuitant, and no guarantee is given that any particular number of monthly payments will be made. Because of the absence of any benefit after death, this type of single life annuity provides the largest monthly income per dollar of purchase price outlay.[12]

The annuity may promise that a certain number of monthly payments will be made whether the annuitant lives or dies, with payments to continue, of course, if the annuitant lives beyond the guaranteed period. In insurance circles, this type of annuity is referred to as a "life annuity certain and continuous," and the annuitant may elect 60, 120, 180, or 240 guaranteed installments.[13] The cost of the annuity increases with the number of guaranteed installments, since life contingencies are not involved during the guaranteed period.

The refund type of single life annuity includes any annuity that guarantees the return in one manner or another a portion or all of the purchase price of the annuity. An "installment refund annuity" promises that, if the annuitant dies before receiving monthly payments equal to the purchase price of the annuity, the payments shall be continued to the annuitant's beneficiary until the full cost has been recovered. If the contract promises, upon the death of

---

[12]In this generalized description of annuities, the monies committed to the annuity will be called the price or purchase price, following insurance terminology. Under a pension plan, assets equal to the actuarial reserve for benefits payable to a retiring employee are set aside, in theory or in fact, to be liquidated in accordance with a stipulated form of annuity.

[13]Such a range of options is not usually provided under a pension plan.

the annuitant, to pay to the annuitant's beneficiary in a lump sum the excess (if any) of the purchase price of the annuity over the sum of the monthly payments, it is designated a "cash refund annuity." The only difference between the "cash refund annuity" and the "installment refund annuity" is that, under the former, the unliquidated purchase price is refunded in a lump sum at the time of the annuitant's death; whereas, in the latter case, the monthly installments are continued until the purchase price has been recovered. These two types of annuities are more costly than the straight-life annuity, with the "cash refund annuity" being somewhat more costly than the "installment refund annuity" because of the loss of interest. A "modified cash refund annuity" promises to refund only a portion of the purchase price, usually the accumulated employee contributions.

The joint and survivor annuity provides periodic payments as long as either of two persons shall live. For most combinations of ages, this is the most expensive of all annuity forms. This type of contract is primarily designed to provide old-age income to a husband and wife. The income may be reduced upon the death of either annuitant to either one half or two thirds of the original amount, on the theory that the survivor does not require as large an income as do the two annuitants. Under some plans, the reduction is made when either annuitant dies. Under others, the reduction is made only if the retired participant dies first. This latter arrangement is often called a "contingent annuitant option."

### Normal and Optional Annuity Forms under Pension Plans

The benefits under a pension plan, and their cost, are calculated on the assumption that the benefit payments will conform to a particular pattern. This pattern is known as the "normal annuity form," and it is the third component of the benefit formula, the other two being the benefit amount and the age at which the payments will commence. The normal annuity form specified in most noncontributory plans is the straight-life annuity, although it is not unusual to guarantee a certain number of installments. Contributory plans usually adopt a modified cash refund annuity. This form promises that, should the employee die before receiving retirement benefits equal to the accumulated value at retirement of his contributions, with or without interest, the difference between his benefits and this accumulation will be refunded in a lump sum to his estate or to a designated beneficiary. Some contributory plans prescribe a life annuity with payments guaranteed for 5 or 10 years, either form of which will, in the typical case, assure the return of the employee's accumulated contributions.

Pension plans have traditionally given the participant the option of electing, before or at retirement, and at his own expense, an annuity form different from that prescribed in the plan document. The range of options has differed, some plans offering a wide choice and others being rather restrictive; but it has been customary to offer some form of joint and survivor annuity so the participant might assure his spouse of a life income in some amount. The amount of benefit payable under an optional annuity form is usually calculated to be actuarially equivalent to the amount payable under the normal form. The factors used, or the actuarial assumptions used to compute them, must be specified in the plan or defined by reference to some independent source, for example, insurance company annuity purchase rates or interest rates published by the PBGC.[14]

All pension plans must provide that retirement benefits payable as a life annuity to an employee married to his or her current spouse for at least one year will be automatically paid in the form of a "qualified" joint and survivor annuity unless the participant elects otherwise with the consent of the spouse. The spouse's consent must be in writing and must be witnessed by a plan representative or a notary public.[15] A "qualified" joint and survivor annuity is defined as a type that provides income to the surviving spouse in an amount equal to at least one half of the income payable during the time that the employee and his spouse are both alive. The participant must be given a reasonable time before the annuity starting date to elect in writing not to have the retirement benefits provided under a joint and survivor annuity.

In the absence of a provision to the contrary, the spouse would lose any interest in the joint and survivor annuity if the participant were to die before retirement. This is considered to be a peculiarly inequitable consequence, if the participant dies after becoming eligible for early retirement but before entering on the joint and

---

[14]Rev. Rul. 79–90.
[15]ERISA §205, I.R.C. §401(a)(11).

survivor annuity. In the past, many plans have voluntarily embodied a provision making a presumption that any participant who dies
after the early retirement date, but before actual retirement, had
entered on a joint and survivor annuity of a specified type (or some
other kind of refund annuity) on the day of his death. A qualified
pension plan must provide a "qualified" preretirement survivor
annuity benefit to the spouse of any participant who dies after
becoming entitled to a vested benefit but before the annuity starting date. This benefit is described with other death benefits in
Chapter 8.

The law permits the employer to place the cost of the joint and
survivor annuity on the participant and his spouse in the form of
reduced benefits. The actuarial reduction usually depends on the
age of the individuals and on the assumptions used. Under typical
assumptions, the reduction in benefits provided upon retirement
under a joint and one-half survivor annuity is 10 percent for an
employee age 65 with a spouse age 65, when compared to the
benefits under a comparable straight-life annuity payable in respect
of the participant. Many plans use an approximate factor, such as
10 percent, which applies in every case regardless of age.

The benefits can be further reduced under the present law to
reflect the cost of the preretirement survivor annuity protection
enjoyed by the spouse before retirement. Some plans reduce the
pension payable at age 65 by 0.5 percent for each year of preretirement survivor annuity coverage. The participant is required to
receive notice, and to have the right to elect, with the spouse's
consent, not to have the protection of the preretirement survivor
annuity. But most plans make no charge for the preretirement protection and provide it to all participants automatically, avoiding the
cumbersome notice and election requirements.

It may be only a matter of time before organized employees and
other groups demand that some type of joint and survivor annuity
benefits be provided at no cost to the participants. This would be
a demand that the joint and survivor annuity be the normal annuity
form under the plan. Some groups have already protested against
the cost (in the form of reduced benefits) of joint and survivor
annuity benefits and have negotiated the use of benefit reduction
factors that are less than those actuarially equivalent. This is comparable to the negotiation of subsidized early retirement factors.

Under the joint and one-half survivor annuity, most plans use the type of joint and survivor annuity that reduces the income only if the spouse is the survivor. If the employee survives his spouse, he continues to receive the same income that was payable when both annuitants were alive. Some plans, generally those that utilize the settlement options of individual insurance or annuity contracts, use the type that reduce when either spouse dies. Either type of joint and survivor annuity may be made available under ERISA.

An option that is available only in the case of early retirement is the so-called Social Security adjustment option. The purpose of the option is to have the benefit from the pension plan plus Social Security be a level benefit throughout the period of retirement, notwithstanding the fact that the full amount of the Social Security old-age insurance benefit is not available until age 65 or later. To accomplish this the original amount of annuity payable upon early retirement is replaced by two other annuity amounts which in the aggregate are actuarially equivalent to the original amount. One of these annuity amounts is a temporary annuity payable to age 65 equal to the expected Social Security benefit, while the other is an annuity payable for life.[16]

If the benefit is provided in any form other than the normal form, the amount of monthly payment will be adjusted to be actuarially equivalent to the payments under the normal form, so that the present value of the expected payments will be the same as if the normal form had been elected. Table 2, based upon one particular set of actuarial assumptions, shows the amount of monthly income under some of the commonly used annuity forms for each $100 of monthly income that would have been provided under the normal form for a participant retiring at various retirement ages. All plans are required to include in the plan document either the actuarial factors used or the assumptions upon which they are based.[17] The factors may not differ by sex.

---

[16]Consider the example of an employee eligible to receive a monthly benefit of $600 from the plan at age 60 and a $500 monthly benefit from Social Security at age 65. A benefit of $500 per month from age 60 to age 65 would have the same actuarial value as a lifetime benefit of $200 per month from age 60. Therefore, to provide a level lifetime benefit, the plan's lifetime benefit is reduced by $200 to $400, making possible a $500 monthly supplement from age 60 to age 65.

[17]I.R.C. §401(a)(25).

**TABLE 2**
**Monthly Benefits Provided at Various Retirement Ages under Commonly Used Annuity Forms for Each $100 Provided under a Straight-Life Annuity***

| Age at Retirement | *Life Annuity* | | | *100 Percent Joint and Survivor Annuity†* | *50 Percent Joint and Survivor Annuity†* |
| | *No Period Certain* | *5-Year Certain* | *10-Year Certain* | | |
| --- | --- | --- | --- | --- | --- |
| 55 | $100.00 | $99.16 | $96.84 | $86.54 | $92.79 |
| 60 | 100.00 | 98.55 | 94.69 | 84.23 | 91.44 |
| 65 | 100.00 | 97.43 | 91.16 | 81.83 | 90.01 |
| 70 | 100.00 | 95.62 | 85.91 | 79.59 | 88.64 |

*Rate basis: UP-1984 Table and 6 percent interest.
†Contingent or joint annuitant assumed to be the same age as the employee in each case.

## Cash Option at Retirement

A perennial issue in plan design is whether a participant upon reaching retirement should be permitted to take the actuarial value of his retirement benefit in the form of a lump sum, rather than in monthly payments spread over his remaining lifetime. There may be a certain amount of pressure from employees for the so-called cash option, and some plans permit employees to make a full or partial withdrawal of the commuted value of their pension benefits.

Justification for the cash option is generally couched in terms of flexibility of financial planning. It is argued that some employees have a more urgent need for a lump sum than for a life income. They may need the money for medical treatment or to buy a retirement home. Some may want to invest in a business of their own. Others may feel that they can invest their share of the plan assets more profitably than the investment manager or in a way that will provide more protection against inflation. Rollover of the lump-sum value into an IRA may be especially attractive. In some cases, the pension benefit may be too small to justify installment payments, while in others it may be so large that the participant should be permitted to draw some of it in a lump sum. Under some plans, the cash option may be the only way that an employee in poor health can preserve his pension for the protection of his spouse or other dependents.

The primary arguments against the lump-sum option are that (1) the employee might squander the lump sum or invest it unwisely, leaving him dependent upon society; (2) the employee would give up the benefit of a life annuity that would protect him against outliving his income; (3) the distribution is based on book value, rather than on the more proper and equitable market value; and (4) the plan would be exposed to adverse selection by healthy persons electing a life income and those with health impairments electing a lump sum.[18]

The basic issue is whether a pension plan is to be regarded as a general savings program, with all the flexibility that one would want in such a program, or as an instrument of business and social policy designed to ensure a dependable source of income throughout the remaining lifetime of retired workers.

Under a defined benefit plan, when a vested benefit is to be paid in a lump sum, its value must be determined on the basis of assumptions regarding interest and mortality. The interest rates used may not exceed the interest rates used by PBGC in determining plan termination liabilities, unless the distribution determined on this basis would exceed $25,000. In this latter case the plan administrator may use any interest rates that do not exceed 120 percent of the PBGC rates, but the resulting lump sum value paid may not fall below $25,000.[19]

## Assignment, Alienation, and Qualified Domestic Relations Orders

The law requires a qualified pension plan to contain a general prohibition against the assignment or alienation of vested benefits. To provide a degree of flexibility that would otherwise be lacking, the law permits the plan to give a retired employee the right to make a voluntary, revocable assignment of a portion of his retirement benefits not to exceed 10 percent of any benefit payment. However, there is a specific prohibition in the law against alienation of any vested benefits for the purpose of defraying the administrative costs of the plan.[20]

---

[18]Some plans that permit a full withdrawal of the actuarial value of the accrued benefits attempt to protect themselves against adverse selection by requiring the participant to elect the cash option some years in advance of retirement.

[19]ERISA §203(e)(2); I.R.C. §§ 411(a)(11)(B); 417(e)(3).

[20]ERISA §206(d), I.R.C. §401(a)(13).

The nonalienation provision generally prevents pension benefits from being attached by a court order. An exception to this, however, is the qualified domestic relations order (QDRO).[21]

For the above purpose a domestic relations order is defined as a court order or court approval of a property settlement agreement that is made pursuant to a state domestic relations law and which relates to the provision of child support, alimony payments, or marital property rights to a spouse, former spouse, child, or other dependent of a participant. A qualified domestic relations order (QDRO) gives an alternate payee the right to receive part or all of the benefits payable with respect to a participant under a plan. In order to be a QDRO a domestic relations order must meet several requirements. A QDRO must clearly specify certain facts and it may not require a plan to pay any type or form of benefit not otherwise provided under the plan. Complex procedural requirements must be satisfied.

## Questions

1. What is the significance of the "normal retirement age" specified under the terms of a defined benefit pension plan?
2. Under what circumstances might it be said that there is more than one normal retirement age under a defined benefit pension plan?
3. A participant in a defined benefit pension plan who retires before the normal retirement age typically receives a smaller pension benefit than if he had remained in service until the normal retirement age. Explain why an adjustment is usually made in the benefit payable to a plan participant who retires early.
4. What does it mean for a pension plan to use "subsidized" early retirement factors?
5. Explain the various approaches that have been taken in a defined benefit plan with respect to the retirement benefits of a participant who continues in the plan beyond normal retirement age. Must a plan participant who remains in the employer's service beyond normal retirement age continue to accrue benefit credits?

---

[21]ERISA §206(d)(1),(3); I.R.C. §§401(a)(13)(B), 414(p).

6.  If a participant continues working after his normal retirement age, when must his pension begin?

7.  What is the significance of the "normal annuity form" stipulated in a pension plan?

8.  Describe the characteristics of the qualified joint and survivor annuity under which benefits must be paid in the absence of an election by the employee to the contrary.

9.  What is the nature and purpose of a "contingent annuitant option"?

10. Adjustments in the pension benefit of a plan by reason of early retirement or the election of an optional annuity form are usually based on factors or actuarial assumptions specified in the pension plan. Would it be feasible and equitable to use different mortality and interest assumptions for benefit adjustment purposes than for valuation purposes? Why might a plan sponsor want to use a fixed and independent set of mortality and interest assumptions to calculate benefit adjustments for early retirement and the election of optional annuity forms? Why might approximate factors be used instead of precise actuarial factors?

11. Do you believe that a retiring employee should be permitted to take a lump-sum cash payment in lieu of a life annuity? Why?

12. If a retiring participant is permitted to elect a lump-sum payment in lieu of the pension to which he is entitled, should the cash out value be based on the highest interest assumptions permissible, or should some lower interest assumptions be used? Why?

13. Are there any exceptions to the ERISA-mandated general prohibition against the attachment or seizure of vested pension rights by the creditors of pension plan participants? In your opinion, should there be any exceptions?

# 7 | Withdrawal Benefits

MOST OF THE PARTICIPANTS in a pension plan on any given date will not remain in the service of the employer until retirement. Some will die, some will become mentally or physically incapacitated, some will have their service terminated by action of the employer, while others, for various reasons, will voluntarily sever their connection with the employing firm. These contingencies have to be dealt with in the plan document. The next chapter will describe the impact on benefit rights of death and permanent disability. This chapter deals with the rights of plan participants whose services are terminated prior to retirement for reasons other than death or disability.

In a sense, the title given to this chapter is a misnomer, since withdrawal from service never creates any benefit rights that were not already in existence. The real question is what happens to the benefit credits or funds accumulated in respect of a plan participant when the service of that individual is terminated before retirement.

## Benefits Attributable to Employee Contributions

One of the basic rules of pension plan design is that a participant must be assured that he or his beneficiaries will ultimately recover, in one form or the other, all the contributions that he makes to the plan. This rule applies not only to voluntary contributions but also to those that he is required to make under the terms of the plan. Such a rule is a pragmatic necessity if participation in the plan is optional, since few employees would be willing to have their contributions forfeited upon death or withdrawal from the plan. Even if participation is a condition of employment, equity dictates that the contributions be returnable in the event that the participant does not survive in the employer's service until early or normal retirement.

The law provides that an employee's rights in that portion of his accrued benefits derived from his own contributions are nonforfeitable,[1] which is the generic term used in the ERISA to refer to a vested status. Since no qualifying conditions were imposed, the benefits are vested immediately and fully. Futhermore, they are vested in the event of death, since no exception was made for that contingency, as it was for benefits attributable to employer contributions.

Before ERISA, virtually all contributory plans provided that, if a terminating employee exercised his right to withdraw his own contributions, with interest, if any, he would forfeit all rights to any pension benefits attributable to employer contributions. This was true, even though he had acquired a vested interest in the accrued benefits financed by employer contributions. In legal terms, the withdrawal of his contributions divested the benefits that had been previously vested. Nevertheless, terminating employees, attracted to a lump-sum distribution, almost invariably withdrew their own contributions, in many cases relinquishing rights to deferred pensions having an actuarial present value greatly in excess of the employee contributions recovered.[2]

ERISA continues the privilege of the terminating employees to withdraw their own contributions while denying employers the right to cancel the benefit accruals that they had previously vested.[3] An

---

[1]ERISA §203(a)(1), I.R.C. §411(a)(1).

[2]Under the contribution schedules and actuarial cost methods of some plans, employees at the younger ages contribute at a level in excess of the annual actuarial cost of their currently accruing benefits. If these employees terminate—and the highest rates of termination occur among younger employees—there are no employer-financed benefits to be canceled.

[3]ERISA §203(a)(3)(D), I.R.C. §401(a)(19), §411(a)(3)(D).

exception was made with respect to employees whose benefits are less than 50 percent vested. In those cases, an employer may cancel the vested benefits of those terminating employees who draw down their own contributions. However, if a plan cancels such benefits, it must contain a "buy back" provision under which the employee's forfeited benefits will be fully restored if he repays to the plan the withdrawn contributions. For defined benefit plans, the repayment must include interest, compounded annually. The interest rate must be 5 percent for plan years after ERISA's vesting requirements apply and before 1988, and thereafter must be 120 percent of the federal midterm rate in effect for the first month of the plan year.

Having made the decision to preserve the employer-financed benefits of employees who cash out the benefits financed with their own contributions, Congress found it necessary to develop rules for determining the respective proportions of an employee's accrued benefits allocable to employer and employee contributions.

For purposes of dividing the accrued benefit into employer- and employee-financed portions, the law presumes that all benefits are financed by the employer, except those that can be attributed to employee contributions. Thus, the statutory rules pertain only to the calculation of the benefits attributable to employee contributions, the difference between this amount and the total accrued benefits being those attributable to employer contributions. The rules distinguish between defined contribution and defined benefit plans.

Under a defined *contribution* plan, the amount of accrued benefits derived from the participant's own contributions is determined by reference to the balance in his individual account, reflecting his contributions and the investment earnings, expenses, gains, and losses associated therewith.[4] Under a defined *benefit* plan, the amount is derived by multiplying the employee's accumulated contributions by a "conversion factor" specified by statute or regulations.[5] The conversion factor is the reciprocal of the actuarial present value at the normal retirement age of a single life annuity of $1 per annum. The statute stipulates that the conversion factor for a normal retirement age of 65 shall be 10 percent, which means that, under the mortality and interest assumptions being used, a

---

[4]ERISA §204(c)(2)(A), I.R.C. §411(c)(2)(A).
[5]ERISA §204(c), I.R.C. §411(c).

sum of $10 would have to be on hand at age 65 to provide a single life annuity of $1 per annum. Multiplying the accumulated contributions by the conversion factor is the same as dividing the accumulated sum by the annuity factor of 10, the more conventional approach. For this computation, the accumulated contributions are assumed to be equal to the sum of the employee's actual contributions to the date of the computation with interest at the prescribed rate described above, compounded annually to the normal retirement date.

The conversion factor would be different for a normal retirement age other than 65. Moreover, the Internal Revenue Service requires adjustments in the factor if the pension benefit is payable other than monthly, or in the form other than a single life annuity. The adjustments[6] are designed to produce actuarially equivalent benefits.

The Secretary of the Treasury is authorized to adjust by regulation the conversion factor from time to time as he may deem necessary.[7] However, no such adjustment has ever been made.

These rules for determining the accrued benefits attributable to employee contributions apply only to mandatory contributions. The accrued benefits attributable to voluntary employee contributions are determined in the same manner that they would have been under a money purchase plan.[8]

If the terminating employee receives a refund of his contributions in a lump sum under a defined benefit plan, it must include interest at the prescribed rate described above. However, if this amount would exceed the value of the total accrued benefit, the minimum required distribution is the greater of the value of the total accrued benefit or the employee's own contributions without interest.[9]

## Benefits Attributable to Employer Contributions

The rights of a terminating employee in the benefits provided by the contributions of the employer depend upon the vesting provisions in the plan. In a defined benefit pension plan, vesting refers to the right of a participant to receive his accrued pension benefits

---

[6]Rev. Rul. 76–47.
[7]ERISA §204(c)(2)(D), I.R.C. §411(c)(2)(D).
[8]ERISA §204(b)(2)(A),(c)(4), I.R.C. §411(b)(2)(A),(d)(5).
[9]ERISA §204(c)(2)(E), I.R.C. §411(c)(2)(E).

at normal or early retirement whether or not he is in the service of the employer at that time. It is a narrower concept than the strict legal concept of a vested right, since the right to a pension is contingent upon the employee's survival to the earliest date on which he can validly claim a pension. Thus, a vested pension benefit is usually terminated by the participant's death prior to normal or early retirement.[10] The vesting of a benefit simply removes the obligation of the participant to remain in the plan until the date of early or normal retirement.

## Basic Vesting Concepts

Vesting provisions differ, within permissible limits, as to the *kinds of benefits vested,* the point in *time* when the eligible benefits vest, the *rate* at which the accrued benefits vest, and the *form* in which the vested benefits may be taken.

As to the *kinds* of benefits vested, the broad possibilities are retirement, death, and total disability. All three kinds of these benefits are vested when they enter a payment status. With this exception, however, the traditional approach has been to vest only the basic retirement benefit. Before ERISA, a common practice with respect to participants who terminate their employment prior to retirement was to vest only the *normal* retirement benefit. That is to say, plans typically specified that the vested benefits of a *terminated* participant became payable only at normal retirement, even though active participants were permitted to retire early, possibly with subsidized benefits. Moreover, the early retirement supplements provided under some negotiated plans are not vested. Thus, as a generalization, it may be said that vesting attaches only to the normal retirement benefit.

With the exception of the qualified preretirement survivor annuity benefit described in Chapter 8, it has not been the practice to vest death and disability benefits not in pay status. In other words, protection against the economic consequences of death and total disability is not continued for participants who leave the employer's service. These are considered to be term coverages that

---

[10]ERISA §203(a)(3)(A), I.R.C. §411(a)(3)(A), Treas. Reg. 1.411(a)–4(b)(1). A defined contribution plan is also allowed to provide for forfeiture of amounts not yet paid upon death, but very few such plans do so.

should properly extend only to active and possibly retired participants. However, if the participant terminates after becoming vested and dies before his annuity starting date (with an eligible surviving spouse), a qualified preretirement survivor annuity benefit must be provided.

As to *time,* vesting may occur immediately or at some future date. The dichotomy here is *immediate* versus *deferred* vesting. Immediate vesting is infrequently found among conventional pension plans. Vesting is generally deferred until stipulated service and (sometimes) age requirements are met.

As to the *rate* at which benefits vest, a distinction is made between full and graded vesting. Vesting is said to be *full* when, upon satisfaction of the conditions laid down for vesting, all benefits accrued to that date vest in their entirety, and all benefits accruing thereafter vest in full as they are credited. Plans have favored the full vesting concept, coupled with reasonable age and service requirements. A small minority of plans have provided for *full* and *immediate* vesting. For example, the individual retirement annuity contracts issued by the Teachers Insurance and Annuity Association and College Retirement Equities Fund (TIAA-CREF) for the faculty and staffs of institutions of higher learning provide for full and immediate vesting. Benefits derived from employee contributions are always required to be fully and immediately vested.

*Graded vesting* is the term applied to an arrangement under which only a specified percentage of the accrued benefits vest upon fulfillment of specified minimum requirements. The percentage of vesting increases on a sliding scale as additional requirements are met, until 100 percent vesting is ultimately attained. For example, a plan may specify that 20 percent of accrued benefits will vest after 3 years of service, with an additional 20 percent vesting each year during the next 4 years until after 7 years of service all accrued benefits are vested. Graded vesting avoids anomalous treatment of employees terminating just before and just after meeting the requirements for full vesting, and it minimizes the danger that an employee will be discharged just before his pension benefits vest. In other words, it prevents a situation in which an employee with fairly long service has no vested benefits on a particular day and then, the following day, has all his accrued benefits fully vested. On the other hand, graded vesting is more difficult to explain to plan participants, a matter of some concern, since the law requires that every participant be furnished with a summary of the plan "written in a manner calculated to be understood by the average plan participant." It is also more difficult to administer. Not only may the plan administrator have to keep track of a relatively insignificant vested benefit for a long period of years, but a participant in a defined benefit plan who terminates and receives a lump-sum distribution while partly vested may reinstate the canceled benefit accruals upon reemployment by paying back his distribution to the plan, plus interest at the prescribed rate described above.[11] The same rule applies in contributory plans to a participant who terminates before his benefits are 50 percent vested, who receives a refund of his contributions, and whose vested benefit is canceled.[12] In this latter case, he does not have to be in the employer's service at the time he seeks to restore the benefits that were canceled.

The employer is required by law to furnish the terminated employee with a certificate stating the amount of benefits vested, the annuity form in which they will be paid, and the time when they will become payable.[13] The *form* of the vested benefits depends to some extent on the contractual instrument used to fund the benefits.[14] If a defined benefit plan is funded through a trust, the vested terminated employee generally retains a deferred claim against the trust fund in the amount of his vested benefits. The plan may permit or direct the trustee to purchase a deferred life annuity in the appropriate form and amount for the employee from a life insurer.

If a defined benefit plan is funded through a contract with a life insurance company, the vested benefits may take the form of a paid-up insurance or annuity contract or a deferred claim against the plan. Under group deferred annuity contracts, all benefits are funded in the first instance in the form of paid-up annuities, and when a vested employee terminates he is simply given title to the annuities credited to his account. Under a group deposit administration annuity contract, a vested employee who terminates may be credited with a paid-up deferred annuity in the proper form and amount, or he may be given a certificate indicating that his benefit

[11]ERISA §204(d),(e), I.R.C. §411(a)(7).
[12]ERISA §203(a)(3)(D), I.R.C. §411(a)(3)(D).
[13]ERISA §105(c), 209(a)(1), I.R.C. §6057(e).
[14]See Chapters 21 and 22 for a description of the various funding instruments.

claim will remain an obligation of the plan to be discharged in the normal manner at retirement. The latter procedure would be similar to the deferred claim arrangement of a trust fund plan. If the plan is funded through individual insurance or annuity contracts (an approach generally confined to small firms), the vested terminated employee may be given the option of taking a paid-up contract in the proper amount or continuing, on a premium-paying basis, at his own expense, that portion of the life insurance policy or annuity contract represented by the vested cash values. Some plans permit the terminated employee to continue the contract or contracts in full force by paying the trustee a sum of money equal to the non-vested cash value, a privilege of some significance to a participant whose health has been impaired.

Under defined contribution plans, the vested benefit takes the form of the participant's vested account balance, which is usually paid out upon termination of employment, but may be retained until a later date. Similarly, a defined benefit plan may permit a terminating employee to take the full actuarial value of his vested benefits in cash. At his option, the participant may place some or all of the sum withdrawn, except his own contributions and employer contributions imputed to him, in an individual retirement account (IRA) set up and administered pursuant to applicable law.[15] If carried out within 60 days from receipt, the transfer would be tax free and, in any event, the earnings on the funds in the IRA would be wholly exempt from current income taxation.[16] The employee could leave the funds in the IRA until retirement, or, with the consent of a subsequent employer, he could transfer the funds on a tax-free basis to a qualified pension plan of the new employer. The terminating employee may, with the consent of the successor employer, transfer the "cash out" value of his vested benefits directly to the pension plan of the new employer, and the transfer will be tax free if carried out within 60 days after receipt from the original plan. The employee is under no obligation to preserve the actuarial value of his vested benefits and may dispose of it in any way that he sees fit, except that spousal consent is generally required to receive a benefit in any form other than a qualified joint

---

[15]IRAs are described in Chapter 28.
[16]I.R.C. §402(a)(5),(6).

and survivor annuity.[17] The employer is not under legal obligation to permit a cash out of the vested benefits.

When the actuarial value of the vested benefit of a terminating employee is not greater than $3,500, the employer has the option, without the employee's consent, of discharging the plan's obligation to him by making a lump-sum cash distribution.[18] This privilege is granted to the employer to avoid the expense of keeping track of a relatively insignificant deferred claim against the plan. The rules governing the actuarial assumptions used in calculating such lump sums for terminated vested participants are the same as those described in Chapter 6 with regard to lump-sum payments upon retirement.

### Statutory Vesting Requirements

Before enactment of ERISA, employers were under no legal obligation to provide for vesting of employer-financed benefits prior to retirement, except for unusual circumstances. The law did provide that all accrued benefits of a participant had to vest, to the extent funded, in the event that the plan terminated or the employer permanently discontinued contributions to the plan. In addition to these rules that applied to all plans, the Internal Revenue Service could require any plan to provide for reasonable preretirement vesting if it appeared from the facts of the case that the plan would otherwise discriminate against the rank-and-file employees in favor of the prohibited group (officers, shareholders, supervisors, and highly paid employees). In certain situations, usually involving small plans, the officers and other favored employees would be expected to remain with the firm until normal retirement, while the rank-and-file employees would tend to terminate their employment and fail to qualify for benefits. Vesting provisions keyed to the expected termination pattern could ensure that the plan would operate for the benefit of the employee group in general, rather than just for the proscribed group.

The minimum vesting standards established by ERISA and modified by TRA were premised on the grounds that vesting of accrued

---

[17]ERISA §205(a),(c), I.R.C. §§401(a)(11)(A), 417(a)(1),(2).
[18]ERISA §204(d),(e), I.R.C. §411(a)(7).

benefits after a reasonably short period of service is necessary (1) to assure equitable treatment of all participants; (2) to remove artificial barriers to changes of employment, hence enhancing the mobility of labor; and (3) to assure that private pension plans fulfill their social role of supplementing for a broad segment of the labor force the old-age insurance benefits provided under the Social Security System.[19]

The minimum vesting standards require benefits derived from employee contributions to be fully and immediately vested. For plan years beginning after 1988 they require benefits derived from employer contributions to be fully vested at normal retirement age, and also to meet either one of two permissible standards.[20]

**1.**   The simplest standard provides for full vesting of all accrued benefits after the participant has accumulated five years of recognized service, irrespective of his attained age. *No* degree of vesting short of five years of service is required under the standard.

**2.**   The second standard, sometimes called the three-to-seven year standard, embodies the progressive or graded vesting concept. Under this standard, the plan must vest at least 20 percent of a participant's accrued benefits by the end of three years of recognized service, and an additional 20 percent each year during the following four years. This means that the benefits must be fully vested after seven years of recognized service, irrespective of the participant's attained age. An exception applies to collective bargaining employees under multiemployer plans, for which full vesting is required after 10 years of recognized service.

Generally speaking, all years of service, including that rendered before entitlement to participation in the plan and before enactment of ERISA,[21] are to be taken into account in determining a participant's place on the vesting schedule. However, the plan may ignore (1) service before the employer maintained the plans or a predecessor plan (so-called past service); (2) service before age 18; (3) service during periods when the employee declined to make man-

---

[19]See Dan M. McGill, *Preservation of Pension Benefit Rights* (Homewood, Ill.: Richard D. Irwin, 1972), Chapter 2, for a discussion of the public policy considerations involved in the vesting issue. Chapter 5 of that volume provides a detailed analysis of the factors affecting the cost of vesting and the various ways in which the cost of vesting may be measured and expressed.

[20]ERISA §203(a), I.R.C. §411(a).

[21]ERISA §203(b)(1), I.R.C. §411(a)(4).

datory contributions; (4) seasonal or part-time service not taken into account under the rules for determining a "year of service"; and (5) service broken by periods of suspension of employment to the extent permitted under the breaks in service rules. It must be emphasized that the foregoing are rules for determining the participant's place on the vesting schedule (i.e., the number of years accrued toward satisfaction of the service requirement) and not for determining the *amount* of accrued benefits.

The pattern of vesting that occurs under the two basic standards is quite dissimilar, but the overall cost impact on a plan with a representative group of participants is remarkably similar. This suggests that they provide about the same amount of vesting, in the aggregate, although the distribution of vested benefits will vary. Young entrants into a pension plan will achieve a fully vested status more quickly under the five-year standard than under the three-to-seven-year standard. A higher percentage of participants will have *some* vesting under the three-to-seven-year standard than under the five-year standard, since vesting commences after three years of service, but less will have 100 percent vesting.

Top-heavy plans are required to have either 100 percent vesting after three years of service or 20 percent vesting after two years of service increasing 20 percent per year to 100 percent after six years.[22]

The law permits the Internal Revenue Service to require more rapid vesting than that required under the minimum schedules if (*a*) there has been a pattern of abuse under the plan, such as firing of employees before their accrued benefits vest; or (*b*) it appears that there have been, or are likely to be, forfeitures of accrued benefits under the plan that have the effect of discriminating in favor of the highly compensated employees.[23]

It should be realized that the standards described above are *minimum* standards, and employers are permitted to provide vesting under more liberal rules than those required by law.

Once vested, the benefits are nonforfeitable, except upon the death of the participant before retirement (and in the absence of a provision for joint and survivor annuities), and except for the circumstances noted below.[24] If a participant in a contributory plan

[22]I.R.C. §416(b).
[23]I.R.C. §411(d)(1).
[24]ERISA §203(a)(3), I.R.C. §411(a)(3).

withdraws his own mandatory contributions before his employer-financed benefits are at least 50 percent vested, the latter can be canceled under a plan provision of general applicability. Moreover, if a participant retires and then returns to work for the same employer, his retirement benefits can be suspended during his period of reemployment. Benefits required to be vested can no longer be forfeited in the event of misconduct by a participant or terminated vested participant (the so-called bad boy clause) or in the event that such persons accept employment with a competitor.

Upon request not more often than once per year, or upon termination from the plan, the participant must be provided with a statement of his accrued benefits and their vesting status.[25] Information concerning vested deferred benefits of a terminated participant must be furnished to the Internal Revenue Service, which transmits it to the Social Security Administration.[26] The Social Security Administration will provide this information to the participant or his beneficiary upon request, and automatically when application is made for Social Security old-age benefits.

## Pattern of Benefit Accruals for Vested Participants

For defined benefit plans, ERISA set out three alternative tests, designed to set limits on the extent of back loading in benefit formulas, against which benefit accruals for vested participants must be measured.[27] The tests are defined in terms of a retirement benefit payable at normal retirement age, which cannot be later than age 65 or the 10th anniversary of the date on which the participant entered the plan (the 5th anniversary in the case of employees who become participants within five years of the normal retirement age), whichever occurs last.[28] Ancillary benefits are excluded from the tests, as well as early retirement supplements that do not continue beyond the participant's normal retirement age.[29] The tests were developed for the purpose of determining the minimum benefit amount that must be credited to a participant who terminates from the plan in a vested status. They are not intended to require that

---

[25]ERISA §§105, 209(a)(1), I.R.C. §6057(e).
[26]I.R.C.§6057, Form 5500, Schedule SSA.
[27]ERISA §204(b)(1), I.R.C. §411(b)(1).
[28]ERISA §§3(22), (24), 204(c)(2)(B), I.R.C. §411(a)(7)(A),(8),(9).
[29]Treas. Reg. 1.411(a)–7(c)(3).

a terminated vested participant in all cases receive the same benefit at normal retirement age that he would have received with the same credited service and same compensation had he been in service at the time of retirement. For purposes of the tests, Social Security benefits and all other relevant factors affecting the benefits under the plan are assumed to remain constant, at current year levels, for all future years. It is necessary that the plan satisfy only one of the three alternative tests.

**1.** The first alternative, called the *3 percent rule,* requires that each participant's accrued benefit at least equals the product of his years of participation times 3 percent of the benefit that would have been payable if he had commenced participation at the earliest possible entry age and had served continuously to age 65, or the normal retirement age under the plan, whichever is earlier (maximum 100 percent after 33 1/3 years). The projected benefit at age 65 must be computed on the assumption that the participant's future compensation is equal to his actual average salary over a period of not more than 10 consecutive years. The test is applied on a cumulative basis, which means that any amount of front loading is permitted. A plan that provides exactly $10 monthly per year of participation with no maximum years of participation and no minimum entry age would not satisfy the 3 percent rule, because the minimum monthly accrued benefit would have to be $19.50 per year of participation (3 percent times $10 times the theoretical maximum of 65 years of participation from entry age 0). The test is also cumulative when the benefits of the plan are increased retroactively. For example, assume that during the first 10 years of an individual's participation the plan provided a flat benefit of $200 per month payable at age 65 and was then amended to provide a flat benefit of $400 a month. The participant's accrued benefit at the end of his 11th year of participation must be at least $132 (3% × $400 × 11).

**2.** The second alternative, called the *133¹/₃ percent rule,* states that the benefit accrual rate for any participant for any future year of service may not be more than one third higher than the accrual rate for the current year. Like the first test, this one also permits an unlimited amount of front loading. The benefit accruals under this test may be expressed in the form of dollar amounts or a specified percentage of compensation. If the plan is amended to increase the rate of benefit accrual, it is assumed (for the purposes of this test) that the new benefit schedule was in effect for all previous plan years. For example, if the plan has been providing an annual benefit accrual of 1 percent of compensation and is amended to provide 2 percent for future service only, it will continue to meet this test, even though 2 percent is more than one third greater than 1 percent. Also, if the plan has a scheduled increase in the rate of accruals that will not take effect for any participant until future years, as may be the case under collective bargaining, the scheduled increase is not taken into account for purposes of the back loading restrictions until it goes into effect. This 133⅓ percent rule governs all plans using a career average formula.

**3.** The third alternative is known as the *fractional rule*. It provides for proration of the projected normal retirement benefit over the years of plan participation. For purposes of this test, the benefit accrual for any particular year of service is based upon the assumption that the participant will continue to earn until normal retirement age the same rate of compensation that would have been taken into account under the plan had the employee retired in that year (but not more than the last 10 years). For example, if the normal retirement benefit is based upon five-year final average pay, it is assumed that the participant will continue to earn until retirement his average pay for the past five years. The plan must first determine the projected benefit that would have been payable at normal retirement age if the participant's service had continued to that date at the compensation indicated above. The minimum accrued benefit required under the fractional rule equals this projected benefit multiplied by a fraction whose numerator is the number of years that he actually participated in the plan and whose denominator is the number of years of participation that he would have had if he had continued in the plan to normal retirement.

Instead of the three foregoing tests, the accrued benefit of a participant in a plan funded exclusively through level premium life insurance or annuity contracts is the cash value of the contracts, determined as though the funding requirements of the plan had been fully satisfied.

Alternative rules are available for benefits accrued before the effective date of ERISA's vesting requirements.[30]

---

[30]ERISA §204(b)(1)(D), I.R.C. §411(b)(1)(D).

## Early Retirement Benefits for Terminated Vested Participants

ERISA provides that a terminated vested participant must be permitted to receive early retirement benefits on the basis of the same age and service requirements applicable to an active participant.[31] This provision was designed to prohibit the practice of requiring a terminated vested participant to wait to normal retirement age for commencement of benefits, when active participants were permitted to retire early, subject to age and service conditions. The benefit payable to a terminated vested participant starting at an early retirement age must be at least actuarially equivalent to the vested benefit he could have received at normal retirement age. However, if a plan uses subsidized early retirement factors for active employees who retire early, it need not use the subsidized factors for terminated vested participants.[32]

## Break in Service

Benefit accruals that have not vested may be lost—temporarily or permanently—through a break in service. *Years of service* and *breaks in service*—or *periods of service* and *periods of severance* if the elapsed time method is used—are generally subject to the same rules for vesting requirements as they are for participation requirements.[33] No benefit accrues for the period or periods during which a break in service occurs or exists. The crucial issues for the reemployed worker are whether prebreak service is counted in determining eligibility for vesting after the break and whether the benefit accruals that were credited before the break in service are forfeited.

All service before and after the break is aggregated in determining years of service, unless a particular exception applies.[34] Service before a one-year break in service can be disregarded until the participant has completed one year of service after the break.[35] If the participant had no vesting before the break, service before the

---

[31]ERISA §206(a), I.R.C. §401(a)(14).
[32]Treas. Reg. 1.411(c)–1(e)(1).
[33]See Chapter 4.
[34]ERISA §203(b)(1), I.R.C. §411(a)(4).
[35]ERISA §203(b)(3)(B), I.R.C. §411(a)(6)(B).

break can be disregarded if the number of consecutive one-year breaks in service equals the greater of five years or the years of service before the break.[36] For defined contribution plans, service after five consecutive one-year breaks in service can be disregarded when determining eligibility for vesting with respect to the benefit accrued before the break.[37]

The aggregated service just described is used to determine eligibility for vesting for benefits accrued after the break. In a defined benefit plan, if the participant was not fully vested before the break, his aggregated service will also be used to determine eligibility for vesting of benefits accrued before the break, but only if he repays any distribution he had received.[38] In a defined contribution plan, any nonvested benefits accrued before the break are permanently lost if there are five consecutive one-year breaks in service.[39]

Many plans use more liberal rules than the requirements described here, partly to simplify the plan.

---

## Questions

1. Explain why ERISA draftsmen found it necessary to specify a procedure for determining the amount of pension benefits attributable to employee contributions.

2. What happens to the employer-financed vested benefits of a terminating employee who elects to withdraw his own contributions in cash? What was the pre-ERISA practice in this regard?

3. Why is it not customary to vest death and disability benefits provided under a pension plan?

4. Describe the various *forms* that a vested pension benefit may take?

5. In what way can an individual retirement account (IRA) be used to preserve a vested pension benefit?

6. May a plan administrator on his own initiative and without the employee's consent discharge the plan's obligation to a terminating vested employee through a lump-sum cash payment?

---

[36]"Rule of parity," ERISA §203(b)(3)(D), I.R.C. §411(a)(6)(D).
[37]ERISA §203(b)(3)(C), I.R.C. §411(a)(6)(C).
[38]ERISA §204(e), I.R.C. §411(a)(7).
[39]Ibid.

7. Describe the vesting rules to which qualified pension plans were subject prior to the enactment of ERISA. In other words, under what circumstances were accrued pension benefits required to be vested?

8. Contrast the two alternative vesting standards set forth in ERISA.

9. Are there any circumstances under which the IRS may impose more rigorous vesting requirements than those reflected in the two statutory standards?

10. Must a terminated vested participant receive the same benefit at normal retirement age that he would have received with the same credited service and with the same compensation had he been in service at the time of retirement?

11. Is a terminated vested participant entitled to the same early retirement benefits that he would have received with the same credited service and compensation had he entered early retirement directly from an active employment status?

12. Explain the purpose and describe the nature of the three alternative tests set forth in ERISA to determine whether a pension plan is in compliance with the prohibition against "back loading" of benefits for participants who terminate from the plan in a vested status.

# 8 | Death and Disability Benefits

## Death Benefits

An EMPLOYER may provide death benefits through group life insurance, a pension plan, a profit sharing plan, or some combination of these. In addition, death benefits are provided by Social Security. Benefits from all these sources should be considered in the design of an overall death benefit program.

Prior to ERISA a plan was not required to make death benefits available. Now the law requires the plan to make a qualified preretirement survivor benefit available for vested married participants, and if the plan is contributory it must provide for the return of the participant's contributions with interest in the event of his death before retirement. In considering death benefits of a pension plan, one's perspective is sharpened if a distinction is made between the benefits payable upon the participant's death before retirement and those payable upon his death after retirement.

The IRS has a long-standing rule that the death benefit of a pension plan, other than the required joint and survivor benefit and preretirement survivor annuity benefit, must be incidental to the primary purpose of the plan, which must be to provide systematically for the payment of definitely determinable benefits to the participants over a period of years, usually for life, after retirement.[1] This constraint has been imposed in recognition of the special tax status accorded pension plans.

### Postretirement Death Benefits

Postretirement benefits may take the form of lump-sum payments or income benefits.

Lump-sum benefits tend to be modest in amount and are often designed to meet the last illness and funeral expenses of the deceased employee. They are regarded to be incidental to the retirement benefit if they are not greater than one half of the participant's salary at date of retirement and account for less than 10 percent of the cost of the plan exclusive of the death benefit.[2] They often range from $1,000 to $3,000. Some plans provide a lump-sum benefit upon the death of the *spouse* of the retired employee to relieve him of the financial burden of paying the last illness and funeral expenses. Many plans provide no postretirement lump-sum death benefit.

The postretirement income death benefit is strictly a function of the annuity form under which the retirement benefits are payable. As was indicated earlier, the retirement benefits of noncontributory plans have traditionally been stated in terms of an annuity form that did not provide a benefit to survivors. Contributory plans have used annuity forms that assured the participant that he or his beneficiary would receive benefits that, in the aggregate, would be at least equal to his contributions. Most plans have permitted the participant to elect annuity forms that would provide death benefits of varying magnitude, at the expense of the retirement benefits.

The law now requires every qualified plan, other than a profit sharing plan or stock bonus plan which does not provide benefits in the form of a life annuity, to include a qualified joint and survivor annuity. A qualified joint and survivor annuity is an annuity that pays the participant's surviving spouse an income for life at least 50 percent, but not more than 100 percent, of that payable during the joint lives of the participant and his spouse and that meets

---

[1]Treas. Reg. 1.401–1(b)(1)(i); Rev. Rul. 74–307.
[2]Rev. Rul. 60–59.

certain other requirements.[3] The amount payable must be actuarially equivalent to the single life annuity that would have been payable to the participant. Thus, the cost of this survivor income is borne by the participant and his spouse through a reduction in the retirement benefits that would otherwise be payable. If a married participant (married at least one year) retires and does not elect any other form of annuity with the consent of the spouse, the benefit must be paid as a qualified joint and survivor annuity, unless the benefit would otherwise have been payable in a form other than a life annuity. Many plans have extended this provision to apply to all married participants, regardless of the period of marriage. The participant must have the opportunity to elect, with the spouse's consent, not to have the retirement benefits provided under a joint and survivor annuity. The employee must be supplied with a written explanation of the joint and survivor annuity, couched in laymen's language, that points out the effect on him and his spouse of a decision to accept or reject the provision. The election must be in writing but is subject to revocation. Regulations specify timing limitations for notification, election, and revocation.[4]

## Preretirement Death Benefits

Preretirement death benefits may take the form of a refund of employee contributions or an explicit benefit embodied in the plan for the specific purpose of providing protection to the dependents of participants who die before retirement. The first type of benefit is available only under a contributory plan. It is generally paid in a lump sum to a designated beneficiary or to the estate of the deceased participant. It had been the custom of contributory plans to refund the contributions of a deceased participant, but the practice is now mandatory.[5] Accumulated mandatory employee contributions under a defined benefit plan must include interest.[6] Accumulated mandatory employee contributions under a defined contribution plan, and accumulated voluntary employee contributions under any plan,

---

[3]ERISA §205, I.R.C. §401(a)(11).
[4]Treas. Reg. 1.401(a)–11(c), 1.401(a)–11T, 1.417(e)–1T.
[5]ERISA §203(a)(1),(3)(A), I.R.C. §411(a)(1),(3)(A).
[6]ERISA §204(c), I.R.C. §411(c)(2),(d)(5).

must reflect their share of the plan's total investment return, positive or negative.

The explicit death benefit may, in turn, be broken down into two types: lump-sum payments and income payments.

**Lump-Sum Benefits.**   A lump-sum death benefit may be provided under a plan funded through one or more life insurance or annuity contracts or one funded through a trust. Almost all defined contribution plans provide a death benefit equal to the account balance. But most defined benefit plans funded through trusts or group annuity contracts provide no preretirement lump-sum death benefit, other than a refund of employee contributions. On the other hand, plans funded through individual or group permanent life insurance contracts typically provide a preretirement death benefit. A contract form often used in the past is one called the "retirement income" (or "income endowment") policy, which provides a face amount of $1,000 for each $10 of monthly income at retirement. Under this contract, the cash value eventually exceeds the face amount and becomes payable in the event of the participant's death before retirement. Some plans use a contract form that provides only a $1,000 death benefit for each $10 unit of monthly income payable under the plan. To permit the use of these contract forms, which have served as the funding instrument for tens of thousands of small pension plans, the Internal Revenue Service has held in a series of rulings[7] that a lump-sum death benefit provided through a life insurance contract is "incidental" to the principal purpose of the plan if it does not exceed a sum equal to 100 times the expected monthly pension benefit or, if greater, the reserve for the pension benefit. This constraint is obviously patterned after the benefit structure of a retirement income contract.

Alternatively, the life insurance feature is deemed to be incidental if the aggregate of the premiums paid for the life insurance on any particular participant is less than one half of the aggregate contributions allocated to his account as of any given time.[8] It is assumed, somewhat arbitrarily, that only one half of a life insurance premium, irrespective of the issue age or the plan of insurance (except term),

---

[7]Rev. Rul. 61–121.
[8]Rev. Rul. 74–307.

is applied to the cost of protection, the other half going into the policy reserve. Thus, in essence, this rule states that no more than 25 percent of the funds available may be used to provide pure life insurance protection.

These limitations have been extended by administrative interpretation to lump-sum death benefits provided under any type of pension plan, whether or not life insurance contracts are used. In other words, the death benefit must not exceed the greater of 100 times the monthly annuity or the reserve for the pending benefit or, alternatively, its cost must not exceed 25 percent of the total cost of the plan.[9] Operating under this authority, pension plans funded through a trust frequently provide lump-sum death benefits. The benefit may be a stated amount, such as $5,000, or a multiple of the deceased employee's annual compensation. A benefit equal to one or two times salary is fairly common.

All of the incidental death benefit limits described above include the value of any qualified preretirement survivor annuity benefit payable. Thus the maximum limit on lump-sum death benefits which would otherwise apply must be reduced by the value of any qualified preretirement annuity benefit payable.

**Survivor Income Benefits.** Before ERISA there was increasing interest in an income type of benefit payable to the surviving spouse or other dependents of a deceased participant. The initial stimulus for this type of benefit was recognition of the need to protect a wife's inchoate interest in her husband's pension during a period when he was eligible to retire and elect a joint and survivor annuity. Under the usual plan provisions, the joint and survivor annuity option would become operative only if the participant retired before his death. If he continued in employment beyond the point where he was eligible for early or normal retirement the spouse's potential annuity benefit was jeopardized. Before ERISA some plans attempted to deal with this problem by stating that, if a participant were to die before retirement but during the period when he would have been eligible for early or normal retirement benefits, the surviving spouse would receive a benefit equal to the amount that would have been payable had the participant retired and elected a joint and last survivor annuity option immediately prior to his death.

---

[9]Ibid.

Reflecting the concern for the spouse's interest in the participant's accruing pension rights, the law now requires that a plan
include a qualified preretirement survivor annuity benefit.[10] However, no survivor annuity is generally required for a profit sharing
plan or stock bonus plan that pays the vested account balance to
the spouse upon death.

The qualified preretirement survivor annuity benefit must be
available to a married participant from the time that he becomes
vested in any accrued benefit until his annuity starting date. The
benefit is not required unless the participant has been married at
least one year at the date of his death. In the case of a participant
who dies while eligible for early retirement, the benefit payable to
the spouse is the amount that would have been payable if the participant had retired under the plan's early retirement provision on
the day before his death and had elected the qualified joint and
survivor annuity. Thus the amount of benefit reflects the reduction
of the accrued benefit by the early retirement reduction factor,
further reduction by the actuarial factor of the joint and survivor
form, and finally, if the plan uses the customary 50 percent joint
and survivor annuity, multiplication by 50 percent.

If the participant dies before becoming eligible for early retirement, the qualified preretirement survivor annuity payments are
computed on the basis of the benefits accrued to date of death but
do not begin until the date that the participant would have reached
his earliest retirement age, that is, the age he would have been
eligible to retire under the plan's early or normal retirement provision. In this case the amount of survivor annuity is determined
as though the participant had terminated employment immediately
prior to his actual date of death, had survived to his earliest retirement age, had then elected to retire under qualified joint and
survivor option, and had then died.

Plans have a choice of providing this qualified preretirement
survivor annuity automatically to all married participants who are
vested in an accrued benefit, or allowing any such participants to
elect, with the consent of the spouse, not to have this protection.
If automatic, the plan sponsor bears the cost of the survivor annuity
benefit. If elective, the cost is borne by electing participants in the

---

[10]ERISA §205, I.R.C. §§401(a)(11),417.

form of reductions in their benefits otherwise payable at normal or early retirement. Some plans reduce the accrued benefit by .5 to 1 percent for each year the protection is provided.

Regulations[11] provide complex and cumbersome requirements for notification of participants eligible to make the election, periods for making elections and revocation, and the elections. These requirements are avoided if the survivor annuity is provided automatically. In part to avoid the administrative requirements of election, and in part to avoid inequities between electing and nonelecting participants, the majority of defined benefit plans provide the benefit automatically.

As indicated earlier, some plans provided ERISA-type survivor annuity benefits before ERISA. Some such plans had extended this provision to cover all participants who had accumulated a specified period of service, such as 20 or 25 years, and had reached a stipulated age, such as 50. The next stage of development was to provide an explicit benefit not related to a joint and survivor annuity and applicable to all participants or to all who meet certain service requirements.

Formerly, many plans provided survivor benefits to widows but not to widowers. However, the Equal Employment Opportunity Commission (EEOC) ruled that a survivor income benefit payable only to the surviving widow or other dependents of a male employee constitutes discrimination against female employees and, hence, is in violation of Title VII of the Civil Rights Act, which prohibits discrimination on the basis of sex.[12] By force of this ruling, employers have had to convert the surviving *widow's* benefit into a surviving *spouse's* benefit. Some employers, reluctant to provide a lifetime benefit to an able-bodied widower of a female employee, attempted to limit the survivor benefit to a spouse who was financially dependent on the deceased employee at the time of his or her death. The EEOC has taken the position that a dependent spouse's benefit is also violative of Title VII of the Civil Rights Act inasmuch as there is a higher *probability* that the surviving widow of a male employee will be dependent than that the widower will be dependent. The survivor annuity mandated by ERISA must be provided irrespective of sex or dependency.

---

[11]Treas. Reg. 1.401(a)–11(c), 1.401(a)–11T, 1.417(e)–1T.

[12]See *Arizona Governing Committee* v. *Norris,* 463 U.S. 1073(1983).

It was often necessary to coordinate the qualified preretirement survivor annuity required by law with a previously existing spouse's benefit. Some plans maintain the two benefits separately and others combine them. In some cases, the existing spouse's benefit already provided benefits as liberal as those required by law, and no addition was required. In other cases, the spouse's benefit provision was modified so that it would meet the requirements for the new survivor annuity. In other cases, the qualified preretirement survivor annuity benefit was added separately, with a provision that benefits under the earlier spouse's benefit would be offset by any benefit payable under the new survivor annuity provision.

Today any spouse's benefit in excess of the mandated qualified preretirement survivor annuity tends to be an explicitly stated benefit, described below, payable to the surviving spouse as long as she or he lives but sometimes subject to termination in the event of remarriage prior to a stipulated age, such as 60. The mandatory survivor annuity may not be terminated upon remarriage.

The spouse's benefit is often restricted to a surviving spouse who had been married to the deceased employee for a specified period, such as one year, or is the parent of a child of the deceased. If there is no surviving spouse, the benefit may be payable to dependent parents. In recognition of the fact that unmarried employees may not have dependent children, some plans permit the survivor benefit to be payable to any dependent relatives of the deceased, including, especially, brothers and sisters and parents. The benefit is usually payable in respect of all participants, but it may be restricted to those with long service or those eligible to retire.

The amount of a nonmandatory survivor benefit may be determined by reference to the participant's compensation at date of death or his accrued or projected pension benefit. If the former approach is used, the amount of the benefit is usually set at about 20 to 25 percent of the participant's monthly compensation rate. The monthly amount tends to be the same irrespective of the spouse's age. The present value of future benefits tends to be higher for the younger annuitant, except that the remarriage rate is much higher at the younger ages, reducing the actuarial value of the annuity if benefits cease on remarriage. There may be additional benefits for dependent children, in the order of 10, 15, or 20 percent of compensation. The overall benefit allowance may be subject to adjustment for Social Security survivor benefits.[13]

The more common approach is to relate the nonmandatory spouse's benefit to the pension of the deceased employee. This may be done in terms of the pension accrued to date of death or the pension that would have been payable had the employee survived in employment until normal retirement age. In neither case is there a reduction in the amount of the benefit because of the spouse's age at the commencement of the income payments, except in some plans when the spouse is younger than the employee by more than a specified number of years, commonly 5 but sometimes 20. An upward adjustment may be made if the spouse is older than the employee.

The benefit based on the accrued pension may be illustrated in terms of an employee who dies at age 55, leaving a spouse age 50. The spouse's benefit would be a specified percentage of the pension that would have been payable at the employee's normal retirement age, on the basis of the benefit credits accumulated to date of death. There would be no reduction to reflect the fact that the spouse is only age 50 and that the benefits will thus be paid over a longer time than was originally contemplated. Under Treasury rules, the maximum spouse's benefit may be expressed in terms of the deceased's *accrued* pension benefit or his *projected* pension benefit.

The qualified preretirement survivor annuity benefit mandated by law is always deemed to be an incidental death benefit. In considering the limits that might logically be imposed on any other spouse's benefit, the Internal Revenue Service took as its guide an earlier ruling on money purchase pension plans, which stated that, for any individual, the cost of the death benefit must not exceed 25 percent of the total cost. It made a series of actuarial calculations to determine what limits should be imposed to keep the cost of the spouse's benefit from exceeding 25 percent of the total cost with respect to the individual participants. The limits might logically have been related to the age of the spouse at the time the income commences. Instead, since the Internal Revenue Service was considering a test case that reduces the benefit actuarially if the spouse

------

[13]See Chapter 10 for a discussion of Social Security integration.

is more than five years younger than the participant, it chose to impose limits in terms of the earliest age at which the participant could qualify for the spouse's benefit. It developed one set of limits for plans that express the benefit as a percentage of the *accrued benefit* and another for plans that provide benefits on the basis of the *projected benefit*. The limits that were promulgated by the IRS are shown in Table 3.[14]

It will be noted that the full amount of the participant's projected pension can be paid only if the participant must be age 55 or more to qualify for the benefit. On the other hand, half of the projected benefit, the percentage generally used today, can be provided if eligibility is established at age 25.

The scale allows a larger percentage when the spouse's benefit is based upon the participant's *accrued* pension benefit. The full accrued benefit can be provided if eligibility for the benefit is not established before the participant's age 50. The scale grades down to 75 percent for an eligibility age of 25 years or less.

While the qualified preretirement survivor annuity itself is always deemed to be incidental, the above limits apply to any combination of this mandatory benefit and an additional spouse's income benefit. Thus, any spouse's income benefit which supplements the qualified

**TABLE 3**
**Maximum Percentage of Participant's Accrued or Projected Pension That May Be Considered an Incidental Death Benefit***

| Earliest Age at Which Participant Becomes Eligible for Spouse's Benefit | Maximum Percentage | |
|---|---|---|
| | Accrued Pension | Projected Pension |
| 20 or less | 75% | 45% |
| 25 | 75 | 50 |
| 30 | 80 | 55 |
| 35 | 80 | 60 |
| 40 | 85 | 66⅔ |
| 45 | 90 | 75 |
| 50 | 100 | 90 |
| 55 and over | 100 | 100 |

*These percentages apply only to a unit benefit pension plan providing a spouse's benefit in the form of a straight-life annuity commencing immediately upon the participant's death, with the benefit being actuarially reduced if the spouse is more than five years younger than the participant.

[14]Rev. Rul. 70–611.

preretirement survivor annuity is not allowed to cause the combination to exceed the above limits.[15]

**Relative Advantages and Disadvantages of Providing Preretirement Death Benefits from Pension Plan.** Preretirement death benefits other than the mandated qualified preretirement survivor annuity can be provided outside the pension plan through a conventional group term life insurance contract or a group survivor income contract, so a policy decision has to be made on whether death benefits are going to be provided through the pension plan or through a group insurance contract. There are both advantages and disadvantages in using the facilities of a pension plan to provide preretirement death benefits, as compared to the use of a separate group insurance plan.

*A. Advantages.* The first advantage is that a pension plan is not subject to state laws that impose a limit on the face amount of group term life insurance that may be placed on any one employee. These limits, once common, now apply only to policies delivered in California, Texas, and Wisconsin.

The second advantage is that the preretirement death benefit can be coordinated with the pension benefit with somewhat more facility and precision. Group survivor income contracts generally express the benefit in terms of the employee's current compensation, which offers certain advantages but may bear little relationship to the accruing pension benefit. If the survivor benefit under a pension plan is expressed as a percentage of the participant's *projected* pension, the preretirement and postretirement survivor benefit can be very similar, there being no discontinuity.

The third advantage is that the assets of the pension plan can be invested with more latitude than the reserves under a group insurance contract offering the possibility of a higher rate of investment return and, hence, lower costs. The assets backing the reserves of a life insurer must be held in the company's general account, which must by law be invested predominantly in fixed-income instruments, while the assets of a pension plan can be held in a separate account of a life insurer, devoted entirely to equity investments, or in a trust whose manager can be given virtually unlimited investment authority, subject to fiduciary requirements.

---

[15]Rev. Rul. 85–15.

The other two advantages involve tax considerations. In the first place, there are no state premium taxes on contributions to pension plans, while group life insurance premiums are generally taxed.[16] Second, employer contributions to a pension plan are not taxable to the participants (except when applied to the cost of death benefits under individual or group life insurance contracts), whereas employer premium payments on that portion of group term life insurance on the life of one employee in excess of $50,000 is taxable income to the employee to the extent that they exceed the employee's own contributions.

**B. Disadvantages.**    There are disadvantages to providing pre-retirement death benefits from a pension plan. The first is that the death benefits must be incidental to the main purpose of the plan: the payment of retirement benefits. This may rule out the use of a particular formula for death benefits. For example, it would not be permissible to provide a surviving spouse's benefit equal to the participant's accrued pension, if the benefit becomes payable in the event of the participant's death before age 50. A separate group life or survivor income plan would not be subject to this constraint.

A second disadvantage is that lump-sum and income death benefits payable from a pension plan are subject to federal income taxation, while benefits paid in the form of life insurance proceeds are fully excludable from federal income taxation. The first $5,000 of a death benefit paid as a lump-sum distribution from a pension is free of federal income tax,[17] and the excess is taxable on a favorable basis as a lump-sum distribution.[18] The income benefits are taxed under the so-called annuity rule that permits the annuitant to recover his cost over his life expectancy without income tax liability.[19] If he made no contributions to the plan, he would have no investment in the contract and, therefore, all benefits would be taxed in full.[20] Large death benefits under a pension plan are subject

---

[16]There will be premium taxes on premiums paid in respect of individual or group permanent life insurance contracts and in some states group annuity considerations are subject to the premium tax.

[17]I.R.C. §101(b).

[18]See Chapter 29.

[19]See Chapter 29.

[20]The survivor is permitted to consider up to $5,000 as her or his investment in the annuity contract to the extent that the deceased employee's rights to this amount were nonforfeitable and the exclusion was not applied against a lump-sum benefit payment. Rev. Rul. 71–146.

to a special 15 percent estate tax in addition to the regular estate tax.[21] A group survivor income contract is treated as group life insurance,[22] but the monthly payments would be taxed under the annuity rule, in accordance with which the interest component of each monthly payment would be treated as fully taxable ordinary income, with the remainder being treated as a refund of principal and hence not taxable.

A third problem is that pension plan death benefits substantially larger than the accrued liability for pensions can cause substantial fluctuations in the employer's cost, particularly for smaller plans.

Both pension plans and group life insurance are subject to the pervasive prohibition against discrimination in favor of highly compensated employees. In various situations one or the other of these bodies of restrictions may prove more troublesome, making this either an advantage or disadvantage for pension plans. Of course, a group life insurance plan can be provided that does not satisfy the nondiscrimination requirements, but in that case highly compensated employees lose the benefit of exclusion of the cost of the first $50,000 of insurance.[23]

## Disability Benefits

All well-designed pension plans contain provisions that protect the accrued benefits of participants who are temporarily unable to work because of illness or injury. Temporary disability is a type of break in service that must be considered in any plan document. A problem of more serious consequence is presented when a participant becomes permanently unable to work because of injury or disease.

As a minimum, the plan may vest the accrued benefits of a permanently disabled participant, irrespective of the normal vesting requirements. If he has reached the early retirement age, some plans provide him an immediate annuity based upon his benefits accrued to date, without reduction for age. Some plans provide for early retirement benefits at an earlier age and with fewer years of service than would be applicable to an able-bodied participant.

---

[21]I.R.C. §4981(d).

[22]*Helvering* v. *Legierse,* 312 U.S. 531(1941).

[23]I.R.C. §89(a)(1).

The most direct way to deal with the disability contingency is to provide a separately identified disability benefit. Like the survivor income benefit, the disability benefit may be expressed as a percentage of the participant's compensation at the onset of disability or as a percentage of his accrued or projected pension benefit. In choosing among these three alternatives, the plan designer is faced with the same considerations as those pertaining to the spouse's benefit. For example, there is the question of coordination with the retirement benefit and also the question of benefit adequacy for the participant who becomes permanently and totally disabled at a young age. The probability of total disability at the younger ages is very low, but the economic consequences to the participant and his family can be catastrophic. This has led many employees to base the disability benefit on the participant's projected pension, without actuarial reduction for age. If the benefit is expressed as a percentage of the accrued pension benefit, a minimum benefit may be provided.

There are some special considerations involved in the providing of a permanent and total disability benefit. Because of the possibility of adverse selection and abuse, some thought must be given to the problem of entry into the plan by an individual who knowingly or unknowingly is afflicted with a health impairment. If the employer requires a preemployment physical examination, the problem is ameliorated but not necessarily eliminated. Three alternative ways of dealing with this problem are to (1) withhold the protection of the disability provision for a period of years after entry into the plan, such as three to five years or longer; (2) exclude benefit payments for disability arising out of a preexisting condition that manifests itself within a specified period, such as one or two years, after the participant enters the plan; or (3) to exclude permanently from the coverage of the disability clause any disability arising out of a preexisting condition. These approaches, of course, do not solve the problem for the employee who becomes disabled without benefits, nor for the employer faced with the difficult choice of providing ad hoc benefits or providing no assistance whatsoever.

A second consideration that arises when the disability is a percentage of compensation at the onset of disability is whether the disability benefit should continue throughout the individual's remaining lifetime (assuming that he does not recover) or only to normal retirement age, with the disabled person then becoming entitled to a retirement benefit. This again is a question of coordination of benefits, viz., the relationship between the disability and retirement benefits. If the disability benefit is to terminate at normal retirement age, the plan usually provides that the disabled person will continue to accrue pension credits on the regular basis, but based on his compensation at the onset of disability, to normal retirement age. Under these circumstances, the disabled participant will receive the same retirement benefit, except for the frozen wage base, to which he would have been entitled had he not become disabled.

A third consideration involves the relationship between the disability benefit and the early retirement benefit. If the disability benefit is a percentage of compensation or a percentage of the projected pension, it may be a more attractive benefit to a person contemplating early retirement than the nondisability benefit, since the latter reflects only accrued pension benefits. Thus, there would be an incentive for participants beyond the early retirement age to seek a disability status and, at that stage, it is easier to establish a disability claim than in earlier years. To counteract this tendency, a plan can stipulate that, if a participant becomes disabled after having met the requirements for early retirement, he will receive the regular early retirement benefit.

Finally, it is vitally important that the total benefits received by a disabled participant and his family be less than what he could earn if he were not disabled. Otherwise, there might be a tendency for some participants to seek a disability status, and there would certainly be no economic incentive for the disabled person to try to rehabilitate himself. This suggests that the disability benefit formula must take into account, by offset or otherwise, the disability benefits provided under Social Security, workers' compensation, and possibly veterans' legislation.

Long-term disability income benefits may be provided under a separate group insurance contract. The tax treatment of the benefits is the same whether they are paid from a pension plan or a group insurance contract. The total benefit package can perhaps be better coordinated if all benefits are provided by one plan. The limitations on integration of disability benefits under a pension plan may be more restrictive than desired, both in the amount of disability benefit and in the definition of disability. Integration of pension plan disability benefits with benefits payable under Social Security, worker's compensation, and other programs is discussed in Chapter

10. Group long-term disability benefits are subject to nondiscrimination requirements which may be difficult to satisfy. Some employers choose to insure the long-term disability benefit in order to transfer the risk to the insurance company and to reap the advantage of the insurer's experience and objectivity in disability claims administration.

Employers that provide benefits before 65 under long-term disability insurance often provide a benefit from the pension plan beginning at age 65, determined as though employment had continued to age 65.

## Questions

1. Why do the federal tax laws limit the amount of death benefits that can be provided under a qualified pension plan? What reasons are there for removing the limits?

2. Contrast the postretirement death benefits that are made available under the various annuity forms of a pension plan, including a qualified joint and survivor annuity.

3. Describe the limitations on preretirement lump-sum death benefits that may be provided under a qualified pension plan, distinguishing between defined benefit and defined contribution plans.

4. Describe the statutory qualified preretirement survivor annuity benefit. Explain the various bases that may be used by a pension plan to determine the amount of other preretirement survivor income death benefits to be paid.

5. What approaches may be used by a pension plan in meeting the cost of providing the protection of a qualified preretirement survivor annuity for vested participants?

6. What is the rationale behind the *specific* limits imposed by the IRS on the income benefits that may be provided by a qualified pension plan to a surviving spouse of a participant who dies before retirement?

7. Outline the relative advantages and disadvantages of providing preretirement death benefits from a pension plan, as contrasted with providing such benefits from a separate group life insurance plan.

8. Describe the various arrangements that may be provided under a qualified pension plan to deal with employees who become totally disabled prior to retirement.

9. From what sources other than a pension plan may disability benefits be provided? Should all disability benefits be provided by these other sources and none from the pension plan?

10. What are the different ways of dealing with preexisting health impairments under a total disability provision of a pension plan?

# 9 | Financial Considerations

## Source of Contributions

THE PRIMARY SOURCE of financial support of a pension plan is periodic contributions, which may be made monthly, quarterly, or annually. Contributions may be made by the employer or the employees, or both. Employee contributions may be divided between mandatory contributions and voluntary contributions. Employee contributions are considered to be mandatory contributions if they are required as a condition of employment, as a condition for participation in the plan, or as a condition for obtaining any benefits under the plan attributable to employer contributions.[1] A plan that includes mandatory employee contributions is characterized as contributory. If only the employer contributes to the plan, it is described as noncontributory. Participation in a contributory plan is generally voluntary, especially when it commences operation, but employees hired after the plan was established may be required to participate as a condition of employment.

---

[1]Treas. Reg. 1.411(c)–1(c)(4).

In the past, contributory plans predominated but noncontributory plans are now in the majority. A contributory plan has the obvious and, in some cases, controlling advantage of making possible larger benefits to the employees or lower costs to the employer. In many cases, the employer's financial position is such that he cannot assume the entire cost of pensions; and unless the employee group is willing to contribute toward the program, no plan will be installed. In other cases, employee contributions are required to enlarge the benefits. Finally, some plans are made contributory on the assumption that the members have a fuller appreciation of the plan if they bear a part of its cost.

The philosophical case for noncontributory plans rests largely on the deferred wage concept, which was discussed earlier. If retirement benefits can be regarded as the equivalent of wages, then, logically, the employer should assume the total cost of the program. If that view is rejected, the argument for unilateral financing loses much of its strength.

Entirely apart from the philosophical or moral aspects of the question, there are strong practical considerations in favor of having the employer bear the total cost of the program. Employee contributions greatly complicate the administration of a plan. Unless participation is a condition of employment, each participant must apply for membership in the plan and authorize the employer to deduct the required contributions from his pay. An individual account must be established and maintained for each participant.

Under defined contribution plans, employee contributions must be credited with their share of the plan's investment earnings, including any increases and decreases in market values. Under defined benefit plans, the interest rate credited to mandatory employee contributions generally must be 5 percent for plan years after ERISA's vesting requirements apply and before 1988, and thereafter must be 120 percent of the federal midterm rate in effect for the first month of the plan year.[2]

Policies must be developed (and enforced) to deal with participants who initially reject participation but later decide they want to join the plan. A policy is also needed with respect to temporary or permanent discontinuance of a participant's contributions. And

[2]ERISA §204(c)(2)(C),(D), I.R.C. §411(c)(2)(C),(D).

if a long-service employee who failed to join the plan reaches an age when he can no longer work effectively, it may be very difficult for an employer to dismiss him with no pension, even if it was his own election. Under contributory plans, the accrued benefit must be divided between employee-derived and employer-derived portions,[3] requiring buy-back provisions for employees who quit and later return. All these and similar problems can be avoided by making the plan noncontributory.

If the plan is noncontributory, all eligible employees are automatically enrolled, facilitating the accomplishment of the employer's business objectives. Furthermore, there is somewhat more flexibility in funding and investment policies when no employee contributions are involved. Finally, the contributions that an employer makes toward a qualified pension plan are deductible as an ordinary business expense for income tax purposes and, in the short run at least, a substantial portion of the cost is shifted to the federal government. On the other hand, mandatory employee contributions are not deductible and, as a consequence, are made from net income after taxes.[4] Dollar for dollar, therefore, mandatory employee contributions are more burdensome than employer contributions. An employer with a contributory plan considering an across-the-board pay increase can boost take-home pay more by reducing employee contributions than by adding the same number of dollars to wages.

There are no objective standards that can serve as a basis for allocating pension costs between the employer and the employees. The allocation must be made in the light of the circumstances surrounding the particular case, with an eye to the practices in other similar cases. The primary consideration is how much each party can afford to pay, given a particular set of benefits. The employee contribution rate should be set in the light of both equity and the desirability of achieving a high degree of participation. Under any plan, the objectives of the program and its qualification[5] can be defeated by inadequate participation. The capacity and willingness of the employer to support the anticipated level of contributions

[3]ERISA §204(c), I.R.C. §411(c).

[4]But elective contributions by employees under CODAs are excluded from taxable income. See Chapter 27.

[5]Mandatory contributions in excess of 6 percent of pay are presumed burdensome and, hence, discriminatory. Treas. Reg. 1.401–3(d), Rev. Rul. 59–185.

through good times and bad, and through periods of greater and lesser tax incentives, must also be taken into account.

In a defined benefit plan, an employee's contribution rate is often set at a multiple of his retirement benefit. The most common practice has been to establish employee contributions at two to three times the rate at which future service benefits accrue. If annual future service benefits accrue at the rate of 1 percent of each year's compensation, for example, the employee contribution rate would usually be set at 2 to 3 percent of each year's compensation. The portion of retirement benefits that such contributions will provide varies with the attained age of the employee and other factors, and the employer then contributes the remainder of the cost of the future service benefits as well as the full cost of the past service benefits.

Under a defined contribution plan, the employee's rate of contribution often bears a fixed ratio to the contribution rate of the employer, both normally being expressed as a percentage of the employee's compensation. Employers often match the employee's rate, with each, for example, contributing 5 percent of the employee's compensation. In some plans, however, the employer contributes at a rate of two or three times that of the employee.

The employee's rate of contribution on that portion of his compensation subject to Social Security taxation may be lower than that on the portion above the taxable wage base.[6]

Mandatory employee contributions to a qualified pension plan generally cannot be withdrawn before normal retirement as long as the participant is in the service of the employer.[7]

A plan may allow a participant to recover his mandatory contributions, with interest, upon withdrawal from the plan, upon termination of the plan itself, or at time of retirement. Many plans allow "cash out" upon withdrawal or plan termination, but not upon retirement. It is permissible under the law for participants to recover all past contributions, with interest, if the plan is converted from a contributory to a noncontributory plan.[8] The plan would rarely, if ever, refer to such a contingency, so in practice the dis-

---

[6]Chapter 10 discusses integration of pension plan contributions with Social Security.
[7]Rev. Rul. 56–693.
[8]Rev. Rul. 70–259.

position of accumulated employee contributions is a matter of employer policy or of negotiation between the employer and employees. Some plans have returned the contributions in cash, while others have transferred them to the employees' accounts in profit sharing or thrift plans. Usually the elimination of employee contributions is prospective only, and prior employee contributions are not returned at the time of the change.

Some plans of both the contributory and noncontributory type provide for voluntary employee contributions to the plan. These contributions are accumulated in individual employee accounts, credited with their share of the plan's investment return (including any appreciation and depreciation of market values),[9] and at the employee's option may be used to provide additional pension benefits at retirement. The contributions and the investment earnings thereon are nonforfeitable and can be withdrawn by the participant at any time, pursuant to the administrative rules of the plan, without prejudice to any other rights or benefits that may have accrued under the plan. Voluntary contributions may not exceed 10 percent of current or cumulative compensation.[10]

## Nondiscrimination Test for Employer Matching Contributions and Employee Contributions

Allowable employee contributions and employer contributions are constrained by an array of limitations under the Internal Revenue Code. These include the limits on mandatory employee contributions and upon voluntary employee contributions described earlier in this chapter, limits on contributions and benefits for individuals under section 415 (Chapter 5), and limits on deductible contributions under section 404 (Chapters 17 and 27). Further restrictions apply to elective contributions under a cash or deferred arrangement under section 401(k) (Chapter 27).

In addition, a nondiscrimination test called the "contribution percentage requirement" applies to certain employer and employee contributions.[11] This requirement limits the average contribution

---

[9]ERISA §204(c)(2)(A),(4), I.R.C. §411(c)(2)(A),(d)(5).

[10]Rev. Rul. 59–185.

[11]I.R.C. §401(m).

percentage for all highly compensated employees. The purpose of the requirement is to limit the amount of contributions that provide favorable tax treatment for highly compensated employees unless other employees enjoy a comparable level of tax-favored contributions.

The contribution percentage for each participant is determined as the ratio of the amount of the applicable contributions for the participant to his compensation. The applicable contributions include all voluntary employee contributions under a defined benefit plan, or the sum of employer matching contributions and all voluntary and mandatory employee contributions under a defined contribution plan. Employer matching contributions include those that match elective deferrals under a 401(k) plan as well as those that match after-tax employee contributions under any defined contribution plan.

The contribution percentage requirement compares the average contribution percentage of all highly compensated employees with the average contribution percentage of all other employees. All employees eligible to make contributions subject to the test or to have employer matching contributions made for them must be included, regardless of whether any such contributions are actually made. If an eligible employee has no actual contributions, his contribution percentage is 0 percent.

The requirement is satisfied if the average contribution percentage of highly compensated employees is not more than 125 percent of that of other employees. The requirement is also satisfied if the average contribution percentage of highly compensated employees is not more than 200 percent of that of other employees and if the difference between the average contribution percentages of the two groups does not exceed 2 percent. These requirements are illustrated as follows:

| Average Contribution Percentage for Nonhighly Compensated Employees | Maximum Allowable Average Contribution Percentage for Highly Compensated Employees | Ratio | Percentage Difference |
|---|---|---|---|
| 1.00% | 2.00% | 200% | 1.00% |
| 2.00 | 4.00 | 200 | 2.00 |
| 4.00 | 6.00 | 150 | 2.00 |
| 8.00 | 10.00 | 125 | 2.00 |
| 10.00 | 12.50 | 125 | 2.50 |

For purposes of satisfying the contribution percentage requirement, regulations are to allow employers to include not only the contributions described above, but also (*i*) elective deferrals under a 401(k) plan and (*ii*) employer "qualified nonelective contributions." Qualified nonelective contributions are employer contributions other than elective contributions under a 401(k) plan, provided that such contributions are fully and immediately vested and are subject to the restrictions on distribution that apply to elective deferrals.

If two plans have been aggregated for purposes of satisfying the coverage tests (see Chapter 4), they must also be treated as one plan for this test.

A plan may pay out to highly compensated employees any "excess aggregate contributions," that is, any contributions higher than the maximum amount that would satisfy the tests, together with income allocable to the excess aggregate contributions. Such excess aggregate contributions may be paid out without any restriction or penalty. The employer must pay a 10 percent tax on any excess aggregate contribution not paid out within two and a half months after the end of the plan year.[12] If excess aggregate contributions are not corrected by the end of the plan year following the contribution, the plan may be disqualified.

Ordinarily the voluntary contributions of highly compensated employees are substantially higher than for other employees. The contribution percentage requirement often makes it difficult to allow voluntary employee contributions without severely limiting these contributions for highly compensated employees. Because of this difficulty and problems imposed by Code section 415 as amended by the Tax Reform Act, many plans that previously allowed voluntary employee contributions have eliminated them.

## Limitations on the Employer's Commitment

It is customary for the sponsor of a single employer, nonbargained pension plan to hedge his commitment under the plan through the inclusion of certain provisions that have become fairly standardized. The first provision, not found in all plans, makes it a matter of record that neither the establishment of the plan nor participation

---

[12]I.R.C. §4979.

in the plan by a particular employee shall create any obligation on the part of the employer to provide continued employment to the employee in order that he may qualify for proffered benefits.

The second provision, which is found in almost all plans, gives the employer the unilateral right to alter, modify, or terminate the plan at any time. However, no action under the authority of this provision can operate to curtail, modify, or terminate any accrued benefit,[13] except as may be necessary under IRS regulations to prevent discrimination in favor of the 25 most highly paid employees upon early plan termination.[14] Moreover, IRS may attempt to retroactively disqualify the plan for termination during the first few (possibly as many as five) years of the plan's existence for a reason other than "business necessity."[15]

A third provision, more critical in some respects than the foregoing, either provides the employer complete freedom to decide whether and how much to contribute, or reserves to the employer the right to suspend, reduce, or discontinue contributions to the plan at any time and for any reason. During the first five years the reason for a complete discontinuance of contributions must be "business necessity," if danger of retroactive tax penalties is to be avoided. Implicit in this provision is the right of the employer to discontinue contributions to the plan, even though the accumulated assets may not be sufficient to provide all the benefits already accrued. For plans subject to ERISA's minimum funding requirements, the freedom to determine the amount of contributions or to suspend contributions is limited.

A fourth clause in defined benefit plans implements the third by stating that, in the event of termination of the plan, or the discontinuance of contributions thereunder, the employer shall have no liability for the payment of accrued benefits beyond the contributions already made. In other words, if the plan were to be terminated, the participants and their beneficiaries would have to look to the assets in the plan, including any annuities that may have been purchased from life insurers, for the satisfaction of their claims.

---

[13]ERISA §204(g), I.R.C. §411(d)(6). Restrictions also apply to any change in the vesting schedule. ERISA §203(c), I.R.C. §411(a)(10).

[14]I.R.C. §411(d)(3), Treas. Reg. 1.401–4(c)(2).

[15]Treas. Reg. 1.401–1(b)(2). *Howard S. Davis Est.* (1954) 22 TC 807 (Acq.) Rev. Rul. 69–24.

The employer might voluntarily make additional contributions to the plan—or pay the benefits out of its own resources—but it would have no legal obligation to do so. If the plan assets proved to be inadequate—as they are likely to be for years after the plan is established or retroactively liberalized—the benefits of all claimants would have to be scaled down or priorities established, with the possibility that some participants would receive nothing. Some plans do not contain an express limitation on the employer's liability, reliance being placed on the employer's reserved right to discontinue contributions. Plan benefits insurance guarantees certain benefits and restricts the employer's ability to limit its liability.[16]

A final limitation on the employer's undertaking, of a general nature and not found in all plans, is a statement that, except for willful misconduct or lack of good faith, no legal or equitable rights against the employer shall be created or exist under the plan. The primary purpose of such a provision is to protect the firm and its agents against legal or equitable action arising out of the administration of the plan; but the language seems broad enough to be invoked against a participant or beneficiary seeking to compel the employer to make good on the benefit rights accrued under the plan.

The employer does not generally have all the foregoing rights under a pension plan subject to collective bargaining. A bargained plan cannot be altered, modified, or terminated without the consent of the bargaining agent, unless such rights have been reserved to the employer—an unlikely situation[17]—or to a joint board of trustees. As a matter of fact, the employer's legal commitment under these plans is not always clear. Generally, however, the employer commits himself to one or the other of two types of undertakings: (1) to maintain the plan with specified benefits during the period of the labor agreement or (2) to make contributions to the plan—a single employer plan or a multiemployer plan—at agreed upon rates, usually expressed in cents per hour worked. The first type of agreement is often supplemented by the employer's commitment to fund

---

[16]See Chapters 24 and 25 for the details of the pension plan benefits insurance program.

[17]An employer does not need a provision in a collectively bargained plan giving him the right to alter, modify, or terminate the plan or to suspend, reduce, or discontinue contributions, since the continued existence of the plan depends upon the continued existence of a related collective bargaining agreement.

the plan on some acceptable basis, but under both undertakings ERISA's minimum funding requirements apply. Under both arrangements, it is always tacitly assumed that the pension plan will be continued indefinitely through successive labor contracts. The basic legal question is what would be the effect of termination of the plan, or of the labor agreement(s) under which it was established and operated, on the benefit rights that were created during the term of the labor contract or contracts.

Under a single employer plan, if the collective bargaining agreement expires without renewal, the employer generally has the right to continue, modify, or terminate the plan, the same as under a nonbargained single employer plan. Under a multiemployer plan, upon expiry of the collective bargaining agreement, the employer stops making contributions and employees accrue no further benefits; in some cases, accrued benefits credited for past service before employer contributions began are cancelled.[18] Upon withdrawal from a multiemployer plan or upon termination of a single employer plan or a multiemployer plan, the employer may be liable for substantial additional payments.[19]

A few prominent companies do not attempt to limit their pension obligations to funds already contributed and promise to pay the accrued pension benefits out of general corporate resources, if necessary. In some cases, this guarantee applies to all classes of accrued benefits, while in others it is limited to vested benefits, benefits in payment status, or some other restricted category. Most of these employer guarantees were unilaterally assumed, one going back to 1904 and another to 1913; but a few were undertaken in response to collective bargaining, in exchange for employer control of funding policy.[20]

---

[18]ERISA §203(a)(3)(E), I.R.C. §411(a)(3)(E).

[19]See Chapters 24 and 25.

[20]Employer guarantees of pension benefits are discussed at some length in Dan M. McGill, *Employer Guarantee of Pension Benefits* (Homewood, Ill.: Richard D. Irwin, 1974), pp. 19–35.

## Questions

1. Outline the arguments in favor of a noncontributory pension plan.

2. Why might an employer, despite the foregoing arguments in favor of a noncontributory plan, conclude that its plan should be contributory?

3. If you were setting up a contributory pension, how would you decide how much the employees should be required to contribute toward the cost of the plan?

4. Do you believe that participants in a contributory pension plan should recover their past contributions in one form or the other if the plan is converted into a noncontributory plan? Why?

5. Explain the difference in status and treatment of *mandatory* and *voluntary* employee contributions to a qualified pension plan.

6. Why should there be any legal limits to the amount of *voluntary* contributions that a participant may make to a pension plan? What is the current limit?

7. What limits apply to employer matching contributions and employee contributions? What is the practical effect of the limits?

8. In what ways have sponsors of single employer pension plans attempted to limit their obligations to the plans and the participating employees and their beneficiaries?

9. To what extent has ERISA affected an employer's ability to limit his obligation to his pension plan and its participants?

10. (*a*) In what way do the rights and obligations of an employer sponsor of a collectively bargained pension plan differ from the rights and obligations that it would have under a noncollectively bargained pension plan?
    (*b*) What is the legal relationship between a collectively bargained single employer pension plan and the collective bargaining agreement to which it owed its origin and under which it continues to function? Specifically, does the plan have a legal existence apart from that of the collective bargaining agreement?

11. In your opinion, should the corporate sponsor of a defined benefit pension plan pledge its general corporate resources to assuring the ultimate payment of the benefit obligations of the pension plan? Why or why not?

# 10 | Integration of Pension Plans with Social Security

## Purpose of Integration

A WELL-DESIGNED PENSION PLAN will take into account the contributions or benefits under the federal OASDI program, described in Chapter 1. Employers, employees, and self-employed individuals each pay taxes under the Federal Insurance Contributions Act (FICA) to fund the OASDI program and the Hospital Insurance program.[1] The taxes are a percentage of pay based on compensation not exceeding the taxable wage base, $45,000 in 1988.

The basic Social Security benefit, the so-called primary insurance amount (PIA), is based upon the average indexed monthly earnings (AIME), which is an average of earnings not exceeding the taxable wage base for certain past years, indexed to reflect increases in average wages and inflation. The PIA is computed by applying a higher percentage to the first portion of the worker's average indexed monthly earnings than to later portions. The average indexed monthly earnings are divided into three segments, and a downward sloping scale of percentages is applied to the three

---

[1] The Federal Insurance Contribution Act is contained in I.R.C. §§3101–3127. Taxation of self-employment income is contained in I.R.C. §§1401–1403.

segments. In 1988, the PIA is 90 percent of the first $319 of AIME, 32 percent of the next $1,603, and 15 percent of any excess.[2] Earnings above the taxable wage base are excluded in determining the AIME and the PIA.

The general objective of some employers will be to provide combined benefits, those payable under Social Security and the plan, that constitute approximately the same percentage of the employee's disposable income irrespective of his position on the pay scale. In other words, the goal is for the higher-paid employees to enjoy retirement income from Social Security and the pension plan that is about the same percentage of their disposable income as that applicable to lower-paid employees. Other employers may have an objective to make the combined employer contributions for Social Security and the plan to be about the same percentage of pay for all levels of employees.

Both contributions and benefits under the OASDI program are more heavily weighted to lower-paid workers. The integration of pension plans with Social Security offsets this weighting under Social Security by having contributions or benefits under the pension plan more heavily weighted toward the higher-paid employees, as a tactic to achieve the objectives described above.

This approach to plan design not only serves the plan sponsor's concept of equitable treatment of participants at all income levels but operates to reduce the cost of the plan, offsetting to some extent the Social Security taxes paid by the employer in respect of the participants. When a plan's benefit or contribution formula is set up to achieve these objectives, the plan is said to be integrated with Social Security.[3]

## Underlying Concepts of Regulatory Requirements

As indicated above, integration involves weighting pension plan benefits and contributions in favor of highly compensated employees. If there were no limitations upon this, it would be possible for

---

[2]The bend points of $319 and $1,922 and the taxable wage base are subject to upward revision annually in accordance with movements in the general level of earnings.

[3]*Correlation* is perhaps a more descriptive term for the concept and process, but the word *integration* is too deeply imbedded in pension literature and regulatory language to change the terminology.

contributions and benefits to discriminate in favor of the highly compensated and it would be possible for private pension plans to provide little or no benefits for the low paid. Provisions of the Internal Revenue Code are designed to prevent these two consequences.

Integration must be carried out in strict conformity with applicable statutory requirements. The Tax Reform Act of 1986 (TRA) made substantial changes in these requirements.[4] The new requirements, which form the basis of the discussion in this chapter, are generally effective with respect to benefits accruing for plan years beginning after 1988.[5] For earlier requirements one should consult the applicable IRS revenue rulings.[6]

One purpose of the requirements, both before and after the Tax Reform Act, has been to ensure that the combined benefits or contributions of the pension plan and the portion of Social Security funded by employer taxes will not constitute a higher percentage of compensation of the more highly paid employees than of the compensation of the less-favored employees. This is accomplished by limiting the permitted disparity between contributions or benefits for the high paid and those for the low paid.

A second purpose, new under the Tax Reform Act, is to prevent plans from providing little or no contributions or benefits for the low paid. A related purpose is to provide incentives to increase the contributions or benefits for the low paid.

## General Approaches to Integration

There are three general approaches to integrating plan contributions or benefits with Social Security. For defined contribution plans, the employer contributions are integrated with employer FICA taxes for retirement benefits. For defined benefit plans two different approaches to integration are available: the excess plan approach and the offset approach. Under an excess plan approach one layer of benefits is based upon all compensation and a second layer of benefits is added with respect to compensation in excess of a speci-

---

[4]I.R.C. §401(a)(5),(l) as amended by TRA §1111.

[5]Later for certain collectively bargained plans. TRA §1111(c).

[6]Rev. Ruls. 71–446, 72–276, 72–492, 75–480, 78–92, 83–53, 83–97, 83–110, 84–45, and 86–74.

fied dollar amount called the "integration level." Under an offset plan the benefit is first calculated on the basis of total compensation and then an "offset" is deducted to reflect the fact that Social Security benefits are payable.

### Defined Contribution Plans

As was pointed out earlier, a defined contribution plan is one under which contributions of the employer or employees or both, and possibly forfeitures, are allocated to individual accounts for participants. In an integrated defined contribution plan the allocation of contributions and any forfeitures with respect to compensation above the integration level exceeds the percentage below the integration level. The percentage applied below the integration level is called the "base contribution percentage" and the percentage applied above the integration level is called the "excess contribution percentage." The permitted disparity between these two percentages may not exceed either 5.7 percent or the base contribution percentage.[7]

The integration level, commonly called the "breakpoint," must generally be set as equal to the Social Security taxable wage base in effect at the beginning of the plan year ($45,000 for 1988). A higher integration level is not permitted. A lower integration level is permitted only if it is nondiscriminatory. As a practical matter any lower limit that satisfies the nondiscrimination requirement may not meet employer or employee objectives.

**Money Purchase Pension Plan.** The application of these requirements to a money purchase pension plan may be illustrated as follows:

| Base Contribution Percentage | Permitted Disparity | Maximum Excess Contribution Percentage |
|---|---|---|
| 3.0% | 3.0% | 6.0% |
| 4.0 | 4.0 | 8.0 |
| 5.0 | 5.0 | 10.0 |
| 6.0 | 5.7 | 11.7 |

[7]If the portion of FICA taxes attributable to old-age benefits ever rose above 5.7 percent, the allowable percentage would increase, but no such increase is currently scheduled or even contemplated for the future.

For a top-heavy plan, contributions for non-key employees may not be less than 3 percent of their compensation.

**Profit Sharing Plan.**  The application of these requirements to an allocation of contributions under a profit sharing plan may be illustrated as follows:

> First, allocations are made for all participants in proportion to the sum of their total compensation plus their compensation in excess of the integration level, not to exceed 5.7 percent of that sum (which would amount to 5.7 percent of compensation below the integration level plus 11.4 percent above).
>
> Second, any remainder to be allocated is allocated in proportion to total compensation.

But if the plan were top-heavy, requiring contributions of 3 percent of total pay first, the allocation would be accomplished in accordance with the following steps:

> *Step 1*:  Allocations are made in proportion to total compensation, not to exceed 3 percent.
>
> *Step 2*:  Any remaining amount is allocated in proportion to excess compensation, not to exceed 3 percent of such excess (bringing the allocation up to 3 percent below the integration level and 6 percent above).
>
> *Step 3*:  Any remaining amount is allocated in proportion to the sum of total compensation plus excess compensation, not to exceed 2.7 percent of that sum (bringing the allocation up to 5.7 percent below the integration level and 11.4 percent above).
>
> *Step 4*:  Any remainder is allocated in proportion to total compensation.

The allocation can be simplified if the plan uses less than the maximum permitted disparity.

Regulations are expected to allow the integration of a target benefit plan if the target benefit satisfies the requirements for integration of a defined benefit plan, even though a target benefit plan is actually a defined contribution plan.

### Defined Benefit Plans

TRA states that integrated defined benefit plans must base benefits on "average annual compensation."[8] The Code defines average

---

[8]IRC §401(1)(3).

annual compensation to mean the greater of the participant's average compensation for his final three years (or all years if less) or the participant's highest average annual compensation for any other period of at least three consecutive years. The reference to "any other period" presumably means any other period specified in the plan. This would mean that an integrated defined benefit plan would generally be required to base benefits upon the average compensation during the last three years (or all years if less), but a plan could elect to use some alternative definition, such as the average for the highest 5 consecutive years in the last 10, for any participant for whom this would produce a higher average. Such an alternative might be desirable where pay fluctuates up and down from year to year, in order to protect employees from benefits based upon a few low years.

According to the statutory language, it appears impossible to have any integrated defined benefit plan based solely upon five-year-final-average compensation or based upon career average compensation, practices common before TRA. However, a technical corrections amendment is expected to allow such plans.

**Defined Benefit Excess Plans.**  An excess plan is an integrated defined benefit plan that provides a higher percentage of benefits with respect to pay above the integration level than with respect to pay below the integration level. Under prior law it was permissible to have a pure excess plan with no benefit below the integration level; such plans will no longer be permitted. Under TRA all excess plans must be "step-rate" excess plans with a base benefit percentage based upon compensation below the integration level and an excess benefit percentage based on pay in excess of the integration level.

Under an excess plan the permitted disparity is defined in terms of the "maximum excess allowance," which is the difference between the excess benefit percentage and the base benefit percentage. The maximum excess allowance may not exceed any one of three limits:

1. The base benefit percentage;
2. For benefits attributable to any particular year of service, 0.75 percent of excess compensation; and
3. For total benefits, 0.75 percent of excess compensation times years of service (maximum 26.25 percent for 35 or more years).

For the above rule, only years of service during which benefits accrue may be counted. Thus, if a plan uses the fractional rule for determining accrued benefits by prorating projected benefits over years of participation, then years of service during which the employee was not a participant may not be counted.

Examples of determination of the maximum excess allowance are as follows:

| Base Benefit Percentage | Maximum Excess Allowance |
|---|---|
| 0.5% times years | 0.5% times years, maximum 26.25% |
| 1.0% times years | 0.75% times years, maximum 26.25% |

*A. Integration Level.*   The integration level may be set at "covered compensation" as defined by the Act or at any lower level. A higher integration level may be used, but in that case the allowable integration percentage must be reduced in accordance with forthcoming regulations. The integration level may never exceed the taxable wage base. No change in the allowable integration percentage is made if the integration level is less than covered compensation.

*Covered compensation* is defined as the average Social Security taxable wage base for the 35 years ending with the participant's normal retirement age under Social Security (i.e., 65, 66, or 67). A different definition applied under prior law. In making this determination for a participant who has not yet reached his Social Security normal retirement age, a plan must assume that the taxable wage base will remain the same in future years.

Table 4 shows a schedule of covered compensation as defined under the Tax Reform Act based upon the 1988 taxable wage base of $45,000. This schedule is illustrative only, since the new integration rules do not apply until 1989.

As under prior law, a plan can use a schedule of covered compensation varying with age like that in Table 4 or can use for all participants the amount allowable for the oldest possible participant. Similarly, a plan can either freeze the table for all years or can adjust it automatically each year to reflect increases in the taxable wage base by including in the plan document the statutory definition of covered compensation rather than specific dollar amounts. Using integration levels that vary by age and changing

**TABLE 4**
**Covered Compensation Amounts for Integration with**
**Social Security Benefits**

| Year of Birth | 1988 Covered Compensation | Year of Birth | 1988 Covered Compensation |
|---|---|---|---|
| 1923 | $15,709 | 1940 | $36,040 |
| 1924 | $16,891 | 1941 | $37,069 |
| 1925 | $18,057 | 1942 | $38,046 |
| 1926 | $19,223 | 1943 | $38,954 |
| 1927 | $20,389 | 1944 | $39,837 |
| 1928 | $21,554 | 1945 | $40,686 |
| 1929 | $22,703 | 1946 | $41,500 |
| 1930 | $23,851 | 1947 | $42,280 |
| 1931 | $25,000 | 1948 | $42,911 |
| 1932 | $26,149 | 1949 | $43,457 |
| 1933 | $27,297 | 1950 | $43,894 |
| 1934 | $28,446 | 1951 | $44,254 |
| 1935 | $29,594 | 1952 | $44,520 |
| 1936 | $30,691 | 1953 | $44,726 |
| 1937 | $31,789 | 1954 | $44,880 |
| 1938 | $33,914 | 1955 and later | $45,000 |
| 1939 | $34,977 | | |

the levels annually is theoretically the best approach, keeping up with changes in the taxable wage base and allowing more integration. But most employers use a single fixed dollar amount as the integration level for all participants in order to simplify administration and communication of the plan.

**B. Early Retirement.** The maximum excess allowance must be reduced if benefits commence before the Social Security normal retirement age. Before the Social Security Amendments of 1983 age 65 was the age at which unreduced old-age benefits under Social Security could commence for all covered workers (the Social Security normal retirement age). Under the 1983 Amendments the Social Security normal retirement age is 65 for those born in 1937 and earlier, but is gradually increased to age 67 for those born in 1960 and later. In contrast, a pension plan's normal retirement age may not be later than age 65 or 5 years of participation, if later.[9] Most pension plans provide unreduced pensions at age 65 (many

---

[9]ERISA §3(24) and IRC §411(a)(8) as amended by the Omnibus Budget Reconciliation Act of 1986 P.L. 99–509.

plans earlier) and allow early retirement with reduced benefits at earlier ages.

Thus, for participants born after 1937 the maximum excess allowance for any benefits commencing at age 65 must be reduced; and for all participants the maximum excess allowance for any benefits commencing before age 65 must be reduced. The reduction in the maximum excess allowance is one fifteenth per year for the first 5 years prior to the Social Security normal retirement age, one thirtieth for each of the next 5 years, and an actuarial reduction for any years in excess of 10.

For younger participants whose Social Security normal retirement age is 67, the reduction of one fifteenth per year results in the 0.75 percent limit being reduced to 0.65 percent at age 65. Thus, if the plan is to use the same benefit formula for participants of all ages, the allowable integration may not exceed 0.65 percent per year. In this case the appropriate early retirement adjustment would be one thirteenth for each of the first three years prior to age 65 and one twenty-sixth for each of the next five years, with an actuarial adjustment for more than eight years early, since one thirteenth and one twenty-sixth of the limit at age 65 equal one fifteenth and one thirtieth, respectively, of the limit at age 67.

*C. Differences from Prior Law.*   Unlike the rules under prior law, there is no reduction in the maximum excess allowance as the result of the form of annuity, death benefits, disability benefits, or employee contributions, since the rules are based only on Social Security old-age benefits.

Prior law requirements for excess plans were different in many respects. They generally allowed more integration. Most excess plans that satisfied the prior requirements will require amendment of the benefit formula to satisfy the new requirements.

**Defined Benefit Offset Plan.**   The Act defines an offset plan as "any plan with respect to which the benefit attributable to employer contributions for each participant is reduced by an amount specified in the plan." The maximum allowable offset is no longer directly related to Social Security. In a contributory plan the benefit may not be reduced below the benefit derived from employee contributions.

The maximum offset allowance may not exceed any one of three limits:

1. Half of the benefit before the offset;
2. For benefits attributable to any particular year, 0.75 percent of the participant's three-year-final-average compensation; and
3. For total benefits, 0.75 percent of the participant's three-year-final-average compensation times his years of service during which benefits accrue (maximum 26.25 percent after 35 or more years).

In calculating final average compensation any year's compensation in excess of the taxable wage base must be disregarded.

The 0.75 percent factor is to be reduced in accordance with forthcoming regulations for any participant whose final average compensation exceeds the covered compensation previously described. These factors will vary with the level of compensation and age and will change annually.

The maximum offset allowance is reduced for each year that benefit commencement precedes the Social Security normal retirement date, in the same manner as for excess plans. No adjustments are required or permitted for other factors.

A plan may use less than the maximum offset allowance, such as the lesser of the maximum offset allowance or a percentage of the Social Security primary insurance amount, provided this does not discriminate in favor of highly compensated employees and is not inconsistent with the purposes of the integration rules. Future regulations will clarify this.

The new requirements for offset plans under the TRA are very different from prior rules. Under prior law the maximum offset was defined as a percentage of the PIA. The reasons stated for basing the offset on final average earnings rather than the PIA were to eliminate the need to determine the employee's actual Social Security benefit and to provide for parity between offset plans and excess plans.

Under prior rules the offset at times completely eliminated any benefit for lower-paid employees. Limiting the offset to half of the benefit prevents this from occurring.

Every prior offset plan will need to be amended in order to comply with the new integration requirements.

**Comparison of Excess Plans and Offset Plans.**   At the time of this writing exact comparisons of excess plans and offset plans were not possible, since regulations had not yet been published. Under either approach, even when the maximum permitted disparity is fully used in the benefit formula, the combined benefits under the plan and Social Security will replace a lower percentage of after-tax pay for higher-paid employees than for lower-paid employees, and may thus not fully accomplish the objective of replacing the same percentage of after-tax pay for all. But either method will come far closer to that objective than if no integration at all had been used. Under the new requirements an excess plan will be substantially easier to administer and to communicate to employees than an offset plan, particularly because the reduction in the 0.75 percent factor under an offset plan must vary with the level of compensation.

## Questions

1. Explain the fundamental philosophy underlying the integration of a private pension plan with the Social Security program.

2. What is the employer's primary motivation in integrating his pension plan with Social Security?

3. In your judgment, how does the dollar amount of employer cost savings from integration compare with the FICA (Federal Insurance Contributions Act) payroll taxes paid by the employer for Social Security on behalf of his employees who participate in the pension plan?

4. Many employees and employee organizations object to the concept and practice of integration, especially when applied in the form of an offset. What is the philosophical argument against integration?

5. Are the various methods of integrating a pension plan with Social Security the actuarial equivalent of each other? Do they have the same effect on plan benefits and costs in the short run? In the long run?

6. Under a defined contribution plan the permitted disparity in contributions may not exceed 5.7 percent, although the employer's FICA tax under the OASDI program will exceed 5.7 percent in 1988 and later years. Why may not the full FICA tax rate under OASDI be used?

7. Explain the concepts of "covered compensation" and the "maximum excess allowance" and describe the manner in which they may be used to integrate an excess plan with Social Security.

8. Under defined benefit plans the normal retirement age generally may not exceed 65, while the normal retirement age for Social Security is scheduled to increase to 67. How does this affect integration? Should the law specify the same normal retirement age for both purposes? If so, what factors should be considered in determining it?

9. Indicate with respect to each of the following pension plans whether or not the proposed benefit formula meets the integration requirements of the Internal Revenue Service. If the integration requirement is satisfied, tell why it is. If the formula does not meet the integration requirement, indicate the adjustment or adjustments that must be made in order for the plan to qualify from the standpoint of benefits.

   *Plan 1*: The plan proposes to provide an annual retirement benefit at age 65 for each year of service to 1.8 percent of the participant's average compensation for the last 5 years of employment, less 1.5 percent of the Social Security old-age benefit for each year of service up to a total of 40 years of service.

   *Plan 2*: The plan proposes to provide an annual retirement benefit at age 65 for each year of service equal to the sum of 0.75 percent of the participant's year-to-year compensation subject to Social Security taxation and 1.5 percent of the participant's year-to-year compensation in excess of the Social Security taxable wage base.

   *Plan 3*: The plan proposes to provide an annual retirement benefit at age 65 for each year of service equal to 1 percent of the participant's final average salary, as defined, falling within the applicable "covered compensation" limit and 1.5 percent of that portion of the participant's final average salary in excess of the applicable "covered compensation" limit. The plan defines "final average salary" as the 5 consecutive years of highest earnings out of the last 10 years of employment.

   *Plan 4*: The plan proposes to provide an annual retirement benefit *at age 62* equal to 0.75 percent of that portion of the participant's average annual salary for the last *three* years of employment in excess of the Social Security covered compensation multiplied by his total years of service.

   *Plan 5*: The plan is to be operated on a money purchase basis. The employer proposes to contribute 5 percent of that portion of the participant's current annual salary within the Social Security taxable wage base and 10 percent of that portion of the participant's current annual salary in excess of the taxable wage base. Each employee is to contribute 3 percent of his *total* current annual earnings. The benefits are to become payable upon retirement at any age after age 59.

*Plan 6:* The plan proposes to provide an annual retirement benefit *at age 60* equal to 1.5 percent of the participant's final average salary, as defined, in excess of the Social Security covered compensation, multiplied by years of service up to 30.

# 11 | Adjustment of Pensions for Inflation and Productivity Gains

THE UPWARD MOVEMENT of prices over the last 40 years has focused attention on the need to protect accrued pension benefits against the loss of purchasing power. Benefits may accrue over a period of 40 to 45 years and may be in payment status for another 30 years or more. Thus, in a period of steadily rising prices, benefits may lose much of their purchasing power between the time they are earned and the time when the final payment is made to the retired employee or his beneficiary.

Concurrently, improvements in technology and the process of production usually give rise to productivity gains that enhance the standard of living of the working population through wage levels that increase more rapidly than prices. In several recent years, prices have risen faster than wages, but most economists expect the historic relationship between these two economic variables to prevail in the long run. In the absence of a special adjustment feature, retired individuals do not share in the productivity gains that are realized after their retirement, except through the impact of such gains on consumer prices. Some observers believe that the retired population should share fully in the productivity gains in the economy, in addition to having their pension benefits protected against the ravages of inflation. In other words, retired individuals should be able to improve their standard of living over the period of their retirement. Other observers would settle for provisions or

**204**

procedures that would preserve the relative standard of living of a pensioner as it existed at the time of retirement. This approach would limit adjustments in postretirement benefits to those associated with cost-of-living changes. Many, if not most, plan sponsors reject the proposition that the purchasing power of their pension plan benefits should be fully preserved, and possibly enhanced through productivity gains, on the grounds that the threat to the benefits of retired people comes from governmental policies and thus the solution must come from the public sector. On strictly pragmatic grounds, most plan sponsors believe that they could not afford to undertake the preservation of the purchasing power of the benefits of their pension plans.

A number of approaches have been developed to provide protection against the loss of purchasing power and some have the further objective (or effect) of making it possible for the retired population to have a share of the productivity gains that would normally inure only to the benefit of active employees. These approaches may be differentiated as to whether they pertain to the accruing benefits of active participants or to the benefit payments to retired employees or their beneficiaries.

## Protection of Accruing Benefits

### Final Average Salary Formula

A common and reasonably effective approach of protecting the purchasing power of accruing pension benefits under defined benefit plans is to compute the benefits at retirement on the basis of the employee's average annual compensation over the last few years immediately preceding retirement. The shorter the period over which the averaging occurs, the more closely the benefits will reflect the employee's earnings status at the point of retirement. Earnings are seldom averaged over a period longer than 10 years, the modal period being 5 years. Some plans are using a four- or three-year average. Some public employee retirement systems base benefits on the earnings of the individual for the last year of employment and a few use the earnings on the last day of employment.[1]

---

[1]Those systems that base benefits on the earnings of the last year of employment may include overtime and unused sick leave.

Earnings tend to reflect inflationary forces, usually with some lag. Hence, a final average salary formula usually produces a pension benefit that is protected against the erosive effects of inflation *up to the point of retirement.* Moreover, to the extent that wages embody realized productivity gains, the employee's pension will likewise be enriched by this component up to retirement. However, this approach provides no protection against the loss of purchasing power that may occur during the period of retirement. Nor does it channel to retired employees any part of the productivity gains that may have emerged after their retirement. Hence, this approach needs to be supplemented by some other method to provide reasonably effective protection against inflation for the employee's total period of participation.

## *Ad Hoc Adjustments of Salary Base or Flat Benefit Accruals*

A second approach to protecting the accruing benefits of active participants under defined benefit plans is to make ad hoc adjustments in the salary base of a career average formula plan or the benefit accruals of a plan that provides a specified dollar benefit for each year of credited service. The chief characteristic of this approach is that the employer or other plan sponsor does not commit himself in advance to making adjustments in the accrued benefits. He observes the trend of events and then makes whatever modifications that seem to be justified. To the extent that the compensation levels (or the flat dollar derivatives) reflect productivity gains in the economy, this approach is consistent with the twin objectives of protecting purchasing power and enhancing the standard of living.

The underlying premise of a career average formula is that the benefit accrual for any particular year of service will be based on the employee's actual compensation in that year, rather than on his average salary for the last few years of employment. The main reason that an employer chooses a career average formula instead of a final average salary formula is to avoid making a benefit commitment in terms of an unknown future salary base. Yet when wages are rising sharply in response to inflationary pressures, benefits based on the earnings of previous years, many of them in the distant past, become hopelessly out of date.[2] The longer the service of the employee the worse his predicament, a result that cannot be reconciled with sound personnel and social policy. A solution to the problem that does not involve a future commitment of indeterminate magnitude is to amend the plan to recompute all benefits for service prior to that date on the basis of compensation levels in effect at that time or on some stipulated basis that represents an updating of the salary. This is analogous to granting past service benefits at the inception of the plan on the basis of compensation levels in effect at that time. This procedure may be repeated as often as conditions seem to warrant. If the salary base is updated on a systematic basis, the benefit (and cost) results could approach those of the final average formula, but without the advance commitment.

The same principle is involved in updating the benefit accruals of a flat benefit plan. This type of plan is generally subject to collective bargaining, and any change in the benefit accruals would tend to be the result of the collective bargaining process. The updating may take the form of an upward adjustment in the yearly benefit accruals for future years of service or an adjustment in the benefit accruals for all years of credited service, past and future. Periodic retroactive adjustments in the flat dollar benefit accruals may approximate the results obtained through the use of a final average formula, again without the advance commitment.

Each ad hoc adjustment involves a formal plan amendment, an administrative inconvenience avoided by the final average formula approach.

## Automatic Index Adjustments

The benefit accruals of active participants in defined benefit plans may be automatically adjusted in accordance with changes in a specified price or wage index. Thus far, plans using this approach

---

[2]For example, if the compensation of a plan participant were to increase at an annual compounded rate of 3 percent, a modest assumption by today's standard, over a covered period of 35 years, a pension benefit based on his career average earnings would be only 67 percent of that based on a 5-year final average formula and only 65 percent of that based on a 3-year final average formula. If the compounded rate of salary increase were 5 percent, the respective percentages would be 54 and 52 percent.

have designated the consumer price index (CPI) of the Bureau of Labor Statistics as the measuring rod; but an appropriately constructed wage index could serve equally well, but with different results.[3] Beginning in January of 1978 the Bureau of Labor Statistics established two new CPIs: the CPI for All Urban Consumers (designated CPI-U) and a revised CPI for Urban Wage Earners and Clerical Workers (revised CPI-W). Both of the new CPIs tie into the value of the old CPI (unrevised CPI-W), which was discontinued after June of 1978. Plans now need to designate which CPI is intended. Adjustments on the basis of the CPI would be designed to protect accruing pensions only against loss of purchasing power, while wage index adjustments would have the additional purpose of reflecting productivity gains.

When a plan provides for index adjustments before retirement, the benefit that accrues during any particular year of service is adjusted at time of retirement to reflect the changes that have taken place in the specified index since the benefit was credited. For example, the benefit that accrued during a participant's age 35 would be adjusted to reflect the net cumulative change in the index over the next 30 years. The benefit accrual for the following year would be adjusted for the index movement over the next 29 years and so on. There may be a limit on the percentage adjustment for each year of the intervening period.

The index adjustment technique is primarily designed for defined benefit plans that provide a flat dollar benefit for each year of service or a benefit based on career average compensation. It may also be used with a final average formula to adjust the compensation for the years entering into the defined salary base. For example, if the plan formula bases benefits on the average earnings of the last five years of employment, the participant's actual compensation for the fifth, fourth, third, and second years prior to retirement would be adjusted to reflect the changes in the index from those years to the date of retirement. No change would be made in the compensation

---

[3]As was noted earlier, in 1977 the Social Security Act was amended to provide for the indexing of wages (and the earnings of self-employed persons) in the calculation of an individual's average monthly earnings. The wages or earnings of an individual for any particular year are multiplied by a factor reflecting the percentage increase in average covered earnings for all covered persons from that year to the year of entitlement. The average monthly earnings of an individual adjusted in that manner is called the average *indexed* monthly earnings (AIME).

for the year in which retirement occurs. This procedure makes it possible to base the benefits of a retiring employee on his compensation immediately prior to retirement, if there were no merit increases during the preceding five years, without the risk of salary manipulation that would be present if benefits were expressed in terms of the individual's actual compensation during his final year of employment. This type of adjustment would be especially advantageous to a participant in a plan that bases benefits on average compensation during the last 10 years of employment or the average compensation during the 5 consecutive years of highest earnings, wherever they happened to fall. In the latter case, of course, the earnings of each of the five years would be adjusted by the appropriate index factors to the year of retirement.

Annual increases in the accrued benefits of active participants on the order of 3 percent would elevate the long-run cost of the plan by about 75 percent, not counting the cost of adjusting benefits after retirement. These adjustments would be in lieu of ad hoc updating of past benefit accruals which would have about the same cost consequences.

### Linkage of Benefits to Asset Values

A fourth approach to protecting the accruing benefits of active participants and giving them an opportunity to share in the productivity gains of the economy is to provide a direct linkage between the dollar value of the benefit accruals and the market value of the assets accumulated to pay the benefits. All defined contribution plans, as well as some defined benefit plans, use this approach. The composition of the asset portfolio is immaterial to the concept. It may be composed entirely of equities (e.g., common stocks and real estate), entirely of fixed-income instruments (e.g., bonds and mortgages), or of a combination of equity and debt instruments (i.e., a so-called balanced fund). For this approach to meet its objectives, however, the market value of the assets must over time keep pace with increases in the cost of living (and the standard of living) and the participants must be permitted to share fully and directly in the growth of the asset values. But for many plans that link benefits to investment performance, the objective is to credit the participant with the total rate of return on the portfolio investments whether it be more or less than the rate of inflation.

**Asset Portfolio or Portfolios.** There is a difference of opinion among economists and investment experts as to the type of asset portfolio that is most likely to provide a hedge against inflation and pass along productivity gains. Indeed, there is no certainty that any type of portfolio can meet that test. Until recent years, there was a general belief that the total investment return (dividend income, net realized capital gains, and net unrealized capital appreciation) on a wisely selected portfolio of common stocks would over time be at least equal to the rate of growth in consumer prices over the same period.[4] In fact, since capital's share of productivity gains should be reflected in the price of common stock, the long-term growth of common stock values should be greater than the rise in consumer prices. A risk premium in the common stock return would increase the differential.

Uncertainty over the long-term performance of common stock has led some observers to espouse the use of a portfolio of marketable bonds and other fixed-income securities.[5] The presumption behind such a proposal is that market yields on bonds will reflect the inflationary expectations of investors and thus will serve as a reasonably satisfactory hedge against inflation, without the greater risks believed to be associated with common stock investments. The market value of a bond portfolio would, of course, move inversely to changes in the level of interest rates (i.e., falling when interest rates rise and rising when interest rates fall), thus influencing the total rate of return on the portfolio. The total rate of

---

[4]This view was expounded by Dr. William C. Greenough in a book entitled *A New Approach to Retirement Income* (New York: Teachers Insurance and Annuity Association, 1952). Dr. Greenough, who later became chairman of the board of TIAA-CREF, studied the relationship between common stock prices and the consumer price level over the period 1880 to 1950. This study showed that over long periods the market value of a representative group of common stocks conformed faithfully to changes in the consumer price level. He did find periods of several years' duration when these two variables moved in opposite directions, leading him to recommend the use of both equity and fixed-income investments in any pension plan that links benefits to investment performance.

[5]Marketable bonds would probably have to be used to avoid the problem of valuing directly placed securities and real estate mortgages, which would not have a readily ascertainable market value. Avoidance of the latter instruments would undoubtedly reduce the overall yield on the portfolio.

return might go down during an inflationary period and go up during a deflationary period—the exact opposite of the desired results. A fund invested in money market debt instruments would tend to reflect inflation, but the rate of return may or may not be satisfactory in the long run.

In view of the uncertain relationship between consumer price behavior and the total rate of return on different types of asset portfolios, many experts recommend the use of a balanced portfolio, or, alternatively, an appropriate distribution of assets between two different portfolios, one invested wholly in equities and the other entirely in long term fixed-income instruments. A balanced portfolio has the capability of (1) smoothing or moderating the short-term fluctuations in the equity component and (2) stabilizing the long-term results by combining negatively correlated returns on the two components of the portfolio. In other words, the return on the equity component should in theory be high when the yield on the fixed-income component is low and vice versa. There have been many periods over the last hundred years when the consumer price level and common stock prices moved in opposite directions, and the undesirable consequences of this configuration of prices are greatly moderated by a substantial component of fixed-income investments. The same moderating influence would be operative if consumer prices and bond yields should move in opposite directions or in the same direction at different rates.

**Participation Mechanism.**   The process by which the individual participants share in the total return on the investment portfolio or portfolios differs from plan to plan. In all cases, however, the investment experience of the plan is reflected fully and directly in the individual account balances of the participants or, under some plans, in the accumulated benefit accruals. The accounts of the participants may be kept in dollars or, because of the greater convenience in accounting for changes in the market value of the plan assets, in ''units.''

The unit approach to linking benefits and asset values may be used with a defined contribution plan or a defined benefit plan. Small plans tend to use the defined contribution approach and the facilities of a life insurance company while large plans tend to use the defined benefit approach and the investment facilities of a trust.

*A. Defined Contribution Approach.*[6]   Under the defined contribution approach, contributions are allocated to individual accounts
for each participant. If the plan is a qualified pension plan, the
amount of contribution for each may be determined under the traditional money purchase approach or under the target benefit approach. The unit in which the accounts of active participants are
usually expressed and maintained goes by various names. If the
plan uses the same unit for both the accumulation and payout stages
it will usually be called either the "variable unit" or the "annuity
unit." If one unit is used for the accumulation stage and another
for the liquidation stage, a common practice, the former is frequently called the "accumulation unit" and the latter the "annuity"
or "pension" unit. For present purposes, the unit will be referred
to as the accumulation unit, and the use of two units will be dealt
with at a later point in this chapter.

The accumulation unit for a particular portfolio is assigned an
initial value of some arbitrary amount, such as $1, $5, or $10. The
initial contributions are used to purchase units at the designated
value. As of any subsequent valuation date, the value of the unit
is determined by dividing the market value of the portfolio assets
by the aggregate number of units credited to the accounts of the
participants. The unit may be valued monthly or daily. The value
of the unit must be recomputed as of each date on which additional
units are purchased or existing units are cashed out or converted
into annuity units or into a fixed annuity. These unit transactions
are identical in all substantive respects to the purchase or redemption of shares in an open-end mutual fund.

If the plan is funded through the facilities of a life insurance
company, there will usually be a small deduction from each contribution for sales and administrative expenses, and the remainder
is applied to the purchase of accumulation units. There will also
be a fee for asset management, which is normally deducted from
either the investment income or the corpus of the portfolio. If the
plan is funded through a trust, the employer may absorb the investment fee and other charges of the trustee, or he may have them

---

[6]For a technical explanation of the prototype money purchase variable annuity plan
developed by TIAA-CREF, see Robert M. Duncan, "A Retirement System Granting Unit
Annuities and Investing in Equities," *Transactions of the Society of Actuaries* 4 (1952),
pp. 317–44.

deducted from the investment earnings before crediting the individual accounts of the participants.

The current contribution for each participant is divided by the current unit value to determine the number of new units credited to his individual account. The accounts share in the investment experience of the portfolio in one of two ways: change in value of their accumulated units or the crediting of additional units. Unrealized appreciation increases the value of the unit and unrealized depreciation lowers the value. Net realized losses reduce the value of the unit. Investment income and realized appreciation on assets may be permitted to increase the unit value, or they may be used to purchase additional units for the participants. If a participant should die before retirement, the value of his vested accumulated units at date of death may be payable to his beneficiary or beneficiaries, or the accumulation units in his account may be canceled and their current market value credited to the employer, depending upon the terms of the plan.

If the plan has associated with it both an equity portfolio and a debt instrument portfolio, the participants may be permitted to designate the proportion of contributions on their behalf that should go into each of the funds. This may be an unfettered choice or the plan may permit a range of options, subject to an overriding requirement that some monies go into each type of account. Some plans require that a minimum proportion be allocated to the fixed-income fund, with no upper limit. In other words, a participant could direct that all contributions made on his behalf be invested in the debt instrument portfolio, but he would not be permitted to make a similar decision with respect to the equity portfolio. At reasonable intervals, usually once a year, a participant is given the opportunity of changing the allocation of *future* contributions between the two types of portfolios. Many plans do not permit him to reallocate the existing balances in the two subaccounts during his active employment, since that would be an invitation, or at least a temptation, to try to anticipate the future behavior of the securities market.

At retirement, the participant may be given the option of taking his pension in the form of a conventional fixed-income annuity or an annuity whose income varies with the investment performance of an associated asset portfolio. This is especially true when the plan provides both an equity and a debt instrument portfolio, or when the participants have the choice during their working lives of having some portion or all of their individual account balances invested in a conventional fixed-income portfolio operated on an amortized book value basis. If the participant chooses to take some or all of his pension in the form of a fixed-income annuity, an appropriate sum of money must be transferred from his accumulation account to the trust fund or insurance company account used to provide fixed-income annuities. This entails a cashing out of accumulation units, with the risk that the timing may be poor from an investment standpoint. To minimize the risk of poor timing, the plan may specify that any such transfer must be spread over a number of months or years. Under some plans, the transfer may be spread over the last several years prior to retirement.

Conversion of the participant's account balance into a variable annuity does not involve any market risk, since the accumulation units and the units used to discharge the annuity obligation derive their values from the same portfolio of assets. If the market value of the portfolio is depressed at the time of the exchange, for example, the value of the accumulation unit will be down but the value of the annuity unit will be down by the same percentage. Thus, the state of the capital market is immaterial. The conversion process will be explained at a later point in this chapter.

**B. Defined Benefit Approach.**     As was pointed out earlier, the benefit accruals of a defined benefit plan can also be linked to the value of a portfolio of assets. Under a defined contribution plan, *contributions* are converted into units, whereas, under a defined benefit plan, the accruing *benefits* are converted into units.

The conversion of defined benefit accruals into units may be accomplished in either of two ways. Under one procedure, the actuarial present value of the benefit accruing in respect of an individual participant in a given year is divided by the current value of an accumulation unit. For example, if a participant is credited with a benefit of $10 a month payable at age 65, the then actuarial value of that $10 benefit accrual is divided by the value of an accumulation unit, and the result is the number of accumulation units to be credited to the participant. At the same time, a sum of money equal to the actuarial value of the original benefit accrual will be paid to the plan and credited to the participant. The plan then operates on a defined contribution principle with respect to that benefit accrual and any later benefit accruals so converted and funded. With each year of service, the participant will be credited with additional accumulation units, the total value of which at any given time is the product of the number of units times the value of the unit computed in the conventional manner. At retirement, the total dollar value of the aggregate accumulation units can be converted into variable annuity units or a fixed-income annuity, depending upon the terms of the plan.

Under the other procedure, the benefit accrual of a participant for each year of service is converted into units of deferred retirement income that serve not only to account for his benefit credits during his active participation in the plan but also to determine the amount of his monthly income in retirement. That is, the same unit of account is used for both active and retired participants. Under this procedure, the conversion of each benefit accrual is accomplished by dividing the *dollar* value (not the actuarial value) of the accrual by the current value of the annuity unit. Under the previous example, the $10 a month benefit would be divided by the current value of the annuity unit. The annuity units are funded in the same manner as the original benefit accrual (since they had the same dollar value at time of conversion), and the plan operates in all other respects as a defined benefit plan, except for keeping account of benefit credits in units rather than dollars.

The monies set aside to fund the annuity units reflect an assumption as to the rate of investment return. This rate is usually referred to as the "assumed investment return" or AIR. The value of the annuity unit is adjusted on each valuation date by multiplying the current value (or, more accurately, the value at the last valuation date) by the quotient derived from the following formula:

$$\frac{1 + i'}{1 + i}$$

where $i$ equals the AIR and $i'$ equals the actual investment return (income plus net realized capital gains and unrealized capital appreciation or depreciation). For example, if the AIR is 5.5 percent and the actual investment return for the measurement period is 7.5 percent, the annuity value will be adjusted upward by 1.9 percent:

$$\frac{1.075}{1.055} = 1.019$$

The new value will then be adjusted on the next valuation date by the same procedure, the value declining if the actual investment return is less than the AIR. Under this procedure, the unit value reflects only investment results and not mortality and expense experience, as would be the case if the value were obtained by dividing the number of units into the market value of the portfolio.

The number of annuity units standing to the credit of a participant at date of retirement will be carried over into retirement and remains constant in number throughout the individual's remaining lifetime.[7] The units continue to be valued in accordance with the foregoing procedure, the employer being credited or charged with any mortality and expense gains or losses. Under some plans, the gain or loss from mortality, expense, and other factors is instead applied to increase or decrease the unit value. The individual's monthly income is obtained by multiplying the number of annuity units with which he had been credited by the value of the annuity unit on that date. Depending upon the terms of the plan, the participant may, upon reaching retirement, be permitted to convert the annuity units into an actuarially equivalent fixed-income annuity.

Under both procedures for converting a defined benefit accrual into a variable benefit accrual (annuity units or accumulation units), the monies set aside in respect of a particular individual are based upon an assumed investment return, and the employer's cost is determined using the AIR factor. The employer cost recognizes future investment earnings equal to the AIR: the higher the AIR the lower the employer's cost.

When the monies are accounted for by accumulation units, the number of accumulation units credited to a participant in a given year is influenced by the AIR: the higher the AIR the fewer the number of units and vice versa. Thereafter, the employee's account is credited with the full amount of investment earnings (including realized and unrealized capital appreciation) through the periodic valuation of the accumulation unit, but the unit must increase in value at a rate equal to the AIR if the ultimate retirement benefit is to be that called for by the original defined benefit formula. The net effect is that the participant's benefits are enhanced only by the amount of investment earnings in excess of the AIR. If the actual earnings are lower than the AIR, the ultimate benefit will be less than it would have been under the defined benefit plan. Thus, the participant bears the full investment risk.

---

[7]The number of units will be reduced if the participant retires early or elects an optional annuity form.

The same principles are operative when the number of annuity units credited to a participant in a given year is determined by dividing the dollar value of the nominal benefit accruals by the value of the annuity unit. While the number of annuity units credited to a participant is not affected by the AIR (only the employer's cost) the subsequent value of each unit is a function of the ratio between the AIR and the actual investment return. The unit value increases when the actual investment return exceeds the AIR and it declines when the actual rate of return is less than the AIR. Thus, the participant again bears the investment risk and stands to receive larger benefits than those called for by the defined benefit formula only to the extent that the actual investment return is greater than the AIR.

Inasmuch as the participant is credited with the full amount of excess investment earnings under defined benefit variable annuity plans, the benefit is generally expressed originally in terms of career average compensation. That is, full participation by the participant in the excess investment earnings of the plan is considered to be an acceptable alternative to the use of a final average salary approach.

**Funding and Administrative Structure.** The benefit accruals of a pension plan can be linked to a portfolio of assets maintained for the exclusive use of the plan and managed by a life insurance company, a bank trust department, or an investment counselor. Or they can be linked to a pooled asset portfolio operated and managed by a life insurer, bank, or mutual fund for a number of pension plans or other shareholders. The funding instruments may be individual or group annuity contracts of a life insurance company; trust agreements with banks, trust companies, or individual trustees; and shares in a mutual fund. The administrative structure for maintaining accounts for the individual plan participants may be provided by a life insurer, a bank trustee, a mutual fund, an actuarial consulting firm, or a professional employee benefits administrator.

A life insurance company places the assets of a variable annuity pension plan (or the variable component of an overall pension plan) in a separate account, distinct from the general asset account of the company. A company may operate several equity and fixed-income separate accounts with different investment objectives and risk characteristics. The employer selects the particular separate account that seems most compatible with his aims and preferences.

As indicated above, he may arrange to have the life insurer hold the plan assets in a so-called single customer separate account, segregated from all other assets. In the eyes of the Securities and Exchange Commission, a separate account is an investment company and in the absence of special dispensations would be subject to the Securities Act of 1933, the Securities and Exchange Act of 1934, and the Investment Company Act of 1940. This flows from the landmark decision[8] of the United States Supreme Court that an individual variable annuity contract is a security within the meaning of the Securities Act of 1933 and that an organization which offers the contract is subject to the Investment Company Act of 1940 and other applicable statutes. Pursuant to this ruling the SEC first sought to treat a life insurance company in its entirety as an investment company if it offered variable annuities to the general public. In a long series of negotiations and litigation between the SEC and the Prudential Insurance Company, a compromise was reached under which only the separate accounts of a life insurer would be regarded as an investment company. This compromise was first reflected in an administrative ruling but is now contained in the Investment Company Amendments Act of 1970. Under this act, a separate account that is used only for qualified pension plans need not be registered with the SEC and is relieved of compliance with certain general requirements that would be appropriate if the separate account was dealing with individual investors. If a separate account were to be used for the funding of individual variable annuity contracts, it would have to be registered with the SEC and comply with all applicable statutes and rulings.

Pooled or collective trusts established and maintained by a bank or trust company for the funding of qualified pension plans are also exempt from registration with the SEC and other regulatory strictures provided that certain rules are observed.

## Protection of Annuity Payments during Payout Stage

It is not sufficient to protect the purchasing power of pension benefits only during their period of accrual. On the average, the benefit payments to a retired participant will be spread over 15 years or

---

[8]*Securities and Exchange Commission* v. *Valic,* 359 U.S. 65(1959).

more, and the purchasing power of the benefits can be seriously impaired over such a period. Moreover, technological changes may be enhancing the earnings and standards of living of the working population, eroding the relative economic status of the retired population. Thus, enlightened pension planning requires consideration of ways and means of protecting the purchasing power and relative standard of living of retired participants.

Some of the same techniques that are used to protect accruing benefits can be used to protect the benefit payments of retired individuals. There are others that are uniquely suited to the protection of benefit payments.

## Linkage of Benefits to Asset Values

When benefit accruals have been linked to the value of an associated asset portfolio, it is a natural progression to continue the linkage into the retirement stage of the participants. As a matter of fact, the whole arrangement is usually set up in anticipation that the retirement benefits will be linked to the same asset portfolio that regulated the value of the benefits during the accrual stage. However, a participant reaching retirement may be given the option of converting his asset-linked benefits to a conventional fixed-income annuity, and a participant in a conventional defined benefit plan may be given the option of taking his retirement benefits in the form of an asset-linked annuity. The various circumstances under which the benefits of retired participants may be linked to asset values are discussed in this section.

**When Benefits Were Asset-Linked during Accrual Stage.**  A distinction must be made between the procedures applied when the plan uses only one asset-based unit and when the plan uses two units. The one-unit arrangement will be discussed first.

*A. One-Unit Approach.*  The one-unit approach may be used with a defined benefit plan that converts its dollar benefit accruals into units of income (annuity units). The changes in the unit value are brought about by application of the formula set out earlier, namely:

$$\frac{1 + i'}{1 + i}$$

As was stated earlier, when only one unit is used, the participant accumulates pieces of deferred retirement income expressed in units, rather than dollars, and he retains throughout retirement the precise number of units that were in his account on date of retirement. If he retires early or elects an optional form of annuity, the number of units of retirement income will be reduced just as the dollar amount of fixed-income annuity payments is reduced under the same circumstances. However, after the adjustment, the reduced number of units remains constant throughout retirement.

The amount of monthly dollar income payable to a participant is determined by multiplying the number of units credited to his account by the dollar value of the unit. For example, if the participant has been credited with 37.264 units of monthly retirement income and each unit has a value of $15.10, the monthly income would be $562.69. The unit is usually revalued monthly or annually. Plans that revalue annually do so to provide retirement income that is level throughout a given 12-month period. Monthly revaluations reflect money market conditions more promptly and accurately; but they also produce monthly variations in retirement income, a situation that may be unsettling to the retired group, especially if the adjustments are downward. Deviations of actual market behavior over that prevailing at the time of an annual valuation can be smoothed by the use of a moving average of market values.[9]

**B. Two-Unit Approach.** The two-unit approach uses an accumulation unit (units of assets) before retirement and an annuity unit (units of income) after retirement.

When two units are employed, it is necessary to exchange the accumulation units of a retiring employee for annuity units. The number of annuity units that will be acquired by the pensioner depends upon the assumptions as to mortality, investment earnings, and possibly expenses, and, of course, upon the number of accumulation units. Since the accumulation units and the annuity units derive their value from the same asset portfolio, the exchange is not affected by the market value of the assets. The number of annuity units that will be credited to the retiring participant is determined in two steps. The first is to determine the monthly

[9]See James L. Clare, "A Smoothed Equity Unit Annuity," *Transactions of the Society of Actuaries* 14 (1962), pp. 340–47 and discussion on pp. 348–64.

payment that would be made if the participant were taking his retirement benefits in the form of a conventional fixed-income annuity. This amount is obtained by dividing the dollar value of the accumulation units by the present value of a life annuity due of $1 per month at the participant's attained age, using appropriate mortality, interest, and expense assumptions. The second step is to divide the monthly payment determined in the first step by the current value of the annuity unit. This yields the number of annuity units. For example, assume that the market value of the participant's accumulation units is $50,000, the present value of a straight-life annuity of $1 per month at age 65 is $135, and the value of the annuity unit is $20. The monthly life income payable to the participants on a fixed-income basis from age 65 would be $50,000/135 = $370.37. The number of annuity units would be $370.37/20 = 18.519. If the participant were to elect a joint and survivor annuity option or a refund option of any kind, the annuity factor would be greater than 135 and the number of annuity units would be proportionately smaller.

Once determined, the number of annuity units remain fixed throughout the pensioner's years of retirement. The annuity unit will be valued monthly or annually, as with the single unit, and the pensioner's monthly income will be determined by multiplying the number of his units by the current value of the unit.

*1. Assumed Investment Return (AIR).* The assumed rate of investment return is an especially critical component in the formula for computing the annuity factor and, hence, the number of annuity units that will be credited to the retiring participant. It affects not only the amount of the initial payment to a retiring employee but also the pattern of future income payments. It represents an anticipation of future investment experience, and changes in the value of the unit value thereafter will reflect only deviations of actual investment experience from the assumed experience.

The higher the AIR the larger will be the initial payment to an annuitant for any given number of annuity units. For example, a 5.5 percent AIR produces an initial payment that is about 15 to 20 percent higher than that generated by a 3.5 percent AIR. On the other hand, when the total investment return, including variations in the market value of the underlying asset portfolio, is rising, the percentage increase in year-to-year income to the annuitant will be greater under a 3.5 percent assumption than under a 5.5 percent assumption. For example, if the AIR is 3.5 percent and the actual investment return is 7.5 percent, the change in unit value would be:

$$\frac{1.075}{1.035}$$

or 3.9 percent. However, if the AIR is 5.5 percent and the actual rate of return is 7.5 percent, the change in unit value would be only 1.9 percent. By the same token, a decline in investment returns will have a smaller impact on annual income under the lower assumption than on the higher assumption.

Regardless of actual investment results, the monthly income provided under the lower AIR will eventually exceed that provided by the higher AIR, the crossover point depending upon the age of the annuitant, as well as whether there is a joint annuitant. The crossover will usually occur about eight or nine years after retirement. Eventually, perhaps 15 or 16 years after retirement, the total payments under the lower AIR will exceed those under the higher AIR. Thus, on the one hand, the main advantage of a lower AIR to the retired employee is that it develops a greater income later in life than the higher AIR, a time when inflation and rising expectations may create a need for increased income. On the other hand, some employees might prefer a higher AIR to maximize their income during the years that they are more vigorous, mentally and physically, and perhaps more important, during the years that they are more likely to be alive. The AIR for a pension plan is chosen by the employer, with advice from a consulting actuary or a life insurer, from a reasonable range of alternatives (e.g., 3.5, 4, 4.5, 5, and 5.5 percent) in the light of his objectives, the long-term investment expectations, and the cost implications. It would not be feasible to permit each participant to choose his own AIR, since apart from administrative complexity, those in poor health or those who believe themselves to be in poor health would elect the highest AIR available, creating an unacceptable degree of adverse mortality selection against the plan.

*2. Difference in Values of the Accumulation Unit and the Annuity Unit.* The accumulation and annuity units of a pension plan are mere accounting entities and are backed by a common portfolio of assets. However, they have different values, since they serve different purposes. The accumulation unit is the basic instrument for measuring an individual participant's share in the plan's accumulated assets, and its value is affected only by investment results. However, the total investment results are reflected in the value of the unit, since the valuation of the unit does not entail an assumption as to future investment experience. On the other hand, as was just noted, the valuation of the annuity unit does involve an assumption as to future investment experience and its value varies only to the extent that actual investment results differ from the AIR. The respective values may also vary because of differing treatment of dividend and interest income. During the accumulation stage, such income may be applied to the purchase of additional accumulation units (thus having no effect on the unit value),[10] while during the payout stage investment income is invariably treated in such a manner as to affect the value of the annuity unit. This difference in treatment of investment income is dictated by the fact that the use of an assumed investment return in calculating the value of the annuity unit requires the advance commitment of investment income to the extent of the AIR. Moreover, there are technical advantages in determining at point of retirement the number of annuity units to be credited to a participant and keeping the number constant throughout retirement.

The value of the annuity unit may also reflect deviations of actual from expected mortality and expense experience, while the accumulation unit is insulated from such experience. However, some insurers offer variable annuity contracts under which they assume, for a charge, the risk of unfavorable mortality and expense experience. In other words, they offer conventional insurance company guarantees as to mortality and expenses. Under these contracts, the *value* of the annuity unit is not affected one way or the other by actual mortality and expense experience, but the *number* of annuity units standing to the credit of a particular individual may be reduced somewhat by the deduction from periodic contributions of the charge for the mortality and expense guarantees. The charge for the guarantees may be embodied in the price of the life annuity that is divided into the dollar value of the accumulation units to derive the number of annuity units.

An alternative way to insulate the annuity unit from the effects of mortality and expense experience is for the employer to absorb

---

[10]In some plans, dividend and interest income during the accumulation stage are permitted to increase the value of the accumulation unit.

through higher contributions any actuarial losses that may arise out of mortality and expense experience and to take credit through lower contributions for any actuarial gains from that source.

**When Benefits Were Not Asset-Linked during Accrual Stage.** A defined benefit plan whose benefits are not linked to an asset portfolio during the accrual stage may provide retirement benefits in the form of an asset-linked annuity. This is more likely to occur under a plan that uses a final average pay benefit formula to cope with the problems of inflation before retirement. Some plans provide the variable annuity automatically for part or all of the pension, but other plans allow the employee to elect whether to receive a variable annuity.

The retiring participant who elects a variable annuity may be credited with a sufficient number of annuity units to give him the same initial monthly retirement income that he would have received under a fixed-income annuity. However, the AIR used in the calculation of the annuity factor takes on special significance, since it affects not only the employer's cost but the benefits that will ultimately be received by the annuitant. The higher the AIR, the lower will be the cost to the employer, since he is taking advance credit for investment earnings on the assets backing the annuity units that he provides. On the other hand, the higher the AIR the smaller will be the excess investment earnings that serve to increase the annuity income of the retired participant.

The same techniques for dealing with variations in mortality and expense experience are available here. The variations may be assumed by a life insurer for a fee, they may be absorbed by the employer, or they may be permitted to enter into the periodic valuation of the annuity unit.

Under an alternative approach sometimes used for insured plans, a variable annuity may be purchased to have the same cost that the plan would have incurred to purchase a fixed annuity. This usually results in a lower initial monthly income than if a fixed annuity had been elected, and accordingly participants rarely elect variable annuities under such plans.

**Critique of Asset-Linked Pension Benefits.** The potential advantage to a participant in a pension plan that links benefit accruals and benefit payments to the performance of a portfolio of assets is that he is credited with the total investment earnings on the assets allocable to his account or benefits. This is true whether the plan operates on a defined contribution or defined benefit basis. Under a defined benefit plan, benefits are *increased* only if the actual investment return exceeds AIR. In any event, after the number of annuity units has been fixed, the participant receives the full investment earnings on the associated assets.

In many cases the employer's expectation (or, at least, hope) in setting up an asset-linked pension plan is that the total investment return over the long pull will be at least equal to the rate of increase in the consumer price level. If this expectation were to be realized, even over the long term, the asset-linked annuity would be a powerful force for the protection of the purchasing power of an employee's pension benefits. An equity portfolio holds out the possibility that capital's share of productivity gains in the economy may be passed along to the plan participants, thus enabling them to improve their standard of living in retirement. Common stock prices may also reflect a reward for risk-taking on the theory that equities embody a higher degree of investment risk than debt instruments. Thus, there is a chance that the total return on an equity-based portfolio will more than offset the rate of increase in the prices of consumer products and services.

The disadvantage to the participant in an asset-linked pension plan is that he must assume the investment risk. In some years, the return on the invested assets has been less than the AIR, reducing the monthly benefits below the level originally contemplated.

The employer may find an asset-linked pension plan advantageous, in that there will be less pressure on him to provide cost-of-living supplements or other types of inflation hedges. This is an advantage that will exist only if the arrangement proves to be reasonably effective in coping with inflationary price movements. Another advantage to the employer is that he is relieved of the investment risk. His contributions to the plan are not affected one way or the other by deviations of actual from assumed investment results.

The primary disadvantage of an asset-linked pension plan to an employer is the loss of contribution credit for excess investment earnings. Under a conventional fixed-annuity pension plan, the employee takes credit against future contributions for the excess of investment earnings over the rate used in the actuarial calculations. This can be a potent cost-reducing factor, as will be apparent from a later discussion of cost factors. He sacrifices this source of cost savings with respect to the asset-linked component of his pension plan.

This feature of the plan will not be an unmitigated disadvantage to the employer if it eliminates or reduces the need to provide cost-of-living supplements, the burden of which is almost always borne by the employer. As a matter of fact, in plans without automatic adjustments many employers expect to finance cost-of-living supplements out of inflation-induced excess investment earnings. It may be a matter of indifference to the employer whether he meets the benefit cost of inflation through ad hoc adjustments in the benefits of retired employees, financed by his own contributions, or through the advanced allocation of all investment earnings to the individual accounts of the plan participants, as exemplified by the asset-linked approach. A potential disadvantage of the approach is employee disenchantment with the performance of the investment portfolio. Since the employer will have sponsored the plan and selected the investment manager, he will have to take a large degree of responsibility for the outcome. When investment experience is poor, a certain amount of employee ill-will may be inevitable. This had led a number of employers to abandon variable annuity plans and make up the previous losses suffered by participants.

## Automatic Cost-of-Living Adjustments

The most direct and responsive method of adjusting pension benefits of retired persons to changes in the price level is to stipulate in the plan that benefits will be modified in accordance with a prescribed procedure to reflect variations in a specified index of consumer prices. Thus far, plans adopting this approach have designated the consumer price index as the measuring rod, but there are some advocates of the construction of a more specialized index that would show changes in the prices of items affecting the budgets of retired persons. However, a 1982 study by the General Accounting Office concluded that "existing indexes would have provided a reasonable indicator of the impact of inflation on retirees."[11]

---

[11]"A CPI For Retirees Is Not Needed Now But Could Be In The Future", GAO/GGD–82–41, General Accounting Office, 1982.

Some argue that the CPI-U is more appropriate than the CPI-W, since the CPI-U includes retirees in its underlying data while the CPI-W is based solely upon active workers.

The prescribed procedure may provide for both upward and downward adjustments, but the principal plans using the approach make provision only for upward adjustments. An adjustment is made only when the change (increase) in the CPI over the base period exceeds a specified percentage. For example, the plan may provide that benefits will be adjusted upward on a specified date, such as June 1, if during the preceding calendar year the CPI increased by 3 percent or more, the adjustment in plan benefits being for the full amount of the CPI increase, rounded to the nearest 0.1 percent.

The benefits of the Social Security program are subject to adjustment on the basis of changes in the CPI from the third quarter of one calendar year to the third quarter of the succeeding calendar year. More precisely, the adjustment in benefits is based upon the change in the arithmetic average of the CPI for each third quarter of the two calendar years involved. Benefits are adjusted effective on December 1 of the year in question. The benefits of the Railroad Retirement System are subject to cost-of-living increases in accordance with the Social Security formula.

More than half of the states provide for automatic cost-of-living increases for some or all of their public retirement systems. They all use changes in the national CPI as the basis for benefit adjustments, except California, which uses the average of the CPI for the Los Angeles–Long Beach area and the San Francisco–Oakland area. The Commonwealth of Puerto Rico uses the CPI for the San Juan metropolitan area.

The retirement plans of New York City and certain other municipalities tie the benefits of retired employees to the CPI. Relatively few business firms provide for automatic adjustment of benefits on the basis of changes in the CPI.

A plan may place a limit on the amount of benefit increase on any one adjustment date. The limit is usually 3 to 5 percent. Plans that provide for a downward revision in benefits make such adjustments only if the CPI falls substantially below the base, viz, 10 percent below. As with ad hoc adjustments, these automatic increases (or decreases) may apply to all benefits in process of payment, including death and disability benefits.

As its name implies, a cost-of-living adjustment is designed only to protect the purchasing power of the benefits payable under the plan. It does not attempt to provide the retired employees a stake in the expanding economy. Nevertheless, it can be a very costly feature of a pension plan. If it produces annual increases in the benefits of retired employees at the compounded rate of 3 percent, for example, the long-run cost of the plan may be increased by about 25 to 30 percent. The cost would be commensurately higher if the benefit adjustments were greater than 3 percent per year.

## Formula Escalation Factor

A technique sometimes used to provide at least partial protection against the loss of pension purchasing power is a formula escalation factor. Under this approach, the plan stipulates that the benefits of all retired individuals will be automatically adjusted upward each year by a specified percentage, such as 2 or 3 percent. Such an escalator is built into the formula in anticipation of future price increases, but the percentage adjustment is automatic and not linked to any cost-of-living index. This approach avoids the complexity of the index adjustment and limits the obligation of the employer to predetermined benefit increases. Moreover, the annual percentage increase normally applies to the original retirement benefit, rather than to the augmented benefits. This, of course, avoids the compounding effect of the index-related adjustments, reducing the cost somewhat.

A number of states use the fixed escalator approach, some requiring the employees to share the cost of the escalator with the employer. The approach is also used to a limited extent among the plans of private employers. Under one type of arrangement, the retiring participant is permitted to elect, at his own expense, an annuity option with a fixed annual increase factor. The pension benefit that he would otherwise receive is actuarially reduced and then grows each year at the compound rate selected. For example, a male participant retiring at age 65 with a regular pension of $400 per month would start with a monthly benefit of $270.40 if he elected a 5 percent annual increase. By the ninth year of retirement, his benefit would have grown to its original amount and would continue to grow at a compound rate of 5 percent. If the same participant had elected a 3 percent growth factor, his initial pension would be $319.20 and it would regain its original level within eight years. Where such an election is allowed, most employees elect an unreduced level annuity.

## Ad Hoc Adjustments

Another approach to the protection of the purchasing power of benefits in a pay status is that of ad hoc adjustments. The ad hoc adjustment of benefits of retired employees has become a common practice among plans that do not use some other method of preserving the purchasing power of benefit payments. Many plans have increased the benefits of retired employees every two or three years, the amount of the increase sometimes being keyed to changes in the CPI since the date of the last adjustment (or the date of retirement). If several years have elapsed, there may be a series of percentage changes, the percentages varying with the number of years since the employees have retired. If these periodic adjustments reflect the appropriate changes in the CPI, and the benefits were computed originally on the basis of final average compensation, the retired employees enjoy reasonably effective protection against inflation, even though they have no formal assurance that the employer will continue to keep the benefits in line with cost-of-living increases. The protection is not fully effective because of the time lag in the adjustments, which tends to be greater than that under automatic adjustment techniques. Because of cost considerations, most such ad hoc adjustments have been less than the CPI increase.

Some plans apply these periodic adjustments to the vested benefits of terminated employees, but the practice is not at all common. If the plan provides disability and survivor income benefits, the periodic adjustments may be made applicable to these benefits as well. There is no reason, in theory, why the adjustments should not apply to all benefits in process of payment.

During periodic declines in common stock prices over the last several years, some plans with asset-linked benefits have provided temporary benefit supplements on an ad hoc basis. The supplements have been roughly equal to the decline in benefits.

## Supplementation Contingent on Actuarial Gains

Another method for augmenting benefits, largely confined to the public sector, is to provide annual or periodic supplements from actuarial gains, primarily excess investment earnings. This method has been applied primarily to defined contribution pension plans under which it is customary for the governing statute to specify

the rate of interest to be credited to employer and employee contributions and to be used in the conversion of accumulated funds
into annuity benefits. The rate is usually set at a conservatively
low level, so that high-quality portfolio management is likely to
produce earnings in excess of the statutory interest assumption.
This excess provides a source of funds that can be used for a
number of purposes, including supplements for retired employees.
The supplements may be payable for life or for one year at a time.
In most state employee retirement systems employing this strategy,
the actuarial gains are used to provide an additional benefit payment
for the year in question, the supplement sometimes being termed
the "13th benefit check."

The strength of this method is its flexibility. No advance commitments are made and supplements are granted on the basis of
realized experience. It has a number of disadvantages. It is not
easily understood by the participants; it offers no assurance as to
the declaration of size of future supplements; and a portion of the
funds for the supplements comes from investment earnings on the
contributions of the active employees, which it would be argued,
should be credited to their individual accounts.[12] Active employees
might also argue with some validity that the excess earnings on the
employer contributions should be applied to the liquidation of unfunded actuarial liabilities (for past service benefit credits or retroactive benefit liberalizations). Finally, the ERISA requirement
that the plan actuary use "best estimate" actuarial assumptions
may reduce actuarial gains for plans subject to its jurisdiction.

### Wage Index

Another method of dealing with inflation and productivity gains is
to link the benefits of retired individuals and other income recipients
to changes in a specified wage index. The index can be one for the
whole labor force or a more appropriate segment of the labor force,
such as those employed in a given profession, industry, or locality.
Under the recomputation approach, described in the next section,
the index may be constructed in terms of the salary associated with
a given position or rank with a particular employment or employee

---

[12]Under some systems investment return in excess of a low guaranteed rate is credited
to both active and retired employees, eliminating this objection.

group. Recognition may be given to changes in the index after the crediting of each unit of benefit or only the changes that have occurred since retirement.

Inasmuch as wages reflect not only inflationary forces but labor's share of productivity gains, adjustment of pension benefits on the basis of a general wage index would enable the retired population to maintain its relative position on the economic scale. That is, if there are real gains in the gross national product and they are reflected in wages on which the index is based, retired employees would receive their pro rata share of the gains, enhancing their standard of living. A more specific index would pass along the productivity gains, if any, associated with the wages entering into the index. There are some public employee retirement systems that adjust the benefits of retired employees in accordance with changes in an index of salaries currently being paid to the active employees. Thus far, the wage index concept is rarely used by private employers.

The cost of linking benefits to a wage index is expected to be greater in the long run than relating the benefits to the CPI because of the productivity component.

An application of the wage index adjustment technique to broad segments of the working population is found in the so-called *repartition* approach that has been in use in France since the close of World War II.[13]

### Recomputation

The wage index concept is applied to a limited segment of the working population through an approach called *recomputation,* a

---

[13]For a detailed description of the repartition scheme and the institutional framework within which it operates, see Tony Lynes, *French Pensions.* Occasional Papers on Social Administration, No. 21, London School of Economics and Political Science (London: G. Bell & Sons, 1967). For a succinct summary of the system, see Dan M. McGill, *Preservation of Pension Benefit Rights* (Homewood, Ill.: Richard D. Irwin, 1972), pp. 280–94. The philosophical basis of the *repartition* principle is the doctrine of social solidarity. This doctrine was first enunciated in the second half of the 19th century, its principal spokesman being Leon Bourgeois, and it became the ideological basis of the French social security system. In that context, the doctrine connoted the obligation of society to assure a minimum subsistence to each of its members who, by reason of age or infirmity, is physically or mentally incapable of maintaining himself by his own efforts. It has taken on a more specialized meaning in connection with the repartition scheme. Here it means that each generation of workers undertakes to support the preceding generation of workers in the expectation that it will be accorded the same treatment by the succeeding generation. It is solidarity *between* generations rather than among one generation.

literal description of what takes place. It is appropriate only for employee groups with rigidly structured and formally recognized job classifications, as exemplified by the military services and uniformed civilian services.

The principle underlying recomputation is that the pension benefits of the retired members of the group should bear a constant relationship to the current compensation levels associated with the rank or job classification that they held at the time of their retirement. A more direct statement of the relationship is that the pension benefit of a retired member should be expressed in terms of the base compensation, as defined, of an active member of the same rank, or in the same job classification, as that held by the retired individual at the time of his retirement. In the military service, this would mean, for example, that a person who retired at the rank of colonel would receive a pension throughout his period of retirement equal to the appropriate percentage, reflecting his years of service, of the base compensation of a colonel still on active duty. If the regular pay scale of the active members of the military services were to be raised, the pension benefits of all retired members would be recomputed in terms of the new scale applicable to their retired rank. The process would be repeated each time there was a pay increase.

Recomputation was a feature of the military retirement system until 1958, when it was replaced by cost-of-living adjustments. Benefits of retired military personnel are now subject to automatic cost-of-living adjustments in accordance with the formula applied under the Civil Service Retirement System. The military services were not pleased with the removal of the recomputation feature, an economy measure on the part of the Congress, and have made several attempts to have it restored.

In the meantime, recomputation continues to be a feature of many retirement plans for police and fire fighters, which tend to be liberal in other respects, frequently including no age requirement for retirement. The principle seems to be fairly well accepted in that specialized segment of public pensions.

It would seem that recomputation, like a general wage index, would operate to bestow productivity gains on the retired population, in addition to protecting them against loss of purchasing power. It might be questioned whether the concept of productivity gains can be applied in the classical manner to government employees, and especially to members of the Armed Forces, but the benefits associated with the concept tend to spill over into plans using the recomputation technique through another principle of governmental personnel policy known as "comparability." The latter term refers to the concept of keeping governmental pay scales, including those of the military services, in line with the pay in comparable job classifications in the private sector. There are obvious difficulties in applying the concept, of course; but, to the extent that governmental pay scales do reflect the general wage structure of private industry, the recomputation technique would probably keep benefit levels somewhat higher than they would be with only cost-of-living adjustments. The fact that the affected groups put up a strong fight to retain (or to reacquire) the recomputation feature would suggest that this is the case.

## Questions

1. Compare and evaluate against each other the following techniques of adjusting accruing pension benefits prior to the participant's retirement:
   *a.* Final average salary formula.
   *b.* Ad hoc adjustments.
   *c.* Automatic index adjustments.
2. Explain why the sponsor of a pension plan with benefits linked to a portfolio of assets might choose to utilize two units (e.g., an accumulation unit and an annuity unit) rather than only one unit.
3. In connection with an asset-linked pension plan that uses two units, explain:
   *a.* The ways in which the participant may share in the investment experience of the affiliated asset portfolio during the accumulation stage.
   *b.* Why there *is* an investment risk from the standpoint of the participant when the participant's accumulation units are converted into a fixed-income annuity at retirement but there is *not* a similar investment risk when the accumulation units are converted into annuity units whose benefit payments vary with the investment experience of an associated asset portfolio.
4. TIAA-CREF (affiliated corporations that offer investment, administrative, and insurance services to pension plans of colleges and

universities) has operated both a fixed-income investment fund and an equity fund since 1952. Participants in pension plans funded through contracts with TIAA-CREF can decide the respective proportions of their contributions that are to go into the two types of funds. At their option, participants can direct that *all* of their contributions go into one or the other fund. At retirement, the participant is permitted, if he so chooses, to transfer the dollar value of his accumulation units into a fixed-income annuity but he is not permitted to convert his fixed-dollar accumulation (from the TIAA fund) into annuity units whose value vary with the investment experience of the equity portfolio. In your opinion, why does TIAA-CREF treat the fixed-income fund and the equity fund differently from the standpoint of conversion at retirement?

5. The assets backing accumulation units and annuity units in a pension plan with two units are invested in the same portfolio of equity securities. Despite this commonality of asset structure and the fact that the values of the two units are identical at plan inception, on any subsequent valuation date the accumulation unit and annuity unit have different unit values. Why is this so?

6. Contrast the two techniques of procedures for converting benefit accruals under a defined benefit plan into benefit units whose value thereafter depend upon the performance of an affiliated common stock portfolio.

7. Explain why some plan sponsors use a career average formula for a defined benefit pension plan that gives participants the option of converting the benefit accruals into units of account whose values vary with the investment experience of an associated asset portfolio.

8. Explain the significance of the assumed investment return (AIR) to (*i*) the sponsor and (*ii*) the plan participant when:
   *a.* Accumulation units are converted into annuity units under a pension plan using two-unit accounting.
   *b.* The benefit accruals of a defined benefit plan are converted into units whose value vary with the investment experience of an associated asset portfolio.
   *c.* When monies accumulated in a fixed-income account are converted in equity-linked annuity units.

9. Explain the various approaches to dealing with mortality and expense gains and losses under a pension plan whose benefit values are linked to a portfolio of assets.

10. State the potential advantages and disadvantages of pension plans with asset-linked benefits:

      *a.*  To the plan sponsor.

      *b.*  To the participants.

11.  Cost-of-living adjustments in the benefits of retired individuals may be limited in various ways. From a conceptual standpoint, describe the major approaches that could be used to limit the adjustment to benefits in pay status because of changes in the cost of living.

12.  In what ways does the adjustment to benefits in pay status through a formula escalation factor differ from that brought about by an automatic cost-of-living index adjustment?

13.  In your opinion, should automatic and ad hoc adjustments to benefits because of cost-of-living increases be applicable to all types of benefits in payment status, including death and disability benefits? Should such adjustment apply to the deferred benefits of terminated vested employees?

14.  As a pensioner, would you prefer to have your benefits linked to a cost-of-living index or a wage index, assuming that each index is an appropriate and relevant one? State any qualifications to your answer.

15.  Explain the process by which actuarial gains might be used to supplement the benefits of active and retired employees. In all probability, what would be the major source of the actuarial gains that could be used for this purpose?

# Valuation of Pension Plan Liabilities

# Part Three

# 12 | Actuarial Cost Factors

IT WAS POINTED OUT in an earlier chapter that the employer's obligation under a pension plan may take the form of an undertaking to set aside funds on a specified basis (the defined contribution approach) or an undertaking to provide benefits in conformance with a stipulated formula (the defined benefits approach). If the employer's obligation is of the former type, he discharges it fully and completely with the payment of the stipulated sum of money; and if all previous payments were made at the proper time and in the proper amount, his cumulative obligations under the plan are at all times fully and unconditionally met. There is no problem of measuring the employer's obligation for accruing benefits under the plan, because the present value of the benefits as of any given date is, by definition, the exact equivalent of the funds on hand.

On the other hand, where the employer undertakes to provide a predetermined benefit, there is no necessary equivalence between the monetary value of the benefits that have been credited as of any given point and the sums that have been accumulated to pay the benefits. A liability—moral or legal—of measurable value is created with the crediting of each dollar of future benefit, entirely apart from any financial or budgetary arrangements that may have been made to meet the obligation. If the plan is to operate on an acceptable basis, however, the accrual of benefit credits must be offset, over time, by the setting aside of funds estimated to be sufficient, with cumulative investment earnings and the benefit of survivorship in service,[1] to provide the benefits credited under the plan. To guide the funding policy of the employer, it is necessary to estimate the amount of benefits that will eventually be paid under the terms of the plan. Because the benefits will be paid over a period of many years, and funds set aside for the payment of such benefits will earn interest until finally disbursed, it is necessary for proper financial planning to convert the anticipated benefit payments into a single-sum value through the discounting process. The process of deriving the actuarial present value of future benefit payments, which involves other actuarial concepts not yet considered, is referred to as the *valuation of the liabilities* of the plan.

Actuarial valuations are undertaken for a number of purposes, the most common being as follows:

1. To estimate the long-term cost of a pension plan or any proposed changes in the plan.
2. To ascertain the level of benefits that can be provided from a series of stipulated contributions.
3. To indicate the contributions that should be made to fund a given set of benefits.
4. To determine the proper charge to be made against the firm's operating revenues for expense accounting purposes.
5. To determine the maximum contribution that the firm can deduct in any one year for federal income tax purposes.
6. To determine the minimum annual contribution to the plan under federal law.
7. To prepare actuarial reports required under federal law.
8. To establish plan costs and liabilities in connection with corporate mergers and spinoffs.
9. To provide a basis for the allocation of the assets of a terminated plan.
10. To provide information to plan participants concerning the funding status of their benefits.

---

[1]Benefit of survivorship in service is an actuarial concept meaning, in this instance, that the benefits of those employees who are assumed to survive and remain in service to normal retirement age will be provided in part by the nonvested contributions, plus interest, made in respect of those employees assumed to die or withdraw before normal retirement age.

The valuation may take into account only the accrued or prospective benefits of persons currently affiliated with the plan as an active participant, a terminated vested participant, or a retired participant or beneficiary, in which event it is referred to as a *static* or *closed group* valuation. This is the conventional type of valuation, and one that is required under federal law for validating tax deductions and establishing minimum funding levels. Some plans also employ a second type of valuation that takes into account the accrued and prospective benefits of not only the current group of participants but also of those who may enter the plan during some finite future period. The latter type of valuation is called a *dynamic* or *open group* valuation and is primarily designed to provide an employer with information about the future costs, funding obligations, and cash flow of his pension plan.

A distinction is also made between a valuation that is based on the assumption that the plan will continue in operation and one based on the assumption that the plan is being terminated as of the date of valuation. The one is known as a *plan continuation valuation* and the other is called a *plan termination valuation*. The former is routinely required under ERISA and the latter may be performed to indicate what the effect of a plan termination would be.

An understanding of the overall valuation process is enhanced by familiarity with some basic concepts of plan population.

## Basic Concepts of Plan Population

A pension plan that has been in operation for a number of years will be made up of four major components or subsets: (1) active participants (employees still in the active service of the employer); (2) terminated vested participants (former employees who terminated with vested benefits); (3) retired participants; and (4) beneficiaries of retired and deceased participants.[2] Together these four segments constitute the *plan population*.

The broad characteristics of the plan population that have significance from a cost standpoint, and hence make an input into the actuarial liabilities of the plan, are the number of participants (and

---

[2] If the plan provides disability benefits, disabled participants would constitute another distinct subset of the population.

beneficiaries), the male and female mix, the attained age distribution, the distribution by years of service, and the distribution of the population by age of entry into the plan. If the benefits of the plan are related to compensation, the level and distribution of salaries are also relevant characteristics.

The plan population and its characteristics are determined by the flow of persons into and out of the plan. A particularly crucial element is whether the inflow is increasing, decreasing, or remaining constant. If the decremental factors—withdrawals, deaths, total disabilities, and retirements—are constant, and a constant number of new entrants flow into the plan population in a fixed pattern of entry ages, in theory a condition will eventually be reached in which the number of persons in the population and their attained age and service distribution are constant and remain so as long as the basic assumptions are realized. Such a population is described quite aptly as a *stationary population*. If the basic conditions are fulfilled, a stationary population will exist within a period of years equal to the difference between the age of the oldest person in the population and the age of the youngest. If, for example, no retired participant or beneficiary lives beyond 95 and the youngest age at which a person can enter the plan is 21, it will take 74 years from the time the first group enters for a stationary population to be achieved. Once a plan population has become stationary in this sense, its normal cost and accrued liability will remain the same year after year, assuming no change in the benefit structure or other factors that would affect the cost. In practice, no plan will ever have an exactly constant flow of new entrants or an exactly stationary population. The stationary population concept is applicable to each of the segments or subpopulations of the plan population.

Closely akin to the concept of the stationary population is that of the *mature population*. In fact, a stationary population is a special case of a mature population. A mature population is one in which the attained age and service distributions remain constant from year to year but not necessarily the *size* of the population.

A population is considered to be *undermature* when the proportion of the participants at the younger ages and with the shorter periods of service is greater than that within a mature population. Conversely, an *overmature* population is one that contains a greater proportion of older participants and those with longer periods of service than is true of a precisely mature population.[3]

Pension plans characteristically begin their operation with an undermature population, reflecting the fact that most of the participants were hired at the younger ages and spill over into the higher attained ages and service categories over a long period of years.[4] If no new employees were hired after the plan went into operation, the population would gradually move through the various age and service cells, eventually reaching an overmature state without ever having satisfied the precise criteria of a mature population. In the normal situation, of course, new employees would be hired from time to time, which would slow down the maturation process.

If the growth *rate* were to continue to decline, the population would continue its aging process, passing through the mature state into what has been characterized as an overmature state.[5] If a point were to be reached in which no additions were made to the employee group, the population would ultimately be extinguished, the various components disappearing from the scene within the same period of years that it would have taken them to mature with a constant rate of increments and decrements.

The natural tendency of a plan population is to mature. Generally speaking, the only population that would not move toward a more mature state each year would be one growing at an *increasing* rate. No plan population, of course, can grow indefinitely at an increasing rate, since it would ultimately swallow up the entire labor force. However, if a population is to mature systematically in accordance with the time parameters mentioned earlier, persons must enter the

---

[3]It should be recognized that there are an infinite number of possible plan populations, reflecting past hiring practices and varying rates of decrement from the labor force. In fact, there are as many potential plan populations as there are possible combinations of age and service distributions. Thus, in reality, plan populations do not fit neatly into categories that can be characterized as undermature, mature, or overmature. These categories themselves do not have sharply defined boundaries, the whole maturing process being in the nature of a continuum.

[4]Some plans start with a reasonably mature active participant population, that being the primary impetus for establishment of the plan. Likewise, a firm with a dormant, overmature group of active employees might start a pension plan in recognition of the cohorts moving inexorably toward retirement.

[5]In the long run, the rate of growth of most plan populations must decline, even down to zero or near zero. In practice the growth rate (plus or minus) varies from year to year.

population at a constant rate or in constant numbers, the additions at the various ages of entry (i.e., the hiring ages) must be at a constant rate or in constant numbers, and the decrements at the various attained ages in each of the subpopulations must conform to a fixed pattern. If any one of these three broad conditions is not satisfied, the maturation process will be erratic. Changes in hiring patterns, mass layoffs or plant closings, and alterations in retirement practices, for example, would disrupt and distort the process. Cessation of growth in the active employee population would have an important and enduring effect. If the active life population were to remain constant in number, each person leaving the group by death, disability, retirement, or voluntary withdrawal would have to be replaced; but in all likelihood, they would not be replaced by a person of the same age. That being the case, the additions at the various entry ages would not be constant, one of the conditions of a mature population. The net effect of deviations from the prescribed conditions is to slow up the maturation process and to make it more erratic.

As will be seen later, the maturity status of the population has a material affect on the accrued liability of a pension plan and, depending on the actuarial cost method, may have an impact on the normal cost.

## Valuation Factors

Central to the valuation of a pension plan is a determination of the *actuarial present value* of the accrued or projected benefits of the plan. The determination must be made for each type of benefit provided under the plan and for each participant in the plan. The actuarial present value as of a specified date of any given benefit amount payable thereafter is a sum equal to that amount (1) multiplied by the probability of occurrence of the event on which the benefit payment is conditioned, (2) adjusted for the probable effect of intervening events (such as changing compensation levels and marital status), and (3) discounted at a stipulated rate or rates of interest. The aggregate amount derived from these individual determinations constitutes the actuarial present value of the benefits of the plan as a whole.

To gain fuller appreciation of the valuation process, it is necessary to examine in detail the factors that enter into each of the three components of the present value computation. The assumptions regarding these factors must be reasonable (taking into account the experience of the plan and reasonable expectations) and in combination must reflect the actuary's best estimate of anticipated experience under the plan.[6] To sharpen the focus of the discussion, only retirement benefits will be considered in this chapter and in the two following ones that are closely related. The valuation of death, disability, and withdrawal benefits is treated in a later chapter. However, it is essential to keep in mind that most of the actuarial cost factors discussed in the context of retirement benefits are also involved in the valuation of other benefits under the plan.

For purposes of this discussion, retirement benefits will be considered to include only those benefits payable to individuals who enter retirement status from an active participant status. They will *not* include benefits payable to individuals who enter retirement status from either a terminated vested or disabled status. This distinction is made in order to illustrate and give emphasis to the calculation of the expected cost of the different benefit components of the plan.

## Population Decrements

Retirement benefits, as defined above, are payable only to those participants who survive in the service of the employer to early or normal retirement age. Thus, the first step in the valuation of a retirement benefit is the determination of the probability that the participant on whose behalf the benefit has been credited will survive in service to early or normal retirement age. This probability is usually expressed as a decimal, such as .70. The probability of surviving is equal to one less the probability that the person will not survive. The probability that he will *not* survive involves the *forces of decrement*. These forces are terminations (voluntary and involuntary), death, disability, and retirement. The reductions in the plan population that they generate are called *decrements*. The probability that a participant will leave the active life subpopulation because of one of these decremental forces is not independent of the probability associated with the other three forces, and a valuation may take this factor into account.

---

[6]ERISA §302(c)(3), I.R.C. §412(c)(3).

**Terminations.**    Terminations, other than by death, disability, and retirement, tend to be the most important decremental force operating within the active life component of a pension plan population. In the typical situation, they overshadow the decrements attributable to preretirement mortality and disability.

Terminations are taken into account through the use of a schedule of termination rates (also called "turnover" or "withdrawal" rates) contained in a so-called *termination table*. A termination table purports to reflect the rate of termination that can be expected to occur each year at each age in the active life subpopulation from the earliest age of entry into the plan to the youngest age at which retirement with immediate benefits can take place. There may be one set of rates for male participants and another for female participants. Separate schedules may be used for hourly rated employees and salaried employees or for any subset of the active employee population that may be subject to a distinctive pattern of terminations.

In recognition of the fact that termination rates tend to vary inversely with length of service, the termination table may portray termination rates not only by attained age but also by duration of service—up to 5 or 10 years of service. Such a table is described as a *select and ultimate* table, the rates that vary with duration of service being called *select* rates and those that apply after the select period being known as *ultimate* rates, following the terminology of mortality tables. Some tables extend the select period all the way to retirement.

Termination rates should not reflect the proportion of *participants* terminating but rather the proportion of actuarial *liabilities* terminating. Terminations among long-service employees with large accrued benefits have far more effect on costs than terminations among short-service employees. Therefore, if select and ultimate rates are not used, the aggregate rates used for each attained age should be heavily weighted by ultimate experience.

Termination rates may be combined with death or disability rates, or both, to determine the total decrements from the active life population age by age or, conversely, to reflect the proportion of employees at any given age predicted to survive all hazards to continued employment and eventually become eligible for retirement benefits.

The termination rates used in the valuation of a particular plan should ideally reflect the expected experience of the plan population involved. There are usually no reliable experience data on past employment terminations at the inception of the plan, and the actuary, in consultation with the employer, selects a hypothetical schedule of termination rates that he believes will be appropriate for the plan population involved. The rates may reflect the observed experience of an existing plan with population characteristics similar to those of the plan being valued. Over time, a large plan will develop a body of experience that can serve as the basis for the termination schedule, with due allowance for changing circumstances. Many plans, including most small ones, continue to use a hypothetical scale of terminations, whose main virtue is that it shows lower rates of terminations at the various attained ages than those likely to be experienced. Many of these scales show no terminations after age 50 or 55. Select and ultimate rates are not usually used, since they introduce a degree of complexity into the calculations that may not be justified by the crudeness of the termination assumptions employed by many plans.

Termination assumptions can be used only when the plan is being funded through an unallocated funding instrument. Termination assumptions are not appropriate when the plan benefits are funded through insurance company contracts under which all funds are allocated to individual participants. For the purpose of valuation of liabilities—and funding—the tacit assumption under such contracts is that each participant who enters the plan will, barring death, remain a member of the plan until retirement, and, in the event that he does withdraw before his date of full vesting or retirement, the liability for payment of the purchased benefits is canceled and the employer receives an appropriate credit against his next contribution to the plan.[7]

Failure to take anticipated terminations into account overstates the actuarial liabilities of a pension plan as of any given time, unless all liabilities represent fully vested benefits, or unless it is assumed that the plan terminates at that point and all benefits vest in full.

---

[7]Under group deferred annuity contracts, the employer is credited with the value of the canceled annuity only if the terminating participant is in good health because the employee's share of the purchase payment had been discounted for mortality. The presumption is made that an employee who terminates in poor health will not survive to normal retirement age.

Moreover, the condition is not corrected as terminations occur and liabilities are canceled, since, in the normal course of events, offsetting liabilities will have been created in respect of other participants who also will ultimately terminate their membership in the plan before achieving a fully vested or retirement status.

**Death.** A second decremental force within the active life subpopulation is death. Retirement benefits are paid only to those participants who live to early or normal retirement, even when the benefits of the deceased participant had vested prior to death. Thus, to arrive at an estimate of the cost of a pension it is necessary to predict the survival rates of the participants through the use of an appropriate mortality table.[8]

A mortality table can be constructed from the observed experience of any group of lives, adjusted to smooth out irregularities and possibly to provide margins of safety. It typically depicts a death rate per 1,000 for all ages from birth to the oldest age to which people are presumed to live. The terminal age of the mortality table is not intended to reflect the actual extremity of the human life span but the age by which, for all practical purposes, the last survivors of a group of lives will have died. The death rates are applied to the survivors of an arbitrary number of persons, called the *radix,* assumed to be alive at the youngest age in the mortality table. From the number of persons in the original group assumed to be alive at each attained age, it is possible to predict the probability that an individual alive at any given age will survive to any later age. A mortality table clearly lends itself to the prediction of the proportion of active participants in a pension plan who will live to early or normal retirement, as well as to the calculation of the actuarial value of the lifetime benefits payable to persons who reach retirement.

Since mortality rates vary among different segments of the general population, a mortality table used for a particular purpose should reflect that body of mortality experience most appropriate for that purpose. It has been found, for example, that the mortality among

---

[8]Mortality table is the generic name for a table that purports to reflect the probabilities of death and survival at the various ages of the human life span. An annuity mortality table is a type of mortality table used to compute rates and reserves for annuity contracts and retirement benefits provided under a pension plan.

individuals who purchase life insurance tends to be higher, age for age, than that of persons who purchase annuities. This impels the insurance companies to adopt a mortality table for the underwriting of annuities that is different from that used for the writing of life insurance. This practice is dictated not only by the lower death rates among annuitants but by the necessity or desirability of providing a margin of safety in the mortality assumptions. Such a margin is provided in a life insurance mortality table by the use of death rates that are higher than those likely to be experienced, while the converse is true with respect to an annuity mortality table. That is, a conservative annuity mortality table shows lower death rates than those normally expected. Thus, the same table cannot be conservative for both life insurance and annuity purposes. The need for a margin of safety in annuity mortality tables is heightened by the secular improvement in longevity that has occurred in varying degrees at all ages and among virtually all elements of the population. This demographic phenomenon operates to reduce the safety of an annuity mortality table, while it enlarges the original margin of safety in an insurance mortality table.

It has also been found that the mortality among employee groups is lower than that experienced by the general population. This is attributable to the fact that the general population embraces persons in varying conditions of health, including a substantial percentage in an impaired state of health, while a minimum standard of health is required for participation in the active labor force. This superior vitality presumably carries over into retirement, which suggests that an annuity mortality table used for the underwriting or valuation of retirement benefits should lean heavily on the mortality experience of employed lives and of those retired from active employment. Finally, it is a matter of common knowledge that females live longer, on the average, than males. The lower mortality rates occur at all ages, including the first week of life, and this superior longevity appears to flow from a better biological heritage. The superiority of the female has been so pronounced in recent decades that the annuity values for female lives at any particular age have tended to conform rather well to those for male lives five or six years younger. As a result, it has been possible to use the same annuity table for male and female lives by assuming that the female is five or six years younger than her stated age, a device known as an age setback or "rating down."

For the most part, mortality assumptions for the valuation of pension plan benefits have been based upon annuity tables developed by life insurance companies for the writing of individual or group annuities. Some actuarial consulting firms have constructed their own mortality tables from the observed experience among pension plans that they service, while others have modified standard tables by reducing or removing the margins added to the observed mortality rates for safety purposes. Such firms feel that there is little or no need for safety margins in mortality rates used purely for estimating the cost of retirement benefits, when no annuities are formally purchased. This is especially so with respect to the active life population, since preretirement mortality generally has a much less important impact on actuarial liabilities than termination assumptions.

The pattern of mortality among group annuitants is markedly different from that among individual annuitants. The Group Annuity Mortality Table for 1951 (Ga-51)[9] developed by Ray M. Peterson, was the first published table to be based entirely on the mortality experience of group annuitants. Male and female death rates were separately tabulated; but many actuaries found it more convenient to use the male table for both male and female lives, the death rates for females at the various ages being equated to the male rates for ages five years younger. To provide a margin for future improvement in mortality, Peterson developed a projection scale (designated Projection Scale C) that has the effect of reducing the death rate at all ages with each passing calendar year. The table can be used in its basic, static form, without the projection factors. If the projection factors are used without limitation, the expected mortality rate at any given age will vary with the calendar year of birth.

The 1951 Group Annuity Table is still used for the prediction of mortality among some pension plan populations. It is seldom used with unlimited projection factors. A common practice is to project the basic mortality rates of the table to some year, such as 1970, and then use the projected rates as a conventional, static mortality table. Other actuaries use age setbacks rather than the projection factors, the setbacks sometimes varying with the year of birth. A

---

[9]Ray M. Peterson, "Group Annuity Mortality," *Transactions of the Society of Actuaries* 4 (1952), pp. 246–307.

1-year setback is the approximate equivalent of a 10-year projection
of the basic mortality rates according to Projection Scale C; in
other words, a 2-year male setback and a 7-year female setback is
the rough equivalent of the 1951 Group Annuity Table projected to
1971.

By the year 1971, the continued decline in death rates had virtually wiped out the safety margin in the Ga-1951 Table at the
significant ages. As a consequence, a new table, the 1971 Group
Annuity Mortality Table (1971 GAM) was constructed[10] from mortality data generated under certain group annuity contracts. Two
sets of projection factors were developed: scale D for both male
and female lives (with separate percentages), and scale E for male
lives only.

The 1971 GAM Table has been widely used for the valuation of
pension plan liabilities, but is gradually being supplanted by the
1983 GAM Table described below. When only the male table is
used, female ages are set back six years.

In 1976, William W. Fellers and Paul H. Jackson published the
UP-1984 Table.[11] The authors explain that "UP" stands for "unisex
pension," although the full words are not used in the title of the
table. The UP-1984 Table is based on the mortality experience of
pension plans funded through trusts, with mortality improvement
projected to 1984. This table represents the combined experience
of males and females, with about 20 percent of the experience being
for females. It is the first published unisex table and is intended to
be used for groups containing both male and female lives or for
groups containing only males or only females. Because it is based
upon the experience of groups with a particular sex distribution
(the composite mix was 80 percent male and 20 percent female),
it may not represent the experience of groups with a significantly
different sex distribution. The authors recommend that, for a group
made up of female lives exclusively, the table be used with a four-
year set-*back* and that, for a group of male lives, it be used with
a one-year set-*forward*.

---

[10]Harold R. Greenlee, Jr. and Alfonso D. Keh, "The 1971 Group Annuity Mortality
Table," *Transactions of the Society of Actuaries* 23 (1971), pp. 569–604, and discussion on
pp. 605–22.

[11]William W. Fellers and Paul H. Jackson, "Noninsured Pensioner Mortality—The UP-
1984 Table," *The Proceedings, Conference of Actuaries in Public Practice* 25 (1976), pp. 456–
502.

In more recent years the Group Annuity Mortality Committee of the Society of Actuaries has studied rates of mortality improvement from a wide variety of sources. This Committee found that rates of mortality had decreased during the 1970s and that the 1971 GAM Table no longer provides an adequate mortality basis for the valuation of group annuity benefits.

On the basis of data from several sources, the Committee constructed the 1983 Group Annuity Mortality Table (1983 GAM).[12] The 1983 GAM Table was designed as a valuation basis for group annuity contracts. Many pension actuaries have also adopted it for the valuation of pension plans.

The Committee also developed Projection Scale H to project future improvement after 1983.

While separate tables were developed for males and females, the Committee determined that annuity values calculated using the male table with a six-year setback can reasonably approximate annuity values using the female table.

Separate mortality tables are often used for disabled individuals to reflect their higher mortality rates.

**Disability.**    The third source of decrements from active life population of a pension plan is disablement. This decremental force operates just like the other two in preventing plan participants from qualifying for a retirement benefit. The plan might provide a separate disability benefit, but a regular retirement benefit would not become payable unless the individual recovered from his disability prior to retirement. Disablement rates are used to estimate both the number of participants who will receive disability benefits and the number who will *not* receive regular retirement benefits.

Tables are available that show the probability of becoming disabled at various ages within the active life group. The rates depend upon the definition of disability employed and the time period the individual must be so disabled before any benefits become payable. The more liberal the definition and the shorter the waiting period the higher the rate of becoming disabled. The rates are also influenced by the manner in which the definition is interpreted and administered—strictly or loosely.

---

[12]Committee on Annuities, "Development of the 1983 Group Annuity Mortality Table," *Transactions of the Society of Actuaries* 35 (1983), pp. 859–899.

Some disablement tables reflect the morbidity experience of life insurance companies under various types of disability clauses. These tables can be used by pension actuaries for the decrementing of the active life population but may be modified for the valuation of disability income benefits. The experience of a large plan can be tabulated over a period of years and safely used, with adjustments for changed circumstances and provisions, in estimating terminations from disability and determining the actuarial value of the benefits payable to a person who becomes disabled. Disability experience under Social Security and the Railroad Retirement System is used by many pension actuaries.

**Retirement.** Under most pension plans, a participant may retire within a range of permissible ages, running from the youngest age at which early retirement is permitted to the oldest age at which employees actually do retire. Retirement age may affect the amount of monthly benefit payable, the period during which contributions are made to the plan, and the number of years during which the retired participant will receive his pension. Each of these variables is a cost consideration. Therefore, it is necessary to estimate the age or ages at which the plan participants will retire.

A precise procedure is to assume rates of retirements over the full range of ages at which retirement may take place. The highest rate usually occurs at the normal retirement age. Relatively high rates also often occur at the first age at which individuals are eligible for early retirement, at age 62 (when Social Security benefits are first available), and at age 65, even if this is not the normal retirement age. As an approximation to the distribution, the actuary often assumes that all participants retire at normal retirement, or at some estimated average retirement age that may be earlier or later than the normal retirement age. When the plan is funded with an insurance company through an allocated funded type of arrangement, it is assumed that all participants retire at the normal retirement age.

## Population Increments

If the retirement benefits of a closed group of active life participants are being valued, no population *increments* are involved. In fact, it would be a contradiction of terms to talk about population increments in connection with a closed group valuation. On the other hand, it is essential to introduce population increments into an existing group of plan participants if an open group valuation is to be carried out.

Two separate kinds of assumptions are usually made concerning new entrants. The first is the change, if any, in the size of the total active labor force. Even if it is assumed that the firm has reached a stable condition and there will be no growth in the active labor force, it will be necessary to add enough new participants to replace those who will be decremented through termination, death, disability, and retirement. If there is to be some growth in the overall labor force, the increments must exceed the decrements. There would probably be some increments even if the overall labor force of the firm was declining.

The second type of assumption is the distribution of new entrants by age, sex, and salary level. An open group valuation is rather sensitive to the assumption as to the distribution of the new participants brought into the plan. It would be totally unrealistic to assume that each person leaving the active life population would be replaced by a new participant of the same age, sex, and salary. Rather, it is assumed that the distribution of the new participants will reflect the hiring practices of the employer. In the typical situation, most of the new participants would be hired at the younger ages and lower salaries; but there may be some additions throughout the full range of employment ages and salaries. For ease of computation, it may be assumed that all new participants are hired at a few of the younger ages and at the same starting salary each year.

### Economic Based Factors

There is a set of actuarial cost factors that are based upon broad economic forces and reflect predictions as to future economic behavior. They are frequently referred to as "economic assumptions." Cost factors falling within this general category are those relating to salary progression, consumer price levels, and investment earnings. In adopting assumptions about these factors, the plan actuary needs and generally seeks input from the plan sponsor, the investment manager or managers, and others with special insights into economic phenomena.

**Cost of Living.** A cost-of-living increase assumption must be made for the minority of plans that provide for postretirement cost-of-living increases. For integrated plans which offset benefits by a percentage of benefits payable under Social Security, a cost-of-living assumption is also needed to project the primary insurance amount age 65 under Social Security. Also, actuaries often make an assumption about the cost of living, either explicit or implicit, in arriving at the other economic factors.

If cost-of-living increases in the plan are subject to a maximum limit, such as 3 percent per year, this limit will be reflected in valuing projected benefits—even if a higher cost-of-living assumption is used in projecting Social Security benefits or is used for other purposes.

Cost-of-living increase assumptions in current use generally range from 3 percent to 6 percent.

**Salary Progression.**[13] If the retirement benefits of a pension plan are expressed in terms of final average or highest average earnings, it is necessary to project the current earnings of the plan participants to the level expected to prevail during the period of service that will establish the formula salary base—usually the years immediately preceding retirement.[14] If the plan valuation is based upon total prospective benefits, as contrasted with accrued benefits, it is essential to project earnings even when a career average benefit formula is employed. In addition, an assumption must be made about future increases in the Social Security taxable wage base, if the plan is integrated by offsetting by Social Security benefits or by any other approach that automatically recognizes changes in the taxable wage base. The Social Security taxable wage base increases automatically by the percentage increase in average earnings of those employees subject to Social Security.

Compensation for an individual participant (as contrasted with the entire group) is projected through an assumption about the

---

[13]For a provocative and enlightening discussion of the impact of salary changes on pension plan costs, see William F. Marples, "Salary Scales," *Transactions of the Society of Actuaries* 14 (1962), pp. 1–30, and discussion contained in pp. 31–50.

[14]Salary projections are also essential in the valuation of the prospective benefits of participants who will terminate with vested benefits prior to retirement, and here the need is to project current earnings to the level that will prevail during the few years prior to termination.

annual rate at which the individual's compensation will increase over his future working lifetime. The series of projected compensation increases is called a "salary scale." Either explicitly or implicitly, the salary scale usually consists of two elements: the increase in average salary levels, and merit increases.

A salary scale used in the valuation of the liabilities of a pension plan should recognize changes in the compensation of plan participants that will come about from periodic upward shifts in the whole wage structure of the employing firm. These shifts will occur because of labor's share of productivity gains in the economy and responses to inflationary pressures. Such shifts are typically manifested in an increase in the average salary of all employees covered by the plan and in an increase in starting salary rates for new employees.

If the plan is integrated by offsetting Social Security benefits or by otherwise reflecting changes in the taxable wage base, it is necessary to make an assumption about future increases in the taxable wage base, which reflects the average compensation of all workers covered by Social Security. Where a specific assumption is made concerning future increases in the taxable wage base, the same assumption is usually used to represent increases in compensation levels for plan participants, since, in the long run, average increases in compensation for a particular employer will usually be close to the average increases for all workers of all employers.

The increase in average compensation is often considered in two parts: one part equal to the increase in the cost of living, and the other equal to the excess, if any, of increases in average compensation over increases in average prices. Compensation levels tend to reflect the cost-of-living increases in response to the needs of employees to maintain their standard of living, to the demands of collective bargaining, and to competition for employees in the marketplace.

Increases in average compensation in excess of average price increases are generally attributable to productivity gains. The amount of this excess has varied greatly over time. In some recent years, price increases have exceeded compensation increases. While there is considerable uncertainty over the magnitude of future productivity gains in the American economy—and some concern that there may be no such gains in the foreseeable future—there is fairly strong support for the view that there should be some labor-hour productivity gains over the long term. If this forecast is correct, and it is assumed that a portion of these gains will find their way into wages over a time period, the wage scale of a firm should increase from this factor. Actuaries usually assume that increases in average compensation will exceed the assumed increase in prices by 0 percent to 2 percent.

In addition to the increases in average compensation, salary scales should also reflect merit increases: those that reward a participant for the acquisition of greater skills, the assumption of broader responsibilities, or simply the rendering of additional years of loyal service to the employer. These upward movements of earnings occur within a wage or salary structure existing as of a given time and are independent of changes that may occur as the whole wage structure is adjusted upward in response to broad economic forces. Merit salary scale increases are usually more rapid at younger ages than at older ages.

The proper approach to the construction of a merit salary scale is to examine the historical relationship between the average compensation of employees at the various attained ages from 20 to 65 and the average compensation of the entire covered group of employees of the firm. For example, if in 1988, the average compensation for 26-year-old male participants with at least one year of service is 52 percent of the average compensation of all participants in that year, and if in 1987 the average compensation of these same individuals (who were then age 25) was 50 percent of the average compensation of all participants, then the rate of merit salary increase during 1987 for 25-year-old employees was 1.04 (52/50). This would mean that, in 1987, the average 25-year-old employee had his compensation increase 4 percent more than the average increase for all participants. If this was a stable relationship, established by historical observation of compensation rates within the employing firm, the merit salary scale would show 1.04 for age 25.

An actuary may use more than one salary scale in valuing the liabilities of a plan. He may use one scale for male employees and another for females. Also, special scales may be constructed for executives and other employees whose pattern of compensation growth is likely to vary from that of the rank-and-file employees.

Table 5 shows excerpts for illustrative ages for a hypothetical salary scale that assumed 3.5 percent inflation, 0.5 percent productivity increases,[15] and merit increases, which vary by age.

Often the actuary does not explicitly identify the separate elements of the salary scale.

In an open group valuation, salary scales should be used with any type of benefit formula, including one that provides a flat dollar benefit for each year of service. The usual purpose of an open group valuation is to estimate the cost and project the liabilities of a pension plan over some future period, such as the next 10 or 20 years. In today's inflationary economy, the wage base, whether expressed as a career average or a final average, is certain to rise, and flat benefit formulas are likely to be adjusted upward to keep pace with rising wages, including benefits for retired participants.

As might be surmised, salary scale assumptions have a potent influence on cost and liability estimates.

**Interest Rate.**    The present value of a series of future contingent payments is a function of the rate of investment return, or of interest at which the payments are discounted. The higher the interest assumption, the smaller the present value. Pension plan costs and liabilities are extremely sensitive to the interest assumption in the valuation formula because of the long time lapse between the accrual of a benefit credit and its payment. The precise impact of the

**TABLE 5**
**Salary Scale**

| Age | Inflation | Productivity | Merit | Total | Ratio of Salary at Attained Age to Salary at Age 20 |
|---|---|---|---|---|---|
| 20 | .035 | .005 | .068 | .108 | 1.000 |
| 21 | .035 | .005 | .062 | .102 | 1.108 |
| 22 | .035 | .005 | .057 | .097 | 1.221 |
| . | | | | | |
| . | | | | | |
| . | | | | | |
| 64 | .035 | .005 | .001 | .041 | 14.033 |
| 65 | | | | | 14.603 |

---

[15]The 3.5 percent inflation plus 0.5 percent productivity increases assumes a 4.0 percent annual increase in the Social Security taxable wage base.

interest assumption depends upon the plan population characteristics, the rates of decrement, the salary scale, and the assumption
as to the pattern of cost accruals (as determined by the actuarial
cost method); but it is a fairly sound generalization that, in respect
of a typical plan, a change (upward or downward) of 1 percent in
the interest assumption (e.g., an increase from 6 to 7 percent) alters
the long-run cost estimate by about 25 percent.[16] This relationship
seems to hold within any reasonable range of interest assumptions.[17]

Because of the sensitivity of the cost estimates to the interest
assumption, the rate must be chosen with great care. Consultation
with the employer and the agency investing the plan assets concerning present and future investment policy may assist the actuary
in estimating the future investment return. The rate should represent the expected rate of return on plan assets over the long term.
It should not be changed to reflect fluctuations in the financial
market that appear to be transitory or of short-term duration. Consideration must be given to the concept of investment return to be
employed. It should be the total expected long-term return on invested assets, including expected changes in market value.

The treatment of unrealized gains or losses on the equity portion
of the investment portfolio is a matter of perennial concern, and
there is no consensus on how such gains or losses should be handled. For purposes of enforcing funding standards, the law requires
that common stocks and other equity investments be valued on a
reasonable actuarial basis that takes into account fair market value.[18]
There is no direct comparable requirement on the measurement of
investment return, but in the long run, investment return will include any appreciation and depreciation of assets, so changes in
asset values should be reflected in the interest assumptions.

---

[16]For a mathematical demonstration of this relationship and the constraints that must
be observed, see Warren R. Adams, "The Effect of Interest on Pension Contributions,"
*Transactions of the Society of Actuaries* 19 (1967), pp. 170–83, and discussion, pp. 184–
93. See also M. T. L. Bizley, "The Effect on Pension Fund Contributions of a Change in
the Rate of Interest," *Journal of the Institute of Actuaries Students' Society* 10 (1950),
pp. 47–51.

[17]It should be understood that the impact on the *actual* cost of the plan depends upon
the rate of contributions to the plan, the extent to which the accrued liabilities have been
funded, and the rate of actual investment return on the invested assets. The suggested
relationship is based upon the tacit assumption that the ultimate fund of plan assets is 25
times the ultimate annual contribution.

[18]ERISA §302(c)(2)(A), I.R.C. §412(c)(2)(A). See Chapter 20 for discussion of asset
valuation.

In the past, it has been common practice in the interest of conservatism to use an interest assumption somewhat lower than the expected long-term rate of return. This, of course, overstates the expected cost of the plan and generates larger contributions and a larger accumulation of plan assets (in the short run) than would be the case if the interest assumption were to conform to the higher rate of actual investment return. (Precise conformity of the two sets of rates over a period of time is, of course, not to be expected.) Any excess of investment earnings over the assumed rate shows up as an actuarial gain for the year in question, but there continues to be an overstatement of actuarial liabilities for all future years of operation.

In today's economic environment, the basic issue involved in the choice of interest assumption is what allowance should be made for future inflation. In theory, there is a "pure" rate of interest for a riskless investment, reflecting only the lender's time preference; and, in the absence of inflation, the long-run return on a portfolio of assets should be a rate equal to the pure rate of interest plus whatever premium is demanded by investors for the possibility of loss of principal or income. For a particular portfolio, the risk premium would reflect the quality mix of the individual holdings. Under inflationary conditions, prudent investors can be expected to demand an investment return that will include an allowance for anticipated price increases during the term for which they relinquish control over their capital.

There are widely differing views among economists about the pure rate of interest on riskless investments. For the period 1926 to 1987, the annual rate of return on long-term U.S. Treasury bills exceeded the rate of inflation by only 0.5 percent. The inflation-adjusted return for this period was 1.2 percent for long-term government bonds, 1.8 percent for long-term corporate bonds, and 6.6 percent for common stocks.[19] The risk premium for the type of portfolio held by the typical pension plan is probably in the order of 1 to 4 percent. Many actuaries currently assume an interest rate of 1 to 4 percent above the assumed cost-of-living increase. Whether or not the cost-of-living increase assumption is explicitly stated, the total interest assumption used for funding is typically 6 to 8 percent.

---

[19]*Stocks, Bonds, Bills and Inflation: 1988 Yearbook*, R. G. Ibbotson Associates, Inc., Chicago, 1988.

If benefits are related to compensation, the allowance for price inflation should be the same in the interest assumption and the salary scale. However, the two inflation increments do not "wash out" or neutralize each other in a valuation of liabilities. The salary scale applies only to active participants, while the interest assumption affects the estimated cost of benefits for all segments of the plan population, including, especially, participants in a retired status. For each one percentage point added to both the interest and salary scale assumptions for inflation, the estimated cost of a representative plan without cost-of-living adjustments goes down about 10 percent.[20] For example, if inflation of 1 percent per year is assumed, and added to both the interest and salary scale assumptions, the projected cost of the plan would be reduced about 10 percent. If there are cost-of-living adjustments after retirement, an increase of one percentage point in the interest, salary scale, and cost-of-living assumptions would have little effect upon the cost of the plan.

Additional statutory constraints that apply to the interest assumption used for certain special purposes will be discussed later in connection with those uses.

## Immediate Annuity Factors for Retired Participants

The valuation of retirement benefits requires the use of immediate annuity factors. As used herein, an *immediate annuity factor* is the actuarial present value of an amount of $1 per annum payable monthly from a specified age to a retired participant under the normal annuity form or any of the unsubsidized optional annuity forms available under the plan. An immediate annuity factor or rate must be computed for each age at which retired persons or their joint annuitants may be found. Specifically, there must be a factor for each age in a spectrum that begins with the earliest age at which retirement can occur and ends with the attained age of the oldest annuitant. For each age, there is usually one factor for male annuitants and another for female annuitants, the latter being larger because of the longer life expectancy of females.

The immediate annuity factor usually reflects only two assumptions: the probability of survival from age to age and a rate of

---

[20]This percentage will vary with a variety of factors.

interest for discounting the future contingent payments.[21] Both of these assumptions are of critical importance since they are operative during the crucial payout stage. An overstatement of the rates of decrement during this period, or of the rate of return on the underlying assets, could have serious cost consequences. The mortality assumptions are usually taken from the same annuity mortality table that is used to predict the probabilities of survival among the active life population, although separate tables are sometimes used for the two subsets of the population. If separate death rates are to be used for female lives, they may be taken from a separate female annuity table, such as the one prepared in connection with the 1983 GAM Table, or assumed to be equal to male rates for setback ages. The same interest rate is generally used in the computation of the annuity factors that is used in the discounting of the projected retirement benefit back to the date of valuation.

Usually, there is no separate actuarial assumption regarding immediate annuity factors, since these factors are typically the result of computations based upon the mortality and interest assumptions. But sometimes, a separate assumption is made concerning the immediate annuity factors, independent of the mortality or interest assumptions underlying them. Where used, the immediate annuity factors are usually set equal to guaranteed annuity purchase rates of insurance or annuity contracts used to fund the plan.

Annuity factors must be computed for each optional form of annuity under which benefits are being paid to retired participants and beneficiaries. If the benefits payable under the optional forms of annuity are the actuarial equivalent of the normal retirement benefit, no allowance need be made for active participants who may choose an optional annuity form. On the other hand, if the optional annuity forms are subsidized, special annuity factors must be computed for each form of subsidized annuity, and an estimate must be made as to the percentage of the retiring participants who will elect each of the options.

A more detailed description of the process by which the annual cost of the plan is computed must be deferred until actuarial cost methods are considered.

---

[21]For plans with automatic cost-of-living adjustments, a cost-of-living assumption is also used. An expense assumption may be used.

## Expenses

The foregoing factors are concerned only with the valuation of the *benefits* under a pension plan; if an estimate of the total *cost* of the plan is to be derived, expenses must be taken into account.

The expenses associated with a pension plan may be broadly classified as: (1) developmental, (2) legal, (3) actuarial, (4) financial, and (5) general administrative. They may be incurred in the first instance by a number of different agencies, but the cost ultimately falls upon the employer (and possibly the employees, if the plan is contributory).

Investment expenses may be considered an offset to investment income, in which case the interest assumption reflects this reduction. Other expenses paid directly from plan assets may be recognized by a specific expense assumption, either as a fixed dollar amount or as a percentage of some other account (e.g., a percentage of other costs or contributions). If expenses are paid directly by the employer, rather than from the plan assets, no expense assumption will be used in the actuarial valuation. Often, no expense assumption is made, even when expenses are paid by the plan assets, particularly if the expenses are relatively small. Any excess of actual expenses over those assumed results in an actuarial loss.

If the plan is insured, the bulk of the expense may be borne by the insurance company. Under some types of annuity contracts, the insurer recovers part or all of its expenses by a direct charge to the individual plan's account balance. Under other contracts, the insurer recovers its expenses by deductions from the investment income otherwise payable or from the margins in premiums charged under the contract.

---

## Questions

1. With respect to each purpose for which an actuarial valuation may be undertaken, indicate whether the valuation would be carried out on a *plan continuation* basis or a *plan termination basis*.
2. Contrast the *nature* and *purposes* of a closed group valuation and an open group valuation. Is either of these types of valuation approach inherently more conservative than the other? Explain.

3. Explain the difference between a *stationary population* and a *mature population*, and indicate which concept is more relevant to the valuation and costing of pension plans.

4. For a pension plan with a typical population (age and sex distribution), which of the preretirement decremental forces has the greatest impact on the cost of the plan?

5. Why do many pension actuaries favor the use of termination tables that reflect withdrawal rates by both attained age and duration of service? What is the term applied to such rates and to a table containing such rates?

6. Why is it not feasible to use termination assumptions in connection with allocated funding instruments?

7. Explain the different ways that an annuity table with projection factors can be used to protect a life insurance company or a pension plan against the financial consequences of future improvement (reduction) in annuitant mortality.

8. Explain why the use of preretirement death and disability rate assumptions in projecting the cost of a pension plan may have both positive and negative cost impacts.

9. What are the components of a properly constructed salary scale used for the estimating of pension costs?

10. Is it necessary or desirable to use a salary scale in estimating the costs and liabilities of a pension plan that provides a flat dollar benefit for each year of service or a benefit based on career average salary?

11. What component of the salary scale should be reflected in the interest assumption? Explain.

12. Do the inflation components of the salary scale and the interest assumption cancel out each other? Explain why or why not.

13. In developing actuarial cost estimates for a pension plan, does the actuary assume that all surviving and persisting participants retire at normal retirement age? Is your answer the same for a pension plan that utilizes allocated funding investments?

14. What kinds of assumptions enter into immediate annuity factors for retired participants?

15. In projecting the actuarial costs of a pension plan that permits the participants to elect optional annuity forms, must the actuary estimate the proportion of participants who will elect each type of permissible option? Explain.

# 13 | Benefit Allocation Actuarial Cost Methods

THE PRECEDING CHAPTER described the factors and outlined the types of assumptions that enter into the valuation of the benefits (and expenses) of a defined benefit pension plan. It also provided a generalized description of the procedures used to determine the actuarial present value of the accrued or prospective retirement benefits.

This chapter defines some fundamental terms and concepts involved in the valuation of a defined benefit pension plan and describes the basic actuarial cost methods associated with one generic approach to apportioning the actuarial present value of benefits to the years of service of the plan participants. The other generic approach with its associated cost methods is considered in the following chapter.

## Terminology

The literature contains much variety in the terms that describe actuarial concepts. The terminology most widely used is the collection of terms found in ERISA, the Internal Revenue Code, and IRS publications (not always internally consistent). Another set is that contained in the 1981 report of the Joint Committee on Pension

Terminology and adopted by the American Academy of Actuaries, the American Society of Pension Actuaries, the Conference of Actuaries in Public Practice, and the Society of Actuaries. In addition, a number of other terms, not contained in either of these two sets, are widely used. This text generally follows the terminology of ERISA, the Code, and IRS publications when they are applicable, but otherwise follows the Joint Committee terminology. Alternative terms are generally identified in the footnotes. A comparative summary of the terminology is found in Table 10 in Chapter 14. Still different terminology is used for accounting purposes, as discussed in Chapter 18.

## Fundamental Concepts

The actuarial present value of future benefits is the discounted amount which, together with future interest, is expected to be sufficient to pay those benefits. The term *actuarial present value*[1] is intended to connote that the derivation of such a value involves population decremental factors, salary scales, and other functions, in addition to an interest discount for the time value of money.

### Normal Cost

For funding, accounting[2], and tax purposes, it is necessary to assign or allocate—in a systematic and consistent manner—the expected cost of a pension plan for a group of participants to the years of service that give rise to that cost. The technique used to accomplish this purpose is called an *actuarial cost method* (or sometimes *funding method*)[3] of which there are several basic types. The general objective of an actuarial cost method is to assign to each fiscal or plan year the cost assumed to have accrued in that year. The portion of the actuarial present value of benefits assigned to a particular year with respect to an individual participant or the plan as a whole is called the *normal cost*.[4] Since the various actuarial cost methods

---

[1]ERISA §3(27).
[2]Accounting for pension costs is discussed in Chapter 18.
[3]ERISA §3(31).
[4]ERISA §3(28).

allocate benefits and actuarial present values according to different patterns, the normal cost of a plan is a function of the actuarial cost method employed. The term *normal cost* originated because, under some methods, the normal cost is defined as the cost that would be assigned to a given year of the plan's operation if, from the earliest date of credited service, the plan had been in effect and costs had been accrued in accordance with that actuarial cost method—and all actuarial assumptions had been exactly realized. The significance and implications of this definition will be more fully grasped as actuarial cost methods are examined in greater detail.

The normal cost is usually determined for the year following the valuation date.

## Actuarial Liability

Actuarial cost methods generally (but sometimes imprecisely) divide the present value of future benefits into two portions, the part attributable to the past and the part attributable to the future. The part attributable to the past is called the "actuarial liability" while that attributable to the future is called the present value of future normal costs.

From a retrospective point of view, the cumulative normal cost of the plan, increased by the valuation rate of interest, decreased by benefit and expense disbursements, and adjusted for actuarial gains and losses (explained below) equals the *actuarial liability* of the plan.[5] Viewed prospectively, the actuarial liability is the actuarial present value of future benefits less the actuarial present value of future normal cost accruals. The actuarial liability of a plan increases each year until the plan population reaches a mature state, if ever, after which it would remain constant if the population and benefit distribution were to remain stable.

The terms *accrued liability*[6] and *actuarial accrued liability* are synonymous with *actuarial liability* (the latter being favored in this

---

[5]The pension plan obligation here described as an actuarial *liability* is not necessarily a legal or accounting liability of the plan or its sponsor. Accounting liabilities are discussed in Chapter 18. Legal liabilities upon plan termination are described in Chapters 24 and 25.

[6]ERISA §§3(29),302(c)(1),(7),I.R.C. §412(c)(1),(7).

text). The term *initial actuarial liability* or *initial accrued liability* refers to the actuarial liability existing at the inception of a plan because of provision for past service credits. It equals the normal costs, increased by interest at the valuation rate, that would have accrued in respect of that service had the plan been in continuous operation from the date of the earliest credited service. The term *past service liability*[7] or *past service cost* is frequently used to refer to the initial actuarial liability, and it is sometimes used to refer to (*a*) any additions to the actuarial liability brought about by retroactive benefit increases after the plan has been in operation, or (*b*) (erroneously) the actuarial liability at the current date. The terms *prior service liability* or *prior service cost* may be used in a sense synonymous with actuarial liability or may be used to indicate the actuarial liability on the valuation date attributable to benefits credited for service prior to the effective date of the plan. These terms with ambiguous meanings are avoided in this text.

That portion of the liability offset by plan assets is referred to as the *funded* actuarial liability, and the ratio of assets to liabilities is called the *funded ratio*. The portion of actuarial liability not offset by plan assets is quite naturally called the *unfunded actuarial liability* or *unfunded accrued liability*,[8] an item of significance and concern.

The actuarial liability may be divided into two segments: the *normal cost liability* and the *supplemental cost liability,* although this differentiation is not usually made in practice. (See Figure 1.) The normal cost liability is retrospectively the sum of all normal cost accruals *since inception of the plan,* increased by interest at the valuation rate and decreased by benefit and expense disbursements allocable to the normal cost accruals.[9] Prospectively, the normal cost liability is equal to the actuarial present value of future benefits minus the actuarial present value of future normal cost

---

[7]ERISA §302(b)(2)(B), I.R.C. §412(b)(2)(B).

[8]ERISA §3(30).

[9]This description applies to the normal cost liability for the plan as a whole. The normal cost liability in respect of an individual participant must also recognize the benefit of survivorship in service.

It should also be pointed out that the normal cost accruals in question are those that would be applicable under the current plan design and current actuarial assumptions, which might be different from those originally determined.

**FIGURE 1**
**Actuarial Present Value of Future Benefits and Its Components**

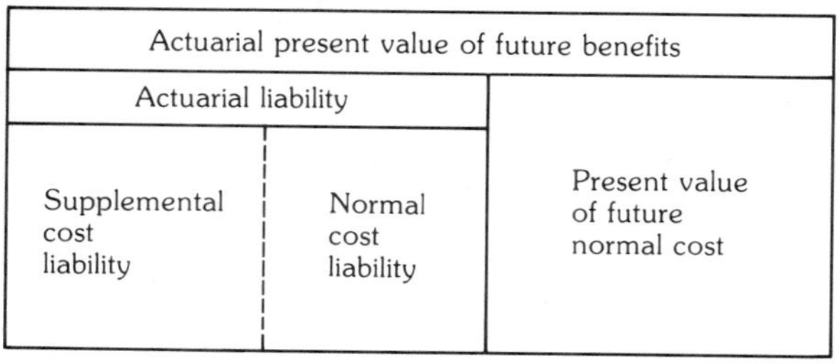

| Actuarial present value of future benefits | | |
|---|---|---|
| Actuarial liability | | Present value of future normal cost |
| Supplemental cost liability | Normal cost liability | Present value of future normal cost |

accruals and supplemental cost accruals. The supplemental cost liability is equal to the difference between the actuarial liability and the normal cost liability. In other words, it is the residual or balancing item in the equation. It is present whenever the actuarial cost method establishes future normal cost accruals whose actuarial present value is less than the actuarial present value of the total projected benefits of the plan.

A significant source of a supplemental cost liability is the granting of benefit credits for service prior to inception of the plan. This is so since there were no normal cost accruals for years prior to establishment of the plan. The supplemental cost liability attributable to past service benefits is equal to the actuarial accumulation of the normal costs that would have accrued in respect of such benefits had the plan been in operation from the earliest date of credited service. This means that, at the inception of the plan, the *actuarial liability,* the *supplemental cost liability,* and the *initial past service liability* are all equal. By the end of the first plan year, the actuarial liability will have increased by the normal cost for the year plus interest at the valuation rate on the supplemental cost liability and less benefit payments; while the supplemental cost liability will have increased only by an amount equal to interest at the assumed rate, less benefit payments attributable to the supplemental liability. Never again will the two values be the same, the disparity becoming larger with each passing year.

Another component or layer of supplemental cost liability is created when the benefits of the ongoing plan are retroactively liberalized. This layer of liability has the characteristics identical to those of the first, representing the actuarial accumulation of the *additional* normal costs that would have accrued from the inception of the plan had the new level of benefits been in effect from the beginning. The actuarial liability would increase by the amount of the additional layer of supplemental cost liability *plus* the normal cost for another year and another year of aging of all actuarial liabilities. Additional layers of supplemental cost liability are created by the adoption of actuarial assumptions more conservative than those that underlay the prior cost accruals. (A *negative* supplemental liability is created by the adoption of less conservative actuarial assumptions.)

### Funding the Supplemental Cost Liability

Supplemental cost liability must be funded in accordance with various schedules laid down in ERISA, the schedules being discussed in a later chapter. Each layer of supplemental cost liability has its own amortization schedule; but the plan sponsor may merge the various schedules into one, with proper weighting of the actuarial values and remaining time periods involved, after regulations regarding this are issued.[10]

The annual cost accrual associated with amortization of the plan's supplemental cost liability is called the *supplemental cost,*[11] paralleling the normal cost that is associated with the benefit accruals for the current year of a plan's operation. For purposes of ERISA's minimum funding requirements this supplemental cost is called an *amortization charge* if positive or an *amortization credit* if negative. The normal cost and supplemental cost together constitute the *annual cost* of the plan.

### Actuarial Gains and Losses

Only by coincidence will the actual experience of the plan conform to the assumptions that underlie the actuarial cost estimates. If the experience of the plan is financially more favorable than the underlying assumptions, *actuarial gains* emerge. If the experience is financially less favorable than that assumed, *actuarial losses* emerge.

---

[10]I.R.C. §412(b)(4).
[11]Also called amortization payment (Joint Committee).

These concepts are applicable to each of the underlying assumptions, as well as to the assumptions taken as a whole. For example, if fewer participants die than were expected to do so according to the underlying mortality assumptions, there is an actuarial loss with respect to retirement benefits but an actuarial gain with respect to any death benefits in the plan. On the other hand, if there were more withdrawals than expected, there would be an actuarial gain with respect to retirement benefits and a partially offsetting loss with respect to the benefits of terminated vested participants. An inadequate salary scale would produce an actuarial loss, while an investment result more favorable than the valuation interest rate would give rise to an actuarial gain. There may be actuarial gains with respect to some factors and actuarial losses with respect to others in the same year. The experience status of the plan as a whole for a given year of operations reflects the net balance of actuarial gains and losses among the various actuarial cost factors. Actuarial gains and losses arising out of deviation of actual from expected experience are frequently referred to as *experience gains and losses,* to distinguish them from gains or losses resulting from a *change in the underlying actuarial assumptions.*

Some actuarial cost methods, called *spread gain* methods, automatically spread all gains and losses over the normal cost for the current and future years. Under all other actuarial cost methods any actuarial gain or loss results in a change in the unfunded actuarial liability of the plan, which may be amortized over a period of years. The choice of amortization period may be influenced by legal and accounting requirements, the actuarial cost method, the funding instrument, plan provisions, collective bargaining agreements, and the fiscal objectives of the plan sponsor. For purposes of determining compliance with minimum funding standards (described in Chapter 17), the law now requires that experience gains and losses be amortized over 15 years for multiemployer plans, or over 5 years for other plans. Changes in the unfunded liability arising out of modifications in the actuarial assumptions must be amortized over 30 years for multiemployer plans, or over 10 years for other plans. To determine the maximum deductible limit for income tax purposes, actuarial gains and losses can be amortized over 10 years.[12]

---

[12] I.R.C. §404(a)(1)(A)(iii).

## Desirable Characteristics of an Actuarial Cost Method

Those concerned with pension plans may seek various properties or characteristics in an actuarial cost method. Some would want the method to develop a normal (or annual) cost that would be a level percentage of covered payroll over the years, assuming no change in the benefit formula or other substantive features of the plan, and assuming actual experience in precise conformity with the underlying actuarial assumptions. Some would want the method to generate an actuarial liability that would be at least equal to the actuarial present value of all accrued benefits, vested and non-vested, that would be payable in the event of plan termination. Some—and this is related to the second characteristic—would want the method to generate an actuarial liability that is not grossly in excess of the plan termination liability, to avoid what they contend is a distortion in the allocation of total plan costs over time. Finally there are those who would want the method to provide sufficient flexibility to meet the short-term fiscal needs of the employer or other plan sponsor. In other words, they would want some room for varying the year-to-year contributions in recognition of the firm's earnings and cash flow situation.

It will be recognized that these four objectives are inherently contradictory and no actuarial cost method yet devised can satisfy all four. In the following discussion, attention will be paid to the extent to which the various cost methods satisfy these objectives. It might be said here that flexibility may be provided through the creation of a supplemental cost component and through the treatment of actuarial gains and losses.

## Classification of Actuarial Cost Methods

Actuarial cost methods may be classified in various ways, depending upon the particular characteristic of the methods that one wishes to emphasize by the classification. From both a conceptual and operational standpoint, one of the most fundamental bases for classification is whether the method allocates the *benefits* of the plan to various plan years and then determines the actuarial present value associated with the benefits themselves or whether it allocates the *actuarial present value* of all prospective benefits to the various plan years without allocating the benefits themselves. Thus, to calculate the actuarial liability under a *benefit allocation* actuarial cost method one first determines the amount of each future monthly pension payment (together with any other potential payments such as death benefits) to which each participant may become entitled and which is attributable to service prior to the valuation date; then one determines the actuarial present value of those benefits. But to calculate the actuarial liability under a *cost allocation* actuarial cost method, the actuarial present value of all projected future benefits under the plan is allocated among the periods before and after the valuation date without determining the portion of the specific monthly benefits attributable to service before and after that date.

Those methods that allocate the *benefits* to particular plan years may be further divided as to whether they allocate the benefits according to the plan's provisions describing the benefit that accrues each year or whether they project the total benefit to become payable at normal retirement age and then allocate the projected benefit to each year of a participant's service in portions that constitute either a level dollar amount or a level percentage of pay. Likewise, those methods that allocate *costs,* rather than *benefits,* may be further classified as to whether the portion of the total projected cost (actuarial present value) assigned to each year of a participant's service is a level dollar amount or a level percentage of pay.

Another basis for classification is whether the method develops a supplemental cost liability, which, as noted earlier, is usually related to past service benefits or to plan amendments that increase accrued benefits. If a method does not generate a supplemental cost liability, then the actuarial present value of all benefits, including past service benefits and other retroactively granted benefits, must be assigned to particular years of service in the form of normal costs.

Another basis for classification is whether the accruing costs of the plan are computed with reference to the entry ages of the various participants or the attained ages. If normal costs are computed on the basis of the participants' actual or assumed entry ages, a supplemental cost liability will be produced by past service and other retroactively granted benefits. If all costs are apportioned from the participants' attained ages to the year of retirement, the annual (normal) cost charges may meet the total cost of the plan, in which case no supplemental liability will develop.[13]

Yet another basis for classification is whether the normal cost and actuarial liability for the plan are determined separately for each individual participant or for the group of participants as a whole, without reference to the individual participants. Under an *individual* actuarial cost method, the normal cost and actuarial liability are calculated for each participant, and these values for the entire plan are simply the sum of the respective values for all the participants. Under an *aggregate* method, the costs (but not necessarily the actuarial liability) are determined for the group as a whole in such a manner that the cost for an individual participant cannot be separately identified. As will be noted later, the cost of the plan determined on an aggregate basis is not the same as the sum obtained by adding the individually determined costs for the various participants. However, under an individual method, it would be possible (although laborious, perhaps) to determine the costs for each individual participant, whereas it would be completely impossible (in theory and in fact) to do so under an aggregate method.

Finally, actuarial cost methods can be distinguished as to the manner in which they determine and deal with actuarial gains and losses. Under some actuarial cost methods, actuarial gains and losses are directly and explicitly computed as the difference between the actual unfunded actuarial liability as of the date of current valuation and the unfunded actuarial liability that would have existed at that date if all actuarial assumptions had been exactly realized. A gain or loss so determined is then amortized over a period of years. This is quite logically known as the *direct* method of determining and dealing with actuarial gains and losses. Under other actuarial cost methods, especially those characterized as *aggregate* methods, gains and losses are not directly computed. In effect, actuarial gains and losses are automatically, and without separate identification, spread over the future working lifetimes of all active participants as a component of the normal cost. This

---

[13]It will be noted later that actuarial present values under benefit allocation cost methods are computed as of the participants' attained ages, but a supplemental cost liability is typically developed from past service benefits and retroactive benefit increases.

approach is referred to as the *spread* method of dealing with gains and losses and will be more comprehensible after the structure of aggregate cost methods has been examined.

Those features of actuarial cost methods that have been described in this section as *bases* for classifying cost methods may also be termed *characteristics* of actuarial cost methods. Any one method may have several of these characteristics and, thus, the dichotomous classifications overlap. The cost method being employed for a given pension plan cannot be conclusively identified until its principal characteristics are given. It is not sufficient to know only whether the plan's costs and actuarial liabilities are computed on the basis of *benefit* allocations or *cost* allocations. It is necessary to know also whether benefits or costs are assigned to plan years in quantities that constitute level dollar amounts or level percentages of payroll, whether or not supplemental cost liabilities are generated, whether entry ages or attained ages are used, whether the computations are made on an individual or aggregate basis, and how actuarial gains and losses are handled. If there is a supplemental cost liability, there needs to be a statement about how it is being handled, including, if appropriate, the period over which it is being amortized.

A full identification of one widely used actuarial cost method would indicate that it is an individual level percentage entry age cost allocation method with supplemental liability and with immediate recognition of actuarial gains and losses. Some authorities would incorporate into the description a reference as to closed group or open group valuation. Whether a closed group or open group approach is used would seem to be more a matter of actuarial assumptions than a cost method characteristic. It is undeniably a vital piece of information about the overall valuation process. Except where otherwise indicated, all descriptions and illustrations of actuarial cost methods in this text assume a closed group of participants.

## Benefit Allocation Cost Methods

A number of actuarial cost methods are in common use, each generating a different normal cost and actuarial liability for the same set of underlying data and actuarial assumptions. For pedagogical purposes, they are subsumed in this text under two broad classes, the dominant basis for the classification being whether *benefits* or *costs* are assigned to the various plan years. Those methods that allocate benefits and then derive the actuarial present value of the benefits are called *benefit allocation cost methods*.[14] Those methods that compute the actuarial present value of the total benefits to be paid and then assign a portion of that value (or cost) to each plan year are called *cost allocation cost methods*. These two approaches are quite distinctive, from both a philosophical and computational standpoint. Benefit allocation cost methods are described in this chapter, with those based on cost allocations being treated in the following chapter.

The distinctive characteristic of any benefit allocation cost method is that a discrete unit of retirement benefit is allocated to each year of credited service of a plan participant, and the actuarial present value of that unit of benefit is separately computed and assigned to the year during which it accrued or is presumed to have accrued. The benefit allocation and actuarial value determination are made with respect to each individual participant, with the resulting values being summed to determine the annual cost and actuarial liability for the plan as a whole. In other words, the aggregate approach by which plan costs and liabilities are determined directly and without specific reference to individual participants is not applicable to benefit allocation cost methods. The actuarial value determination is always made as of the participants' *attained* ages, but a supplemental cost liability may be—and typically is—developed.

There are two distinct types of benefit allocation cost methods in common use, being differentiated only by the manner in which the unit of benefit assigned to a participant's given year of service is determined. In all other respects, they are identical. Both are called the *accrued benefit cost method* or *unit credit method*.

## Traditional Accrued Benefit Cost Method

Under the traditional accrued benefit cost method the benefit assigned to a participant's given year of credited service is determined by direct application of the plan's benefit formula. The *traditional*

---

[14]Also called accrued benefit cost method (by ERISA), unit credit method (by ERISA), unit credit actuarial cost method (by Joint Committee), single premium method, and step-rate method.

accrued benefit cost method is sometimes called the *traditional unit credit* method. This method is often used when the annual benefit accrual is expressed as a flat dollar amount or a specified percentage of the participant's *current* compensation for each year (which, of course, means a *career average* formula). It is technically possible to use the traditional accrued benefit cost method in connection with a final average pay plan, but IRS regulations do not permit its use for *funding* such a plan.[15] However, in order to assist readers to grasp the differences among the various actuarial cost methods, it seems desirable to show the application of all methods under the same hypothetical plan; so all actuarial cost methods are illustrated in this text by a final average pay plan.

Under the traditional accrued benefit cost method the benefit assigned to a given year of credited service is defined as the expected *increase* in the participant's accumulated plan benefit during the year. Under a final average pay plan the increase in a participant's accumulated benefit during a given year of service is a combination of that year's benefit accrual and the adjustment of all previous years' accruals to reflect the moving (presumably upward) salary base. In other words, each year the benefit accruals for all previous years are recomputed in terms of the new salary base, such as the average for the last five years, including the current year.

The plan accrued benefit is required to be ascertainable at all times. Even if the plan provides a composite benefit at normal retirement, subject to a minimum period of service, equal to a specified percentage of defined compensation (such as 40 percent of the participant's average salary during the last five years of service) or a specified dollar amount, the total prospective benefit must be arbitrarily assigned by the plan document to the participant's potential years of service. It will be recalled that, for purposes of determining *vested* benefit accruals, ERISA requires that such a composite benefit be prorated over the total potential years of service or be apportioned in such a fashion as not to result in excessive "back loading."

**Normal Cost.** The first step in deriving the normal cost in respect of a given participant under the traditional accrued benefit

---

[15]Treas. Reg. 1.412(c)(3)–1(e).

cost method is to determine the dollar amount of benefits allocated to the participant during the year in question. This amount is the *increase* in the participant's accumulated plan benefit during the year, as defined by the plan document. Needless to say, an increase in the participant's accumulated benefit because of a plan amendment would not be a part of the normal cost calculation, but would give rise to an increase in the actuarial liability.

The second step in deriving the normal cost for a given participant is to multiply the dollar amount of benefit allocated to the participant for the year in question by the actuarial present value of $1 of benefit. The actuarial present value of $1 of benefit at any given attained age is equal to the present value (at normal retirement age) of a life annuity due in the amount of $1 per year payable monthly beginning at normal retirement age (here assumed to be age 65), multiplied by the probability that the participant will survive in service to normal retirement age and discounted back to the participant's current age at the valuation rate of interest. The probability of survival takes into account decrements from death, disability, and withdrawal.[16] The actuarial present value of each $1 of benefit increases with each advance in age, since the probability that the participant will survive in service is enhanced and the discount period is shortened.

On the basis of the 1971 GAM Table and interest at 6 percent, the actuarial present value at age 65 of a straight-life annuity due of $1 per year payable monthly to a male age 65 is $9.27.[17] In other words, the plan would have to have assets of $9.27 on hand at a

---

[16]For present purposes, withdrawal of vested participants is treated as a decrement, since the examples are concerned with calculations of the actuarial value of a *retirement* benefit. Benefit accruals preserved through vesting have their own cost and must be separately valued. Some actuaries do not make this distinction and include the cost of terminated vested benefits with the cost of retirement benefits. Under this procedure, terminations of vested participants are not treated as decrements.

When the traditional accrued benefit cost method is used by life insurers in connection with group deferred annuity contracts, no allowance is made for terminations by disability and withdrawal. All participants are assumed to remain in service until retirement, or their earlier death, and all terminations of nonvested participants, other than from death, result in actuarial gains whenever they occur. This same procedure is often used by trust fund plans.

[17]The cost illustrations in this text assume that all participants retire at age 65. In practice, the actuary may assume that a percentage of participants retire at each age at which retirement is possible.

male participant's age 65 to pay him a lifetime benefit of $1 per year, the first monthly payment due at date of retirement. According to the mortality, disability, and withdrawal assumptions employed in the derivation of survivorship functions (in Appendix B), the probability that a male participant now age 30 will survive in service until age 65 and, hence, become entitled to a retirement benefit is .1416 and the present value at age 30 of $1 payable at age 65 at 6 percent is .1301. Thus, the actuarial present value at a male participant's age 30 of a lifetime benefit of $1 per year payable monthly from age 65 under a 6 percent interest assumption is $9.27 × .1416 × .1301 = $0.171. With interest at 6 percent and the benefit of survivorship in service, this amount would accumulate to $9.27 at the participant's age 65. If a male participant age 30 should be credited with a benefit for his year of service at that age of $100 per year payable monthly from age 65, the actuarial present value of that benefit at age 30 would be $0.171 × 100 = $17. This would be the normal cost for this participant in this year under this particular cost method. The normal cost for the same benefit credited to a female participant of the same age would be $23, since the actuarial value of her benefit at age 65 would be about 20 percent larger and her probability of surviving in service from age 30 to 65 would be greater than that of a male participant of the same age, if withdrawal rates for females are assumed to be the same as those for males.[18]

If the foregoing male participant should be credited with another $100 of annual benefit during his next year of service at age 31, the actuarial present value or normal cost of the benefit would be $21, reflecting the slightly higher probability of survival to normal retirement and a one-year shorter discount period. Again, this sum invested at 6 percent interest and improved by the benefit of survivorship in service would accumulate to $927 at age 65, the amount that would have to be on hand at that time, according to the mortality and interest assumption, to provide a life income of $100 per year payable monthly from age 65.

---

[18]The use of differing withdrawal rates and salary scales for females, in some instances, may cause the normal cost for a female to be less than for an equally compensated male of the same age.

The foregoing process for determining the normal cost under the traditional accrued benefit cost method for an individual participant with a normal retirement age of 65 may be summarized as follows:[19]

$$\text{Normal cost} = \left(\begin{array}{c}\text{Benefits allo-}\\ \text{cated to at-}\\ \text{tained age for}\\ \text{current year}\end{array}\right) \times \left(\begin{array}{c}\text{Probability}\\ \text{of surviving}\\ \text{in service to}\\ \text{age 65}\end{array}\right) \times \left(\begin{array}{c}\text{Interest}\\ \text{discount}\\ \text{from at-}\\ \text{tained age}\\ \text{to age 65}\end{array}\right) \times \left(\begin{array}{c}\text{Annuity factor at}\\ \text{age 65 for \$1 per}\\ \text{year payable}\\ \text{monthly for life}\end{array}\right)$$

This same formula is used to derive the normal cost under all benefit allocation cost methods, the only difference among the methods being the dollar value of the benefits allocated to the participant in the current year.

The values involved in determining *future* normal costs of the retirement benefits of a male participant entering the plan at age 30 (under the assumptions employed in Appendix B) are set out in Table 6.[20] The retirement benefit is assumed to be 1 percent of the participant's average salary during the last five years of service for

**TABLE 6**
**Calculation of the Normal Cost for an Individual Male Participant at Various Attained Ages under the Traditional Accrued Benefit Cost Method**

| (1) | (2) | (3) | (4) | (5) | (6) |
|---|---|---|---|---|---|
| | | | Interest Discount | Annuity Factor at Age 65 for | |
| | Benefits Allocated | Probability of Surviving in Service | from Attained Age to | \$1 per Year Payable Monthly | Normal |
| Attained Age | to Attained Age | to Age 65 | Age 65 | for Life | Cost |
| 30 | \$  164 | .1416 | .1301 | \$9.268 | \$    28 |
| 40 | 447 | .3809 | .2330 | 9.268 | 368 |
| 50 | 959 | .6646 | .4173 | 9.268 | 2,465 |
| 60 | 1,751 | .8592 | .7473 | 9.268 | 10,420 |

---

[19]All the cost illustrations in this chapter are in terms of normal retirement benefits only. It would unduly complicate the discussion to demonstrate how the cost of withdrawal, death, and disability benefits is derived or how multiple retirement ages would affect plan costs. It should be kept in mind, however, that the normal cost and actuarial liability for the plan as a whole reflects the cost and actuarial value of all benefits under the plan, not just retirement benefits.

[20]The figures in this chapter may not total due to rounding.

each year of credited service, with no explicit integration with Social Security. The participant's salary, currently $15,870, is assumed to increase in accordance with the merit scale (shown in Table B-5 in Appendix B, part of which was reproduced in Table 5 of Chapter 12), plus an annual compound rate of increase of 4 percent to reflect inflation and real wage gains. The total projected benefit at normal retirement age is $31,903.

It will be noted that the normal cost for the illustrative participant, expressed in dollar terms, increases in astronomical proportions over time. This is due to three factors, as may be clearly seen from the table: the dollar benefit allocated to each attained age increases manyfold because of the growth in the salary base, the probability of surviving in service to age 65 improves, and the period over which the prospective benefit is discounted shrinks, leading to a smaller discount. The annuity factor at age 65 remains constant, of course.

The increase in the individual participant's normal cost is not quite so shocking when expressed as a percentage of the participant's growing salary. The normal cost curve of a male participant entering the plan at age 30 remaining to age 65, under the set of actuarial assumptions used in this text, is depicted in Figure 2. The normal cost is only 0.18 percent of the participant's salary at age 30, but it rises each year, eventually reaching 19.1 percent of current salary. The annual increase is especially sharp after about age 45. Because of such sharply increasing costs, regulations do not permit use of the traditional accrued benefit cost method for minimum funding requirements for final average pay plans.[21]

The normal cost of retirement benefits for the plan as a whole is the sum of the separately computed normal costs of the benefits allocated to the individual participants at the various attained ages. Since the actuarial value of each unit of benefit in respect of a particular participant goes up each year, for reasons previously noted, it might appear that the normal cost for the plan as a whole must also increase from year to year. This is not necessarily so. The normal cost of benefits for the participants in any given attained age cohort increases from one year to the next only by an amount reflecting the one-year shorter period of interest discount and by

---

[21]Treas. Reg. §1.412(c)(3)–1(e)(3).

**FIGURE 2**
**Normal Cost Curve as a Percentage of the Salary of a Male Participant**
**Entering the Plan at Age 30 under the Traditional Accrued Benefit**
**Cost Method**

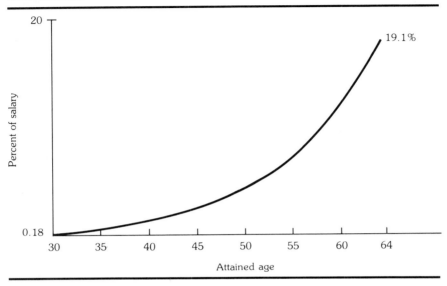

the increased probability of surviving to retirement age, and, of course, any increase in benefit accruals. The annual increase in the normal cost from the discount factor is equal to the interest rate assumed in the valuation formula. In a particular case, the entry of new participants into the plan with their relatively low normal cost, and the retirement of the oldest participants with their relatively high normal cost, might offset or more than offset the increased cost associated with surviving participants. However, as the plan population matures, the normal cost for the whole group *tends* to increase in absolute dollar amount and as a percentage of covered payroll.

The normal cost curve under the traditional accrued benefit cost method for a hypothetical pension plan is shown in Figure 3. The normal cost as a percentage of covered payroll was simulated on an open group basis over a 50-year period, beginning with a relatively immature plan population. The population was assumed to grow from an initial level of 1,000 to 1,895 by the end of 25 years, declining thereafter to the original number of 1,000 by the 50th

**FIGURE 3**
Normal Cost as a Percentage of Covered Payroll of a Hypothetical
Pension Plan over a 50-Year Period under the Traditional Accrued Benefit
Cost Method

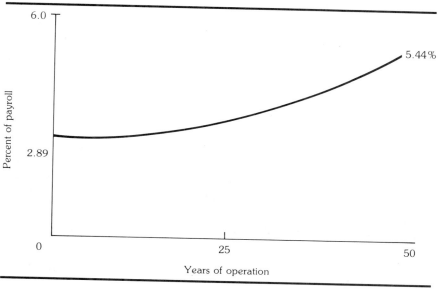

year. New entrants to replace those leaving active service were
introduced at various realistic entry ages. The average age of the
participants increased from 40.2 to 46.6 years during the period,
and the average period of service increased from 6.7 years to 13.8
years. This change in the attained age and service composition of
the plan population caused the plan normal cost to increase during
the period from 2.89 percent of covered payroll to 5.44 percent of
covered payroll, an overall rise of 88 percent. The normal cost, *as
a percentage of payroll,* was not affected by the increase in the
dollar amount of benefit accruals arising from growing salaries. The
covered payroll grew at the same rate as the benefit accruals, the
relationship remaining constant. Differing assumptions could, of
course, produce results quite different from these.

**Actuarial Liability.**   The actuarial liability in respect of a given
participant under the traditional accrued benefit cost method is at
all times precisely equal to the actuarial value of the cumulative
benefit allocated to the participant on the date of the valuation.

The process of determining the actuarial value of a participant's accumulated plan benefit is identical to that employed in the calculation of the normal cost, the only difference being the use of the *total* accumulated plan benefit, rather than the annual *increase* in the accumulated plan benefit. Thus, if only retirement benefits are considered, the basic calculation is as follows:

$$\begin{pmatrix} \text{Actuarial} \\ \text{liability} \end{pmatrix} = \begin{pmatrix} \text{Benefits} \\ \text{allocated} \\ \text{to date} \end{pmatrix} \times \begin{pmatrix} \text{Probability} \\ \text{of surviving} \\ \text{in service to} \\ \text{age 65} \end{pmatrix} \times \begin{pmatrix} \text{Interest} \\ \text{discount} \\ \text{from at-} \\ \text{tained age} \\ \text{to age 65} \end{pmatrix} \times \begin{pmatrix} \text{Annuity factor} \\ \text{at age 65 for \$1} \\ \text{per year payable} \\ \text{monthly for life} \end{pmatrix}$$

If a male participant age 40 with a salary of $20,290 at the inception of the plan described above had been credited with 10 years of service and if his past salary increases had followed the assumed rates, he would have a composite annual benefit of $1,809 beginning at age 65 standing to his credit. Each dollar of this benefit would have the same actuarial value at age 40 as a dollar of benefit accruing at that age. Thus, the actuarial liability associated with this one individual at plan inception would be:

$$\$1,809 \times .3809 \times .2330 \times \$9.268 = \$1,488$$

The actuarial liability in respect of this participant at age 41 would be $1,976. The increase of $488 would represent the combined effect of the normal cost of the benefit allocation for age 40, interest on the initial actuarial liability of $1,488 at the valuation rate, and the benefit of survivorship in service.

The computation of the actuarial liability in respect of this individual participant at quinquennial ages beginning at age 40 is shown below.

| Attained Age | Benefits Allocated | Probability of Surviving in Service to Age 65 | Interest Discount from Attained Age to Age 65 | Annuity Factor at Age 65 for $1 per Year Payable Monthly for Life | Actuarial Liability |
|---|---|---|---|---|---|
| 40 | $ 1,809 | .3809 | .2330 | $9.268 | $ 1,488 |
| 45 | 3,607 | .5248 | .3118 | 9.268 | 5,470 |
| 50 | 6,247 | .6646 | .4173 | 9.268 | 16,057 |
| 55 | 9,951 | .7910 | .5584 | 9.268 | 40,736 |
| 60 | 14,966 | .8592 | .7473 | 9.268 | 89,060 |
| 65 | 21,552 | 1.0000 | 1.0000 | 9.268 | 199,744 |

The actuarial liability for the plan as a whole is the sum of the separately computed actuarial liabilities for all the participants, including the retired and terminated vested participants. The actuarial liability for the entire plan is at all times precisely equal to the actuarial present value of all benefits actually credited to date. The traditional accrued benefit cost method is the only actuarial cost method that produces such an equality.

If the plan should terminate, or for some purpose is assumed to terminate, the benefits would be valued on the basis of the traditional accrued benefit cost method. This would be known as a *plan termination liability*. Dependent upon the purpose to be served, this type of valuation may be based upon all accrued benefits, all vested accrued benefits, or all guaranteed accrued benefits. A plan termination valuation differs from a plan continuation valuation in that, under the former, no account is taken of future decrements from disability or withdrawal, future salary increases, or future death and disability benefits that are not part of the accrued benefit payable after plan termination. In other words, a plan termination valuation assumes that benefits under the plan are fixed in amount for all time and are fully vested. The plan termination liability may be larger or smaller than the ongoing plan liability, depending upon the relative cost impact of the differences in treatment of the various cost factors.

**Supplemental Cost.** *Supplemental cost* or *amortization charge* was defined earlier as the annual cost accrual associated with amortization of the plan's supplemental cost liability. This definition needs to be refined at this point to recognize that, under some plans, the supplemental cost liability is not amortized. The objective of the plan sponsor may be limited to preventing the *unamortized* (or *unfunded*) portion of the supplemental cost liability from growing by crediting interest to it at the rate assumed in the actuarial valuation. In this situation, the interest credited to the supplemental cost liability (and paid to the plan) may be regarded as a form of supplemental cost. Counting the crediting of interest only as a method, there are three general approaches to determining the supplemental cost for a given year of pension plan operation. These approaches are applicable to the supplemental cost liability generated under any actuarial cost method and should not be uniquely associated with the traditional accrued benefit cost method.

**A. *Interest Only Supplemental Cost.*** This is the simplest method of dealing with the supplemental liability and is usually the least costly method in the early years. The aim is not to amortize (and fund) the supplemental liability but only to prevent its unfunded component from growing in dollar amount. The only pension expense recognized under this procedure is the interest credited to the account and funded. Specifically, the expense or cost is precisely equal to the original amount of supplemental liability, possibly adjusted for actuarial gains and losses, multiplied by the rate of discount used in determining the present value of plan benefits. This is known (and has been previously referred to) as the *valuation rate of interest*. Technically, this interest payment is due at the end of the plan year. If it is paid at the beginning of the plan year, the amount is discounted for one year at the valuation rate of interest.

Over time, several layers of supplemental liability may develop from retroactive benefit liberalizations, actuarial losses, and changes in actuarial assumptions, each with its own original value and its own valuation rate of interest. The various layers of supplemental liability may be dealt with differently. Some may be funded on an "interest only" basis, with some being amortized over a period of years. For example, the initial supplemental liability, created at plan inception through the granting of past service benefits, may be administered on an "interest only" basis, with all future layers of supplemental liability being amortized over a period of years.

The principal weakness of the approach is that the plan never becomes fully funded, and in the event of its termination the accrued benefits of the plan participants and their beneficiaries cannot be paid in full. To combat this weakness and to protect the plan benefits insurance program (discussed in a later chapter), ERISA prohibited the interest-only approach for pension plans subject to the minimum funding standards.[22] It can still be used by governmental plans, church plans, and other plans not subject to the funding requirements of ERISA.

**B. Level Dollar Supplemental Cost.**   A second method, the one usually used, for deriving the supplemental cost of a pension plan is to determine the level dollar amount that would have to be expensed (and presumably funded) each year to fully amortize the supplemental liability over a given number of years, recognizing that the liability is a discounted value and, hence, bears interest.

---

[22]See Chapter 17.

This is accomplished by dividing the original dollar amount of the supplemental liability by the present value at the valuation rate of interest of an annuity certain of $1 per year for the period over which the liability is to be amortized. The value of $1 per period payable for a specified number of periods without reference to death or any other contingency is an *annuity certain*.

For example, if the supplemental liability was derived in the first instance on the basis of a 6 percent interest assumption and is to be amortized in 30 equal annual installments payable at the beginning of each year, the divisor would be the present value of $1 payable immediately plus 29 subsequent annual payments of $1, all discounted to the present at a 6 percent interest rate. This value can be obtained from a conventional compound interest table that gives the present value of $1 per annum for varying periods and at varying rates of interest. The amortization process is precisely analogous to the repayment of a mortgage on a home. Each annual installment is part principal and part interest, with the interest component dominating in the early years. The proportion of the annual installment representing repayment of principal increases each year.

During a period of expanding payrolls, each level annual charge against (or contribution toward) the supplemental liability constitutes a declining percentage of covered payroll. This is graphically illustrated in Figure 4, which shows the level dollar supplemental cost as a percentage of covered payroll for the simulated pension plan used for illustrations in this text when the supplemental liability is assumed to be fully amortized over a 30-year period. (The dollar amount of the supplemental liability and the manner in which it was derived are immaterial for the purposes of this illustration.) This is the maximum amortization period permitted under ERISA for future increases in the unfunded actuarial liabilities arising from establishment or amendment of a plan or from a change in actuarial assumptions. ERISA prescribes level dollar amortization of supplemental liabilities as the minimum standard.

The dominance of the interest factor in a long-term amortization schedule is strikingly displayed in Figure 5. This figure portrays the unamortized portion of the supplemental liability of the illustrative pension plan from year to year as a percentage of the original value of the liability under a 30-year amortization schedule. The amount of amortization is modest through the first 15 years.

**FIGURE 4**
**Supplemental Cost as a Percentage of Payroll under 30-Year Level Dollar Amortization**

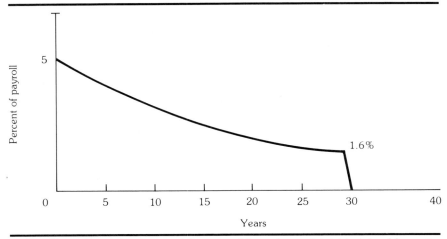

Note: These values are based upon a stationary population and a growth in total salaries of 4 percent per year.

**FIGURE 5**
**Unamortized Supplemental Liability as a Percentage of the Original Dollar Value under a 30-Year Level Dollar Amortization Schedule**

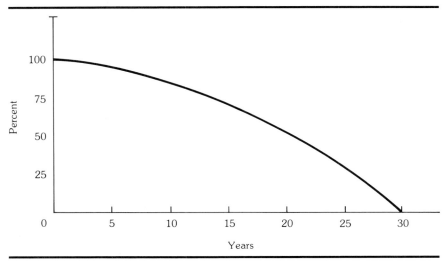

*C. Level Percentage Supplemental Cost.* A third method of deriving the supplemental cost of a pension plan is to amortize the supplemental liability over a period of years in annual installments that constitute a level percentage of the covered payroll. The procedure for determining this amount is somewhat more complicated than that involved in deriving the level dollar amount to be amortized. It is necessary to determine the present value of the future covered payroll expected to be paid during the amortization period. The future covered payroll may be projected by using an open group method that reflects new entrants, or it may merely be assumed to equal the current payroll increasing by a fixed percentage annually.

The present value of the future covered payroll for the amortization period is then divided into the supplemental liability to determine the supplemental cost as a percentage of the payroll. The percentage so derived is applied to the projected payroll for each of the years in the amortization period, to determine a fixed schedule of annual supplemental cost charges (and funding contribution) for the amortization period. The dollar amount of the annual charge will rise with the assumed increase in payroll, but the percentage charge will be level. The initially derived percentage may be applied to the *projected* payroll, rather than to the *actual* payroll that emerges in the future to assure that the scheduled dollar charges (and contributions) will actually amortize the supplemental liability over the period desired. Otherwise, if the actual payroll turned out to be smaller than the projected one, there would be a shortfall in the future charges and contributions, and the supplemental liability might never be fully amortized without an upward adjustment in the percentage charge. Contrariwise, if the actual payroll were to grow more rapidly than assumed, the supplemental liability would be amortized over a shorter period than planned, not necessarily an undesirable result.

Since the covered payroll is assumed to increase over time, the level percentage supplemental cost will be smaller than the level dollar supplemental cost during the early years of the amortization period and greater during the later years. Moreover, depending on the length of the amortization period, the assumed rate of growth in covered payroll, and the valuation rate of interest, the level percentage supplemental cost may be *less than the interest only* supplemental cost during the early (or possibly a substantial) portion of the amortization period, in which event the unfunded component of the supplemental liability would grow for a time. For this reason and others, pension plans subject to the minimum funding standards of ERISA are not permitted to use the level percentage supplemental cost method. The method continues to be used by some plans not subject to ERISA's funding standards.

Figure 6 shows the supplemental cost under the level dollar and level percentage methods for the illustrative pension plan under a 30-year amortization schedule. The two curves are actuarially equivalent but, as was pointed out earlier, amortization proceeds at a faster pace under the level dollar method during the early portion of the amortization period.

Figure 7 delineates the unamortized portion of the supplemental liability from year to year as a percentage of the original value under the level dollar and level percentage supplemental cost methods, when the amortization period is 30 years. It will be noted that with a 6 percent interest assumption, which underlies all actuarial illustrations in this text, the *unfunded* component of the supplemental liability *increases* for about 10 years under the level percentage method. In fact, the unfunded component of the

**FIGURE 6**
**Supplemental Cost as a Percentage of Payroll under 30-Year Level Dollar and Level Percentage Methods**

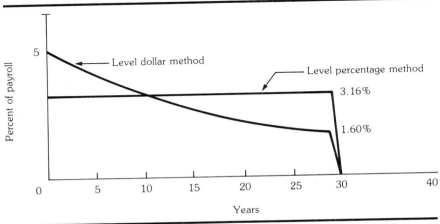

Note: These values are based upon a stationary population and a growth in total salaries of 4 percent per year.

**FIGURE 7**
**Unamortized Supplemental Liability as a Percentage of the Original Dollar Value under 30-Year Level Dollar and Level Percentage Amortization Schedules**

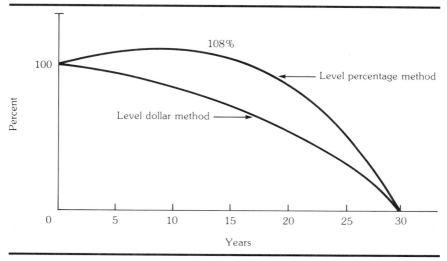

supplemental liability in the 17th year is about the same as it was in the first year. Thereafter, it declines rapidly to zero.

Even though the *dollar* value of the unamortized portion of the supplemental liability increases for a time under the level percentage method, its *relative* value declines throughout the period. That is, as a percentage of the total actuarial liability for the plan, the unamortized supplemental liability declines steadily. This may be observed in Figure 8 in respect of the actuarial liability and unamortized supplemental liability under the traditional accrued benefit cost method.

## *Projected Accrued Benefit Cost Method*

The traditional accrued benefit cost method fails to satisfy the criteria of an "ideal" actuarial cost method postulated earlier, in that (1) the normal cost of the plan is likely to rise from year to year, and (2) the actuarial liability may fall short of the plan termination liability. Both of these shortcomings are moderated by the projected accrued benefit cost method. A modification of the

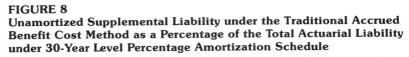

**FIGURE 8**
**Unamortized Supplemental Liability under the Traditional Accrued Benefit Cost Method as a Percentage of the Total Actuarial Liability under 30-Year Level Percentage Amortization Schedule**

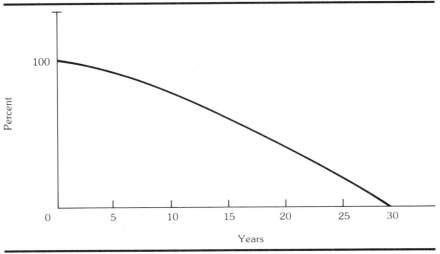

traditional accrued benefit cost method described later in this chapter *assures* that its actuarial liability will be equal to the plan termination liability.

**Normal Cost.** The normal cost under the projected accrued benefit cost method (also called the projected unit credit method), is computed by the same formula as that used for the traditional accrued benefit cost method. The only difference between the two methods is the manner in which the annual benefit accrual is determined. Under the projected accrued benefit cost method a total prospective retirement benefit is projected for each participant in the plan, a salary scale being used if the benefit is based on the participant's compensation. It is necessary to project the participant's current salary, whether the benefit is based on career average or final average salary. This is especially important if the plan is integrated with Social Security. Once the total prospective benefit has been estimated, a pro rata portion is allocated to each year of service. This is done by dividing the prospective retirement benefit by the number of years for which benefits are credited.[23]

---

[23]Treas. Reg. 1.412(c)–(e)(3).

If benefits are related to compensation, this results in a larger allocation of benefits to the earlier years of service and a smaller allocation to the later years of service than that which occurs under the traditional accrued benefit cost method. The total prospective benefit, which reflects the effect of rising earnings from merit, inflation, and real wage gains, is simply leveled out over the participant's entire period of credited service. If benefits under the plan do not accrue uniformly, as when the benefit formula applicable to years of prior service is less than that for future service, the allocation of the projected benefits must be adjusted to reflect the difference.

The benefit allocations that occur under the previously illustrated hypothetical pension plan at selected ages and the manner in which their normal cost is derived are shown in Table 7. With a salary of $15,870 at age 30 and an annual growth rate of approximately 5 percent, a benefit of 1 percent of the participant's average salary during the last 5 years of service for each of the 35 years of service would add up to a total annual benefit of $31,903. This amount divided by 35 produces a benefit allocation of $912 to each year of credited service. The actuarial values in columns (3), (4), and (5) are identical to those in Table 6. The normal cost of the benefit allocated to any of the attained ages is obtained by multiplying the benefit times the values in columns (3), (4), and (5). Thus, the normal cost associated with the benefit allocation at attained age 30 is $912 × .1416 × .1301 × 9.268 = $156.

It will be noted that the normal cost rises from $156 at age 30 to $5,427 at age 60, compared to $28 and $10,420, respectively,

**TABLE 7**
**Calculation of the Normal Cost for an Individual Male Participant at Various Attained Ages under the Projected Accrued Benefit Cost Method**

| (1) Attained Age | (2) Benefits Allocated to Attained Age | (3) Probability of Surviving in Service to Age 65 | (4) Interest Discount from Attained Age to Age 65 | (5) Annuity Factor at Age 65 for $1 per Year Payable Monthly for Life | (6) Normal Cost |
|---|---|---|---|---|---|
| 30 | $912 | .1416 | .1301 | $9.268 | $ 156 |
| 40 | 912 | .3809 | .2330 | 9.268 | 750 |
| 50 | 912 | .6646 | .4173 | 9.268 | 2,344 |
| 60 | 912 | .8592 | .7473 | 9.268 | 5,427 |

under the traditional accrued benefit cost method. The moderation of the cost incline produced by the projected accrued benefit cost method is graphically depicted in Figure 9. The figure shows the normal cost as a percentage of salary under both the projected accrued benefit cost method and the traditional accrued benefit cost method. The normal cost, as a percentage of salary, starts at 0.98 percent and rises to 8.08 percent at age 64, the comparable percentages for the traditional method being 0.18 and 19.10 percent, respectively.

A more meaningful measure of the cost characteristics of the projected accrued benefit cost method is the normal cost curve for an entire plan over a period of years. Figure 10 presents such a 50-year curve based upon the same hypothetical pension plan and actuarial assumptions as those underlying Figure 3. For purposes of comparison, the normal cost pattern for the traditional method is juxtaposed with the projected accrued benefit cost method curve. It will be noted that the projected accrued benefit cost method normal cost curve is flatter than that of the traditional method, rising from 3.24 percent of covered payroll to 4.27 percent over the 50-year period.

**FIGURE 9**
**Normal Cost as a Percentage of the Salary of a Male Participant Entering the Plan at Age 30 under the Two Accrued Benefit Cost Methods**

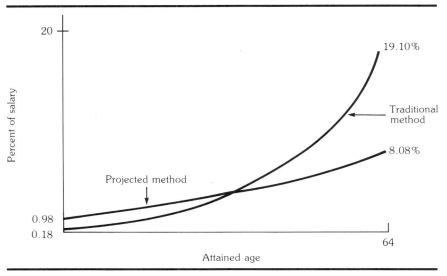

**FIGURE 10**
**Normal Cost as a Percentage of Payroll of a Hypothetical Pension Plan over a 50-Year Period under the Two Accrued Benefit Cost Methods**

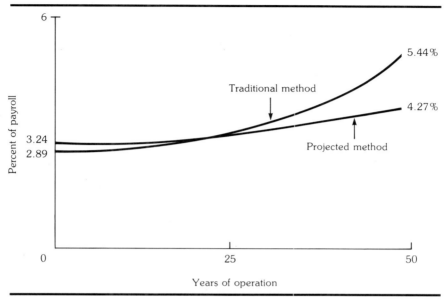

**Actuarial Liability.** Like the normal cost, the actuarial liability under the projected accrued benefit cost method is calculated in precisely the same manner as under the traditional method, except for the determination of the benefits allocated to date of valuation. The benefit allocated to date under the projected accrued benefit cost method in respect of an individual participant, when early retirement and ancillary benefits are ignored, is determined as follows:

$$
\begin{matrix} \text{Benefit} \\ \text{allocated} \\ \text{to date} \end{matrix} = \begin{pmatrix} \text{Projected} \\ \text{benefit at} \\ \text{retirement} \end{pmatrix} \times \begin{pmatrix} \text{Years of service to date} \\ \text{Potential years of service} \\ \text{from entry age to normal} \\ \text{retirement age} \end{pmatrix}
$$

To use the example of the male participant who entered the plan at age 30 and expects a retirement benefit of $31,903 per year at age 65, the benefit allocated up to his age 40 would be:

$$
\$31,903 \times \frac{10}{35} = \$9,115
$$

The actuarial liability in respect of this illustrative participant at his attained age 40 would be:

$$\$9,115 \times .3809 \times .2330 \times 9.268 = \$7,497$$

This is a larger actuarial liability than would have been developed under the traditional accrued benefit cost method, since a greater cumulative benefit had been allocated to the participant's first 10 years of service.

In the following year's actuarial valuation the projected benefit for this participant would be recalculated based upon his then current salary rate and the salary scale, and the portion of the projected benefit based upon service to this new valuation date would be determined as in the prior year. To whatever extent this new cumulative benefit differs from the sum of the cumulative benefit calculated the prior year plus the benefit allocated for the intervening year, an actuarial gain or loss will result.

### Projected Accrued Benefit Cost Method with Level Percentage Allocation

The total prospective benefit can be allocated to a participant's year of service in dollar amounts that represent a level percentage of the participant's pay in the year in which the benefit allocation is made, rather than in level dollar amounts as described above. This approach has strong theoretical justification, being based on the concept that a participant's annual benefit accruals should reflect his current economic worth to the employer. If it is assumed that the cash compensation of an employee is a rough measure of his worth to the firm, then it may be argued that his annual benefit accrual should bear a constant relationship to his current compensation.[24] A unit of benefit that constitutes a level percentage of the participant's current cash compensation meets this test.

Since an employee's cash compensation usually increases each year, this method of benefit allocation would produce annual benefit accruals that increase in *dollar* amount from year to year, or, at least, periodically. If an employer's funding contributions should

---

[24]This rationale and a set of cost accounting principles based on it were developed by Hall and Landsittel in *A New Look at Accounting for Pension Costs* (Homewood, Ill.: Richard D. Irwin, 1977). See especially pp. 47–48.

follow the pattern of benefit allocations, the rate of funding would be slower than that which occurs under any of the cost methods approved for final pay plans. Believing that the method would produce an unacceptably slow rate of funding, the IRS has prohibited the method for funding purposes. Moreover, in developing Statement 87, the Financial Accounting Standards Board rejected the method, despite its theoretical underpinning, in favor of the more pragmatic method that allocates the total prospective benefit in level *dollar* amounts. In view of the fact that the method is not currently being used for any purpose, its manner of generating the normal cost and actuarial liability of a pension plan will not be described herein.[25]

## Plan Termination Cost Method

In some instances, it is appropriate and meaningful to compare the actuarial liability under any actuarial cost method calculated on a plan continuation basis with the liability that would exist if the plan should be terminated on the valuation date. The two sets of values will be different. As was pointed out earlier, a plan termination valuation omits salary projections, withdrawal assumptions, and ancillary benefits that would not be paid in the event of a plan termination. Whether a plan termination liability will be larger or smaller than a plan continuation liability depends upon the interaction of several opposing cost factors. There is a greater probability that the plan continuation liability will be less than the plan termination liability under a benefit allocation cost method than under a cost allocation cost method, since the latter, to produce level annual costs, *implicitly* allocates larger benefit accruals to service to date than a benefit allocation cost method. Since the smallest cumulative benefit allocations are made under the traditional accrued benefit cost method, this method has the greatest probability of producing an ongoing plan liability smaller than the plan termination liability.

This undesirable result can be avoided by defining the normal cost in terms of the progression of year-to-year values of the actuarial liability determined on a plan termination basis. This mod-

---

[25]The method is described in detail on pp. 291–96 of the Fifth Edition of this text.

ification of the traditional accrued benefit cost method is called the "plan termination cost method."[26] The plan termination cost method definition of normal cost is in contrast to all other cost methods, where the normal cost is an independent quantity derived by applying appropriate actuarial present values to an assumed pattern of benefit allocations. The normal cost at any age under the plan termination cost method is the liability for accrued benefits at the next higher age less the actuarial accumulation of the current year's liability for accrued benefits to the next year. If there are no gains and losses, this formulation is equally applicable to an individual participant and the plan as a whole.

In effect, the normal cost for the plan or an individual participant in any given year is the actuarial value of the benefits accruing in that year plus the increase in the actuarial value of all previously accrued benefits attributable to a rise in the salary base—all actuarial values ignoring future withdrawals and ancillary benefits that would not be paid in the event of a plan termination. The updating of previous benefit accruals occurs only when the plan uses a final average benefit formula. If the plan provides benefits on the bases of the average salary during the last five years preceding retirement, the plan-termination cost method calculates the accrued benefits of each participant annually on the basis of his average salary for the preceding five years.

## Questions

1. Define each of the following terms encountered in the valuation of a pension plan:
   a. Actuarial cost method.
   b. Normal cost.
   c. Supplemental cost.
   d. Actuarial liability.
   e. Supplemental cost liability.

---

[26]First developed in Dan M. McGill and Howard E. Winklevoss, "A Quantitative Analysis of Actuarial Cost Methods for Pension Plans," *Proceedings of the Conference of Actuaries in Public Practice* 23 (1974). This is not one of the six methods listed in ERISA §3(31) as acceptable for minimum funding requirements.

2.   Identify the various occurrences that give rise to supplemental cost liability under a pension plan.

3.   Identify the various cost factors that enter into a computation of experience actuarial gains and losses and, with respect to each factor, indicate the direction or nature of the deviation of actual from assumed experience that would give rise to an *actuarial gain*.

4.   Distinguish between the *direct* and *spread* methods of determining actuarial gains and losses.

5.   Explain why none of the generally recognized actuarial cost methods can satisfy all of the criteria of an "ideal" cost method.

6.   Identify and briefly explain each of the elements involved in a complete description of a particular actuarial cost method. In other words, what are the characteristics of the method that must be known before a full identification can be made?

7.   Contrast the procedures involved in determining the unit of benefit allocated to a particular year of service under the three *benefit allocation* cost methods.

8.   Under the benefit allocation cost methods, in what respect or respects does the derivation of the actuarial liability differ from the derivation of the normal cost?

9.   Describe the three basic procedures for computing the supplemental cost of a pension plan.

10.  What change in the procedure for determining the normal cost of a pension plan under the projected accrued benefit cost method would have to be made to eliminate a supplemental liability when there are past service or other retroactively granted benefits? What effect would such a modification have on the ability of the method to satisfy the criteria of an "ideal" actuarial cost method?

11.  The cumulative retirement benefit payable at age 65 of a male participant now age 37 for all years of credited service is $3,000 per year as of his current year of service. The comparable benefit for his five immediately preceding years of service was $2,500, $2,150, $1,825, $1,400, and $1,150, respectively. Using the appropriate actuarial functions and values set out in Appendix B, compute the (*a*) normal cost, and (*b*) actuarial liability in respect of this participant for the current year under the traditional accrued benefit cost.

12.  A male participant now age 48 entered the plan at age 26. His projected benefit at age 65 is $20,800. Using the appropriate actuarial functions and values set out in Appendix B, compute (*a*) the normal cost, and (*b*) the actuarial liability in respect of this participant under projected accrued benefit cost method.

13.  Assume that a pension plan has an initial supplemental liability of $5 million and the plan sponsor wishes to amortize it in 30 equal installments payable at the beginning of each year. Using the appropriate values from Appendix B, indicate the annual supplemental cost that would emerge from this amortization schedule.

14.  What would be the supplemental cost for the first year of the plan's operation if the $5 million initial supplemental liability were to be amortized in 30 annual installments of such size that they constitute a level percentage of covered payroll: Assume that the annual covered payroll at the inception of the plan is $8 million and that it will increase 4 percent per year.

# 14 | Cost Allocation Actuarial Cost Methods

COST ALLOCATION ACTUARIAL COST METHODS are built around a completely different principle than benefit allocation methods. Through the use of salary projections (if the benefits are salary-related), the participant's total prospective benefit at retirement is estimated, the actuarial present value of that benefit at the participant's entry age or attained age (depending upon the method) is determined, and this value (or cost) is allocated to each year of the participant's total prospective service (from entry age or attained age) in an amount that is constant in dollars or a constant percentage of the participant's estimated salary from year to year. Costs are generally allocated as a percentage of salary when a salary projection scale has been used to project plan benefits. Under all other circumstances, costs are typically allocated in level dollar amounts.

The cost may be computed in respect of the individual participants and summed to obtain the normal cost and actuarial liability for the plan as a whole, in which event the cost method is referred to as an *individual* method. Or the cost may be computed directly for the entire plan without attribution on any theoretically precise basis to the individual participants, in which event the approach is called an *aggregate* method. Finally, under both the individual and aggregate approaches, there are methods that develop a sup-

301

plemental liability and those that do not. Thus, a full identification of these methods must indicate whether they are *with supplemental liability* or *without supplemental liability.*

## Individual Cost Allocation Methods

### Level Dollar Cost Method

The individual level dollar cost methods are typically used for a pension plan that provides a flat dollar benefit for each year of service. It is not considered appropriate for a plan that provides benefits on the basis of final average salary. As before, a distinction must be made between the derivation of the normal cost and the actuarial liability. The procedure for calculating the normal cost determines whether or not there will be a supplemental liability.

**Normal Cost.**   Four steps are involved in the derivation of the normal cost for retirement benefits under the individual level dollar cost methods. The first is to estimate the participant's total prospective benefit at retirement. This is done in exactly the same way as it is under the projected accrued benefit cost method, salary projections being used if the benefit is salary related. The second step is to determine the actuarial present value of the total prospective benefit of the participant. If the individual entered the service of the plan sponsor after the plan had been established, this present value calculation would be made as of the individual's entry age (which in the first year would, of course, also be his attained age). If the plan has just been established and this is the first valuation, or if a newly created set of retroactive benefits is being valued for the first time, a decision must be made as to whether a supplemental liability is to be generated. If so, the actuarial present value calculation will be as of the employee's entry age into the plan (in a newly established plan, the age from which past service benefits are credited), the method being called the *entry age normal cost method.* If not, the calculation will be as of the participant's attained age, the method being called the *individual level premium cost method.*[1]

---

[1] The individual level premium cost method is called the *individual level actuarial cost method* by the Joint Committee.

The verbal formula for the second step of the entry age calculation is as follows:

$$
\begin{array}{c}
\text{(1)}\\
\begin{pmatrix}
\text{Actuarial}\\
\text{present}\\
\text{value of}\\
\text{projected}\\
\text{benefit at}\\
\text{participant's}\\
\text{entry age}
\end{pmatrix}
\end{array}
=
\begin{array}{c}
\text{(2)}\\
\begin{pmatrix}
\text{Projected}\\
\text{annual}\\
\text{benefit at}\\
\text{age 65}
\end{pmatrix}
\end{array}
\times
\begin{array}{c}
\text{(3)}\\
\begin{pmatrix}
\text{Probability}\\
\text{of surviving}\\
\text{in service}\\
\text{from entry}\\
\text{age to age}\\
65
\end{pmatrix}
\end{array}
\times
\begin{array}{c}
\text{(4)}\\
\begin{pmatrix}
\text{Interest}\\
\text{discount}\\
\text{from}\\
\text{entry}\\
\text{age to}\\
\text{age 65}
\end{pmatrix}
\end{array}
\times
\begin{array}{c}
\text{(5)}\\
\begin{pmatrix}
\text{Annuity}\\
\text{factor at}\\
\text{age 65}\\
\text{for \$1}\\
\text{per year}\\
\text{payable}\\
\text{monthly}\\
\text{for life}
\end{pmatrix}
\end{array}
$$

This is the same formula as that used to compute the normal cost under the benefit allocation cost methods, except that here the total projected benefit is inserted in column (2) and the values in columns (3) and (4) are computed as of the participant's entry age, rather than his attained age. It should be noted that the actuarial present value of the participant's projected benefit is frequently referred to as the "present value of future benefits" and abbreviated as PVFB. The expression generally comprehends all benefits to which the participant or his beneficiary might become entitled, rather than just the retirement benefit.

The same formula is used for an attained age valuation of the projected benefit, except that the values in columns (1), (3), and (4) reflect the participant's attained age at plan inception or amendment.

The third step in the normal cost calculation is to determine the actuarial present value of a *temporary employment based life annuity* of $1 per year payable from the participant's entry age or attained age. This is an annuity assumed to be paid at the beginning of each year that the participant is alive and still in the service of the plan sponsor. Its present value reflects the probability (involving life contingencies and withdrawal rates)[2] that the participant will survive in service from year to year all the way to retirement, with the annual probabilities being discounted back to the participant's entry or attained age at the valuation rate of interest. Again, the choice of entry age or attained age depends upon whether a supplemental liability is desired.

---

[2]In the valuation of smaller plans, the actuary may use only the mortality decrement and discount factor because of the unpredictability of withdrawals. If the plan is very small (e.g., less than 10 participants), even the mortality decrement may be omitted.

Finally, as a fourth step, the actuarial present value of the projected benefit (PVFB) is divided by the value of the temporary employment based life annuity of $1 per year. This is a matter of simple proportion. If the value of $1 per year payable as long as the participant is in service is known, then the number of dollars that would have to be paid in that manner to have a present value equal to another previously determined quantity, the PVFB, is obtained by dividing the unit value of the temporary employment based life annuity into the PVFB. The result is the normal cost for the participant in question. It is assumed to remain fixed and level to the participant's normal retirement age, but it may be recomputed from time to time to reflect changing circumstances.

The process by which the normal cost is computed under the individual level dollar cost methods can be illustrated in terms of a male participant in the hypothetical pension plan postulated earlier, with a current salary of $20,290, whose attained age is 40 but who has 10 years of credited past service, giving him an entry age of 30. It is assumed that the plan has just been established and that this is the initial valuation. The first example calculates the individual level premium cost method normal cost as a level dollar cost from *attained age* to retirement age.

**A. Attained Age Calculation.** The projected benefit of the participant at retirement is $21,552. Each dollar of projected retirement benefit has an actuarial present value of $0.823 at the participant's *attained age 40,* the product of columns (3), (4), and (5) of the formulation set out below.[3] Thus, the actuarial present value, or PVFB, of the total benefit is $21,552 × $0.823 = $17,737. The actuarial values and process employed in arriving at this PVFB are as follows:

| (1) | | (2) | | (3) | | (4) | | (5) |
|---|---|---|---|---|---|---|---|---|
| PVFB at participant's attained age | = | $\begin{pmatrix} \text{Projected} \\ \text{annual} \\ \text{benefit at} \\ \text{age 65} \end{pmatrix}$ | × | $\begin{pmatrix} \text{Probability} \\ \text{of surviving} \\ \text{in service} \\ \text{from} \\ \text{attained age} \\ \text{to age 65} \end{pmatrix}$ | × | $\begin{pmatrix} \text{Interest} \\ \text{discount} \\ \text{from} \\ \text{attained} \\ \text{age to} \\ \text{age 65} \end{pmatrix}$ | × | $\begin{pmatrix} \text{Annuity} \\ \text{factor at} \\ \text{age 65} \\ \text{for \$1} \\ \text{per year} \\ \text{payable} \\ \text{monthly} \\ \text{for life} \end{pmatrix}$ |

---

[3]Figures in this chapter may not total due to rounding.

$$\$17,737 = \$21,552 \times .3809 \times .2330 \times \$9.268$$

Note that the values shown in columns (3) and (4) are *attained age* values.

The actuarial present value at male age 40 of a temporary employment based life annuity of $1 per year, under the actuarial assumptions used for the hypothetical plan, is $8.954. Thus the

$$\text{Normal cost} = \begin{pmatrix} \text{Attained} \\ \text{age} \\ \text{PVFB} \end{pmatrix} \div \begin{pmatrix} \text{Temporary employment} \\ \text{based life annuity of \$1 per} \\ \text{year from age 40 to age 65} \end{pmatrix}$$

$$\$1,981 = \$17,737 \div \$8.954$$

As before, the normal cost for the plan is the sum of the normal cost values calculated for each of the participants.

There is no supplemental liability under this attained age derivation of costs, since all prospective benefits are taken into account and, at the establishment or amendment of the plan, the actuarial present value of future benefits is offset fully and precisely by the actuarial present value of future cost accruals. Neither is there any *initial* actuarial liability, for the same reason. After the first year of the plan's operation, there is an actuarial liability which, retrospectively, is the actuarial accumulation of past annual cost accruals less benefit disbursements and which, prospectively, is the actuarial present value of total prospective benefits (the PVFB for the plan) less the present value of future cost accruals.

The normal cost under this method is not solely attributable to benefit accruals after the attained age, since it includes a component for the amortization of past service benefit costs which under certain other actuarial cost methods would be separately identified as a supplemental cost. Over time, the proportion of the annual cost attributable to past service will decrease under the individual level premium cost method, since for new entrants the annual level cost is determined on an entry age basis. As will be illustrated later, the annual cost under the individual level premium cost method, in the absence of retroactive benefit liberalizations, will merge into the entry age normal cost, and thereafter be identical to it, after the youngest participant with past service or other retroactive benefit credits has retired. In this sense, the individual level premium cost method is a transitional cost method. The long-run or ultimate level dollar cost method normal cost is that derived on an entry age basis.

Because the level-dollar-cost-method normal cost is computed as a level annual dollar cost, it is larger than the normal cost developed under benefit allocation cost methods during the early years of a participant's service. If there are past service or other retroactive benefit credits, however, the actuarial liability under the individual level premium cost method may be less than the plan termination liability for all benefits accrued under the terms of the plan. This is so, since the *implicit* supplemental liability created by the past service or retroactive benefit credits under this method is not fully amortized until the participant reaches normal retirement age. There is little accounting or fiscal flexibility under this method, since there is no *explicit* and *separately amortized* supplemental liability. The only element of flexibility is found in the treatment of actuarial gains and losses, which may be recognized immediately or spread over a period of years.

The individual level premium cost method is sometimes used in combination with the traditional accrued benefit cost method to provide a supplemental liability and, hence, more flexibility. Under this combination approach, the initial actuarial liability (and supplemental liability) is determined under the traditional accrued benefit cost method. Similarly, any increase in actuarial liability arising out of subsequent benefit improvements is determined under the traditional accrued benefit cost method. Then, the excess of the PVFB over this supplemental liability is amortized in equal annual accruals (constant dollar amount or level percentage of pay) over the participant's future service lifetime, as determined by the individual level premium cost method. This combination is sometimes referred to as the *attained age normal cost method*,[4] a term also used, confusingly enough, for a similar approach utilizing an *aggregate* method.

*B. Entry Age Calculation.*    The individual entry age normal cost calculation differs from the attained age calculation only in the use of the participant's entry age in computing the PVFB and the actuarial present value of a temporary employment-based life annuity of $1 per year. The projected benefit for the illustrative male participant age 40 with 10 years of past service is still $21,552, and the actuarial present value at age 65 of each $1 of benefit is still

---

[4]ERISA §3(31).

$9.268. However, since the intent of the calculation is to determine what would have been the normal cost of the participant's accruing benefits had the plan been in operation at the beginning of his credited service and the normal cost recognized each year thereafter, it is necessary to ascertain the actuarial present value of the participant's total projected benefit, or PVFB, as of the participant's theoretical age of entry into the plan. Moreover, since the objective is to amortize the entry age PVFB in level annual dollar amounts over the participant's total years of credited service, it is necessary to compute the value of a temporary employment-based life annuity of $1 per year payable from the participant's earliest date of credited service and divide that sum into the PVFB.

The actuarial values that would be used in this illustrative entry age computation are as follows:

| (1) | | (2) | | (3) | | (4) | | (5) |
|---|---|---|---|---|---|---|---|---|
| PVFB at participant's entry age | = | $\begin{pmatrix} \text{Pro-} \\ \text{jected} \\ \text{annual} \\ \text{benefit} \\ \text{at age 65} \end{pmatrix}$ | × | $\begin{pmatrix} \text{Probability} \\ \text{of surviving} \\ \text{in service} \\ \text{from entry} \\ \text{age to age} \\ \text{65} \end{pmatrix}$ | × | $\begin{pmatrix} \text{Interest} \\ \text{discount} \\ \text{from} \\ \text{entry} \\ \text{age to} \\ \text{age 65} \end{pmatrix}$ | × | $\begin{pmatrix} \text{Annuity} \\ \text{factor at} \\ \text{age 65} \\ \text{for \$1} \\ \text{per year} \\ \text{payable} \\ \text{monthly} \\ \text{for life} \end{pmatrix}$ |

$$\$3{,}680 = \$21{,}552 \times .1416 \times .1301 \times \$9.268$$

The entry age PVFB is smaller than the attained age PVFB, since the probability of the participant's surviving in service to normal retirement age is lower at age 30 than at age 40, and the period over which the prospective benefit is discounted is 10 years longer. The entry age temporary employment-based life annuity of $1 per year, $7.059, is also smaller than its attained age counterpart, despite the fact that the annual payments are assumed to continue over a period 10 years longer than that under the attained age calculation.[5] The net result is still a smaller normal cost than the attained age normal cost, as may be observed:

---

[5]This anomaly results from the relatively high termination rates at ages 30 to 40. This is not an unusual phenomenon at the lower ages, especially when select termination rates are assumed.

$$\text{Normal cost} \ = \ \left(\begin{array}{c}\text{Entry age}\\ \text{PVFB}\end{array}\right) \ \div \ \left(\begin{array}{c}\text{Temporary employment-based}\\ \text{life annuity of \$1 per year}\\ \text{from age 30 to age 65}\end{array}\right)$$

$$\$521 \ = \ \$3,680 \ \div \ \$7.059$$

The lower annual cost accruals under this method are due solely to the fact that the total projected cost is spread over a longer period of years, resulting in more accruals, more interest credits, and greater benefit of survivorship in service. Another way to view the matter is that the individual level premium cost method includes in each annual cost accrual a pro rata portion of the cost that is treated as a supplemental cost under the entry age normal cost method.

**Actuarial Liability.**    The actuarial liability under the individual level dollar cost methods can be determined retrospectively or prospectively. Retrospectively, the actuarial liability *for the plan as a whole* is the sum of all normal cost accruals to date plus interest at the valuation rate of interest and less all benefit disbursements, the total being adjusted for actuarial gains and losses. *For an individual participant* still in the active service of the plan sponsor, the retrospective actuarial liability is the sum of normal cost accruals to date plus interest at the valuation rate of interest and the benefit of survivorship in service. The latter increment is the participant's pro rata share of the cumulative normal cost accruals "forfeited" by those participants who entered the plan at the same age and in the same year as the participant but who died or terminated with nonvested benefits prior to the valuation date. For the plan as a whole and the individual participants, the normal costs that are accumulated are those that *should have accrued* based upon circumstances existing at the date of valuation and not necessarily those that were initially computed. In other words, if in the interim there has been a change in benefits, actuarial assumptions, or actuarial cost methods, the actuary constructs a new schedule of normal costs from the participants' various entry ages, and these revised normal costs are accumulated to determine the retrospective actuarial liability. For all cost and liability illustrations in this book, it is assumed that the original cost calculations remain valid.

It can be demonstrated mathematically and logically that the actuarial present value of a participant's total prospective benefit at any date is equal to the actuarial value of his normal cost accruals to date plus the actuarial value of the normal cost accruals that will be allocated to future years of service. This is so because the normal cost allocations must add up to the total cost of the projected benefits. This is true for the plan as well as the individual participant. This relationship is shown below:

$$
\underbrace{\begin{array}{l}\text{Actuarial value of}\\\text{projected benefits}\\\text{(PVFB)}\end{array}}_{(1)} = \underbrace{\left(\begin{array}{l}\text{Actuarial value}\\\text{of normal costs}\\\text{allocated to date}\\\text{(actuarial liability)}\end{array}\right)}_{(2)} + \underbrace{\left(\begin{array}{l}\text{Actuarial value}\\\text{of future normal}\\\text{cost accruals}\end{array}\right)}_{(3)}
$$

If the dollar value of items (1) and (3) is known, then the dollar value of item (2) can be easily derived. Transposing items, the following relationship is obtained:

$$
\begin{array}{l}\text{Actuarial value of normal}\\\text{costs allocated to date}\\\text{(actuarial liability)}\end{array} = \left(\begin{array}{l}\text{Actuarial present}\\\text{value of projected}\\\text{benefits (PVFB)}\end{array}\right) - \left(\begin{array}{l}\text{Actuarial value}\\\text{of future normal}\\\text{cost accruals}\end{array}\right)
$$

This happens to be the verbal formulation of the prospective approach to the valuation of a pension plan. The formula is usually shortened to read as follows:

$$
\text{Actuarial liability} = \left(\begin{array}{l}\text{Present value of}\\\text{future benefits}\\\text{(PVFB)}\end{array}\right) - \left(\begin{array}{l}\text{Present value of}\\\text{future normal}\\\text{costs}\end{array}\right)
$$

In this formulation, future benefits include benefits credited for service to date, benefits to be credited for future service, benefits of terminated vested participants, and benefits payable to retired participants. If the valuation is for the plan as a whole it will also include, if appropriate, benefits payable to disabled participants and beneficiaries of deceased participants. Because of computational advantages, the prospective valuation formula is generally used.

**A. Attained Age Calculation.** Under the individual level premium cost method, the present value of future normal cost accruals at the inception of the plan is precisely equivalent to the present value of future benefits; hence, there is no actuarial liability at that point. For the same reason there is no supplemental liability. The actuarial present value of future benefits at age 40 for a male participant entering the plan at age 30 is $21,552 × $0.823 = $17,737. The normal or annual cost for such a participant is $1,981. The present value of a temporary employment-based life annuity of $1 per year is $8.954. The actuarial liability in respect of the illustrative participant is:

$$(\$21,552 \times \$0.823) - (\$1,981 \times \$8.954) = 0$$

There will be an actuarial liability at the end of the first year, representing for the male participant now age 41 the normal cost for the year, plus interest and the benefit of survivorship in service. At the participant's age 41, the PVFB has moved up to $20,173 ($21,552 × $0.936), the temporary employment-based life annuity has increased to $9.053, and the normal cost remains at $1,981. The actuarial liability thus becomes:

$$(\$21,552 \times \$0.936) - (\$1,981 \times \$9.053) = \$2,239$$

The actuarial liability for the individual participant and the plan as a whole increases from year to year, not only because of additional normal cost accruals but because the group of participants moves ever closer to the normal retirement age. This upward movement in attained ages increases the probability of surviving in service to retirement and shortens the period over which future benefit payments are discounted at compound interest.

On the other hand, no supplemental liability ever arises under the individual level premium cost method, since the costs associated with retroactive benefit increases, changes in actuarial assumptions, and so forth continue to be amortized on an attained age basis. The actuarial present value of the benefit changes will be exactly offset by the present value of the future normal costs associated with those changes.

*B. Entry Age Calculation.*   The situation is different whenever the normal cost accruals are computed on the assumption that the accruals were initiated prior to the establishment or amendment of the plan, as is the assumption under the entry age normal cost method. In the example of the male participant age 40 at the inception of the plan, with 10 years of credited past service and a total projected benefit of $21,552 per year, the PVFB at plan inception is $21,552 × $0.823 = $17,737. The present value of future normal cost accruals is $521 × $8.954, or $4,665, with $521 representing the annual cost accrual and $8.954 the present value of each dollar of cost charges to be made between that date and the participant's normal retirement age. The difference, $13,072, is the initial actuarial liability (and supplemental liability) attributable to this one participant. In terms of the formula, this would appear as follows:

$$(\$21,552 \times \$0.823) - (\$521 \times \$8.954) = \$13,072$$

It must be apparent that the initial actuarial liability (and supplemental liability) is derived by using in the formula the annual cost accrual for age 30, rather than the one for age 40. All other figures in the two equations (one for the attained age individual level premium cost method and one for the entry age normal cost method) remain the same.

Retrospectively, the initial actuarial liability in this particular case is the sum of the annual cost accruals of $521 for the 10-year period of credited past service, improved at 6 percent interest and with the benefit of survivorship in service. There is a theoretical presumption that these cost accruals were actually made, but it is clearly a presumption contrary to fact. No cost accruals could have been made prior to the establishment of the plan, although some provision with respect to the supplemental liability may be made at date of plan inception.

Both the actuarial liability and the supplemental liability in respect of the participant in question will increase from year to year. Ten years after establishment of the plan, the actuarial liability for the individual, then age 50, would be:

$$(\$21,552 \times \$2.570) - (\$521 \times \$8.750) = \$50,830$$

The projected benefit and the normal cost accrual would remain the same, the present value of each dollar of benefit would be larger (since retirement is closer), and the present value of the employment-based temporary life annuity due of $1 would be smaller (since fewer payments remain). The result is an actuarial liability $37,758 greater than at the inception of the plan. In the meantime, the supplemental liability would have increased by $27,774, as a result of interest and the benefit of survivorship in service.

The nature of the initial actuarial liability (and supplemental liability) under the entry age normal cost method can perhaps be more fully grasped by comparing it with the initial actuarial liability (and supplemental liability) under the traditional accrued benefit cost method. In the discussion of the latter method, it was pointed out that the initial actuarial liability at plan inception for a male participant age 40 with cumulative benefit credits of $1,809 per year payable monthly at age 65 is $1,488. It was further pointed out that this sum represents the present value at age 40 of a projected benefit of $1,809 per year—the precise amount of benefits credited under the plan for 10 years of service prior to establishment of the plan. In contrast, the initial actuarial liability for the same participant under the entry age normal cost method is $13,072. Thus, it is larger than the value of the benefits attributable to service prior to inception of the plan. The explanation of this difference lies in the leveling of cost accruals under the entry age normal cost method. Since for any particular individual, the cost of each $1 of benefits at age 65 (or any other designated age) goes up with each increase in age, the level costs are more than the cost of benefits accruing in the earlier years and less than the cost of benefits accruing in the later years. Hence, the costs allocated to past service benefits are always greater than the present value of past service benefits at the effective date of the plan. Since retrospectively, the initial actuarial liability (and supplemental liability) is merely the sum of the normal cost accruals for the years of credited past service, plus interest and the benefit of survivorship in service, it follows that the entry age normal cost method will produce a larger initial actuarial liability (and supplemental liability), other things being equal, than the traditional accrued benefit cost method.

The initial actuarial liability (and supplemental liability) for the entire plan is the sum of such liability attributable to each of the participants in the plan. Yet the liability need not be computed in terms of the specific periods of service of such individuals. Rather than compute the annual cost accrual from a participant's earliest date of credited service, some actuaries use an arbitrary age at which the participant is assumed to have entered the plan. For example, the cost calculations may be based on the assumption that all individuals enter the plan at age 28. If this assumption had been made in the case of the hypothetical male age 40 with 10 years of actual credited service, the costs would have been leveled from age 28, producing a lower normal cost and a larger initial actuarial liability. In lieu of *one* assumed entry age, the actuary may use an assumed entry age for each quinquennial grouping of ages. Thus, all individuals entering the plan at ages 25 to 29 may be assumed to have entered at 27. The assumed entry age or ages may be based on the observed or anticipated experience of the group—or may be rather arbitrary in nature, particularly if the group is small. However, the assumption about the entry age or ages must be reasonable and, in combination with other assumptions, must represent the actuary's best estimate of future experience. Such uses of an assumed entry age were developed to reduce the computational burden before modern computers, and are still used by some actuaries.

The use of assumed or average entry ages will produce a supplemental liability for individuals entering the plan after its establishment at ages above the assumed entry age. Hence, the concept of a supplemental liability should not be associated exclusively with the process of establishing a plan. Individuals entering the plan at ages lower than the assumed entry age bring with them a *negative* actuarial liability, offsetting the positive actuarial liability of those entering at higher ages.

A supplemental liability may also arise out of: a retroactive increase in benefits (identical in principle to granting past service credits at plan inception); a class of benefits, such as disability benefits or a minimum retirement benefit, not envisioned or properly provided for by the normal cost accruals; an unfavorable deviation of actual from expected experience not offset by an increase in the normal cost accruals; a change in actuarial assumptions; or a change in the method by which costs are computed.

Unless modified by actuarial gains and losses, a given layer of supplemental liability increases each year by an amount equal to the assumed rate of interest, reduced by expected benefit payments. For the entire group of participants whose benefit accruals give rise to the supplemental liability, the probability of survival in service has already been discounted. Thus, the aggregate value of the supplemental liability does not increase because of the benefit of survivorship in service if the actuarial assumptions are realized.

## Level Percentage Cost Methods

The individual level *percentage* cost methods differ from the individual level *dollar* cost methods only in that the normal cost is defined (and derived) as a level percentage of salary (or payroll), rather than as a level dollar amount. It is suitable only for plans that express the benefit as a percentage of salary. In contrast, the level dollar cost methods are used mainly for plans that express the benefit as a flat dollar amount for each year of credited service.

The level percentage cost methods can function on either an attained age or entry age basis. In practice, they are usually structured on an entry age basis, thus generating a supplemental liability. The term *entry age normal cost method* refers to individual cost allocation methods based upon entry age regardless of whether the normal cost is determined as a level dollar amount or as a level percentage amount. Both approaches are widely used.

**Normal Cost.**  In deriving the level percentage to be used in the normal cost calculation under the entry age normal cost method, the actuary, once again, starts by estimating the total cost of the participant's projected annual retirement benefit as of the participant's entry age. This value, the PVFB, is determined in exactly the same manner as it is under the level dollar entry age normal cost method and, in fact, is the same value. However, rather than dividing the PVFB by the actuarial present value of a temporary employment-based life annuity of $1 per year payable from entry age to retirement age, the actuary divides by the present value of such an annuity for $1 at entry age to age 65, increasing each year at a rate equal to what the participant's salary is assumed to increase. The dollar value of this annuity is divided into the PVFB to determine the normal cost at entry age. The participant's entry age salary (i.e., his current salary divided by the salary increase ratio expected under the actuarial assumptions)[6] is divided into the first-year normal cost to determine the *normal cost percentage*. For each year of subsequent service, the normal cost in respect of the participant is obtained by multiplying the participant's attained age salary by the normal cost percentage.

This process is summarized below and illustrated in terms of the familiar male participant age 40 at plan inception with 10 years of credited service:

---

[6]The actual salary at entry age is not used, and indeed should not be used even if known, since it would in all likelihood contradict the stated salary scale assumption.

$$(\text{PVFB}) \div \left( \begin{array}{l} \text{Present value of a temporary em-} \\ \text{ployment-based life annuity of \$1} \\ \text{at entry age increasing annually} \\ \text{at salary scale to age 65} \end{array} \right) = \begin{array}{l} \text{Normal cost} \\ \text{at entry age} \end{array}$$

$$\$3,680 \div 11.97 = \$307$$

$$\left( \begin{array}{l} \text{Current annual} \\ \text{salary} \end{array} \right) \times \left( \dfrac{\begin{array}{l} \text{Salary scale factor*} \\ \text{for entry age} \end{array}}{\begin{array}{l} \text{Salary scale factor} \\ \text{for attained age} \end{array}} \right) = \begin{array}{l} \text{Assumed salary} \\ \text{at entry age} \end{array}$$

$$\$20,290 \times \dfrac{\$2.349}{\$4.446} = \$10,720$$

$$\left( \begin{array}{l} \text{Normal cost} \\ \text{at entry age} \end{array} \right) \div \left( \begin{array}{l} \text{Participant's assumed annual} \\ \text{salary at entry age} \end{array} \right) = \text{Normal cost percentage}$$

$$\$307 \div \$10,720 = 2.86 \text{ percent}$$

$$\left( \begin{array}{l} \text{Normal cost} \\ \text{percentage} \end{array} \right) \times \left( \begin{array}{l} \text{Participant's annual} \\ \text{salary at attained age} \end{array} \right) = \begin{array}{l} \text{Normal cost for each} \\ \text{subsequent year} \end{array}$$

*See Appendix Table B-5.

An alternative approach is to ascertain the normal cost percentage directly by determining the actuarial present value at entry age of the participant's future salary earnings and dividing that quantity into the entry age PVFB. One way of determining the present value of the participant's future salary is to multiply his assumed entry age salary by the actuarial value at entry age of a temporary employment-based life annuity of $1, increasing annually by the projected salary scale. Another approach is to compute the actuarial present value at entry age of the salary expected to be received by the participant during each year of credited service, taking into account the probabilities of death and termination and the passage of time before the salary is received. The sum of these seriatim present values is the present value of the participant's career salary.

The level percentage individual level premium cost method would be computed in the same manner as the level percentage entry age normal cost method, except that all values would be computed as of the participant's attained age. In this case, the actual salary at attained age would be used, with no need to calculate the salary at entry age. Since the attained age normal cost would fully amortize the expected cost of all benefits, there would be no supplemental liability and, of course, no supplemental cost.

The normal cost for the entire plan that would develop under several cost methods over a 50-year period under the previously described hypothetical pension plan is shown in Figure 11. The normal cost curve of the traditional accrued benefit cost method is repeated to show the contrast with the level percentage entry age normal cost method and other cost allocation methods. Several significant relationships may be observed in Figure 11. As might be expected, the lowest normal cost, as a percentage of payroll, during the first several years of the hypothetical plan simulation is that generated by the traditional accrued benefit cost method; true

**FIGURE 11**
**Normal Cost Curves for Hypothetical Pension Plan over a 50-Year Period under Individual Cost Allocation Methods and the Accrued Benefit Cost Method**

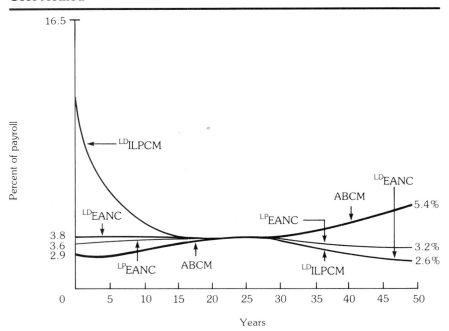

ABCM = Traditional accrued benefit cost method.
LDEANC = Entry age normal cost method using a level dollar approach.
LPEANC = Entry age normal cost method using a level percentage approach.
LDILPCM = Individual level premium cost method using a level dollar approach.

to the characteristics of the method, however, the plan normal cost rises during each year of the 50-year simulation and eventually exceeds by a wide margin the normal cost under any other method.

The individual level premium cost method using the level dollar approach generates the largest initial normal cost because, among other reasons, it amortizes the *implicit* supplemental liability as a component of the normal cost. The normal cost declines over time as participants with past service benefits retire, eventually being identical with the entry age normal cost method using the level dollar approach. The latter represents the true long-run normal cost of the plan when expressed as a level dollar amount. Its ultimate level is lower than the entry age normal cost method using the level percentage approach, since it generates a larger actuarial liability than the level percentage approach and, hence, the investment earnings on the plan assets (real or theoretical) assume a larger share of the total cost burden than under the level percentage approach.

The entry age normal cost method using the level percentage approach represents the long-term normal cost of the plan when measured as a percentage of payroll. It develops an initial normal cost (under the illustrative plan) lower than that of the level dollar approach under either the entry age normal cost method or the individual level premium cost method, but its ultimate normal cost is second only to that of the traditional accrued benefit cost method. Because its initial entry age normal cost is smaller using a level percentage approach than using a level dollar approach, it develops a smaller actuarial liability, as can be appreciated on a retrospective look. The normal cost declines until a stable plan population has been achieved, after which it continues as a level percentage of payroll but on a higher plane than the level dollar cost methods because of smaller investment earnings.

**Actuarial Liability.** The actuarial liability under the entry age normal cost method using the level percentage approach is derived in the same manner as that under the level dollar cost methods. It can be derived either retrospectively or prospectively, the latter being the standard approach. The initial actuarial liability (and supplemental liability) in our example of a male participant of age 40 with 10 years of credited service is computed prospectively as follows:

$$PVFB = \$21,522 \times \$0.823 = \$17,737$$

$$\text{Present value of future normal costs} = \$20,290 \times .0286 \times 13.79$$
$$= \$8,002$$

$$\text{Actuarial liability} = PVFB - \text{Present value of future normal costs}$$
$$= \$17,737 - \$8,002 = \$9,735$$

It will be noted that this is a smaller actuarial liability than that developed under the entry age normal cost method using the level dollar approach. The difference is accounted for entirely by the substitution of a larger normal cost for future years in the formula. All the other values are the same as those for the other individual level cost methods and will be in each future valuation. It should be remembered that after the first, inception-of-plan, valuation all the values in the formula are *attained age* values, except the normal cost rate, which is always determined on the basis of the participant's entry age.

The actuarial liability that develops under the entry age normal cost method using the level percentage approach and the other individual level cost methods under the previously illustrated hypothetical pension plan is given in Figure 12 as a percentage of payroll. As with the normal cost, the traditional accrued benefit cost method is included to give further perspective. The plan termination liability curve is given to indicate whether the actuarial liability under each method is deficient or excessive, compared to that particular standard of adequacy.

There are no surprises here. The lower the ultimate normal cost developed by a plan, the larger is the actuarial liability. The greater the actuarial liability, the larger the portion of the total cost borne by investments on the real or assumed plan assets. Both approaches to the entry age normal cost method generate an actuarial liability that greatly exceeds the plan termination liability. In a sense, this is the price that has to be paid for their level normal cost. The traditional accrued benefit cost method actuarial liability conforms closely to (but in this example is lower than) the plan termination liability, but does so at the expense of a normal cost that tends to rise over time.

## Aggregate Cost Allocation Methods

The second broad approach to determining the annual cost of a pension plan through an allocation of the total projected cost is the

**FIGURE 12**
**Actuarial Liability Curves as a Percentage of Payroll for a Hypothetical Pension Plan over a 50-Year Period under Individual Cost Allocation Methods and the Accrued Benefit Cost Method, Compared to the Plan Termination Liability**

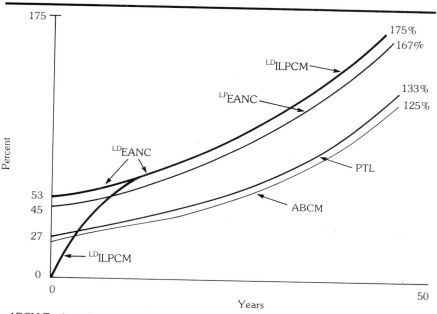

ABCM Traditional accrued benefit cost method.
LDEANC Entry age normal cost method using level dollar approach.
LPEANC Entry age normal cost method using level percentage approach.
LDILPCM Individual level premium cost method using a level dollar approach.
PTL Plan termination liability.

*aggregate method.* The portion of the total projected cost to be allocated to each plan year is generally expressed as a percentage of covered payroll if benefits are related to pay, and as a stipulated dollar amount per active participant if benefits are not related to pay. The annual cost accrual (normal cost plus supplemental cost) can be computed with or without supplemental liability.

It is one of the peculiarities of this approach that no actuarial liability ever directly emerges.[7] The normal cost is defined and

[7]Some argue that the aggregate method develops an actuarial liability that is precisely equal to the present value of future benefits less the present value of future normal costs, which also equals the assets plus the unfunded liability. IRS has said that under the aggregate cost method the actuarial liability is not *directly* calculated.

derived in such a way that the present value of future benefits, less plan assets and any unfunded liability, is always fully and precisely offset by the actuarial present value of future normal cost accruals. If the plan sponsor desires a supplemental liability, it must be computed under one of the individual forms of actuarial cost method. In its pure form, the aggregate method is simply incapable of producing its own supplemental liability.

### Level Dollar Cost Method

The basic concept underlying the aggregate cost method without supplemental liability is that the remaining *unfunded* projected cost of the pension plan is to be amortized over the remaining service lifetimes of the active participants in level annual dollar amounts or in annual amounts that constitute a level percentage of covered payroll. The dollar or percentage cost accrual so determined would accomplish this purpose only if there were no new entrants into the plan, no benefit changes were made, and actual experience conformed precisely to the projected experience. In fact, there are new entrants to any sizable plan every year, there are likely to be actuarial gains and losses, and there may be other developments that affect the cost of the plan. Consequently, it is necessary to recompute the annual cost accrual every year (or every two or three years), the sum derived always being the amount expected to be required to amortize on a level basis the then *unfunded* cost over the remaining service lifetimes of the new "closed" group. The process can be viewed as one involving the determination of a series of temporary annual cost accruals for a succession of closed groups.

As its name suggests, the aggregate level dollar cost method determines the level annual *dollar* cost accrual that would be needed to amortize the unfunded projected cost of the plan if the postulated conditions were to be realized. The first step in the overall computation for the first year is to determine the actuarial present value of future benefits, the PVFB. If there is to be no supplemental liability, this calculation takes into account all projected benefits, irrespective of their type or the period of service to which they are attributable. The actuarial present value is determined exactly as it would be under one of the individual level cost methods. The second step is to determine the actuarial present value of a temporary employment-based life annuity of $1 per year for each active participant, the values being computed as of the participants' attained ages.[8] The third step consists of dividing the *sum* of the individual participant unit annuity values into the PVFB. This step yields the dollar amount of cost that must be accrued or amortized in respect of each active participant. It is a weighted average cost per participant and does not represent the actual annual cost for any particular individual. The process is summarized below and illustrated with values derived from the hypothetical pension plan used in previous examples.

$$
\begin{pmatrix} \text{Annual cost} \\ \text{per active} \\ \text{participant} \end{pmatrix} = \begin{pmatrix} \text{Present value of} \\ \text{future benefits} \\ \text{at participant} \\ \text{attained ages} \\ \text{(PVFB)} \end{pmatrix} \div \sum \begin{pmatrix} \text{Temporary employment-} \\ \text{based life annuity of \$1} \\ \text{per year for each par-} \\ \text{ticipant from attained} \\ \text{age to age 65} \end{pmatrix}
$$

$$\$1,727 = \$12,096,492 \div \$7,005$$

First year total cost = (Cost per employee) × (Number of employees)

$$\$1,727,000 = \$1,727 \times 1,000$$

After the first year, the formula must be modified to reflect the asset values that have been accumulated to offset the cost accruals for the first and subsequent years. Hence, as of any date after establishment of the plan, the level dollar cost accrual is derived by dividing the present value of future benefits (including those payable to retired participants), *less any plan assets,* by the sum of the individual participant unit annuity values. This amount must be recalculated annually (or every two or three years) and, with a stable group and no change in the benefit structure or the actuarial assumptions, will decline from year to year until the implicit cost of any past service benefits has been completely amortized. Indeed, whether or not there are any past service benefits, the ratio will tend to fall as new participants enter the plan at the younger ages, the cost amortization period being thereby lengthened. The cost

---

[8]In theory, the remaining unfunded cost at any point in time could be amortized through any pattern of assumed cost accruals that would meet the fiscal needs of the employer and the funding requirements of federal law. This concept was explored in C. L. Trowbridge, "The Unfunded Present Value Family of Pension Funding Methods," *Transactions of the Society of Actuaries* 15 (1963), pp. 151–69. The aggregate cost method is a special case of the unfunded present value family of methods.

of past service benefits, retroactive benefit increases, or any other plan development that would normally give rise to a supplemental liability is amortized over the remaining service lifetimes of the active participants.

Actuarial gains and losses are not explicitly recognized under this type of cost method, being merged indistinguishably into the remaining unfunded cost to be amortized over the remaining service lifetimes of the active participants, like any element of cost.

A supplemental liability can be created under the aggregate level dollar (or level percentage) cost method in a variety of ways, the most common being to assume the recognition of cost accruals prior to the effective date of the plan. The approximate effect of this is to make no allowance in the regular or normal cost accrual for benefits attributable to past service. This can be accomplished by excluding past service benefits from the present value of future projected benefits. In practice, the actuary may assume a supplemental liability equal to that produced under the accrued benefit cost method or one of the individual level cost methods.[9] Regardless of how it is arrived at, the unfunded portion of the supplemental liability is subtracted (along with plan assets) from the present value of future benefits in calculating the annual cost. Thus, the annual cost accrual under the aggregate level cost method with supplemental liability is derived by multiplying current covered payroll by the percentage obtained from dividing the present value of future benefits, less *the unfunded liability and plan assets,* by the sum of the individual participant unit annuity values. Like the aggregate level cost method without supplemental liability, this method allocates costs over the remaining service lifetimes of the active participants.

After the first year, the unfunded liability is not calculated directly, being determined as if the actuarial assumptions had been exactly realized. That is, the unfunded liability for any year after the first is assumed to be equal to the unfunded liability for the previous year plus interest for one year and the annual cost for the current year, less contributions to the plan during the current year.

---

[9]Under the aggregate cost approach, the actuary frequently computes the first-year cost accrual on the basis of the entry age normal cost method. The supplemental liability would thus be available as part of the regular costing procedure.

Thus, actuarial gains and losses are not reflected in the unfunded liability but are automatically spread over the remaining service lifetimes of the active participants.

When the supplemental liability was calculated to be precisely equal to the present value at plan inception of the past service benefits, this procedure is known as the "attained age normal" cost method, like its individual counterpart.[10] When the supplemental liability was derived by techniques that assumed an average age of entry into the plan, or a set of assumed entry ages, the method is identified as the frozen initial liability method.[11]

### Level Percentage of Payroll Method

This form of aggregate cost method differs from the one described in the preceding section only in that the annual cost accrual is defined and derived as a level percentage of payroll, rather than as a dollar amount per participant. This is the form of aggregate cost method used by plans that have salary-related benefits.

The cost accrual for the first year of a plan's operation under this method, assuming no supplemental liability, is determined by dividing the aggregate present value of future benefits by the present value of the estimated future earnings of the active participants in the plan at the time of the valuation. The present value of future salaries is obtained by summing the present value of the future salary of each individual in the "closed" group. The latter value is derived by multiplying the participant's current salary times the actuarial present value at the participant's *attained age* of a temporary employment-based annuity of $1 per year to age 65, increasing each year at a rate equal to that at which the participant's salary is assumed to increase. This is the same procedure used to value future salaries under the individual level premium cost method using the level percentage approach.

Dividing the present value of future salaries into the present value of future benefits yields a percentage called the *normal cost percentage* or *annual cost accrual rate*. This percentage is multiplied

---

[10]ERISA §3(31). The Joint Committee terminology is *frozen attained age actuarial cost method.*

[11]ERISA §3(31). The Joint Committee terminology is *frozen entry age actuarial cost method.*

times the current covered payroll to obtain the annual cost (in dollars) for the plan.

This process and illustrative amounts are set out below:

$$\begin{matrix} \text{Annual} \\ \text{cost} \\ \text{accrual} \\ \text{rate} \end{matrix} = \left( \begin{matrix} \text{Present value of} \\ \text{future benefits} \\ \text{at participant} \\ \text{attained ages} \\ \text{(PVFB)} \end{matrix} \right) \div \sum \left( \begin{matrix} \text{For each participant,} \\ \text{temporary employ-} \\ \text{ment-based life annu-} \\ \text{ity of \$1 per year,} \\ \text{increasing annually at} \\ \text{salary scale, from at-} \\ \text{tained age to age 65} \\ \text{times current salary} \end{matrix} \right)$$

$$.0781 = \$12,096,492 \div 154,931,392$$

First year normal cost = Current covered payroll × Cost accrual rate

$$\$1,171,500 = \$15,000,000 \times .0781$$

The cost accrual rate must be recomputed each year (or every two or three years), taking into account the growing plan assets and other changed circumstances, and applied to the then current payroll.

A supplemental liability can be created in the same manner and with the same consequences as under the aggregate level dollar cost method.

## Individual Aggregate Cost Method

The *individual aggregate cost method,* as the name suggests, blends some of the characteristics of an individual cost method and an aggregate cost method. This method is widely used for small plans.

Under the individual aggregate cost method, sometimes referred to as the *individual spread-gain cost method,* the PVFB is first calculated for each individual participant. The total plan assets, if any, are allocated (see later discussion) among all participants. The assets allocated to each participant are subtracted from his PVFB to obtain the present value of future normal costs for the individual. Since this present value of future normal costs must be paid by the normal costs of future years, it is divided by a temporary employment-based life annuity of $1 per year from attained age to age 65 to obtain the individual's normal cost. If a level percentage approach is used rather than a level dollar method, the temporary employment-based life annuity will be for $1 per year increasing annually in accordance with the salary scale.

At the inception of the plan, when there are no plan assets, this method is identical to the individual level premium cost method. Because the PVFB is expected to be funded entirely by future normal costs, there is no supplemental liability under this method. Like the aggregate cost method without supplemental liability, the individual aggregate method never has an unfunded liability. The individual aggregate cost method automatically spreads actuarial gains and losses over the future working lifetimes of participants through the normal cost.

Various methods are used to allocate plan assets among participants for purposes of the method. If the method is first applied to a plan at some time after the plan's effective date, plan assets are usually allocated in proportion to each participant's PVFB.[12] Thereafter regulations require only that the allocation be ''reasonable.'' One commonly used approach is to increase the amount of assets allocated to each participant on the prior anniversary by the individual's normal cost of the intervening year, and then to allocate the total plan assets in proportion to this adjusted total. If the plan includes participants or beneficiaries who are not active employees, this approach may be modified to first allocate assets to such participants and beneficiaries equal to their PVFB, and then to allocate the remaining plan assets in accordance with the previously described procedure.

## Summary of Actuarial Cost Methods

The characteristics of the principal actuarial cost methods are presented in schematic form in Figure 13. Actuarial gains and losses can be determined on either a *direct* or *spread* basis under any of the cost methods, except the aggregate, which always spreads such gains and losses.

Table 8 compares the classification used to describe the principal actuarial cost methods in this text with the terminology of ERISA and the terminology of the Joint Committee on Pension Terminology.

---

[12]Treas. Reg. 1.412(c)(3)–1(c)(5), Rev. Proc. 80–50.

**FIGURE 13**
**Schematic Summary of Characteristics of the Principal Actuarial Cost Methods**

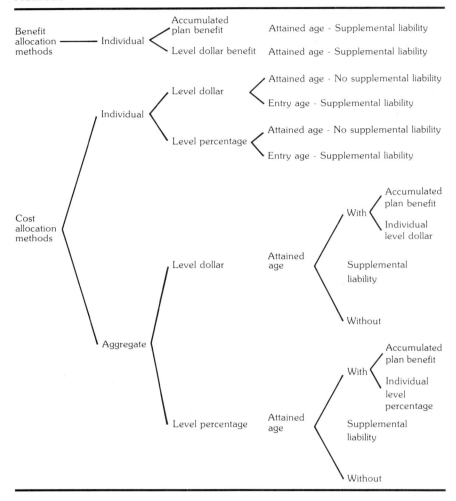

**TABLE 8**
**Classification and Comparative Terminology of Actuarial Cost Methods**

| Classification | ERISA | Joint Committee |
|---|---|---|
| **Benefit Allocation Cost Methods** | | |
| Accumulated Plan Benefit Method | Accrued Benefit Cost Method or Unit Credit Method | Unit Credit Actuarial Cost Method |
| Level Dollar Benefit Method | Same as above | Same as above |
| **Cost Allocation Methods-Individual** | | |
| Level Dollar Cost Method: | | |
| Attained Age–No Supplemental Liability | Individual Level Premium Cost Method | Individual Level Actuarial Cost Method* |
| Entry Age–Supplemental Liability | Entry Age Normal Cost Method | Entry Age Actuarial Cost Method |
| Level Percentage Cost Method: | | |
| Attained Age–No Supplemental Liability | Individual Level Premium Cost Method | Individual Level Actuarial Cost Method* |
| Entry Age–Supplemental Liability | Entry Age Normal Cost Method | Entry Age Actuarial Cost Method |
| **Cost Allocation Methods-Aggregate** | | |
| Level Dollar Cost Method: | | |
| With Benefit Allocation Cost Method Supplemental Liability | Attained Age Normal Cost Method | Frozen Attained Age Actuarial Cost Method |
| With Entry Age Normal Cost Supplemental Liability | Frozen Initial Liability Cost Method | Frozen Entry Age Actuarial Cost Method |
| Without Supplemental Liability | Aggregate Cost Method | Aggregate Actuarial Cost Method |
| Level Percentage Cost Method: | | |
| With Benefit Allocation Cost Method Supplemental Liability | Attained Age Normal Cost Method | Frozen Attained Age Actuarial Cost Method |
| With Entry Age Normal Cost Supplemental Liability | Frozen Initial Liability Cost Method | Frozen Entry Age Actuarial Cost Method |
| Without Supplemental Liability | Aggregate Cost Method | Aggregate Actuarial Cost Method |
| **Mixed Methods** | | |
| Attained Age–Benefit Allocation Cost Method Supplemental Liability | Attained Age Normal Cost Method | Attained Age Actuarial Cost Method or Frozen Attained Actuarial Cost Method |

*If spread gain: Individual Spread-Gain Actuarial Cost Method.

## Questions

1.  In what fundamental respects do *individual* cost allocation cost methods differ from benefit allocation cost methods?
2.  Indicate the role played by each of the following actuarial functions, and explain the rationale behind the use of each function:
    *a.*  Probability of surviving in service to age 65.
    *b.*  Present value of $1 payable in *n* years hence.
    *c.*  Present value of $1 per annum for *n* years.
    *d.*  Present value of $1 per annum for *n* years increasing by *x* percent per year compounded.
    *e.*  Present value of a temporary employment-based life annuity of $1 per annum.
    *f.*  Present value of a temporary employment-based life annuity of $1 per annum increasing annually by percentage equal to the total salary scale.
    *g.*  Present value of $1 per year payable monthly for life from age 65.
3.  Compare the normal cost that is generated with respect to (*a*) an individual participant, and (*b*) the entire plan, under the principal actuarial cost methods.
4.  Compare the actuarial liability generated by
    *a.*  The traditional accrued benefit cost method.
    *b.*  The entry age normal cost (level dollar or level percentage) method, other things being equal.
5.  Are there any actuarial cost methods that do not develop an actuarial liability? Explain.
6.  Is there any actuarial cost method that would develop an actuarial liability precisely equal to the actuarial present value of the benefits that would become payable in the event of plan termination? Explain.
7.  What actuarial cost method is used to value the liabilities of the nonactive participants in a pension plan?
8.  What are the *advantages* and the *disadvantages* of the entry age normal cost method, as compared to the benefit allocation cost methods when considered from the vantage point of (*a*) the plan participants, (*b*) the plan sponsor, (*c*) present and future shareholders of the plan sponsor, and (*d*) broader societal interests?
9.  On the date his pension plan was established, a male participant of age 38 was receiving an annual salary of $20,000. The plan provides

for each year of credited service an annual retirement benefit payable monthly equal to 1 percent of the participant's average annual salary during the last five years of service, with no offset or other form of integration with Social Security. The participant is credited with 10 years of past service, with an annual benefit for each year of past service of 1 percent of his annual salary at plan inception. The participant's annual salary increases are expected to average 6 percent. Using the above facts and the appropriate actuarial functions from Appendix B, compute in respect of the foregoing male participant at age 38:

a. The first-year *annual cost* under the individual level premium cost method (level percentage approach).

b. The first-year *normal cost* and *supplemental cost* under the entry age cost method (level percentage approach), assuming that the initial supplemental liability is amortized in 30 equal annual dollar installments.

c. The first-year *annual cost* under the aggregate cost method (level percentage approach) without supplemental liability (assuming for this purpose that all the participants are age 38 and have the same salary and benefit expectations as the individual cited in the facts).

d. The first-year *annual cost* under the attained age normal cost method (level percentage approach), with the supplemental liability being amortized in 20 level annual installments. (Assume for this purpose that all the participants are age 38 and have the same salary and benefit expectations as the individual cited in the facts.)

10. How would the supplemental liability for the plan as a whole, however calculated, at the beginning of the second plan year compare with the initial supplemental liability (assuming the actuarial assumptions were exactly realized)?

11. How would the actuarial liability for the plan as a whole, whether calculated under a benefit allocation cost method or an individual cost allocation method, at the beginning of the second plan year (assuming the actuarial assumptions were exactly realized) compare with:

a. The actuarial liability at the inception of the plan?

b. The supplemental liability at the beginning of the second plan year?

# 15 | Pension Cost Illustrations and Forecasts

THE DYNAMICS OF A PENSION PLAN and the long-run characteristics of the various actuarial cost methods can be portrayed through simulation of the plan's operations over successive generations of participants, with appropriate assumptions as to future experience. Such a simulation of an actuarial plan, with alternative assumptions about future experience, can provide the plan sponsor with valuable insights as to the potential normal cost, actuarial liability, cash flows, and asset accumulations under various scenarios. It can also indicate the potential financial consequences of any plan changes that might be under consideration, taken individually or collectively. Large pension plan sponsors have shown increasing interest in projections of pension costs and associated cash flows. These projections can extend far into the future, but because of the difficulty of predicting the behavior of the various cost factors, especially population size and characteristics, salary levels, and rate of investment return, the reliability of the results diminishes with the duration of the projection. This is especially true of the dollar values obtained.

In this chapter, a 50-year simulation of a hypothetical pension plan is presented for the dual purpose of demonstrating the dynamics of three basic actuarial cost methods and illustrating the types of financial information that can be made available to plan sponsors through long-term actuarial forecasts. The period of the simulation is much longer than would usually be used for an actual plan. The typical forecast would extend about 10 years into the future, some going out as far as 25 years. A 50-year simulation is used in this example to carry the plan through the 30-year amortization of the supplemental liability and into durations where long-term cost characteristics come to the surface. The forecast component of the illustration can be considered as constituting the first 10 or 15 years of the simulation. After the supplemental liability has been amortized, the simulation shows only normal costs. With an actual plan, additional layers of supplemental liability are almost certain to be created during a period of 50 years, and their amortization would add to the plan's annual costs.

## Pension Cost Illustrations

The pension costs and liabilities generated in this simulation are based upon a plan that begins with a relatively immature population of 1,000 male participants, with no retired participants, and grows at a rate of 5 percent during the first year of the plan's operation, the rate of growth grading downward to zero in the 25th year. Beginning in the 26th year the population starts to decline at the same rate at which it was assumed to grow in the 25th year, with the annual decline mirroring the assumed annual growth during the first 25 years and reaching the original population of 1,000 at the end of the 50th year of the forecast. With this pattern of growth and decline the plan population moves in continuous progression from a relatively immature state to a fully mature state and eventually to a relatively overmature state.

The plan is assumed to provide a retirement benefit at age 65 of 1 percent of the participant's average annual compensation during the last five years of employment multiplied by the years of credited service, with no explicit integration with Social Security. Retirement benefits are assumed to vest in full after 10 years[1] of credited service. The normal annuity form is the single-life annuity, and in

---

[1]Beginning in 1989 plans subject to ERISA's vesting requirements may no longer use 10-year vesting.

the interest of simplicity, it is assumed that there are no death, disability, or early retirement benefits.

The benefits under the plan are valued in accordance with the actuarial functions and values set forth in Appendix B, all present values being derived on the basis of a 6 percent interest assumption. For simplicity it is assumed that the actual experience during the 50-year simulation conforms in all respects to the actuarial assumptions, there being no actuarial gains or losses.[2] The supplemental liability under the traditional accrued benefit cost method and entry age normal cost method is assumed to be amortized in equal annual dollar installments over a 30-year period, the maximum period permitted for single employer plans established after January 1, 1974. It is also assumed that the annual cost (normal cost plus the allocable portion of the supplemental liability, if any) is funded currently, the contributions being made at the beginning of the year in which the cost is incurred. The assets are assumed to earn interest at the rate of 6 percent per year compounded.

The 50-year simulation is, in essence, a series of 50 closed group valuations based upon the plan population, benefit accruals, and asset accumulations pertaining to the years in question. The deferred benefits of terminated vested participants and the benefits payable to retired participants are also reflected in the successive valuations.

Table 9 provides some data that serve as points of reference for a pension cost forecast. It shows, for example, the number of retired participants year by year, starting with 12 at the beginning of the second year of operation and rising to 738 at the beginning of the 51st year. Thus, by the end of the period there are three retired participants for each four active participants, a very high ratio reflecting the advanced maturity of the group. In addition,

---

[2]In an actual simulation, experience economic assumptions may differ from those used for valuation purposes, producing actuarial gains and losses. Indeed, best estimate economic assumptions may be used for both valuation (simulation only) and experience purposes, again eliminating actuarial gains and losses but possibly projecting a markedly different financial scenario. Generally, the most realistic and satisfactory approach is to assume that contributions to the plan during the forecast period, typically 10 years, will be made in accordance with the actuarial assumptions currently used for valuation purposes but that experience gains will emerge in consonance with a less conservative set of economic assumptions, producing year-to-year adjustments or corrections in the cost and cash flow projection.

**TABLE 9**
**Background Data for Pension Cost Simulation**

| Year of Plan Operation | Number of Active Participants at Beginning of Year | Number of Terminated Vested Participants at Beginning of Year | Number of Retired Participants at Beginning of Year | Salary at Beginning of Year | Benefit Payments during Year | Plan Termination Liability at Beginning of Year |
|---|---|---|---|---|---|---|
| 1 | 1,000 | 0 | 0 | $ 15,000,000 | $ 35,387 | $ 4,068,186 |
| 2 | 1,050 | 8 | 12 | 16,566,823 | 73,237 | 4,756,150 |
| 3 | 1,100 | 16 | 24 | 18,235,208 | 113,763 | 5,493,712 |
| 4 | 1,151 | 25 | 36 | 20,010,094 | 157,088 | 6,284,862 |
| 5 | 1,202 | 34 | 48 | 21,896,025 | 203,385 | 7,133,998 |
| 6 | 1,252 | 44 | 61 | 23,896,620 | 252,846 | 8,045,862 |
| 7 | 1,302 | 54 | 74 | 26,014,612 | 305,961 | 9,025,980 |
| 8 | 1,352 | 65 | 87 | 28,246,163 | 362,727 | 10,079,117 |
| 9 | 1,400 | 76 | 101 | 30,598,486 | 423,357 | 11,211,083 |
| 10 | 1,448 | 87 | 115 | 33,072,230 | 488,138 | 12,428,045 |
| 11 | 1,494 | 99 | 128 | 35,667,204 | 557,399 | 13,736,443 |
| 16 | 1,699 | 165 | 202 | 50,340,547 | 989,348 | 21,862,354 |
| 21 | 1,839 | 238 | 282 | 67,420,585 | 1,602,420 | 33,217,720 |
| 26 | 1,895 | 308 | 368 | 85,811,157 | 2,465,786 | 48,529,944 |
| 31 | 1,839 | 368 | 460 | 102,983,071 | 3,657,722 | 68,192,975 |
| 36 | 1,699 | 412 | 553 | 117,546,095 | 5,238,598 | 91,967,955 |
| 41 | 1,494 | 434 | 636 | 127,738,707 | 7,230,321 | 118,825,132 |
| 46 | 1,252 | 434 | 700 | 132,214,891 | 9,594,626 | 146,788,975 |
| 51 | 1,000 | 410 | 738 | 130,461,442 | 12,154,692 | 173,188,580 |

**TABLE 10**
**Annual Cost, Liability, and Asset Accumulation under the Traditional**
**Accrued Benefit Cost Method**

| | Normal Cost | | Supplemental Cost | |
|---|---|---|---|---|
| Year | In Dollars | As Percent of Salary | In Dollars | As Percent of Salary |
| 1 | $  433,645 | 2.89% | $234,532 | 1.56% |
| 2 | 475,289 | 2.87 | 234,532 | 1.42 |
| 3 | 520,636 | 2.86 | 234,532 | 1.29 |
| 4 | 569,968 | 2.85 | 234,532 | 1.17 |
| 5 | 623,547 | 2.85 | 234,532 | 1.07 |
| 6 | 681,918 | 2.85 | 234,532 | 0.98 |
| 7 | 744,537 | 2.86 | 234,532 | 0.90 |
| 8 | 812,233 | 2.88 | 234,532 | 0.83 |
| 9 | 885,309 | 2.89 | 234,532 | 0.77 |
| 10 | 964,035 | 2.91 | 234,532 | 0.71 |
| 11 | 1,048,659 | 2.94 | 234,532 | 0.66 |
| 16 | 1,557,870 | 3.09 | 234,532 | 0.47 |
| 21 | 2,224,209 | 3.30 | 234,532 | 0.35 |
| 26 | 3,043,591 | 3.55 | 234,532 | 0.27 |
| 30 | 3,778,449 | 3.79 | 234,532 | 0.24 |
| 31 | 3,971,828 | 3.86 | 0 | 0.00 |
| 36 | 4,943,685 | 4.21 | 0 | 0.00 |
| 41 | 5,862,498 | 4.59 | 0 | 0.00 |
| 46 | 6,607,582 | 5.00 | 0 | 0.00 |
| 51 | 7,096,745 | 5.44 | 0 | 0.00 |

there are 410 terminated vested participants with deferred claims against the plan. Thus, by the end of the period there are more inactive participants with claims against the plan than there are active participants.

The annual salaries for the active participants rise from $15,000,000 to $130,461,442, reflecting a per capita rate of growth in excess of 4 percent per year.[3] Benefit payments to retired participants start off slowly because of the small number of persons in that subset of the plan population. By the third year of the plan, benefit payments exceed $100,000 per year and thereafter increase rapidly, reaching $12 million after 50 years. It is interesting and

---

[3]The salary of each participant is assumed to grow in accordance with a merit scale plus 4 percent per year for inflation and productivity increases. Per capita average salaries rise at a rate more than 4 percent per year because of the maturing of the population.

| Annual Cost | | | Assets | | |
|---|---|---|---|---|---|
| In Dollars | As Percent of Salary | Actuarial Liability Beginning of Year | In Dollars* | As Percent of Actuarial Liability | As Percent of Plan Termination Liability |
| $ 668,178 | 4.45% | $ 3,421,997 | $ 0 | 0% | 0% |
| 709,821 | 4.28 | 4,050,548 | 671,835 | 17 | 14 |
| 755,169 | 4.14 | 4,721,984 | 1,389,153 | 29 | 25 |
| 804,501 | 4.02 | 5,440,051 | 2,155,855 | 40 | 34 |
| 858,079 | 3.92 | 6,208,889 | 2,976,246 | 48 | 42 |
| 916,450 | 3.84 | 7,032,985 | 3,854,987 | 55 | 48 |
| 979,070 | 3.76 | 7,917,476 | 4,797,403 | 61 | 53 |
| 1,046,766 | 3.71 | 8,866,728 | 5,808,054 | 66 | 58 |
| 1,119,841 | 3.66 | 9,886,248 | 6,892,658 | 70 | 61 |
| 1,198,567 | 3.62 | 10,981,977 | 8,057,377 | 73 | 65 |
| 1,283,191 | 3.60 | 12,160,204 | 9,308,732 | 77 | 68 |
| 1,792,402 | 3.56 | 19,494,723 | 17,080,215 | 88 | 78 |
| 2,458,741 | 3.65 | 29,823,285 | 27,993,535 | 94 | 84 |
| 3,278,123 | 3.82 | 43,903,164 | 42,855,952 | 98 | 88 |
| 4,012,981 | 4.03 | 58,208,250 | 57,973,718 | 100 | 91 |
| 3,971,828 | 3.86 | 62,213,487 | 62,213,487 | 100 | 91 |
| 4,943,685 | 4.21 | 84,651,057 | 84,651,057 | 100 | 92 |
| 5,862,498 | 4.59 | 110,338,647 | 110,338,647 | 100 | 93 |
| 6,607,582 | 5.00 | 137,453,843 | 137,453,843 | 100 | 94 |
| 7,096,745 | 5.44 | 163,431,351 | 163,431,351 | 100 | 94 |

*Figures in this column represent the assets at the beginning of each year before the contribution for that year is made. The plan begins without assets, the first contribution being made immediately thereafter.

instructive to compare these yearly cash outflows, which, of course, are not affected by the actuarial cost method, with the yearly contributions under the three actuarial cost methods employed in this simulation. Throughout the first 30 years, when supplemental costs are being funded, contributions under all three cost methods are well in excess of benefit payments. Benefit payments eventually overtake contributions but investment income from accumulated plan assets is available to absorb the deficiency. In each year of the simulation, investment income must be added to contributions to arrive at the total flow of funds into the plan. Under all three cost methods plan assets continue to grow throughout the period.

The plan termination liability is shown to measure the adequacy or redundancy of the asset accumulations under the various actuarial cost methods if the plan were to terminate. The plan termination liability purports to reflect the actuarial present value of all retirement benefits accrued to date,[4] with no allowance for future salary increases or employee withdrawals. If the accumulated assets, properly valued, equal the plan termination liability, the plan could on the date of valuation discharge all of its obligations for accrued benefits without further contributions.

The projection of costs, liabilities, and assets under the traditional accrued benefit cost method is portrayed in Table 10. Projections under this method are shown for instructional purposes only, since in practice the traditional accrued benefit cost method would not be used for a plan with benefits based upon final average compensation. In absolute terms, the normal cost increases from $433,645, in the first year of the plan's operation to $7,096,745 in the 51st year. As a percentage of salary, however, the growth in normal cost is much less spectacular, the percentage going from 2.89 percent to 5.44 percent, an increase of 88 percent over the 50-year period. The supplemental liability is amortized in 30 equal annual installments of $234,532, which because of rising salary levels constitute a declining percentage of payroll. The supplemental cost ranges from 1.56 percent of payroll in the first year down to a relatively insignificant 0.24 percent in the 30th year, when the final installment is paid. The normal and supplemental costs combined range downward from 4.45 percent in the first year to 3.56 percent in the 16th year, then rise to 4.03 percent in the 30th year, with the normal cost continuing its upward climb to 5.44 percent in the 51st year. These costs are lower than they would have been had ancillary benefits been provided by the plan.

The assets accumulate rapidly during the period when the supplemental liability is being amortized and funded. As would be expected, by the end of the amortization period the plan assets are precisely equal to the actuarial liability and will remain in that relationship until another layer of supplemental liability is created or actuarial gains and losses emerge. At all durations, however, the plan assets fall short of the plan termination liability. Such a deficiency is to be expected until the supplemental liability has been fully funded, but in the example there is still a deficiency at

---

[4]This exceeds the plan termination liability under Title IV of ERISA, which is based on that portion of accrued benefits guaranteed by the Pension Benefit Guaranty Corporation. See Chapter 24.

the end of 30 years and thereafter to the end of the simulation. After 30 years of the plan's operations the plan termination liability is $68,192,975, whereas the plan assets amount to only $62,213,487, a deficiency of 9 percent. A deficiency of 6 percent remains after 50 years. This indicates the cost-inflating impact of omitting employee withdrawal assumptions in the derivation of the plan termination liability.[5]

The trend of costs, liabilities, and asset accumulations under the individual entry age normal cost method using the level percentage approach is shown in Table 11. In absolute terms the normal cost rises from $535,562 in the first year to $4,235,883 in the 51st year. However, as a percentage of salary, the normal cost declines from 3.57 percent to 3.25 percent, reflecting a downward shift over time in the average entry age of the plan participants.[6] The supplemental liability is amortized in 30 equal annual installments of $466,435, which because of rising salary levels constitute a declining percentage of payroll. These annual charges are much larger than under the traditional accrued benefit cost method, since the supplemental liability itself is much larger. In the first year the supplemental cost is 3.11 percent of salary, declining to 0.47 percent in the 30th year. The combined normal and supplemental costs range from 6.68 percent of payroll in the first year to 3.96 percent in the 30th year. Thereafter, the normal cost drifts downward to 3.25 percent of payroll, as compared to 5.44 percent under the traditional accrued benefit cost method. In other words, since the entry age normal cost method allocates a larger proportion of the total prospective cost of the plan to the supplemental liability component, the normal cost ultimately becomes smaller in absolute terms than the traditional accrued benefit cost method normal cost.

---

[5]Whether the actuarial liability under the traditional accrued benefit cost method would be more or less than the plan termination liability for any particular plan may depend upon the plan provisions and the actuarial assumptions used. In addition, in the case of an actual plan termination, the liability might be redetermined on the basis of different actuarial assumptions than those used for an ongoing plan, resulting in different percentages than those shown.

[6]Under the individual entry age normal cost method the normal cost percentage for a particular participant remains constant throughout his active membership, barring changes in assumptions, but the normal cost percentage for the plan as a whole may move upward or downward in response to changes in the entry age distribution of the active participants, as occurred in the present simulation.

**TABLE 11**
**Annual Cost, Actuarial Liability, and Asset Accumulation under the Entry Age Normal Cost Method**

| Year | Normal Cost | | Supplemental Cost | |
|------|-------------|-----------------------|-------------------|-----------------------|
|      | In Dollars  | As Percent of Salary  | In Dollars        | As Percent of Salary  |
| 1    | $ 535,562   | 3.57%                 | $466,435          | 3.11%                 |
| 2    | 591,261     | 3.57                  | 466,435           | 2.82                  |
| 3    | 650,822     | 3.57                  | 466,435           | 2.56                  |
| 4    | 714,387     | 3.57                  | 466,435           | 2.33                  |
| 5    | 782,060     | 3.57                  | 466,435           | 2.13                  |
| 6    | 853,923     | 3.57                  | 466,435           | 1.95                  |
| 7    | 929,582     | 3.57                  | 466,435           | 1.79                  |
| 8    | 1,009,558   | 3.57                  | 466,435           | 1.65                  |
| 9    | 1,093,866   | 3.57                  | 466,435           | 1.52                  |
| 10   | 1,182,487   | 3.58                  | 466,435           | 1.41                  |
| 11   | 1,275,367   | 3.58                  | 466,435           | 1.31                  |
| 16   | 1,795,563   | 3.57                  | 466,435           | 0.93                  |
| 21   | 2,392,055   | 3.55                  | 466,435           | 0.69                  |
| 26   | 3,020,850   | 3.52                  | 466,435           | 0.54                  |
| 30   | 3,480,708   | 3.49                  | 466,435           | 0.47                  |
| 31   | 3,587,169   | 3.48                  | 0                 | 0.00                  |
| 36   | 4,038,929   | 3.44                  | 0                 | 0.00                  |
| 41   | 4,318,116   | 3.38                  | 0                 | 0.00                  |
| 46   | 4,386,254   | 3.32                  | 0                 | 0.00                  |
| 51   | 4,235,883   | 3.25                  | 0                 | 0.00                  |

The asset buildup is much more rapid than under the traditional accrued benefit cost method. By the end of the supplemental liability amortization period, the actuarial liability and asset accumulation are in balance and remain so thereafter. After nine years, the asset accumulation surpasses the plan termination liability and the margin increases in absolute terms with each passing year. By the 30th year, the assets have grown to $88,409,890 while the plan termination liability is only $64,008,760, an excess of 38 percent. With the completion of the supplemental liability amortization the percentage margin of plan assets over the plan termination liability declines, dropping to 25 percent by the end of the period. This excess results from the leveling of future costs that is characteristic of individual level cost methods.

| Annual Cost | | | Assets | | |
|---|---|---|---|---|---|
| In Dollars | As Percent of Salary | Actuarial Liability Beginning of Year | In Dollars* | As Percent of Actuarial Liability | As Percent of Plan Termination Liability |
| $1,001,998 | 6.68% | $ 6,805,627 | $ 0 | 0% | 0% |
| 1,057,696 | 6.38 | 7,745,227 | 1,025,684 | 13 | 22 |
| 1,117,257 | 6.13 | 8,761,275 | 2,132,981 | 24 | 39 |
| 1,180,822 | 5.90 | 9,859,697 | 3,328,127 | 34 | 53 |
| 1,248,495 | 5.70 | 11,046,797 | 4,617,754 | 42 | 65 |
| 1,320,358 | 5.53 | 12,329,191 | 6,008,827 | 49 | 75 |
| 1,396,017 | 5.37 | 13,713,780 | 7,508,615 | 55 | 83 |
| 1,475,993 | 5.23 | 15,206,957 | 9,123,904 | 60 | 91 |
| 1,560,302 | 5.10 | 16,816,055 | 10,862,440 | 65 | 97 |
| 1,648,923 | 4.99 | 18,548,644 | 12,732,233 | 69 | 102 |
| 1,741,802 | 4.88 | 20,412,431 | 14,741,457 | 72 | 107 |
| 2,261,998 | 4.49 | 31,947,959 | 27,146,015 | 85 | 124 |
| 2,858,490 | 4.24 | 47,802,160 | 44,163,176 | 92 | 133 |
| 3,487,285 | 4.06 | 68,606,792 | 66,524,109 | 97 | 137 |
| 3,947,144 | 3.96 | 88,876,325 | 88,409,890 | 99 | 138 |
| 3,587,169 | 3.48 | 94,406,042 | 94,406,042 | 100 | 138 |
| 4,038,929 | 3.44 | 124,338,932 | 124,338,932 | 100 | 135 |
| 4,318,116 | 3.38 | 156,653,862 | 156,653,862 | 100 | 132 |
| 4,386,254 | 3.32 | 188,688,487 | 188,688,487 | 100 | 129 |
| 4,235,882 | 3.25 | 217,242,613 | 217,242,613 | 100 | 125 |

*Figures in this column represent the assets at the beginning of each year before the contribution for that year is made. The plan begins without assets, the first contribution being made immediately thereafter.

The annual cost and asset accumulation under the aggregate level cost method without supplemental liability are depicted in Table 12. There is no actuarial liability in the conventional sense under this method since the accumulated assets plus the present value of future annual costs at all times equal the present value of future benefits. Under this method, the adequacy of the asset accumulation may be measured against the plan termination liability.

The annual cost, whether expressed in dollars or as a percentage of payroll, is higher in the early years under this method than under the other two methods, and the asset accumulation is commensurately greater. This stems from the fact that for this particular plan population and this set of actuarial assumptions the unfunded future costs during the early years of the forecast are being am-

**TABLE 12**
**Annual Cost and Asset Accumulation under the Aggregate Cost Method**
**without Supplemental Liability**

| | Annual Cost | | Assets | |
| --- | --- | --- | --- | --- |
| Year | In Dollars | As Percent of Salary | In Dollars* | As Percent of Salary |
| 1 | $1,171,147 | 7.81% | $        0 | 0% |
| 2 | 1,199,101 | 7.24 | 1,204,982 | 25 |
| 3 | 1,231,743 | 6.75 | 2,472,925 | 45 |
| 4 | 1,269,297 | 6.34 | 3,809,822 | 61 |
| 5 | 1,311,933 | 5.99 | 5,222,135 | 73 |
| 6 | 1,359,738 | 5.69 | 6,716,715 | 83 |
| 7 | 1,412,747 | 5.43 | 8,300,719 | 92 |
| 8 | 1,470,622 | 5.21 | 9,981,267 | 99 |
| 9 | 1,533,715 | 5.01 | 11,765,552 | 105 |
| 10 | 1,601,979 | 4.84 | 13,661,350 | 110 |
| 11 | 1,675,339 | 4.70 | 15,676,561 | 114 |
| 16 | 2,111,636 | 4.19 | 27,804,030 | 127 |
| 21 | 2,644,987 | 3.92 | 43,996,038 | 132 |
| 26 | 3,231,811 | 3.77 | 64,922,662 | 134 |
| 31 | 3,778,412 | 3.67 | 90,682,840 | 133 |
| 36 | 4,232,751 | 3.60 | 120,496,473 | 131 |
| 41 | 4,530,884 | 3.55 | 152,706,598 | 129 |
| 46 | 4,625,108 | 3.50 | 184,734,757 | 126 |
| 51 | 4,449,301 | 3.45 | 213,435,153 | 123 |

*Figures in this column represent the assets at the beginning of each year before the contribution for that year is made. The plan begins without assets, the first contribution being made immediately thereafter.

ortized over a period of about 16 years, as compared to 30 years under the other two methods.[7] By the eighth year the annual cost drops below the combined normal and supplemental costs of the entry age normal cost method, but the normal cost of the latter understandably remains below the annual cost under the aggregate method to the end of the 50-year period. The annual cost under the aggregate method moves below the combined costs of the traditional accrued benefit cost method around the 26th year and below the traditional accrued benefit cost method *normal* cost around the 29th year.

Consistent with the characteristics of this cost method, the growth in assets is even more rapid than under the entry age normal cost

[7]The period over which the remaining unfunded costs is amortized declines as the average attained age of the plan population increases.

method and much more vigorous than under the traditional accrued benefit cost method. After one year the plan assets are more than one fifth of the plan termination liability, and after three years they have grown to 61 percent. Within eight years the accumulated assets exceed the plan termination liability, the margin reaching 34 percent after 25 years. The excess declines thereafter, being 23 percent by the end of the simulation.

The most significant ratios from the preceding tables are summarized in Table 13 for easy comparison among the three actuarial cost methods.

In addition to its use in projecting costs, assets, and liabilities for funding purposes, forecasts can be used to project amounts for accounting purposes.

## Forecast as an Actuarial Cost Method

The amount of pension cost to be recognized and funded each year could be determined by a long-term forecast of the plan's liability. Such a cost determination would not be carried out through a series of annual closed group valuations, as in the foregoing simulation, but through a form of open group valuation.

The first step might well be the selection of a funding objective. The length of the forecast period, e.g., 25 years, is a key element of the funding objective. One possible objective might be to accumulate assets equal to the actuarial liability on an ongoing plan basis by the end of the forecast period. Another objective might be to accumulate assets equal to the plan termination liability within a specified time, possibly shorter than the forecast period. The funding objective might include a contribution pattern for reaching the ultimate objectives, such as contributions that are a level percentage of salaries during the forecast period.

The second step in the process would be to project the existing plan population ahead to the end of a selected period, using best estimate assumptions as to increments and decrements, especially the age and sex distribution of the new entrants. This projection would include, for each year, the active participants and their compensation, as well as the terminated and retired participants and beneficiaries and the amounts of their benefit payments.

The third step would be to calculate the amount of the funding objective at the end of the forecast period. For example, if the

**TABLE 13**
**Summary of Costs and Asset Accumulations under Three Actuarial Cost Methods**

| Cost Method | Year of Plan Operation | Annual Cost as Percent of Payroll | | | Assets as Percent of | |
|---|---|---|---|---|---|---|
| | | Normal Cost | Supplemental Cost | Total | Actuarial Liability | Plan Termination Liability |
| Traditional accrued benefit cost method with supplemental liability | 1 | 2.89 | 1.56 | 4.45 | 0 | 0 |
| | 6 | 2.85 | 0.98 | 3.83 | 55 | 48 |
| | 11 | 2.94 | 0.66 | 3.60 | 77 | 68 |
| | 16 | 3.09 | 0.47 | 3.56 | 88 | 78 |
| | 21 | 3.30 | 0.35 | 3.65 | 94 | 84 |
| | 26 | 3.55 | 0.27 | 3.82 | 98 | 88 |
| | 31 | 3.86 | 0.00 | 3.86 | 100 | 91 |
| | 36 | 4.21 | 0.00 | 4.21 | 100 | 92 |
| | 41 | 4.59 | 0.00 | 4.59 | 100 | 93 |
| | 46 | 5.00 | 0.00 | 5.00 | 100 | 94 |
| | 51 | 5.44 | 0.00 | 5.44 | 100 | 94 |
| Entry age normal cost method with supplemental liability | 1 | 3.57 | 3.11 | 6.68 | 0 | 0 |
| | 6 | 3.57 | 1.95 | 5.52 | 49 | 75 |
| | 11 | 3.58 | 1.31 | 4.89 | 72 | 107 |
| | 16 | 3.57 | 0.93 | 4.50 | 85 | 124 |

| | | | | | |
|---|---|---|---|---|---|
| 21 | 3.55 | 0.69 | 4.24 | 92 | 133 |
| 26 | 3.52 | 0.54 | 4.06 | 97 | 137 |
| 31 | 3.48 | 0.00 | 3.48 | 100 | 138 |
| 36 | 3.44 | 0.00 | 3.44 | 100 | 135 |
| 41 | 3.38 | 0.00 | 3.38 | 100 | 132 |
| 46 | 3.32 | 0.00 | 3.32 | 100 | 129 |
| 51 | 3.25 | 0.00 | 3.25 | 100 | 125 |

Aggregate cost method without supplemental liability

| | | | | | |
|---|---|---|---|---|---|
| 1 | — | — | 7.81 | — | 0 |
| 6 | — | — | 5.69 | — | 83 |
| 11 | — | — | 4.70 | — | 114 |
| 16 | — | — | 4.19 | — | 127 |
| 21 | — | — | 3.92 | — | 132 |
| 26 | — | — | 3.77 | — | 134 |
| 31 | — | — | 3.67 | — | 133 |
| 36 | — | — | 3.60 | — | 131 |
| 41 | — | — | 3.55 | — | 129 |
| 46 | — | — | 3.50 | — | 126 |
| 51 | — | — | 3.45 | — | 123 |

funding objective were to accumulate assets equal to the actuarial liability under the entry age normal cost method at the end of 25 years, then such a liability would be determined as of that date based upon the projected population of active, terminated vested, and retired participants and beneficiaries as of that date. Such a valuation would be made using the same methods previously described.

The final step would be to determine the amount of contributions required to meet and satisfy the funding objective. The assets of the plan at the beginning of the forecast period plus the contributions paid during the forecast period must be sufficient, together with investment earnings, to provide the benefits projected to be paid during the forecast period and to accumulate a balance of assets at the end of the forecast period equal to the funding objective at that time. The determination of the present value of future contributions is accomplished by determining the present value, as of the beginning of the forecast period, of the respective items as follows:

$$\begin{array}{c} \text{Present value} \\ \text{of future} \\ \text{contributions} \end{array} = \begin{array}{c} \text{Present value} \\ \text{of benefit payments} \\ \text{during forecast} \\ \text{period} \end{array} + \begin{array}{c} \text{Present value} \\ \text{of forecast} \\ \text{objective} \end{array} - \begin{array}{c} \text{Initial} \\ \text{plan} \\ \text{assets} \end{array}$$

If it is desired that future contributions be a level percentage of compensation, this percentage can be determined by dividing the present value of future contributions by the present value of future compensation during the forecast period.

This determination is illustrated for an employer whose funding objective is to accumulate the actuarial liability under the entry age normal cost method at the end of 25 years by a level percentage of compensation. The data and assumptions are those shown earlier in this chapter.

The benefit payments for certain years were shown in Table 9. The total benefit payments during the 25-year period are $21,613,778. The present value of these payments, discounted at 6 percent interest to the beginning of the period, is $8,321,978.

The actuarial liability under the entry age normal cost method at the end of the 25 years, as shown in Table 11, is $68,606,792. The present value of this amount, discounted at 6 percent interest for 25 years is $15,985,314.

In the example the initial plan assets were assumed to be $0. Thus, the present value of future contributions is $24,307,292 ($8,321,978 present value of benefit payments plus $15,985,314 present value of funding objective less $0 assets).

The projection of future salaries for certain years is shown in Table 9. The total salaries projected to be paid during the 25-year period is $1,095,182,065. Discounted at 6 percent interest, the present value of this amount is $484,587,847. The contribution percentage required to satisfy the funding objective equals the present value of future contributions ($24,307,292) divided by the present value of future compensation ($484,587,847) and is 5.02 percent.

The employer could not actually contribute this amount unless it were sufficient to satisfy the minimum funding requirement but not greater than the maximum deductible limit during each year. Table 11 shows that 5.02 percent contributions would not be sufficient to satisfy the minimum funding requirement in the early years if the entry age normal cost method were used for the funding requirements. This would force the employer either to modify the initially proposed funding pattern or to adopt a different actuarial cost method for purposes of determining the minimum funding requirements.

One or more years after the initial forecast a new forecast can be made, taking account of then current asset values and participant data and an updated forecast of anticipated experience. It would not be necessary to make annual forecasts, but they could be undertaken every few years, or whenever there are significant new developments.

This technique of establishing cost accruals and funding contributions might come close to satisfying the four objectives of an actuarial cost method postulated in Chapter 13, if actual experience follows the projections. The annual cost and funding contributions could be calculated as a level percentage of covered payroll or level dollar amounts, whichever is desired. The actuarial liability and associated assets would not need to exceed the plan termination liability. In fact, the accumulation of assets equal to the plan termination liability after a reasonable period of years could be the central funding objective, which would satisfy the third objective mentioned. There would be flexibility in the choice of the period over which the funding objective is to be accomplished, and there could be provision for modification of the costing and funding schedule in the event of fiscal exigencies. On the other hand, it can be argued that assumptions regarding new entrants over a long future period are likely to be too unreliable to serve as a basis for a plan's funding.

The forecast actuarial cost method, as it might be termed, is not one of the approved cost methods for determining the maximum tax deductible limit upon contributions or for complying with the minimum funding standards. Indeed, some persons believe that the approach is too unstructured even to justify characterization as an actuarial cost method. It is clearly a management tool that, properly used, could provide useful insight into both near-term and long-term fiscal implications of a pension plan. In some circumstances it would seem practicable, and perhaps highly desirable, to have cost forecasts made for the guidance of plan sponsors, while determining the income tax deductions and funding requirements on the basis of conventional and officially recognized cost methods.

## Stochastic Forecasting

The simulations set forth above are *deterministic* in nature (i.e., the results are determined by a single set of economic experience assumptions).[8] If there is a high probability that the assumptions will be realized over time, a deterministic forecast with one set of assumptions can be a useful management tool. Financial forecasts can be developed with respect to various combinations of plan specifications, economic and demographic assumptions, actuarial cost methods, and funding policies. However, great uncertainty attaches to any assumptions that purport to reflect future economic developments, especially the rate of inflation. The rate of *expected* inflation is a component of the salary scale and the rate of investment return and serves as the basis of postretirement benefit adjustments.

---

[8]It will be recalled that a forecast of pension plan costs, liabilities, cash flow, and asset accumulations usually utilizes two sets of actuarial assumptions: (1) the *valuation* assumptions, which establish the plan's actuarial liabilities, cost, and funding contributions (and hence the employer's tax deductions for the plan) before adjustment for experience gains and losses; and (2) the *experience* assumptions, which produce annual adjustments in costs and contributions through actuarial gains flowing from more realistic assumptions, especially those of an economic character. Stochastic forecasting is concerned with experience assumptions and their variability.

In recognition of uncertainty over future economic events, the plan actuary may prepare several deterministic simulations, each based upon a separate set of economic experience assumptions. For example, he may prepare projections based upon three sets of economic assumptions, characterized as optimistic, pessimistic, and most probable. Nevertheless, for each projection the assumptions are fixed throughout the forecast period or follow a predetermined pattern, such as a downward graded schedule of interest rate assumptions.

On the other hand, the simulation may be made on a basis that reflects the observed variability of the economic forces that form the foundation of the economic assumptions. Such a simulation employs Monte Carlo techniques and is generally referred to as a *stochastic forecast*. Since, in theory, economic forces are infinitely variable, it is necessary to construct and parameterize a model that will track the behavior of the forces shaping the economic experience assumptions.

The most basic economic assumption for a pension plan is that pertaining to the annual rate of investment return. Unfortunately, the rate of return on the portfolio of a given pension plan can vary greatly from year to year, reflecting broad market forces as well as forces specific to the individual portfolio holdings. For instance, during the 10 years 1978 to 1987, the aggregate annual rate of return on the 500 common stocks making up Standard & Poor's Composite Index ranged from a high of 32.4 percent to a low of $-4.9$ percent. The total annual rate of return on portfolios of intermediate and long-term bonds has also displayed considerable volatility.

To generate a pattern of returns on the portfolio of a particular pension plan, it is necessary to partition the portfolio into various broad classes of assets, such as equities, intermediate and long-term bonds, and cash equivalents (money market instruments). Each component of the portfolio has its own distribution of returns, but there is no extant probability distribution that precisely describes the historically observed pattern of return for any class of assets. Experience suggests, however, that the pattern of annual returns on a portfolio, or any of its major components, can be modeled by a normal distribution (in statistical terms). The various portfolio components vary in the mean and dispersion of their normal distribution. For example, the normal distribution of possible returns on debt instruments is characterized by a smaller expected return and narrower dispersion than that for common stock. Once these distributions have been quantified, Monte Carlo techniques can be used to create sequences of random returns for the portfolio and any of its components.

The distribution of returns for any portfolio, or subset thereof, is determined by assumptions about its *mean* return and its *standard deviation* or other measure of dispersion. These two values are derived from observation of historical experience, tempered by judgment as to the course of future events. The area beneath the curve of the probability distribution is partitioned into, say, 100 segments of equal area, with the segments being assigned numbers from 1 to 100. For each year in the forecast, a large quantity of random numbers from 1 to 100 are generated and then associated with their corresponding segment, thereby establishing a pattern of random returns. Typically, 200 to 500 expected returns are generated for each year of the forecast, with a full gamut of related values, such as asset accumulation, being projected with each of the random returns. These randomly generated returns take the place of the fixed, predetermined rate (or rates) of return associated with a deterministic simulation model. The net effect is that a stochastic forecast can be characterized as a set of deterministic forecasts in respect of which the economic assumptions of each forecast are determined randomly by statistical technique, rather than by exercise of subjective judgment.

More realism can be introduced into the simulation if account is taken of the variability of inflation. As indicated above, inflation impacts benefit payouts through the salary scale and cost-of-living adjustments and both nominal and real rates of return. Expected inflation can be built into the projections on a deterministic and judgmental basis, but *unexpected* inflation is a disruptive influence. Unexpected inflation can be randomly generated in a manner similar to the random generation of expected returns, based on assumptions about the potential range of unexpected inflation. Also, serial correlation may be involved in the year-to-year inflation rates, and appropriate weights must be assigned to the randomly generated annual rates of inflation and the assumed long-run rate to develop the expected rate of inflation for successive years. An algorithm based on historical relationships must be developed to measure the impact of simulated inflation on the *real* and *nominal* rates of return on the various subsets of the portfolio and, through an assumed *mix* of asset classes, on the real and nominal rates of return on the entire portfolio. This impact is, of course, created through the process of randomly generated unexpected rates of inflation.

Once a stochastic forecast has been developed, it can be analyzed to ascertain statistical probabilities of various results and to assess the volatility of those results. For example, in contrast to the deterministic forecast illustrated in Table 11, which projects an asset accumulation of $14,741,457 at the end of 10 years, a stochastic forecast would have the capability of indicating the statistical probability that the assets of the plan at that time would be greater or smaller than that amount or fall within a range of, for example, $13 million to $16 million.

The primary function of a stochastic simulation is to make the plan sponsor aware of the potential range of outcomes over the forecast period, with an indication of the probabilities and volatility involved, in contrast to predicting a specific future result. The simulations may vary greatly as to the scope and sophistication of the assumed relationships among the economic cost factors and their impact on other elements. Needless to say, the results of a stochastic forecast are no more reliable than the validity of the assumed relationships among the relevant variables and the potential range of the fluctuations, as constrained by the parameters.[9]

## Questions

1. Contrast a conventional open group valuation of a pension plan (or national old-age insurance program) with a forecast of pension costs, liabilities, cash flows, and asset accumulations that employs a series of closed group valuations with dynamic population and salary assumptions.
2. Describe the items of information typically provided under a pension plan cost forecast.

---

[9]For a fuller and more general treatment of stochastic processes, the interested student should consult Frederich S. Hillier and Gerald J. Lieberman, *Introduction to Operations Research* (San Francisco: Holden-Day, 1967), pp. 439–76.

3.  Explain in terms of the actuarial functions involved why the normal cost of the simulated pension plan increases over time under the traditional accrued benefit cost method whereas the normal cost under the entry age normal cost method remains constant for many years and then declines.

4.  Why is the annual cost of the simulated pension plan under the aggregate cost method greater in the early years than the annual cost under the traditional accrued benefit cost method and individual entry age normal cost method?

5.  Why is the aggregate cost method characterized as a *level* cost method despite the fact that the annual cost changes with each valuation?

6.  Will the asset accumulation under the traditional accrued benefit cost method *always* be less than the plan termination liability? Will the ultimate asset accumulation under the individual entry age normal cost method be greater than the plan termination liability under all circumstances? Explain.

7.  In your opinion, what should be the funding objective of a pension plan sponsor when annual costs and funding contributions are to be determined under the forecast approach? Answer in terms of the *measure of liability* to be employed at the end of the forecast period and the *number of years* over which the liability is to be amortized.

8.  Describe the difference in methodology in determining the plan termination liability of a pension plan and the actuarial liability at the same point in time under one of the entry age normal cost methods.

9.  To what extent could the forecast type of actuarial cost method be made to satisfy the characteristics or properties of an "ideal" actuarial cost method postulated earlier?

10. Why might the IRS have reservations about approving the forecast approach as a method for determining minimum funding requirements or tax-deductible contributions to a pension plan?

11. How do stochastic forecasts differ from deterministic forecasts?

# 16 | Valuation of Ancillary Benefits, Employee Contributions, and Small Plans

THE FOUR PRECEDING CHAPTERS have been concerned with the valuation of the retirement benefits of a defined benefit pension plan. However, all plans must by law provide withdrawal benefits and survivor benefits and, at the option of the employer or other plan sponsor, disability benefits and additional death benefits may be provided. The cost of these ancillary benefits must be recognized in the valuation process. Procedures for determining the cost of these benefits are discussed in this chapter. The special problems associated with contributory plans and small plans are also considered.

## Ancillary Benefits

### Withdrawal Benefits[1]

Withdrawal benefits are those payable to participants who leave the plan before early or normal retirement age. They are payable

---

[1]For a detailed discussion of the cost of withdrawal benefits, see Dan M. McGill, *Preservation of Pension Benefits Rights* (Homewood, Ill.: Richard D. Irwin, 1972), pp. 141–76; and Dan M. McGill and Howard E. Winklevoss, "A Quantitative Analysis of Actuarial Cost Methods for Pension Plans," *Proceedings of the Conference of Actuaries in Public Practice* 23 (1974), pp. 212–43.

only to participants who had achieved a fully or partially vested status prior to termination, which in the case of a contributory plan encompasses all participants, in respect of benefits attributable to their own contributions. The benefits may be payable in the form of cash (often limited to refund of employee contributions) or a deferred claim to income payments commencing at early or normal retirement age. The following discussion is addressed primarily to income benefits.

The valuation of the withdrawal benefits of a pension plan must recognize the expected or actual benefits of three subsets of the plan population: active participants, terminated vested participants, and retired participants. The valuation of the benefits of the active population is by far the most complex.

**Active Participants.**    The valuation of withdrawal benefits is basically the same as the valuation of retirement benefits except that, in the determination of both the normal cost and the actuarial liability, the present value of withdrawal benefits is used in lieu of the present value of retirement benefits.

The first step in calculating the present value of the expected withdrawal benefits of an active participant is to calculate the annual amount of projected accrued benefit for each age at which the participant can potentially terminate with vested benefits. This projection will ordinarily reflect future years of credited service and projected salary increases up to the potential termination date. But if the traditional accrued benefit cost method is used, instead of the projected accrued benefit, the benefit accrued to the valuation date and the benefit to be accrued during the year following the valuation date are determined for purposes of the actuarial liability and the normal cost respectively.

The second step is to calculate the vested accrued benefit for each age at which the participant can potentially terminate with vested benefits. This is done by multiplying the accrued benefits determined in the preceding step by the vesting percentage applicable to each age.

The third step is to determine what the value of such benefits at each age would be if the participant were to terminate at such age. This value is calculated by multiplying the amount of annual vested accrued benefit by the value of a deferred annuity of $1 beginning at the normal retirement age. This value of a deferred annuity equals the value of an immediate annuity as of the normal retirement age discounted to the age of possible termination by interest and by the probability of surviving in the interim years.

The fourth step is to discount, with interest, back to the date as of which the present value of withdrawal benefits is to be determined, the values found in the third step (which were as of the dates of possible termination). This provides the value, at the date as of which the present value of withdrawal benefits is to be determined, of the vested accrued benefit potentially payable at each age at which the participant can possibly terminate with vested benefits.

The fifth step is to multiply this potential value with respect to each age at which the participant might terminate by the probability that he will actually do so. This probability equals the probability that he will (1) survive in service to that age,[2] and (2) terminate his service during that age. The first component of that probability reflects the impact of the three decremental forces discussed earlier (in connection with retirement benefits), and the same assumptions as to the rates of termination, death, and total disability would be made. The second component involves only the probabilities of withdrawal and death for the year in question.

The sixth step in calculating the present value of the expected withdrawal benefits of an active participant is to sum for the participant the values just computed of withdrawal benefits payable upon termination at each possible age. While this process has been described as a series of steps, the computer, of course, accomplishes them successively in moments, producing the final result for the individual and combining it with the results for all other active participants. To simplify the computation it is usually assumed that all terminations will occur at either the beginning or the end of the year.

The actuarial present value of withdrawal benefits in respect of active participants can be, and usually is, allocated to the participants' years of service in accordance with the same actuarial cost method that is used to allocate retirement benefits. When an individual cost allocation cost method is used, the actuarial liability

---

[2]For a participant who has already achieved a vested status, this probability for the *current* year is 1, or certainty.

for withdrawal benefits may be negative for many active participants and, indeed, the actuarial liability for the entire group of active participants may be negative. The explanation for this seemingly anomalous result is that the probability of termination decreases with age and a level normal cost may be less than the actual annual cost at the younger ages. This negative actuarial liability for withdrawal benefits will automatically decrease the actuarial liability for the plan as a whole, if the cost of retirement benefits and the cost of withdrawal benefits are computed in a single operation, as they frequently are. If separate calculations are used, any negative actuarial liability for withdrawal benefits is subtracted from the positive actuarial liability for retirement benefits.

When the traditional accrued benefit cost method is used, and the benefit that accrues in a particular year is a definitely fixed quantity, it is not necessary to make a separate calculation of the cost of withdrawal benefits. The cost can be accurately reflected in the cost of retirement benefits by assuming no terminations among the participants whose benefits have fully vested. If a vested participant should, in fact, terminate, the actuarial value of his withdrawal benefit generally would be precisely the same as the actuarial value of his accrued retirement benefit at the moment before termination. Thus the termination would have no effect on the actuarial liability of the plan. Since it is expedient to use the same termination rates for all participants who are at the same attained age, regardless of their entry age, the termination assumption may be eliminated at all ages above the *average* age at which full vesting is achieved. The shortcut, of course, yields only the approximate cost of vesting. An even less precise, but more conservative, approach is to assume that there will be no withdrawals at any ages, with an actuarial gain being produced whenever a participant terminates with a nonvested accrued benefit. This technique is especially associated with allocated funding instruments, since it is impracticable to use termination assumptions with individual allocation of funds.

The technique of assuming no withdrawals among fully vested participants is also sometimes used in connection with the projected accrued benefit cost method or with cost allocation cost methods, but the cost of vesting (or withdrawal benefits) is overstated. If a participant were to terminate after having achieved a fully vested status, the actuarial liability for this vested benefit would be less than his actuarial liability as an active participant just prior to termination, resulting in an actuarial gain of the difference.

**Terminated Vested Participants.** The valuation of the vested benefits payable to terminated participants is somewhat simpler. These individuals have already satisfied two of the requisite conditions for benefit entitlement. They survived in service to vesting and then later severed their employment relationship. The only remaining requirement is that they survive to early or normal retirement. Moreover, the amount of their benefits is fixed, unless subject to cost-of-living adjustments. The actuarial present value of the benefits of a terminated vested participant is derived by: (1) multiplying the benefit amount by the probability of survival to normal retirement age, (2) multiplying the sum so derived by the annuity factor for the normal retirement age, and (3) discounting the value obtained in (2) to the date of valuation. All the factors and assumptions are identical to those used for active participants. In effect, the valuation is accomplished in accordance with the principles of the benefit allocation cost method.

**Retired Vested Participants.** The valuation of the benefits of terminated vested participants who have begun to receive income payments is the simplest procedure of the three. The actuarial liability associated with a particular individual is determined by multiplying the dollar amount of his benefits by the annuity factor for his attained age. This is done for each individual in the retired group, using the annuity factor appropriate for the participant's sex and attained age. Terminated vested participants who have later retired are usually combined with all other retired participants for valuation purposes.

The sum of the actuarial liability of the withdrawal benefits associated with active, terminated vested, and retired vested participants constitutes the actuarial liability for withdrawal benefits for the plan as a whole.

### Death Benefits

The actuarial present value of preretirement death benefits provided under a pension plan is usually determined in accordance with the principles governing the net single premium of an individual life insurance contract. There is one important difference. Whereas the net single premium takes into account only the probability of death and an assumed rate of interest, the actuarial present value of pension plan death benefits must also recognize the probability that the participant may withdraw from the plan and no longer be exposed to the possibility of death in service.

**Preretirement Lump-Sum Benefit.**    The actuarial present value of a preretirement lump-sum benefit is determined by multiplying the amount of the benefit by the separate probabilities that the participant will die in service in each year from the date of valuation to retirement age and discounting the expected value of the benefit for each year back to the date of valuation at an assumed rate of interest. The sum of the discounted yearly values represents the actuarial present value of the benefit. The calculation for each year must reflect the probability that the participant will survive in service to that year and then die in that year. This requires recognition of the combined probabilities of death, withdrawal, and total disability prior to each year in the computation. This is accomplished, as with retirement benefits, by applying the yearly probabilities of these occurrences to the plan population cells and showing the survivors year by year. Then the appropriate death rate is applied to the surviving members of the cell. The rates of decrement are usually assumed to be the same as those used in the valuation of retirement and withdrawal benefits.

When the retirement benefits of a plan are being valued on the basis of a cost allocation cost method, the actuarial present value of the preretirement death benefits will be allocated to years of service in the same manner as the cost of retirement benefits. However, if the basic benefits are being valued on the basis of a benefit allocation cost method, a special procedure may be used for the valuation of the death benefit. Under this procedure, a portion of the lump-sum death benefit is assumed to accrue each year and the single premium cost of that "piece" of death benefit is charged to expense for the year. If the death benefit does not vary with years of service, the unit of benefit accrued each year is arbitrarily determined and an actuarial loss will ordinarily occur in the year of death, since the full cost of the death benefit will not have been accrued.

Another general approach to the valuation of a preretirement death benefit is the so-called one-year term insurance method. Under this method, the current year's cost for death benefits is assumed to be an amount equal to the death benefits expected to be paid during the year, discounted back to the beginning of the year at the valuation rate of interest. There is no actuarial liability under this method. If actual benefit disbursements exceed those expected, there will be an actuarial loss; and if the disbursements are less than expected, there will be an actuarial gain. Under a modification of this method, all actuarial gains are accumulated in a special reserve for future adverse experience.

In some plans, the preretirement death benefit is approximately or precisely equal to the actuarial liability for retirement benefits. In that case, the additional cost of the death benefit may be obtained indirectly by omitting the mortality assumption in the valuation of the pension benefit. There is no additional cost or loss upon death, since the benefit paid equals the actuarial liability for retirement benefits, which is released. In those small plans where no preretirement mortality is assumed in the valuation of pensions (see below), it is considered appropriate to ignore the cost of uninsured preretirement death benefits if they do not significantly exceed the actuarial liability.

**Preretirement Income Benefit.** Preretirement income death benefits may include both ERISA's required survivor annuity and other survivor income benefits. They are valued in the same way as lump-sum death benefits except that the value of the income benefit changes each year. The lump-sum benefit for a given year is a known quantity, but the amount at risk under an income benefit in any given year is the present value of an immediate or deferred life annuity in the amount stipulated. Survivor annuity benefits not required by ERISA sometimes terminate with the remarriage of the spouse before a specified age. Benefits to children usually cease at a stated age, such as 18. The present value of the immediate or deferred life annuity is calculated in the same manner as any other annuity, reflecting the yearly probabilities of survival and discounting of each benefit payment; but if benefits cease on remarriage, the value must be reduced by the yearly probabilities that the income recipient will remarry before a stipulated age. Many actuaries use the remarriage rates of female income beneficiaries of the Railroad Retirement System. The yearly probabilities of marriage, by years since widowhood, for quinquennial ages at widowhood 30 through 55 are shown in Table 14.[3]

An assumption may be made concerning the proportion of participants who are married, since only these will be covered for benefits payable to a spouse. Some experience supports the assumption that 80 percent of male workers and 50 percent of female workers are married. An assumption may be made that all participants are unmarried, in effect eliminating the valuation of survivor benefits for living participants; such an assumption may be justified if other actuarial assumptions are conservative in nature and the resulting combination of assumptions satisfies the "reasonable in the aggregate" requirement. If survivor benefits are payable to children, an assumption may be made concerning the number and ages of children.

For purposes of computing the annuity factor, remarriage (if relevant) is treated as a decremental factor, having the same effect as death. Thus, each payment is contingent upon the annuitant

**TABLE 14**
**Yearly Probabilities of Remarriage of Widows under the Railroad Retirement System, according to the 1980 Railroad Retirement Board Remarriage Table**

| Age at Widowhood | Number per 1,000 Remarrying during Year | | | | | | Attained Age* |
|---|---|---|---|---|---|---|---|
| | 0 | 1 | 2 | 3 | 4 | 5 | |
| 20 | 76.00 | 131.82 | 86.31 | 73.35 | 66.58 | 40.70 | 25 |
| 25 | 58.58 | 115.40 | 77.03 | 67.83 | 62.23 | 36.11 | 30 |
| 30 | 39.27 | 97.45 | 71.44 | 64.02 | 58.61 | 34.09 | 35 |
| 35 | 28.78 | 74.22 | 61.40 | 41.03 | 36.55 | 25.85 | 40 |
| 40 | 15.20 | 47.15 | 41.91 | 26.32 | 24.87 | 14.00 | 45 |
| 45 | 8.35 | 23.22 | 23.89 | 17.61 | 13.80 | 6.29 | 50 |
| 50 | 5.03 | 9.94 | 12.43 | 8.56 | 5.85 | 4.06 | 55 |
| 55 | 3.56 | 7.60 | 7.56 | 6.78 | 5.06 | 3.95 | 60 |

*Remarriage rates for the attained ages below are those shown for the fifth year of widowhood. Attained age rates, known as "ultimate" rates, are the ones used by actuaries in valuing benefits subject to a remarriage provision.

[3]*Sixteenth Actuarial Valuation,* Table S–7, U.S. Railroad Retirement Board. See also Francisco Bayo, "Mortality and Remarriage Experience for Widow Beneficiaries under OASDI," *Transactions of the Society of Actuaries* 21, part 1 (1969), pp. 59–80.

being alive in an unmarried state. Most plans remove the restriction on remarriage after the annuitant reaches age 60.

**Survivor Income Benefits for Deferred Vested Participants.** ERISA requires survivor income benefits to be provided upon the death of terminated participants entitled to deferred vested benefits. The value of such benefits needs to be determined for all individuals who have already attained such status. This involves computations similar to the computation of the value of survivor income benefits for active participants.

In addition, the value of such survivor benefits payable upon the death of a terminated vested employee while eligible for a deferred vested pension must also be computed for all active employees, since all active employees may potentially enter deferred vested status with such accompanying survivor benefit coverage. The valuation of these benefits combines the techniques of valuation for active participants of the deferred retirement benefits payable upon withdrawal and the valuation of survivor income benefits payable with respect to those who have already withdrawn.

The valuation of survivor benefits related to death during the period of entitlement to deferred vested benefits is quite complex, while the magnitude of the value of the benefits may be so small as to be of little significance. This has led some actuaries to adopt one of the several alternative simplifications:

1.  Assume no deaths among terminated participants during the period of deferral (increasing the value of deferred pensions while eliminating the value of survivor benefits), a conservative approach; or
2.  Assume that all terminated employees will be immediately paid in a lump-sum distribution (eliminating the value of survivor benefits payable upon death after termination of employment); or
3.  Assume that all participants are unmarried (eliminating the value of survivor benefits both before and after retirement), an unconservative approach which may be justified if other actuarial assumptions are conservative.

**Postretirement Death Benefits.** Postretirement lump-sum death benefits are valued in the same manner as preretirement lump-sum benefits, except that there is no possibility of loss of coverage through withdrawal or total disability. The only probability taken into account is death, and it increases with each increment in attained age, reaching 1, or certainty, with the last age in the annuity table. The costs are recognized and accrued during the working lives of the participants.

Postretirement income death benefits are a function of the annuity form under which the retirement benefits are being paid and are reflected in the calculation of the annuity factor for that type of annuity.

### Disability Benefits

Disability is one of the three decremental forces taken into account in the valuation of retirement, withdrawal, and death benefits. If an explicit, independently determined benefit is payable under the plan in the event of total disability it, too, must be valued as part of the overall valuation of the plan.

**Valuation of Disability Benefits in Respect of Active Participants.** There are three steps in the valuation of a disability benefit for active participants. The first is the determination of the yearly probabilities of the occurrence of disability as defined in the plan. These probabilities are not independent of the probabilities of death and withdrawal and must be combined with them to form a multiple decrement table, as in the valuation of the other types of benefits under the plan. The rate of disablement increases with attained age and varies by sex.

The second step is to determine the present value of the benefits that would be payable should a participant become disabled. The amount of monthly benefit that would be payable is multiplied by a disabled life annuity factor for an annual benefit of $1 payable monthly. The value of a disabled life annuity is usually computed on the basis of a mortality table that reflects higher rates of mortality than those associated with active lives. It should, in theory, also reflect the probability that the disabled person will recover from his disablement. However, since the cost reduction associated with recovery would be partially offset by the cost of restoring the accrued benefits of the individual as an active participant, the probability of recovery is often ignored in the interest of simplicity.

Even if the recovery probability is recognized, the cost of restoring the accrued retirement benefits may be ignored. A disabled life annuity factor must be computed for each age at which a participant could qualify for disability benefits under the plan. In this regard, it is similar to the survivor annuity described in the preceding section. Like the probability of disablement, the value of a disabled life annuity varies with the attained age and sex of the disabled person.

The third step is to multiply the disability benefit that would be payable at each potential age of disablement by the probability that the participant will survive in employment to that age and *then become disabled at that age,* with the result being multiplied by the value of a disabled life annuity at that age and discounted back to the valuation date at the same rate of interest used for other valuations. These calculations are made for all active participants and summed.

Disability benefits for active participants can be, and frequently are, valued on the basis of the same actuarial cost methods and assumptions (except for mortality after disablement) as those used for the normal retirement benefits. The normal cost and actuarial liability for disability benefits may be independently determined or they may be derived in combination with the other benefits under the plan. If the latter procedure is used, the present value of disability benefits expected to be paid in the future is added to the present value of all other benefits and the combined values are assigned to years of service in accordance with the characteristics of the actuarial cost method employed in the valuation. If a benefit allocation cost method is used, an allocation of disability benefits can be made to particular years, similar to the allocation of normal retirement benefits. If a disabled participant continues to accrue retirement benefits, the actuarial present value of these accruals can be recognized annually as they occur or in their entirety at the time of retirement.

Disability benefits can also be valued on a one-year term insurance basis. Under this method, the current year's cost is assumed to be equal to the actuarial present value of all disability benefits ultimately to be paid to all participants who are expected to become disabled during the year. No actuarial liability is set up for participants not disabled. If the present value of future disability benefits for those participants who actually become disabled is greater than the expected present value, an actuarial loss is sustained. If the actual present value is less than the expected, there would be an actuarial gain. There could also be actuarial gains or losses in the future in respect of the disablements of a given year if the duration of the disabilities (reflecting deaths or recoveries) is different from the actuarially predicted durations. In other words, actuarial gains and losses may emerge in connection with either the *expected rate of disablement* or the *expected value of the disabled life annuity.* Actuarial gains may be accumulated in a reserve for future adverse experience with respect to either the rate or duration of disability.

Some plans, especially those so small that no one is likely to become disabled in a particular year, do not use a disability decrement in valuing normal retirement benefits and do not calculate any cost for disability benefits in respect of active participants. If and when a disablement actually occurs, the actuarial present value of the benefits payable to the disabled participant is set up as an actuarial liability, creating an actuarial loss in that amount in the year of disability. This loss, like other gains and losses, may be amortized over a period of years.

**Valuation of Disability Benefits in Payment Status.**  The actuarial present value of the benefits payable to a participant in a disabled state at the time of valuation is derived by multiplying the amount of the benefit by the disabled life annuity factor for the participant's attained age, sex, and (sometimes) duration of disability. This calculation is carried out for all disabled persons, the sum of the present values constituting the actuarial liability for benefits in payment status.

# Valuation of Employee Contributions

Employee contributions to a pension plan may be made on a mandatory basis, as a condition for participation and possibly even as a condition of employment, or on a voluntary basis. Voluntary contributions present no valuation problems since they are accumulated in the participants' individual account and administered on the money purchase principle. The monies in the account are withdrawable in the event of the participant's death, disability, or termination prior to retirement and are payable to the participant at retirement in the form of a lump-sum distribution or supplemental retirement income. On the other hand, mandatory employee contributions may necessitate special valuation procedures because of the employee's right to a refund of his contributions, usually with interest, upon his termination or death before retirement.

Mandatory employee contributions create no valuation problems when the contributions are administered on the money purchase principle and applied to provide retirement benefits supplemental to those financed by employer contributions. However, special valuation procedures must be used when employee contributions are applied to the reduction of employer costs. The new dimension added to the valuation process under this circumstance consists of estimating the probability that a refund of an employee's contributions will have to be made in each of the future years of his participation in the plan and determining the amount of each potential refund. The employer's cost is obviously reduced by employee contributions, but the gross savings is reduced by the refunds that have to be made. The basic purpose of this valuation procedure is to determine the *net* effect of employee contributions on the employer's cost. For this purpose, the employee's right to a refund of his contributions is considered to be an additional benefit of the plan.

In determining the present value of future benefits for active employees, the actuary generally assumes that a refund will be made if an employee dies when no survivor annuity is payable, or if an employee terminates employment before becoming eligible for a vested pension attributable to employer contributions. But if an employee dies when a survivor annuity is payable or terminates employment with a vested pension, it is usually assumed that no refund will be paid, and the entire vested pension or survivor annuity is valued accordingly.

The crucial actuarial function in this valuation procedure is the actuarial present value of the employee's right to a refund of $1, plus accumulated interest, in any future year in which he might die or terminate his employment and receive a refund. The actuarial present value of the refund right for each such future year is the probability of payment (i.e., the probability that the employee will continue in the plan to the beginning of such year and then terminate and receive a refund during the year) times the amount of the payment times the interest discount factor.

An actuarial liability is associated with past employee contributions. Under all actuarial cost methods, this liability is equal to the actuarial present value of the employee's right to a refund of all his prior contributions with interest. If the interest rate credited to employee contributions is the same as the interest rate used in the interest discount factor, the two interest rates offset each other and the present value of any potential refund of $1 is simply the probability of payment times $1. In this case, the present value of the refund of past employee contributions for all future years combined is the accumulated employee contributions with interest as of the valuation date times the probability that the employee will die or terminate employment when a refund is payable. For example, if an employee 35 years of age has $1 of accumulated employee contributions and the probability that he will receive a refund is .60, the present value at age 35 of his right to a refund of the $1 contribution is $1.00 × .60 = $0.60. This simplifies the calculations to such a degree that offsetting interest is sometimes assumed as an approximation even when the two interest rates differ.

Under the traditional accrued benefit cost method, the normal cost should include the value of refunds associated with the current year's contribution. This is calculated in the same manner as the value of refund of past employee contributions, using the current year's contribution in place of the accumulated employee contributions. The total normal cost, including the value of future refunds of the current year's employee contributions, is reduced by the amount of employee contributions for the current year to determine the employer's normal cost for the year.

Under cost allocation cost methods, employee contributions for all years, past and future, and the cost of refunding them, are taken into account. In the valuation equation, the present value of future benefits includes the present value of refunding both accumulated *prior* contributions and *future* contributions. The amount of refund potentially payable in each future year must be projected, multiplied by the probability that it will be paid, and multiplied by the interest discount factor to determine the present value of future refunds. The actuarial liability for the plan equals the present value of future benefits (including refund of employee contributions) minus the present value of future employee contributions and the present value of future employer normal costs. In effect, the present value of future benefits is reduced by the present value of future employee contributions in determining the actuarial liability and the present value of future employer normal costs. Rather than adding the cost of refunding employee contributions to the present value of future benefits, such cost may be offset against the present value of future employee contributions on an exact or approximate basis.

There is a hybrid valuation method under which a cost allocation cost method is used for all items except future employee contributions. In this case, the actuarial liability is determined as if there were not future employee contributions, and the calculated normal cost is reduced by the current year's net employee contributions (contributions less the related cost of refund). The refund cost for prior accumulated employee contributions would be included in the present value of future benefits.

The normal annuity form for most contributory plans is a modified cash refund annuity, which assures ultimate payment of an amount not less than the accumulated contributions of the employee, with interest. The present value of the refund feature can be determined directly and precisely for each employee under such an annuity. However, the additional cost of the refund feature can be approximated by calculating an average ratio of death benefits to monthly income at normal retirement and by using this ratio for all employees irrespective of their particular circumstances.

## Valuation of Small Plans

The great majority of pension plans cover fewer than 25 employees, and the valuation of such small plans involve certain special considerations. In the first place, the experience of the plan is less predictable than that of a larger plan. A plan with 10,000 active participants, for example, may, depending upon the age and sex distribution, experience about 50 deaths per year, or a composite death rate of 0.5 percent, with relatively little annual variation. The number of deaths within an active population of 100 participants would normally be either none, one, or two per year, constituting 0 percent, 1 percent, or 2 percent, respectively, of the active life group. On the other hand, there would normally be no deaths among an active life group of 10 persons; but if a death occurs, the death rate for that year would be 10 percent. There may be equally large variations in the year-to-year rates of withdrawal. Not only will the smaller plan have wider variations in the death and withdrawal rates, but for the very small plan the most probable assumption for any given year may be that there will be no deaths or withdrawals.

Second, it is important to minimize the cost of actuarial valuations for a small plan. The cost of actuarial services should constitute only a small part of the overall cost of the plan. Through the use of computers, complex methods and assumptions may be applied to a large plan at a low cost per employee, whereas the use of the same methods and assumptions for a small plan may produce burdensome costs per employee.

Third, many small plans (but by no means all) have actuarial valuations carried out by persons with limited actuarial skills who may not be qualified to use the more complex methods and assumptions.

Any or all of the foregoing considerations may affect the actuary's choice of actuarial methods and assumptions. He may decide to assume no deaths, no withdrawals, and no disablements prior to retirement, or he may assume no deaths but some withdrawals or vice versa. Even when benefits are based on final average earnings, he may use the individual level premium cost method with no salary scale, accruing the cost of actual salary increases on a level annual cost basis from the participant's attained age to normal retirement age. He may use a simplified approach to determining the cost of withdrawal, death, or disability benefits, or he may ignore such costs altogether. He may be conservative with respect to some assumptions (e.g., no deaths and no withdrawals and a low interest rate) and unconservative with respect to others (e.g., no salary scale with a final average salary formula), expecting that gains from one source will offset losses from another.

However, for even the smallest plans, the assumptions must be reasonable and, in the aggregate, must represent the actuary's best estimate of future experience.[4]

---

[4]ERISA §302(c)(3), I.R.C. §412(c)(3).

## Questions

1. Contrast the valuation of withdrawal benefits for:
   a. Active participants.
   b. Terminated vested participants.
   c. Retired vested participants.

2. Explain the concept of a *negative* actuarial liability that sometimes emerges in the value of withdrawal benefits of active participants.

3. Explain why it may not be necessary to make a separate calculation of the cost of withdrawal benefits when the retirement benefits are valued on the basis of the traditional accrued benefit cost method.

4. When pension plan benefits are valued on the basis of the entry age normal cost method, failure to assume any withdrawals among fully vested participants results in an overstatement of the cost of vesting (or withdrawal benefits). Explain why this is so. Why does it not happen under the traditional accrued benefit cost method?

5. Contrast the "present value" and one-year term insurance approaches to valuing death and disability benefits.

6. Under what circumstances would it be appropriate to ignore the probability of death before retirement in the valuation of a pension plan?

7. Why is it *necessary* to value *mandatory* employee contributions to a defined benefit pension plan and *unnecessary* to value *voluntary* employee contributions to the same plan?

8. What normal annuity form is usually associated with a pension plan that requires contributions from the participants?

9. Describe the actuarial shortcuts that may be taken in the valuation of a small pension plan and give the reasons for the shortcuts.

# Financial Management of a Pension Plan

# Part Four

# 17 | Approaches to Meeting Financial Obligations of a Defined Benefit Plan

THE DOMINANT FUNCTION of an actuarial cost method is to apprise the employer of the rate at which the obligations under a defined benefit plan are accruing, to the end that appropriate financial arrangements may be made to meet such obligations. Unless satisfactory arrangements are made to discharge the obligations of a plan, the benefit rights created thereunder may prove to be illusory. This chapter is devoted to an analysis of the various approaches that may be utilized to meet the obligations of a defined benefit pension plan as they accrue or become due.

## Current Disbursement Approach

The simplest approach that can be used to meet the financial obligations of a pension plan is for the employer to disburse the benefits as they become due. This is commonly referred to as the pay-as-you-go approach, but throughout this volume the more accurate expression "current disbursement approach" is used to describe the arrangement.

Under the current disbursement arrangement, retirement benefits are paid directly to the pensioner by the employer in the same manner as payroll. Such benefits, if reasonable in amount, are

**371**

deductible from the employer's gross income as a necessary business expense and are taxable to the recipient as ordinary income. For this purpose, no distinction is made between past service and future service benefits, since under this arrangement such a distinction would be meaningless.

The outlay under this method is normally low during the early years of an employer's existence, or at the start of the pension program, since the number of retired employees is relatively small and no provision is being made to meet the accruing benefits of those employees who are still working. As the employee group matures, however, constantly increasing numbers of persons are added to the retired rolls until, eventually, retirement benefits constitute a significant percentage of the payroll cost. In fact, the annual outlay under this arrangement, expressed as a percentage of payroll, ultimately reaches a level that is considerably higher than that of any other financial method.

To anticipate the heavy drain on cash resources that this method ultimately entails, an employer may set up a special reserve for pensions. This action may involve the earmarking of specific assets for the payment of pension benefits, or only the placing of a restriction against surplus, similar to a reserve for depreciation. Whatever the nature of the action taken, it does not place any assets beyond the control of the employer and fails, therefore, to insulate the pension benefits against the financial vicissitudes of the employer. Moreover, the reserve is usually not established or maintained on the basis of actuarial estimates of the liabilities of the plan. An unattractive feature of the special reserve arrangement from the standpoint of any taxable employer is that the sums transferred to the reserve are not deductible as an ordinary and necessary business expense.[1] To be deductible, such sums would have to be placed beyond the control of the employer, as by transfer to a trustee under a suitably drawn trust agreement or by payment to an insurance company for the purchase of benefits. The benefits, nevertheless, are deductible in the tax year in which paid.

Prior to ERISA, there were no restrictions on the use of the current disbursement approach to financing, and it was used in

---

[1] In some countries, West Germany, for example, sums set aside in a balance sheet reserve are deductible for income tax purposes.

connection with a substantial number of plans. Many, if not most, of these plans provided benefits that were supplemental to those of a basic underlying plan. However, with specified exceptions, the approach can no longer be used for pension plans subject to ER-ISA's funding requirements.[2] This is true whether or not the plan seeks a qualified status under the tax provisions of the law administered through the Internal Revenue Service. Hereafter, the current disbursement approach can be used within interstate commerce only for (1) plans maintained by an employer primarily to provide deferred compensation for a select group of management and highly paid employees; (2) supplemental plans that provide benefits or contributions in excess of the limitations imposed by law; (3) plans which have not provided for any employer contributions since enactment of ERISA (i.e., plans of unions funded exclusively by member contributions); (4) governmental and church plans; (5) nonqualified plans of employers not engaged in interstate commerce, or plans of employee organizations whose membership is not interstate in character;[3] and (6) plans for certain other organizations and classes of employees.

## Funding

The conventional approach to the financing of pension benefits is for the employer (and employees, if the plan is contributory) to set aside funds for the payment of such benefits with a trustee or insurance company in advance of the date on which the benefits become payable. This practice is known as *funding,* a term to which frequent reference has been made in earlier sections of this book. The amount of funds set aside each year usually bears a definite relationship to the pension costs assumed to have accrued in that year. As a matter of fact, most employers annually set aside enough funds to meet the costs attributable to that year, plus a portion of the initial actuarial liability, with a view toward having all obligations fully funded at the earliest practicable date.

Pension plans have traditionally been funded through cash contributions, and that is still the dominant practice. In recent years,

---

[2]ERISA §§3(31),4,301, I.R.C. §412(a),(h).

[3]Courts have interpreted "interstate commerce" extremely broadly to include almost all business and industry.

however, some large firms, to conserve their working capital and reduce their liquidity requirements, have met some or all of their funding requirements through the transfer of real property or property rights to the pension plan. Some firms have contributed shares of common or preferred stock in their own companies to the pension plan. This type of funding is permissible so long as the assets transferred constitute *qualifying* employer real property or *qualifying* employer securities, it is prudent for the plan to hold such assets, and, in the case of defined benefit plans and most money purchase pension plans, the securities and real property of the plan sponsor do not constitute more than 10 percent of the pension asset portfolio.[4] Other firms have transferred mineral rights or royalty interests to their pension plans. Some commercial airlines have transferred their aircraft to their pension plan and then leased back the aircraft. Assets of this type do not fall within the 10 percent limitation, as they are not in the form of employer securities or real estate.

These transactions would normally be prohibited, since they involve parties in interest.[5] The plan sponsors, however, have been able to obtain exemptions from the Department of Labor. To procure the exemption, the plan sponsor usually agrees to buy back the property at any time at a price equal to the value at which it was transferred to the plan. In addition, it may agree to indemnify the plan against any loss of principal that it might suffer from holding the asset. Naturally, the repurchase and indemnity agreements are no more secure than the fiscal viability of the firm. Indeed, the holding of employer stock and reliance on employer repurchase and indemnity agreements do not insulate the pension plan against the financial vicissitudes of the plan sponsor. If held in moderation, however, they pose no serious threat to the well-being of the plan and lend an element of flexibility to the firm's financial management.

Under some plans no assets are set aside for active participants, but as each participant reaches retirement his benefits are funded in full. This practice is known as *terminal funding* and is usually a compromise between no funding (as represented by the current

---

[4]ERISA §407. See Chapter 2 for fiduciary requirements.
[5]ERISA §406, I.R.C. §4975. See Chapter 2 for prohibited transactions.

disbursement approach) and approximate full funding.[6] Terminal funding can be accomplished through the purchase of an immediate annuity in the appropriate amount for each employee as he reaches retirement or by the transfer to a trustee of a principal sum actuarially estimated to be sufficient to provide the benefits to which the participant is entitled. The principal sums required for such purchase or transfer sums normally come out of the operating revenue of the employer, since by definition the employer makes no advance provision, other than through the possible creation of a special reserve, for the accumulation of the sums needed. The annual contribution required for terminal funding will tend to increase each year, both absolutely and as a percentage of payroll, until a stable population is achieved, after which it will level off (in the absence of inflation).

Like the current disbursement approach, terminal funding is no longer an acceptable method of meeting the cost of qualified pension plans and other plans subject to the funding provisions of ERISA.[7]

The remaining discussion of funding will be concerned with those budgetary arrangements that have as their objective the orderly accumulation over a period of years of the sums needed to provide benefits to retiring employees. These arrangements are sometimes referred to as *advance* funding, meaning the setting aside of funds in advance of the date of retirement.[8]

## Purposes of Funding

**Security of Benefits.** The primary purpose of funding is to enhance the security of the benefit rights of the plan participants. In

---

[6]In a small plan with some participants close to retirement at the time the plan is established, terminal funding may require larger contributions in the early years than would be required if funds were being set aside in accordance with one of the conventional actuarial cost methods, under which supplemental liabilities could be amortized over many years. In this situation, especially under an arrangement where annuities are purchased for participants as they reach retirement, the employer will contribute the larger terminal funding amounts.

[7]ERISA §3(31).

[8]For the sake of completeness, the concept of postretirement funding should be mentioned. Under the practices of some insurers, the benefits of employees at or near retirement at date of plan inception or liberalization may be spread over a period extending 5 to 10 years beyond retirement. The same technique may be used in trust fund plans.

the absence of funding, the participants are completely dependent upon the employer's future willingness and ability to honor their claims, except to the extent such benefits are guaranteed by the PBGC (see below). Moreover, with no advance provision for the payment of benefits, the employer's ability—and perhaps even his willingness—to meet the burden of pension claims will be weakened with the addition of each new name on the pension roll. On the other hand, if a funding program is in effect, the employees can look to a segregated fund, irrevocably committed to the payment of benefits and administered by an independent third party, for the satisfaction of their claims. The higher the ratio of assets in the fund to the actuarial liabilities of the plan, the greater the assurance that the claims of the participants and pensioners will be satisfied. If each dollar of actuarial liability is matched by a dollar of assets in a segregated fund or the promise of a life insurer to pay, a high degree of assurance obtains with respect to the benefit rights that have been created as of any given time.

**Protection of the Pension Benefits Insurance Program.**    A related purpose of funding is to protect the pension benefits insurance program against abuse. Under ERISA, the Pension Benefit Guaranty Corporation (PBGC) insures the vested benefits of plan participants subject to certain limits.[9] If an insured event occurs and the plan assets are less than the actuarial present value of the insured benefits, the Pension Benefit Guaranty Corporation must make good on the deficiency. It clearly would be impracticable to insure the vested benefits of a pension plan if the employer were under no obligation to set aside funds in a systematic manner to meet the accruing costs of the benefits. He could promise any permissible level of benefits, make no contributions other than those necessary to pay benefits to retired participants or their beneficiaries and eventually terminate the plan with no further financial obligation. To prevent this type of abuse and to instill a sense of responsibility in the setting of benefit levels, ERISA requires pension plans to conform to specified minimum funding schedules. These funding standards are benefit security devices in themselves, but they are also an essential element in a feasible program of plan benefits insurance.

---

[9]See Chapters 24 and 25.

**Enforcement of Fiscal Responsibility.**    A third purpose of funding is to ensure a measure of fiscal responsibility on the part of those charged with the design and administration of a pension plan. Another way of expressing the thought is that funding forces the employer to face up to the costs of his pension plan. Before the accounting profession adopted the principle of accrual accounting for pension plan costs, the only way in which such costs got reflected in the financial statements of the firm was through the funding process. If in a particular fiscal year no contribution was made to the plan, no pension cost appeared in the operating statements. This, of course, distorted the operating results of the firm and affected the apportionment of pension costs over different generations of shareholders, employees, consumers, and taxpayers. With accrual accounting, pension costs of business firms get reflected in operating statements somewhat independently of funding, but for plans of governmental agencies and organizations not affected by accounting standards funding still serves as the primary force for cost recognition and fiscal discipline.

Advance recognition of pension costs is especially critical for state and local governments. If a plan were to be operated on a current disbursement basis, its initial cost and that of any benefit improvements would become apparent only over a long period of years. There would be a strong temptation for the elected officials to seek political advantage through the granting of excessively liberal pension benefits, since it would not require a current increase in taxes or other revenue, as might an increase in wages and salaries. On the other hand, if the granting of pension benefits must be accompanied by appropriate funding contributions, the pension demands of the employees are more likely to receive critical scrutiny.

**Reduction of Employer Outlay.**    One of the most persuasive arguments in favor of funding, from the standpoint of the employer, is that it will reduce the ultimate out-of-pocket cost of the plan. If an employer were to provide $600 a month to an employee who retires at age 65 and lives 15 years thereafter, it would pay $108,000 on the current disbursement basis ($600 times 12 months times 15 years). However, if the sum required to provide the benefit was to be accumulated through a series of level annual installments, extending from age 30 to age 65 discounted for interest at 5 percent but not for mortality, the outlay would aggregate only $28,322 (about

$809 per year for 35 years) or about one fourth of the cost under the current disbursement basis.

The difference in the outlay under the two methods of financing is, of course, wholly attributable to the interest factor. Under the current disbursement method, the employer's contributions obviously earn no interest, and the total cost is the sum of the individual payments. Under the advance funding scheme, each annual installment is credited with interest (5 percent in the above example) from date of payment until the time it is disbursed as a retirement benefit. Over the period of years, the sums contributed to the plan are credited with $79,678 in interest. If the funding agency earns more than the assumed 5 percent, the employer's outlay would be reduced to an even greater extent than that indicated.

While investment earnings on the funds set aside for the payment of benefits reduce the employer's outlay for pensions, they should properly be viewed as part of the true cost of the pension plan. They represent money which presumably would have been earned if the funds transferred to the plan had been invested elsewhere. In fact, the counter argument for nonfunding is that such funds will earn more in the employer's business than in the hands of a separate funding agency. While this may be true on a gross yield basis, allowance must be made for the tax deferred status of the investment income of a qualified pension plan. An employer would have to enjoy an earnings rate, before taxes, substantially higher than that of the funding agency to net the same rate.

## Disadvantages of Funding

From the standpoint of the employees, there appear to be no disadvantages to funding unless the financial burden involved would discourage an employer from adopting a pension plan in the first instance or would lead it to provide less generous benefits than would otherwise be provided or would cause it to pay lower cash wages. From the standpoint of the employer, however, there are possible disadvantages, which in a given case may or may not be important.

The most obvious potential disadvantage of funding is that the agency to which the funds are transferred may earn a lower investment return than the employer could have obtained through retention and investment of the funds in his own business, (or less than the employer pays as interest on borrowed funds), even after income taxes. This situation has undoubtedly prevailed in a number of cases in the years gone by and may still prevail to some extent.

A second possible disadvantage of funding is that the accumulation of large sums of money in the hands of the funding agency may create such an aura of affluence that the participants will demand liberalization of the pension plan. Financially unsophisticated employees do not understand why a pension plan must accumulate large sums of money, and they tend to equate a large buildup of assets with ability to provide higher benefits. Some groups interpret an excess of plan income over plan outgo as grounds for plan liberalization. An employer with a well-funded plan must be prepared to explain to its employees, or to their bargaining agents, why such a large accumulation of assets is necessary.

A third disadvantage, of a minor nature, is that a funded plan involves more actuarial, legal, and investment expenses than a plan operated on a current disbursement basis.

## Statutory Funding Standards

Congress has long imposed *upper* limits on the amount of pension plan contributions that an employer can deduct as an ordinary and necessary business expense for federal income tax purposes.[10] These limitations are designed to prevent an employer from timing his contributions in such a manner as to minimize his income tax liability over the years. Before ERISA, Congress never set any *lower* limits on plan contributions, although the IRS promulgated some rules through PS 57 that were construed by some to require a minimum level of funding. ERISA articulated new guidelines for both *maximum* and *minimum* contributions. The minimum standards are especially significant and will be described first.

**Minimum Standards.**    The plan's supplemental liability or liabilities must be amortized over a specified time, in addition to the funding of the normal cost.[11] The amortization period depends upon

---

[10]I.R.C. §404.
[11]ERISA §302(b), I.R.C. §412(b).

whether the plan was already in existence on January 1, 1974. There are separately articulated amortization schedules for experience gains and losses and for liabilities created by plan amendment or change in actuarial assumptions. Changes in the actuarial liability of an integrated pension plan attributable to changes in Social Security benefits or the wage base subject to Social Security taxation are treated as experience gains or losses.

The requirement to amortize the supplemental liability applies only to defined benefit plans, since a pure money purchase plan cannot have a supplemental liability. The minimum amount that is to be contributed under a money purchase plan is the amount called for by the plan formula. A collectively bargained multiemployer plan that calls for a specified level of contributions and an agreed level of benefits during the contract period is considered to be a defined benefit plan. On the other hand, a target benefit plan is to be treated as a money purchase plan for purposes of the minimum funding rules.

Compliance with minimum funding requirements is demonstrated on the annual report form, Form 5500, for defined contribution plans. For defined benefit plans, compliance is demonstrated on Schedule B, which is prepared by the enrolled actuary and attached to Form 5500.

For the general purpose of the minimum funding standards, the liabilities of a plan are to be calculated on the basis of actuarial assumptions and actuarial cost methods which, in the aggregate, are reasonable and which, in combination, offer the actuary's best estimate of anticipated experience under the plan.[12] Requirements for the valuation of assets are discussed in Chapter 20.

Unless the employer elects to meet the alternative minimum funding standard as described later, the same actuarial assumptions and cost method must be used for determining the minimum annual contribution to the plan and the maximum amount that can be currently deducted for federal income tax purposes.[13]

The funding requirements for multiemployer plans differ in certain respects from those applicable to all other plans. In this chapter all plans other than multiemployer plans are referred to as *single employer plans*, although the category actually includes multiple employer plans that are not multiemployer plans as defined by law.

---

[12]ERISA §302(c)(3), I.R.C. §412(c)(3).

[13]I.R.C. §404(a)(1)(A), Treas. Reg. §1.404(a)–14(d)(1).

**Basic Amortization Periods.**[14]    Unfunded actuarial liabilities in existence on the effective date of the minimum funding standards must be amortized in equal annual installments, taking into account both interest and principal, over a period of years. For purposes of the minimum funding requirements, the amortization period for each portion of the unfunded actuarial liabilities depends on its source. For new unfunded liabilities and changes in unfunded liabilities with amortization periods commencing after January 1, 1988, the amortization periods are as follows:

| | |
|---|---|
| Initial unfunded liability | 30 years |
| Plan amendments | 30 years |
| Actuarial gains and losses | |
| Single employer plans | 5 years |
| Multiemployer plans | 15 years |
| Changes in actuarial assumptions | |
| Single employer plans | 10 years |
| Multiemployer plans | 30 years |

Longer amortization periods applied to unfunded liabilities for which the amortization commenced on certain earlier dates, and these longer amortization periods continue to apply to such amounts. This shorter amortization period for actuarial losses was prescribed to encourage realism in the choice of actuarial assumptions. Actuarial valuations, including the determination of experience gains and losses unless a spread gain method is used, must be made at least every three years, and in some circumstances more frequent determinations are required.[15] Legislation proposed in 1988 would require all plans to have annual actuarial valuations.

Neither statutes nor regulations define the amortization period applicable to changes in unfunded liabilities resulting from changes in actuarial cost methods and asset valuation methods.

Amounts to be amortized under the various schedules may be combined (with offsets for any amortizable credits) into a composite amortization schedule, weighted by the amounts and remaining years associated with each of the individual schedules.[16]

---

[14]ERISA §302(b)(2), (3), I.R.C. §412(b)(2), (3).
[15]ERISA §103(D), 302(c)(9), I.R.C. §412(c)(9), 6059(a).
[16]ERISA §302(b)(4), I.R.C. §412(b)(4).

**Funding Standard Account.**   Each plan subject to the minimum funding standards must set up and maintain a special account called the "funding standard account," which provides a cumulative comparison between actual contributions and those required under the minimum funding standard.[17] The primary purpose of the funding standard account, apart from its record-keeping function, is to provide some flexibility in funding through allowing contributions greater than the required minimum, accumulated with interest, to reduce the minimum contributions required in future years.

Each plan year the funding standard account is charged with the normal cost for the year and the share of the actuarial liabilities that must be amortized annually under the rules set forth above. It is credited each year with the current year's amortization of any decreases in the unfunded actuarial liabilities resulting from experience gains, changes in actuarial assumptions or methods, or plan amendments. Some special rules apply to multiemployer plans.[18] Interest is added to all charges and credits from their effective date to the end of the plan year.[19] If the contributions to the plan, adjusted for actuarial gains and losses, exactly meet the minimum standards, the funding standard account will show a zero balance. If the contributions exceed the minimum requirements, the account will have a credit balance at the end of the year available to reduce the minimum requirement for the following year. If the contributions for a plan year are less than the minimum requirement, the account will show a deficiency, called the "accumulated funding deficiency," which will accrue interest at the valuation rate.

**Full Funding Limitation.**   Despite the foregoing rules, the employer is under no obligation to contribute more than required to satisfy the full funding limitation. The full funding limitation is the excess of the lesser of the plan's actuarial liability determined for funding purposes or 150 percent of its *current liability* over the value of plan assets.[20] If the actuarial liabilities cannot be directly determined on the basis of the actuarial cost method used for reg-

---

[17]ERISA §302(b)(1), I.R.C. §412(b)(1).
[18]ERISA §302(b)(6),(7), I.R.C. §412(b)(6),(7). See Chapter 25.
[19]ERISA §302(b)(5), I.R.C. §412(b)(5).
[20]ERISA §302(c)(6),(7), I.R.C. §412(c)(6),(7).

ular valuations, the liabilities are to be calculated on the basis of the entry age normal cost method.

For this purpose the *current liability* is the plan's liability determined on a plan termination basis. The interest rate used in the determination of the current liability must fall within a permissible range. The permissible range is between 90 percent and 110 percent of the weighted average yield on 30-year Treasury securities during the four-year period immediately preceding the plan year, except that regulations may extend the lower bound of the range to 80 percent. The interest rate is also required to be a reasonable estimate of the interest rate that is implicit in the price of deferred and immediate annuities available to discharge the current liability. However, this second requirement may not cause the interest rate used to fall outside the permissible range.

If the actuarial liability for funding purposes has been used in determining the full funding limitation because it is less than 150 percent of the current liability, the asset value used must be the lesser of the fair market value of plan assets or the actuarial value of the plan assets. But if the current liability has been used, the asset value must be the actuarial value of the plan assets.

To whatever extent use of the current liability reduces required contributions below the level that would have been required if the full funding limitation had been determined on the basis of the regular actuarial liability of the plan, regulations may require increased contributions in future years.

**Additional Funding Requirements for Single Employer Plans.** Beginning in 1989 additional funding requirements apply to a single employer plan with more than 100 participants that has an *unfunded current liability* for a year.[21] A plan's *unfunded current liability* is the excess of the plan's current liability over the actuarial value of plan assets. For this purpose the current liability is determined as described above except that, for any participant who became a participant after 1987 and has less than five years of participation, a stipulated percentage of the participant's service prior to participation may be disregarded in determining his accrued benefit.

---

[21]ERISA §302(d), I.R.C. §412(1).

Every new plan that provides accrued benefits on its effective date for prior service will, as a result, have an unfunded current liability during its first plan year.

The additional funding requirement ordinarily equals the excess, if any, of the *deficit reduction contribution* over the plan's net charges and credits for amortization of unfunded liabilities arising from establishment of the plan, plan amendments, funding waivers, or the switch back from the alternative minimum funding requirement (described later in this chapter).

The *deficit reduction contribution* consists of two parts: the unfunded *old* liability amount and the unfunded *new* liability amount. The unfunded old liability amount is the annual amount required to amortize over 18 years the unfunded current liability as of the beginning of the plan year beginning in 1988, based upon the plan provisions in effect on October 28, 1987. The unfunded new liability amount ordinarily is a percentage of the excess of the unfunded current liability over the unamortized portion of the unfunded old liability amount. The applicable percentage is 30 percent for a plan with no assets, grading down to as little as 13.75 percent as the funded ratio of the current liability increases.

The required deficit reduction contribution is illustrated below for a new plan that, as of its effective date, has a normal cost of $250,000, an actuarial liability for funding purposes of $3 million, a current liability of $2 million, and plan assets of $0.

---

*Regular minimum funding requirement*

| | | |
|---|---:|---:|
| Normal cost | | $250,000 |
| Amortization amount (30-year amortization of $3,000,000) | | 205,606 |
| Total | | $455,606 |

*Additional funding requirement*

| | | |
|---|---:|---:|
| Deficit reduction contribution (30 percent of $2,000,000) | $600,000 | |
| Less amortization amount above | 205,606 | |
| Additional funding requirement | | $394,394 |
| Total minimum funding requirement | | $850,000 |

---

This additional funding requirement may discourage employers from establishing plans that provide accrued benefits as of the effective date with respect to prior service.

The additional funding requirement may be increased if an *unpredictable contingent event* occurs. Such an event is one that is not reasonably or reliably predictable and that is not contingent upon the age, service, compensation, or disability of participants. An example of an unpredictable contingent event might be a plant closing that, under the terms of the pension plan, triggers an increase in benefits.

The additional funding requirements do not apply to plans with fewer than 100 participants. For plans with fewer than 150 participants the additional requirement is reduced. In determining the number of participants for this purpose all defined benefit plans of the same employer and of other employers in the same controlled group must be aggregated. In addition, special rules apply to certain collectively bargained plans and certain steel industry plans.

If a plan is amended to increase the current liability by more than $10 million and the plan assets are less than 60 percent of the current liability at the end of the year of the amendment, requirements for bonding or other security apply.[22]

**Shortfall Method.**   Special provision has been made for plans, usually of the multiemployer type, that are maintained pursuant to collective bargaining agreements that call for a predetermined level of contributions over a period longer than a year, such as a specified dollar amount per hour of covered service by an employee or a specified dollar amount per ton of coal mined.[23] The purpose of the exception is to permit the employers to base their contributions upon the terms of the labor agreement during the period to which the agreement relates (but generally not longer than three years), irrespective of any experience gains or losses that might emerge during the period. If the actuarial assumptions were reasonable and the actuarial calculations were correct at the beginning of the labor contract period, and the agreed upon contributions were made when due, no deficiency in the funding standard account would develop during the term of the collective bargaining agreement. This would be the case even if the contributions turned out to be less than was reasonably expected at the beginning of the contract term, because

---

[22]ERISA §307, I.R.C. §401(a)(29).
[23]Treas. Reg. §1.412(c)(1)–2.

of a decline in employment, for example, or a reduction in output. In that event, any difference between anticipated and actual contributions would be treated as an actuarial loss, to be amortized in 20 equal annual dollar installments. At the option of the plan, amortization of the contribution "shortfall" may be deferred for 5 years and then amortized over 15 years. An excess of actual over anticipated contributions would be treated as an actuarial gain, to be amortized in the same manner as an actuarial loss.

**Overriding Minimum Funding Standards for Multiemployer Plans.** A special minimum funding standard applies to a multiemployer pension plan in *reorganization,* as defined below. Referred to as the minimum contribution requirement (MCR), this provision stipulates that the annual contributions to the plan must be sufficient to fund the benefits of all *retired* participants over a period of 10 years and *all other vested benefits* over a period of 25 years.[24] This requirement becomes operative whenever it would produce larger annual contributions to the plan than would be required under the basic funding standard (essentially, normal cost plus 30-year amortization of supplemental liabilities). The plan is deemed to be in *reorganization* whenever the annual contributions under the MCR would exceed those under the normal funding standard.

If, for a plan in reorganization, the number of *pay status participants* (participants receiving retirement benefits) in a given year (the base year) exceeds the average number of active participants in that year and the two preceding years, the plan is said to be "overburdened" and is entitled to an *overburden credit* against the contribution called for by the MCR.[25] The amount of the credit is one half of the average guaranteed benefit (the average annual benefit insured by the Pension Benefit Guaranty Corporation) multiplied by the *overburden factor.* The factor is simply the excess of the average number of pay status participants over the average number of active participants for the base year and two preceding years. In effect, the plan is credited with one half of the average insured annual benefit payable in respect of an unidentified group of retired participants considered to be excess to a normal cohort

---

[24]ERISA §4241, §4243, I.R.C. §418B.
[25]ERISA §4244, I.R.C. §418C.

of retired persons. "Normal" is implicitly defined as a number equal to the average number of active participants. This is obviously a crude measure of an overburden, but it was not intended to be anything more than that. The credit merely reduces the contribution required in the plan year in question and does not relieve the participating or signatory employers of their obligation ultimately to fund all insured benefits. Moreover, an overburden credit is not available for any plan year in respect of which the contribution base was reduced through collective bargaining, unless there was a corresponding reduction in the plan's unfunded vested benefits attributable to pay status participants.

A multiemployer plan in a reorganization mode is permitted to reduce accrued benefits retroactively to the level of benefits guaranteed by the PBGC, subject to a number of restrictions safeguarding the interests of the participants.[26] Benefits must not be proportionally reduced more for inactive participants (retired and terminated vested) than for active participants.

As explained in Chapter 24, a plan sponsor may not terminate a single-employer plan before all benefit commitments (generally vested benefits) are funded unless the employer is in "distress."[27] Even in a distress termination the employer is required to continue funding certain benefit commitments.

**Alternative Minimum Funding Standard.**[28]    In lieu of the regular minimum funding requirements described above, some plans that use the entry age normal cost method for the regular funding requirements may use an alternative funding standard. Under the alternative funding standard the minimum annual contribution to the plan would be the normal cost plus the excess (if any) of the actuarial value of the benefit accruals over the fair market value of the assets. Under this standard all assets, including equities and fixed-income instruments, would be valued at their actual market value on the date of valuation, without benefit of averaging or amortization. The normal cost for this standard would be the lesser of the normal cost generated by the actuarial cost method used for

---

[26]ERISA §4244A, I.R.C. §418D.

[27]ERISA §4041.

[28]ERISA §305, I.R.C. §412(g).

the plan and the normal cost that would be developed under the traditional accrued benefit cost method. Compliance with this standard would assure that the plan at all times would have assets, valued at market, at least equal to the actuarial value of all accrued benefits, whether vested or not. This provision was added because many persons maintain that there is no need for a plan to hold assets in excess of its liabilities for accrued benefits, computed on a plan termination basis, and that there is no justification for the law to require a more rapid buildup of assets than that needed to meet the accrued benefits, realistically valued. The law restricts the alternative standard to plans that use the "entry age normal" actuarial cost method (to use the language of the law).

Having elected to use the alternative method, a plan must maintain an alternative funding standard account. The account will be charged each year with the normal cost plus the excess of the actuarial value of accrued benefits over plan assets (but not less than zero) and will be credited with contributions. There is no carryover of contributions over the required minimum from one year to the next, since the excess contributions become a part of the plan assets for the next year's comparison of assets and liabilities. On the other hand, any shortfall of contributions will be carried over from year to year, with interest, and an excise tax will be payable on the cumulative deficiency (or on the funding deficiency existing in the basic funding standard account, if smaller).

A plan that elects the alternative funding standard must maintain both an alternative funding standard account and the basic funding standard account. The basic account is credited and charged under the usual rules, but an excise tax will only be levied on the smaller of the accumulated funding deficiencies of the two accounts, if any. A plan making this choice is required to maintain both accounts since the minimum required contribution is the lesser of the contributions called for by the basic and alternative standards.

The required contributions under the alternative standard may exceed those required under the basic method for a particular year or period of years, if there is a substantial increase in liabilities, as through a plan amendment. If the minimum required contributions under the basic standard become lower than those under the alternative standard, the employer is likely to switch back to the basic standard.

If a plan switches back from the alternative to the basic funding standard, it is generally given five years in which to amortize the excess of charges over credits that may have built up in the basic funding standard account over the years during which the alternate standard was being used. However, if there should be a funding deficiency in the alternative funding standard account in the year before the switchback, it must be paid off immediately (not over a period of five years). Such a deficiency would have to be corrected within the permissible period whenever it occurred, not only at the time of the switchback.

Whenever an employer switches back from the alternative to the basic funding standard, he is relieved of the obligation of maintaining the second account. If in some subsequent year the employer should return to the alternative standard, he would have to establish a new account with a zero balance.

**Variances from the Prescribed Standards.**   If an employer would otherwise incur substantial business hardship,[29] and if enforcement of the minimum funding requirements would be adverse to the interests of plan participants in the aggregate, the Internal Revenue Service may waive for a particular year payment of part or all of the plan's funding requirements.[30] This type of waiver can be made for both single employer and multiemployer plans. For single employer plans, no waiver will be granted unless the business hardship is expected to be temporary. Security may be required if the waiver exceeds $1 million. If a waiver is to be granted for a multiemployer plan, there must be a finding that 10 percent or more of the employers contributing to the plan would suffer a substantial business hardship if required to make the funding contributions for the year in question. No more than three (five for multiemployer plans) waivers may be granted to a plan within any consecutive 15-year

---

[29] The law provides that the factors to be taken into account in determining business hardship shall include, but not be limited to, whether or not (1) the employer is operating at an economic loss, (2) there is substantial unemployment or underemployment in the trade or business and in the industry concerned, (3) the sales and profits of the industry are depressed or declining, and (4) it is reasonable to expect that the plan will be continued only if the waiver is granted.

[30] ERISA §303(a), I.R.C. §412(d)(1).

period. The amount waived, plus interest, must be amortized not less rapidly than ratably over 5 years (15 years for multiemployer plans). The contributions waived by the IRS, of course, increase the exposure of the PBGC, a matter of some concern since the waivers are generally granted to the weaker plans and plan sponsors.

A plan may also request an extension for up to 10 years in the amortization period for unfunded actuarial liabilities.[31] In practice, this extension is rarely if ever requested, since the waiver previously described provides more effective relief.

During the time that a variance is in effect, whether it be in the form of year-by-year waiver of funding contributions or an extension of the time to amortize unfunded actuarial liabilities, there can be no plan amendments that increase the benefits or accelerate the rate of vesting, except as noted below.[32] Under exceptions to the general rules, amendments that increase plan liabilities may be permitted if (1) they are *de minimis* in nature, as determined under regulations of the Secretary of Labor; (2) they are required as a condition for the plan to retain its qualified status; or (3) they merely repeal, in whole or in part, a previous decrease in benefits.

**Contributions.** For plan years beginning after 1988, contributions to single employer defined benefit plans to satisfy the minimum funding requirements must be paid in four quarterly installments, similar to the estimated tax payments for income tax. The *required annual payment* is the lesser of 90 percent of the amount required to satisfy the minimum funding requirements for the current plan year or 100 percent of the amount required to satisfy the minimum funding requirements for the prior plan year. If the plan year is a calendar year, 25 percent of this required annual payment must be paid by April 15, July 15, and October 15 of the plan year and by January 15 of the following year. Comparable dates apply when the plan year is not a calendar year. This requirement to contribute 25 percent of the required annual payment is reduced to 6.25 percent for plan years beginning in 1989, 12.5 percent for plan years beginning in 1990, and 18.75 percent for plan years beginning in 1991.

---

[31]ERISA §304(a), I.R.C. §412(e).
[32]ERISA §304(b), I.R.C. §412(f).

Contributions made after the close of the plan year may be credited to that year in satisfaction of the minimum funding requirements. They may be retroactively credited if made within eight and a half months after the end of the year.[33]

**Enforcement.**  Any accumulated funding deficiency will be subject to an excise tax of 5 percent (100 percent if not "corrected" or paid off within a limited period).[34] In addition to the excise tax, the employer may be subject to civil action in the courts for failure to meet the minimum funding standards.[35]

**Exemptions from the Prescribed Standards.**  In general, the funding requirements apply to qualified pension plans, as well as to nonqualified plans of private employers in interstate commerce and of employee organizations with members in interstate commerce.[36] Profit sharing and stock bonus plans are exempt. Staff retirement plans of the federal government and those of state and local governments are also exempt from the requirements. Church plans are also exempt unless they elect to comply with the participation, vesting, and plan termination provisions, in which event they must also comply with the funding requirements.

Other plans specifically exempt from the funding standards are (1) those established and maintained outside the United States primarily for the benefit of persons substantially all of whom are nonresident aliens; (2) those maintained by an employer primarily to provide deferred compensation to a select group of highly compensated employees; (3) those that provide supplemental benefits on an unfunded, nonqualified basis; and (4) those to which the employer does not contribute.

**Maximum Deductible Contributions.**  An employer can deduct for income tax purposes only such contributions to a pension plan as fall within the permissible limits set forth in the law.[37]

---

[33]ERISA §302(c)(10), I.R.C. §412(c)(10), Treas. Reg. §11.412(c)-12.

[34]I.R.C. §4971.

[35]ERISA §502(b).

[36]ERISA §3019(a), I.R.C. §412(h). Courts have interpreted interstate commerce so broadly as to include almost all business and industry.

[37]I.R.C. §404(a).

The most general rule on deductibility of employer contributions is that the firm may deduct any amounts that were required to meet the minimum funding standards. Beyond this general rule there are two specific limitations for defined benefit plans that have long been part of the tax law on pensions.

Under the first rule, sometimes called the "straight-line" rule, the employer is permitted to deduct any sum necessary to provide with respect to all the plan participants the remaining unfunded cost of their past and current service credits distributed as a level amount, or a level percentage of compensation, over the remaining future service of each such employee. This simply means that an employer can deduct each year such sum, computed in accordance with applicable regulations, as is needed to provide on a level contribution basis (dollars or percentage of covered payroll) the total projected benefits payable under the plan. The calculation can be made with respect to each individual participant or the employee group as a whole.

The second rule, known as the "normal cost" or "normal cost plus 10-year" rule, permits the employer to deduct annually an amount equal to the normal cost of the plan, plus, if there are supplemental liabilities, an amount necessary to amortize such supplemental liabilities in equal annual dollar installments over 10 years. Deductions for contributions toward the amortization of the supplemental liabilities are available, obviously, only so long as there are unamortized amounts. Both the normal cost contributions and the amortization payments must be determined in accordance with relevant regulations.[38]

If there are more than 100 employees of an employer covered under one or more defined benefit pension plans, the maximum deductible limit for each plan of the employer is not less than the plan's unfunded current liability. In some circumstances this rule results in deductible contributions substantially larger than the rules described above.

A general rule that overrides all the others is that the tax deduction for any particular year cannot exceed the amount needed to bring the plan to a fully funded status. That is, no deductions can be taken for contributions that would raise the plan assets to

---

[38]Treas. Reg. §1.404(a)–14.

a level above the actuarial value of plan liabilities. It follows, of course, that no deductions could be taken for contributions made while a plan was in a fully or overly funded condition. Full funding for tax deduction purposes is determined in the same way as full funding under the funding requirements.

As explained in Chapter 29, a 10 percent excise tax is imposed on all employer contributions made for a year that exceed the maximum deductible limit, even if the employer is otherwise tax-exempt. In addition a penalty is imposed if it is determined that an employer's deduction exceeded the deductible limit because of an error in the actuarial computations or because the actuarial assumptions used were too conservative.

Limitations on the deductibility of contributions to profit-sharing and stock bonus plans, and limitations that apply when an employer maintains both a defined benefit plan and a defined contribution plan covering the same employees, are described in Chapter 26.

## Patterns of Funding

As a normal practice, an employer will not make contributions to a pension plan in any one year in excess of the amount that he can deduct as an ordinary and necessary business expense for federal income tax purposes. Yet, in order to avoid penalties, the amount to be contributed must comply with the minimum funding standards described in the preceding pages. Within these parameters, the actual amount of the employer's annual contributions will depend upon the actuarial cost method that it chooses to use and, in certain circumstances, on the funding instrument employed. As a matter of fact, the minimum and maximum constraints are themselves expressed in terms of the actuarial cost method used by the employer, except for the alternative minimum standard and the full funding limitation.

Any of several actuarial cost methods may be selected if the actuary certifies that the method and assumptions are reasonable in the aggregate. ERISA lists six acceptable actuarial cost methods,[39] but it is possible that additional methods may be designated

---

[39] ERISA §3(31), Treas. Reg. §1.412(c)(3)–1.

as acceptable by the Internal Revenue Service. Any change in the method used may be made only with the prior approval of the Internal Revenue Service.[40] The choice of method will be influenced by the nature of the benefit formula, the type of funding instrument, and the degree of funding flexibility desired. These factors are interrelated, and a decision with respect to one may dictate the course of action with respect to the other two. The choice of funding instrument may even dictate the actuarial cost method, as well as the type of benefit formula and the degree of funding flexibility. Having selected (consciously or by indirection) the actuarial cost method, the employer must set aside funds on a cumulative basis equal to the normal (or annual) cost of the plan and the statutorily prescribed portion of the supplemental liability, if any. Thus, the actuarial cost method and the funding policy are inextricably intertwined.

The interplay between the actuarial cost method, the funding instrument, the benefit formula, and the funding policy is delineated briefly in this section.

**Benefit Allocation Actuarial Cost Methods.** Benefit allocation actuarial cost methods assume that the normal cost of a pension plan for any particular year is precisely equal to the present value of the benefits allocated to the participants for service during that year. They are best suited to the type of benefit formula that attributes a specifically identifiable unit of benefit for each year of credited service, including service prior to inception of the plan.

If a plan's funding policy is geared to a benefit allocation cost method, the cost of each dollar of future service benefit (actual or estimated) will be met in full in the year in which it accrues by a contribution to the pension plan. This is especially true of the traditional accrued benefit cost method, which allocates benefits on the basis of actual, realized benefit accruals, without projections. Benefits attributable to service prior to establishment of the plan are funded in accordance with a policy especially adopted for that purpose by the employer or dictated by an insurer. Because of the statutory limitations discussed earlier, past service benefits are seldom funded in full at the inception of the plan, contributions in

---

[40]ERISA §302(c)(5), I.R.C. §412(c)(5). Rev. Proc. 85–29 grants automatic approval for certain changes in funding methods.

respect of them generally being spread over a number of years. The sharp differentiation between past and future service benefits, with the former giving rise to a supplemental liability, provides a desirable degree of financial flexibility.

The traditional accrued benefit cost method of funding is virtually always used in connection with group deferred annuity contracts and may be used with other types of arrangements. It is equally appropriate for a benefit formula that provides a definite benefit and one that utilizes the money purchase concept. From a structural standpoint, it is not well suited for a plan that provides a flat composite benefit or one that provides for the deduction of Social Security benefits. Some question whether it is appropriate for a plan that bases benefits on the earnings of some future period, such as the last five years of service, because of its structural inability to take future salary increases into account. The complications associated with all such formulas can be accommodated by the other two forms of benefit allocation cost methods, since they project or estimate benefits.

If the traditional accrued benefit cost method is used in connection with a group deferred annuity contract, the periodic contributions are applied to the purchase of single premium deferred life annuities, the contributions covering not only the present value of the deferred benefits but also the charge levied by the insurer to take care of its expenses and to accumulate a contingency reserve. The future service contributions are allocated to the participants on the basis of the benefits earned during the time interval involved. Past service contributions are allocated in accordance with a formula prescribed in the contract, annuities generally being purchased in the order of nearness to normal retirement date.

Under trust fund plans and group deposit administration annuity contracts, contributions are determined in respect of specific individuals for specific units of service; but deferred annuities in the appropriate amounts are generally not purchased for such individuals. Consequently, in the event of termination of the plan, the previous contributions plus interest would be allocated among the pensioners[41] and participants in accordance with the termination formula set forth in the plan or the provisions of ERISA.

---

[41]In the case of a deposit administration plan, annuities for pensioners would already have been purchased.

Since the present value of each dollar of benefits to be paid at retirement increases with the attained age of the participant, there is a tendency for future service contributions for the plan as a whole to rise each year until the employee group matures. However, this tendency is offset to some extent by new entrants to the plan, withdrawals, deaths, and retirements. As a result, the average cost per dollar of annuity credited may show only a slight percentage increase or, under certain circumstances, an absolute decrease. If the initial past service liability is liquidated over the first 20 or 30 years, as is generally the objective, the total contributions will level off after maturity of the plan at a rate equal to the cost of future service benefits. Under a group deferred annuity contract, the initial past service liability must be fully funded upon attainment of normal retirement age by the youngest participant with prior credited service.

**Cost Allocation Actuarial Cost Methods.**   Cost allocation cost methods can be used with any type of benefit formula, being especially adaptable to the type of formula that provides a composite benefit (as opposed to a series of unit benefits). Within this family of methods, there exist procedures that are suitable for any type of funding instrument, with the possible exception of the conventional group deferred annuity. Likewise, there are available procedures that provide a high degree of flexibility in funding policy. The specific approaches within the family of cost allocation cost methods have such diverse characteristics, however, that it is necessary to consider each one separately.

*A. Individual Level Premium Cost Method.*   The individual level premium cost method is closely identified with plans funded exclusively by individual and group permanent contracts of life insurers. Under these arrangements, the contract or certificate for a particular participant is written in an amount exactly adequate to provide the benefits that would be payable to the participant if his rate of compensation remains unchanged to normal retirement age, and the payment of premiums on the contract meets the funding requirements. As is true of all insurance or annuity contracts, the premium is calculated as of the attained age of the employee on the effective date of the contract or certificate. If the rate of compensation increases, with an attendant change in benefits, an adjustment in the amount of coverage is made in the manner described in a later chapter, and the funding of the increase in benefits is accomplished by a separate and additional level premium, payable from the date of increase.

Inasmuch as the insurance contracts are written in amounts designed to provide benefits for the entire period of credited service, no distinction is made between past and future service costs. The sums necessary to amortize the initial actuarial liability are merged distinguishably into the annual premium and are not identifiable as past service contributions. The total amount funded each year is simply the sum of the premiums on all contracts issued under the plan, less dividends and surrender credits, if applicable.

In the event of termination of the plan, all participants would be entitled to take over the contracts (individual) being maintained on their lives. They could continue the contracts in full force through the assumption of premium payments or surrender them pursuant to their terms. The degree to which the anticipated retirement benefits would be funded as of any given date would depend upon the age at which the employee became a member of the plan, the amount of past service benefits, if any, and the length of time during which premiums have been paid. If no portion of the benefits of a particular employee is attributable to service prior to establishment of the plan, the "accrued" benefits on any given date would tend to be overfunded to some extent because of the leveling out of costs that would otherwise be increasing each year. After a point, the cost of each year's "unit of benefit," if the total benefit can be so apportioned, will exceed the annual premium and the degree of overfunding will begin to decline. At retirement, the assets (represented by the reserve under the contract) will be in exact balance with the present value of the benefits payable. Any benefits attributable to past service will be fully funded only upon maturity of the insurance contract. Benefits for participants at or beyond normal retirement age at inception of the plan can be funded with a single-sum payment equal to the present value of future benefits plus an allowance for the insurer's expenses, or through a series of contributions extending beyond actual retirement.

This pattern of funding is not confined to individual and group permanent insurance contracts or to insurance contracts in general. It can be, and frequently is, used to fund trust fund plans. If it is used with a group deposit administration annuity contract or trust fund plan, the annual level cost may be determined and funded as a level percentage of payroll, rather than as a level dollar amount. With these unallocated funding instruments, the prospective benefits payable to specific individuals serve only as a measuring rod for the determination of the sums of money to be set aside periodically. The monies are paid into an unallocated fund, and an individual participant has no vested interest in, nor prior claim to, the contributions attributable to his benefit expectations. In the event of early termination of the plan, the assets might, and in all likelihood would, be distributed among the employees in a manner quite different from the pattern by which contributions were computed. However, once the implicit initial actuarial liability is funded, which these methods contemplate, there should be enough assets upon termination to meet the accrued benefit claims of all participants.

Irrespective of the funding agency employed, contributions under this approach to funding will be relatively high during the early years of the plan, especially under the level *dollar* cost method, when the initial actuarial liability is being amortized at a rapid rate. The amortization of the initial actuarial liability slows down gradually with the retirement of employees who had large past service credits (or whose period of future service was relatively brief), and after the retirement of the last employee with prior service the contributions level off at a rate equal to the cost of future service benefits.

**B. Individual Entry Age Normal Cost Method.** The individual entry age normal cost method serves as the funding guide for many trust fund plans and deposit administration contracts, and sets the pattern of funding for plans that cover a large number of employees. The rationale of this funding policy is that the prospective benefits of a participant should be funded at a uniform percentage of compensation or in uniform annual increments over his entire working lifetime. With respect to any particular pension plan, the individual's working life span is usually assumed to extend from the earliest date of employment recognized for benefit purposes to the normal retirement age, or, alternatively, the average age at which the participants under the plan are expected to retire. Thus, the "normal" cost of benefits for any specific participant is conceived to be that uniform annual amount or percentage of compensation that would have to be paid from the earliest date of credited service to the assumed age of retirement to accumulate the capital sum needed to provide the anticipated benefits. In practice, the funding contributions are sometimes based on an assumed age or ages of entry into the plan, rather than the actual age or ages, but the underlying principle is the same.

If the individual enters the service of the employer after the effective date of the plan, the annual funding payments with respect to the employee could, depending upon the assumptions, be identical with those under the individual level premium cost method. If, however, the employer's actual or assumed credited service antedates the establishment of the plan, the funding contributions would be smaller than under the aforementioned method and a supplemental liability would be created—for reasons explained earlier.

The employer has great flexibility with respect to the funding of the initial actuarial liability generated under this approach. It can be funded over a period as short as 10 years or over a period as long as 30 or 40 years, depending upon the effective date of the plan. Supplemental liabilities associated with plan liberalizations can be funded over a period of 30 years, while those arising out of actuarial losses must be funded within a 5-year or 15-year period.

Normal cost contributions under this method tend to be fairly level, changing slightly if the average entry age changes. Total contributions depend upon the funding policy adopted relative to the initial actuarial liability and subsequently emerging supplemental liabilities.

This funding approach may be used with any type of benefit formula and any type of funding instrument that does not allocate contributions to individual participants before retirement.

*C. Aggregate Level Cost Method.* The aggregate level cost methods are analogous to the individual level cost methods, except for the calculation of costs and contributions on a collective, rather than individual, basis. If the annual cost accruals are computed on the basis of total anticipated benefits, including those attributable to past service, there is no supplemental liability and, in effect, a portion of each annual contribution will go toward the funding of benefits credited for service prior to inception of the plan. This makes for a higher initial level of contributions than might otherwise be necessary and deprives the employer of the flexibility associated with a supplemental liability. In this form, the aggregate cost method dictates a rather inflexible funding policy.

To provide more flexibility in funding and to lower the level of contributions in the early years of the plan, the actuary may create a supplemental liability under this approach. Such a liability may be produced in various ways, including the calculation of first-year costs on the basis of either the accumulated plan benefit method or one of the individual level cost methods (with supplemental liability, of course). The resulting supplemental liability can then be funded at a pace consistent with the employer's overall financial policy and applicable law.

This approach to funding has found its widest use among trust fund plans. It is equally adaptable to group deposit administration annuity contracts. It is not appropriate for use with allocated funding instruments.

## Questions

1.  Compare the *initial* and *ultimate* annual outlay under the current disbursement approach to financing a pension plan with that of a financial approach based on one of the conventional actuarial cost methods.
2.  What is meant by terminal funding?
3.  Are the interests of the plan sponsor and the plan participants the same with respect to funding policy? Explain.
4.  Must the enrolled actuary of a pension plan use the same actuarial assumptions and the same actuarial cost method to determine the minimum annual contribution to the plan and the maximum amount that can be currently deducted for federal income tax purposes?
5.  What is the minimum amount that must be contributed to a pension plan in respect of a particular plan year to avoid a violation of ERISA minimum funding standards?
6.  With respect to variances from ERISA prescribed funding standards, explain:
    a.  The *types* of variances that may be granted.
    b.  The *conditions* that must be met before a variance can be granted.
    c.  The *restrictions* that are imposed on the plan while a variance is in effect.
7.  State the purpose and nature of the funding standard account (FSA) prescribed by ERISA.

8.  Describe the alternative minimum funding standard available to pension plans under ERISA. Why might a plan sponsor be reluctant to elect the alternative minimum funding standard?
9.  What constraints, legal or otherwise, does a plan sponsor face in choosing an actuarial cost method initially and in changing from one method to the other after the plan has gone into operation.
10. Explain the relationship among (*a*) the actuarial cost method, (*b*) the funding instrument, and (*c*) the funding policy for a pension plan.
11. With respect to each of the following types of funding instruments, indicate the actuarial cost method or methods that you would expect to be used with it:
    *a.*  Individual life insurance or annuity contract.
    *b.*  Group deferred annuity contract.
    *c.*  Group deposit administration annuity contract.
    *d.*  Trust instrument.
12. Which of the foregoing funding instruments impose constraints on the funding policy of the plan sponsor beyond those imposed by law? Explain.

# 18 | Pension Accounting

HISTORICALLY, PENSION ACCOUNTING has been concerned with measuring the impact of a pension plan on the earnings and financial condition of the business firm that sponsors the plan. More precisely, it has been concerned with measuring and recording the cost of accruing pension benefits and with recognition of the unfunded actuarial liabilities of the pension plan, especially those arising out of the granting of benefit credit for service prior to inception or amendment of the plan.

A succession of committees of the American Institute of Certified Public Accountants and its predecessor organizations have grappled with the problem of developing an acceptable set of principles to guide the actuarial profession in accounting for pension costs and liabilities and to bring about some degree of uniformity in practice. Each of these committees has issued authoritative, officially endorsed statements of recommended practice, all of which are reviewed briefly in this chapter. With the enactment of ERISA in 1974, which imposed certain reporting and disclosure requirements on the pension plans subject to its jurisdiction and charged the accounting profession with responsibility for certifying the appropriateness and accuracy of the financial information in the reports, it became necessary for the profession to develop generally accepted accounting principles for the plans themselves, as contrasted to their sponsors. In response to this challenge, the Financial Accounting Standards Board (FASB), the current arbiter of accounting practices and standards, launched two projects, one to develop generally accepted accounting principles for pension plans themselves and the other to develop such principles for the business and nonprofit entities that sponsor the plans. The product of these projects will be examined in due course.

Pension cost accounting is concerned primarily with *defined benefit* plans. For any given accounting period, the employer's expense for a defined contribution plan is usually known with exactitude. Some defined contribution plans have a formula that specifies precisely how much must be contributed by the employer for the period in question. Other defined contribution plans provide complete discretion to the employer; but by the time the financial statements for the period are prepared, the contribution ordinarily has been paid or at least has been determined. For defined contribution plans, the employer's charge to expense for a period is the actual amount contributed to the plan for the period. Any portion of the required contribution not paid by the end of the period is shown on the employer's balance sheet as an amount payable. Since the employer makes no benefit commitment, there is no basis for any other pension liability to show up on the employer's balance sheet.

Unless otherwise indicated, the remainder of this chapter is concerned only with accounting for defined benefit plans.

## Accounting for the Plan

### Form 5500 and Related Forms

Titles I and IV of ERISA and the Internal Revenue Code require a pension plan sponsor or plan administrator to submit certain information about the plan to the Department of Labor, the Pension Benefit Guaranty Corporation, and the Internal Revenue Service.[1] To ease compliance with this requirement, the three regulatory agencies developed a joint annual report form, designated Form 5500. Form 5500 is filed with the IRS, which provides a copy to the Department of Labor and transmits certain extracted data to

---

[1] ERISA §§103, 4043, I.R.C. §6058.

the Pension Benefit Guaranty Corporation. Simplified Form 5500-C was developed for plans with fewer than 100 participants,[2] and an even more abbreviated Form 5500-R may be filed by these small plans for two out of every three years. Form 5500 and Form 5500-C include a statement of assets and liabilities and a statement of changes of fund balance, and require the attachment of certain additional financial information.

Form 5500 and Form 5500-C show the plan assets and liabilities as of the beginning and end of the plan year. Assets are generally shown at current value,[3] which is the market value of an investment if an active market exists, as it does for most pension plan investments. The value of any portion of an allocated annuity or insurance contract that fully guarantees any benefit payments is excluded from the assets shown. Thus, the assets shown generally exclude the value of any annuities that have been purchased for retired employees, as well as any amounts individually allocated under an annuity contract to guarantee benefits for active employees. The liabilities shown on Form 5500 include liabilities for amounts payable, including any benefit payments currently due and unpaid, but do not include any actuarial liabilities for benefits that will become payable in the future. These liabilities are subtracted from the total assets to produce the net assets available to pay future benefits and expenses.

Form 5500 and Form 5500-C include a statement that reconciles the net assets at the beginning and end of the year. This includes a summary of income, expenses, and other changes in net assets, including the change in unrealized appreciation and depreciation of assets.

Form 5500 requires a number of attachments:

- Schedule A—Insurance Information: This schedule provides financial information concerning any insurance or annuity contracts used to fund the plan.
- Schedule B—Actuarial Information: This schedule, prepared and signed by the enrolled actuary for any defined benefit plan subject to ERISA's funding requirements, presents information con-

---

[2]ERISA § 104(a)(2)(A).

[3]An exception applies to annuity contracts with unallocated funds, other than separate accounts, which may be shown at their contract value.

cerning compliance with the funding requirements, as well as the present value of vested and nonvested accrued benefits as of the beginning of the plan year.[4] For this purpose "accrued benefits" generally means the retirement benefits earned to date as defined by the plan. It must also include, if significant, the value of subsidized early retirement benefits, death benefits, and disability benefits related to the accrued benefits. Each significant actuarial assumption used to calculate the value of accrued benefits is required to "reflect the best estimate of the plan's future experience solely with respect to that assumption," unlike the actuarial assumptions used for funding purposes which are only required to be "reasonable in the aggregate."[5]

- Schedule SSA—Annual Registration Statement Identifying Separated Participants with Deferred Vested Benefits: This schedule is used when participants who will be entitled to benefits in future years terminate. A copy of Schedule SSA is forwarded to the Social Security Administration, which reminds the participants of their benefits when they become eligible for their social security benefits.
- Schedule of all investments: Not required with Form 5500-C.
- Schedule of any party-in-interest investments.
- Schedule of any loans or leases in default.
- Schedule of all transactions exceeding 3 percent of the current value of plan assets: Not required with Form 5500-C.
- Opinion of an independent qualified public accountant: Not required with Form 5500-C. While the law apparently permits the accountant to express his opinion with respect to the financial statements included on the form, almost all accountants actually prepare an additional balance sheet and income statement as part of their report.

Except for Schedule B, all of the above requirements apply to both defined benefit and defined contribution plans.

Almost all plans with at least 100 participants[6] are required to have an annual audit by an independent qualified public accountant,

---

[4]This value of accrued benefits may be omitted for plans with less than 100 participants if it has not been calculated.

[5]Instructions for Schedule B.

[6]An exception applies to certain plans funded exclusively with allocated insurance or annuity contracts. 29 CFR §2620.104–44.

following generally accepted auditing standards. This audit provides the basis for the accountant's opinion referred to above.

The financial statement and schedules required for the annual report of a plan with 100 or more participants must be examined by an independent qualified public accountant retained by the plan on behalf of its participants.[7] The accountant must render an opinion on whether the financial statements and supporting schedules are presented fairly in conformity with generally accepted accounting principles. Such an opinion has to be based upon an examination carried out in accordance with generally accepted auditing standards.

## Generally Accepted Accounting Principles

Inasmuch as there were no generally accepted accounting principles for pension plans at the time that ERISA imposed this statutory responsibility on the accounting profession, FASB launched a project, referred to above, to develop a set of accounting principles for pension plans as soon as possible. After several years of discussion, debate, and consultation with all interested groups, FASB in March 1980 promulgated *Statement of Financial Accounting Standards No. 35* "Accounting and Reporting by Defined Benefit Pension Plans," and made it effective for plan years beginning after December 15, 1980.[8] Financial statements for defined benefit plans must be prepared in accordance with *Statement 35,* if they are to receive an unqualified opinion from the plan auditor.[9] Information developed in accordance with the principles of *Statement 35* is acceptable for related items on Schedule B of Form 5500.

In developing *Statement 35,* the Board and staff focused on the informational needs of the plan participants, with an eye on the needs of others, such as investors, creditors of the plan sponsor,

---

[7]ERISA §103(a)(3).

[8]The background of this statement is set out in a *FASB Discussion Memorandum,* "Accounting and Reporting for Employee Benefit Plans" (Stamford, Conn., October 1975). See also the *FASB Exposure Draft,* "Accounting and Reporting by Defined Benefit Plans," issued in July 1979.

[9]*Statement 35* applies to all ongoing defined benefit pension plans, including plans not subject to ERISA and plans not qualified under the Internal Revenue Code, other than social insurance programs. However, *FASB Statements* 59 and 75 have indefinitely deferred its effective date for pension plans of state and local governmental units, in the expectation that the Governmental Accounting Standards Board will publish standards for these plans. *Statement 35* does not apply to plans expected to be terminated.

and those who advise or represent participants. The primary function of the financial statements prepared on the basis of *Statement 35* is to provide financial information useful in assessing the plan's present and future ability to pay plan benefits when due. While *Statement 35* is based on the assumption that the plan is ongoing, the intent is to portray the financial condition of the plan at a given moment on as realistic a basis as possible. The result is a series of cross-sectional snapshots of the plan over time, as contrasted with a longitudinal long-run view of the financial needs of the plan as reflected in funding decisions of the plan sponsor.

*Statement 35* stipulates that the financial statement for a defined benefit plan must include information about:

- Net assets available for benefits as of the end of the plan year.
- Changes during the year in the net assets available for benefits.
- Actuarial present value of accumulated plan benefits.
- Significant effects of such factors as plan amendments, plan merger or spinoff, and changes in actuarial assumptions on the actuarial present value of accumulated plan benefits.

The benefit information may be presented as of either the beginning or end of the plan year. If a beginning-of-year date is chosen, net assets must be shown as of that date (in addition to end-of-year information), along with the changes in net assets for both years.

Plan assets must be reported on the accrual basis of accounting. They must include contributions receivable as of the reporting date, if they are payable pursuant to a formal commitment or a legal or contractual requirement. Most assets must be presented at their "fair value" which is basically the same as "current value" (i.e., market value) used by ERISA. Unlike the IRS asset valuation rules for funding, *Statement 35* does not authorize any smoothing or averaging of asset values. This, of course, makes for sharp variations in year-to-year reported values, which may be partially or fully offset by changes in the actuarial present value of plan obligations. Insurance and annuity contracts are valued on the same basis as for Form 5500. This is generally the contractual account balance for a group deposit administration or IPG annuity contract and the contractual cash value of individual contracts. For contracts that provide for the purchase of annuities for some or all of the participants, the value of the purchased annuities is excluded from both the plan assets and the accumulated plan benefits. Operating assets owned by the plan, such as buildings and equipment employed in the administration of the plan, are valued at cost less accumulated depreciation or amortization.

In developing *Statement 35,* the Board concluded that accrued benefits should be measured in a uniform manner, irrespective of the type of benefit formula contained in the plan document. In pursuit of this objective, the Board stipulated that plan benefits should be measured on the accumulated plan benefits basis. As noted earlier, accumulated plan benefits are benefits reasonably expected to be paid under the provisions of the plan in exchange for services already rendered by the participants. Measurement of the accumulated benefits is based primarily on the participant's pay history, service, and other appropriate factors as of the date of measurement. Future salary changes are not considered (a decision that has been roundly criticized by pension actuaries and others) and future years of service are considered only in determining expected eligibility for particular types of benefits such as early retirement, death, and disability benefits. *Automatic* cost-of-living adjustments are taken into account, but a mere expectation of such adjustments on an ad hoc basis without a prior contractual commitment is not recognized. In summary, accumulated plan benefits include vested and nonvested benefit accruals, as determined by plan provisions, and a pro rata portion of other benefits, such as supplemental early retirement benefits, death benefits, and disability benefits.

The accumulated plan benefits are valued on the assumption that the plan is ongoing. This means the various decrements that affect the probability of payment of the benefits—death, disability, withdrawal, and retirement—are taken into account. The resulting values are reduced to present values through the use of a realistic interest assumption. Under *Statement 35* guidelines, the assumed rate (or rates) of investment return must reflect the expected rates of return during the periods for which payment of the benefits is deferred, and must be consistent with returns realistically achievable on the type of assets held by the plan and with the plan's investment policy. Many plans use a higher interest assumption for *Statement 35* purposes than for funding purposes, reflecting among other things the fact that the average deferral period for benefits already *accrued* is shorter than the average deferral period for *projected* benefits, which are usually used in funding computations.

Stated differently, the actuarial present value of accumulated plan benefits is more heavily weighted toward those participants already retired and those close to retirement, for whom the deferral period is shorter, than is the value of all projected benefits used for funding purposes.

Under *Statement 35,* the actuarial present value of accumulated plan benefits must be shown separately for three categories: benefits in payment status, other vested benefits, and nonvested benefits. Accumulated employee contributions for active participants must be separately identified.

*Statement 35* also requires the statement of a defined benefit plan to include a description of the significant actuarial methods and assumptions used to determine the actuarial present value of accumulated plan benefits, as well as any significant changes in those methods and assumptions. A brief, general description of the plan agreement must be provided, as well as the funding policy for the plan. *Statement 35* also lists other items which must be disclosed where applicable.

*Statement 35* values may differ substantially from those developed for other purposes, especially the values used for funding in the valuation balance sheet and Schedule B of Form 5500 because of different asset valuation rules, interest assumptions, or measures of benefit accruals. Even though the two sets of values serve different purposes, the uninitiated may be confused by the discrepancies between the two balance sheets. Many actuaries and others question the value of the *FASB 35* exercise, while others, conceding some value to the approach, question whether the benefit to the users equals the extra cost and effort of preparing a second financial analysis.

*FASB Statement 35* does not apply to defined contribution plans. These plans are subject to the generally accepted accounting principles that apply to all financial statements generally.

## Accounting for Pensions by Employers

Employer accounting is concerned with the impact of a pension plan on the financial statements of the entity that sponsors the plan. This is a separate question than that of how the asset and liability values of the plan itself are determined and presented, although some common issues and subissues are involved. The central issues in employer pension accounting are determining the proper charge against operations for pension expense and deciding whether the obligation assumed by the sponsor of a defined benefit plan is of such nature that it should be reflected on the balance sheet of the sponsor, and if so, how it should be reflected. Several philosophical, legal, and accounting questions are involved in the resolution of these two controlling issues.

## Practice Prior to Opinion No. 8

Prior to publication in 1966 of *Opinion No. 8* by the Accounting Principles Board of the American Institute of Certified Public Accountants, the prevailing practice was to treat the contribution to a pension plan in any given year as the pension expense for that year. This was the accepted practice, despite the fact that the contributions to the plan reflected financial and tax judgments more than accounting considerations. This was a form of *cash* accounting, as contrasted with *accrual* accounting used for most business transactions. The accounting treatment of the contribution was the same, whether it represented normal cost only, normal cost plus interest on the unfunded supplemental liability, or normal cost and a portion of the supplemental liability. Similarly situated business firms could show widely varying pension expense solely because of differences in actuarial assumptions, actuarial cost methods, or funding policies. A business firm could improve its earnings statement for a given year simply by omitting or reducing its contribution to the pension plan. Over the years many firms, some of them prominent, showed no pension expense in their financial statements for a year or two, despite the fact that pension benefits continued to accrue in the normal manner. On the other hand, a firm could understate its true earnings by making a disproportionately large contribution to its pension plan in a particular year, to take advantage of a favorable cash or tax position. All this obviously impaired the comparability of financial statements and the validity of any analyses based on the statements.

The accounting treatment of costs associated with benefits credited for service prior to inception of a pension plan or retroactive benefit liberalizations was a subject of continuing study and debate within the accounting profession. In theory, there were three ways in which these costs could be handled: (1) they could be charged to retained earnings (then called earned surplus) as payments for services performed in the past; (2) they could be charged to income in the year of the plan's inception (or benefit liberalization) as a current cost of establishing or liberalizing the plan; or (3) they could be amortized by charging them to operations over a period of future years on the assumption that the plan sponsor will receive *future* benefit from plan benefits bestowed in recognition of *past* service. The third approach was the only one recognized by the IRS for tax-deduction purposes.

## Accounting Research Bulletins

The first authoritative pronouncement on this subject was issued by the Committee on Accounting Procedure of the American Institute of Certified Public Accountants in 1948 in the form of *Accounting Research Bulletin No. 36,* ''Pension Plans: Accounting for Annuity Costs Based on Past Services.'' In paragraph 4 of *ARB 36,* the committee expressed its opinion as follows:

> The committee believes that, even though the calculation is based on past services, costs of annuities based on such services are generally incurred in contemplation of present and future services, not necessarily of the individual affected but of the organization as a whole and, therefore, should be charged to the present and future periods benefited. This belief is based on the assumption that although the benefits flowing from pension plans are intangible, they are nevertheless real. The element of past services is one of the most important considerations of most pension plans and costs incurred on account of such services contribute to the benefits gained by the adoption of a plan. It is usually expected that such benefits will include better employee morale, the removal of superannuated employees from the payroll, and the attraction and retention of more desirable personnel, all of which should result in improved operations.

The Committee went on to say in paragraph 5 that:

> (a) Costs of annuities based on past services should be allocated to current and future periods; provided, however, that if they are not sufficiently material in amount to distort the results of operations in a single period, they may be absorbed in the current year. (b) Costs of annuities based on past services should not be charged to surplus.

The committee had nothing to say about normal costs and the practice of treating plan contributions for a period as the pension expense for that period.

In 1953, the Committee on Accounting Procedure issued *ARB No. 43*, "Restatement and Revision of Accounting Research Bulletins." Chapter 13A of that Bulletin carried forward the language and content of *ARB 36* unchanged.

In 1956, the Committee on Accounting Procedure issued *ARB No. 47*, "Accounting for Pension Costs." This was the first official publication of the accounting profession to address the entire subject of pension cost accounting, the previous bulletins having dealt solely with accounting for past service costs. In *ARB 47*, the committee reaffirmed the previous opinion that past service benefit costs should not be charged to earned surplus *at the inception of the plan*, but indicated that it might be appropriate for an *existing plan* to charge to earned surplus that portion of the initial past service liability that should have been charged to income since plan inception but for any reason was not so charged.

The committee recognized two prevailing but conflicting views as to the proper basis for accounting for pension costs. One view held that the accrual of pension costs should not "necessarily" be dependent upon the funding arrangements of the plan or be governed by a strict legal interpretation of the sponsor's obligations under the plan. According to this view, normal costs should be systematically accrued during the expected period of active service of the covered employees, and the cost of past service benefits should be charged off in a systematic and rational basis over some reasonable period without distorting the operating results of any one year. The second view was that to accrue pension costs in excess of the plan contributions could lead to a recorded pension liability in excess of the amount that the plan would have to pay in benefits if the plan should terminate. Some persons of this persuasion expressed concern that "in the case of an unfunded or partially funded plan the accumulation of a substantial accrual would lead to pressure for full funding, possibly to the detriment of the company and its security holders, and that the fear of this might deter management from entering into pension arrangements beneficial to employees."[10]

---

[10]Par. 6 of *ARB Bulletin No. 47*.

## APB Opinion No. 8

Notwithstanding the preferences expressed in *ARB 47*, accounting for pension costs continued to vary widely among plan sponsors and sometimes resulted in wide year-to-year fluctuations in the provision for pension costs of a particular plan sponsor.

Because of the growing importance of pensions and continuing lack of uniformity in accounting for them, the Accounting Principles Board commissioned a study by Ernest L. Hicks, a partner in the Arthur Young accounting firm, that led to the publication in 1965 of a book, *Accounting for the Cost of Pension Plans* by Hicks, and the subsequent issue, in 1966, of *APB Opinion No. 8* of the same title, based on the reasoning and recommendations in the Hicks treatise.

*Opinion No. 8* was a landmark development in the quest for comparability in pension cost accounting and served as the official guide to pension accounting by plan sponsors for 20 years, until superseded by *FASB Statements 87* and *88* (described later). It established the principle that accounting for pension costs should not be discretionary with the plan sponsor and that the cost should be recognized annually, whether funded or not. It set the parameters for a basic accounting method, identified actuarial cost methods acceptable for determining pension costs, prescribed the accounting treatment of actuarial gains and losses, and identified the employees who should be included in the cost calculation. It also required footnote disclosure of many important aspects of the pension plan, including its major features, the funding policy, the annual charge to operations for pension expense, the basis for determining the annual charge, and the plan amendments.

*Opinion 8* took the position that the entire cost of benefit payments ultimately to be made should be charged against income subsequent to adoption or amendment of the plan, and that no portion of the cost should be charged directly to surplus. The APB members held such differing views on how to measure the cost of ultimate benefit payments that they settled for merely *narrowing* the range of practices by establishing rules for determining *minimum* and *maximum* pension cost accruals that bracketed their differing views.

The basic charge to expense for pension cost under *Opinion 8* equaled the sum of the annual normal cost, an amount equal to interest on any unfunded prior service cost, and, if indicated, a provision for vested benefits. No provision for vested benefits was required if the benefits were fully funded or if the unfunded value of vested benefits decreased at least 5 percent during the year. If a provision for vested benefits was required, the minimum provision for vested benefits was the lesser of the amount needed to bring about a 5 percent reduction in the unfunded vested benefits or the amount needed to amortize the entire unfunded prior service cost over 40 years.

The minimum *funding* requirement for a year, before recognizing any credit balance in the funding standard account, usually equals or exceeds the minimum *charge to expense* for accounting purposes under *Opinion 8*. But a credit balance could reduce or eliminate the minimum funding requirement, resulting in a minimum charge to expense that exceeded the minimum funding requirement. The basic maximum charge to expense was the sum of the normal cost plus 10 percent of any initial past service cost or any prior service cost arising from plan amendments.

*Opinion 8* allowed the minimum and maximum charge to expense to be determined on the basis of any reasonable set of actuarial assumptions and any reasonable actuarial cost method not specifically banned in *Opinion 8*. The *Opinion* specifically banned the terminal funding and pay-as-you-go approaches. The employer's discretion as to choice of actuarial cost method and actuarial assumptions was clearly at odds with the objective of uniform treatment of pension costs. The *Opinion's* approach to this critically important aspect of pension accounting represented a compromise between the actuary's (and plan sponsor's) desire for flexibility and the accountant's desire for comparability.

As was noted in an earlier chapter, some actuarial cost methods automatically spread actuarial gains and losses over the future working lifetime of employees through an adjustment in the normal cost. If such a spread-gain method was not being used, actuarial gains or losses had either to be spread over a period of 10 to 20 years or merely added to the unfunded liability and made subject to whatever amortization procedure was being used. But if a gain or loss arose from a single occurrence not directly related to the operation of the plan, and not in the ordinary course of the employer's business (e.g., a plant closing), the entire gain or loss had to be recognized immediately.

As a general proposition, unfunded actuarial liabilities did not have to be shown on the balance sheet as a liability. There were two exceptions to this general rule. If the plan sponsor had a legal obligation to provide the benefits under the plan and if the actuarial value of the accrued benefits exceeded the amounts paid or accrued, the excess had to be shown in the balance sheet as both a liability and a deferred charge. Likewise, if the actual contributions paid to a plan during a given year were less than the charge to expense for pension cost for that year, the difference had to be included in the balance sheet as a liability for accrued pension cost. On the other hand, if the contributions exceeded the charge to expense the excess was reflected on the balance sheet as an asset for prepaid pension cost.

As with all accounting standards, deviations were allowed without disclosure if they were deemed not material. When *Opinion 8* was adopted, the maximum deductible contribution for past service was 10 percent of the past service base. ERISA changed this to allow amortization of the past service base over 10 years, which, with interest, may allow contributions of 13 or 14 percent. Subsequent IRS regulations changed the methods used in determining the base itself. Accountants usually considered any contribution that was within the deductible limits to be acceptable as a charge to expense, even if it exceeded the amount described by *Opinion 8.* This difference was allowed either because the accountant determined that the difference was not material or because he believed, rightly or wrongly, that *Opinion 8* could reasonably be interpreted to allow past service liabilities to be amortized at the same rate at which they could be funded on a tax deductible basis. For whatever reason, it was unusual for the pension expense for an accounting period to be different from the contributions to the plan for the period.

## FASB Statement 36

Pending completion of the project on employer accounting for pensions (see below), FASB issued *Statement No. 36,* "Disclosure of Pension Information." The *Statement* amended *Opinion 8* to require plan sponsors to disclose in notes to their financial statements much of the same information that *Statement 35* requires of the plans themselves. If the employer maintained more than one plan, the information could be reported in total for all plans, separately for each plan, or combined in useful groupings. For both defined benefit and defined contribution pension plans the following items were required:

    a.  A statement that a pension plan existed, identifying or describing the employee groups covered,

    b.  A statement of the company's accounting and funding policies,

    c.  The provision for pension cost for the period,

    d.  Nature and effect of significant matters affecting comparability for periods presented, such as changes in accounting methods (actuarial cost method, amortization of past and prior service cost, treatment of actuarial gains and losses, etc.), changes in circumstances (actuarial assumptions, etc.), or adoption or amendment of a plan.

For defined benefit plans the notes also had to disclose the actuarial present values of vested and nonvested accumulated plan benefits, the interest rates used in determining them and the date as of which they were determined, and the plan's net assets available for benefits.

*Statement 36* made no change in the basic provisions of *Opinion 8* that governed measurement of pension cost and pension liabilities.

## FASB Statement 87

Despite the fact that *Opinion 8* was a major step forward in the evolution of rational accounting for pension costs by sponsors of defined benefit pension plans, dissatisfaction with it gradually developed within the financial community and certain segments of the accounting profession. The principal criticisms of the opinion were that it:

- Accepted a variety of actuarial cost methods and amortization practices.
- Permitted artificial leveling or smoothing of pension expense.
- Failed to recognize certain obligations as liabilities of the plan sponsor.
- Provided too much latitude in the choice of actuarial assumptions.
- Ignored postretirement benefits not provided within the framework of a pension plan.

In recognition of these perceived flaws in *Opinion 8*, FASB undertook a broad scale project to develop a new set of pension accounting principles for plan sponsors that would be acceptable to all segments of the business and financial communities, especially the accounting and actuarial professions. Over a period of several years FASB produced a background paper on the subject,[11] a discussion memorandum,[12] a set of tentative conclusions entitled *Preliminary Views*, an exposure draft,[13] and finally, in 1985, a *Statement of Financial Accounting Standards No. 87*, "Employers Accounting for Pensions," familiarly known as *FASB Statement 87*, or, simply, *Statement 87*. At various stages in the long drawn-out process, public hearings were held and extensive consultations were undertaken with interested constituents and knowledgeable professionals. Many persons and groups have been critical of the final document or portions of it.

**Underlying Propositions.** Certain fundamental concepts or propositions underlie *Statement 87*.

**A. Deferred Compensation.** The first proposition is that pensions are a form of deferred compensation. The plan participant exchanges a portion of his service to the employer for the latter's promise to pay him certain benefits at a later date, if certain conditions are met. By participating in the plan, the participants implicitly (or, in certain collective bargaining situations, *explicitly*) agree to accept lower current compensation in return for the promise of pension plan benefits, subject to the terms and conditions of the plan, and the employer incurs a parallel obligation independent of any contributions that the employer may be making to the plan.

**B. Obligation to Individuals.** The second proposition is that the employer's obligation for ultimate payment of the "deferred wages" runs to the employees, as individuals, rather than to the plan or to the plan participants collectively. Under this view, the plan and its associated trust are merely the vehicles or instrumentalities through which the employer discharges his obligation to the individual employees. This view rejects the notion that the employer discharges his obligation by making the required contributions to the plan trustee. Despite the fact that the employer can

---

[11]FASB "Accounting for Pensions by Employers: A Background Paper" (Stamford, Conn., March 1980)

[12]*FASB Discussion Memorandum*, "Employers' Accounting for Pensions and Other Post-retirement Benefits" (Stamford, Conn., February 1981)

[13]*FASB Exposure Draft*, "Employers' Accounting for Pensions" (Stamford, Conn., March 1985)

recapture his contributions to the plan only under severely restricted conditions, he retains a financial stake in the plan assets. If the total return on the assets exceeds the assumed rate of return, he can reduce future contributions to the plan; if the investment experience of the plan is unfavorable, he must make larger contributions to the plan than anticipated. Indeed, in the long run, he must make up any loss of principal that the assets may suffer.

Because of the contingencies involved in qualifying for a benefit, notably employee turnover and deaths, some respected observers hold the view that the employer's obligation under the plan is to the covered employees, as a group. As a practical matter, the difference between the two views may be more conceptual than real.

*C. Indefinite Continuance.*    The third proposition is that the plan will continue indefinitely. The significance of this assumption is that all the benefits that accrue under the plan will, subject to the actuarial experience, ultimately have to be paid. The employer cannot look only to the benefits that have vested as of a given point in time. If the plan were to terminate, some nonvested benefits might not be paid; but if the plan continues, both vested and nonvested benefits will qualify for payment, again subject to diminution through population decrements.

*D. Benefit Earned Proportionately.*    The fourth proposition is that a plan participant earns a pro rata proportion of his total prospective benefit with each year of service. This has to do with the *measurement* of benefit accruals. It is also an essential element in the venerated accounting concept of matching *revenue* and *expense*. Presumably an employee's service during a given accounting period produces revenue to the employer. The pension cost component of the total compensation package of the individual for that period should be recognized and charged to operations in the same manner as cash wages and current fringe benefits. Thus, it is necessary to determine on some rational basis the rate at which an employee earns his total pension over the various accounting periods of his employment.

The actuarial profession has generally preferred to allocate or attribute the total prospective pension in such a manner as to produce a level annual *cost,* in dollars or as a percentage of compensation, the *benefit* allocation being grossly distorted in many cases. In theory, the employee should earn his pension at the same rate at which he earns his wages or salary. This would mean that the dollar amount of prospective pension benefit allocated to each accounting period should constitute a *level percentage of pay.* For practical reasons, FASB chose to prorate the total pension over the total years of service, which, obviously, produces a constant *dollar* amount of benefit accrual for each year of service.

**E. Future Value of Prior Service Benefits.**   The fifth proposition is that the granting of benefit credits for service prior to inception or amendment of the plan will produce future economic benefits to the firm in the form of reduced employee turnover, improved productivity, lower cash compensation, and enhanced prospects for attracting additional qualified employees. This proposition provides the rationale for charging the cost of such "prior service benefits" (which may include postretirement cost-of-living benefit increases) to future earnings, rather than to retained earnings, and for recognition of an intangible asset offsetting the future cost of such benefits. It is further presumed that the economic benefits from prior service benefits will be realized from the future efforts and attitudes of the employees with the firm at the time the benefit credits are bestowed. Thus, it follows that the intangible asset should be amortized or written off over the average remaining service period of the active employees.

**F. Pension Plan Autonomy.**   The sixth and final proposition is that a pension plan is a sufficiently autonomous legal entity that it would be inappropriate to include its assets and liabilities on the balance sheet of the business firm or other organization that sponsors the plan. The plan participants have first claim to the assets of the plan, and those assets are not available to the plan sponsor as long as the plan is in existence. The assets, however, are properly regarded as an offset to the plan's benefit obligations. Thus, FASB has concluded that the net difference between the plan's assets and liabilities should be reflected in the sponsor's balance sheet, in the manner described hereafter.

**Provisions of *FASB Statement 87.*[14]   A. Measurement of Benefit Obligation.**   *Statement 87* uses several different measures of the value of benefits attributable to the past, which it calls the *benefit obligation.*

---

[14]*Statement of Financial Accounting Standards No. 87* "Employers' Accounting for Pensions" (Financial Accounting Standards Board, Stamford, Conn., 1985). Study of the statement itself, including the illustrations of its Appendix B, is essential for a comprehensive knowledge of its contents. This text uses various phrases from the *Statement* without any indication of quotation of the particular phrase.

The term *accumulated benefit obligation* is essentially the same as the term *actuarial present value of accumulated plan benefits* of *FASB Statement 35* and the term *present value of accrued benefits* used by Form 5500. It is the actuarial present value of benefits attributed by the pension plan's benefit formula to employee service rendered before a specified date, based upon employee service and compensation prior to that date. The "vested benefit obligation" is the actuarial present value of vested benefits. This is the vested portion of the accumulated benefit obligation.

The "projected benefit obligation" is the actuarial present value as of a specified date of benefits attributed by the pension plan's benefit formula to employee service rendered prior to that date. Unlike the accumulated benefit obligation, the projected benefit obligation utilizes salary projections to estimate the amount of benefits that will ultimately be payable and to determine the proportion of those projected benefits that are related to service to date. For a plan in which benefits are not related to pay, the accumulated benefit obligation and the projected benefit obligation are the same.

The "service cost" is the actuarial present value of projected benefits attributable to the single year (or other fiscal period) for which the financial statement is prepared. Like the projected benefit obligation, the service cost is based upon projected future salaries.

If future benefits increases have been contractually promised, as under a collective bargaining agreement for hourly employees, such increases must be reflected in both the accumulated benefit obligation (assuming retroactive application of the benefit increases) and the projected benefit obligation and in the service cost. This requires recognition of the participants' expected year of retirement.

If an employer has a history of regular increases in nonpay-related benefits or in the past service benefits under a career-average-pay plan, this may indicate that the employer has a present commitment to make future amendments and that the substance of the plan is to provide benefits attributable to prior service that are greater than those described by the plan document. If so, the substantive commitment must be used in determining the projected benefit obligation and the service cost.

**B. Measurement of Plan Assets.** *Statement 87* uses two different measures of plan assets, "fair value" and "market-related value." Fair value is the amount that a pension plan could reasonably expect to receive for an asset in a current sale between a willing buyer and a willing seller, that is, other than in a forced or liquidation sale. If an active market exists for the asset, fair value is the market value. Plan assets used in the operation of the plan, such as buildings and equipment, are valued at their cost less accumulated depreciation or amortization.

The "market-related value of plan assets" may be either the fair value or a calculated value that recognizes changes in fair value over not more than five years, such as a five-year-average-market-value method.

Plan assets include amounts held in a trust or annuity contract to provide benefits but do not include other employer assets or reserves that may have been designated for pension funding but not effectively restricted to such use.

*C. Annuity Contracts.* A number of special rules apply to annuity contracts under which the insurer has guaranteed to provide specified benefits to specific participants. Benefits funded through such contracts are generally excluded from all three measures of benefit obligation, and the value of such contracts is excluded from the plan assets. For participating annuity contracts under which future dividends are anticipated, however, the excess of the purchase price over the cost of a comparable nonparticipating contract is treated as the purchase of a right to future dividends. The statement provides rules for valuing such an asset in future years.

The treatment of annuity contracts described above does not apply to annuity contracts that do not guarantee specified benefits to specific participants or to annuity contracts under which the employer remains subject to all or most of the risks and rewards related to future experience. Such contracts are treated as investments and are valued at fair value. The contract's cash surrender value or conversion value, if determinable, is considered its fair value.

*D. Assumptions.* Each significant assumption used in calculating the benefit obligations and the service cost must reflect the best estimate of anticipated experience solely with respect to that specific assumption.

The salary increase assumption should reflect estimated compensation changes for the present participants, including changes related to price inflation, productivity, seniority, promotions, and other factors. Projected Social Security benefits used to calculate benefits in Social Security offset plans should reflect estimates of the future increases in price and wage levels that affect Social Security benefits. Projected benefits should be based on the assumption that any automatic future increases in the maximum limits on benefits under Section 415 of the Internal Revenue Code will occur (to the extent the plan document reflects such future increases), in contrast to the Code's requirement that these increases be ignored for minimum funding purposes.

The interest assumption used to calculate each of the benefit obligations and service cost, called the "discount rate," must reflect the rates at which the pension benefits could be effectively settled. In estimating these discount rates, the actuary would find it appropriate to consider information about interest rates used in current annuity purchase rates (including rates published by the Pension Benefit Guaranty Corporation). PBGC periodically surveys annuity purchase rates and publishes regulations stating the interest rates implied in the annuity purchase rates. The computations required by *Statement 87* and their explanation are simplified if the employer uses a single interest rate as the discount rate, but the PBGC rates consist of one interest rate for retired participants and a series of rates applicable to different years for participants not yet retired. Some plan sponsors have adopted either the PBGC rate applicable to retired employees or a composite level rate that would approximately reproduce the service cost generated by the series of PBGC rates. Instead of using interest rates reflecting annuity purchase rates, employers may look to rates of return on high-quality fixed-income investments currently available and expected to be available during the period to maturity of the pension benefits. Such fixed income rates are generally higher than the PBGC rates and other annuity purchase rates. Material changes in long-term interest rates may not be ignored. Thus if interest rates fluctuate, it could be necessary to change the discount rate almost every year.

In addition to the discount rate used to calculate benefit obligations and service cost, *Statement 87* requires an investment return assumption to be used to estimate the expected return on plan assets. This investment return assumption, called the "expected long-term rate of return on plan assets," may or may not be the same as the discount rate. In selecting this rate the plan sponsor must consider the returns currently being earned by the plan assets and rates of return expected to be available for reinvestment. Because of the extreme volatility of common stocks as a class, past rates of return on the common stock component of a pension plan investment portfolio may be an unreliable guide to future performance. Long term bond rates may be a better indicator of future portfolio returns. Some employers have adopted the discount rate as the expected long-term rate of return on plan assets, and illustrations included in *Statement 87* indicate that using the same rate for both purposes is acceptable, at least in some circumstances.

**E. Recognition of Net Periodic Pension Cost.** The "net periodic pension cost" (which *Opinion 8* termed *annual provision for pension cost*) to be charged as an expense against income for a year (or other fiscal period) consists of six components:

- Service cost.
- Interest cost.
- Actual return on plan assets.
- Amortization of unrecognized prior service cost, if any.
- Gain or loss (including the effects of changes in assumptions) to the extent recognized.
- Amortization of unrecognized obligation at the date of initial application of *Statement 87*.

The combination of these six elements may result in the net periodic pension cost being negative, although it will usually be positive. Each of the six elements needs explanation. For simplicity, this text assumes that the fiscal period is a year.

*1. Service Cost.* The service cost is the cost associated with the benefits attributable to the particular year for which the financial statement is prepared. It is the actuarial present value of benefits attributed to services rendered by employees during that period, calculated as of the last day of that period. Pension benefits are to be attributed to particular years in accordance with the plan's benefit formula, except that, like the projected benefit obligation, benefits are to be based on projected salaries rather than actual compensation prior to the statement date. If the plan benefit formula is the same for all years of service, the benefit attributed to any particular year would equal the participant's anticipated benefit calculated on the basis of projected salary and service, divided by the projected years of service.[15] But if the benefit formula is not the same for all years, such as 1 percent of pay per year of prior service and 1.5 percent of pay per year of future service, the allocation of the projected benefit among the years of service would be similarly prorated. Special rules apply to benefits not related to years of service, such as death, disability, or supplemental early retirement benefits that are not a function of service.

*2. Interest Cost.* The interest cost component represents the amount by which the projected benefit obligation is expected to grow during the year because of interest. It normally represents the discount rate multiplied times the projected benefit obligation at the beginning of the year, perhaps adjusted to reflect interest on benefits paid during the year.

*3. Actual Return on Plan Assets.* The actual return on plan assets is the total investment income for the year, including realized and unrealized appreciation and depreciation of the fair value of plan assets. It equals all of the increase in the fair value of plan assets during the year except the portion resulting from the excess of contributions over benefits.

*Statement 87* provides that the *expected* return on plan assets is based upon the expected long-term rate of return on plan assets and the market-related value of plan assets. As noted below, the net periodic pension cost includes a credit equal to the excess of the actual return on plan assets over the expected return on plan assets. Thus, while the net periodic pension cost appears to include the actual return on plan assets, the effect of this offsetting credit is that the net periodic pension cost actually includes only the expected return on plan assets. This enables the net periodic pension cost to be closely predicted at the beginning of the year, before the actual return on plan assets is known.

The actual return on plan assets is a negative element, to be subtracted from the positive elements of the net periodic pension cost. If the interest rate used for the expected return on plan assets (a negative element) is the same as the discount rate applied to the

---

[15]This is comparable to the unit credit actuarial cost method with benefits prorated by years of service, also called the "projected unit credit" method. Unlike IRS minimum funding regulations for plans using the unit credit method, *Statement 87* requires that career average pay plans, like final average pay plans, use projection of benefits with projected salary increases.

projected benefit obligation (a positive element), the net effect of these two elements of net periodic pension cost is to charge interest on the unfunded portion of the projected benefit obligation, similar to the inclusion of interest on the unfunded liability required under *Opinion 8*. But the two interest rates may differ.

*Statement 87* applies to unfunded nonqualified plans, such as excess benefit plans, as well as to funded plans. For an unfunded plan, of course, there is no actual return on plan assets.

*4. Amortizaton of Unrecognized Prior Service Cost.* A new pension plan usually credits benefits based on service prior to the effective date, creating a projected benefit obligation on the effective date. Plan amendments frequently result in an increase in the projected benefit obligation. The increase in projected benefit obligation resulting from establishment or amendment of a plan is termed *prior service cost*. Occasionally an amendment can decrease the projected benefit obligation, resulting in a negative prior service cost. Amounts of projected benefit obligation established before the effective date of *Statement 87* are not treated as prior service cost, but are separately accounted for.

The entire prior service cost is not included in the net periodic pension cost in the year that it is created. Rather it is amortized over the expected future period of service of present active participants expected to receive benefits under the plan.[16] By using rates of death, retirement, disability, and other forms of withdrawal, the actuary can project the periods of service expected to be worked in future years by present participants.

For example, for 1,000 participants expected to receive benefits under the plan at the beginning of a year when a prior service cost is created, the actuary may project that 980 years of service will be credited during that year, that 940 will be credited the following year, and so forth. Totaling these projections for all future years, he may determine that the total number of years of service to be credited in all future years is 15,000 years of service. Of these 15,000 years, 980, or 6.53 percent of them, will be credited during the first year. Therefore 6.53 percent of the prior service cost would

---

[16]If all or almost all of the participants are inactive, their remaining life expectancy is used instead of the remaining service period for this purpose and other requirements of *Statement 87*.

be included in the net periodic pension cost for the first year as amortization of unrecognized prior service cost. The next year the amount of unrecognized prior service cost included in the net periodic pension cost would be 6.27 percent (940/15,000) of the amount of prior service cost that was determined at its creation.

This complex approach to amortization can be avoided by adopting an alternative approach that amortizes the prior service cost more rapidly, such as straight-line amortization over the average remaining service period. In the above example, the average remaining service period is 15 years (15,000/1,000); thus one fifteenth of the prior service cost could be treated as the amortization amount each year.

It should be noted that the amortization amount does not include any interest. Interest on the prior service cost has already been included as part of the interest cost based on the total projected benefit obligation described earlier.

5. *Gain or Loss (Including the Effects of Changes in Assumptions) to the Extent Recognized.* For purposes of *Statement 87,* a gain or loss is a change in the amount of projected benefit obligation or plan assets resulting from actual experience different from that expected or from changes in assumptions. This differs from funding requirements and traditional actuarial practice, which do not treat changes in assumptions as gains and losses.

The gain or loss component included in net periodic pension cost consists of two parts, (*a*) the difference between the actual return on plan assets and the expected return and (*b*) the amortization of the unrecognized net gain or loss from previous years.

The first of these, the difference between the actual return on plan assets and the expected return, has the effect of removing from the net periodic pension cost the current year's gain or loss on assets that is included in the component for actual return on plan assets.

Determining the second part of the gain or loss component, the amortization of the unrecognized net gain or loss from prior years, requires several steps. The total net gain or loss for all prior years after the effective date of *Statement 87* is adjusted by the amount of such gain or loss recognized in prior years. This unrecognized net loss (negative if a net gain) is then increased by the excess of the fair value of plan assets over the market-related value of plan assets (a negative amount if the fair value is smaller), thus deferring asset gains not yet included in the market-related value. The amortization amount to be included in the gain or loss component can be based upon this adjusted unrecognized net gain or loss, but it is permissible to first reduce its magnitude by 10 percent of the larger of the projected benefit obligation or the fair value of plan assets, basing the amortization on the excess, if any. If amortization is required, this net amount is divided by the average remaining service period of active employees expected to receive plan benefits to obtain the amortization amount included in the gain or loss component of the net periodic pension cost. The amortization amount of the gain or loss component is positive if there is a net loss and negative if there is a net gain. This process of determining the gain or loss component results in substantial deferral of recognition of gains and losses and in smoothing cost fluctuations between years.

6. *Amortization of Unrecognized Obligation at the Date of Initial Application of Statement 87.* At the beginning of the first year to which *Statement 87* applies, there exists an unrecognized obligation equal to the excess, as of the end of the previous year, of (a) the pension benefit obligation over (b) the fair value of plan assets plus any accrued pension cost included in the liabilities of the employer's balance sheet (or less any asset for prepaid pension cost included in the employer's balance sheet). The component for amortization of unrecognized obligation is determined by dividing this difference by the average remaining service period for active employees expected to receive plan benefits. The employer may elect to use 15 years if this is longer than the average remaining service period. The component for amortization of unrecognized obligation at the date of initial application of *Statement 87* is a positive element of the net periodic pension cost if the initial projected benefit obligation exceeds the fair value of plan assets adjusted for balance sheet accruals, and otherwise it is a negative element of the cost.

*F. Recognition of Liabilities and Assets.* The amount of employer contributions to the plan will ordinarily differ from the net periodic pension cost. The cumulative difference between these two is recognized on the employer's balance sheet as an asset for prepaid pension expense if employer contributions exceed the net periodic pension cost, and as a liability for unfunded accrued pension cost if less.

An additional liability may be required on the employer's balance sheet if there is an unfunded accumulated benefit obligation. The term *unfunded accumulated benefit obligation* means the excess, if any, of the accumulated benefit obligation over the fair value of plan assets. This additional liability for unfunded accumulated benefit obligation equals the excess, if any, of the unfunded accumulated benefit obligation over the unfunded accrued pension cost, increased by any asset for prepaid pension expense. Thus the combination of this additional liability and any prepaid pension expense or unfunded accrued pension cost is equivalent to a net liability on the employer's balance sheet equal to the unfunded accumulated benefit obligation.

Any such additional liability is generally offset by adding an "intangible asset" of equal amount to the balance sheet.[17]

**G. Disclosures.**   *Statement 87* describes extensive disclosures required in the employer's financial statements regarding the employer's pension plans, their funding and their accounting. The net periodic pension cost must be broken down between the service cost component, the interest cost component, the actual return on assets for the period, and the net total of other components. All three measures of benefit obligation must be shown. A detailed schedule is required reconciling the funded status of the plan with amounts reported in the employer's balance sheet. *Statement 87* provides examples of such disclosure statements.

**H. Employers with Two or More Plans.**   If an employer sponsors more than one defined benefit plan, the net periodic pension cost, asset and liability items for the employer's financial statement must be calculated separately for each plan. The employer's financial statement combines amounts for all such plans in the statement, but it does not offset them. Thus an excess of plan assets over the accumulated benefit obligation for one plan cannot reduce the unfunded accumulated benefit obligation of another plan, and the prepaid pension cost of one plan does not offset the unfunded accrued pension cost of another. For purposes of the required disclosures, all of an employer's defined benefit plans may be aggre-

---

[17]However, the intangible asset may not exceed the unrecognized prior service cost plus the unrecognized net obligation arising before the effective date of *Statement 87*. If the additional liability exceeds this amount, a decrease in the net worth shown on the balance sheet results.

gated or they may be aggregated in groups to provide the most useful information. However, plans with unfunded accumulated benefit obligations may not be aggregated with other plans for purposes of the required schedule reconciling the funded status of the plan with amounts reported in the employer's balance sheet.

*I. Defined Contribution Plans.* *Statement 87's* requirements with respect to defined contribution pension plans are quite simple. The net periodic pension cost equals the required employer contributions to the plan. Any difference between the net periodic pension cost and the actual employer contributions results in either a liability for unfunded accrued pension cost or an asset for prepaid pension cost, the same as under defined benefit plans. Brief and simple disclosure requirements apply to defined contribution plans.

*J. Multiemployer Plans.* The requirements for accounting for the costs of a multiemployer plan in the financial statement of a contributing employer are usually comparable to the requirements with respect to defined contribution plans. However, if it is either probable or reasonably possible that the employer will withdraw from a multiemployer plan with resulting withdrawal liability, other requirements apply.[18]

*K. Other Rules and Effective Dates.* Special rules apply to non-U.S. pension plans and to a variety of special situations not described herein.

*Statement 87* is generally effective for financial statements for fiscal periods beginning after December 15, 1986. But for a business whose securities are not publicly traded and which does not sponsor any defined benefit plan with more than 100 participants, the *Statement* is effective for fiscal periods beginning two years later. That later effective date also applies to foreign plans, and to all plans with respect to the requirement that any unfunded accumulated benefit obligation be shown on the balance sheet.

Earlier application is encouraged for all employers, and many have decided to comply early. The advantages and disadvantages of adopting the new rules before the mandatory dates differ from employer to employer, causing employers to reach differing decisions concerning early adoption.

---

[18]Requirements in this case are determined by *FASB Statement No. 5.* See Chapter 25 for a description of withdrawal liability under multiemployer plans.

## FASB Statement 88: "Plan Terminations, Settlements, Curtailments and Termination Benefits"

*FASB Statement No. 88* establishes requirements for the way in which an employer's financial statements reflect the effect of certain special events in defined benefit plans, such as a plan termination or curtailment, settlements of benefit obligations by purchase of annuities or lump-sum payment, and provision of certain termination benefits. *Statement 88* describes the amount of gains and losses required to be recognized immediately in the employer's financial statements for these events. These requirements supplement the requirements of *Statement 87* and become effective at the same time as *Statement 87*. Thus, a decision to adopt *Statement 87* early will automatically trigger the early adoption of *Statement 88*.

**Settlements.** *Statement 88* defines a settlement as "a transaction that (*a*) is an irrevocable action, (*b*) relieves the employer (or the plan) of primary responsibility for a pension benefit obligation, and (*c*) eliminates significant risks related to the obligation and the assets used to effect the settlement." A settlement will occur if a plan's obligation to provide benefits is discharged by paying a lump-sum distribution or by purchase of a nonparticipating annuity contract.

If a participating annuity contract is purchased, this constitutes a settlement only if the employer is no longer subject to all or most of the risk and rewards associated with the annuity. But if a purchase of a participating annuity is a settlement, the portion of the premium that exceeds the cost of a similar nonparticipating annuity is treated as an investment in the asset of future dividends.

Even the discharge of the benefit obligation for a single participant by payment of a lump-sum distribution or purchase of an annuity constitutes a settlement, but the employer may elect not to recognize settlements if the total of all settlements in a year is less than the sum of the service cost component and the interest cost component of net periodic pension cost for the year. Thus in a large plan the settlements resulting from routine benefit distributions will not ordinarily require recognition, but in a small plan the retirement of a single participant may require recognition as a settlement.

**Curtailments.**   A curtailment is an event that significantly reduces the benefits that would ordinarily be expected to be earned in the future by present participants. Any event which significantly reduces the expected years of future service, such as a plant closing that results in a significant number of terminations of employment, would constitute a curtailment. A plan amendment reducing or eliminating benefits to be accrued in the future would also be a curtailment.

**Plan Terminations.**   A plan termination usually involves both a curtailment and a settlement. Therefore it is usually subject to the requirements for both events.

**Termination Benefits.**   Some pension plans provide special termination benefits triggered by a particular event such as a plant closing. Other employers have agreed to provide such benefits outside the pension plan under the terms of a collective bargaining agreement. *Statement 88* defines "contractual termination benefits" to include both types, and establishes requirements for accounting for them.

In a temporary effort to encourage early retirements, some employers have offered special termination benefits to certain employees if they retire or terminate employment during a limited period of time, often called a "window period." *Statement 88* establishes rules for accounting for these "special termination benefits."[19]

---

# Questions

1. Explain why pension cost accounting is almost exclusively concerned with *defined benefit* pension plans.
2. What role has ERISA played in the accounting profession's emphasis on accounting and reporting standards for pension plans?

---

[19]Accounting for such special termination benefits prior to the effective date of *Statement 88* is governed by *FASB Statement No. 74.*

3. *FASB 35* has been sharply criticized by many actuaries, plan administrators, and other members of the pension community. Some are of the opinion that the plan financial statements prepared in accordance with *FASB 35* are not worth the cost and effort involved. What features of *FASB 35* might cause a pension professional to question its usefulness?

4. What is the relationship, if any, between *FASB 35* and *FASB 87?*

5. The proper treatment of "prior service costs" of a pension has been a real challenge to the accounting profession over the years and is the subject of lively debate.
   a. How does *FASB 87* define "prior service costs"?
   b. Identify the three basic approaches to the expensing of prior service costs that would have some justification in accounting theory and explain the theory or rationale behind each of the approaches.
   c. Describe the *specific* treatment of prior service costs that has been prescribed under *FASB 87.*

6. Why do the actuarial and accounting professions tend to disagree over pension accounting issues or, at least, find it difficult to reach an accommodation of each others' views?

7. Identify the various propositions that underlie FASB's approach toward employer pension accounting and point out how each of the propositions are reflected in *FASB Statement 87.*

8. Explain each of the following terms and indicate how their values would be determined for a particular plan:
   a. The pension benefit obligation.
   b. The accumulated benefit obligation.
   c. The vested benefit obligation.
   d. The service cost.
   e. The market-related value of plan assets.

9. *Opinion 8* prescribed the minimum and maximum charge to expense for pension cost. Does *FASB 87* provide for such a range?

10. Describe the elements of net periodic pension cost under *FASB 87.*

11. Can an employer's net periodic pension cost be negative? Explain.

12. What is the difference in use of the discount rate and the expected long-term rate of return on plan assets? Would you expect these two rates to be equal? Why or why not?

13. Should the FASB prescribe uniform actuarial assumptions to be used for determining pension cost? Why or why not?

14. *FASB 87* allows amortization of any gain or loss over a period of years. Some have argued that gains and losses should be fully and

immediately recognized in the year that they occur. What are the arguments for and against such a change?

15. In your view, should FASB require employers to show the unfunded actuarial liability of a defined benefit pension plan on their balance sheets? Would you expect such a change in accounting practice to have an adverse effect on the attitudes of the firm's creditors and current and prospective investors in the firm? Why or why not? In forming your opinion, take account of the fact that the amount of unfunded pension liability is now shown in the notes to the sponsor's financial statements.

16. Under *FASB Statement 87,* are an employer's contribution to its defined benefit plan year treated as the firm's pension expense for the year? Why or why not?

17. One goal of the FASB has been to achieve comparability of financial statements of different employers. Has *Statement 87* accomplished this?

18. What events does *FASB 88* relate to?

19. How does an employer account for its obligation under multiemployer pension plans?

20. Do you believe that an employer's unfunded obligation for the payment of postretirement benefits other than those contained in its pension plan should be reflected on its balance sheet? What other postretirement benefits might be involved?

# 19 | Management of Pension Plan Assets: Policy

THE FUNDING OF A PENSION PLAN, whether in response to regulatory requirements or the dictates of sound financial management, leads to the accumulation of assets dedicated to the payment of plan benefits and administrative expenses. Productive deployment of these assets reduces the direct cost of a defined benefit plan and increases the benefits that can be paid under a defined contribution plan. For example, if the assets of a fully funded defined benefit plan can be invested in such a manner as to earn a total rate of return of 6 percent in a stable economic environment, on the average, about 70 percent of the plan's benefits will be paid out of investment earnings, leaving only 30 percent to be met out of contributions to the plan. With a given level of contributions, investment earnings play a comparably significant role in generating benefits for participants in a defined contribution plan. Plan assets and their capacity to generate future investment earnings are the primary source, as of any given point in time, of benefit security, the assurance that the accrued benefit rights of the plan participants will ultimately be honored. Thus, the management of pension plan assets is a major concern of both plan sponsors and those regulatory authorities charged with the responsibility of protecting the interests of plan participants and their beneficiaries.

**434**

## Regulatory Constraints

The management of pension plan assets is subject to regulation and oversight at both federal and state levels. Federal constraints are found primarily in the statutory prescriptions of ERISA and the implementing regulations promulgated by the Department of Labor and the Internal Revenue Service. State constraints are contained in the statutes, regulations, and court decisions relating to the investments of life insurance companies, banks, trust companies, and fiduciaries of various sorts. The general preemption of applicable state law by ERISA does not extend to state laws regulating the investments of banks, trust companies, and life insurance companies.

### Federal Regulation

The rules and regulations of various federal agencies have some relevance to the investment of pension plan assets; but the primary regulatory responsibility in this area lies with the Department of Labor, the Internal Revenue Service, the Securities and Exchange Commission, the Federal Reserve System, and the Comptroller of the Currency. The authority of the DOL and IRS derives mainly from ERISA.

**ERISA.** The constraints imposed by ERISA on the management of pension plan assets flow from and are an integral part of the basic fiduciary responsibilities imposed by the act on any person or persons who exercise any discretionary authority or control over the management of a pension plan, especially the management of its assets.[1] Full responsibility for all aspects of the plan's operations, including the management of its assets, ultimately rests upon the directors and senior management of the sponsoring entity. For operating purposes, that responsibility will usually be vested in a specific individual or a committee, known as the retirement, pensions, or benefits committee. Either the plan sponsor[2] or such person or committee is usually designated as the plan administrator.[3]

---

[1] ERISA §3(21).
[2] ERISA §3(16)(B).
[3] ERISA §3(16)(A).

ERISA requires the plan to have a named fiduciary,[4] which is typically either the plan administrator or the plan sponsor. Some of the technical and administrative functions may be contracted out to specialists, but the ultimate responsibility for the overall operation of the plan and compliance with applicable law remains with the plan sponsor.[5]

Under an individual account plan which permits individual participants and their beneficiaries to exercise control over their own accounts, no fiduciary is liable for the actions of the participants or beneficiaries.[6]

**A. Segregation of Plan Assets.**  Both ERISA and the Internal Revenue Code require that the assets of a pension plan be held in trust or under a comparable arrangement.[7] There are at least three reasons for this requirement: (1) to remove the assets from the control of the plan sponsor and assure their ultimate application to the payment of plan benefits and reasonable expenses of administering the plan; (2) to prevent the commingling of the plan assets with the assets of other plans (except under approved conditions) or the assets of the institution or individual providing trust or investment services; and (3) to facilitate the identification, management, and control of the plan assets by the trustee or trustees.

Qualified pension plans funded through insurance or annuity contracts issued by a domestically licensed life insurance company have always enjoyed a statutory exemption from the general requirement that their assets be held in trust.[8] This is true whether the insurer guarantees all funded benefits through individual or group annuity contracts or merely holds the assets in unallocated fashion in its general asset account or in one or more separate accounts. The assets of the insurer issuing such contracts are likewise exempt from the trust requirement. Assets in individual retirement accounts (IRAs) held in certain custodial accounts[9] are also exempted from the trust requirement, as are the assets invested

---

[4]ERISA §402(a).
[5]ERISA §402(b),405(c).
[6]ERISA §404(c).
[7]ERISA §403, I.R.C. §401(a)(1).
[8]ERISA §403(b)(1), I.R.C. §403(a), Treas. Reg. 1.403(a)–l(d).
[9]I.R.C. §408(h).

in mutual funds or other regulated investment companies and held in custodial accounts in respect of Section 403(b) annuity contracts (individual tax-deferred annuities, or TDAs).[10] Section 403(b) annuities funded through life insurers have been exempt from the trust requirement from their inception. There are exemptions for other less common arrangements,[11] and the Secretary of Labor has authority under ERISA to grant other exemptions.

In an important ruling of general application, the Secretary of Labor, by regulation,[12] has held that registration of securities of a pension plan in the name of a nominee or its street name ("street name" registration) is not violative of the trust requirement if the securities are held on behalf of the plan by a bank, trust company, broker-dealer, or clearing agency, or their nominees. The plan trustee or trustees must maintain control over such securities and evaluate the safeguards against loss from such an arrangement, including the financial stability of the nominees, adequacy of insurance, and so forth.

The plan sponsor appoints the trustee or, if the plan is to be funded through a life insurer, selects the insurer and the contractual arrangement.[13] The trustee or trustees must be named in the plan document or the trust instrument, or appointed by the named fiduciary for the plan.[14] After acceptance of the trusteeship and acknowledging in writing a fiduciary status with respect to the plan, the trustee or trustees have exclusive authority and discretion to manage the assets of the plan, unless: (1) the plan document or trust instrument expressly provides that the trustee or trustees are subject to the direction of a named fiduciary (not a trustee in this sense) or (2) authority to manage, acquire, or dispose of assets of the plan is delegated to one or more asset managers.

Investment responsibilities can be legally delegated only to an investment adviser registered under the Investment Advisers Act

---

[10]ERISA §403(b)(5), I.R.C. §403(b)(7).

[11]ERISA §403(b).

[12]29 CFR 2550.403a–1.

[13]Under a negotiated multiemployer pension plan, the plan sponsor is the board of trustees, composed of an equal number of labor and management representatives, which is responsible for the plan's operation and determines investment policy and chooses asset managers.

[14]ERISA §403(a).

of 1940, a bank (as defined in that act), or an insurance company qualified under the laws of two or more states to provide investment management services.[15] To be qualified, an asset manager must acknowledge in writing that it is a plan fiduciary, as that term is defined by ERISA. The plan sponsor must exercise prudence in selecting and retaining asset managers.

When authority to manage some or all of the plan assets is delegated to other investment entities, the assets subject to delegation retain their identity as plan assets, title to which remains with the plan trustee or trustees.

**B. Definition of Plan Assets.** Identification of plan assets has crucial significance in fixing the scope of the trustee's authority and responsibility. When a plan invests in another entity, there is an issue of whether the plan's asset consists only of its investment in the entity itself, or whether the underlying assets of the entity are also deemed to be plan assets. For example, if the plan purchases shares of a mutual fund, the issue is whether the plan assets consist only of the shares of the mutual fund or whether the plan assets include an undivided interest in the underlying investments of the mutual fund. The manager of such a pooled investment vehicle would be a plan fiduciary if retained directly by the plan to invest a portion of the plan assets and, it may be argued, it should make no difference that the manager is retained indirectly through the acquisition of an ownership interest in the pool.

In attempting to discern and implement the will of Congress in this matter, the Department of Labor[16] has embraced the general proposition that, where a pension plan invests in an equity interest of another entity, the underlying assets of that entity are properly viewed as plan assets and must be managed in accordance with the fiduciary responsibility provisions of ERISA, unless there are circumstances that make these provisions unnecessary or inappropriate. As a practical matter, it is argued, the plan is retaining the manager of the other entity, generally a pooled investment vehicle, to manage that portion of the plan's assets which is so invested.

Whenever a plan invests in any entity, if the underlying assets of the entity are construed to be plan assets, the manager of the

---

[15]ERISA §§3(38), 402(c)(3), 405(d).
[16]29 CFR 2510.3–101.

entity will be a fiduciary with respect to the pension plan and the plan fiduciaries will have fiduciary responsibility for the prudent investment of the underlying assets.

Congress recognized the importance of the issue and included a provision in ERISA that was intended to clarify the status of a pension plan's contractual arrangements with investment companies and life insurance companies.[17] That provision declares that the underlying assets of a mutual fund or other investment company registered with the SEC under the provisions of the Investment Company Act of 1940 are *not* to be construed as assets of a pension plan holding securities of the investment company. Congress reasoned that the supervision of the investment company by the SEC provides sufficient protection to the pension plan and its participants. This conclusion does not relieve the plan trustee from the obligation of exercising prudence in the acquisition and retention of investment company shares, which constitute plan assets. Regulations have extended this relief with respect to all publicly-offered securities that are freely transferable, widely held, and registered under federal securities laws.[18]

The same ERISA provision states that the assets of a life insurer's general account, against which most contractual guarantees and other general obligations are enforceable, shall not be construed to be assets of a plan which owns a guaranteed benefit contract. Rather, only the contracts or policies issued to the plan trustee by the life insurer are to be treated as plan assets. The rationale for this exemption, apart from its inherent logic, is that the general account operation, including its investment activities, are adequately supervised by state regulatory authorities.

The same issue has arisen in connection with the acquisition by a pension plan of certificates or securities backed by mortgages guaranteed or insured by various housing agencies of the federal government, such as GNMA, FNMA, or FHLMC. The question is whether the plan assets include the mortgages in the government-backed pool, or only the certificates that evidence a pro rata ownership of the pool. Concluding that the real security behind these pass-though certificates is the government guarantee, rather than

---

[17]ERISA §401(b).
[18]29 CFR 2510.3–101(a),(b).

the individual mortgages in the pool, the DOL has taken the position that only the certificates are the plan assets, and not the underlying mortgages.[19] Thus, the sponsor or manager of a governmental mortgage pool would not be a fiduciary of a plan merely by reason of the plan's investment in the pool.

Under another rule, if a plan has an equity interest in an operating company that is primarily engaged, directly or through majority owned subsidiaries, in the production or sale of a product or service, the underlying assets of the operating company, such as property and equipment, are not deemed to be plan assets.[20]

The rule for operating companies described above also applies to certain equity investments in a venture capital operating company (VCOC). Generally a limited partnership or corporation, a VCOC raises money through the sale of its own securities or participation shares and then invests the money in selected securities of small operating companies. As part of the investment arrangements with portfolio companies, the VCOC management may participate or be given the right to participate in the management of the portfolio companies. By regulation[21] the Department of Labor has stipulated that investment by a pension plan in a VCOC will not result in the assets of the VCOC being classified as plan assets so long as certain conditions are fulfilled. The same principle applies to a real estate operating company which satisfies certain criteria.[22]

Apart from the special rules explained above, the underlying assets of an entity in which a plan has an equity interest are deemed to be plan assets unless the equity participation in the entity by all benefit plan investors is less than 25 percent of the particular class of equity interests.

In the case of any plan investment in a group trust or a common or collective trust of a bank which pools the investments of more than one plan, or any investment in a separate account of an insurance company, the plan assets are deemed to include the underlying assets of the entity, except where the entity is a registered investment company, regardless of any other rules.

---

[19]29 CFR 2510.3–101(i).
[20]29 CFR 2510.3–101(a)(2),(c).
[21]29 CFR 2510.3–101(d).
[22]29 CFR 2510.3–101(e).

In summary, unless the entity is a registered investment company, plan assets will always be deemed to include the underlying assets in the following situations:

- A group trust;
- A common or collective trust fund of a bank; or
- A separate account of an insurance company.

Otherwise, if a plan has an equity interest in an entity, the underlying assets will be treated as plan assets unless less than 25 percent of the equity interest of the company is held by benefit plan investors or unless the entity is one of the following:

- A registered investment company;
- A publicly offered security that is freely transferable, widely held, and registered;
- An operating company, including a venture capital operating company or a real estate operating company; or
- A governmental mortgage pool.

*C. Statement of Investment Policy.*   Some observers believe that the plan sponsor is under a fiduciary obligation to develop and adopt a set of written policy guidelines for the investment of the plan assets. It should keep the guidelines under continual review and make whatever modifications that seem to be called for in the light of the economic and plan circumstances then prevailing. The guidelines should be communicated to the asset managers and reasonable efforts made to ensure compliance with the guidelines by the managers.

*D. Diversification of Investments.*   The plan sponsor and its investment managers are under specific mandate to diversify the plan assets and thereby minimize the risk of large losses, unless under the circumstances it is clearly prudent not to do so.[23] The degree of diversification must be determined by the facts and circumstances of the particular case, including the purposes of the plan, the amount of plan assets, and financial and industrial conditions. A highly diversified portfolio might reflect diversification by (1) type of investment—stocks, bonds, mortgages and the like; (2) geographic location; (3) industrial sector; and (4) dates of ma-

---

[23]ERISA §404(a)(1)(C).

turity of fixed-income instruments. If the assets are allocated to more than one asset manager, with each manager being instructed to hold specific classes of investments, such as common stocks only or bonds only, the managers are not liable for failure to diversify their holdings by type. Instead, the diversification test is applied to the deployment of plan assets as a whole. The diversification requirement can be satisfied by placing all the plan assets in a pooled investment account, if the latter is itself properly diversified. Thus, it is permissible to have the plan assets held in a pooled trust fund, a pooled separate account of a life insurance company, or shares of a mutual fund. Alternatively, the assets may be invested wholly in insurance or annuity contracts guaranteed by a life insurance company or wholly in the securities of the federal government or its agencies, since these require no diversification to minimize the risk of large losses.

In addition to the general diversification requirement, defined benefit plans and most money purchase pension plans are prohibited from acquiring or holding more than 10 percent of the plan assets in the securities or real property of the employer.[24]

***E. Prudence Standard.*** In managing the assets of a qualified pension plan, an individual or organization must act "with the care, skill, prudence, and diligence under the circumstances then prevailing that a prudent man acting in a like capacity and familiar with such matters would use in conducting an enterprise of like character and with like aims."[25] This is a variation of the "prudent man" standard that derives from the classic rule first enunciated in 1830 by the Supreme Judicial Court of Massachusetts in the famous case of *Harvard College* v. *Amory.* The original rule was enunciated as a standard for a trustee in managing the assets of a personal trust or an institutional endowment. The new federal standard, which applies to all pension plan fiduciaries, whether or not they have investment responsibilities, is intended to measure the behavior of a pension plan asset manager against the behavior of other such managers, rather than against the investment behavior of individuals managing their own funds or professional managers

[24]ERISA §407.
[25]ERISA §404(a)(1)(B).

handling the assets of personal trusts or other aggregation of funds not associated with a pension plan. This has caused some to characterize the new benchmark as the "prudent expert" standards. It is also intended that the overall investment performance of the portfolio be judged, rather than the performance of specific portfolio holdings.

The federal courts will have the ultimate responsibility of determining the meaning and full ramifications of this standard of prudence for pension plan fiduciaries. The Department of Labor has promulgated a regulation[26] to provide some guidance on the interpretation of "prudence" in the ERISA context. The regulation was not intended to serve as the exclusive method for satisfying the prudence rule, but as a "safe harbor" approach, namely, one officially sanctioned method of complying with the law.

The regulation is couched in general language and provides little additional guidance as to the suitability of a particular course of investment conduct. The primary contribution may well rest on its support of risk/return tradeoff and other tenets of modern portfolio theory. It states in the preamble that no specific investment or investment course of action is prudent per se or imprudent per se, but must be judged by the role that it will play within the overall plan portfolio. In determining the prudence of a particular investment or investment course of action, an asset manager must consider with respect to that portion of the total plan portfolio which he manages:

- The composition of the portfolio, with regard to diversification.
- The liquidity and current return of the portfolio, relative to the cash flow requirements of the plan.
- The projected return of the portfolio, relative to the funding objective of the plan.

In assessing these factors, an asset manager may rely and act upon information provided by or at the direction of the appointing fiduciary, if the manager does not know and has no reason to know that the information is incorrect. This is an especially important provision from the standpoint of an asset manager who manages only a portion of the plan portfolio.

---

[26]29 CFR 2550.404a–1.

While endorsing the concept of total portfolio performance, DOL expresses its view in the preamble of the regulation that no relevant or material attributes of a contemplated investment may properly be disregarded nor any particular investment be deemed prudent solely by reason of the propriety of the aggregate risk/return characteristics of the overall portfolio. The DOL approves the use of an index fund, if the fund filters out the securities of companies subject to adverse financial developments, and the use of the fund is consistent with the plan's needs and investment objectives. It also expressed the view that "prudence" does not require that every item in a plan portfolio be income-producing under all circumstances. In effect, DOL accepts the "total return" concept of portfolio performance.

**Federal Securities Laws.**[27]  The investment operations of a pension plan (and other employee benefit plans of the asset accumulation type) are subject to the Securities Act of 1933, the Securities Exchange Act of 1934, and the Investment Company Act of 1940, as these important pieces of legislation have been interpreted by the SEC and federal courts. The Securities Act of 1933, which regulates the offer and sale of securities, is of most relevance, especially its registration (disclosure) and antifraud provisions. A critical question, which has generated much disagreement and controversy, is whether any aspect of pension plan operation gives rise to an interest that might be characterized as a "security" and, hence, should enjoy all the investor safeguards embodied in the 1933 act and other securities laws. To be more specific, the question is whether a participant in a pension, profit sharing, or similar plan has made an investment, or—another issue—whether the acquisition by the plan of a fractional interest in a pool of assets managed by a bank or insurance company is tantamount to the purchase of a security.

With respect to the first issue, the Securities and Exchange Commission has long applied a test first enunciated in the landmark case of *SEC* v. *W. J. Howey Co.*[28] Under the *Howey* test, an in-

---

[27]Much of the material for this section was drawn from *SEC Release No. 33–6188* (February 1, 1980) [45FR8960] and *SEC Release No. 33–6281* (January 15, 1981) [46FR8446].
[28]328 U.S. 293 (1946).

vestment contract (security) requires: (1) the investment of money (or its equivalent in goods or services), (2) in a common enterprise, (3) with an expectation of profit (a return in excess of the cash contribution), (4) from the managerial efforts of others.

Since 1941, the SEC has held the general view that the interests of employees in pension, profit sharing, and similar plans are investment contracts in the generic sense, since such plans are capital accumulation vehicles designed to produce a "profit" to the employees in the form of retirement benefits or a cash distribution.[29] However, with the exception noted below, the Commission has taken the position that the plans need not be registered and in compliance with all relevant provisions of the 1933 act.[30]

The SEC has consistently maintained that a voluntary, contributory pension or profit sharing plan meets all the *Howey* tests of an investment contract and should be registered if employee contributions are to be invested in employer securities, as they frequently are in profit sharing plans and may be in a pension plan. It contends that when an employee elects to participate in a voluntary, contributory pension, or other similar plan, he has made an investment decision motivated by an expectation that the ultimate return on his contributions in the form of cash or retirement benefits will exceed the return on alternative investment opportunities. The need for full disclosure is magnified when employer securities are to be acquired. The SEC position was ratified by Congress in the 1970 amendments to Section 3(a)(2) of the 1933 Act. When participation in the plan is involuntary, no investment contract is involved, even though employee contributions are required, since the expectation of profit or gain is not a motivating factor.

The applicability of federal securities laws to employee interests in pension and profit sharing plans has been before the federal courts on various occasions—one case, *International Brotherhood of Teamsters* v. *Daniel*,[31] reaching the Supreme Court. This case involved a noncontributory multiemployer plan in which participation of eligible employees was automatic and, hence, involun-

---

[29]Opinion of Assistant General Counsel, CCH Fed Sec L. Rep. 1941–44.

[30]This administrative practice was affirmed by Congress in 1970 and codified in §3(a)(2) of the 1933 act.

[31]99 S. Ct. 790, *International Brotherhood of Teamsters* v. *Daniel* (1979).

tary. The Court held that the interest of the employee, Daniel, in the plan was not a security because Daniel had no choice as to participation, made no contribution other than his labor, and had no realistic expectation of profit at time of plan entry in view of the 20-year service requirement for vesting. This was a rather narrow case and the courts are yet to speak on some of the broader issues.

The question of registration of pooled asset accounts maintained by banks and insurance companies for the investment of pension plan assets was largely resolved by the aforementioned amendments to Section 3(a)(2) of the 1933 act, which were proposed by interested banks and insurance companies. The amended Section 3(a)(2) exempts from registration bank collective trust funds and insurance company separate accounts maintained for the exclusive use of qualified pension, profit sharing, and stock bonus plans. The justification for this broad exemption, which the SEC staff interprets to include interests of the plan participants themselves, is that these pooled investment vehicles are available only to plan trustees who are presumed to be possessed of sufficient financial sophistication to assess the investment characteristics of the pooled funds. These unregistered funds are prohibited from dealing directly with the public. Pension plans may acquire shares in investment companies that offer their investment services to the general public, but such funds must be registered with the SEC and comply with the Investment Company Act of 1940.

The amended Section 3(a)(2) also exempts any security arising out of a contract issued by an insurance company to qualified plans. This provision is broad enough to encompass guaranteed income contracts, annuity contracts, and any other security relating to an insurance company contract issued to an employee benefit plan.[32]

Interests of participants in voluntary, contributory Keogh plans and IRAs are deemed by the SEC staff to be securities, but separate registration of the interests has not been required. Most such plans can rely on an exemption from registration for the offer and sale of employee interests. Securities acquired by these plans must meet the usual requirements of the 1933 act, no special exemptions being available.

[32]*SEC Release No. 33–6281* (January 15, 1981) [46 FR 8446].

**Banking Laws.** Pension plans that utilize the investment facilities of banks and trust companies may be affected by the laws and regulations pertaining to national banks, member banks of the Federal Reserve System, and members of the Federal Deposit Insurance Corporation. These laws are administered by the Comptroller of the Currency, the Board of Governors of the FRS, and the FDIC, respectively. They are designed to ensure the general soundness of the banking system and the solvency of individual banks.

Pension plans deal primarily with the trust departments of commercial banks and trust companies and would tend to be most affected by the laws regulating the trustee functions of those institutions, including the investment of trust assets. Both the Federal Reserve authorities and the Comptroller of the Currency have issued regulations pertaining to collective trust funds, which are widely used by small- and medium-size plans for the investment of the total plan assets. Specialty collective trust funds are commonly used for a portion of the assets of larger funds, especially money market funds utilized for cash management. In combination with the securities laws administered by the SEC, these regulations are designed to ensure that collective trust funds are operated in a sound and equitable manner.

## State Regulation

ERISA preempts state law with respect to most matters bearing directly on the operation of a pension plan. An exception is made of those state laws that regulate banks, trust companies, and insurance companies. Nevertheless, there may be overlapping jurisdiction in the investment of assets that fall into the DOL classification of "plan assets."

**Trust Investments.** All states have laws that regulate the investment of assets held in a fiduciary capacity. These laws tend to be rather restrictive and may limit investments to a so-called legal list of fixed-income instruments. The more enlightened laws prescribe standards to be observed and permit the fiduciary to acquire and hold any assets that fall within those standards. The laws of many states permit a portion of the assets to be invested in common stocks, sometimes under the discretion afforded by the "prudent man" test. In all states, these statutory restrictions can be set aside in respect of trust assets by agreement between the trustee and the person or entity creating the trust. It is common practice for the parties to a pension trust agreement to waive the statutory restrictions and to confer on the trustee whatever discretion the grantor is willing to grant and the trustee is willing to accept. However, the plan trustee and any persons or institutions providing investment advice or management in respect of plan assets are fiduciaries under the plan and must conduct their investment operations in accordance with the federal prudent man standard enunciated in ERISA.

The common law of trusts, frequently codified in state statutes, requires that the assets of any given trust be held separate and apart from the assets of every other trust administered by the trustee and from the assets of the trustee itself. To provide greater diversification of risk and operating economies, most states have modified the common law doctrine to permit commingling of trust assets, at the direction of the trust grantors involved. The laws may make provision for one commingled pool for small personal trusts and estates, generally called a *common trust fund* and subject to a 10 percent limit on participation by one entity, and another such pool, called a *collective trust fund,* for employee benefit plans, with no restrictions on the amount of plan assets that may be placed in the pooled trust. Federal banking authorities have granted permission for the pooling of trust assets in respect of banks subject to their jurisdiction.

**Insurance Company Investments.**  Investments of the general asset account of a life insurer are regulated by the laws of the state in which the company is domiciled and, if it does business in the state of New York, by the laws of that state. The standards vary greatly from state to state. The proportion of the general asset account that can be invested in common stocks is limited in most states, although the restrictions have been relaxed somewhat in recent years in a number of states, including New York. Indeed, there has been a significant relaxation of investment restrictions in some important states in order to permit insurers to take advantage of new investment instruments, strategies, and markets and to pursue more aggressive investment policies generally. The general asset account of an insurer is not subject to ERISA's investment standards, since the assets therein are not regarded to be plan assets.

Life insurer separate accounts are also subject to regulation by state insurance authorities, but they are free of the limitations on common stock holdings and certain other strictures applicable to the general asset account. The assets in these accounts are regarded as "plan assets" by the Department of Labor and must be managed in accordance with the federal prudence standards.

## Investment Characteristics of Pension Plans

Pension plans have a number of distinctive characteristics that influence investment policies and strategies. These characteristics vary by sponsorship and type of plan. Thus, it is useful to distinguish between those plans that promise a determinable retirement benefit and usually commingle the plan assets, at least with respect to active employees, and those that make specific contributions on behalf of the plan participants, with the contributions being accumulated, with investment earnings, in individual accounts and the benefits at retirement being determined by the account balances.

### Defined Benefit Plans

A dominating feature of the investment policy of a defined benefit plan is that the plan sponsor bears most of the investment risk. As was noted earlier, ultimate contributions of the plan sponsor are reduced by investment earnings on the plan assets. Contributions are calculated initially on the assumption that the plan assets will earn a certain rate of return. If the return is greater than that assumed, future contributions will be smaller than anticipated. If the return is smaller than assumed, contributions will be greater. The amount of benefits payable to plan participants or their beneficiaries is not affected by investment experience (except in the event of plan termination, and only then under certain circumstances).[33] It follows that a plan sponsor (employer or employers) can pursue riskier investment strategies without breaching its fiduciary obligations than if unsatisfactory investment results were going to diminish the benefits of the participants.

A second important feature of the investment environment is that the plan assets can be invested with a long time horizon.

---

[33]See Chapters 24 and 25.

Corporate pension plans are usually established with the intention that they be permanent undertakings, and, except for the employees near retirement, the obligations of the plan will not mature for many years. Thus, the investment managers have the option of ignoring short-term convolutions in the financial markets and concentrating on long-term results. Of course, the plan may have a strategy of active, aggressive asset management that would call for efforts to anticipate interest rate movements and short-term developments in the stock market. Moreover, the asset managers may feel that they are under pressure to show favorable performance (as compared to other managers), for each review period, sometimes as short as a calendar quarter. The point is that, under normal circumstances, the cash flow and liability characteristics of a plan provide the investment managers with the latitude to pursue any strategies that seem to be called for, including investing for the long pull.

A related characteristic is that, under normal circumstances, a plan has a positive cash flow and can invest its assets with only minimal regard for liquidity. Since the bulk of its obligations are deferred to the participants' retirement and then consist of income payments spread over the individual's remaining lifetime, while contributions to finance the distant benefit payments are made throughout the employees' period of employment, large accumulations of assets are amassed. Current contributions, investment earnings on the plan assets, and maturing investments exceed benefit and expense disbursements for many years. There may be a minor need for liquid assets within each plan year because of the timing of cash flows (many employers make their contribution for the entire year at the end of the year, for example), but this need can be met through money market instruments. A contributory plan requires somewhat more liquidity than a noncontributory plan, since a terminating participant is entitled to a lump-sum refund of his contributions with interest. Plans that provide lump-sum death benefits and permit "cash out" of accrued benefits at retirement obviously have more need for liquidity than those without those features, but the payments can generally be made out of cash flow. An exception might occur with a small plan that has to make a large lump-sum settlement with a terminating or retiring employee. Another exception would be an old plan with few if any new entrants for the last several years. The plan population could become so mature that its benefit payments could exceed its income from all sources. Finally, a unique liquidity need would arise if the plan should be terminated and closed out through lump-sum distributions or the purchase of paid-up annuities for all active and retired employees.

Another significant investment characteristic of a qualified pension plan is that the investment earnings are exempt from federal income taxation. This is true not only of dividend and interest income but also of capital gains. This means that tax-exempt securities should not be attractive to a pension plan, since the lower yields usually associated with such securities have no offsetting tax advantage. Moreover, the plan need have no tax preference, as among dividend and interest income, realized gains and losses, and unrealized appreciation. A decision as to whether to invest in low-dividend growth stocks or higher-dividend securities with little growth potential need not be influenced by tax considerations as it must be for tax-paying entities. Similarly, a decision to sell or hold a security with unrealized appreciation or depreciation can be made strictly on the basis of investment merit, since there is no tax effect from realizing the gain or loss. Despite this tax neutrality, it has been observed that most plans subject to public scrutiny are reluctant to realize losses, although such action might offer distinct investment advantages through asset redeployment.

A final characteristic is that the plan trustee need not distinguish between *principal* and *income* beneficiaries in the investment of plan assets and the allocation of investment earnings. The trustee of a personal trust must balance the conflicting interests of the trust beneficiaries who are to receive the current income and who naturally want to see the income maximized, even if the principal is jeopardized, and the parties—individuals or organizations—who are to receive the trust corpus upon termination of the trust. The dominant interest of the latter is to see the trust corpus preserved and even enhanced by investment in growth stocks and other assets that offer the potential of capital gains but may generate relatively low levels of income. In a pension plan, all trust beneficiaries are of the same class, and, if the plan is of the defined benefit type, have no direct interest in or claim to the investment returns. This provides much more flexibility to the asset managers than if they had to deal with conflicting interests. In a contributory plan, the trustee may perceive a duty to invest employee contributions in a more conservative fashion than employer contributions but that is a relatively minor consideration.

### Individual Account Plans

In an individual account plan, the participants bear the investment risk, in that their ultimate benefits vary directly with the plan's investment results. The employer's contributions are not at all affected by the plan's investment experience, at least in the short run. The plan trustee invests the plan assets on behalf of the participants and may feel a keener sense of fiduciary responsibility than if it was investing for the employer's account. Whether the trustee, in fact, has a heavier fiduciary burden when investing for the accounts of individual participants has not been tested in the courts. As a practical matter, the trustee is more vulnerable to class action suits and to derivative and individual suits from disgruntled participants unhappy over investment performance.

There may be conflicts of interest among the plan participants comparable to those found in personal trust situations. There will almost certainly be differences among the participants as to risk averseness and degree of financial sophistication. Participants nearing retirement may prefer a more conservative investment policy than those just entering the plan. Those who anticipate a lump-sum settlement may be more interested in preserving the book value of the assets than do those who expect to have their interests liquidated over a long period of time. Some plans accommodate these differing objectives by allowing each participant to allocate his own account balance among two or more investment funds with different objectives, such as an equity fund and a fixed-income fund.

Many individual account plans permit a terminating or retiring employee to take his account balance in a lump sum. This increases the liquidity requirements of the plan and may impinge on investment policy.

## Investment Policy and Strategy

Many plans, especially the larger ones, develop a statement of investment policy for the plan and communicate that policy to the managers of the plan assets. It is customary to keep the policy under regular review, and to make whatever modifications seem to be called for by the changing economic and capital market developments. Not all plans have adopted a formal statement of investment policy, and some of the statements adopted have been rudimentary in scope and substance. Many sponsors delegate development of the investment policy to the trustee or insurer.

It is not sufficient that a statement of investment policy be developed, whether thoughtfully or purely for the record. Consideration must be given to ways to accomplish the stated objectives. Implementation of policy goes under the rubric of strategy. What follows in this section is not a comprehensive and theoretically rigorous treatment of investment policy and strategy but an outline of the factors that should be considered and some of the alternatives available—all described in nontechnical terms.[34]

## Elements of Investment Policy

As a minimum, a statement of investment policy has to address three components: rate of return objective, acceptable risk parameters, and liquidity requirements. A fourth component, diversification, is frequently included in deference to the ERISA mandate that investments be diversified. The statement may also specify the types of investments that are to be included or excluded from the portfolio.

**Rate of Return Objective.**     The rate of return objective may be stated in various ways. One is to state it in very general terms without quantification, such as to maximize the return consistent with preservation of principal and the need for liquidity. Few could disagree with that formulation as a statement of principle, but it provides little guidance to the asset managers. Most statements attempt some quantification of the return objective. The simplest but perhaps least satisfactory approach is to state the goal in terms of a specific nominal rate of return on the aggregate investment portfolio. This ignores the asset allocation formula as well as the

---

[34]The literature on investment policy and operations is voluminous, much of it highly technical and statistical in nature. Two very readable but authoritative books that can be consulted on various investment topics treated in this volume are Sidney Cottle et al., *Pension Asset Management: The Corporate Decisions,* (New York: Financial Executives Research Foundation, 1980), and Arthur Williams III, *Managing Your Investment Manager,* (Homewood, Ill.: Dow Jones-Irwin, 1980).

projected rates of return on different types of investment instruments and in various sectors of the capital markets. This approach is sometimes refined by setting separate return objectives for the equity and fixed-income segments of the portfolio. A similar—and equally simplistic—approach is to set as a target an overall nominal rate of return equal to that assumed in the actuarial valuation of the plan's liabilities. This obviously should be the minimum aggregate rate of return over the long run but, under normal circumstances, it does not represent a challenging target to the investment managers.

A more enlightened and more common approach is to express the income goal in relative terms. For example, the target for the cash equivalent segment might be the index of returns on 90-day Treasury bills, which is designed to serve as a proxy for the risk-free return available to investors. The target for the equity portion of the portfolio might be the return on the Standard & Poor's 500 Composite Stock Index, while the target for the fixed-income segment might be the return on the S&P High-Grade Corporate Bond Index or the Salomon Brothers High-Grade Long-Term Bond Index.[35] Such goals would signal a willingness to accept investment results equal to that of the "market," which could be obtained from investment in appropriately structured stock and bond index funds with greater certainty and a lower outlay for investment management services. In the hopes of enjoying an incremental return from active portfolio management, many plans specify a return objective somewhat higher than that of the designated indexes, possibly 200 basis points (2 percent) higher for the equity and fixed-income segments of the portfolio, which, of course, entails greater risk.

A more sophisticated approach sometimes used is to establish a goal in terms of the anticipated return on a "bench mark" or baseline portfolio, reflecting a supposedly optimal mix of stock, bond, and short-term securities characterized by a particular risk/return relationship. The asset managers for the plan would participate in the construction of the baseline portfolio, an indexlike fund, which would be reflective of, and consistent with, the plan's broad investment objective. Performance would be measured against this standard.

[35]These indexes and others are described in Chapter 21.

Finally, disheartened by years of *negative real* rates of return on pension portfolios, a plan may establish an objective of earning a *real* rate of return of a specified magnitude. Operationally, the policy statement would stipulate that the portfolio should be managed in such fashion as to produce a *nominal* rate of return of 2, 3, or 4 percent over and above the long-term rate of inflation. Alternatively, the goal might be stated in terms of an index, such as the S&P 500, which is assumed to reflect an inflation component.

**Risk Tolerance.** A second element of investment policy is determination of the amount of portfolio risk that the plan sponsor is willing to tolerate. Risk in connection with a common stock portfolio is generally viewed as a variation of actual return from expected return. Return variance may be due to broad economic forces, such as recession, unemployment, and inflation, which can cause unexpected results in the entire universe of common stocks, or it may be attributable to causes that are peculiar to the individual portfolio companies. The first type of variance is called *market* or *systematic* risk, while the second is generally designated as *residual* risk, although it is sometimes known as *specific, nonmarket,* or *nonsystematic* risk.

The most common measure of systematic risk is "beta," which is a measure of the price volatility of a stock or entire portfolio relative to the overall market, with Standard & Poor's Composite 500 Index generally being treated as a proxy for the market.

A beta of 1.0 signifies that the variability of return or riskiness of the portfolio is the same as that of the market—that volatility, up or down, in the market will be reflected in the portfolio. A beta of less than 1.0 indicates that the portfolio is less sensitive to broad economic forces than the market generally, while a beta of more than 1.0 indicates greater sensitivity than the market. By definition, this element of risk is endemic to investment and cannot be eliminated by diversification. Since systematic risk cannot be eliminated, economic theory postulates that an investor should be rewarded for assuming it. The expected systematic return of a portfolio is the portfolio beta times the expected market return.

That portion of the total variability or risk not explained by beta is termed *residual risk*. Residual risk is present in any portfolio that deviates from the market portfolio. Since this form of risk usually arises from an asset manager's making a "bet against the market" by holding a portfolio different from the market, it can be considered the risk of *active management*. One theory holds that, in the aggregate, there is no reward for assuming residual risk. This means that the positive incremental returns from the assumption of residual risk by successful active managers must be offset by negative relative returns for unsuccessful managers. Residual risk can be reduced through diversification and, in fact, can be effectively eliminated in an index fund.

The extent to which residual risk has been diversified away in a given stock portfolio is designated by $R^2$, the coefficient of determination. $R^2$ indicates the proportion of the total variance in a portfolio's return accounted for by market moves. A portfolio with an $R^2$ of 1.00 will have all of its variability explained by market movement. It would be perfectly diversified, as exemplified by an index fund. A portfolio with an $R^2$ of .90 will have 90 percent of its volatility explained by market forces.

Residual risk can be further subdivided into the risk of investment strategy (extra market covariance risk) and the risk of security selection (specific risk). Extra market covariance risk refers to the observed tendency for the returns on certain groups of securities to move in tandem, apart from overall market variability. For example, price changes of international oil stocks tend to be in a uniform direction, creating an element of nonmarket risk for a portfolio holding such securities. Other examples might include pharmaceutical stocks, consumer product stocks, and interest sensitive stocks. Investment managers assume this form of risk when, for reasons of strategy, they overweight or underweight certain groups of securities with common characteristics, as compared to the weighting of these securities in the market portfolio. This risk element would be present, for example, if a particular group of securities made up 12 percent of a given portfolio, while on a capitalization basis that group constituted only 8 percent of the market portfolio.

Variability in return resulting from changes in the circumstances surrounding an individual firm exposes a portfolio holding stock of that firm to specific risk, the risk associated with selection or "stock picking." Examples of events that might affect the specific risk associated with the holding of the stock of a particular firm would be a change in management, a change in ownership (as through a merger or acquisition), a technological breakthrough by a major competitor, a prolonged work stoppage, and so on.

The relative importance of these various components of risk depends upon the body of assets involved. In terms of an individual stock, specific risk is the most important component, possibly accounting for more than half of the total risk, followed by systematic risk and extra market covariance, in that order. As the number of securities in a portfolio increases the levels of extra market covariance and specific risk diminish from the diversification effect—the combining of stocks with varying risk characteristics that are negatively correlated. Thus, for an entire portfolio, especially one assembled by an institutional investor, systematic risk is by far the dominant element, with extra market covariance and specific risk following in that order. As an extreme, in a well-designed index fund, the residual risk component is virtually eliminated, leaving only market or systematic risk.

There is a theoretical relationship between risk and expected return at any given time that can be represented in optimal terms by an upward sloping line (the efficient frontier) when risk is shown on the horizontal axis and return on the vertical axis. A plan sponsor can express portfolio objectives quantitatively by identifying the point along the efficient frontier at which it would like to have the common stock portfolio located. Its decision reflects its risk aversion. The more risk (volatility or beta) it is willing to assume, presumably the greater the expected return. The policy statement should indicate the common stock beta that the plan sponsor favors. This, of course, should be consistent with other elements of investment policy, especially the rate of return objective for the entire pension portfolio. The statement might also quantify the degree of diversification sought by setting an $R^2$, or market correlation, target.

The beta and $R^2$ concepts are as relevant to fixed-income securities as they are to common stocks, but are more difficult to implement. Fixed-income securities are subject to three basic types of risk: (1) credit risk or the risk of default (or delay) on principal and interest payments; (2) the risk of interest rate changes, which affect the market price of a fixed-income security and the rate at which cash flows can be reinvested; (3) the risk of nonparallel changes in bond yield curves on both maturities and market sectors (e.g., Treasuries versus corporates), which could reduce (or enhance) the attractiveness of a given bond or portfolio of bonds.

Generally speaking, there is no systematic attempt to quantify the total risk associated with a portfolio of fixed-income securities. Bonds and commercial paper are rated as to credit risk by a number of rating organizations. It is customary for the investment policy statement to speak to the quality of the fixed-income securities that are to be held in the portfolio. The statement may set a quality floor below which the managers are not to venture, or it may designate a weighted average quality rating as a general target or guideline.

Credit risk and a portion of interest rate risks, like common stock volatility, can be reduced by judicious diversification. Likewise, the risk of nonparallel yield curve shifts can be reduced by diversifying the portfolio in market sector, quality, and maturity. Thus, the policy statement may contain directions on diversification of the fixed-income portfolio. This would normally be done by specifying portfolio holding limits by issuer and issue. The statement may also set a duration target for the portfolio. (Duration is explained later.)

**Liquidity Requirements.**    As was noted earlier, the typical pension plan has only minimal liquidity needs, which can usually be met out of the plan's cash management program. If there are any special liquidity needs, the asset managers should be alerted through an appropriate provision in the investment policy statement. If the asset managers are not to be constrained by liquidity considerations, the policy statement and instructions to the managers should so indicate.

**Diversification.**    Many policy statements contain a reference to diversification, in part because of the explicit mandate in ERISA that the plan assets be diversified. Diversification is one method of attempting to achieve the three substantive objectives of portfolio management: acceptable return, preservation of principal, and adequate liquidity. Thus, in a sense, it is inappropriate to regard diversification as a goal of *investment policy*. It may be more properly regarded as a strategy consideration. In that regard, there is a trade-off between the stabilizing effect of diversification and the promise of higher risk-adjusted returns from more highly concentrated stock and bond selection.

The diversification component of a policy statement may be no more than a generalized commitment to the principle, or it may contain specific guidelines as to diversification by types of assets, sectors, quality ratings, and the like.

## Elements of Investment Strategy

Investment strategy is that complex of approaches, techniques, tools, and devices used to achieve the investment goals of the pension plan—as determined by the plan sponsor, trustee, and insurer. There are many factors to consider in developing an overall strategy for the investment of a pension plan portfolio, and the alternatives are becoming increasingly more complex and challenging. The major decisions that are involved in the implementation of any given investment policy are set out below, proceeding from the general to the specific.

**Active versus Passive Portfolio Management.** The most fundamental decision to be made is whether the portfolio is to be actively or passively managed. Active portfolio management implies asset concentration, frequent trading, and risk and return objectives higher than those of the market portfolio. Passive management connotes a well-diversified portfolio with infrequent trading, and market level risk and return expectations. The ultimate in passive management is investment in index funds of various types, a subject treated in Chapter 21.

The common stock component of any institutionally managed portfolio has traditionally been actively managed. Implicit in this approach is the belief that, at any given time, some stocks are overpriced and some are underpriced in terms of the capital asset pricing model. While the issues of some dominant blue-chip companies are sometimes held indefinitely, with little thought being given to their replacement, most portfolio companies are kept under periodic if not continual review to determine their suitability for retention, not only in absolute terms but in comparison with other issues available for acquisition. In a volatile business environment, a third or half of a common stock portfolio may turn over within a one-year period. In the process, the portfolio may become "unbalanced" in the sense that certain groups of stocks may be overweighted or underweighted, as compared to their representation in the market portfolio. This is an almost inevitable result of identifying underpriced and overpriced stocks and abandoning the concept of perfect diversification.

Until recent years, the bond component of an institutional portfolio was typically managed in accordance with a different concept, characterized as *buy* and *hold*. In an era of low and stable interest rates, debt instruments of financially strong, well-entrenched corporations promised preservation of capital, a modest but predictable cash flow, and ample liquidity. The only risk in holding a debt instrument was the probability of delay or default on payment of interest and principal, the so-called credit risk. With a normal, upward sloping (as to maturity) yield curve, long-term debt instruments were attractive because of their higher yields. Long-term bonds—and the buy-and-hold strategy—seemed especially well suited to the needs of pension plans. The liabilities of the latter were expressed in nominal terms, were highly predictable, and were, on balance, long term in nature. Coupon income and the proceeds of maturing bonds were reinvested at prevailing interest rates that did not vary much from year to year. If the plan sponsor was dissatisfied with the long-term bond yields available, it could seek higher returns through investment in common stocks.

The profound changes in the capital market interest rate structure that accompanied the virulent inflation of the late 1960s and 1970s wrought drastic changes in the investment characteristics of fixed-income securities, especially long-term bonds. Spiraling interest rates for all maturities produced a general decline in the prices of all outstanding debt securities, the sharpest declines being associated with the longest maturities. While coupon payments and proceeds of maturing securities could be reinvested at the higher interest rates, the bulk of the bond portfolio could not be switched to higher-yielding securities without unacceptably large capital losses. Inflation was eroding the purchasing power of the coupon payments to such an extent that the *real* return on bond investments turned negative. In the meantime, the benefit obligations of pension plans were beginning to assume real, as opposed to nominal, character as they kept pace with inflation through final-average salary formulas and ad hoc cost-of-living adjustments for retired participants. These concurrent developments focused attention on the need for a *real* return on the pension portfolio and a strategy that would produce such a result.

By 1970, active bond management was well on the way to supplanting the buy-and-hold philosophy. It was developed more as a response to unprecedentedly *volatile* interest rates than to unprecedentedly *high* interest rates. Sharp and rapid changes in the level and structure of interest rates create opportunities as well as challenges for bond managers. While active bond managers rely on a number of stratagems and techniques to achieve better results than those of an unmanaged portfolio, success depends primarily on the ability to forecast future interest rate movements. There is little evidence that any manager can do so consistently. Nevertheless, there is a widespread belief that active bond managers as a group will over time outperform the long-term market indexes on a cumulative basis.

**In-House versus External Management of Portfolio.** The plan sponsor must decide whether the pension plan assets are to be managed "in-house"—by the financial staff of the plan sponsor—or by outside money managers. In the early days of pension programs, there was a natural tendency for the plan sponsor to invest the pension plan assets within the organization. As the industry grew and the asset accumulations became sizeable, banks, trust companies, insurance companies, and investment counseling firms developed special staffs and facilities to manage the assets, and external management became common. Today an overwhelming proportion of the vast accumulation of pension assets is managed by professional money managers.

However, in response to the mounting sums paid to outside firms for investment services, and the unimpressive performance of the investment community over the last decade or so,[36] more and more firms are evaluating the situation, and many have taken some or all of the pension portfolio management back in-house. Another response to the same phenomenon is to place some or all of the

---

[36] In any given time period, a substantial percentage of investment managers fail to match the performance of the market indexes, and very few *consistently* outperform the market when transaction costs and management fees are taken into account.

plan assets in an index fund or funds. A significant number of large plan sponsors perform cash management services for their pension plans with the staff that performs that corporate function.

**Allocation of Assets.** A third strategy that must be made or affirmed at each meeting of the pension investment committee or similar body is the allocation of assets among (1) cash or cash equivalents (instruments with original or remaining maturity of less than one year), (2) intermediate and long-term fixed-income instruments, and (3) equities, predominantly common stocks and real estate holdings. In some respects, this is the most challenging investment decision that the plan sponsor must make, and it must be made on a continuing basis as the economic and financial outlook changes. It involves a judgment as to the relative investment merits of equities and fixed-income securities over the near term under a projected economic scenario. Cash and cash equivalents provide flexibility in investment decision making and a hedge against unforeseen developments. They maximize liquidity and minimize the risk of principal loss. Of course, they may be held for their own investment merit, as in recent years when they outperformed every other category of investment. A common reason for holding cash equivalents today is to enable the plan sponsor to postpone an allocation decision until it can be made with increased insight and confidence. Under "normal" economic circumstances with a normal yield curve, cash and cash equivalents will be held primarily for market timing purposes.

In recent years a typical allocation of assets might be 20 percent in cash equivalents, 30 percent intermediate and long-term bonds, and 50 percent in equities. An alternative approach is to make a basic allocation between equity and fixed-income managers and let them make the strategic decision as to how much "cash" to hold. A 50-50 split between these two classes of assets is not uncommon, or a 40-60 percent split, some allocating the larger percentage to equities and others to debt securities. Some plans allocate all the assets to equities, realizing that some proportion will be held in cash equivalents at any given time, while others want all assets in debt securities, even obligations of the federal government or its agencies.

An adjustment in the asset allocation can be accomplished through transactions and through the channeling of cash flow. The latter is the preferred method, if it can accomplish the purpose, since one set of transaction costs can be avoided. Depending upon the time available, a major shift in allocation may have to be carried out through dispositions and new acquisitions.

There is a difference in philosophy with respect to distortions in the allocation formula produced by market action. For example, a decision may be made to hold 60 percent of the portfolio assets in equities at a time when somewhat less than that percentage is in that form. What if a bull market develops and the *market value* of *existing* equity holdings causes the proportion to rise to 65 or 70 percent of the total portfolio? Some plan sponsors take the position that, under such circumstances, no part of current cash flow should be allocated to the equity component as long as it exceeds the specified target, but that no holdings should be disposed of to bring the allocation back into balance. Others would instruct the equity managers to sell enough stock to restore the target ratio, on the theory that this form of discipline assures the capturing of some of the gains associated with the market rise.

The asset allocation may extend beyond the broad divisions discussed above and direct assets into various sectors of the capital markets. Typically, however, sector decisions are left to the asset managers, since they are paid to exercise their judgment on such matters.

**Choice of Sector and Quality.**   The capital markets are stratified into various sectors and subsectors, with issues of varying quality being found in each sector of the market. The fixed-income market sectors generally recognized are transport, telephone, utility, financial, industrial, and government (including agencies). Aggregations of common stocks, such as Standard & Poor's Composite 500 Index, and those listed on the New York Stock Exchange, are also broken down into a number of sectors by industry. Portfolio managers typically spread their investments among sectors in order to lessen extra market covariance.

Fixed-income securities and common stocks are classified by their investment characteristics, which may strongly influence the terms on which they are traded in the capital markets. Bonds and commercial paper are rated by such organizations as Moody's and Standard & Poor's, which publish the quality ratings according to certain standardized classifications. Asset managers and brokerage houses, for internal purposes, may classify common stocks by their investment characteristics, such as growth, income, speculative, and so on.

There are yield differentials among fixed-income securities that reflect sector, quality, maturity, call feature, and so on, and from time to time these differentials spread in such a manner as to create trading or swapping opportunities for capital gains or higher yields. Likewise, the attractiveness of a common stock issue in the market-place may change overnight with an unfavorable development or a disappointing earnings report. For these and other reasons, al-location of assets by sector, quality, and so forth is generally left to the asset managers who can be expected to follow financial developments closely and act promptly when circumstances require it.

**Maturity Spacing.**    This is a strategy issue that is unique to fixed-income instruments. It is a function of that most difficult of all investment exercises—predicting future interest rate behavior and the term structure of interest rates. If the asset manager concludes that interest rates for intermediate and long-term bonds are going to rise, it will want to hold most of the fixed-income portfolio in cash or cash equivalents to minimize the effects of price erosion and to maximize the quantity of assets available to ''go long'' near the peak of the interest rate climb (price decline). A portion of the portfolio may be allocated to other maturities as a partial hedge against a forecasting error. If intermediate and long-term interest rates are expected to decline, the portfolio manager will want to ''lock in'' the existing yields and maximize capital gains by com-mitting most of the portfolio to long-term bonds, unless it thinks that the interest rate decline is only temporary and that rates will shortly soar to new heights.

Some bond portfolio managers, as a hedge against unpredictable interest rate behavior, utilize a ''laddered'' approach—allocating assets in some systematic fashion, possibly proportionally, to various available maturities. This approach sacrifices the probability of great gains from a major commitment to the ''right'' maturity (in retrospect) and avoids the probability of a serious loss from a bad timing decision. It is also useful in meeting any liquidity needs of the pension plan. The same objectives can be pursued through application of the immunization concept.

Maturity spacing and other timing decisions are generally left to the fixed-income managers.

**Selection and Trading of Securities.** The most specific and operational phase of investment strategy is the selection and trading of the portfolio securities. In a sense, it is the "bottom line" of the whole operation. It must be carried out within the framework of the broader policy and strategy decisions examined above. The asset managers select the securities to be acquired or sold and normally execute the trades. In some situations, depending upon the nature of the asset manager(s) and the entire investment apparatus, the trades may be executed by a master trustee upon instructions from the asset manager. The *timing* of purchases and sales is a critical element of portfolio management and is the responsibility of the asset manager or managers. How well this function is carried out has a vital bearing on the overall performance of the investment manager.

## Nontraditional Investment Objectives

In recent years, various groups have sought to have pension plan assets invested in a manner to promote certain economic, social, and political goals, some of which are in conflict with the traditional objective of maximizing return within acceptable risk levels. These interest groups are diverse in nature—including *inter alia* labor unions, church organizations, state and local governments, and ethnic constituencies—and their goals are diverse.

The AFL–CIO and certain of its constituent international unions are on record as favoring the investment of "union" pension funds in ways to create jobs, promote unionism, provide housing, and increase the pool of funds for mortgage lending. By and large, organized labor takes the position that pension assets are "owned" by the plan participants (since they represent deferred wages) and should be invested in a manner that is supportive of their general welfare and, as a minimum, not in direct conflict with their interests. Labor argues that its general investment goals can be achieved with little or no loss of investment return (it cites the poor performance of professional asset managers over the last 10 years or so); but some international unions, the Teamsters union being one, advocate investing pension funds below market rates for certain purposes, especially for residential mortgages.

Various church groups, working through the Interfaith Center for Corporate Responsibility, oppose the investing of pension funds (and other institutional portfolios, such as university endowments) in companies that do business in South Africa, produce socially questionable goods (e.g., liquor and tobacco products), engage in certain marketing practices in Third World countries, have discriminatory employment practices (against women and blacks, in particular), or manufacture certain military equipment, especially nuclear components.

Many state and local government officials favor investing the assets of their public employee retirement systems in ways that will stimulate the local economy, rebuild the inner core of their cities, reduce borrowing costs, and achieve other local goals. Several states have modified their investment statutes to make it lawful for public retirement systems to respond to some of these capital needs. A dramatic example of the use of retirement system assets to help solve a particular problem was provided by New York City, when the city retirement systems were asked to purchase a special issue of New York City bonds of questionable investment merit.

Corporations sometimes employ the assets of their pension plans to achieve corporate goals that are only tenuously related to the interests of the plan participants. Recent examples involve the use of plan assets to purchase outstanding common stock of the plan sponsor to ward off a takeover by another corporation.

Whether the assets of pension plans should be invested to achieve these collateral goals involves a number of issues. The first is where legal and beneficial ownership of the plan assets lies and what authority should attend such ownership. A second issue is whether ancillary investment objectives should be pursued only if they are not in conflict with the primary investment objectives, or whether they should be followed even if they involve a potential reduction in yield or an increase in risk. If there is a known or potential cost, a third issue is which party will bear the direct loss and whether there are to be any cost trade-offs. A fourth issue is the process by which decisions will be made as to the nontraditional goals that will be pursued and at what cost to the parties involved. A fifth issue is whether ancillary investment goals are compatible with the prudent man standard and with the ERISA mandate that the plan assets be employed for the sole and exclusive benefit of the plan participants and their beneficiaries.

The answer to some of these questions is known. Legal title to the plan assets is vested in the plan trustee (or insurer, if no trustee is used), while the equitable title (or beneficial ownership) is shared by all the plan participants and their beneficiaries. The legal relationships are similar to an irrevocable personal trust. The plan sponsor relinquishes title to its contributions the moment they are paid to the trustee or insurer and can recover them, with certain minor exceptions, only if the plan is terminated and the accumulated plan assets are more than adequate to satisfy all claims against the plan. No plan participant or beneficiary has legal claim to any particular plan assets. Participants and beneficiaries have certain claims, ripened or unripened, against the plan as a legal entity and, thus, fall into the creditor classification. The status of plan assets under defined contribution individual account plans may be different, but the question of nontraditional investments is largely, if not entirely, confined to defined benefit plans.

Under a defined benefit plan, the plan sponsor is the primary risk bearer. It commits itself to contribute whatever sums are needed, along with investment earnings, to provide all benefits that accrue under the plan. Earnings on the plan assets are a direct offset to the plan sponsor's contributions, and any change in investment policy or strategy that would reduce that stream of income to the plan would have to be made up by additional contributions. Since the plan sponsor can normally deduct its pension contributions for federal income tax purposes, it follows that taxpayers as a body bear much of the cost of an investment policy that diminishes the rate of return on plan assets. If the plan continues indefinitely, the plan sponsor and the general body of taxpayers absorb any cost of a nontraditional investment policy. If the plan were to terminate with inadequate assets because of diminished investment income, the Pension Benefit Guaranty Corporation would sustain the initial loss but would ultimately recoup the loss from the sponsor or through higher premium payments from other sponsors of defined benefit plans. In some cases the loss of investment income would fall upon plan participants whose benefit claims exceed the amount insured by the PBGC.

Clearly, the parties who stand to lose from a course of action that would impair the flow of income to pension plans—plan sponsors, plan participants, taxpayers, and the general corporate community—should have something to say about whether such a course is to be pursued. In theory, an employer could negotiate a curtailment of benefits, a wage cut or freeze, or some other type of trade-off in exchange for its willingness to forego some investment income through targeted investments. Under collectively bargained multiemployer plans, employees have a voice—weak though it may be—in investment policy through union representatives on the joint board of trustees. The only way that taxpayers and other plan sponsors (which support the PBGC) can make their voices heard on this issue is through the legislative process.

The Department of Labor, which has the primary responsibility under ERISA for safeguarding the interests of plan participants and beneficiaries, has not provided much guidance on this delicate issue. Its spokesmen have reaffirmed the primacy of interests of plan participants and beneficiaries. On the other hand, they have endorsed the concept of targeted investments of a social nature if such investments do not adversely affect earnings or the level of risk. They make a distinction between "exclusionary" and "inclusionary" investment policies, finding the former acceptable if it does not unduly restrict the pool of eligible investments and the latter objectionable because it may become too restrictive, making it difficult to achieve proper diversification and a proper balance among investment criteria. In a nutshell, DOL's present position seems to be that socially motivated and regionally focused investments are in conflict with the Congressional mandate that pension plans be managed for the sole and exclusive benefit of plan participants and their beneficiaries if they reduce portfolio earnings or increase portfolio risk. It interposes no objection to consideration of social and related benefits in choosing among investment alternatives that satisfy the prudence standard and other traditional criteria. It is worth noting that, if a proposed investment meets standard criteria for risk and expected return, there is no special benefit to the socially desired project. If the capital market functions the way it is supposed to, socially desirable projects can gain only at the expense of present and prospective pensioners or of all plans through the operations of PBGC.

It seems likely that the twin issues of who shall control pension plan assets and how they are to be invested will become increasingly important over the next decade or so.[37]

## Questions

1. As a general rule, the assets of a qualified pension plan must be held in trust.
   a. What is the rationale behind this general requirement?
   b. What are the principal exceptions to this general rule? What is the justification for these exceptions?
2. Explain the process by which an organization or organizations, other than the plan trustee, may be given authority to manage assets of a pension plan.
3. Identify the property or property rights acquired and held in respect of a qualified pension plan that under Department of Labor regulations (a) are deemed to be plan assets and (b) are *not* deemed to be plan assets. What is the practical significance of classifying some holdings of a pension plan as "plan assets" and some as not "plan assets"?
4. Many pension experts believe that ERISA's prudent man rule requires the administrator or trustee of a pension plan to adopt a written statement of policy for the investment of the plan assets. This articulated policy would be communicated to and serve as a guide to the investment manager or managers. What is meant by a statement of investment policy? Is there any distinction between investment policy, investment objectives, and investment strategy?
5. Must the trustees of a pension plan vote the proxies of common stock held by the plan, or can that function be legally delegated to the investment manager?
6. ERISA imposes a specific mandate upon pension plan trustees to diversify the investment of plan assets, unless it is clearly prudent not to diversify. In your view, would it be a violation of the diversification requirement if all the plan assets were invested in corporate

[37]For a comprehensive and rigorous analysis of the issues involved in the broad topic, see Dan M. McGill, editor, *Social Investing of Pension Plan Assets* (Homewood, Ill.: Richard D. Irwin, 1984).

fixed-income instruments and no equities? In equities exclusively? In an investment type contract with one life insurance company? In federal government bonds?

7. Is it consistent with the diversification requirement to permit an administrator to invest 10 percent of the plan assets in securities or real estate of the sponsoring employer?

8. Why might it be argued that the standard of fiduciary behavior imposed by ERISA is the prudent *expert* standard?

9. The preamble of a Department of Labor regulation states that no relevant or material attributes of a contemplated acquisition for a pension plan investment portfolio may properly be disregarded, nor that any particular investment may be deemed prudent solely by reason of the propriety of the aggregate risk/return characteristics of the overall portfolio. Is this statement consistent with DOL's endorsement of modern portfolio theory as a guide to the management of pension plan assets? Explain.

10. In your opinion, is the interest of a pension plan participant in the benefits that may be provided by the plan a "security," in the sense that term is used in the various federal securities laws?

11. What advantages does a *pooled* or *collective* trust fund of a bank or trust company offer a pension plan, as contrasted to a trust fund that stands on its own feet?

12. Identify and explain briefly the distinctive characteristics of a defined benefit pension plan that may influence the plan's investment policies and strategies.

13. Describe the various ways in which the rate of return objectives of a pension plan may be expressed. Which of these approaches do you personally favor? Why?

14. *a.* Distinguish among the following categories of risk involved in the active management of a pension plan equity investment portfolio:
    (1) Market risk.
    (2) Residual risk.
    (3) Extra market covariance risk.
    (4) Specific risk.
    *b.* Which of these types of risk would be eliminated through the use of an index fund?

15. What is the relationship, if any, between beta, a measure of volatility, and $R^2$, the coefficient of determination?

16. Describe the risks involved in the management of a fixed-income investment portfolio and the techniques or instruments that may be used to minimize those risks.

17. In your opinion, is it a legitimate exercise of fiducial responsibility for the trustees of a pension plan to invest all or a portion of the plan assets to promote certain social objectives, such as housing for low-income persons, jobs for racial or ethnic minorities, the unionization of the work force, or preservation of the fiscal viability of a city or state?

18. May the trustees of a pension plan legally use some of the plan assets to prepare and file a stockholder resolution with the management of a company whose stock it holds, for the purpose of changing a corporate policy or practice considered by some to be socially undesirable? Would your answer be any different if the policy or practice in question involved a purely business decision?

19. Assume that 10 percent of the assets of a particular pension plan consist of shares of common stock of the plan sponsor held by an independent trustee. What should be the response of the plan trustee to a tender offer for those shares of stock by a corporation attempting an unfriendly takeover of the plan sponsor? Would your answer be any different if the plan trustee was a committee of executive officers of the plan sponsor? Why?

20. Certain unions in the construction trades, notably those representing carpenters and bricklayers, have invested the bulk of the assets in their multiemployer pension plans in pools of residential mortgages on the grounds that such investments stimulate home construction and hence increase the flow of contributions to the plans. The investments are limited to mortgages on homes built with union labor. Is this investment practice in compliance with the fiduciary standards set forth in ERISA?

# 20 | Management of Pension Plan Assets: Operations I

## Forms of Investment

PENSION PLANS invest in a wide array of tangible and intangible assets. Under the prudent man concept and the current philosophy of judging investment performance in terms of the total portfolio, rather than its individual components, there are few *classes* of assets that are not suitable for a pension plan portfolio. Trustees are generally freed by plan sponsors of the strictures of fiduciary investment statutes, and the separate accounts of life insurers offer a variety of investment approaches. Competition among investment managers and the desire of plan sponsors to hold portfolio assets that will outperform inflation (and, hence, produce a real return) have broadened the search for productive investments and boosted the tolerance of plan sponsors to investment risk and unconventional holdings.

Despite periodic publicity concerning various "exotic" investment opportunities, the great bulk of pension plan portfolios remains invested in common stocks, intermediate and long-term bonds, money market instruments, group annuity contracts, and other conventional investments. Modest percentages may be found in real estate equity and mortgages, oil and natural gas properties, collectibles, options, futures contracts, foreign securities, and other

472

innovative investment opportunities believed to offer the prospect of higher-than-average returns.

## Common Stocks

Since common stocks have historically offered a higher rate of return than fixed-income securities, they have occupied a prominent place in the portfolios of most pension plans over the last 25 to 30 years. Many plans have a long-term program of holding at least half of their assets in common stocks. There is a broadly held opinion that, in the long run, common stocks will outperform inflation, giving the plan a real rate of return. That faith is shaken from time to time by depressed conditions in the common stock market, but many plan sponsors believe that, in the long run, common stocks will outperform fixed-income securities. Some plan sponsors are committed to 100 percent investment in common stocks, except for cash equivalents held for market-timing purposes. At the other extreme, some plans have never invested in common stocks, relying entirely on fixed-income securities, sometimes only obligations of the federal government or its agencies.

## Intermediate and Long-Term Debt Instruments

Along with common stocks, intermediate and long-term debt instruments (the latter in particular) have served as the foundation of pension plan portfolios, especially long-term bonds. If call or refunding features are not exercised, long-term bonds offer the chance of locking up a high level of steady cash flow for the life of the bond, as well as an opportunity to garner extraordinary capital gains if interest rates decline. Furthermore, long-duration bonds may be used to immunize pension liabilities for relatively long periods.[1] These bonds may lose attractiveness in periods of volatile and rising interest rates.

Intermediate bonds, especially those in the 4–10-year maturity range, are more appealing to investors than long-term bonds during periods of high and gyrating interest rates. They are less volatile in price than longer-term bonds and offer more stable income than

---

[1] See pp. 490–92.

the short-term alternative. Some of these bonds have been issued with very low or zero interest coupons to reduce or eliminate the coupon reinvestment risk. Such bonds are issued at a substantial discount, the purchase price determining the yield to maturity date of the bond, which sometimes extends as far as 30 years. Some recently issued bonds of this type permit the issuer to call, or the holder to redeem, the bond at par at specified intervals. Called "extendibles," these bonds, if called or redeemed, are usually reissued at current coupon rates, the intent and effect being to make them variable coupon bonds, protecting both the issuer and investor against adverse changes in the interest structure.

Most of the corporate debt instruments are publicly traded and, hence, are marketable—at a price. Many plans hold some privately placed securities, directly or through participation in pools of such instruments managed by insurance companies or banks. Private debt instruments usually command a somewhat higher yield than comparable public debt, partly because of limited marketability. The limited marketability of privately placed debt instruments is partly offset by a more rapid and systematic return of cash to the investor through scheduled interest and principal (sinking fund) payments.

Pension plans also hold sizeable quantities of debt issued by the federal government or its agencies. Much of the debt is represented by Treasury bills or certificates, but some is in Treasury notes and bonds. The major appeal of government debt instruments is their risklessness (no default risk) and their liquidity, the latter being heightened by the very active futures market that utilizes Treasury issues as the underlying or deliverable securities.

Some pension plans have acquired holdings in the foreign bond market. Bonds issued by foreign governments or business concerns may be denominated in dollars or in foreign currencies. American pension plan sponsors have been primarily interested in Eurobonds and Yankee bonds. Eurobonds are bonds issued by one country in a second country and denominated in the currency of a third country, usually the United States. Yankee bonds are dollar-denominated bonds issued by foreign concerns and registered with the Securities and Exchange Commission for sale in the United States. These foreign bonds appeal to some portfolio managers as a way of achieving greater diversification of risk and earning a superior return because of perceived inefficiencies in the foreign bond market.

Some plans prefer bonds denominated in selected foreign currencies to have an opportunity of gains from currency fluctuations. (Of course, there is also the chance of loss from currency fluctuations.)

## Short-Term Debt Instruments

In recent years, short-term debt instruments, those with maturities of less than one year, have been significant components of many pension plan portfolios. Domestic short-term debt instruments are issued by corporations, financial institutions, and the federal government. Collectively these are referred to as money market instruments.

U.S. Treasury bills, generally 90 days or 6 months in maturity, are auctioned each week. T-bills, as they are generally known, are quoted on a discounted basis, with selected government security dealers essentially bidding for an effective yield. They provide no interest payments but, at maturity, pay a lump sum at par value.

A variety of short-term instruments can be purchased from banks. Certificates of deposit (CDs) are receipts for short-term time deposits in a bank, which may be issued in negotiable or nonnegotiable form.[2] Interest and principal are generally paid in a lump sum at maturity. CDs normally range in maturity from one to four to five years. Some pension plans buy dollar-denominated CDs from European banks or European branches of American banks, which yield a slight margin over domestic CDs because of reserve requirement differentials and different risk perceptions. Some plans buy CDs payable in foreign currencies to take advantage of currency fluctuations. Most CDs are issued at fixed-interest rates, but some longer-term CDs of both the domestic and Eurodollar variety are offered on a floating rate basis.

Bankers' acceptances are time drafts drawn on a bank by a customer to be used in settlement of a domestic or international commercial transaction. The bank accepts the draft for a fee and honors it at maturity, thus substituting its credit for the customer's credit. The bank is reimbursed by the customer for assuming its

---

[2]Nonnegotiable CDs are usually issued in amounts not exceeding $100,000. They are attractive to many small pension plans because in those amounts they are fully insured by the FDIC.

obligation. The bank, which will collect the trade debt from its customer at the maturity of the time draft, may retain the instrument as an earning asset or may realize cash on the instrument before its due date by offering it for sale in the secondary market at the going rate of discount for the time period involved. Bankers' acceptances generally sell at a slight risk premium above the T-bill/CD rate.

A repurchase agreement (a REPO) is an instrument under which the purchaser, normally an institutional investor, acquires ownership of a debt security and the seller, usually a security dealer, agrees at the time of the sale to repurchase the obligation at a mutually agreed upon time and price, thereby determining the yield during the purchaser's holding period.[3] This results in a fixed rate of return insulated from market fluctuations during the period. Any security can serve as the basis of the repurchase agreement, but T-bills and GNMA certificates are generally used. If the seller defaults on its promise to repurchase the security, the purchaser can sell the security to other investors. The risk to the purchaser is that its recovery under the transaction will be less than it would have been under the repurchase agreement, because of a decline in the market price of the underlying security and legal costs involved in enforcing its rights. Repurchase agreements are usually for short periods, such as one week or even one day, but they may be longer. REPOs of 15 or fewer days duration are characterized as "short" and those of 16 or more days duration are termed "long." Reverse REPOs are agreements under which lending institutions themselves borrow from security dealers or other institutions by means of a sale and repurchase of a particular security.

Many large corporations, including financial institutions, raise money in the capital market by selling their negotiable, short-term unsecured promissory notes, known as commercial paper. Creditworthy firms avail themselves of this source of funds in lieu of more expensive bank loans. The paper is usually sold at a higher rate than that payable by T-bills, but lower than the prime rate of banks. Maturities run from 30 to 270 days. Moody's and Standard & Poor's

---

[3]Many people describe a repurchase agreement as a loan from the investor (purchaser) collateralized by the underlying security. The distinction between a purchase and a collateralized loan can be significant in case of the seller's default or bankruptcy.

rate the credit quality of this commercial paper, using three investment grade classifications.

Predictably, in a portfolio of short-term debt instruments, maturities produce a high rate of turnover. As each instrument matures, it is usually replaced by another of short-term maturity. The yield on the portfolio reflects recent and current capital market conditions and may fluctuate substantially, unlike the current yield on a portfolio of long-term bonds. But the fluctuation in yield of a short-term portfolio has only a minimal effect on market values, particularly if the portfolio is limited to instruments having a remaining maturity of 90 days or less. The instruments themselves are generally marketable, with only minimal risk of capital losses. Such a portfolio is well suited to a defined contribution plan that seeks to provide participants both liquidity and preservation of principal. It is also useful as a temporary haven for pension assets when the manager is awaiting more favorable investment opportunities in stocks or bonds.

A number of major banks have established collective trust funds invested in money market instruments. These funds are used both for regular investment of a portion of the portfolio and as a temporary investment to facilitate cash management. All cash in the trust, which originates from contributions, investment income, and sale of securities, may be swept into the money market fund daily to be kept there temporarily until it is permanently invested, in order to keep the trust assets fully invested at all times. Other banks use money market mutual funds for this purpose.

Historically, long-term debt instruments have typically provided a higher return than short-term instruments. At various times during the last several years, however, an "inverted" yield curve has prevailed, meaning that short-term investments of the types described above have generally yielded higher rates of return than those available from longer-term and, thus, presumably riskier investments. Investment in these instruments also provided a "safe harbor" for principal in periods of high market volatility and protected the plan against the price hazards of taking a "long" position in the debt sector before interest rates had peaked. In periods of high short-term interest rates, this "hedge" against interest rate volatility costs the investor little or nothing in foregone returns. Of course, the investor takes the risk of matching long-term liabilities with assets having short-term maturities. Many plans hold a fourth or third of their portfolio in these short-term debt instruments and some have, at times, had all their money invested in that manner.

## Real Estate Investments

Real estate equity investments have become popular in recent years, stimulated by rising real estate values and the success of certain real estate pools of life insurers. Monies may be placed in specific real estate properties (frequently through limited partnerships) or in real estate pools managed by life insurers, banks, and trust companies. The great preponderance of pension plan real estate equity investments, which still constitute a relatively small percentage of total pension assets available for investment, is in commercial properties—office buildings, industrial parks, and shopping centers. Some investment managers are touting investment in farmland and farm properties, offering their management services for such properties.

A growing (but still small) percentage of pension plan assets is invested in real estate mortgages. These investments tend to be concentrated in large commercial properties. Some insurance companies offer separate accounts for mortgages, and the general account of insurance companies often includes substantial mortgage investments. There is a strong interest in many quarters in channeling pension funds into residential mortgages to stimulate the housing industry and to relieve the growing shortage of living accommodations. Legislation has been introduced into Congress from time to time to force pension plans to invest a stipulated percentage of their assets in residential mortgages, possibly at interest rates below the market. As might be expected, building contractors, materials suppliers, mortgage bankers, and organized labor—especially the building trades unions—have been supportive of such legislation, none of which has been enacted as yet.

Pension plans have been reluctant to go into individual residential mortgages because of the administrative problems involved in originating and servicing the mortgages. They have also wished to be insulated against direct dealings with borrowers, especially their own plan members. Some plans have been attracted to pass-through certificates of participation in government-insured pools of residential mortgages or bonds backed by such mortgage pools. These certificates or bonds offer yields somewhat higher than those available from competing investments and minimize the administrative problems, but they lack marketability, which accounts for the higher yield. As noted earlier, the Department of Labor has tacitly approved investment in these mortgage pools and has issued a regulation designed to encourage investment in the pools. Real estate investments in general tend to be illiquid and cannot prudently dominate a plan's portfolio.

## Leased Property

Some pension plans purchase or acquire tangible assets of various sorts and then lease them to industrial and commercial users. Examples of assets acquired for the purpose of leasing include offshore drilling rigs, aircraft, and railroad rolling stock. These arrangements are usually subject to approval by the IRS (via private letter rulings), since the leasing or rental income might otherwise be subject to taxation as unrelated business income.[4] As was pointed out in an earlier chapter, some airlines have made their pension plan contributions in the form of aircraft, which they subsequently leased back from the plan. The investment return on these leasing activities of pension plans has generally been much higher than that on more traditional investments.

## Tangible Personal Property

When it became apparent during the decade of the 1970s that common stocks once again were not a satisfactory hedge against inflation, except with a long lag, investment managers began searching for assets that seemed to offer a potential for appreciation in value greater than the rate of inflation. This search led to so-called collectibles—tangible personal property, such as precious metals, jewelry, oriental rugs, art objects, coin and stamp collections, and antiques of various kinds. Enterprising dealers sometimes assembled pools of such items and offered shares of participation in the pools. Other dealers offered individual items as investments. Some pension plans invested a small portion of their portfolio in these objects in the interest of diversification and as a modest hedge

---

[4]See Chapter 29.

against inflation. With a decline in the prices of many collectibles and an adverse change in their tax treatment,[5] interest in them on the part of pension plans seems to have diminished.

### Options and Interest Rate Futures Contracts

Pension plan sponsors have recently developed interest in *options* and *futures,* two risk-management vehicles that serve the same general purpose for pension plan sponsors. An option is the right to buy or sell a security at a specified price (the "striking" price) during a stipulated period generally not exceeding one year. The right to buy is a *call* option, while the right to sell is a *put* option. A call option is purchased when the investor believes that the price of the security will rise, whereas a put option is purchased when he believes that the price of the security will decline. A put can be used to lock in a portion of an unrealized capital gain on a portfolio holding, whereas a call gives the investor an opportunity to realize a capital gain in an up market with a minimum investment of funds. Thus, an option can be viewed as a hedge or as a speculation. An investor may *sell* call options against certain securities in its own portfolio ("covered" call options), realizing earnings from the option price at the risk of giving up some capital gains, or it may buy a put as a hedge against sustaining some capital losses. There is a highly developed options market that is both complex and sophisticated.

When authorized and disposed to use options, pension portfolio managers generally write (sell) calls and buy puts against certain of their equity holdings as a means of reducing the variability of returns or earning incremental returns. Such portfolios are sometimes considered bond substitutes, because they are expected to show returns that are 30 to 40 percent less variable than a common stock portfolio without giving up all of the potential excess return. Options may also be written in the course of liquidating positions in individual stocks, or they may be written in the expectation that the underlying security will not be "called" away (i.e., the option

---

[5]If the investment of individual accounts under a defined contribution plan is individually directed, investment of such individual accounts in collectibles is generally treated for tax purposes as though the investment had been distributed to the participant; this effectively precludes collectibles from individually directed accounts. I.R.C. §408(m).

will expire unexercised, the option premium serving as incremental income).[6]

The futures market originally developed to serve the needs of suppliers and users of various types of commodities. The concept has been adapted to fixed-income securities as a mechanism for reducing the impact on a bond portfolio of anticipated interest rate changes.

Futures trading takes place in certain standardized securities, namely, long-term U.S. Treasury bonds, GNMA modified pass-through mortgage-backed securities, 90-day T-bills, and 90-day commercial paper. A futures contract *sale* obligates the seller to deliver a specified amount of one of the foregoing types of instruments (as specified in the contract) at a specified future time and at a specified price. A futures contract *purchase* obligates the buyer to take delivery of the specified instrument at a specified future time at a specified price. Although futures contracts by their terms call for actual delivery or acceptance of securities, it is customary for the contract to be closed out before the settlement date by an offsetting transaction, without actual delivery or receipt of the securities. Thus, closing out a futures contract *sale* is effected by the original seller entering into a futures purchase contract for the same aggregate amount of the stipulated security and the same delivery date. If the price in the sale exceeds the price in the offsetting purchase, the seller realizes a gain. If the sale price is less than the offsetting purchase price, the seller sustains a loss on the transaction. A *purchase* contract is settled by an offsetting *sale* contract.

When commodity futures contracts are traded, both buyer and seller are required to post margins with the brokers handling their transactions as security for the performance of their undertakings to buy and sell and to offset losses in their trades due to daily fluctuations in the market. The *initial* margin, posted at the time of the trade, is in the nature of a good-faith deposit, and must not be smaller than the mininum amount specified for that size and type of transaction by the commodity exchange through which the trade was made. The broker may permit certain customers to deposit Treasury bills or other securities, rather than cash, as margin.

---

[6]For a comprehensive treatment of options, see Lawrence G. McMillan, *Options as a Strategic Investment* (New York: New York Institute of Finance, 1980).

The traded security is marked to market daily and the "loser" must post an additional margin with the broker equal to the change in market value. Called the *variation* margin, this deposit is always made in cash.

Since the only current commitment of funds is that involved in the maintenance of the required margins, futures transactions are highly leveraged. Consequently, any movement in the market price of the leveraged security produces a disproportionate immediate gain or loss to the investor. The risk of loss can be minimized if futures contract sales are restricted to those made against existing portfolio holdings. This practice treats the futures contract as a hedge rather than a speculation.

Futures contract *sales* are made when the owner of the securities believes that interest rates may rise, while *purchase* contracts are entered into when the buyer believes that interest rates may decline. If futures operations are not used (or cannot be used), a portfolio manager, expecting an interest rate rise and wishing to position the portfolio to take advantage of the change, would shorten the maturity structure of the portfolio and then reverse the move when the interest rate rise appeared to reach its peak. With a normal yield curve, this type of portfolio shift would cost the portfolio income during the time the proceeds were being held in short-term instruments and large transactions costs would be incurred. With a futures market, and the assumption that yield differentials in the "cash market" among various securities will continue at approximately the same levels in the near term, the same general objective could be achieved by entering into an agreement to sell a particular type of security or securities at some specified future date. Futures contracts can also be used to smooth the commitment of funds to the capital markets when cash flows, principally contributions, are excessively uneven.

### Foreign Securities

Reference was made earlier to the interest of pension portfolio managers in the bonds of foreign governments and foreign business firms. There is parallel interest in the common stock of foreign corporations, especially those in Western Europe and Japan, which have an aggregate dollar value approximately equal to that of the common stock in U.S. corporations. Extension of the geographical boundaries for investment activities expands the universe of available securities, affording the opportunity of earning higher returns, achieving broader diversification of risk, and capturing foreign exchange gains from strong currencies. These potential advantages of foreign investing must be evaluated against the additional risk of currency fluctuations.

If selected in accordance with normal investment criteria, foreign investments do not violate the ERISA prudence standard. The more prevalent the practice becomes among pension plan investors, the more consistent it will be with the ERISA definition of prudence, which is a relative rather than absolute standard.

## Valuation of Assets

The basis used for valuing the assets of a pension plan has both operational and public policy implications. The value placed on the assets impacts the funding standard account and the required contributions to the plan. Measurement of portfolio performance on a total return basis requires a consistent and uniform method of determining asset values. Likewise, disclosure of the financial condition of the plan to its participants, the business community, and the regulatory agencies requires a realistic basis of asset valuation. The basis of valuation may depend upon the purpose for which the valuation is being made.

Assets are valued at fair market value for many purposes. It may be difficult or impossible, however, to determine the fair market value of some assets, such as insurance and annuity contracts, privately placed fixed-income securities, real estate, and "collectibles," that are not traded in an organized market. In these cases, an approximation or alternative value must be used. For individual insurance and annuity contracts, the cash value is the market value. For group annuity contracts of the deposit administration (DA) or of the immediate participation guarantee (IPG) types, the contractual account balance is generally used. Separate accounts under annuity contracts use market value.

### Funding Defined Benefit Plans

For purposes of funding a defined benefit plan, it can be argued that the most appropriate asset value is the fair market value. This is the true value of the assets, in the sense that it generally represents the value for which the assets could be sold. As indicated above, for some assets fair market value is difficult or impossible to determine.

But even when fair market value is known exactly, there may be problems in using it for purposes of funding. Fair market value is subject to sharp fluctuations that can be disruptive of funding patterns and budgetary projections. And changes in asset values attributable to shifts in the interest structure would have to be offset by compensating or commensurate changes in the actuarial interest assumption, a practice at variance with American actuarial tradition. In recognition of these practical difficulties, pension actuaries have tended to use asset values other than fair market value in preparing actuarial balance sheets and determining funding contributions.

One alternative approach is to value all assets at cost. This has the advantages of simplicity and of stabilizing asset values. But if market values differ substantially from cost, the cost value may be unrealistic. And if market values are rising, the plan may be forced to sell assets to realize the appreciation and reflect it in plan costs.

A modification of the cost approach is sometimes used for bonds and other debt instruments purchased at a premium over, or a discount under, their maturity value. The current book value of the bond may be obtained by amortizing the premium or discount over the period between its purchase date and its maturity date or earliest call date.

Such methods can smooth asset value fluctuation and gradually recognize appreciation and depreciation in market values.

Over the years, actuaries have developed a number of approaches to stabilizing the market value of assets for actuarial purposes. The most common approach is to use a moving average of year-end market values for a specified period, typically five years. Another approach is to capitalize at a realistic discount rate the anticipated stream of dividend income from the equity assets. Still another approach is to increase the initial cost of an equity asset by an assumed rate of long-term growth. A variation of that approach is to assume asset growth equal to actual inflation plus a subjectively determined real rate of return. Yet another is to increase the aggregate value of the equity assets at the previous year-end, adjusted for changes in the portfolio, by the percentage change in some designated stock index. With any of these procedures, the actuary may set upper or lower limits on the percentage variation from actual market value that would be acceptable.

Any asset valuation method other than *actual* fair market is termed an *actuarial* valuation method, and the values derived thereunder are called *actuarial* values to distinguish them from actual values.

For purposes of the minimum funding standard, ERISA requires that the value of the plan assets be determined on the basis of a "reasonable actuarial method of valuation which takes into account fair market value" and is permitted under regulations.[7] These asset valuation procedures were designed to mitigate the effect on the funding standard account of short-run changes in the fair market value of plan assets.

In due course, the IRS promulgated a regulation[8] stipulating that the asset valuation method must take account of fair market value, either directly in the calculation of the value itself or indirectly in determining the outside limits of the value. The method must be consistently applied and must produce an actuarial value falling within a corridor of 80 to 120 percent of the fair market value of the assets as of the applicable valuation date. Fair market value is defined as "the price at which the property would change hands between a willing buyer and a willing seller, neither being under any compulsion to buy or sell and both having reasonable knowledge of relevant facts." Alternatively, prior to 1989, a plan could use a procedure that produces an aggregate value falling within a corridor of 85 to 115 percent of the *average value* of the assets as of the valuation date.

The asset valuation method cannot be designed to produce a result consistently above or below fair market value or average value. The method has to be applied on a consistent basis and cannot be changed without advance IRS approval.[9]

The plan administrator for a multiemployer plan may elect to value all bonds and other evidences of indebtedness (e.g., mortgages, notes, and the like) at amortized cost, rather than under the

---

[7]ERISA §302(c)(2)(A), I.R.C. §412(c)(2)(A).

[8]Treas. Reg. 1.412(c)(2)–1.

[9]The IRS takes the position that an asset valuation method is an actuarial cost method (a view contested by some) and that advance approval is, therefore, required for any change. However, a change in the method to reflect a type of asset not previously held by the plan is not construed to be a change of actuarial cost method, requiring IRS approval.

general rule described above. The election is made by a statement attached to Schedule B of Form 5500, and must apply to all bonds and evidences of indebtedness not in default. Once elected, the election may be revoked only with IRS consent. Most plans have not made such an election.

Regulations may allow use of an alternative approach for single employer plans with a dedicated bond portfolio (discussed later).

The method of asset valuation affects the amount of the gain or loss from investment return each year. This becomes part of the plan's total actuarial gain or loss.

The asset valuation method must be specified in an attachment to Schedule B of the plan's annual actuarial report and be described in such detail that another actuary employing the method would arrive at a reasonably similar result.

### Defined Contribution Plans

Under defined contribution plans, the fair market value of plan assets is used to determine the value of each participant's individual account. Valuations must be made at least annually.[10]

### Accounting Requirements

The valuation of plan assets for accounting purposes must be determined under generally accepted accounting principles, a subject addressed in Chapter 18.

### Other Uses of Asset Valuation

For purposes of determining the financial condition of a terminated pension plan, the Pension Benefit Guaranty Corporation values all assets at fair market value and the liabilities on the basis of the current interest rate structure.

For internal management purposes, a plan sponsor may value the assets and liabilities of the plan on any basis that it chooses. It is customary to use different assumptions for funding purposes than for reporting in accordance with the FASB prescriptions.

---

[10]Rev. Rul. 80–155.

## Asset Managers

As was noted earlier, the assets of a pension plan may be managed by the staff of the sponsoring firm or by outside firms that specialize in providing investment services. The decision is one to be made by the plan sponsor. As a practical matter, only firms with a large and sophisticated financial staff can safely undertake the investment of pension assets. The sponsoring firm may manage certain types of assets, such as cash equivalents, in which it has special skills, leaving the remaining assets to external managers. Assets managed in-house must still be held in trust, but an individual or group of individuals may be designated as the plan trustee under the trust agreement.

The remaining discussion of this section relates to external asset managers.

### Bank or Trust Company

Trust companies and banks with trust powers manage a substantial proportion of all pension plan assets. They may perform this function as a trustee of the pension plan or as a professional asset manager engaged by the trustee to manage a portion of the pension portfolio. Whatever the role, the function falls within the purview of the trust division of the bank.

**Traditional Functions.**   As a trustee-investment manager, the bank or trust company performs the traditional services of a trustee, all in accordance with the trust indenture entered into between the plan sponsor and the trustee. It receives contributions from the plan sponsor, invests and reinvests the accumulated assets, and renders periodic accounting of its stewardship to the plan sponsor. As a minimum, the trustee provides the plan administrator with all the financial information called for in governmental reports, notably Form 5500. It may make benefit payments on instructions from the plan sponsor.

The trustee is under legal obligation to invest the funds received under a pension plan. In the absence of any specific instructions in the trust instrument, the trustee would have to invest the funds in accordance with any applicable state statute governing fiduciary investments. It is customary, however, for the plan sponsor to free the trustee of the constraints of the state fiduciary investment statute and to bestow on the trustee varying degrees of authority over the investments of the trust. Many trust agreements give the trustee complete discretion in the performance of its investment function, with the trustee being held to a commensurate degree of responsibility for the investment results. It is common for the trust indenture to contain some limitations on the trustee's investment behavior, especially on the proportion of the portfolio to be invested in broad classes of assets. In practice, instructions of this sort may come from the plan sponsor in periodic written form.

In acting as an asset manager but not as plan trustee, a bank or trust company would perform all the conventional services of a trustee except the disbursement function. Benefits are paid by the trustee or by the plan sponsor, acting as the trustee's agent. Under these circumstances, of course, the bank is responsible only for the assets entrusted to it, but is a fiduciary under ERISA with respect to those plan assets.

As an asset manager, a bank is subject to the basic principle of trust law that the assets (or the records of ownership of the assets) of each trust must be segregated from the assets of all other trusts administered by it and from its own assets. This feature of trust administration makes it difficult for a small pension plan to achieve adequate diversification of investment risks unless some relief is provided. To make the advantages of diversification available to small plans, all states have modified the common-law rule as to segregation of trust assets by authorizing the pooling of plan assets, subject to certain restrictions. Banks active in the pension field offer one or more commingled trust funds designed for the special needs and exclusive use of pension plans, with no limit on the extent of participation. The investment of plan assets in a commingled trust must be specifically authorized by the plan sponsor.

Further information on the trustee's function is provided in Chapter 23.

**Master Trusteeship and Custodianship.**     A trust company or a bank with trust powers may perform other trust services that are supportive of the investment function. The plan trustee, usually a bank or trust company, must hold legal title to and possession (or "indicia" of ownership) of specifically identifiable plan assets. Holding and accounting for plan assets is a custodial function that is not the exclusive jurisdiction of a trustee but is frequently combined with the trustee function.

With the advent of multiple investment managers[11] of the assets of a single pension plan has come the need for a master trustee and custodian, a service offered by many large banks in money market centers. Such a fiduciary may offer a broad range of services logically associated with that function, but the plan sponsor need not avail itself of all the services. As a minimum, the master trustee holds legal title to, and effective possession of, all plan assets. In practice, it (and any other plan trustee) may choose to delegate the custodial function to a central depository such as the Depository Trust Company in New York City that would hold the indicia of ownership of registered securities in the United States, under an agency agreement, and issue electronic records against them. Subcustodians may have to be appointed to hold foreign securities. It is generally immaterial to the plan sponsor who performs this ministerial function, so long as it is efficient and surrounded by sufficient safeguards. Upon instructions from the plan sponsor, the master trustee allocates plan assets and cash flow among the various asset managers and monitors their activities. The master trustee makes timely collection of dividends, interest, and proceeds from sales, redemptions, and maturities; settles securities transactions; often computes and compares the investment performance of the asset managers; and submits consolidated (as well as detailed) financial results to the plan sponsor.

The master trustee may perform cash management services for the plan. Located in a financial center and in receipt of the plan's cash flow, the master trustee is the logical party to see that cash balances are continuously and favorably invested and that the cash needs of the plan are met. The master trustee normally disburses benefits for the plan on instructions from the plan sponsor. If the plan sponsor has authorized the lending of securities to brokers and to other capital market participants—a low-risk activity (if done properly) that may produce enough income to meet the total fee of the master trustee and custodian—the master trustee will perform that function.

The master trustee may manage some of the plan assets, but it is not a customary arrangement. It can perform its other functions

---

[11]See Chapter 21.

more objectively if it is not competing with the other managers on the very case that it is monitoring. Some master trustees do not offer asset management services to pension plans.

**Immunization of Portfolio against Risk of Interest Rate Changes.** In an effort to match the popularity of insurance company guaranteed income contracts (discussed later) and to meet a perceived need of many plan sponsors, a number of banks offer a bond management service usually described as immunization of plan liabilities or dedication.[12] The basic objective of the technique is to eliminate the interest rate risk associated with reinvesting the income (and the proceeds of maturing investments) from a fixed-income portfolio.[13] More broadly, it is an attempt to match the assets of the portfolio to the liabilities of the pension plan (or other financial entity). Since, for various technical reasons, it is usually not possible to immunize the entire portfolio, the asset manager "partitions" the liabilities into various subsets having identifiable time horizons that lend themselves to the immunization technique. In the pension field, the technique has been largely confined to the actuarial liabilities of a closed group, such as the already retired segment of the plan population.

There are two basic approaches to immunization: the laddering of maturities, and duration mangement.[14] Under the first approach,

---

[12]The concept of immunization has been around for many years having been introduced into economic literature in the late 1940s. The pioneering paper on the subject in the context of pension plans was F. M. Redington, "Review of the Principles of Life Insurance Valuation," *Journal of the Institute of Actuaries* 78 (1952), pp. 286–340.

[13]Another approach to this objective is the purchase of zero coupon bonds, which provide no payoff until maturity and sell at a deep discount. There is no income to be reinvested until maturity, and the purchase price determines the yield to maturity, which is assured—barring credit risks. Zero coupon bonds are not yet available in the quantity and range of maturities to be used to immunize large-scale liabilities.

[14]"Duration" is one of the most frequently used concepts in fixed-income markets. It has two meanings. First, it denotes the (present value-weighted) average time until cash payments are received from an asset. As a measure of time until payment, duration is a more comprehensive concept than maturity, because maturity is the time until the final payment only; and the final payment may represent a relatively small fraction of the asset's total present value. The maximum duration of financial instruments in the marketplace today is about eight years. Secondly, duration is a gauge of interest sensitivity. The "longer" duration of an asset, the greater its price reaction to a movement in interest rates. The duration of a bond is shorter than the remaining period to maturity, since it recognizes intervening coupon payments. The longer the maturity of a bond, the lower its coupon rate; and the lower the current level of market interest rates, the longer the duration of the bond and the greater the rate of return volatility of the bond. Thus, duration is a measure of bond return volatility and, as such, is a proxy for risk.

the asset manager constructs a dedicated portfolio that will throw off a cash flow (including proceeds of maturing investments) approximately equal to that of the immunized liabilities. In the case of retired lives, for example, the portion of the portfolio dedicated to that segment of actuarial liabilities is expected to generate a cash inflow to the plan that matches the highly predictable cash outflow for benefit payments to the retired participants. There is no reinvestment risk of any consequence, since the cash inflow goes out with a short time lag to the benefit recipients.

Under the second approach, the asset manager constructs a dedicated portfolio with a duration such that, with no change in the yield curve, a given nominal return will be realized over a particular time horizon, related to the "partitioned" liabilities to which the assets are dedicated.[15] If the future reinvestment rate of return deviates from what is implicit in the current yield curve, the increase or reduction in reinvestment income, as the case might be, would be precisely offset by capital losses or capital gains, respectively—unless there are nonparallel shifts in the yield curve. If there are nonparallel shifts in the yield curve, the dedicated portfolio must be reimmunized to achieve the desired balance of yields and maturities, as measured by the duration. This approach requires sophisticated computer programming and active management.

The primary appeal of immunization to the plan sponsor is that it may permit the use of a higher interest rate in valuing the immunized liabilities of the plan, thus lowering required contributions to the plan over the immunized holding period. The chief drawback of the technique, apart from its complexity, is that it may produce a duration or maturity structure that is not optimal in terms of expected or actual interest rate behavior. In effect, the liability structure dictates the asset structure, which might not be the one that the portfolio manager would have preferred in the light of its interest rate forecasts. Furthermore, actual results from immunization may deviate from expectations because of nonparallel shifts in the yield curve, calls, and other unexpected events. This risk can be minimized through frequent reimmunization, a technique

---

[15]As a practical matter, the time horizon cannot extend much beyond eight years, since the durations (not maturities) of bonds currently on the market do not exceed eight years.

involving burdensome administrative procedures and some transactions costs. An intermediate approach is to pursue an active
management strategy, unless the return on the portfolio declines
to a predetermined level. At that point, the portfolio would be
immunized as promptly as feasible. This approach or strategy is
called *contingent immunization*. In effect, a "safety net" is placed
under an actively managed portfolio to assure that the return will
not drop below a preselected floor. In the meantime, the portfolio
manager can pursue the added returns potentially available from
active management.

## Life Insurance Companies

Life insurance companies compete head-on with banks and trust
companies for the management of pension plan assets. They offer
a number of contractual arrangements (to be described later), under
which the insurer assumes legal responsibility for the payment of
all plan benefits that have been fully funded with the insurer. Insurance or annuity contracts representing the insurer's obligations
become assets of the pension plan. The investments of the insurance company are not assets of the plan, although, under certain
contractual arrangements, they may be deemed to be plan assets
for purposes of fiduciary responsibility under ERISA. The insurer,
not the plan sponsor, has all rights to possession, control, and
disposition of the investments acquired with the sponsor's contributions. Life insurers offer certain contractual arrangements that
do not contemplate the purchase of annuities for vested or retired
employees and are designed to be purely investment vehicles for
pension plan assets. The assets under these contracts may be held
in the general asset account of the insurer or in one or more separate
accounts. In some cases, the assets are placed in the general asset
account of a fully owned subsidiary.

**General Asset Account.**    Under a life insurer's traditional mode
of operation, all of its assets are held in one commingled account
and are available for the satisfaction of any and all obligations of
the company, regardless of their nature or source. The account is
not labeled, since it is constituted of all the insurer's assets which
are not earmarked for any particular obligations or segmented in
any way. Traditionally, net investment income has been allocated

to the various lines of business on a pro rata basis, without regard for the timing of the cash flows or for the rate of return at which particular cash flows are invested. This composite rate of return, computed in accordance with the rules of the National Association of Insurance Commissioners on the basis of amortized book values, is referred to as the *portfolio rate of return*. It serves as the basis for the crediting of interest to participating individual insurance and annuity contracts, under the insurer's dividend formula and the crediting of investment earnings to group insurance and annuity contracts for experience rating purposes.

The portfolio basis of crediting interest is a generally equitable, simple, and satisfactory way of allocating investment earnings when interest rates are stable and monies remain with the insurer over a long period of time, encompassing any interest rate cycles that might develop. However, in a period of volatile interest rates, with large pools of money seeking the highest rate of return, the portfolio basis of allocating investment earnings becomes inequitable and possibly even impracticable, except for individual lines of insurance. Thus, in the early 1960s, life insurers active in the group insurance and pension business—in order (1) to allocate investment earnings more equitably, (2) to eliminate adverse financial selection, and (3) to meet competition—introduced the investment generation method of allocating such earnings. Each company has its own distinctive procedure for this exercise, but the general objective is to allocate investment earnings in such a way as to recognize the rate of interest at which the net cash inflows are invested and reinvested. The method generally keeps track of cash flows and investment returns by calendar year generation, causing the approach to be called the "investment year method" (IYM); but some companies have used a longer accounting period, especially for individual lines of insurance. The general approach is commonly described as the "new money" method.[16]

Even with a more equitable and realistic basis for allocating investment earnings, the companies found that the general asset account (or general account), as the general purpose commingled account has become known to distinguish it from various special or separate accounts, was not a completely satisfactory vehicle for

---

[16]The investment year method is described in detail on pp. 555 ff.

the investment of pension plan assets. In the first place, the general asset account is subject to the investment constraints imposed by state law, which, among other restraining features, frequently imposes severe limits on the amount of common stock that can be held. Second, the general asset account is subject to the liquidity requirements of the company's individual insurance and annuity business, particularly the strains imposed by policy loans and cash surrenders. Third, as the residual repository of assets, the general asset account holds various types of low-yielding assets, such as old real estate mortgages, the company's home office and regional office buildings, and policy loans, which were frequently made at what today seem to be unrealistically low contractual interest rates. Fourth, the investment earnings on assets backing the benefit obligations of qualified pension plans held in the general asset account of an insurer must bear a share of the insurer's federal income tax. Fifth, a portion of the investment earnings of the general asset account must be set aside in the Mandatory Security Valuation Reserve. Finally, the investment policy appropriate for the mix of business backed by the general asset account may not be appropriate for pension plans or may not meet the objectives of particular pension plans.

**Separate Accounts.** Because of the foregoing drawbacks of the general asset account as a vehicle for the investment of pension plan assets, particularly the limitation on the use of common stock, a number of insurers, under the authority of special legislation or administrative interpretation of existing law, took the momentous step in the early 1960s of establishing separate accounts for the investing of pension assets. The companies continued to make their general asset account available to those plans that wanted traditional insurance company interest and annuity rate guarantees or simply found the investment services of the general asset account suitable for their purposes, even when annuity purchases were not contemplated.

In the beginning, most of the insurers contemplated the establishment of only one separate account, which would commingle the assets of a number of pension plans. In response to the widely held view that common stocks were an excellent inflation hedge, it would be invested exclusively in common stock (and cash equivalents). As the full capabilities of the separate account approach became apparent, many insurers set up more than one common stock separate account, with the accounts having different investment objectives and assets of varying risk characteristics, as well as separate accounts for other types of assets. Today there are separate accounts for publicly traded bonds, direct placement bonds, real estate mortgages, real estate equity, oil and natural gas properties, money market instruments, and perhaps other classes of assets. The largest pension insurers operate 10 or 12 separate accounts, covering a wide range of investment objectives, each tailored to meet a specific objective. These accounts are pooled accounts, the assets being commingled on a basis similar to that of a collective trust fund.

Contributions to a pension plan are placed in a separate account only upon written agreement with the plan sponsor or the plan trustees. The agreement may specify the percentage of plan assets and future contributions to be allocated to the various accounts, or it may permit the plan sponsor to give directions for the allocation of each individual contribution. The agreement may permit the plan sponsor to reallocate past contributions and associated investment earnings from time to time. The plan sponsor is under no obligation, of course, to allocate contributions to all of the separate accounts.

Under some agreements the insurer may be given authority to provide total management of the plan assets, with the right to distribute the assets among the various accounts. Under none of these arrangements does the insurer make any guarantee of its investment performance. It promises neither preservation of principal nor a minimum rate of return. It is obligated, however, to invest the assets in accordance with applicable law[17] and the stated investment objectives of the account. The account is maintained on a market value basis, and the actual investment experience (including realized and unrealized capital gains and losses) is reflected directly and immediately in the status of the account.

Transactions between the plan sponsor and a pooled separate account are carried out in terms of units, which are identical in

---

[17]In general, a separate account of a New York licensed insurer is subject to the same investment restrictions as the general account. However, all separate accounts are permitted to invest up to 10 percent of their assets in a manner not authorized for the general account, and an equity separate account may be invested entirely in common stocks and other equity interests.

principle to those used in connection with equity-based annuity contracts and mutual funds. When the plan sponsor makes a contribution to the separate account, its plan is credited with an appropriate number of units (determined by dividing the dollar value of the contribution by the current market value of one unit), and, when funds are withdrawn from the separate account for benefit payments, transfer to the general account, another separate account, or another funding agency, an appropriate number of units are redeemed. The same procedure is followed when the insurer, under its discretionary authority, reallocates plan assets. Investment earnings operate to increase the *value* of the unit, rather than increasing the *number* of units credited to the participating plans.

If the plan assets are large enough to permit an appropriate degree of diversification, the sponsor or trustee may arrange to have all the assets managed in an individual account, independent of the general account and any other separate account. Such arrangement is known as an ''individual customer'' separate account. It permits a closer working relationship between the sponsor and the asset manager than is possible under a pooled separate account. As an example, the plan sponsor may specify the allocation of assets among broad classes of investments, as well as quality levels. In all cases, however, the choice of specific assets to be acquired and held rests with the insurer.

The assets in a separate account may be held by the insurer under a group annuity contract which obligates the plan sponsor to purchase annuities for retiring participants from an unallocated contractual fund so long as the contract remains in effect. Alternatively, they may be held under a type of contract that merely offers the plan sponsor the opportunity to purchase annuities in accordance with a stipulated schedule of annuity rates but does not obligate it to do so. If fixed-income annuities are purchased under either arrangement, the sums required are transferred to the general asset account, which normally underwrites all guarantees of the insurer. Sums set aside for asset-based (variable) annuities are held in a separate account maintained for the writing of such annuities. If the plan holds funds in the general asset account, the purchase payments may be taken from that source, or they may be drawn from one or more of the separate accounts to which contributions have been made. Transfers between and among the various accounts, including the general account, are made in cash (obtained in the case of separate accounts through the redemption of units) rather than in kind. Transfers from a single customer separate account to another separate account of the same insurer can be made in kind if permitted by state law and if the securities are acceptable to the insurer.

Funds under these contracts can usually be withdrawn by the plan sponsor upon relatively short notice, usually 90 days. Withdrawals from separate accounts (other than guaranteed income contracts described below) are on a market value basis and are generally payable in a single sum. Withdrawals from the general asset account, if large in amount, may have to be spread ratably over a period as long as 10 years. If paid in a single sum from the general asset account, the book value is adjusted (upward or downward) to a "market value" equivalent determined by a bond-yield calculation, reflecting the average period to maturity and the yields currently available on new money invested in securities of a quality comparable to that of the securities in the general account portfolio.

A separate account is regarded to be an investment company by the Securities and Exchange Commission and, in the absence of special statutory or administrative exemptions, it would have to be administered in conformity with the Investment Company Act of 1940, the Securities Act of 1933, the Securities and Exchange Act of 1934, and the Investment Advisers Act of 1940. However, through a series of SEC administrative rulings and eventually a statutory enactment (the Investment Company Amendments Act of 1970), separate accounts available only to qualified pension plans (other than Keogh plans) have been given an exemption from the most burdensome provisions of the foregoing laws and implementing regulations. This exemption applies to all qualified plans, irrespective of size and the presence of employee contributions, and irrespective of whether the plans provide fixed-income annuities or asset-based (variable) annuities.

**Guaranteed Income Contract.**  As one facet of its asset management services, the insurer may accept a block of funds and guarantee a rate of return reflective of the yields currently available on the type and quality of assets acquired with the funds. Contracts containing such an interest guarantee have various appellations, depending upon the insurer, but they tend to be known under the generic name of "guaranteed income contract," or GIC. This approach to crediting investment earnings is a variation of the investment year method. Under the latter, interest is credited to contract experience accounts in accordance with the composite rate at which monies were invested by the insurer during the entire calendar year. Under a GIC, the insurer may guarantee a rate of return for a specified time period only slightly lower than the rate currently obtainable in the capital market. The insurer bases its guarantee on the bonds or other securities that are purchased with the new monies and, in effect, earmarked for the plan's account. The insurer seeks call protection for the period during which its interest guarantee will be in effect, but, depending upon the contract terms, it may assume the risk of not being able to reinvest the investment income at the guaranteed rate. The insurer's commitment may take the form of a series of interest rate guarantees, the rates declining with the length of the guarantee. The insurer may accept a series of deposits over a period of years, in contrast to a single sum (presumably one-time) deposit, in which case the interest guarantee is graded downward over time; reflecting the insurer's uncertainty over the interest rate structure that may prevail in the future, beyond the period for which loan commitments have been made.

There are many variations among the guaranteed income contracts on the market and some of the variations can be of crucial importance. The most important feature, of course, is the minimum rate of interest to be credited. A second feature is the time over which the guarantee is to apply. Perhaps the most common period is 5 years, but some insurers offer guarantees, cautiously fashioned, that extend up to 20 years.

A third factor, related to the term of the guarantee is the timing of the insurer's repayment of the monies to the contract-holder or other disposition of the assets. Under some contracts, the original sums deposited plus accumulated interest are paid in a lump sum at the end of the guarantee period, or otherwise disposed of in accordance with instructions from the plan sponsor. Other contractual arrangements call for the deposited sums and accumulated interest to be paid to the plan sponsor in monthly or annual installments throughout the term of the contract. This type of arrangement reduces the reinvestment risk of the insurer. The contract-holder may be permitted to specify the pattern of the payout.

A fourth factor to be considered is whether the interest income that is accruing at a guaranteed rate can itself be reinvested at the guaranteed rate during the term of the contract. Some insurers provide for the compounding of interest at the guaranteed rate, while others credit the accruing interest with the new money rate applicable to the period during which the interest accrued. In some cases the interest is paid out annually, to be reinvested by the plan sponsor on the best terms available or applied to the payment of benefits.

A fifth consideration is whether the contract-holder is credited with its share of investment earnings in excess of the guaranteed rate. In technical parlance, the question is whether the contract is participating or nonparticipating. Some insurers guarantee the highest rate of interest that their circumstances can justify but make no provision for participation by the plan sponsor in excess investment earnings. The margin between the guaranteed and actual rate of return, if positive, may be viewed as the price or penalty paid for the guarantee feature. When the contract is nonparticipating, there is no explicit charge for the guarantee. Some insurers prefer to ''hedge their bets'' by offering conservative interest guarantees but providing for participation in excess investment earnings.

A sixth factor is the nature and magnitude of the charge made for the guarantee. The ''charge'' may take the form of nonparticipation in excess investment earnings, a conservative (favorable to the insurer) algorithm for computing excess interest earnings, or an explicit charge. Normally, the charge, expressed as a percentage of the assets and ranging up to 25 basis points, is applied as a deduction from the excess investment earnings that would otherwise have been credited to the contract. Under some contracts, the charge can reduce the effective yield on contract assets below the minimum rate guaranteed.

A seventh area in which differences in practice may be found is the manner in which the market value is computed for partial withdrawals under the contract. Under the terms of most contracts, no market value adjustment is made in respect of sums deposited in the first year of the contract or for monies withdrawn to pay benefits in any year. Under all other circumstances, a market value adjustment is usually made. Some insurers assume that the sum withdrawn was spread pro rata over all investment year cells, producing a ''coupon'' rate for the withdrawn segment equal to the composite rate on all the investment year cells. Other insurers assume that the monies are withdrawn from the most recent investment year cells beginning with the cell for the immediately preceding year.

This procedure is generally referred to as the last in, first out (LIFO) method. Still other insurers assume that all withdrawals are made from the current year's cell, even if this creates a negative balance for the cell, causing the cell to be credited with negative interest thereafter. This procedure avoids the need for a market value adjustment. At least one insurer computes the market value on the assumption that the withdrawn amounts came from the oldest investment year cells, starting with the first. Quite logically, this is known as the first in, first out (FIFO) method. Some companies apply the LIFO concept to withdrawals in a given calendar year not in excess of a specified limit, such as 10 percent of the contract-holder's beginning balance, with amounts in excess of that limit being spread ratably over all investment year cells.

Another aspect of this same question is whether the algorithm permits a market value in excess of book value. In theory, the market value of the withdrawn sums should be greater than book when the "coupon" rate on that segment of the investment portfolio from which the withdrawn funds were assumed to come is higher than the rate at which monies are currently being invested or committed. Most companies let the adjustment go in either direction, but there are some that do not recognize a market value in excess of book value.

Another aspect alluded to earlier is whether interest earnings accumulated at a guaranteed, minimum rate of interest can be withdrawn or transferred at the end of the contract term without a market value adjustment. This would be a concern only if interest rates were higher at the end of the term than the rate at which interest was credited. There is also the question of whether the principal can be withdrawn or transferred intact (i.e., at book value) at the end of the contract period.

A final issue is whether the guarantee of principal and interest is funded through the general asset account or a fixed-income separate account. Guarantees have traditionally been associated with the general asset account, but a few insurers are in a position to offer them through a separate account, passing along certain federal income tax savings and a potentially higher yield. The separate account may be an attractive mechanism for this purpose, but the plan sponsor should assure itself that the guarantee has the ultimate backing of the general asset account.

For a plan sponsor with a substantial body of retired participants, the guaranteed income contract may be an appealing alternative to the purchase of single-sum immediate annuities for the retired employees. Under this alternative, the plan sponsor deposits with the insurer a single sum calculated to be the approximate equivalent of the actuarial value of the retirement benefits in pay status, at the rate of interest proferred by the insurer. The insurer credits the deposit with a fixed, guaranteed rate of interest and returns the money over a period of years in monthly or annual installments that roughly "track" the pattern of benefit payments to the retired persons. In this way, the plan sponsor avoids the charge that the insurer would justifiably make for its mortality guarantee and the disbursement of monthly checks. Of course, the plan sponsor will incur a benefit disbursement expense in one form or the other. A GIC used for this purpose is a form of liability immunization from the standpoint of the plan sponsor.[18] The ultimate form of immunization is the actual purchase of annuities for the retired lives, or some other segment of the plan population.

The total volume of outstanding GICs has reached such proportions that a secondary market for the instruments has developed. While relatively thin at the present time, this market has grown up to accommodate the changing needs of pension plan portfolios. There are firms that specialize in the active management of GICs; indeed, some do nothing else. GICs are being actively managed to guard against credit risk; achieve broader diversification; smooth out cash flows, thus minimizing the reinvestment risk and meeting liquidity needs; and enhance the rate of return. Currently, some of these firms are holding out the possibility of adding 20 to 30 basis points to the net return, while achieving some of the other goals of active management. These various goals are pursued through such strategies as renegotiating maturities, stretching out payments from the GICs into smaller units, such as $1 million to $5 million denominations. Smaller units, or denominations, can create a broader market, fill in plan liquidity gaps, and achieve other purposes.

**Segmentation of the General Asset Account.**    It was stated earlier that by law and tradition all assets of a life insurer are available to meet the contractual and other obligations of the insurer. This concept was breached when pension insurers, with the approval

---

[18]The insurer may, in turn, immunize its own liability created by the sale of the GIC.

of regulatory authorities or state legislatures, dedicated certain assets of the company to particular contract-holders through the device of legally constituted separate accounts, established by action of the insurer's board of directors. Since these separate accounts are viewed by the SEC as investment companies, certain formalities must be observed to avoid the full burdens of registration and regulatory oversight that attach to a full-fledged investment company. These formalities themselves can be burdensome and restrictive.

The same objectives could be achieved through the creation of a series of fully owned subsidiaries, but they pose their own administrative, financial, and regulatory burdens. Nevertheless, a number of companies have established subsidiaries to offer investment services or to service particular kinds of pension plans.

Recently, several pension insurers have obtained regulatory approval to partition their general asset account without going through the legal formalities of establishing separate accounts or chartering fully owned subsidiaries. This procedure is called *segmentation*. By this device, the insurer can allocate general account assets to various lines of business or to defined classes of contract holders by merely setting up and maintaining *memorandum* accounts. The segmentation must be carried out and maintained on an equitable and consistent basis. Claims of a particular segment of contract-holders are not limited to assets dedicated to that segment but are enforceable against the entire general asset account.

Segmentation is a powerful and flexible tool for asset management and allocation of investment earnings. It permits the matching of assets and liabilities in a way not possible under other approaches. Assets can be segmented in ways to meet the differing investment objectives of various groups of contract holders. It is a way to introduce the investment year method of allocating investment earnings when the insurer does not want to do it in a formal fashion or for all purposes. In the hands of an unscrupulous management, it could become an instrument of gross favoritism of one class over another or unfair discrimination among the various classes of contract holders.

The issuance of a GIC based upon a particular lending transaction, a commonplace occurrence, is an extreme form of portfolio segmentation. The GIC is supported by an identifiable set of securities, with a claim against the insurer's surplus if the two sets of cash flows do not mesh. It may also be argued that a GIC is an extreme form of the new money approach to allocating investment earnings.

## Registered Investment Advisers

There are hundreds of firms and individuals who provide investment advice to pension plans, institutional endowments, financial institutions, and other individuals. The adviser may be an individual operating under his own name or a business name, or it may be a firm with dozens or hundreds of specialists and supporting staff and the most sophisticated computer hardware and software. It may be an independent entity or a subsidiary of a bank, insurance company, or other financial institution. Often the investment advisor is also designated *investment manager* for part or all of a plan's assets, with authority to make investment decisions within investment policy guidelines. Any investment manager of a pension plan who is neither a trustee nor named fiduciary of the plan must be registered under the Investment Advisers Act of 1940. Like a bank or insurer managing pension assets, it must acknowledge in writing that it is a fiduciary under ERISA.[19]

Many of these firms, large and small, offer their services to qualified pension plans. Some specialize in one sector of the capital market. For example, one firm may specialize in common stocks, one in conventional bonds, and another in convertible bonds. There may be specialization within a sector. Thus, one firm may be a specialist in growth stocks, while another emphasizes stocks with superior dividend performance.

Some investment advisers offer a full range of investment services, including execution of trades. Others merely advise the plan sponsor or trustee on investment policy, investment strategy, and stock or bond selection but leave execution, custodianship, and record-keeping to the trustee. Some advisers also manage stock or bond mutual funds or an index fund, which can be used by pension plans.

In one form or the other, investment advisers play an important role today in the management of pension plan assets.

---

[19]ERISA §§3(38), 402(c)(3).

## Questions

1. Describe and, where necessary, explain the techniques and practices used by pension asset managers to reduce or eliminate the risk associated with the reinvestment of investment income.

2. What difference does it make to a pension plan, as an investor, whether a repurchase agreement is viewed by the courts as a straightforward purchase and sale of the security in question or a loan from the investor collateralized by the underlying security?

3. Contrast the following short-term debt instruments used by commercial banks to obtain loanable funds or to enhance their liquidity and evaluate them in terms of their attractiveness and suitability as investments for pension plans:
    a. Certificate of deposit.
    b. Commercial paper.
    c. Bankers' acceptance.

4. Describe the traditional and current role of intermediate and long-term bonds in the investment portfolio of pension plans.

5. What role have short-term financial instruments played in the investment portfolios of pension plans, historically and in recent years?

6. Explain the concept of yield curves in respect to debt instruments, indicating what is meant by an "inverted" yield curve.

7. The trustees of a multiemployer pension plan have been advised by one of their investment managers to consider investing a portion of the plan's assets in real estate. The trustees have been reluctant to move any assets into the real estate sector, since they are unfamiliar with the types of real estate investments available and have heard that such investments are very illiquid.
    a. Describe the various types of real estate investments available to pension plans.
    b. If you were an investment adviser to this plan, what advice would you offer the plan trustees with respect to investing in real estate?
    c. Are real estate investments more illiquid than other classes of investment?

8. Compare and contrast *options* and *financial futures* as instruments for the hedging of risks in financial transactions.

9. Evaluate the arguments *for* and *against* the use of *cost* and *fair market* value in the valuation of the assets of a
    a. Defined benefit pension plan.
    b. Defined contribution pension plan.

10. Two students are engaged in an argument over the impact of pension plan asset valuation on the plan's funding requirements. One student argues that asset valuation is of significance only in the preparation of an actuarial balance sheet for the plan and has no bearing, directly or indirectly, on the employer's funding requirements. The other student argues that a net change in the value of a pension plan asset during a particular plan year is reflected fully and directly in the employer's contribution to the plan in the next plan year. Which of these two students is correct? How would you explain the significance to funding of changes in the value of plan assets?

11. What are the requirements of the Internal Revenue Service with respect to the valuation of pension plan assets?

12. Describe the various services available from bank trustees in connection with the investment of pension plan assets.

13. The sponsor of a defined benefit pension plan has read in *The Wall Street Journal* and other financial publications that a plan sponsor can reduce its contributions to the plan by adopting an immunization strategy. The sponsor is unfamiliar with the concept of immunization and is puzzled that the strategy can reduce required contributions to the plan.
    a. How would you explain the immunization concept to the plan sponsor?
    b. Why may immunization lead to a reduction in plan contributions?
    c. Is it feasible to immunize all of the liabilities of a pension plan? Why or why not?
    d. What is *contingent immunization* and why might it be adopted?

14. Describe the two principal approaches employed by life insurance companies in allocating investment earnings among its various lines of business and contract-holders. In your opinion, which of the two approaches is the more equitable from the standpoint of the contract-holders?

15. Explain why the general asset account of a life insurer may not be a completely satisfactory vehicle for the investment of pension plan assets.

16. Three devices that may be used by a life insurance company to make its investment services more attractive to pension plan sponsors are (a) separate accounts, (b) segmentation of the general asset account, and (c) wholly owned subsidiaries. As a life insurance company executive responsible for pension plan investment services, which of these three approaches would you favor? Why?

17. Describe the characteristics of a life insurance company separate account that would cause the SEC to regard it as an investment company.

18.  By what rationale did the SEC grant an exception from registration to those bank and life insurer pooled investment accounts that restrict their services to qualified pension and other employee benefit plans?

19.  Identify and explain the significance of the variations found among guaranteed income contracts (GICs).

20.  Why might a GIC be characterized as a form of liability immunization?

# 21 | Management of Pension Plan Assets: Operations II

## Use of Multiple Managers[1]

WHEN A PENSION PLAN has accumulated assets of a certain size, such as $50 to $100 million, it may employ more than one investment manager. Many large plans use as many as 20 or 25 managers and at one time AT&T used more than 100. Many plan sponsors are reluctant to entrust more than $50 million to any one manager. On the other hand, many managers are unwilling to manage less than $5 or $10 million for any one account.

There are three basic reasons—all related—why a plan sponsor might decide to use more than one manager. The first—and most obvious—is to broaden the diversification of risk. Since successful investing is very much an art and not a science, and involves a high degree of subjective judgment, risk can be reduced by reflecting the judgment and skills of more than one firm. A portfolio put together by three investment managers, for example, even when

---

[1]For a much more complete discussion of this topic, see Arthur Williams III, *Managing Your Investment Manager* (Homewood, Ill.: Dow Jones-Irwin, 1980), pp. 71–107, or Sidney Cottle et al., *Pension Asset Management: The Corporate Decisions* (New York: Financial Executives Research Foundation, 1980), pp. 207–26.

operating under the same guidelines will inevitably be different, and more diversified, than if it had been assembled by one manager.

A second reason for using multiple managers is to have the benefit of the research resources, contacts, and innovative ideas of several firms. These things get reflected, of course, in the stock and bond selections that make up the portfolio.

A third reason is to blend the investment styles and strategies of several managers in such a way as to reduce risk and take advantage of the special skills that they may have. As indicated above, many investment advisers choose to concentrate their research and resources in a particular sector of the capital market and become extremely knowledgeable and adroit in that area. The only way that a plan can avail itself of this special expertise is to use a number of such specialists, perhaps mixed in with some generalists. Some managers may be selected for distinctive types of investments, such as common stocks, bonds, or convertibles, or all managers may be permitted to invest in all types of investments. The strategies developed by some investment advisors work better in one kind of market environment than another; if some of these conflicting strategies are reflected in the same portfolio, the portfolio is insulated to some extent from unexpected movements in the market. It will be recognized that this blending of styles and strategies is a form of diversification.

As with all forms of human activity, there are certain disadvantages in using multiple managers. It is standard practice for the investment management fee to be expressed as a percentage of the assets under management, with the percentage declining as the size of the portfolio increases. The annual fee, which is customarily paid in monthly or quarterly installments, generally is applied in accordance with a sliding scale that declines with the magnitude of assets under management. For example, the fee often starts at 1/2 percent and declines to 1/10 percent, but for some asset managers the scale starts at 3/4 percent or even higher. The highest percentage is often applied to the first $5 million and the minimum is often paid on amounts in excess of $100 million. The fee of each manager is based on its share of assets and may never reach the lowest percentage if the plan assets are divided among too many managers. The total annual fee paid for investment services is almost certain to be larger for multiple managers than it would have been for one manager.

The second disadvantage is the administrative burden placed on the plan sponsor in monitoring the performance of the various managers and making allocation decisions. The monitoring may be delegated to a master trustee or some other firm, but a fee must be paid for this service. This, of course, adds to the cost disadvantage of using several managers. The additional cost may be offset many times over by better investment performance, but it may not be. Allocation of net cash flow of the plan to the various managers involves frequent judgments as to relative performance and possibly emotionally upsetting reallocations of assets.[2] If only one manager is employed, there are no subsequent allocations to consider. Since cash flow allocations involve both policy decisions and delicate business relationships, they should engage substantial amounts of top-management attention.

The third disadvantage may be the most serious of the three. This is the possibility that the strategies and investment decisions of the various managers may work at cross-purposes and cancel each other out. This probability takes on more reality if the managers are chosen because of diversity of styles and strategies, as is becoming more common. The greater the number of managers and variety of styles, the greater the possibility that their special skills will be neutralized and the overall performance will approach that of an index fund. Some practitioners believe that this neutralizing effect becomes serious if more than three or four managers are employed.

There are investment consultants whose primary or even exclusive service is evaluating the qualifications of other investment counselors and asset managers. In effect, they are search firms.

---

[2]There is no prescribed formula for deciding how to allocate new contributions among existing managers. The simplest procedure is to give each manager an equal amount, but that would change the proportions of the portfolio allocated to each manager. To maintain existing proportions, each manager could be given a pro rata share of new money. The cash flow could be apportioned in terms of performance; but, depending on market conditions and anticipated changes, this philosophy could lead to favoring the *best* performer or the *worst performer.* Another basis of allocation is to maintain or achieve a preferred mix of asset categories, particularly if the various managers invest in different types of assets. Another is to assign a disproportionate share to the manager or managers whose asset category appears to be undervalued. Under some conditions, assets are allocated on the basis of a pattern designed to create a baseline portfolio over some time period. Finally, the allocation may be done on the basis of pure judgment. The reverse process, liquidating assets to meet benefit payments or choosing assets to transfer to a new manager, involves many of the same judgments.

They make in-depth studies of the portfolio managers, research staff, and traders of the leading firms, looking for distinctive philosophies, strategies, market specializations, and decision-making processes. For a fee, they assist plan sponsors in selecting a coordinated group of outside managers whose special expertise and interests are optimally suited to the investment goals and objectives of the plan sponsor. They may also advise the plan sponsor on policy and strategy. Some firms' services include the monitoring and continuing evaluation of the outside managers engaged on their recommendation to manage a portion of the plan portfolio.

## Index Funds

Disillusioned by the apparent inability of active money managers to consistently outperform (or even equal) the market averages and desiring to reduce investment management fees and transaction costs, a few years ago a number of plan sponsors developed a strong interest in the concept of an index fund. An *index fund* is a portfolio of securities constructed in such a manner that its risk and return patterns are identical to or closely replicate those of a selected market index or some other standard. In its pure form, an index fund holds every security in the index and in the same proportion as its weight in the index. To reduce the cost and inconvenience of holding all securities in the index in the proper proportions, some index funds hold only those securities selected by a sampling procedure intended to replicate the risk and return patterns of the whole market index.

By placing assets in an index fund, an investor enjoys perfect diversification within the marketplace bounded by the index, and is reasonably assured of a rate of return equal to that of the marketplace less transaction costs and the management fee. Both transaction costs and management fees are much lower than for a comparable actively managed portfolio.[3] For these advantages, the investor forgoes the opportunity of earning a higher rate of return than that of the market and may give up some flexibility in adapting the overall investment program to its needs. Investment in an index

---

[3]Nevertheless, these and other costs have caused many "sample" index funds to underperform the "market" to a noticeable degree.

fund is the extreme manifestation of a passive investment strategy with respect to the assets so deployed.

In theory, the ideal index fund would be one that holds all the stocks, bonds, and other financial instruments in the marketplace, and in the precise proportions in which they appear in the marketplace.In practice, such a fund could not be created or maintained. It would be too cumbersome to operate, and most of the advantages of such a comprehensive fund can be obtained from a much smaller and narrower set of assets. If an investor has a large enough body of assets under its management, it could construct and maintain its own index fund, at considerable expense and inconvenience. In reality, investors have turned to the index funds operated by professional money managers—banks, brokerage houses, and investment advisers.

The index fund concept is applicable to both common stocks and bonds, but it is much more difficult to construct and maintain a bond index fund.[4] Hence, most index funds in operation at the present time are stock funds. While a number of common stock indices are available, the vast majority of index funds attempts to track the returns of the Standard & Poor's Composite 500 Index, including reinvested dividends. The companies included in the S&P 500 Index are so dominant in the economy that an index fund patterned after the S&P 500 Index is considered to be an acceptable proxy for the entire universe of U.S. common stocks.

The largest proportion of pension plan indexed assets are in pooled funds. Because of economies of scale, these permit the manager to charge lower management fees than under any arrangement. The plan sponsor decides what proportion of plan assets should be in the index fund and then purchases shares or participation units in the fund. The manager of the pooled index fund assumes the responsibility of maintaining the proper balance of common stock by capitalization through appropriate sales and pur-

---

[4]Due to the dynamic nature and size of the fixed income securities universe, it is not possible to hold all the issues in a fixed income index fund in their capitalization weighted proportions relative to the bench mark, such as the Shearson Lehman Government Corporate Index or the Salomon Brothers Broad Investment Grade Index. This means that a sampling strategy must be utilized, the index fund being constructed of a large number of "cells" that in combination reflect the risk/return characteristics, duration, and weights of the targeted universe. Constant monitoring of these cells and their interdependence is necessary to replicate the results of the selected index. The first bond index fund was introduced in 1983 and today a number are in operation.

chases. Management fees on the order of 1/10 percent of assets under management and transaction costs are charged to the fund and will probably cause the overall return to be slightly less than that of the S&P 500. Fortunately, index fund portfolio turnover tends to be extremely low, rarely exceeding 5 percent per year, compared to 25 to 30 percent for a conventionally managed stock portfolio.

Some index fund managers will operate an individual customer index fund for a minimum size fund, possibly as low as $10 million but usually closer to $25 million. The management fee for a separately managed index fund is somewhat higher than for a similar pooled fund. The plan sponsor might want a separate fund for a number of reasons. One reason, exemplified by church denominational plans, is to exclude stocks of companies that engage in controversial business practices or in manufactured products of questionable social utility. Another reason is to exclude the stock of companies known or believed to be in serious financial condition.[5] An index fund that has been purged of such stocks is known as a "filtered" fund, and may have a better chance of meeting the prudence standard of ERISA than one that has done no screening. A third reason for a separate index fund is to save administrative transaction costs by reducing the number of stocks in the portfolio. Studies have shown that a capitalization weighted portfolio of 250 of the largest capitalization securities should track the S&P Index within 50 basis points (0.5 percent) on an annual return basis before transaction costs. The 25 largest companies by capitalization account for 40 percent of the S&P Index, and the smallest 200 companies have such minimal impact that many index funds exclude them. It must be recognized, of course, that any "tinkering" with the S&P Index on the basis of social considerations, investment judgment, or transaction cost control weakens the link to the S&P Index and erodes to some extent the reason for utilizing the index approach.

Few pension plans invest all of their assets in an index fund. Such a fund is viewed as another vehicle in the total range of investment alternatives. The marketing pitch of firms merchandising their index funds is that a pension plan should use an index

---

[5]Most pooled index funds engage in such purging, the practice not being confined to individually managed funds.

fund to achieve the desired degree of portfolio diversification and to assure the plan of a market rate of return on a portion of the portfolio (the so-called passive core) to free it to pursue a more venturesome and, presumably, more remunerative active investment policy with respect to the remainder of the portfolio. To the extent that risk is rewarded by higher returns, this combination of passive and active investment strategy would produce a composite return in excess of market indexes. Correspondingly, it also dampens return volatility relative to a totally active portfolio.

The index fund concept can be applied to various subsets of capital market instruments, and a number of specialized funds are in operation, such as "dividend tilt" funds, which cater to the tax motivations of broad classes of investors, and funds containing stocks of foreign corporations. The case for indexing international equity investments rests on the assumption that it is more difficult to add value from selection in those markets.

## Accountability for Investment Results[6]

As was pointed out earlier, a pension plan sponsor has a fiduciary responsibility to invest the plan assets in a prudent manner and for the sole benefit of the plan participants and beneficiaries. If it delegates the investment function, as is the custom, it has a fiduciary responsibility to use prudence in selecting the asset managers and in continuing their services after the original selection process is completed. This means that there must be a system by which the various asset managers account periodically for their investment results and the plan sponsor can evaluate their absolute and relative performance. This is something that a prudent and concerned plan sponsor would do in the absence of a legal obligation, purely out of self-interest, if for no other reason.

### Time Horizon

When an investment manager is engaged, there is generally a tacit understanding that it will be retained for a sufficiently long period to demonstrate its competence (or lack thereof). In most cases the

---

[6]For a more detailed and technical analysis of this subject, consult Williams, *Managing your Investment Manager*, pp. 117–40, or Cottle, *Pension Asset Management*, pp. 229–58.

parties are thinking of a time horizon that encompasses a number of up markets and down markets. This period seems reasonable since it allows for differences in risk postures and investment styles. The market does not favor, or go against, all investment strategies or risk postures at the same time. Instead, there is a different market environment in each cycle, during which different types of stocks and bonds may perform differently. Over the years, market cycles have averaged 52 months in duration. Thus, this approach contemplates a time horizon of about four years.

The second most frequent approach is to set an explicit time horizon, generally in the range of three to five years. These time horizons undoubtedly reflect the parties' consciousness of market cycles and are intended to relate to them.

These time horizons are informal understandings and not at all in the nature of a contractual commitment. The plan sponsor can terminate the arrangement at any time, with reasonable notice. Termination before the end of the contemplated time horizon would normally occur only because of dismal, if not calamitous, results clearly attributable to the manager or of changes in the organization or professional staff of the asset manager that presage changes in the nature and quality of the investment services that could be expected in the future. There is much turnover of skilled performers in the investment community, and the character of a particular firm, especially a small one, may change overnight with the departure or death of one or two key persons. Thus, the plan sponsor must retain the capability of adapting to changed circumstances.

### Frequency of Reporting

The investment managers report periodically on their stewardship of the assets entrusted to them. The most common reporting frequency is quarterly, although some joint trust pension plans review results annually. The managers report in a format that either shows various performance measurements or permits the plan sponsor to make its own calculations. For the larger plans, performance data are generally submitted to a firm that provides performance measurement services, and the analysis and comparative performance data will be furnished by the latter in connection with the periodic review. If the assets under management are sizable, the portfolio manager and supporting staff will generally present the results in person, explaining why the portfolio performed well or poorly during the period under review. These presentations usually include economic and market forecasts and an explanation of the strategies to be pursued during the next few months. These presentations and their accompanying economic analysis may cause the plan sponsor to revise its overall strategy, especially the mix of assets.

## Measurement of Investment Performance

As noted, the investment results are generally presented in a format that permits comparisons with the return on various stock and bond indexes, and possibly with other pension portfolios. Two measures of performance are critical to these comparisons: the *dollar-weighted* rate of return, and the *time-weighted* rate of return.

Both of these measures are based on the *total* rate of return, reflecting not only dividend and interest flows but *realized* and *unrealized* capital gains and losses. Both measures require that the market value of the portfolio be known as of the beginning and end of the time period for which the rate of return is being computed.

The *dollar-weighted* rate of return for a given period is the percentage rate of change (positive or negative) in the market value of the portfolio assets during the period, when recognition is given to the timing and magnitude of external cash flows. It is the rate that will discount the end-of-period value of the portfolio back to the beginning-of-period portfolio plus interim contributions and less withdrawals. It is logically identical to the interest rate at which the beginning portfolio and all net cash flows must be invested to arrive at the ending value of the portfolio. This measure is also known as the *internal* rate of return and as the *discounted cash flow* rate of return. It is a measure of the actual performance of the portfolio during the period, reflecting both the skills of the portfolio manager and the timing effect of contributions to, and withdrawals from, the pension fund.

The *time-weighted* rate of return is the percentage change in the market value of a unit of assets (e.g., $1 or $100) invested continuously for the entire measurement period. More simply, it is the rate at which a dollar invested at the beginning of a period would have compounded during that period, regardless of interim cash flows. Computation of this rate requires the use of ''units'' or ''shares,'' and the determination of the net asset value per unit at the beginning and end of the measurement period and on any date when a cash flow transaction occurs. To account for a contribution or withdrawal during the year, units are "bought" or "sold" at the then-prevailing net asset value per unit. Investment income (dividends and interest) is not converted into units but serves to increase the net asset value of existing units. At year-end, the ending portfolio value divided by the outstanding units gives an ending net asset value per unit that can be compared directly with the beginning value or with any interim value. The concept is identical to that used in mutual fund accounting.

The essential contribution of the time-weighted rate of return is that, contrary to the dollar-weighted rate of return, it eliminates the effect on return of the *timing* of external cash flows (i.e., contributions and withdrawals).[7] The two measures of return are identical for any period when there are no external cash flows or, irrespective of cash flows, when the rate of return throughout the period is constant. The two rates differ only when additions to the portfolio are invested at a different yield than the existing assets or net withdrawals force the liquidation of assets having a different return than the remaining assets. Since the portfolio manager has little, if any, control over the external cash flow of the portfolio, the time-weighted rate of return is considered to be the better measure of the *manager's* performance. The *dollar-weighted* return is the better measure of the *portfolio's* performance. If the portfolio manager, under a discretionary grant of authority, has control over the cash flow of a particular segment of the portfolio, such as the equity component or the bond component, the dollar-weighted rate of return is the appropriate measure of the manager's performance for the segment of the portfolio. Each measure is significant and makes a distinctive contribution to the evaluation of investment results.

It was noted above that, to compute a time-weighted rate of return for a portfolio, or segment of a portfolio, the market value of the relevant assets must be known on the date of each external transaction. This would create no difficulties if transactions occurred only at the end or beginning of calendar quarters, at which

---

[7]For a comprehensive and technical explanation of the time-weighted rate of return, see *Measuring the Investment Performance of Pension Funds for the Purpose of Inter-Fund Comparison* (Park Ridge, Ill.: Bank Administration Institute, 1968).

point portfolio valuations usually take place. In reality, contributions and withdrawals can occur at any time during the calendar year. To overcome this practical problem, an approximation of the time-weighted rate of return can be derived by determining the *internal* rate of return for each period between portfolio valuations, and linking the results to obtain an annual (or annualized) rate of return.[8] This modification of the pure method assumed that the return within the period (quarter) is uniform, which will not be true if there are significant cash flows within the period. The shorter the period between valuations, the less violence the approximation does to the pure rate.[9]

The investment results of each of the asset managers are combined to produce dollar-weighted and time-weighted rates of return for the entire pension portfolio, as well as for each of its major components: equities, bonds, and short-term instruments. There are some definitional problems and differences in custodian accounting practices that may cause the computed rates of return not to be precisely comparable to those of other pension plans and market indexes.

Performance results are more meaningful if they can be related to the total risk of the portfolio. There is a theoretical relationship between risk and return for all types of capital assets. Some observers contend that if one portfolio outperforms another only because it took greater nonsystematic risk, no credit is due the portfolio manager. They assert that the real measure of a manager's performance is whether it was able to earn a superior return when recognition is given to differences in risk and that it is necessary to look at *risk-adjusted* rates of return.

For a common stock portfolio, a statistical measure of "value added" from active management is called *alpha*. It is the intercept

---

[8] This linking is accomplished by multiplying the separate internal rates of return times each other, with equal weight being assigned to each period. For example, if the internal rate of return per quarter for four quarters were 2 percent, 8 percent, 5 percent and $-6$ percent, the time-weighted rate of return for the year would be 8.73 percent ($1.02 \times 1.08 \times 1.05 \times .94 - 1.00$, converted to a percentage).

[9] Some measurement services estimate the market value of the portfolio at each month-end by regression analysis and then compute monthly internal rates of return. The estimation is carried out by applying the portfolio's beta to the rate of return on the market during the monthly subinterval. There are technical problems with the estimation process, but this approach can produce more accurate results than the linking of quarterly returns.

of the regression line of return on the portfolio and that of the market when the market return is zero. Both are adjusted for the return on a risk-free asset. If the alpha is equal to 0.0, there is a zero risk-adjusted rate of return, and the manager added no non-systematic value from its efforts. If the alpha is greater than 0.0, there is a positive risk-adjusted rate of return. An alpha of less than 0.0 indicates that there is a negative risk-adjusted rate of return. There may be a *negative* risk-adjusted return even when the nominal rate of return is *positive,* and vice versa. As with beta, it is possible to measure the statistical significance of the derived values, and this item is included in some performance analyses.

The alpha factor is not a wholly satisfactory measure of the value added from active bond management, primarily because the risk characteristics of a bond or aggregation of bonds continually change as the maturity date approaches. However, an approximation to the alpha can be derived by the same statistical techniques used to determine the alpha for common stock portfolios. The risk level and rate of return is compared with a "market line" portraying various percentage combinations of riskless Treasury bills and a slice of the overall bond market. The line reflects various combinations of risk and return, and any combination of risk and return for a particular portfolio above that line suggests a positive risk-adjusted return, or value added from active management. Any point below the line indicates a negative risk-adjusted return.

The impact of active management on a bond portfolio can also be ascertained, with some limitations, through use of the duration model. Duration, it was noted earlier, is a measure of the average time to receipt of discounted cash flows from a fixed-income instrument. It is a measure of the sensitivity of a bond's price to changes in interest rates. With this information for all the portfolio securities, it becomes possible to attribute the sources of the portfolio's return to the market, the policy effect, the interest rate anticipation effect, the analysis effect (the selection of issues with better-than-average long-term prospects), and the trading effect (the difference between the total management effect and the effects attributable to analysis and interest rate anticipation). This is a complex process and the rates of return must be precisely measured to attribute return to various effects. Moreover, duration is not a measure to the total portfolio risk, since it ignores the quality factors. There are other conceptual flaws that limit the usefulness of this approach.

A more recent approach to determining value added to a bond (or stock) portfolio by management is to compare actual investment results with market results and with the results that would have obtained had the beginning portfolio been held without change throughout the measurement period, the so-called naive alternative. The difference between the rate of return on the market and the theoretical return on the beginning portfolio is considered to be the management differential, as reflected to the beginning of the period. The yield on the beginning, or buy-and-hold, portfolio will equal its beginning yield to maturity if nothing else changes. However, interest rates may change during the period, and sector and quality differentials may broaden or narrow, with unequal effects on the market portfolio and the buy-and-hold portfolio. The difference between the total rate of return on the beginning portfolio and the sum of the beginning yield to maturity, the interest rate effect, and the sector/quality effect, is called the "residual" or "other selection" effect. Finally, the difference between the return on the beginning portfolio and the return on the actual portfolio is called the "activity" or "swapping" factor. It measures the effect of active management during the measurement period.

The total riskiness of an equity or bond portfolio when the asset manager has discretionary control over cash flow may be estimated by the mean absolute deviation (MAD) of the time-weighted rate of return. The MAD is the average of the absolute difference in the time-weighted rate of return on each portfolio holding and the time-weighted return for the entire portfolio. In this context, "absolute" means without regard to sign, a deviation of $-3$ having the same value as $+3$. The MAD is a useful value to have when comparing investment results with market indexes and other portfolios.

Rates of return and risk factors are computed not only for the latest measurement period but for various time intervals and on a cumulative basis. It is customary to show results for the most recent calendar year; the last 2, 3, 4, and 5-year periods; the last 10 years; and for individual managers the whole period of their stewardship on a cumulative basis. Rates of return may be shown separately for principal (changes in market value) and income (or principal and income combined).

## Comparisons with Other Pension Portfolios and Market Indexes

Absolute rates of return, especially internal rates of return, are important to a pension plan sponsor in terms of its investment goals and objectives and actuarial interest assumption. However, they can be viewed with more perspective if they are compared with the investment results of appropriate market indexes and other pension plans with similar investment objectives. This is especially important when the rates of return are disappointing or even negative, as they have been in some years.

It is customary for asset managers to include comparisons with widely recognized market indexes in their periodic reports of investment performance. The best known common stock indexes are those maintained by Standard & Poor's, Dow Jones, the New York Stock Exchange, the American Stock Exchange, Value Line, and Wilshire Associates. These indexes differ as to their composition, the weighting of the stock issues, changes in the list of securities, the treatment of income, and the frequency and timing of index available. The most widely used stock indexes for comparison purposes is Standard & Poor's Composite 500 Index, which, as its name suggests, contains the common stock of 500 large corporations, weighted by the market value of the outstanding shares of the constituent companies (referred to as capitalization weighted). Standard & Poor's also maintains an index of the stock of *industrial* corporations, also weighted by market capitalization. The second most frequently cited index is that maintained by Dow Jones concerning 30 industrial stocks (actually the stocks of 29 industrials and AT&T). The stocks are weighted by price, and the published value is derived by dividing the aggregate market value of the outstanding stock by a constant that was originally 30 but has been adjusted downward over the years to reflect stock splits and other changes in capitalization. The denominator is published each Monday in *The Wall Street Journal*. Thus, strictly speaking, the resulting value is an *average* not an *index*. Dow Jones also computes separate averages for 15 utilities and 20 companies in transportation, and then combines the 65 companies into a composite average.

The indexes of the two stock exchanges contain the stocks of all listed companies, weighted by market capitalization. The Wilshire index reflects the market value of about 5,000 stocks, with changes in the group being made monthly. The Value Line index contains about 1,700 stocks, which are given equal weighting, and reflects the geometric mean of daily price relativities.

There are a number of bond indexes. The index of returns on 90-day Treasury bills is designed to serve as a proxy for the risk-free return available to investors. The returns are computed on the assumption of continuous reinvestment on a tax-free basis in 90-day T-bills. Standard & Poor's High Grade Corporate Bond Index is widely used for long-term bonds. In effect, this is a hypothetical high-quality bond portfolio with a 20-year maturity and 4 percent coupon rate, priced to reflect current interest rates. The Salomon Brothers High Grade Long-Term Bond Index and the Lehman Brothers Kuhn Loeb Corporate Long-Term Bond Index each reflect the coupon rates and current prices of a broad group of outstanding bond issues (almost 4,000 issues), weighted by market capitalization. They are regarded to be superior indicators of market return and are widely used for evaluative purposes. Their primary drawback is that they consider only bonds with a remaining maturity of at least 20 years. The Lehman Brothers Kuhn Loeb Bond Index is a capitalization weighted return index on more than 4,000 issues of more than one-year maturity. Moody's, Merrill Lynch, and Dow Jones also publish a number of specialized bond indexes.

An investor can construct its own hybrid index by combining several of the published indexes with weightings reflecting the composition of its own bond portfolio.

Comparisons of the investment results of a particular pension portfolio with certain market indexes can be misleading, if the investment objectives of the plan are significantly different from those implicit in the market results. It may be more meaningful to compare results with other large pension plans that are more likely to be pursuing investment policies similar to those of the plan under review. A number of firms in the financial field offering investment performance and analysis services have created and maintain a data bank that contains performance data on several hundred pension plans of various types. These firms offer risk and return comparisons, not only with standard market indexes but with the pension plans in their data bank and possibly with the commingled funds of banks and insurance companies operated for qualified pension, profit sharing, and savings plans. These comparisons are becoming very sophisticated, reflecting several risk/return measures and showing the relative ranking of the client plan against all other plans in the universe by quartile or quintile groups. Risk-and-return measures are given by broad asset categories—equities, bonds, and short-term securities—and possibly by sector groupings. Performance data are furnished for past periods of varying duration and for various ending dates which, of course, can be crucial.

There are reasons to believe that these performance analyses are helping plan sponsors to reassess their investment objectives and strategies on a continuing basis and to evaluate the performance of their asset managers against that of their peers.

## Questions

1. The trustees of a defined benefit pension plan, having seen the plan assets grow to $110 million through contributions and investment earnings, are wondering whether it would be advisable to use more than the one asset manager that has managed the assets from plan inception.

   a. Outline the arguments for and against the use of multiple asset managers.

   b. Under what circumstances might it be advisable for the plan sponsor to bring the investment "in-house"?

2. Many investment professionals believe and assert that the use of an index fund by a pension plan is a denial of the potential benefits of active portfolio management and, indeed, constitutes an attack on the whole theoretical foundation of modern portfolio theory. How do you respond to this attitude?

3. What potential advantages does a properly constituted index fund offer to the sponsor of a defined benefit pension plan? Would these advantages have equal appeal to the sponsor of a defined contribution pension plan?

4. To what extent, if any, does the "screening" or "filtering" of a portfolio serving as a proxy for the market (a) undermine the rationale or theory of an index fund? and (b) affect the performance of the modified portfolio?

5. Explain the difference between a *dollar-weighted* rate of return and a *time-weighted* rate of return. Indicate the distinct role each plays in the measurement of investment performance.

6. Explain how the use of "units" in determining the time-weighted rate of return eliminates the effect on the rate of return of the timing of cash flow.

7. In determining the time-weighted rate of return by the "unit" technique, what transactions would you include in the cash flow? How could investment income, including realized capital gains and losses, be treated?

8. One acceptable method of computing the time-weighted rate of return is to determine the internal rate of return for various measurement periods, such as a month or a quarter, and link these results through a mathematical formula to obtain the annualized rate of return for longer periods, such as a year, three years, or five years. Since the internal rate of return reflects the timing of the portfolio's cash flow, how can it be said that a time-weighted rate of return calculated by this procedure eliminates the effect of cash flow timing?

9. Explain the role of each of the following statistical values in evaluating the performance of a portfolio manager: (a) alpha, (b) beta, and (c) R or coefficient of determination.

10. Identify and explain briefly the various types of risk that may be found in the common stock portfolio of a pension plan.

11. Which of the foregoing types of risk would be found in a "pure" or unmodified index fund?

12. Identify five commonly recognized clusters of common stock which, if found in disproportionate weight in a common stock portfolio, might give rise to extra market covariance risk.

13. Describe the various techniques or approaches that may be used to isolate the effect of risk on the total investment return of a common stock portfolio.

14. Identify and explain briefly the types of risk associated with fixed-income instruments.

15. Other things being equal, what effect should a general decline in interest rates have on the market price of (a) outstanding debt instruments, and (b) issued common stocks, as a class? Why?

16. What, in theory, is the best measure of the price sensitivity of a bond to a change in the level of interest rates?

17. Describe the various *types* of bench marks against which the *absolute* performance of a pension asset manager may be measured.

18. Over what time period (horizon) and with what frequency should the performance of a pension asset manager be measured? Justify your answer.

# 22 | Allocated Funding Instruments

As NOTED IN EARLIER SECTIONS of this volume, the assets of a qualified pension plan must either be held in trust or be transferred to a life insurance company in exchange for its promise either to pay the plan benefits when they become due or to provide stipulated investment services. The financial institution—bank, trust company, or life insurer—to which plan contributions are paid is referred to herein as the *funding agency.* The legal document that defines the obligation of the funding agency is designated as the *funding instrument.* The funding instrument serves as a conduit through which contributions intended for benefit payments are channeled to the ultimate recipient—the participants or their beneficiaries. It also provides the legal and institutional framework within which accumulated plan assets are invested.

Funding instruments may be broadly classified as to whether they represent agreements with life insurance companies or with trustees, normally banks and trust companies. A more meaningful classification for many purposes can be derived from the manner in which plan contributions to the funding agency—and accumulated plan assets—get applied to the satisfaction of individual benefit claims. Within this context, funding instruments can be classified as *allocated* funding instruments or *unallocated* funding instruments.

524

An *allocated funding instrument* is one under which all past and current contributions are credited to individual plan participants in such a manner as to give them a legally enforceable claim to the benefits that can be provided by cumulative contributions, contingent on satisfaction of certain stipulated conditions. An *unallocated funding instrument* is one under which *some or all* of the current and accumulated contributions are held by the *funding agency* in a pooled account, until disbursed in benefit payments or applied to the purchase of paid-up annuities at retirement or on earlier termination of employment with vested benefits. This distinction is of crucial significance to plan design, administration of plan assets, and security of benefit expectations.

## General Characteristics

As a practical matter, only certain types of insurance and annuity contracts issued by life insurance companies can satisfy the above definition of an allocated funding instrument. The assets of a defined benefit plan funded through a trust are commingled and are allocated to individual participants only when paid to them in lump-sum or income benefits or used to purchase annuities in the names of terminated vested or retired employees. Under a money purchase pension plan funded through a trust, the *plan sponsor* maintains individual *memorandum* accounts on behalf of the participants to which contributions and associated investment income are currently credited; but these individual accounts are not funding instruments. The funding instrument is the trust agreement, and the trustee does not ordinarily[1] partition the trust fund into subaccounts, one for each participant, against which the participants would have legally enforceable rights, including the right of a periodic accounting. The trust fund is a pooled account held and invested for the collective benefit of the participants and their beneficiaries.

Sometimes a bank, in addition to its role as trustee, provides recordkeeping services for the employer and maintains the individual accounts on behalf of the employer; but in such instances,

---

[1]Trust assets are partitioned in the case of participant directed individual accounts, described in Chapter 23.

the bank is acting in the role of administrative assistant to the plan sponsor, rather than in its role of trustee.

Premiums and annuity considerations paid to the insurer under allocated funding instruments generally flow into the general asset account and lose their identity as pension assets, except for tax apportionment purposes. This is in accordance with the general principal and tradition that all contractual guarantees of a life insurer are obligations of the general asset account. The guarantees are fixed-dollar obligations, payable without adjustment for fluctuations in the market value of the underlying assets. The premium rates for individual life insurance contracts remain fixed throughout the premium-paying period of the contracts; but the annuity purchase rates under group contracts are normally guaranteed for only the first five years of the contract, being subject thereafter to the risk of adverse rate changes that would apply only to *future* annuity purchases. Group annuity rates may be adjusted downward for favorable experience; and the nominally fixed premiums of participating individual life insurance contracts are adjusted annually through so-called dividends, a refund of a portion of the premiums for favorable experience.

The primary appeal of an allocated funding instrument to the plan sponsor is the transfer of risk to the insurer. For an appropriate consideration, a life insurer will assume the legal responsibility of paying part or all of the benefits under the plan on behalf of the sponsor. Every dollar paid to a life insurer under an allocated funding instrument carries with it the insurer's unconditional guarantee that a retirement benefit of a specified amount will be paid pursuant to the terms of the plan. The risk transferred to the insurer is that of unfavorable deviations from assumed experience with respect to mortality, investment earnings, and expenses of administration. To the extent that the benefit obligations of the plan have been funded by allocated funding instruments and, thus, assumed by the insurer, the participants look to the insurer, rather than to the sponsor, for the payment of their benefits. It is an unsettled question whether, under ERISA, the plan sponsor retains a residual, contingent liability for the benefit claims under the plan if the insurer, because of insolvency, could not meet its contractual obligations.

An important corollary to the risk transfer that occurs under an allocated funding instrument is that, as of any given time, the plan sponsor's cost for benefits accrued to that date is *known* and *fixed*.

The accrued benefits and their maximum cost are fixed at all times. As noted above, the nominal cost may be reduced retroactively through dividends and experience rate credits.

Another appeal of the allocated funding approach to the sponsor is that the insurance or annuity contract may be part of a comprehensive package of services needed to establish and maintain a pension plan. In the process of assuming responsibility for benefit payments, the insurer may provide all actuarial, investment, disbursement, accounting, and reporting services associated with a plan. The insurer may either prepare or supply the information for reports going to regulatory authorities and participants. It generally keeps the plan sponsor informed about all legislative, legal, or tax developments that may affect the operation of the plan. A representative of the insurer usually designs the plan, not always an objective exercise. The only service that the sponsor may have to seek from other external sources is legal and tax advice.

Finally, the allocated funding approach appeals to some plan participants, a factor that may contribute to the overall morale of the work force, with resulting benefits to the employer. Plan participants may respond favorably to the idea of individual insurance or annuity contracts (or units of paid-up annuities, under a group deferred annuity contract) being issued in their name, even though they cannot take possession of the contracts until they leave the service of the employer with vested rights. Except for past service benefits under group deferred annuity contracts, the benefits are at all times fully funded and are usually not subject to divestment through reallocation of assets upon termination of the plan. In other words, the allocation of plan contributions that takes place when each contribution is made usually remains in effect when the plan terminates and the ERISA allocation formula becomes applicable to previously unallocated plan assets. The owner-participant in a small plan may find this feature of an allocated funding instrument very appealing. If the allocations under a group deferred annuity are in conflict with the plan termination allocation formula of ERISA (an unlikely occurrence), deferred annuities and those in pay status might have to be cancelled or reduced in amount.

There are two major disadvantages of the allocated funding approach: inflexibility and cost. The contracts used by life insurers to accommodate allocated funding are highly structured. The individual and group permanent insurance contracts were designed for other purposes and were adapted, with minor modifications, if any, to funding pension plans. The other contract used for allocated funding, the group deferred annuity contract, was developed specifically for pension plans but utilizes a rigid system of contribution allocation. Under defined benefit plans funded solely with allocated funding instruments, the result is that the plan must be designed to fit the contract forms, rather than the other way around. The benefit formula, in particular, is highly constrained. It is not feasible, for example, to utilize benefit formulas that recognize final pay, offset benefits by Social Security, or provide early retirement benefits not based on full actuarial equivalence. Final-pay formulas may produce an undesirable cost pattern. (Some plans that employ a final-pay formula do not recognize pay increases that occur within five years of the individual's normal retirement age.) Contributions are shaped by schedules of premium and annuity purchase rates and do not recognize anticipated turnover, retirements at other than the normal retirement age, and other developments that might affect the amount of contributions. Transfer of the accumulated funds to another funding agency is awkward, if not impossible.

The cost per unit of benefit is likely to be higher under an allocated funding instrument than under an unallocated funding instrument, for a number of reasons. The first, not the fault of the instrument, is that allocated funding tends to be used with small groups, limiting the opportunity to spread fixed costs. Furthermore, distributions costs associated with the marketing of individual contracts are incurred, the principal item being commissions to the soliciting agent or broker. Installation costs are incurred in connection with any type of pension plan, and commissions to agents or brokers under individual contracts may be offset to some extent under other funding instruments by payments to an actuarial firm or to an employee benefit consultant. State taxes have to be paid on premiums paid on individual insurance contracts, and may be payable under group annuity contracts. Administrative expenses are higher because of the issuance of individual contracts or the maintenance of individual annuity accounts, a source of expense not found under unallocated funding contracts. Finally, the cost may be higher in the long run because the plan is funded through the general asset account and does not have access to the potentially higher investment returns of the various separate accounts maintained by the insurer. In some circumstances these higher costs may cause the purchase of individual contracts to be determined to be a breach of fiduciary responsibility by the plan sponsor, the trustee or other fiduciaries.[2]

These disadvantages of allocated funding instruments are so serious that their use is largely confined to small plans and situations where the sponsor believes that the advantages of the approach may outweigh the disadvantages. Individual insurance or annuity contracts are extensively used to fund small defined contribution plans, Section 403(b) annuities, IRAs, and other individual account arrangements. These arrangements are typically operated on a *money purchase* basis, which does not require the degree of adaptability that a defined benefit plan does.

To explain these funding instruments, and to provide a better appreciation about why life insurers found it necessary to develop more flexible funding instruments, the essential features of the various allocated funding instruments of life insurers will be briefly described in the following sections.

## Individual Insurance or Annuity Contract

### General Characteristics

The prime characteristic of this form of allocated funding is that individual insurance or annuity contracts are purchased on the lives of persons eligible to participate in the plan. The contracts may be held by the employer or by a trustee or custodian acting under the terms of a trust or custodial agreement executed by the employer. If a trust is used, the provisions of the plan are usually incorporated in the trust agreement, and the trustee—frequently an officer of the employer firm—is charged, along with the plan administrator, with the responsibility of administering the plan.

Many insurance companies have developed a master or prototype plan that the employer can adopt by executing a joinder agreement.[3] Under this arrangement, all ownership rights are vested in the trustee or the employer for the purpose of carrying out the

---

[2]*Brock* v. *Shuster,* Civil No. 87–2759 (D. DC, filed Nov. 3, 1987).

[3]There is a technical distinction between a master plan and a prototype plan. See Rev. Proc. 84–23. Master and prototype plans have also been developed by banks, investment companies, and trade or professional associations.

terms and conditions of the plan, except the right of participants to name a beneficiary to receive the death benefit and the manner in which the benefit will be paid. The master or prototype plan may permit the employer to select various options relating to such basic provisions as employee coverage, contributions, benefit schedules, and vesting. A master or prototype plan must be approved by the Internal Revenue Service, which assigns a serial number to it; but such approval does not constitute a ruling or determination on the qualification of the plan of a particular employer who adopts the master or prototype plan.

The plan usually calls for the purchase of insurance policies or annuity contracts similar to the individual policies or contracts offered to the general public. If an insurance policy is used, evidence of insurability satisfactory to the insurer may be required; but the more common practice is to underwrite the plan on a "guaranteed issue" basis, which means that no evidence of individual insurability is required, subject to certain limitations determined by the nature of the group and the aggregate amount of insurance involved. The *no-evidence* basis of underwriting is to be distinguished from the *nonmedical* basis, under which an individual health statement is always required and a medical examination may be requested at the option of the insurer. A minimum number of five lives is usually required for guaranteed issue underwriting, and there may be other requirements, as well. Amounts of insurance in excess of that provided under the guaranteed issue formula will be made available, subject to the normal underwriting requirements of the insurer. If the insurer employs regular underwriting procedures, a medical examination or other evidence of insurability is required for each participant as he enters the plan or becomes entitled to another policy because of an increase in benefits. If the participant who has to show evidence of insurability cannot qualify for insurance at standard rates, the contract may be issued on a substandard or classified basis, with the extra cost being borne by either the employer or the employee, or shared in some proportion. Alternatively, substandard risks may be issued policies at standard rates providing the same retirement benefits but with reduced death benefits, called "graded death benefits." When the participant is not insurable on any basis, a retirement annuity contract may be used in lieu of an insurance policy.

To permit more flexibility in plan specifications and a more liberal underwriting approach, as exemplified by the guaranteed issue device, some companies have developed special policy series for use in connection with pension plans. These policies usually contain provisions especially adapted to the needs of a pension plan and, moreover, are accorded different actuarial treatment from that of policies in the conventional series. Premiums, cash values, settlement options and other features under the contracts must not permit plan benefits to differ by sex. Commission scales are lower, cash values and death benefits are different, and special dividend classifications are created.

The plan may be contributory or noncontributory. In either case, the employer periodically pays the premiums on the insurance or annuity contracts, either directly or through a trustee. Benefit payments are generally made directly by the insurance company, upon certification of entitlement by the employer, plan administrator, or trustee.

## Types of Contracts

**Level Premium Retirement Annuity Contract.** Under a level premium retirement annuity contract level annual premiums are used to accumulate a cash value that may be converted into annuity payments at the time of retirement. The guaranteed cash value under a retirement annuity is the equivalent of the premiums paid less a charge for expenses, accumulated with interest at a guaranteed rate, sometimes reduced by a surrender charge. Frequently dividends or interest in excess of the guaranteed rate is added to increase the cash value.

Upon retirement or earlier termination of employment (or earlier if permitted by the plan) the contract may be surrendered for its cash value or the cash value may be applied to provide a monthly annuity to the participant. The amount of monthly annuity that can be provided for each $1,000 of cash value depends upon the form of the annuity and, if payments are contingent upon the survival of the annuitant, upon the age of the annuitant. It was formerly common practice to have the amount of monthly annuity differ by sex to recognize the longer average lifetime of females, but this practice is no longer allowable under employee plans. The settlement option provisions of the contract specify the minimum guaranteed monthly income per $1,000 applied. Under the provisions of one leading company, each $1,000 applied is guaranteed to provide a monthly life income of $5.61 to an annuitant age 65, with payments guaranteed for 10 years.

Under the practices of many companies, if the annuity rates associated with insurance and annuity contracts currently being issued for immediate annuities under qualified plans are lower than those guaranteed in the settlement options provision of the policy, these more favorable *current* rates are substituted for the guaranteed *contract* rates.

Should the participant die before the contract has been surrendered or applied to provide an annuity, a death benefit equal to the cash value, but not less than the considerations paid, is available.

**Flexible Premium Retirement Annuity.**  Flexible premium retirement annuities function essentially the same as level premium retirement annuities, except that there is almost complete flexibility to vary the premium from year to year. As under the level premium retirement annuity, the guaranteed cash value under a flexible premium retirement annuity equals the premiums paid less a charge for expenses, accumulated with interest at a guaranteed rate, sometimes reduced by a surrender charge. Dividends or interest in excess of the guaranteed rate increase the cash value.

If it is desired to increase the amount of contributions for a participant using level premium retirement annuities, it is necessary to issue an additional contract. But if flexible premium annuities are used instead, the amount of premium under the existing contract is simply increased. While a plan funded with level premium contracts may have many contracts on the life of one participant, only one flexible premium annuity contract is needed. This reduces the administrative costs of both the insurance company and the employer. It reduces the commissions payable because there are fewer first-year premiums with their higher commission rate. Likewise it generally increases the cash values because a lower expense charge is deducted from renewal premiums than from first-year premiums in determining the cash value. The disadvantages of level premium annuity contracts have caused many plans to replace them with either flexible premium retirement annuities or with some other funding instrument.

**Variable Annuity Contracts.**[4]    Under individual variable annuity contracts, the assets representing the contract reserves are invested in a separate account or in a unit investment trust, which in turn is invested in common stocks or mutual funds. The benefits provided by the contract depend upon the investment performance of the underlying assets.

During the accumulation years before benefit payments begin, the variable annuity contract is similar to a mutual fund. The premiums, less an expense charge, are applied to purchase units. The value of the unit reflects the total investment return of the underlying assets, including investment income and realized and unrealized appreciation and depreciation of market values, reduced by a charge for expenses. When benefits become payable, the value of the units may be paid as a lump sum or may be applied to provide a fixed annuity or a variable annuity.

Individual variable annuity contracts may be used in any of the ways that flexible premium annuities are used.

**Retirement Income Policies.**    The retirement income policy is identical with the level premium retirement annuity contracts, except that the former incorporates an insurance feature.[5] Whereas the retirement annuity contract, in the event of the participant's death before retirement, only returns the premiums paid or the cash value, whichever is larger, the retirement income policy pays $1,000 for each $10 unit of monthly income that would be provided under the policy at age 65, or the cash value, whichever is greater. The excess of the death benefit over the cash value represents the insurance element. The amount of insurance protection decreases as the cash value increases and eventually declines to zero when the cash value equals or exceeds the face amount of insurance under the policy. The type of insurance involved is decreasing term, since it is both limited in duration and reducing in amount. After the term insurance has expired, the contract becomes an annuity contract, in effect, and its cash value continues to increase until at maturity the proceeds are sufficient to provide the stated amount of monthly income.

---

[4]Variable annuities are described in more detail in Chapter 11.

[5]Technically, the retirement annuity contract contains a minor insurance element during the first few years after issue, measured by the excess of the accumulated premiums over the cash value of the contract.

**Term Life Insurance.** Term life insurance usually provides a level amount of death benefit protection for a limited period. The term of the policy may be a single year, a period of years such as 5 years, or a period of years extending to some stipulated age such as age 65. At the end of the term the policy expires with no value.

Traditionally the premium remains level during the stipulated period. At the end of the period most policies provide for automatic renewal for a new period of the same length. Under many policies no renewal is allowed to extend the insurance beyond some maximum age such as 70, but after 1986 any such limitation on the right of active employees to continue coverage would violate age discrimination requirements. The premium for the new period will be higher than for the original period, based upon the attained age of the insured. Many policies include the right to convert the policy to another form of insurance without evidence of insurability.

Term life insurance has lower initial premiums than any other form of life insurance, but future increases in premiums result in higher annual premiums than other forms in later years.

**Whole Life Insurance.** A whole life policy, sometimes called a "straight life" policy, provides a level amount of death benefit throughout the lifetime of the insured, with premiums that continue for life. Traditionally the premiums remain level for all years, although some insurers offer a modified form that has reduced premiums for the first few years.

Whole life insurance develops a cash surrender value. If the policy is surrendered prior to the death of the insured, the cash value may be paid in a lump sum or may be applied under the settlement options of the policy to provide a monthly annuity. Some whole life policies also allow additional amounts to be added to the cash value at the time of retirement to increase the amount of monthly annuity that can be provided.

**Limited Payment Life Insurance.** A limited payment life insurance policy is the same as a whole life policy except that premium payments are limited to a certain number of years, although the insurance continues throughout the remaining lifetime of the policyholder. Many pension plans have used limited payment life policies with premiums payable to age 85, 90, or 95. Such policies are essentially whole life policies.

**Universal Life Insurance.** A universal life insurance contract functions somewhat like a savings account plus term life insurance. Premiums paid are deposited in an account. Each month the account is increased by interest and is decreased by an expense charge and the cost to purchase term insurance. The account balance may be called the "gross cash value" or simply "cash value." If the policyholder surrenders the contract, he will receive the "cash surrender value," which equals the gross cash value less any surrender charge. After the early policy years any surrender charge is generally reduced to $0. Some contracts have no surrender charge.

The initial face amount of insurance will be the amount that was applied for, provided the insurance company agrees to insure this amount. Thereafter the face amount of insurance will generally remain the same, except that the policyholder has the option to reduce the amount of insurance at any time. The policyholder may also increase the amount of insurance if evidence of insurability (i.e., good health) is provided.

Universal life insurance offers two alternative patterns of death benefits, often called "level death benefit" and "increasing death benefit." Under the level death benefit method the death benefit generally equals the face amount of insurance. This level death benefit includes the policy's cash value plus a pure term insurance element. Thus, for each month term insurance is purchased equal to the face amount of insurance less the cash value. The cost of insurance deducted from the account is the cost to purchase this amount of term insurance.

Under the alternative method of "increasing death benefits," the death benefit equals the sum of the face amount of insurance *plus* the cash value. Under this method each month term insurance is purchased for the full face amount of insurance, and the cost of insurance is determined accordingly. Since more insurance is purchased under this method than under the level death benefit method, less of the premiums are available to add to the savings element of the policy. The total death benefit will increase or decrease with any increase or decrease in the cash value.

The premium payable under a universal life policy is usually completely flexible. The first premium must be at least sufficient to pay the expense charge and cost of term insurance for the first month. Thereafter the policyholder may pay any amount desired, so long as the amount paid each month plus the surrender value is sufficient to pay the monthly expense charge and the cost of insurance.

Although the amount of premium payable is flexible, a level "target premium" or "planned premium" is usually established. Sometimes the target premium is established at a level that would be expected to be sufficient to maintain the cost of insurance until some advanced age such as 90 or 100 and to gradually increase the cash value to equal the face amount of insurance at that age. However, many other ways to determine the target premium are in use. Thus, for any particular face amount of insurance, the purchaser has great flexibility in determining the premium level. Federal regulations establish a maximum on the ratio of premiums to face amount that is required to prevent adverse tax consequences.

The level of costs and benefits under universal life is controlled by four cost elements:

1.  The expense charge specified in the policy.
2.  The rates used for cost of insurance.
3.  The rate of interest credited.
4.  The surrender charge.

The cost of insurance is based upon a set of rates. The insurance company maintains two sets of rates, current rates and guaranteed rates. The current rates are the rates actually used to determine costs of insurance under the contract. The current rates do not appear in the contract and may be changed by the insurance company without prior notice. The guaranteed rates are rates specified in the contract that place a guaranteed maximum on the current rates. The guaranteed rates are established on a conservative basis. One would not ordinarily expect the current rates to ever rise to the level of the guaranteed rates.

The interest credited is also subject to two rates, a current rate and a guaranteed rate. The current rate is the rate actually used, while the guaranteed rate is a minimum guarantee. The guaranteed rate is specified in the policy. The current rate generally reflects currently available interest rates and may be changed from time to time.

Any expense charges and surrender charges are stated in the policy and are guaranteed.

## Benefit Structure and Funding

Some defined benefit plans and some defined contribution plans are funded entirely with individual insurance and annuity contracts. In this case the benefit structure and funding of the plan are shaped by the characteristics of the contracts used. In other cases individual contracts are used to fund part of the benefits under the plan; in these plans also the characteristics of the contracts may have a significant effect upon the benefit design and the funding of the plan.

**Defined Benefit Plans Fully Funded with Individual Contracts.** In earlier years it was common to fully fund defined benefit plans with retirement income policies, retirement annuity contracts, or both.

The level premium retirement annuity contract may be used to accumulate through the payment of level annual contributions a maturity value at a stipulated age sufficient to provide a life income of a specified amount. The income objectives are usually expressed in units of $10 per month. Under the actuarial assumptions of one leading company, a maturity value of $1,828.18 is needed to guarantee a monthly life income of $10 to a participant aged 65, with payments guaranteed for 10 years. If a participant in a pension plan should be entitled to a retirement benefit of $100 a month at age 65, with 120 guaranteed payments, an insurance company using the rates cited would have to have $18,281.80 on hand when the participant reaches retirement age. Theoretically, it would be immaterial to the insurer whether the $18,281.80 was paid to it in a lump sum at the time of the employee's retirement or was accumulated over a period of years by a series of payments. If, however, a retirement annuity should be purchased for the participant at age 45, an annual deposit of $557.66 with the insurer would be guaranteed to accumulate to the required sum of $18,281.80 at the participant's age 65. At that time annuity payments would begin at the normal rate of $100 per month, unless the participant elects an option with a more generous refund feature.

Dividends or interest credits exceeding the guaranteed interest rate could be applied to reduce the required employer contributions. If the *current* annuity purchase rates are substituted for the *contract* rates stated above, the maturity value of the policies would be *larger* than the sum needed to provide the plan benefits. In that event, the excess maturity value may be credited to the employer to reduce its future contributions under the plan or be applied to increase the amount of monthly pension.[6]

The retirement income policy could be used in the same manner as indicated above for the retirement annuity contract. The only differences would be the slightly higher premiums under the retirement income policy and the higher death benefit.

Retirement income policies were once commonly used as the sole funding instrument for many defined benefit plans. They are no longer commonly issued, but many previously issued policies remain in force, either on a premium paying or paid-up basis, continuing to fund part of the benefits under plans.

The retirement benefits of a defined benefit plan fully funded through individual insurance or annuity contracts are typically expressed as a flat percentage of salary or as a percentage of compensation for each year of service. Under plans funded with level premium retirement annuities and retirement income policies, the benefit formula was often designed to produce units of benefit commensurate with those of the underlying contracts, partly to avoid issuing additional contracts for very small increments of benefit. If the benefit is expressed as a flat percentage of compensation, salary brackets may be set up and the stipulated percentage applied to the midpoint of each bracket to produce benefit units in multiples of $10, or whatever sum is envisioned in the benefit formula.

If the benefit formula provides for a percentage of compensation for each year of service, the projected benefit may be rounded off to the highest, or nearest, multiple of the basic benefit unit.

Under both types of formula, the participant's compensation at any given time is assumed to continue at the same level until normal retirement age, and the premiums or considerations are adjusted to the total anticipated benefit. For example, the initial contract in respect of a participant is issued in an amount guaranteed to provide the monthly benefit that would be payable to the participant should he remain on the payroll at his current salary until he reaches retirement. If a subsequent increase in compensation should entitle

[6]Rev. Rul. 78–56.

the participant to an increase in his projected retirement income, a premium increase is made in the case of a flexible premium retirement annuity, or an additional level premium policy in the appropriate amount is purchased for him. Each such increase is assumed to remain in effect until normal retirement age. If level premium policies are used, over a period of years the trustee or employer may purchase half a dozen or more policies for a single participant, each one, after the original, representing an additional increment to the employee's retirement income.

Benefits payable to a participant upon his withdrawal from the plan prior to retirement are derived from the cash values of the contracts on his life at the time of termination. If the cash values are less than the benefit required to be vested by ERISA, a supplemental amount must be provided by the plan. If the vested benefit is not paid as a lump-sum distribution, the deferred vested benefit must satisfy the qualified preretirement survivor annuity requirements.

Under ERISA, a defined benefit plan funded exclusively with individual level premium insurance and annuity contracts is defined as an "individual contract plan," provided no premiums are in default and there are no policy loans or other security interests against the contracts. Such a plan is not subject to the usual rules defining the required amount of accrued benefit, if the accrued benefit at least equals the policy cash value. In such case, the cash value must be determined on the assumption that there are no premiums in default and no policy loans.[7] Because of the general decline in the use of level premium retirement annuity and retirement income contracts, combined with problems of complying with sex discrimination and qualified preretirement survivor annuity requirements, few if any plans still meet the requirements for "individual contract plans" as defined in ERISA.

The terminating participant may be given the right to continue in force, on a premium-paying basis, that portion of the life insurance policy or annuity contract represented by the vested cash values. Some plans permit the former employee to continue the contract or contracts in full force by paying to the trustee a sum of money equal to the nonvested cash values. To prevent the former

---

[7]ERISA §§204(b)(1)(F), 301(b), I.R.C. §§411(b)(1)(F), 412(i).

employee from converting his vested benefits into cash (through surrender or assignment of the paid-up policy vested in him), some plans stipulate that the paid-up policy will be retained by the trustee, as an earmarked trust asset, until the individual attains the normal retirement age, at which time the contract will be released to the prospective annuitant. Another approach to the same objective is to turn over the vested policy to the terminating employee, but with an endorsement prohibiting surrender of the policy for cash or assignment of the policy as collateral, until the individual reaches the normal retirement date specified in the plan. The endorsement may provide that, upon maturity of the policy, the proceeds are to be paid to the employee only in the form of a life income.

It is customary for the individual contract pension plan to provide for the payment of a death benefit in the event that the participant should die before retirement. Such a benefit is inherent in the types of contracts used to fund the retirement benefits. If the deceased was covered under a level premium or flexible premium retirement annuity contract, the death benefit would be equal to the gross considerations paid, without interest, or the cash value, whichever is greater. The death benefit under a retirement income insurance policy is even more generous. This type of policy typically provides a minimum death benefit of $1,000 for each $10 unit of monthly life income, the cash value being paid if greater. This is a definitely planned death benefit, clearly intended to be supplemental to the arrangement for retirement benefits.

Death benefits after retirement depend upon the form of annuity specified by the plan or elected by the participant. The normal annuity form for most individual contract pension plans is a life income with payments guaranteed for 120 months; but a number of other forms are made available by the insurer for election by the participant, with an actuarially equivalent amount of benefit. Pursuant to ERISA, the actual retirement benefits for married participants must be paid in the form of a qualified joint and survivor annuity, regardless of the normal form of retirement income, unless the participant elects in writing, with spousal consent, to have them paid in some other available form. In the event of his death before his actual retirement date, the policy proceeds may be applied to satisfy the requirements for a qualified preretirement survivor annuity (see Chapter 8).

Various arrangements are made to protect a participant who becomes totally disabled before reaching the normal retirement age.

A minimum step is to provide that the cash values shall be vested in the participant and become available for withdrawal. Retirement benefits would be diminished by any sums withdrawn by the participant. A somewhat more generous arrangement is to include a waiver of premium provision, at an extra premium, in all contracts issued under the plan. This would preserve all accumulated values in the contracts of the disabled participant and, through annual increments to the cash values, would ensure that the participant, if still alive at the normal retirement age, would receive full retirement benefits.

The funding of a defined benefit plan exclusively through conventional individual insurance and annuity contracts is inextricably tied to the premium structure of the contracts. If the plan remains in operation and premiums are timely paid, all participants are assured of receiving all of their benefits in full. Current service benefits are fully funded at all times, and all past service and other retroactively granted benefits are ultimately funded in full if the contracts remain in force. Thus, there is a high degree of benefit security associated with this funding instrument.

Insurance contract plans are exempt from the minimum funding requirements.[8]

Individual insurance or annuity contracts used to fund pension benefits are kept in force through level dollar contributions payable during the participant's continued employment until normal retirement age. While called "premiums" (in the case of life insurance contracts) or "annuity considerations" (in the case of annuity contracts), these payments are derived in accordance with the principles of the individual level premium cost method. The leveling of costs is characteristic of this method, along with the absence of withdrawal assumptions in the premium computations.

As is true of all individual insurance and annuity contracts, the premium and annuity purchase rates of any particular contract are guaranteed for the lifetime of the contract. The plan sponsor knows at the outset the maximum cost of providing the set of benefits in effect under the pension plan as of any given time. The insurance company, however, makes no guarantee as to the rates that will apply to contracts issued in the future to new participants or to current participants who qualify for additional retirement benefits.

---

[8]ERISA §301, I.R.C. §412(h)(2), (i).

Such contracts are subject to the rate basis currently being applied by the underwriting insurer.

All pension plans underwritten by a life insurance company provide for certain credits (actuarial gains) to the employer, which, under the requirements of the Internal Revenue Code, cannot be paid in cash but must be applied against future premiums or contributions. If the pension plan is funded through "participating" contracts, policy dividends will become payable within a few years after issue. Companies that use a special policy series for pension plans set up separate dividend classifications for such policies. This practice is dictated by the special actuarial and underwriting treatment accorded the policies.

Whenever a participant terminates his service with the employer before all cash values have vested in him, the nonvested values are applied to reduce future premiums. This, of course, involves surrender of that portion of the insurance or annuity contract represented by the nonvested cash values.

As under any type of pension plan, the participant in an individual contract pension plan may continue in service beyond the normal retirement date, but the normal retirement benefits must become payable to the participant no later than April 1 following the year of attainment of age 70 1/2, even though he is still working.

The most common arrangement is to defer commencement of the annuity payments until the participant actually retires, subject to the age 70 1/2 limitation. The proceeds of the matured policies are credited with interest, which may be accumulated for ultimate distribution to the retired pensioner in the form of augmented annuity payments or may be applied to reduce future premiums. At actual retirement, the participant may become entitled to a retirement benefit that reflects his attained age and the retained policy proceeds, possibly augmented by accumulated interest. If larger, he must receive a benefit calculated using the plan's benefit formula, but recognizing his service and compensation after normal retirement age in the same manner as service and compensation before normal retirement age. The employer is credited with any difference between the accumulated cash value and the sum required for an annuity for the amount of benefit specified in the plan. This credit is allowed in one sum at date of actual retirement, rather than in a series of annual adjustments.

Flexible premium annuities have sometimes been used as a substitute for individual retirement income insurance policies. The traditional death benefit under a defined benefit plan of 100 times the projected monthly pension will exceed the cash value of the annuity contract. To fund this death benefit, a yearly renewable term insurance contract is issued to each participant. The amount of death benefit under the term insurance fluctuates each year, and equals the death benefit provided for under the plan, less the death benefit payable under the flexible premium annuity as of the beginning of the year. The insurance contracts may be issued to the trust as part of the pension plan, or may be purchased outside the pension plan.

This combination of flexible premium annuity and yearly renewable term insurance separates the funding of the pension and the funding of the death benefit. This allows for greater flexibility in designing the amount of death benefit, compared to retirement income insurance. Death benefits are not required to be a multiple of the amount of retirement income. But if the term insurance is issued to the pension trust, usual rules concerning incidental death benefits apply.

**Defined Contribution Plans Fully Funded with Individual Contracts.** Some defined contribution plans are fully funded through the use of individual contracts. Flexible premium retirement annuity contracts or variable annuity contracts may be used for this purpose. If it is desired to provide life insurance under the plan, a combination of flexible premium retirement annuity contracts and either whole life policies or term insurance policies may be used. It is possible to allow the individual participant to elect what portion, if any, of the contributions to his account are to be invested in insurance contracts, subject to the limitations upon incidental death benefits described in Chapter 8.

**Plans Partially Funded with Individual Contracts.** Some small defined benefit plans and defined contribution plans are funded by a combination of individual insurance policies and an unallocated funding instrument. The insurance contracts used are usually whole life policies, limited payment life policies, or universal life policies, although term insurance is also sometimes used. Uses of such combinations of funding instruments are discussed in Chapter 23.

# Group Permanent Insurance Contract

## *General Characteristics*

The use of individual contracts under pension and profit sharing plans is normally confined to a group of employees that is not large enough to qualify for coverage on a group basis. Many large plans originally funded on an individual contract basis are now being funded through group contracts issued by life insurers or by trusts administered by banks. The group approach that most closely resembles the individual contract approach—and into which some individual contract pension trusts have been converted—is known as the group permanent plan. It originated with group life insurance outside of pension plans, in which area it represented an attempt to provide life insurance protection beyond the working years of the participants. It derived its name from the fact that so-called permanent forms of insurance, such as retirement income insurance and whole life, were substituted for the more conventional group term insurance. Since these contracts developed cash values, which could be used for retirement benefits, it was a logical and simple step to adapt the mechanism of the group permanent life insurance plan to the funding of pension benefits.

A group permanent whole life, universal life or retirement income insurance contract is very similar to the collection of individual insurance contracts of the same type it was designed to replace. Similarly, group level premium annuity contracts, sometimes called group permanent annuities because of their similarity to group permanent insurance, are essentially a collection of individual level premium annuities.

Plans fully or partially funded through group permanent insurance or annuity contracts tend to have the same general characteristics and design features as those utilizing individual contracts. By way of reinforcement, it may be noted that a group permanent insurance contract under a defined benefit plan can be adapted to any type of benefit formula; but it is most widely used with a formula that relates the benefit to compensation, either as a flat percentage of earnings or as a unit of benefit for each year of service. The benefits are normally payable under a life income option with payments guaranteed for 5 or 10 years. Vesting provisions are similar to those found in plans funded through individual contracts and must meet the minimum standards of ERISA.

For profit sharing plans group permanent insurance may be used to replace individual insurance contracts for employees who elect to have part of their account invested in permanent insurance.

Disability benefits can be provided in the form of accelerated vesting, early retirement provisions, waiver of premium, or even disability income payments independent of sums accumulated for retirement.

## Funding

The partial or total funding of a pension plan through a group permanent insurance contract may be determined by the premium structure of the contract like those funded through individual insurance or annuity contracts. Premiums tend to conform to those for individual insurance contracts, except that the expense component may be smaller because of economies of scale and a lower commission scale. Premium and annuity rates are guaranteed for the lifetime of each amount of insurance or annuity. As with a plan funded through individual contracts, certain credits, or cost offsets, are generated and credited against future employer contributions to the plan.

# Group Deferred Annuity Contract

## General Characteristics

The earliest contractual arrangement made available by life insurance companies for the funding of pension benefits on a group basis was the group deferred annuity contract. Few new group deferred annuity contracts have been issued in recent years to fund ongoing plans, but many still remain in force, usually on a paid-up basis. However, many group deferred annuity contracts have been issued to fund benefits in terminating defined benefit plans. While utilizing the group approach, this type of contract is not subject to the statutory rules that regulate the writing of group life insurance.

The underlying legal document of the group deferred annuity is the master contract which, along with the application, if attached, constitutes the entire contract between the employer and the insurer. Each employee receives a certificate setting forth in substance the rights and benefits to which he and his beneficiaries are entitled. This certificate is merely evidence of participation in the plan and is not regarded, in the eyes of the law, as a contract between the employee and the insurer. Nevertheless, the employee is considered to be a third-party beneficiary under the master contract and, as such, can enforce his rights created thereunder.

Since no life insurance mortality risk is involved, no evidence of insurability is required for participation in the plan.

### Benefit Structure

The group deferred annuity contract is designed for the funding and payment of retirement benefits, any other benefits being incidental. For ongoing plans it was best suited to (and was usually used with) a formula that provides a unit of benefit for each year of service. The benefit may be expressed as a flat amount for each year of service or as a percentage of earnings. The typical group deferred annuity contract provided a specified percentage of current earnings for each year of service. For purposes of administrative convenience, a schedule of salary classes was frequently established, and the percentage was applied to the midpoint of the appropriate salary bracket.

The benefits are provided through the medium of a deferred life annuity. This is a type of annuity under which the income payments do not commence until a specified period has elapsed. The typical period of deferment extends from the date of purchase to the attainment of a specified age by the annuitant. A *pure* deferred life annuity refunds no part of the purchase price if the annuitant should die before reaching the specified age, since the rates charged make allowance for anticipated mortality. The *refund* deferred life annuity, on the other hand, returns the purchase price, with or without interest, if the annuitant should die before the annuity payments commence.

When a pension plan that has not been funded with allocated funding instruments is terminated, plan assets are often applied to purchase deferred annuities under a deferred annuity contract for part or all of the accrued benefits. The amount of annuity is the amount that was accrued at the time of plan termination under the plan's benefit formula. The normal form of annuity as well as the qualified joint and survivor annuity must be in accordance with the forms in effect at the time of termination. In addition, the deferred annuity contract must guarantee early retirement benefits, lump-sum distributions, and other options as generous as those in the plan just before termination and must provide for the qualified preretirement survivor annuity. Immediate annuities are purchased under the same group contract for participants and beneficiaries for whom the annuity commencement date has already occurred.

## Funding

**Annuity Purchase Rates.**   For any given group of participants and set of benefits, the amount of the periodic consideration is determined by reference to a schedule of *annuity purchase* rates that determine, for each attained age in the group, the amount of money that must be paid to the insurer for each $1 of monthly benefit payable at normal retirement age under the normal annuity form. These rates reflect assumptions as to mortality, interest, and expenses, including an allowance for contingencies and profit (or contribution to surplus, in the case of a mutual insurer). Mortality assumptions are based on the observed experience of individuals covered under group annuity contracts, with margins for deviations and allowance for future reductions in mortality.

Interest assumptions used in the derivation of group annuity rates to purchase annuities upon plan termination reflect the rates of return that can be obtained at the time of purchase.

An explicit allowance ("loading," in insurance terminology) for expenses, contingencies, and profit (or contribution to surplus) is usually made.

**Experience Accounting.**   All group deferred annuity contracts that were issued to fund ongoing plans and some contracts issued to fund terminated plans make provision for an adjustment in the plan contributions if experience warrants it. In a mutual life insurance company it is usually described as a "dividend," and in a stock life insurance company it is referred to as a "rate credit." Except for the smallest plans, the amount of the refund depends primarily upon the experience of the plan in question. This is accomplished through the maintenance of a noncontractual memorandum account, generally called the "experience account," for each group annuity contract.

During any particular contract year, including the first, this experience account is credited with all contributions under the contract for that year. The accumulated balance, including contributions for the current year, is credited with a rate of interest or a series of interest rates designed to reflect the actual investment earnings of the various segments of the fund, determined by reference to the year in which the monies were invested and reinvested.[9] The account is charged with benefit disbursements under the contract during the current year, as well as with all expenses allocable to it under accepted cost accounting techniques. It may be credited or charged, as the case may be, with a "mortality adjustment," which has the effect of smoothing mortality fluctuations (1) over the years of the particular contract, and (2) among all group annuity contracts written by the company. A "risk charge" is also deducted from the experience account, as a contribution to the insurer's profits or surplus.

At the end of the contract year, the insurer calculates the present value of the benefits that are payable under the annuities that have been purchased and are still in force. The minimum basis for this valuation may be specified in the contract; but the actual valuation may be more stringent than the minimum and may include various contingency reserves. Nevertheless, whatever basis is used is normally applied to all group deferred annuity contracts, regardless of when they were issued.

The difference between the amount shown in the experience account and the contractual liabilities, as revealed by the periodic valuation, reflects the gain or loss under the contract. After appropriate amounts have been allocated to the contingency reserve, and, in some companies, to the reserve for future expenses, the gain, if any, may be returned to the plan sponsor in the form of a dividend or rate reduction. The insurer is under no contractual obligation to pay a dividend, if earned, and the sponsor has no legal right to an accounting.

Strictly speaking, a group annuity contract is not terminated until the insurer has fulfilled all its obligations under the contract. Therefore, in the usual circumstances, the contract will not be fully terminated until the last annuitant dies. If a situation arises, however, under which there is no entity to act as a contract-holder, the

---

[9]See p. 555 ff. for an explanation of the rationale and technique for allocating investment earnings in accordance with the calendar year in which the plan assets were invested or reinvested.

contract may be terminated, and thereafter the insurer's obligations for the benefits purchased to the date of termination will be to the covered employees directly.

## Questions

1.  What are the principal advantages and disadvantages of an allocated funding instrument?

2.  In your opinion would the purchase of individual insurance or annuity contracts by a pension or profit sharing plan be a breach of fiduciary responsibility? Always? Never? Under certain circumstances? Give reasons for your answer.

3.  What is the potential appeal of a master or prototype plan to an employer considering the adoption of a pension plan? Would you expect a large- or medium-sized employer to be attracted to a master or prototype plan?

4.  Is it feasible to fund a money purchase pension plan through individual insurance or annuity contracts? Why?

5.  Is there assurance that the cash values of the individual insurance or annuity contracts used to fund a pension plan will be sufficient to satisfy the vested benefit rights of employees who terminated from the plan?

6.  To what extent are the premium rates and annuity benefits associated with individual insurance or annuity contracts used to fund a pension plan guaranteed with respect to a particular employee?

7.  Describe the advantages of a flexible premium annuity in the funding of a pension plan compared to an annual premium retirement annuity.

8.  What is the principal advantage of term insurance over other forms of insurance? What are the disadvantages?

9.  How is the surrender value of a universal life policy determined?

10. How is the amount of premium under a universal policy determined?

11. Why might an employer choose to fund his pension plan through a group permanent insurance contract, rather than through individual insurance or annuity contracts?

12. What is the principal use of group deferred annuity contracts currently being issued?

13. Explain the process by which a life insurance company determines the dividend or retroactive rate adjustment under a group deferred annuity contract.

# 23 | Unallocated Funding Instruments

## General Characteristics

THE TERM *unallocated funding* is applied to any arrangement under which contributions are held in an undivided fund until used to meet benefit payments as they come due or used to purchase deferred or immediate annuities. There are two general types of unallocated funding instruments: unallocated group annuity contracts, and *trust agreements* with banks and trust companies (or, in some cases, natural persons). There are several versions of unallocated group annuity contracts, but they have certain basic characteristics in common.

The distinguishing characteristic of an unallocated funding instrument is its flexibility. It accommodates any policy or practice permitted by law. Subject only to legal constraints, it provides almost complete flexibility in benefit structure, actuarial assumptions, and funding procedures, and often investment policy as well. Any type of benefit formula can be used, since the amount of benefit to be paid to a participant need not be determined until he retires or terminates with vested benefits. Thus, it accommodates a final average pay formula, with such otherwise complicating features as integration with Social Security, subsidized early retirement benefits, alternative normal retirement ages, and minimum benefits.

Actuarial assumptions can be more flexible than those underlying the insurance and annuity rates of a life insurer shouldering the legal responsibility for paying the plan's benefits and, in the process, offering guarantees that extend 50 to 75 years into the future. Allowance can be made for anticipated withdrawals, staggered retirements, and salary progression, and the mortality and interest assumptions can be set more realistically. Contributions to the plan need not be linked to a presumed, unchangeable pattern of benefit accruals, but can be geared to one of a wide range of actuarial cost methods, with their varying presumptions as to the pattern of benefit or cost accruals. Finally, broad latitude about investment policy and strategy is available through the use of life insurance company separate accounts and the various investment vehicles of banks, trust companies, investment advisors, and mutual funds.

## Group Deposit Administration Annuity Contract

The term *deposit administration* may be broadly applied to any type of group annuity contract under which contributions are not currently applied to the purchase of single premium-deferred annuities for individual participants. Group annuity contracts embodying this concept were made available as early as 1929, but did not achieve much popularity until after World War II, when plan sponsors began to seek more flexibility in plan design, funding procedures, and investment policy than those available under conventional insured arrangements. Its use spread until the deposit administration contract and its variants, the immediate participation guarantee contract and the guaranteed investment contract, became the standard contractual form for the funding of large- and medium-sized plans through the facilities of life insurance companies.

The original or basic deposit administration contract has been modified over the years in an attempt to match the flexibility of the trust arrangement. The integrated package of traditional insurance company guarantees and services has been "unbundled" to give plan sponsors the opportunity to forego the purchase of annuities while taking advantage of the investment services of the insurer. Today, many large plans are using only the investment services of the insurer, typically one or more of the separate accounts (see pp. 494–97 ff.) or a guaranteed income contract (see pp. 497–501). These investment services are provided within the conceptual and contractual framework of the group deposit administration contract, although for product differentiation purposes the contracts may bear distinctive names.

## General Characteristics

The central concept of the *conventional* deposit administration arrangement is that all funds intended for the payment of benefits to participants still on the active rolls of the plan sponsor are held in an undivided account, variously called the "active life fund," "annuity purchase fund," or "deposit administration fund." The monies in the account are commingled with the other assets of the insurer and held in the general asset account. The account is credited with all contributions and interest at the rate specified in the contract; it is charged with the purchase price of all annuities provided for retired participants (and possibly vested participants), and with any ancillary benefits (death, disability, and withdrawal) disbursed directly from the account. No expenses are charged against the account, except for the administration or contract charge, expense assessments against cash distributions, and the expense component in the annuity purchase rates.

As each participant reaches retirement, there is withdrawn from the active life fund an amount sufficient to provide, pursuant to the terms of the plan and the group annuity contract, an immediate annuity for the retiring participant. The purchase price includes an allowance (the loading) for expenses and contingencies.

The group deposit administration annuity contract is usually issued directly to the employer; but it may be issued to a trustee or board of trustees, as under a multiemployer pension plan.

## Benefit Structure

The deposit administration arrangement can accommodate any set of benefits, any type of benefit formula, and any form of annuity. Preretirement death and disability benefits are payable directly from the active life fund and need have no particular link to retirement benefits. Postretirement death benefits are a function of the annuity form under which benefits are being paid. Disability benefits are sometimes paid directly by the employer until the disabled person reaches retirement age, at which time an immediate annuity in the proper amount is purchased for the disabled participant with monies drawn from the active life fund.

Refunds or employee contributions, with interest, because of participant withdrawal, are charged directly to the active life fund. Depending upon the terms of the plan, a terminating vested participant may be given a paid-up deferred annuity in the appropriate amount or retain a claim against the plan to be discharged in the normal manner at retirement.

## Funding

The funding of a group deposit administration annuity contract, unlike that of the allocated funding instruments, is not tied to a premium structure. It can be funded in accordance with any of the traditional actuarial cost methods. The required contributions can be determined by the actuarial department of the life insurer or by an actuarial consulting firm retained by the plan sponsor.

The deposit administration contract sets out a schedule of annuity purchase rates and a rate of interest at which the monies in the contractual fund (the active life fund) will be accumulated, both being guaranteed for the first five years of the contract. Yet the contributions to the plan need not bear any fixed relationship to the annuity purchase rates, other than being sufficient in the aggregate to accumulate a fund capable of providing an immediate annuity in the appropriate amount for each participant as he reaches retirement. Moreover, the cumulative contributions must be no less than those called for under the minimum funding standards of the Internal Revenue Code.

The specified (and guaranteed) rate to be credited to the active life fund tends to be well below prevailing rates, and the annuity purchase rates are computed on a very conservative basis. Moreover, after the contract has been in effect for five years, the rates can be changed from year to year as to future contributions. These rate guarantees are intended to put a *ceiling* on the cost of benefits already accrued and funded. The minimum rate of interest and the rate schedules in effect at the time a dollar is paid to the insurer apply to that dollar regardless of when it is withdrawn from the active life fund to provide an annuity. The actual cost of the accrued benefits is determined by experience, and downward adjustments are made through the dividend process.

These adjustments are made through the maintenance of a memorandum experience account that reflects all facets of the plan's operations. It is to be distinguished from the contractual active life fund which, with the exception of dividends on immediate annuities, reflects only those transactions under the contract pertaining to active participants, up to and including the purchase of paid-up annuities. Like its counterparts, the deposit administration experience account is credited with all contributions to the plan, whether originating with the plan sponsor or the participants, and the plan's proper share of the insurer's investment earnings. It is charged with the actual benefit disbursements to date (not with the purchase price of annuities), with the expenses and taxes allocable to the plan under accepted cost accounting techniques, and with a ''risk charge,'' which is a contribution to the insurer's surplus. The balance in the account as of the end of any accounting period, less the estimated present value of the insurer's liabilities under the plan—including the obligation to provide annuities at fixed rates out of the sum in the active life fund—is theoretically available for dividend or rate credit.[1] In determining such credits, however, the insurer generally applies a ''credibility formula,'' to smooth out mortality fluctuations, and withholds a reserve for expenses and contingencies.

The rate of interest credited to the accumulated balance in the experience account has a significant impact on the size of the dividend or rate credit and, hence, on the cost of the plan to its sponsor. For many years, the standard practice was to credit the account with the net rate of interest earned on the insurer's total investment portfolio (or, in some companies, the net rate of return on all investments other than policy loans). This was a natural, but not necessarily inherent, consequence of the commingling of insurer assets for investment purposes.

The yield on the composite portfolio reflects the condition of the capital markets at the time the various assets were obtained and

---

[1]As pointed out in connection with group deferred annuity contracts, the insurer, in valuing its liabilities, may use assumptions more conservative than those underlying the rate guarantees. This is also true of the liabilities attaching to the sums in the active life fund. If the insurer should conclude that the assumptions underlying its rate guarantees are too optimistic, it might place a higher value on its obligations to active participants than the sum credited to the active life fund. Normally, however, the reserve liability with respect to active lives is exactly equal to the amount in the active life fund, less the portion intended for expense reserves and contingencies.

only by coincidence will be equal to the rate of return currently obtainable on new investments. It may be higher or lower than the new money rate. If the rate of asset growth among all classes of contracts is approximately the same, and if no class is in a position to take advantage of the spread between the composite portfolio yield and the return on new investments, the use of an average rate produces no complications and achieves an acceptable degree of equity among the various kinds of contract-holders. In many companies, however, funds generated under pension plans have been growing at a more rapid pace than the general assets of the insurer; and under group annuity plans, especially of the deposit administration type, the plan sponsor is able to exercise considerable control over the flow of funds to the insurer and may have the contractual right to withdraw funds already paid to the insurer (but not committed to the payment of benefits to persons already retired). When the new money rate is lower than the portfolio rate, as it was during the 1940s, for example, the channeling of pension (and all other kinds of) monies to the insurer dilutes the investment return to all classes of contracts. When the opposite condition prevails, the flow of pension monies to insurers is impeded, the funds that might otherwise have gone to life insurers being diverted to bank trustees for investment at current rates of return. Moreover, funds on deposit with insurers may be withdrawn for transfer to bank trustees.

To deal with these problems and to meet the competition of banks for pension monies, group insurers in the early 1960s adopted procedures designed to credit each block of pension money with the rate of interest at which the funds were actually invested. This approach is referred to as the "new money," or "investment year," method of allocating investment earnings.[2]

## Investment Year Method of Allocating Investment Income

Under the investment year[3]—or new money—approach to allocating investment earnings, the net increase (plus, under one account-

---

[2]See Edward A. Green, "The Case for Refinement in Methods of Allocating Investment Income," *Transactions of the Society of Actuaries* 13 (1961), pp. 308–19, and discussion, pp. 320–52, for a development of the rationale of the approach and a general description of the various procedures that may be used.

[3]Some insurance companies use investment generation periods shorter than a year, reflecting the volatility of new money interest rates within a year.

ing method discussed below, the rollover of investments of previous calendar years) during a particular calendar year in the assets of a life insurer, subject to investment year accountability,[4] is treated as a separate cell or component of the general asset account. The net investment income, including realized capital gains and losses, derived from the assets in that calendar year cell is credited to the cell as long as the assets are held by the company. Each year there will be changes in the asset composition of the cell, because of maturities, repayments, redemptions, sales, and exchanges. This, of course, affects the rate of investment return credited to the cell. The effect depends upon whether these developments are being accounted for in accordance with the "declining index" method or the "fixed index" method.

Under the *declining index method,* the portion of a calendar year cell that rolls over in a subsequent year because of maturities, repayments, redemptions, sales, and exchanges goes into the cell for the calendar year in which the reinvestment takes place. Likewise, the investment income from the assets that remain in the cell will be placed in the successive calendar year cells corresponding to the years in which the income is invested. After each annual rollover, the rate of return is adjusted to reflect the yield on the remaining assets. The balance in the original cell (and all other cells) declines as the portfolio turns over and eventually, perhaps in 20 or 30 years, approaches zero.

Under the *fixed index method,* the amount of assets associated with a particular calendar year cell remains constant from year to year, being equal to the sum originally credited to the cell. Reinvestments arising from sales, repayments, redemptions, and maturities are placed back in the cells from which the rolled-over assets came. Account is kept of the rate of interest at which the rolled-over portions of the cell are reinvested. The rate credited to an entire cell is the weighted average of the rates of return at which its various segments were invested and reinvested. If the trend of interest rates is upward, the weighted rate will rise each year, reflecting reinvestment of the cell assets in higher-yielding securities and mortgages. If the trend is downward, the opposite result will obtain. Investment

---

[4]Not all investment income is allocated in accordance with the investment year method. It is customary to exclude the income from real estate, stocks, policy loans, short-term notes and bills, and bank deposits. In other words, the method is used primarily for bonds and real estate mortgages, which, because of definite maturities and repayment schedules, lend themselves more readily to investment year accounting.

income credited to the various cells in any given year is treated as new money for that year and goes into the cell for that year.

The specific manner in which these two methods allocate investment income among investment years may be grasped from the following simplified illustration of the treatment of the new monies received in one particular year, $T$, monies received in subsequent years being ignored. It is assumed that the investable funds generated in a particular year are received at the end of the year and are all invested or reinvested at that time. In reality, of course, investment income and proceeds from portfolio turnover are being received and reinvested throughout the year, the transactions occurring on the average at midyear. Actual investment year allocation formulas make allowance for the timing of the cash flows. Moreover, the illustration ignores outflows due to benefits and expenses.

*Assumptions:*

Year $T$ New Money, including Investment Income $1,000,000

*Interest Rates Credited to New Money*

| Year of Investment | Year of Crediting | | | |
|---|---|---|---|---|
| | $T$ | $T+1$ | $T+2$ | $T+3$ |
| $T$ | 8.50 | 8.48 | 8.45 | 8.40 |
| $T+1$ | — | 8.60 | 8.52 | 8.44 |
| $T+2$ | — | — | 8.56 | 8.51 |
| $T+3$ | — | — | — | 8.58 |

*Rate of Portfolio Rollover*

| Year of Investment | Percent of Assets Rolled Over in | | | |
|---|---|---|---|---|
| | $T$ | $T+1$ | $T+2$ | $T+3$ |
| $T$ | — | 4% | 5% | 6% |
| $T+1$ | — | — | 6 | 7 |
| $T+2$ | — | — | — | 6 |
| $T+3$ | — | — | — | — |

### Declining Index Method

A.  Interest Credited in Year $T + 1$

$1,000,000 \times .0848 = $84,800

Distribution of Total Fund at End of Year $T + 1$

| | |
|---|---|
| $ 960,000 | Year $T$ Cell ($1,000,000 less 4% Rollover) |
| 124,800 | Year $T+1$ Cell ($40,000 Rollover in Year $T+1$ |
| | plus $84,000 Interest Credited in Year $T+1$) |
| $1,084,800 | |

B.   Interest Credited in Year $T+2$

$960,000 $\times$ .0845 = $81,120      Interest on Year $T$ Balance
124,800 $\times$ .0852 =  10,633      Interest on Year $T+1$ Balance
  Total    $91,753

Distribution of Total Fund at End of Year $T+2$

$  912,000     Year $T$ Cell ($960,000 less 5% Rollover)
   117,312     Year $T+1$ Cell ($124,800 less 6% Rollover)
   147,241     Year $T+2$ Cell ($55,488 Rollover from $T$ and
               $T+1$ Cells in Year $T+2$ plus $91,753 Interest
               Credited in Year $T+2$)
─────────
$1,176,553

C.   Interest Credited in Year $T+3$

$912,000 $\times$ .0840 = $76,608     Interest on Year $T$ Balance
117,312 $\times$ .0844 =   9,901     Interest on Year $T+1$ Balance
147,241 $\times$ .0851 =  12,530     Interest on Year $T+1$ Balance
  Total    $99,039

Distribution of Total Fund at End of Year $T+3$

$  857,280     Year $T$ Cell ($912,000 less 6% Rollover)
   109,100     Year $T+1$ Cell ($117,312 less 7% Rollover)
   138,407     Year $T+2$ Cell ($147,241 less 6% Rollover)
   170,805     Year $T+3$ Cell ($99,039 Interest Credited in Year
               $T+3$ plus $71,766 Rollover from Cells $T$, $T+1$,
               and $T+2$ in Year $T+3$)
─────────
$1,275,592

*Fixed Index Method*

A.   Interest Credited in Year $T+1$

    $1,000,000 $\times$ .0848 = $84,800

Distribution of Total Fund at End of Year $T+1$

      $1,000,000     Year $T$ Cell
        84,800     Year $T+1$ Cell
      $1,084,800

B.   Interest Credited in Year $T+2$

    $1,000,000 $\times$ .084528* = $84,528
     84,800 $\times$ .0852   =   7,225
          $91,753

*(.96)(.0845) + (.04)(.0852) = .084528.

Distribution of Total Fund at End of Year $T+2$

| $1,000,000 | Year $T$ Cell |
| 84,800 | Year $T+1$ Cell |
| 91,753 | Year $T+2$ Cell |
| $1,176,553 | |

C.  Interest Credited in Year $T+3$

$$1,000,000 \times .08407048^* = \$84,070$$
$$84,800 \times .084442\dagger = 7,161$$
$$91,753 \times .0851 = 7,808$$
$$\$99,039$$

*(.96)(.95)(.0840) + (.04)(.94)(.0844) + [1 − (.96)(.95) − (.04)(.94)](.0851) = .08407048
†(.94)(.0844) + (.06)(.0851) = .08442.

Distribution of Total Fund at End of Year $T+3$

| $1,000,000 | Year $T$ Cell |
| 84,800 | Year $T+1$ Cell |
| 91,753 | Year $T+2$ Cell |
| 99,039 | Year $T+3$ Cell |
| $1,275,592 | |

It can be seen that the two methods produce identical results and are, in fact, only different ways of looking at the same investment phenomena. The investment income allocation under both methods depends upon the assets that become available for investment in each calendar year, as depicted under the declining index method. In the example, it is assumed that $1 million of new money is received in Year $T$ and is initially invested in that year. It is further assumed that the monies earned 8.48 percent in Year $T+1$, producing investment income of $84,800. This income and the 4 percent of the Year $T$ new money that turns over in the Year $T+1$ are placed in the $T+1$ cell and, under the simplifying assumptions of the example, become available for investment at the end of Year $T+1$. In the meantime, the turnover on Year $T$ investments has reduced the yield on those assets slightly and the $960,000 remaining in the Year $T$ cell is credited with a rate of 8.45 percent in Year $T+2$, or $81,120 in income. The $124,800 in the $T+1$ cell is credited with a return of 8.52 percent in Year $T+2$, resulting in an allocation of $10,633. The $T+2$ investment income and the rollover from the $T$ and $T+1$ cells are placed in the new cell $T+3$ and the process continues, becoming quite involved when the number of accounting cells reaches 20 or 25 as they have in some companies. With the computer, however, the computations are manageable.

The fixed index method assumes that the original inflow of money remains in cell $T$ with the investment income generated by the funds being placed in the cell for the year in which the income is credited. The problem then becomes one of determining the weighted rates of return to be applied to the various cells, each of which has a balance equal to the original input. The weights come from the asset allocations of the declining index procedure and are shown in parentheses in juxtaposition to the rates of return. The weights are simply the percentage of the cell balance invested at the various rates of return. This process is continued beyond the point where any of the original assets remain in cell $T$. In the allocation formula, that calendar year cell, and any subsequent ones that no longer contain any derivative assets from Year $T$, is assigned a weight of zero. Nevertheless, as long as the derivative assets remain with the company, they will be credited with interest in accordance with this principle.

Any assets acquired by the insurer before the effective date of the investment year method may be credited with an aggregate rate of interest appropriate for a generalized ''year'' or cell consisting of all investments made before the effective date of the investment year method. The aggregate rate represents the average yield on all assets not subject to the investment year method, adjusted to reflect the use of ''new money'' rates for the other assets. Whenever the balance in any calendar year cell becomes unduly small, or the spread between the aggregate rate and the new money rate for the cell becomes significant, the cell may be closed out and the remaining assets transferred to the segment of the general account subject to the aggregate rate. Such closeouts are likely to be in the sequence in which the cells were created. Some companies merge all investment years that originated at least 10 years in the past.

The investment year method can be used to allocate investment income among the major product lines of an insurer (e.g., ordinary life insurance, group life insurance, group annuities, individual annuities, and debit life insurance) as well as among the various classifications of contracts within each major line of business. In New York, if the method is to be used *within* any line of business, it *must* be used to distribute investment income *to* the major annual statement lines of business.[5] To the extent feasible, the same method must be used to allocate investment income to each line and within each line. The companies have generally found it feasible to apply the method within only the group lines and the individual immediate annuity line, where the largest and most mobile accumulation of assets is found. The method is of critical importance to the group annuity line of a company.

The concept works the same way for an individual group annuity contract as it does for the entire life insurance company or the group annuity department of the company. In the case of a group annuity contract, the experience account (or fund) serves as the focal point and is divided into investment year components or cells. Under the fixed index method, the new money for any particular calendar year cell is the net increase in the experience fund for that year while, under the declining index method, the new money is the net increase in the experience fund plus the rollover of in-.vestments associated with the experience fund. A new cell comes into existence each calendar year. The investment income and portfolio rollover associated with the original assets of each cell can be accounted for on either the declining index or fixed index basis, the same procedure being used for all cells—and all contracts. This approach is a feature of the experience rating process and does not affect any rate guarantees in the contract. The total amount of investment income credited to group annuity contracts for experience rating purposes in respect of each calendar year cell should correspond to the investment income available to that calendar year cell for the entire group annuity line.

Having once adopted the investment year method, an insurer licensed in New York cannot revert to the portfolio average method—except upon a gradual basis and in accordance with a plan approved by the New York Superintendent of Insurance six months prior to its effective date. Any deviations from the rules laid down for the investment year method in regulations of the New York Insurance Department require the prior approval of the de-

---

[5]Sec. 91.5(2) of the Regulations of the New York Insurance Department.

partment and must be necessary for reasons of feasibility. These rules, and those of other state insurance departments, are designed to ensure equitable treatment of all classes of policyholders, both old and new.

### Discontinuance of the Plan

The discontinuance of a pension plan funded through a deposit administration contract has no effect on the annuities already purchased, except perhaps to accommodate the asset allocation procedure of ERISA.[6] The monies in the active life fund must be allocated.

If the plan itself is not terminated but is to be continued through some other funding instrument, the plan sponsor may wish to transfer the unallocated funds to the new funding agency. This is normally permitted by specific contract provision, and, even when the contract does not specifically grant the transfer privilege, some insurers may be willing to consider a transfer on a basis negotiated at the time of discontinuance. In either event, the assets to be transferred are subject to a market value adjustment. This adjustment, which may be positive or negative, reflects the difference between the fund balance and the market value of assets purchased with deposits to the fund. This adjustment will usually be negative if interest rates are higher at the time of transfer than at the time of investment and reinvestment, and positive if lower.

### Immediate Participation Guarantee Group Annuity Contract

Compared to allocated funding instruments, the conventional deposit administration contract is a wondrously flexible and accommodative funding vehicle. Yet, many plan sponsors, keenly sensitive to cash flow considerations, find certain features of the instrument objectionable. They particularly object to the insurer's control over the experience rating process through which net actuarial gains get credited to the active life fund or against future contributions. They also object to the insurer's holding a contingency reserve, which defers the crediting of a portion of the cumulative actuarial gains.

---

[6]ERISA §4044.

Finally, some feel that investment returns are unduly constrained by the necessity of maintaining the active life fund in the insurer's general asset account, whose characteristics were described earlier.

To meet these objections, life insurers introduced a modification of the conventional deposit administration contract, variously labelled *immediate participation guarantee* (IPG), *pension administration,* or *direct rated* deposit administration contract. As under the basic contract, the modification—hereafter called the IPG contract—calls for the creation and maintenance of a contractual account for the pension plan into which all contributions are deposited. The account is credited annually with interest at the rate applied to all group annuity experience accounts, the rate generally being determined by applying the investment year method to the insurer's actual investment experience. The account is charged directly with its allocable share of insurer expenses and taxes, with a risk charge and, under the practices for some insurers, with all benefit payments, including those to retired participants. In other words, some insurers do not withdraw from the contractual account the sum required to provide annuities for individual participants, although they guarantee the benefits of retired participants and evidence such undertaking by individual certificates. Under the practices of other insurers, the IPG account is debited, as each participant retires, with the actuarial value (or gross single premium) of the annuity benefits to be paid to the individual. In this case, provision is made (usually through annual cancellation and reissue of all outstanding annuities) for an adjustment in the IPG account that has the net effect of fully and currently reflecting the experience of retired lives with respect to all relevant cost factors.

Contributions to the IPG account can be determined by the plan sponsor in accordance with any IRS-approved cost method and must meet ERISA minimum funding standards. The contract usually requires the plan sponsor to maintain the account balance at a level sufficient to provide full benefits to all participants who have retired, plus a specified margin, on the order of 5 percent. This means that the account must at all times be at least equal to the actuarial present value of all benefits payable to retired participants, computed on the basis of the schedule of annuity purchase rates in effect at the time the participants retired. The valuation is on a gross premium basis to assure that the annuities would be self-sustaining in the event of discontinuance of the contract. The contract usually stipulates that, if the account balance should ever fall to a level the insurer has actuarially determined to be necessary to pay guaranteed benefits in full to retired participants, plus the aforementioned margin (a contingency reserve), the contract will become a conventional deposit administration group annuity contract, participating in dividends in the normal manner. Except for very mature plan populations, this insurer-imposed level of funding is likely to be exceeded by that flowing from compliance with ERISA minimum funding standards.

The practical effect of this modus operandi is that the insurer is not able to accumulate a contingency reserve (except for the margin in respect of obligations to retired participants and the margin implicit in conservative rate schedules), and net actuarial gains are reflected directly, fully, and immediately in the IPG account, rather than through the noncontractual dividend or experience rating formula of the insurer. Furthermore, the plan sponsor may elect to have some or all of the IPG account invested in one or more of the insurer's separate accounts, which are maintained on a market value basis.[7]

Some IPG contracts offer no guarantee as to the rate of investment return or the preservation of principal, while others guarantee principal and provide a minimum guarantee of interest, similar to a traditional deposit administration contract. The IPG account is credited with its pro rata share of investment earnings, adjusted for capital gains and losses (only *realized* gains and losses, if the account is invested entirely in the general asset account). The older contracts contain a schedule of annuity purchase rates, guaranteed against an adverse change during the first five years of the contract, and require that the benefits of retired participants be underwritten by the insurer in the form of annuities. Later versions of the IPG contract omit the requirement that annuities be purchased but include a schedule of annuity purchase rates in the event the plan administrator *elects* to purchase annuities for retiring participants.

Certain "investment only" arrangements, such as the guaranteed income contract,[8] while written in the form of an IPG contract, make no pretense of offering annuities and the contract contains no reference to annuity purchase rates.

---

[7]Separate accounts are described on pp. 494–97.

[8]Discussed on pp. 497–501.

## Trust

### *General Characteristics*

A trust is the most flexible of all funding arrangements. Its flexibility stems from the nature of the trust concept and the fact that the trustee, unlike an insurer, makes no long-term guarantees that must be circumscribed by contractual conditions and limitations.

In essence, a trust fund arrangement is one under which contributions to provide pension benefits are deposited with a trustee—usually a bank, but sometimes a natural person or group of persons—which invests the money, accumulates the earnings, and pays benefits directly to eligible claimants or makes funds available to the plan administrator for the payment of benefits. The trustee also renders periodic accountings to the employer or to other sponsoring organization and to the plan administrator. The rights and duties of the trustee are set forth in the trust indenture: a formal, written agreement between the plan sponsor and the trustee. The indenture may, but usually does not, incorporate the terms and conditions of the pension plan itself.

The plan sponsor remits all contributions to the trustee, whether they originate with the participants or the firm. If the plan is noncontributory, contributions may be paid over to the trustee only once a year, although some sponsors prefer to make more frequent payments of smaller size. If the plan is contributory, however, the sponsor may remit after each pay interval the sums withheld from the participants' paychecks. It is not customary for the trustee to distinguish between monies contributed by the sponsor and by the participants or to record the amounts contributed by, or on behalf of, a particular individual. The employer maintains a record of participant contributions and, if circumstances should demand it, can certify to the trustee the amount contributed by any particular person.

In acting as funding agency for a pension plan, the trustee is subject to the basic principle of trust law that the assets of each trust must be segregated from the assets of all other trusts administered by it and from its own assets. This requirement stems from the fact that the relationship among the parties to a trust is essentially fiduciary, rather than contractual in nature. However, in recognition of the need for diversification of investments, regulatory authorities have granted permission to bank trustees to operate commingled trust funds for the exclusive use of qualified pension and profit sharing plans, subject to certain safeguards. Diversification may also be achieved through investment in mutual fund shares.

The trustee is under legal obligation to invest the funds received under a pension fund. In the absence of any specific instructions in the trust agreement, the trustee would have to invest the funds in accordance with any applicable state statute governing fiduciary investments. It is customary, however, for the plan sponsor to free the trustee from the restraints of the state fiduciary investment statute and to bestow on the trustee varying degrees of authority over the investments of the trust. Many trust agreements give the trustee complete discretion in the performance of its investment function, and the plan sponsor holds the trustee to a commensurate degree of responsibility for the investment results. Such sponsors want to take full advantage of the investment skills of the trustee and to relieve their own officers of the burden of participating in the investment decisions associated with the trust. At the other extreme, some trust agreements stipulate that the trustee shall buy and sell only those investments selected by the plan sponsor or by the person or persons designated by the sponsor, and only on written instructions from the sponsor or such person or persons. In such cases, the bank or trust company is not performing the traditional function of a trustee and, except for holding legal title to the assets of the trust, is little more than a custodian. Some plan sponsors charge the trustee with the responsibility of managing the investment portfolio but require the written approval of the pension board, or some other representative of the sponsor before any transactions can be carried out. A variation of this approach, applicable especially to common stocks, is for the plan sponsor to approve a trustee-recommended list of securities eligible for the portfolio, with names being periodically added and deleted upon recommendation of the trustee. Other sponsors specify the classes of investments to be purchased, as well as the percentage of the total fund to be invested in each class, and permit the trustee to select the specific assets to be bought and sold.

In some defined contribution plans the trustee maintains two or more separate portfolios with differing objectives, for example, a common stock fund and a fixed income fund, and the participant is allowed to designate the proportion of his account to be invested in each portfolio.

Some plans allow each participant to direct the investment of his own account.[9] The plan may restrict the allowable investments to certain types, such as mutual funds or securities listed on a major stock exchange, or it may allow any legal investment. Under this approach the trustee performs only custodial functions. This self-directed approach involves substantial administrative problems.

As has been pointed out, the plan sponsor may delegate the investment function to more than one asset manager. In that event, the trustee may be one of several asset managers, or may perform only a trustee and custodial function, managing no assets itself except possibly overnight cash balances.

The disbursement function is strictly routine and involves minimal discretion on the part of the trustee. No benefits are disbursed, except upon written instructions from the pension board or plan administrator. Whenever a participant becomes entitled to benefits, the pension board or plan administrator certifies that fact to the trustee, along with the amount and duration of the payments and mailing instructions. Some plans provide for the purchase of immediate annuities for employees becoming entitled to retirement benefits. In such event, the trustee, upon written instructions from the pension board or plan administrator, transfers a sufficient sum of money to the insurer named in the instructions to purchase an immediate annuity of the proper size for the retiring employee. In many instances, the pension board or plan administrator, acting as agent for the trustee, disburses the benefits directly, requisitioning from the trustee, from time to time, the funds needed to finance the benefits. The payor must withhold federal income tax from the benefit payment unless the payee has directed otherwise, and in any case must report the amount of payment to the Internal Revenue Service.[10]

Periodically—at least once a year—the trustee accounts to the employer or other sponsoring organization and to the plan administrator for the administration of the trust. The completeness of the accounting will, of course, vary from trustee to trustee; but as a minimum, the report will show the balance in the trust at the beginning and the end of the accounting period; contributions received; investment earnings, reflecting realized capital gains and losses; sums disbursed in the form of benefits; charges against the fund, including

[9]ERISA §404(c).
[10]See Chapter 29.

the trustee's fee; assets acquired and disposed of during the period; and a listing of the specific assets owned by the trust, with such details as date acquired, cost, and current market value. The plan administrator incorporates the pertinent portions of this accounting in the annual report Form 5500 and in the summary annual report provided. The trustee's report will also provide other information needed for any schedules required to be attached to Form 5500.

Thus, it can be seen that the role of the trustee in a trust fund pension plan is normally confined to the management and disbursement of the funds accumulated under the plan. It usually does not participate in the development of the plan or in the various activities incident to inauguration and administration of the plan.[11] Finally, it generally does not provide any actuarial services, either before or after the plan is established.

The trustee under a trust fund plan generally levies two types of fees: investment and remittance. The fee for investment services is the principal charge levied by the trustee. It is levied annually or quarterly and is usually expressed as a graded percentage of the market value of the trust fund. The fee is graduated downward as the size of the fund increases, and may be adjusted to the responsibilities placed upon the trustee. The fee for preparing and mailing checks to pensioners and other benefit claimants is usually a specified amount per check, subject to a minimum annual charge.

The trust agreement usually stipulates that the trustee shall be entitled to reimbursement for reasonable expenses, including counsel fees, incurred in the administration of the trust. This would be in addition to the investment and remittance fees discussed above.

The employer may pay the trustee's fees and reimbursable expenses directly or authorize the trustee, usually in the trust agreement, to charge such items against the trust fund.

### Benefit Structure

The funding of a pension plan through a trust imposes no constraints on its benefit structure not found in relevant law. Any type of benefit formula can be used, no matter how complex. The plan can also

---

[11]Banks in the largest financial centers may aggressively solicit pension funds and actively participate in the development of plans. Some banks employ—or maintain an affiliation with—actuaries to help develop new pension business.

provide benefits that vary, after retirement, through linkage with a specified price or wage index or through changes in the market value of plan assets. The plan may provide for a single normal retirement age, or it may permit retirement without actuarial reduction at any age within a specified range of ages, subject to minimum service requirements. Benefits may be provided in the form of an annuity or a single sum payment. Under trust fund defined benefit plans, the normal annuity form is typically the straight-life annuity, without a refund feature (except for participant contributions). Most plans, however, provide the same optional annuity forms as those available under plans funded through life insurers. Plans are subject to ERISA's requirements concerning provision of a joint and survivor annuity.

Some trust fund plans stipulate that the trustee shall purchase an immediate annuity in the appropriate amount for each participant as he reaches retirement. This practice is most often found when the number of participants is relatively small, and when the sponsor wishes to avoid the risks of providing lifetime benefits out of plan funds.

A participant who terminates before becoming eligible for retirement is usually entitled to a refund of his own contributions, with interest; if he has satisfied the vesting requirements, he has a nonforfeitable right to all accrued benefits. The plan may permit the actuarial value of the vested benefits to be paid in a lump sum or to be transferred to an IRA or to the pension plan of a successor employer (with the latter's consent). Under defined benefit plans, the terminated vested participant is entitled to retain a claim against the plan for deferred benefits.

The plan must provide a qualified preretirement survivor annuity benefit, if applicable, and it may provide other death benefits in any amount deemed "incidental" to the retirement benefit by the IRS. Any such benefits may be paid directly from the trust fund. Disability benefits of any kind can be accommodated. Claims are adjudicated by the plan administrator and benefits are paid from the trust fund.

### Funding

The funding of a defined benefit plan through a trust is identical in all material respects with what occurs under a deposit administration contract of an insurer. The determination of actuarial costs and liabilities is performed by an actuarial consultant retained and paid by the plan sponsor (directly or out of the trust fund), but who acts on behalf of the plan participants by mandate of ERISA. The actuarial assumptions are likely to be similar to those used with any unallocated funding instrument, any differences being attributable more to the judgment and temperament of the actuary than to the funding instrument employed. Any allowable actuarial cost method can be used. As under any form of unallocated funding, the suitability of the actuarial assumptions and the cost method must be attested to by an enrolled actuary, one whose professional qualifications have been certified by the Joint Board established by ERISA.

Actuarial gains or losses are reflected directly and immediately in the level or size of the trust fund. Depending upon the actuarial cost method and other considerations, these gains and losses may be amortized over several years for purposes of determining annual contributions to the plan. For purposes of the funding standard account, actuarial gains and losses must be spread in equal dollar installments over a period of years.

### Discontinuance of the Plan

Whenever a trust fund plan terminates, the assets in the trust must be allocated among the active participants, terminated vested participants, retired participants, and other persons in benefit status in accordance with the priorities set out in ERISA (as previously discussed). Within the latitude permitted by regulations, the plan may establish more refined priority classes than those set forth in the law.

The employer or plan administrator may, of course, terminate a trust agreement pursuant to its terms and transfer the plan assets to another trustee without termination to the plan.

## Combination of Funding Instruments

The funding instruments heretofore described may be combined in various ways to accumulate the funds needed to satisfy the obligations of a defined benefit pension plan. One of the most prevalent blends, often used under small plans, is that produced through the coupling of life insurance contracts with an unallocated fund of assets, often called a "side fund" or "auxiliary fund." Another type of blending is achieved through funding a portion of the benefits through a group annuity contract and the other portion through a trust fund. These combinations of instruments are referred to as *split-funding* or as a *combination plan*.

## Life Insurance and Side Fund under Defined Benefit Plans

The core of a combination defined benefit plan is an individual contract pension trust or group permanent life insurance contract that provides life insurance protection to the date of retirement and accumulates cash values that become a part (usually about one third) of the principal sum needed to provide the retirement benefits. The additional sums required for the retirement benefits are accumulated in an unallocated fund administered by a bank under the terms of a trust agreement or by the insurer on the deposit administration principle. At the direction of the plan sponsor, the unallocated monies held by the insurer may be placed in the general asset account or in a separate account. The insurance contracts contain a provision that permits them to be converted into annuity contracts at (or immediately prior to) the participants' normal retirement dates, at annuity rates guaranteed on the original date of issue, or, if more favorable, at current annuity rates. The sums in the side fund are also convertible into immediate annuities on the same basis as the cash values of the affiliated life insurance contracts. Upon retirement, these conversions may be made, or the policies may be surrendered and all benefits paid directly from the trust in the form of a life annuity or a single sum payment. The plan combines the rate guarantees of the life insurance contracts with the funding and investment flexibility of the auxiliary fund. Funding flexibility is provided, whether the unallocated fund is administered by a trustee or the life insurer, but investment latitude is provided only under a trust arrangement or separate accounts of life insurers.

Any type of life insurance contract that promises protection to the date of retirement, accumulates a cash value, and is contractually convertible into an annuity contract can be used with a combination plan. As a matter of practice, some form of whole life or universal life policy is usually used. The policy may be one of the type available to the general public, or it may be one of a series especially designed for combination plans. The coverage may be made available through individual contracts, if the number of employees is small, or through a group permanent contract, if the number of participants is large enough to qualify the plan for group coverage. Individual contracts may be made available on a guaranteed issue basis, just as under individual contract plans funded with retirement income or retirement annuity contracts.

The benefits under a combination plan are essentially the same as those under a fully insured individual contract or a group permanent plan. Retirement benefits are frequently payable in units of $5 or $10 per month, the payments being guaranteed for 120 months. The death benefit prior to retirement is generally $1,000 for each $10 of monthly life income; and it remains level up to the normal retirement date, unlike the death benefit under a retirement income or retirement annuity contract. No part of the side fund is usually paid out as a lump-sum death benefit—all such benefits being provided through the related insurance policies.

Withdrawal benefits must conform to the requirement of ERISA, and, depending upon the circumstances, may be met out of the cash value of the insurance policies on the life of the terminating participant or out of the policy cash values and some of the monies in the side fund. The amount of vested benefit must satisfy ERISA's vesting requirements, regardless of whether this is more or less than can be provided by the policy cash values. The amount of benefit must be definitely determinable under the plan's provisions, independent of the amount of contributions or assets in the side fund. Contributions to the side fund are not premiums, in the technical sense, but do carry with them insurer guarantees as to the rates at which they may be converted into retirement benefits. The actual amount of annual contributions to the fund is subject to the discretion of the employer, subject to ERISA's minimum funding requirements. Actuarial valuations for the plan may be performed by an actuary employed by the insurance company or by a consulting actuary.

The employer is free to adopt any funding pattern for the side fund that suits its desires and circumstances and meets the requirements of ERISA. The funding usually results in the accumulation by the participants' retirement dates of the necessary funds to convert the policies on their lives to annuities of the appropriate amount or to provide the benefits from the trust. The insurer has no responsibility for the management of the side fund, unless the monies are held under a deposit administration arrangement. If the side fund is invested in the general asset account of the life insurer, the assets are guaranteed against loss of principal and are credited with a guaranteed rate of return, plus such excess interest as may be earned and declared on such assets. If the side fund is invested in the insurer's equity separate account, of course, it will reflect increases and decreases in market value. Under no circumstances is the insurer responsible for the adequacy of the fund.

The purchase of life insurance under defined contribution plans is discussed in Chapter 26.

## Group Annuity and Trust Fund

Split-funding with a group annuity contract and trust fund may be entered for several reasons. The employer may want to take advantage of certain insurer guarantees and the investment latitude of a trust. Some employers believe that insurance companies can earn a higher rate of return on fixed-dollar investments than a bank or independent investment manager but are less effective with equity investments. Annuities may be purchased for retirees at a cost less than the plan's calculated liability for them in order to reduce the plan's unfunded liability and thus reduce the current employer contribution and pension expense. Or split-funding may occur because of a change in strategy, with new contributions being placed in one funding medium and old contributions in another. In defined contribution plans, participants may be given a choice between two or more investment media.

The insurance vehicle for split-funding may be either a group deferred annuity contract, a group deposit administration annuity, an immediate participation guarantee contract or a guaranteed investment contract. The group annuity contract may be issued directly to the plan sponsor or to the trust. If the latter, the contract becomes, in effect, an asset of the trust.

Under a defined benefit plan, the allocation of pension contributions between the group annuity contract and trust may be determined by the extent to which equity investments are to be held. Contributions to the insurer are usually placed in the general asset account of the insurer, where they are invested predominantly in fixed-income securities; contributions to the trust may be channeled almost exclusively into common stocks. In practice, the plan administrator may decide what proportion of each employer contribution should go into common stocks, with the remainder going to the insurance company. Under such circumstances, the payments to the insurer would tend to be residual in nature. Participant contributions, if any, may be paid to the insurer, where they enjoy a contractual guarantee as to preservation of principal and minimum rate of return.

The arrangement may contemplate disbursement of retirement benefits by both the insurer and the trustee, by the trustee only, or by the insurer only. If the latter, as each participant reaches retirement, the trustee may purchase from the insurer holding the other assets an immediate annuity of the appropriate amount. The insurer might or might not provide guarantees on rates at which the annuities can be purchased by the trustee. The normal rate and other guarantees would be applicable to the funds held by the insurer.

Split-funding is primarily concerned with the manner in which the plan assets are administered and need have no effect on the substantive features of the plan.

---

## Questions

1. Explain the basic characteristic of an unallocated funding instrument and identify the various advantages associated with such an instrument.
2. At what time and in what fashion are the expenses incurred by the insurer under a group deposit administration annuity contract charged against the contractual fund? Against the experience fund?
3. Are dividend or retroactive rate adjustments charged against the contractual fund of a group deposit administration annuity contract? Why or why not?
4. Other things being equal, would you expect contributions to a group deposit administration annuity contract to be greater or smaller than those payable under a group deferred annuity?
5. Describe the types of rate guarantees available under conventional deposit administration contracts.

6. Other things being equal, how would the employer credits that emerge under a deposit administration contract compare with those associated with a group deferred annuity contract? Why?

7. Contrast the "contractual fund" under a group deposit administration contract with the "experience fund," indicating among other things which fund would be larger after the first few years of the contract's operation.

8. Is the reserve liability under a deposit administration contract (a) *smaller* than, (b) *equal* to, or (c) *greater* than the active life fund? Explain.

9. Do you believe that the investment year (new money) method of allocating investment earnings is more equitable than the portfolio rate method? Why or why not?

10. Does the allocation of investment earnings to the group annuity line of business on the investment year basis necessarily mean that there will be a lesser amount of investment earnings to allocate to the other lines of business, assuming a fixed amount of investment earnings for the year in question?

11. Contrast the "declining index" and "fixed index" methods of accounting for new money flows under the investment year approach to allocating investment earnings.

12. When, if ever, would a particular investment year cell be closed out under the fixed index approach to accounting for new money flows?

13. Explain the necessity and procedure for making market value adjustments to lump-sum withdrawals from a deposit administration contract.

14. Identify the objectionable features (to some employers, unions, and consultants) of the deposit administration contract that the immediate participation guarantee (IPG) contract was designed to overcome and indicate the extent to which the IPG contract, in fact, achieves the purposes for which it was created.

15. Explain, in terms of the various types of separate accounts that may be established and maintained by a life insurer, how the separate account approach enables the insurer to offer a broader and more diversified range of investment services.

16. For the last several years, many life insurance companies have offered pension and profit sharing plans an "investment only" deposit administration contract that may provide a guarantee against loss of principal and provide a minimum rate of investment return. As a prospective "purchaser" of an "investment only" type of contract on behalf of a qualified pension plan, what potential terms of the contract would you want to consider and evaluate?

17. Describe the range of authority that may be vested in a bank trustee in connection with the investment of the assets of a qualified pension plan.
18. Compare the trust approach to funding a pension plan with (*i*) individual insurance contracts, (*ii*) a group deferred annuity, and (*iii*) a group deposit administration annuity with respect to:
    *a.* Adaptability to benefit structure of the pension plan.
    *b.* Flexibility in determining contributions to the plan.
    *c.* Guarantee of investment results and annuity purchase rate.
    *d.* Probability that the plan participants will receive the benefits to which they are entitled, ignoring plan termination insurance.
19. Would you expect to find an auxiliary or side fund in connection with a pension plan funded through a retirement income policy of a life insurer?
20. What is meant by *split-funding?* What is the dominant appeal of split funding to the plan sponsor?

# 24 | Single-Employer Plan Termination and Plan Benefits Insurance

THERE ARE MANY REASONS why an employer might terminate a pension plan. The entire business may terminate and have no more employees, or a particular facility may be closed at which all of the plan participants were employed. The business may be sold to another firm which intends to cover all employees under its own plan. The employer may decide to combine two or more plans, or may decide to replace the plan with one of another type. The employer may not be able to afford to continue funding the plan.

A number of statutory and regulatory requirements affect whether and how a plan may be terminated, and a system of plan benefits insurance guarantees the payment of part or all of the benefits earned to date under covered plans.

## Internal Revenue Code Requirements Affecting Plan Termination

### Permanence Requirement and Discrimination upon Early Termination

In invoking the right to terminate its pension plan, an employer must consider a series of rulings and regulations by the Internal

Revenue Service. Like most other rules of the IRS, these are intended to prevent discrimination in favor of shareholders, officers, and highly paid employees. In the absence of appropriate constraints, it would have been possible for a firm with a small core of officers and permanent employees to establish a plan, make tax-deductible contributions in respect of all employees for several years, and then discontinue further contributions, with only the favored few participants ever qualifying for retirement benefits. This sort of scheme would have been especially attractive during years of high profits and large tax liabilities.

In order to forestall such practices, the IRS took the position that the term "plan" implies a permanent as distinguished from a temporary program.[1] If a plan were to be terminated within a few years after it was established for any reason other than business necessity, such action would be construed as evidence that the plan from its inception was not a bona fide program for the exclusive benefit of employees in general. If the IRS concludes from all the facts that a plan from its inception was not intended to be a permanent and continuing program for the exclusive benefit of employees in general, employer contributions toward the plan are disallowed as federal income tax deductions for all open tax years. Some of the motivating forces for termination that have been recognized by the IRS as valid business reasons include bankruptcy, insolvency, change of ownership, change of management, and financial inability to continue contributions to the plan.

## Limitation on 25 Highest Paid Employees

Another expression of IRS concern that early termination of a defined benefit plan could lead to discrimination in favor of the highly compensated employees is seen in the limitation upon the benefits payable to the 25 highest paid employees within 10 years of the effective date of the plan or of an amendment increasing benefits under the plan.[2] Before these restrictions were adopted in

---

[1]Treas. Reg. 1.401–1(b)(2), Rev. Rul. 69–25. But see *Lincoln Electric Co. Employees Profit-Sharing Trust*, 51–2 USTC, 190 F 2d 326 (1951).

[2]Treas. Reg. 1.401–4(c).

1956, it was possible for a plan to be established and for contributions to be made which were sufficient only to provide large benefits for one or more highly compensated employees retiring in the first few years, leaving few if any assets available to provide benefits for other employees in the event of early plan termination.

The restriction limits the amount of employer contributions that may be used to provide benefits for each employee who was among the 25 highest paid employees upon the effective date and whose anticipated annual pension exceeds $1,500. The limits become applicable if the plan is terminated within 10 years of the effective date. The limits also apply if benefits become payable to one of the 25 highest paid during the 10-year period, except that they do not restrict the payment of benefits in the form of level annuity payments in the plan's normal form or any other form that provides a monthly income no greater than the normal form. If the limits apply, the amount of employer contributions that may be used for a participant is subject to complex limits, but never reduces the accrued benefit below the amount of benefit that is guaranteed in the event of plan termination.

Every qualified defined benefit plan is required to contain intricate provisions containing the above restrictions, unless it is reasonably certain that the restrictions would not affect any employee or unless the IRS determines that the provisions are not necessary to prevent discrimination.

The $1,500 amount referred to has not been adjusted since 1956, in spite of inflation.

## Vesting upon Plan Termination

Upon termination or partial termination of any qualified plan, whatever the cause, the accrued benefit rights of all participants must vest to the extent funded.[3] Under a defined contribution plan all accrued benefits are funded, so this rule results in the full vesting of all accrued benefits. Under a defined benefit plan this rule results in nonvested accrued benefits becoming vested to the extent that plan assets are sufficient to fund them.

---

[3]ERISA §411(d)(3).

## Nondiversion and Exclusive Benefit Requirements

The trust of a pension plan must be established for the exclusive benefit of participants and their beneficiaries.[4] It must be impossible, at any time prior to the satisfaction of all liabilities with respect to employees and their beneficiaries, for any part of the trust assets to be used for or diverted to purposes other than the exclusive benefit of employees and their beneficiaries.[5] Regulations interpret this generally to prohibit any reversion of plan assets to the employer prior to the termination of the plan and related satisfaction of liabilities.[6]

In a defined contribution plan, the plan assets are ordinarily exactly equal to the sum of the individual accounts which represent the liabilities to participants and their representatives. But in a defined benefit plan it is not uncommon for plan assets to substantially exceed the liabilities. Upon plan termination any excess assets generally may either be allocated to increase benefits for participants and beneficiaries or, if the plan so provides, revert to the employer. If the employer maintaining a plan with such excess assets wishes to recover the excess assets, the only way to do so is to terminate the trust.

## Reestablishment Terminations and Spin-Off Terminations

Some employers, desiring to recover the excess assets under a defined benefit plan but also desiring to continue the operation of the plan, have adopted one of two alternative permissible devices to accomplish this result.[7] One of these is called a "reestablishment termination." Under a reestablishment termination the plan is terminated, annuities are purchased from a life insurance company to satisfy all liabilities to participants and beneficiaries, and the residual assets revert to the employer. Simultaneously the employer adopts a new pension plan, usually identical to the plan just terminated except that it specifies that the benefits determined under the plan's benefit formula will be offset by the amount of annuity purchased under the terminated plan.

---

[4]I.R.C. §401(a).

[5]I.R.C. §401(a)(2).

[6]Treas. Reg. §1.401–2(b).

[7]Implementation Guidelines adopted by the Department of the Treasury, the Department of Labor and the Pension Benefit Guaranty Corporation.

The second device is called a "spin-off termination." Under a spin-off termination the plan is split into two plans, one for retired participants and beneficiaries receiving payments and the other for active participants. Annuities are purchased to guarantee all accrued benefits under both plans. All of the excess assets are initially placed in the plan for retirees, which is then terminated with a reversion of the excess assets to the employer.

In both a reestablishment termination and a spin-off termination, participants and beneficiaries generally receive the same benefits that they would have received if there had been no termination at all. However, all accrued benefits become vested and have annuities purchased for them at the time of the event, resulting in benefit payments to those participants who would have terminated employment prior to vesting.

### Taxation of the Reversion

Any reversion of excess assets to the employer upon plan termination is included in the employer's taxable income in the year received. If the employer is subject to federal income tax, this results in either current taxation or reduction of any tax loss carry forward from prior years.

If the employer is subject to federal income tax, a 10 percent excise tax is payable by the employer on the amount of the reversion in the year in which it is received.[8]

## Plan Benefits Insurance

Inasmuch as most pension plans begin operations with a supplemental liability and additional layers of supplemental liability may be created from time to time by plan amendments, actuarial experience losses, and changes in actuarial assumptions—and since the funding of the supplemental liability is generally spread over a long period of years—there is no assurance that the accrued benefits of a typical defined benefit plan could be paid in full if the plan should terminate. Over the years, thousands of plans have terminated, many with loss of some benefits to the participants as a group. To deal with this situation and to assure participants that

---

[8]I.R.C. §4980.

their vested benefits will be paid, up to a limit, irrespective of the funded status of the plan at the time of termination, Title IV of ERISA established a program of plan benefits insurance, officially entitled "plan termination insurance."

The provisions concerning plan benefits insurance for multiemployer plans, which are described in the next chapter, differ substantially from those for other plans. Except as noted, this chapter describes the provisions applicable to plans other than multiemployer plans. These other plans are generally referred to as "single-employer plans," although in fact they include many multiple-employer plans which do not fit into the definition of "multiemployer plan."

### Administering Agency

The plan benefits insurance program is administered by a self-financed public corporation named the Pension Benefit Guaranty Corporation, hereinafter referred to interchangeably as the PBGC or the Corporation.[9] It functions under a board of directors consisting of the Secretaries of Commerce, Labor, and the Treasury, with the Secretary of Labor serving as chairman. The board of directors establishes general policies of the Corporation, while the day-to-day operations of the Corporation are under the direction of an executive director, assisted by a staff of about 450 people. The employees of the Corporation are nonpolitical government employees and are appointed in accordance with federal civil service regulations.

There is an advisory committee that counsels the Corporation on matters of broad policy, especially the investment of funds.[10] It consists of two representatives of employee organizations, two representatives of employers, and three representatives of the public.[11] The members, who serve staggered three-year terms, are appointed by the President, upon recommendation of the board of directors. The committee must meet at least six times a year and may meet at other times determined by the chairman or requested by any three members of the committee.

---

[9]ERISA §4002.

[10]ERISA §4002(h).

[11]The senior author was the first chairman of the advisory committee and served on the committee for two terms.

## Plans Covered

The insurance program covers, with certain exceptions, all qualified defined benefit pension plans and all other defined benefit pension plans affecting interstate commerce that, for the preceding five years, have in practice met all the requirements of a qualified plan.[12] A plan once determined by the IRS to be qualified continues to be a covered plan with respect to all accrued benefits, even if the determination is subsequently deemed to have been unwarranted or if the plan loses its qualified status because of a subsequent amendment. However, benefits accruing after the disqualification are not insured.[13]

Among the classes of plans specifically excluded from coverage are individual account plans (such as money purchase pension plans, profit sharing plans, thrift and savings plans, and stock bonus plans), governmental plans, church plans that have not elected coverage and meet other specified conditions, plans of fraternal societies to which employers of the participants do not contribute, plans for a limited group of highly paid employees, plans that only provide for benefits or contributions in excess of the limitations in the Internal Revenue Code, plans established and maintained outside the United States primarily for nonresident aliens, plans maintained by a "professional service employer" covering not more than 25 active participants, and qualified plans exclusively for "substantial owners" (a "substantial owner" being a person who owns a sole proprietorship, has more than 10 percent interest in the capital or profits of a partnership, or at least 10 percent of either the entire stock or the voting stock of a corporation).[14]

## Plan Termination as the Insured Event

The objective of the plan benefits insurance program is to assure the ultimate payment of vested benefits, within defined limits, irrespective of the funded status of the plan at the time of its termination or the dissolution of the business entity that sponsored

---

[12]ERISA §4021(a).
[13]ERISA §4022(b)(6).
[14]ERISA §4021(b).

the plan. If one accepts the proposition that the sponsor of a pension plan has a moral and legal obligation to fund the benefits that have accrued to date under the plan, it follows that the insured event (i.e., the event or circumstance that triggers the insurance mechanism) should be the liquidation or dissolution of the sponsoring firm. Under this philosophy, the plan sponsor should continue funding the plan on some stipulated basis as long as it continues in operation, even though the plan has been terminated and no additional benefits are accruing or vesting.

This view of the sponsor's obligation was not originally embodied in ERISA. Instead the act provided that a plan termination would activate the insurance mechanism, even though the sponsor continued in business and perhaps established another plan. This meant that the insured event was *plan termination*. The sponsor and all members of its control group were liable to the PBGC for any unfunded insured benefits up to 30 percent of its net worth at the time of plan termination. If the unfunded insured liability exceeded 30 percent of the sponsor's net worth, the PBGC had to absorb the excess and spread the loss over all insured plans.

Prior to enactment of the Single-Employer Pension Plan Amendments Act of 1986 (SEPPAA) plan sponsors generally had an unrestricted right to terminate a pension plan at any time, subject to providing ten days advance notice to the PBGC. An exception to this applied (and still applies) to plans subject to collective bargaining, which generally may not be terminated or modified during the period of the collective bargaining agreement without the union's consent.

This was a flawed concept. Contrary to sound insurance principles, the insured event was largely under the control of the plan sponsor, an interested party. Coupled with this, the law created an incentive for a plan sponsor to terminate the plan at any time the unfunded insured liability exceeded 30 percent of its net worth. It also created a disincentive to fund at the maximum tax-deductible level, since there was always the potential of terminating the plan at some future date under circumstances that would relieve the sponsor of some of its unfunded insured liabilities. Many such plan terminations occurred, creating large liabilities for the PBGC. Some of the firms that terminated their plans were ongoing employers, and some of these immediately set up other pension or profit sharing plans.

SEPPAA substantially restricted the ability of plan sponsors to terminate plans with unfunded guaranteed benefits, as described later in this chapter. While plan termination is still the insured event, an employer is no longer free to terminate a plan with unfunded accrued benefits except in a "distress" situation. If an employer that is not in a distress situation desires to terminate a plan with unfunded accrued benefits, it may need to first freeze the accrual of benefits and continue funding the plan until all accrued benefits are funded, at which time the plan could be terminated. Thus plan terminations with unfunded accrued benefits are now limited to distress situations.

The Omnibus Budget Reconciliation Act of 1987 eliminated the 30 percent limit on the plan sponsor's liability.

An employer can effectively terminate a plan for some of the participants and continue it with respect to others. For example, the plan can be effectively terminated with respect to the employees at a particular plant or facility and be continued for employees at all other locations if the coverage requirements continue to be met. The IRS may regard this as a *partial termination,* but it is not considered to be a termination of any kind for purposes of the plan benefits insurance provisions of Title IV of ERISA.

### Reportable Events

The administrator of any covered pension plan is required to report to the PBGC certain specified developments or changes in circumstances that might be indicative of a deterioration in the financial condition of the plan and, hence, might be a portent of plan termination.[15] These reportable events are: (a) a loss of qualified status under the Internal Revenue Code; (b) a determination by the Department of Labor that the plan is not in compliance with Title I of ERISA; (c) a plan amendment that decreases the benefits of the participants or discontinues the accrual of future benefits; (d) a decrease in active participants to 80 percent of the number at the beginning of the plan year, or 74 percent of the number at the beginning of the previous plan year; (e) an IRS determination that there has been a complete or partial plan termination for tax purposes; (f) a failure to meet the minimum funding standards; (g) an

---

[15] ERISA §4043, 29 CFR 2615.

inability of the plan to pay benefits when due; (*h*) a distribution from the plan of $10,000 or more within a 24-month period to a "substantial owner," for reasons other than death, if there are unfunded vested liabilities after the distribution; (*i*) a merger or consolidation of the plan with another plan, or the granting by the Labor Department of an alternative method of compliance with any requirements;[16] and (*j*) any other event that the Corporation determines may be indicative of a need to terminate the plan, such as the closing of a plant or the cessation of benefit accruals.

The law gave PBGC authority to waive the reporting requirement for some or all of the specified events and to add new events. Under this authority, PBGC added two new events: (1) the granting of a waiver of the minimum funding standards; and (2) certain changes in the plan sponsor's ownership or financial condition, including a sale of the business or a portion thereof, voluntary liquidation, and bankruptcy. ERISA stipulated that reportable events were to be reported within 30 days after their occurrence; but the PBGC has waived this requirement for most events. There is no penalty for failure to comply with these reporting requirements.

The Secretaries of Labor and the Treasury are under obligation to report to the PBGC any other events or developments that raise questions about the soundness of the plan.

## Liability of a Plan Sponsor to PBGC

To foster a sense of prudence and discipline on the part of the plan sponsor; in setting benefit levels and meeting the cost of accruing benefit credits; to discourage termination of underfunded plans; to help finance the insurance program; and to provide accrued benefits in excess of those insured; ERISA requires that the sponsor of a terminated single-employer plan pay the PBGC the amount of any unfunded benefit liabilities.[17]

**General Nature and Determination of the Liability.**　The obligation to reimburse the PBGC attaches not only to the plan sponsor

---

[16]The PBGC does not consider a change in the plan's funding instrument or funding agency a reportable event.

[17]ERISA §4062.

but to all members of its controlled group, as defined in the law. In fact, the plan sponsor and the members of its controlled group are *jointly* and *severally* liable for any such obligation, so that each can be held responsible for the entire liability. The amount of the potential obligation is the excess of (1) the actuarial value of the plan's accrued benefits as of the date of plan termination over (2) the fair value of the plan's assets on the date of plan termination.

The plan sponsor's obligation to the PBGC is payable in a lump sum upon demand from PBGC, except that any obligation in excess of 30 percent of the sponsor's net worth is to be paid under commercially reasonable terms prescribed by the PBGC. However, by written agreement with the PBGC, the firm can arrange to meet the obligation over a period of years. Terms of the installment settlement vary with the circumstances.[18]

The net worth of the plan sponsor and controlled group members is determined as of a date chosen by the PBGC within a corridor bounded by the date of plan termination and a date not more than 120 days prior to plan termination. The law requires the PBGC to determine net worth on whatever basis that best reflects, in its judgment, the current status of the firm's operations and economic prospects. It is computed without taking the PBGC claim into account. It is increased by any asset transfers made by the plan sponsor prior to plan termination, and by any assumption of liabilities deemed by PBGC to have been improper. Since the balance sheet net worth is greatly affected by the methods and bases used by the firm in valuing its assets and liabilities, PBGC does not use balance sheet values. If the firm is in process of dissolution, the net worth may be determined in terms of its liquidation value.

In effect, the employer liability provisions of ERISA supersede certain contract law principles that allowed a plan sponsor to limit its financial obligation for pensions to the amounts already contributed to the plan. Thus, an exculpatory provision in the plan document limiting the employer's liability under the plan, or a provision in a collective bargaining agreement obligating an employer to contribute only specified amounts to the plan, does not modify, substitute for, or extinguish the employer's statutory liability to the PBGC under Title IV of ERISA. Moreover, discharge

---

[18]ERISA §4067.

of an employer's obligation to the PBGC does not override any contractual rights that the plan participants may have against the employer for benefits payable but not insured by the PBGC. For example, there may be contractual rights to vested noninsured benefits under a collective bargaining agreement. These benefit rights would normally be treated as general unsecured claims in a Title 11 or a similar state proceeding.

If two or more sponsors that are not under common control have contributed to the same multiple-employer plan (other than a multiemployer plan) that terminates, ERISA provides a method of allocating the liability to the PBGC among the employers.[19] If an employer withdraws from such a plan while the plan continues, the withdrawing employer may be required to place in escrow the amount that its liability would have equalled had the plan then terminated.[20] The escrowed amount is to be held to offset any liability that the plan incurs in the event it is terminated during the following five years and is returned to the withdrawing employer at the end of the five years if there has been no plan termination in the interim. In lieu of the escrow a withdrawing employer may post bond for 150 percent of the amount required to be escrowed. As an alternative in some situations, the plan may be treated as split into two plans with the plan of the withdrawing employer being treated as terminated.

### PBGC Claim against the Assets of the Plan Sponsor.

The PBGC must have legal recourse against the assets of a plan sponsor or controlled group member with primary or secondary liability if it is to enforce its claim for reimbursement in respect of benefits paid by the PBGC on behalf of a terminated plan. The legal status of that claim is important to all parties concerned, especially the other creditors of the plan sponsor or other controlled group members, both current and potential. Through the years, there has been concern in various quarters over the impact of PBGC's potential claim on the availability of credit to the sponsor of defined benefit plans. This impact is affected not only by the potential magnitude of the claim but also by its relationship to the claims of other creditors in insolvency or bankruptcy proceedings.

---

[19]ERISA §4064.
[20]ERISA §4063.

Conceptually, the PBGC could be treated as a preferred creditor vis-a-vis other unsecured creditors, a general creditor, or a sub-ordinated creditor—one whose claim is subordinate to those of all other creditors but superior to those of preferred and common shareholders. As a preferred creditor, the PBGC would have a prior claim to any assets available after satisfaction of the claims of secured creditors and other unsecured creditors with a higher priority. As a general creditor, it could seek an active role on the creditors' committee in the proceedings but would have to settle for its pro rata share of the assets available to that class of creditors. As a subordinated creditor, it would have only a remote chance of realizing on its claim in reorganization or bankruptcy proceedings and would have minimal influence in trying to protect its interests in competition with other creditors.

If a plan sponsor or its controlled group does not pay or make acceptable arrangements to pay its liability to the PBGC, other than any liability exceeding 30 percent of the sponsor's net worth, the PBGC automatically acquires a lien against all the assets and property rights of the controlled group.[21] The lien remains in effect for six years after termination of the plan, or for the duration of any collection agreement entered into between the plan sponsor (or members of its controlled group) and the PBGC. During that period, PBGC may bring a civil suit in a U.S. district court to collect its claim or to enforce its lien upon the plan sponsor's property. In the event that the plan sponsor becomes insolvent or bankrupt before liquidating its debt to the PBGC, the latter's claim is treated as a judgment lien, with a priority equal to that of a judgment lien of the federal government for unpaid taxes. The only claims with higher priority are those of secured creditors (only with respect to the collateral), mechanics' liens, and a few other special claims.

The PBGC may have other types of claims against the plan sponsor or the plan, such as unpaid contributions and expenses connected with the takeover of the terminated plan. Unpaid contributions are generally treated as *wages due,* which enjoy a limited priority, the balance being general unsecured creditor claims. Any claims for unpaid contributions that arise after the plan sponsor files a bank-

[21]ERISA §4068.

ruptcy petition are accorded the status of *administrative expenses,* a priority category. Expenses incurred by the PBGC in taking over a terminated plan are treated as an offset to the plan assets and, thus, are recovered directly. The offset, however, increases the asset insufficiency, which the PBGC may not be able to recover because of the net worth limitation, the sponsor's insolvency, or other reasons.

### Benefits Insured

The law provides that the PBGC shall guarantee payment of all basic benefits of a terminated pension plan, subject to certain limitations, that had become nonforfeitable (or vested) by the terms of the plan. Since all accrued benefits, to the extent funded, vest upon plan termination by virtue of the termination, it is significant that the insurance coverage is limited to benefits that had vested prior to termination through satisfaction of the service (or age and service) requirements of the plan. Basic benefits so vested are insured, with limitations, even though they achieved that status by plan provisons more liberal than those required by the minimum vesting standards of ERISA.

**Basic versus Nonbasic Benefits.**   The Corporation is authorized to provide insurance coverage for both *basic* and *nonbasic* benefits. Coverage of basic benefits is mandatory, if the benefits are otherwise eligible for protection, whereas insurance of nonbasic benefits is optional with the Corporation. The two types of coverage are to be kept separate and distinct, from a financial standpoint, through the use of separate trust, or guaranty, funds.[22] The law does not define the terms *basic* and *nonbasic,* leaving the matter to regulations.

In a nutshell and as an oversimplification, the PBGC has defined a basic benefit as any type of retirement benefit that was nonforfeitable on the date of plan termination, and any death, survivor, or disability benefit that was owed or was in payment status at date of plan termination.[23] For this purpose, a benefit is nonforfeitable if, by the date of plan termination, the participant has met all of

---

[22]ERISA §4005(a).
[23]29 CFR §§2618.2, 2613.3.

the plan's substantive conditions for entitlement.[24] The fact that a participant had not applied for his benefit or had not completed a waiting period (for a disability benefit, for example) would not be disqualifying. A benefit is not considered *forfeitable* because entitlement ceases if and when the recipient remarries, reaches a specified age, or recovers from disability, although the PBGC would treat the recipient's continued eligibility to receive guaranteed benefits in accordance with the terms of the plan. Moreover, by an explicit provision in ERISA, a retirement benefit is not considered *forfeitable* merely because it can be suspended if the participant returns to active employment with the employer or, in the case of a multiemployer plan, if he returns to work in the same industry, trade, or craft, and in the same geographic area covered by the plan.[25]

The Corporation regards as "basic" only that portion of the normal retirement benefit payable in level monthly installments for the remaining lifetime of the participant.[26] This excludes lump-sum and special supplemental monthly benefits provided under some plans to encourage early retirement or to ease the participant's transition from an active to a retired status. Benefits earmarked for the payment of medical insurance premiums or other purposes are not basic benefits, unless the participant may elect to take them in the form of retirement benefits payable to himself. An otherwise basic benefit is deemed to satisfy the requirement that the basic benefit be one payable in level installments, even though the level of payments may change at some future time as a result of (1) the application of a Social Security, Railroad Retirement, or workers' compensation offset; (2) a joint and survivor annuity option; or (3) cost-of-living adjustments or other increases for retired participants.

A basic benefit may reflect cost-of-living adjustments for active, terminated vested, and retired participants effective prior to termination of the plan. These adjustments may have been on an ad hoc basis or in accordance with a formula escalation factor or a specified cost-of-living index. Such benefit increases that have become effective pursuant to plan provisions prior to termination of

---

[24] 29 CFR §2613.6.
[25] ERISA §203(a)(3)(B), I.R.C. §411(a)(3)(B).
[26] 29 CFR §§2613.2, 2613.4.

the plan are entitled to insurance protection, subject to the phase-in rules; but any increases becoming effective after the termination date are not insurable.

The insurance payments of the Corporation are to be made in the form of monthly benefits, even though the terminated plan may have made provision for the participant to take some or all of his normal retirement benefit in a lump sum.[27] As an exception, the PBGC will pay in a lump sum the value of a participant's guaranteed benefit attributable to his mandatory employee contributions, if the participant so elects and if such payment is consistent with the plan's provisions. The benefit may be paid under any of the annuity forms made available by the Corporation, including joint and survivor annuity options, provided the election is made a specified period prior to retirement. The benefits under the optional annuity forms are to be the actuarial equivalent of the normal annuity form, as computed by the Corporation, using its own mortality and interest assumptions.[28] This principle is to be applied even though one or more of the optional annuity forms made available by the terminated plan were subsidized by the employer. However, any elections of optional annuity forms executed by participants prior to termination of the plan will be honored by the Corporation, the benefit payments being those that would have been made under the terms of the plan.

The normal retirement benefit is regarded as a basic benefit by the Corporation regardless of the age of the participant at the time the income commences. Thus, if the plan provides that the full amount of accrued retirement benefits will become payable upon the participant's retirement after 30 years of service, irrespective of his attained age, such benefits of participants who have elected early retirement prior to plan termination will be insured by the Corporation, up to the applicable limits. The same is true if eligibility for full, unreduced benefits (for service rendered to date of retirement) is conditioned on the total of the participant's attained age and years of credited service equaling some specified number, such as 90. Under both of these types of eligibility requirements, retirement with full, unreduced benefits may (and probably will)

[27]29 CFR §2613.8.
[28]29 CFR §2621.4(a).

take place before age 65, which is regarded by many as a standard normal retirement age. It is worth noting in this regard that the limit on the amount of basic monthly benefits that can be insured (discussed below) is actuarially reduced if the normal retirement benefit becomes payable before age 65. Thus, persons retiring before age 65 may suffer a reduction in insured benefits.

Some negotiated plans provide that, if an employee loses his job because of the closing of a plant or facility, he will be permitted to retire with full, unreduced benefits for service rendered to date with less service or at an earlier age than employees who remain in employment until they satisfy the other eligibility requirements. The Corporation would not regard a benefit payable under these circumstances as a basic benefit unless it was in pay status at the time of plan termination and, even then, the amount insured could not exceed the dollar amount of basic retirement benefits accrued for normal age retirement.

The Corporation regards as basic benefits all early retirement benefits in pay status payable in level monthly installments for the remaining lifetime of the participant, even though they may be greater than the actuarial equivalent of the normal retirement benefit.[29] It does not insure as basic benefits temporary supplemental benefits paid from early retirement date to normal retirement date, or for some other temporary period. An exception is made for benefits payable under the so-called Social Security adjustment option, in connection with which the participant's normal retirement benefit is permanently reduced to provide a temporary life annuity during the early retirement period equal to the estimated Social Security benefit payable at age 65.

In all these cases, the benefits must be vested and nonforfeitable by the terms of the plan before they become insurable. Except for the qualified preretirement survivor annuity benefit, rights to death and disability benefits that have not yet matured are not generally regarded as vested, even though the participant has become vested in his retirement benefits. Thus, if a vested participant dies or becomes disabled after leaving the service of the employer, no benefits other than the qualified preretirement survivor annuity are

---

[29]The Corporation does not insure any portion of early retirement benefits in excess of the dollar amount of basic retirement benefit accrued for normal age retirement.

payable. The PBGC has concluded that other preretirement death and disability benefits not in payment status before termination of the plan are not basic benefits and are not currently entitled to insurance protection unless the benefit constitutes a return of the employee's mandatory contributions to the plan. If, at the time of the plan termination, there are pending death claims payable in a lump sum, the Corporation will honor such claims and pay them in a lump sum.

Nonbasic benefits would presumably include death and disability benefits not treated as basic benefits, monthly retirement benefits in excess of the amount that can be insured as basic benefits, medical insurance premiums and benefits, and other more unusual benefits that might emerge from the collective bargaining process. Thus far, the PBGC has made no arrangements to insure nonbasic benefits and there is no indication that it intends to do so.

**Limitation on Amount of Monthly Benefits.** ERISA imposes a limit on the amount of basic benefit that can be insured by the PBGC. The statutory ceiling for single employer plans is linked to changes in the Social Security contribution and benefit base. Originally $750 per month, the limit had risen to $1,909.09 by 1988.[30] The benefit to which the ceiling applies is a single life annuity (popularly known as a "straight-life annuity") commencing at age 65. If the benefit is payable at a lower age than 65, or in any annuity form other than the straight-life annuity, the limit is actuarially reduced on the basis of actuarial factors prescribed from time to time by the PBGC. The applicable reduction can be substantial in respect of disability income benefits, survivor income benefits, or retirement benefits payable after a stipulated period of service, such as 30 years, irrespective of attained age, since recipients of such benefits may be young at plan termination. The limit is not actuarially *increased* when the participant retires at an age later than 65.

The limit relates to the basic benefits that the PBGC is permitted to guarantee in respect of any one individual, regardless of the number of plans in which benefits might have been earned.[31] The

---

[30]ERISA §4022(b)(3)(B).
[31]29 CFR §2621.3(b).

benefit ceiling in effect on the date the plan terminates is controlling, irrespective of when the participant begins to receive benefits.

In no event can the guaranteed benefit in respect of a given participant be greater than this average gross income from the plan sponsor during the five consecutive years of highest earnings (or, if the period is shorter, the time during which he was an active participant).[32]

**Phase-In of Insurance Coverage.**   To make the plan benefits insurance program less vulnerable to abuse, Congress stipulated that *full* coverage of basic benefits was to be available only after the benefits have been in effect for five years or more. This restriction was aimed not only at newly established plans but also at amendments to existing plans that increase benefits. However, provision was made for the coverage of single employer plan benefits to take effect in graduated steps during the five-year period, unless the Corporation finds substantial evidence that the plan was not terminated for a reasonable business purpose but rather for the purpose of taking advantage of the insurance. Specifically, the law states that 20 percent of the basic benefit, up to the specified limit, shall be insured at the end of the first year, with an additional 20 percent of the benefit becoming insured at the end of each subsequent year until full coverage is available. The first 20 percent of coverage becomes effective 12 months after the later of the adoption date or effective date of the plan (or plan amendment). The successive increments become effective each 12 months thereafter.

To prevent too rapid a phase-in of benefits that exceed the statutory maximum guarantee ($1,909.09 in 1988), the amount of coverage phased in each year is the lesser of 20 percent of the new benefit (or benefit increase) or 20 percent of the statutory maximum guarantee.[33] For example, a plan is amended July 1, 1986, to increase a straight-life annuity commencing at age 65 from $1,700 to $2,000 per month and is terminated two years later on July 1, 1988. The increase guaranteed is $83.64 (40 percent of the excess of $1,909.09 over $1,700).

The law provides a more rapid phase-in of the guarantee of small benefits (under $100 per month) by insuring $20 of the benefit each

---

[32]ERISA §4022(b)(3)(A).

[33]ERISA §4022(b)(7), 29 CFR §2621.5–6.

year, irrespective of the 20 percent limitation, until the full benefit is guaranteed. Thus, a benefit increase of $50 per month would be fully insured after three years.

The law provides a special phase-in rule for substantial owners because they have the greatest incentive to abuse the program. The insurance coverage of the basic benefits of a substantial owner is phased in at the rate of 1/30th per year, without application of the minimum benefit of $20 per month discussed above. This rule applies not only to the benefits of a newly established plan but also to those provided by a plan amendment. The insurance coverage of each set of newly created benefits must be phased in over a 30-year period beginning with the date of the amendment (or, if later, the effective date of the increase).[34]

If a new pension plan covers substantially the same persons that an earlier plan covered and provides essentially the same benefits, the years of existence of the predecessor plan are added to those of the successor plan in determining the insurance coverage of any particular set of benefits.[35]

Any increase in the value of the plan benefit, such as that arising out of a liberalization of vesting or a reduction in the normal retirement age, is subject to the same phase-in rules as those applicable to an explicit benefit increase. Benefits provided under a plan provision calling for automatic cost-of-living adjustments are subject to the phase-in feature, as are ad hoc adjustments in the benefits of retired persons.

### Allocation of Single Employer Plan Assets

Since not all benefits under a pension plan are insured, it was necessary for ERISA to provide a procedure for allocating the assets of a single employer plan that has become subject to an insured event between the benefits that are insured and those that are not insured. The allocation procedure is therefore important to plan participants since it can affect the amount of benefits they receive. It also is important to both the PBGC and the employer, and they both profit from maximizing the proportion of assets going

---

[34]29 CFR §2621.7.
[35]ERISA §§4021(a), 4022(b), PBGC Opinion Letter 86–9.

to insured benefits. The more assets that are assigned to insured benefits, the smaller the amount of PBGC resources that must be applied to the payment of insured benefits. On the other hand, the more plan assets that are allocated to insured benefits, the smaller the amount of noninsured benefits that will be paid from plan assets.

**Priority Classes.**   It might have been assumed that the law would give first priority against the plan assets to insured benefits. However, Congress decided that the benefits payable to participants who had been retired for at least three years on the date of the insured event, or could have been retired for three years, should be given priority over employer-financed benefits of other insured participants, even for amounts in excess of the insurance limit. This meant that some uninsured benefits were to have a higher priority than some insured benefits, making it necessary to establish priority classes even among the insured benefits.

The statutory allocation formula establishes six classes of benefits, in descending order of priority, with the assets for the first four classes being allocated on a pro rata basis, if necessary, within each successive class.[36] The benefit classes are as follows:

**1.**   Benefits attributable to voluntary employee contributions. For participants not yet retired, the claim would be for assets in an amount equal to the balances in the individual accounts. These benefits are not insured by the PBGC, since they are almost invariably provided on a money purchase basis. Because they have first claim to all plan assets, their payment is virtually assured.

**2.**   Benefits attributable to mandatory employee contributions, taking into account those paid out before the date of the insured event.

**3.**   Benefits of a participant or beneficiary that had been in a pay status for at least three years on the date of the insured event, and the benefits that would have been in pay status for three or more years if the participants had retired with normal benefits three years prior to the insured event. In each case, the priority attaches only to the lowest benefit level under the plan during the five years prior to retirement; and for those already retired, the priority attaches only to the lowest benefit level of the three-year period of

---

[36]ERISA §4044.

benefit payments. These restrictions are designed to withhold this high priority from general benefit increases provided within five years prior to the insured event and from participants who become eligible to begin receiving benefits within the three-year period preceding the insured event. Within the limits described, this priority attaches to all benefits falling within this class, irrespective of the amount of the monthly benefit. Thus, uninsured benefits may enjoy this priority.

**4.** All other benefits up to the applicable limitations that would be insured but for the aggregate limitation of $750 (indexed) per month on insured benefits from two or more plans and the special limitation on the coverage of a "substantial owner." The waiver of these special limitations has the effect of giving certain uninsured benefits a priority over other uninsured benefits.

**5.** All other vested benefits, meaning the *uninsured* vested benefits not falling within one of the higher-priority classes. Assets allocated to this category must be applied first to benefits offered by the plan five years before the occurrence of the insured event and then to benefits added later, in the order in which they were made available.

**6.** All other benefits under the plan.

A benefit that could be placed in more than one priority category, such as the vested benefit of a person who retired four years before the insured event, is assigned the highest priority for which it qualifies and is not included in more than one category. A PBGC regulation permits plans to provide for limited subclasses within each priority category—advanced age, seniority, and disability being permissible bases for preference in asset allocation.[37]

The statute is silent about the allocation of plan assets between the insured and uninsured benefits of a participant whose benefit claims fall within one of the priority classes. Obviously, the financial burden on the PBGC would be minimized if the insured benefits were to be given first claim to the plan assets. If the plan assets were to be sufficient to cover the insured portion of the participant's benefits, there would be no drain on the Corporation's resources. By the same token, the proportion of the participant's benefit claims that would be satisfied by the combination of plan assets and in-

---

[37]29 CFR §2618.17.

surance payments would be maximized if the uninsured portion of his benefits were to be given first claim to the assets. ERISA requires plan assets to be prorated among participants on the basis of the value of their total insured and uninsured benefits in the category. The PBGC has made a policy decision that the assets allocated within any category to a particular participant are assigned first to the participant's insured benefits in the category, and the remaining assets are assigned to the participant's uninsured benefits in the category.

The statutory formula supersedes the allocation procedure set forth in the plan, except possibly for any assets that might remain after satisfaction of all vested benefits. The superimposed procedure applies to previously allocated assets, as well as to assets still unallocated at time of termination. In that connection, the amended law states that life insurance or annuity contracts issued by life insurers are plan assets and, as such, are subject to the statutory allocation formula. This could cause a life insurance company to have to reduce or cancel some life insurance and annuity contracts.

**Recapture of Benefit Payments.** Not only does the statutory allocation formula give priority, with the exceptions noted, to insured benefits, including assets previously allocated, but the trustee is authorized to recapture from a retired participant certain payments made during any 12-month period within the three years prior to the occurrence of the insured event.[38] The intent of this provision is to permit the trustee to recover any amounts substantially in excess of the stipulated limits paid out by the plan administrator in the form of a lump sum or in accelerated pension payments in anticipation of the insured event. There is no recapture threat if the participant's entire interest in the plan is taken in the form of a conventional life annuity, but the amount of future annuity payments is subject to reduction in accordance with the asset allocation rules. If benefits were not paid as a life annuity, the trustee may recover any excess of the actual payments during the three years over the sum of (1) the payments that would have been paid in the life annuity form (or if larger, the lesser for each 12-month period of $10,000 or the actual payments) plus (2) the present value

---

[38]ERISA §4045.

at the time of termination of the participant's future guaranteed payments that would have been payable if benefits were paid as a life annuity.

The trustee is not authorized to recover any amounts paid by reason of the death or disability of the participant, provided that the disabled participant is also receiving disability benefits under the Social Security program. The PBGC is authorized to waive any recovery that would cause substantial economic hardship, which, of course, could increase the plan sponsor's liability for unfunded insured benefits.

### Plan Termination Initiated by the Plan Sponsor

The virtually unlimited right of plan sponsors to terminate plans contributed to very large liabilities being placed upon the PBGC, creating substantial deficits in the benefits insurance program. In order to ameliorate the situation SEPPAA was enacted, amending ERISA to limit the sponsor's right to terminate a defined benefit plan. A defined benefit plan may not be terminated voluntarily unless it satisfies the requirements to be either a *standard termination* or a *distress termination*.[39]

**Standard Termination.** A standard termination is a plan termination in which the plan assets are sufficient to cover all *liabilities* for benefits earned to date, protecting participants from the loss of such benefits without imposing any liability upon the PBGC.[40] Benefit liabilities include all accrued benefits.[41] Benefit liabilities also include early retirement supplements and subsidies such as early retirement reduction factors which are more liberal than actuarial equivalent factors, as well as special benefits which become payable only upon plant shutdown or certain other special events. However, plant shutdown benefits are included in benefit liabilities only if at the time of plan termination the participant has satisfied all of the conditions required of him under the provisions of the plan to establish entitlement to the benefits, other than submission of an

---

[39]ERISA §4041(a).

[40]ERISA §4041(b)

[41]ERISA §4001(a)(16), I.R.C. §401(a)(2), Rev. Rul. 85–6.

application for benefits and similar administrative requirements. Benefit liabilities always equal or exceed the amount of guaranteed benefits.

Sixty days prior to the date of a proposed standard termination the plan administrator must send a notice of intent to terminate to each participant and beneficiary and to any labor union representing participants. The notice of intent to terminate must state the proposed termination date.

As soon as practicable after the notice of intent to terminate is provided, the plan administrator must provide a notice to the PBGC. This notice must include a certification by an enrolled actuary stating, as of the proposed termination date, the projected amount of plan assets and the actuarial present value of the benefit liabilities and stating that the plan assets are projected to be sufficient to satisfy the benefit liabilities. The notice to the PBGC must also include a certification by the plan administrator that the data used by the actuary in preparing the actuarial certification was complete and accurate.

No later than the date that the above notice is sent to the PBGC, the plan administrator must provide another notice to each participant and beneficiary. This notice must state the amount and form of the individual's benefit liabilities and the data, such as length of service and compensation, upon which they are based.

Unless the PBGC issues a notice of noncompliance within 60 days of receiving its notice from the plan administrator, the plan administrator generally must begin distribution of the plan assets as soon as practicable after the 60-day period. If the plan administrator fails to make a timely distribution, the termination is void and the plan is treated for all purposes as an ongoing plan. Thus, the employer is always able to abandon a standard termination before its completion. After the distribution has been completed, a final notice must be provided to the PBGC.

**Method of Distribution of Plan Assets.** All benefits that were payable as an annuity under the provisions of the plan must be provided in the form of an annuity after plan termination unless a lump-sum distribution is allowed under one of several exceptions.[42]

---

[42]29 CFR §2617.4.

A lump-sum distribution is permissible if the present value of the benefit is less than $3,500 or if the benefit is smaller than the smallest monthly benefit normally provided by an insurer. A lump sum may also be provided if the plan provided for this form of distribution and if the participant elects it.

The benefit liabilities to be provided as annuities generally must be provided under one or more annuity contracts issued by a life insurance company. This may include any annuities that had been purchased in the normal course of the plan's funding as well as any additional contracts purchased at the time of termination.

The benefit liabilities include benefits payable immediately to some participants and beneficiaries and benefits payable commencing at some deferred date for others. The right to a deferred annuity often includes the right to elect early retirement, with reduced benefits determined on either an actuarially equivalent basis or some subsidized basis. Under some circumstances the plan administrator may not be able to purchase deferred annuities that include the early retirement benefits and which have rates that reasonably take account of the probability of early retirement. In this case the PBGC may provide the early retirement benefits if the plan administrator pays the PBGC the value of the benefits.

Any benefit liabilities to be provided in the form of a lump sum must equal the present value of the benefit liabilities, determined in accordance with regulations.[43]

**Allocation of Excess Assets.**    If the plan assets are more than sufficient to satisfy the allocation requirements for all benefit liabilities, the residual assets are allocable to either the plan sponsor or to participants and beneficiaries.[44] Unless the plan document so provides, all such residual assets are to be allocated to participants and beneficiaries. This allocation must be in proportion to their other allocations of plan assets (other than any allocations for voluntary employee contributions) unless that would be discriminatory. Any plan amendment creating or increasing the amount of reversion to the employer may not become effective until five years after its adoption. If the plan provides for a reversion to the em-

---

[43]29 CFR §2619.26.
[44]ERISA §4044(d), 29 CFR §2618.30–32.

ployer, there must first be determined the amount of residual assets required to be allocated to mandatory employee contributions if the plan is contributory; any remainder of the residual assets may revert to the employer.

**Distress Terminations.**   If plan assets are less than the benefit liabilities, a plan may not be terminated voluntarily unless each contributing employer (and each member of a controlled group with such employers) satisfies the requirements for a distress termination.[45] An employer is in distress if it satisfies any one of four criteria:

1.   A petition for liquidation of the employer has been filed under bankruptcy laws.
2.   The employer is in the process of reorganization under bankruptcy laws, the bankruptcy court determines that the employer will be unable to pay its debts under reorganization and to continue in business outside reorganization, and the court approves the termination.
3.   The employer demonstrates to the PBGC it will be unable to pay its debts when due and unable to continue in business unless the distress termination occurs.
4.   The employer demonstrates to the PBGC that its pension costs have become unreasonably burdensome solely as a result of a decline in the employer's workforce.

To initiate a distress termination the plan administrator must provide a notice of intent to terminate the same as for a standard termination, except that for a distress termination the notice of intent must also be sent to the PBGC.

As soon as practicable after providing the notice of intent to terminate, the plan administrator must provide the PBGC with information it needs to determine whether the criteria for a distress termination have been satisfied. In addition the information must include a certification by the enrolled actuary including, as of the proposed termination date, the projected value of plan assets, the present value of all benefit liabilities, and the present value of the portion of benefits that are guaranteed under the plan benefits in-

---

[45]ERISA §4041(c).

surance program. The certification must state whether the plan assets are sufficient for benefit liabilities or for guaranteed benefits or for neither. The information must also include the name and address of each participant and beneficiary and information needed for the PBGC or the trustee to pay future benefits to them. In addition the plan administrator must certify the completeness and accuracy of the information upon which the actuary's certification is based and the completeness and accuracy of all other information provided.

Unlike a standard termination, a distress termination does not require that participants and beneficiaries be provided with any information concerning their individual benefits.

In a standard termination the plan administrator may proceed with the termination unless the PBGC provides a notice of non-compliance, but under a distress termination the plan administrator may not terminate the plan until the PBGC notifies the plan administrator of its determination.

In a distress termination, if the PBGC determines that the assets exceed the benefit liabilities, the termination is thenceforth treated as a standard termination.

If the plan assets are less than the benefit liabilities, but if the allocation of plan assets results in all guaranteed benefits being fully funded, the plan administrator must proceed to distribute all of the plan assets in the same manner as for a standard termination.

Any payments received by the PBGC for unfunded nonguaranteed benefits (the excess of a plan's unfunded benefit liabilities over its unfunded guaranteed benefits) will be applied to provide the unfunded nonguaranteed benefits of participants.[46] If a plan's unfunded nonguaranteed benefits exceed $20 million, any such payments received will be applied to provide unfunded nonguaranteed benefits under the particular plan. Otherwise, any such payments received will be pooled to provide unfunded nonguaranteed benefits under all other such plans.

If the plan assets are insufficient to provide for all guaranteed benefits, the plan must be brought under the control and administration of a "termination trustee." The termination trustee may be the PBGC, the plan administrator, or an individual appointed

[46]ERISA §4022(c).

by a federal court, possibly from a list of persons submitted by the PBGC. The administrator and the PBGC may agree that the latter is to be the termination trustee. Court approval is not required for such an agreement. It is the policy of the PBGC to seek trusteeship status for itself in virtually all cases, in the interest of uniform administration and operating efficiencies. With few exceptions, the plan sponsor has agreed to the arrangement. When the PBGC has found it necessary to go to court to be appointed trustee, its petition has generally been approved.

As termination trustee, the PBGC assumes responsibility for the further administration and eventual winding up of the plan. It maintains plan records, processes applications for retirement, issues checks to benefit recipients, and responds to inquiries from plan participants and their beneficiaries.

Under present policy, the assets of the plan are transferred to a commingled trust fund maintained by the PBGC for purposes of investment diversification and efficiency. These assets are managed for the PBGC by private-sector investment managers, selected by competitive bidding on the basis of past investment performance and future potential performance. The assets are invested in the private sector under a set of guidelines laid down by the PBGC, with the counsel of the Advisory Committee.

## Plan Termination Initiated by the PBGC

Termination of a pension plan generally occurs at the initiative of the plan sponsor. Under ERISA, however, the PBGC was given the authority to petition an appropriate federal district court to terminate a plan irrespective of the plan sponsor's wishes, under certain specified circumstances.[47] Basically, involuntary termination is authorized when necessary to protect the interests of plan participants or the PBGC. The latter is interested in protecting itself against unreasonable increases in its exposure to loss through continued operation of the plan, against continued accruals of benefit obligations, and possible deterioration of the sponsor's net worth. The PBGC may institute judicial proceedings to terminate a pension plan if it finds that:

---

[47]ERISA §4042.

- The plan is not in compliance with the minimum funding standards of the Internal Revenue Code.
- A reportable event[48] has occurred.
- The ultimate loss to the PBGC with respect to the plan may reasonably be expected to increase unreasonably if the plan is not terminated forthwith.
- The plan is unable to pay benefits when due (in which case termination by PBGC is mandatory).

After approval by the court, an involuntary termination proceeds similarly to a distress termination which has been approved by the PBGC.

### Liability for Accumulated Funding Deficiencies and Waived Funding Deficiencies

At the time of plan termination the amount of any accumulated funding deficiency plus the amount of any previously waived funding deficiencies becomes immediately due and payable to the plan trustee.[49]

### Amendment to Reduce or Freeze Plan Benefits

At times a plan sponsor may desire to make a plan amendment to reduce or discontinue all future benefit accruals, but without terminating the plan. Such a step may be taken for many of the same reasons that a plan termination is undertaken, generally in order either to reduce plan costs or to make changes where reduction or elimination of accruals is appropriate, as in a change to a different type of plan for future service or in a plant closing.

The least disruptive of such courses of action would be a plan amendment (effective only with respect to service thereafter) to reduce the rate at which pension benefits accrue, to decrease or eliminate ancillary benefits, such as those payable upon death or disability, or to cut back on other attractive but costly plan features. This type of action is called a plan *curtailment* and does not involve any official response (other than IRS approval) or penalty.

---

[48]ERISA §4043.
[49]ERISA §4062(c).

A more drastic form of action would be a plan amendment to discontinue all future benefit accruals, but with recognition of future service for vesting and phase-in purposes and with continuation of contributions for the funding of benefits already accrued. With no further change of policy, all accrued benefits of continuing employees would eventually become fully vested and fully funded. This type of action is referred to as *freezing* of the plan or, in the terminology of the IRS, a "suspension" of the plan. In some circumstances, as when it accompanies a substantial reduction of the number of active participants, the IRS may regard a suspension as a *partial termination* requiring that all accrued benefits vest to the extent then funded.[50]

If a plan is frozen without a plan termination, the employer avoids any immediate assessment of liability to the plan's trust for previously waived funding deficiencies, to the PBGC for unfunded guaranteed benefits, or to a 4049 trust for unfunded benefit commitments.

The employer is required to notify participants and beneficiaries at least 15 days before the effective date of any amendment which eliminates or significantly reduces future benefit accruals.[51]

## Financial Structure

The PBGC is intended to be a self-financed entity, not dependent upon the federal government for support. PBGC receives no appropriations from the Congress but has its own sources of revenue, which can be utilized for corporate purposes. However, its budget is subject to the budgetary processes of the federal government, and its revenue and disbursements are included in the totals of the federal budget.

The PBGC has five main sources of funds: premium income, investment earnings, levies against plan sponsors subject to liability for unfunded insured obligations, monies borrowed from the U.S. Treasury, and assets of terminated insufficient plans. Under present practices, premium payments and Treasury borrowings, if any, flow into two statutory guaranty funds, while assets from insufficient terminated plans and employer liability collections are held in trust

---

[50]I.R.C. §411(d)(3).
[51]ERISA §204(h).

funds managed by or for the PBGC. Investment earnings are added to the assets that generated them.

**Guaranty Funds.**   ERISA originally made provision for four revolving funds, but only two of these have been established.[52] One fund is operated for the insuring of basic benefits of single employer plans, while the other fund holds the monies accumulated for the insurance of basic benefits of multiemployer plans. Representatives of multiemployer plans insisted upon a separate guaranty fund—and a lower scale of premiums—in the belief that such plans rested on a firmer financial foundation than single employer plans and offered a lower probability of termination. Statutory provision was made for another revolving fund for each of these two categories of plans to account for monies associated with the insurance of nonbasic benefits. Since no programs have yet been established for nonbasic benefits, these guaranty funds have not been activated.

Amendments to ERISA have added three more funds, two related to multiemployer plans and the other to segregate premiums for single employer plans resulting from premium increases becoming effective after 1987. Having two separate funds for single employer plans has the same practical effect as having only one fund.

Premium payments by pension plan sponsors are credited directly to the appropriate revolving funds.[53] Benefit payments by the PBGC to participants in terminated plans and operating expenses of the Corporation are initially charged to the revolving funds, with periodic reimbursement from the trust funds for their pro rata share of benefit payments and expenses.

Each revolving fund is intended to be self-sufficient, except that transfers will be made from the newer single employer fund to the older single employer fund as needed. With this exception, the resources of one fund are not to be used to pay the insurance losses or expenses of another fund. The overhead expenses of the Corporation are allocated to the funds in accordance with accepted cost accounting procedures. Any amount borrowed from the Treasury must be allocated to one or more of the funds and must be repaid by monies withdrawn from the same funds.

---

[52]ERISA §4005(a).
[53]ERISA §4005(b).

ERISA states that the Corporation *may* invest any monies in excess of its current needs in obligations issued or guaranteed by the federal government. The Treasury Department has taken the position that the monies in the guaranty funds, derived essentially from premium payments and investment earnings thereon, *must* be invested in government securities. The Treasury at one stage argued that the assets of terminated plans taken over by the Corporation as trustee should also be invested in government securities; but a compromise was eventually worked out, under which the trusteed assets are invested in the private sector in the expectation of higher yields and, thus, lower premiums for the plan sponsors.

The financial officers of the PBGC manage the investments of the revolving funds within the scope permitted. At their discretion, they may negotiate with the Treasury for the purchase of special nonmarketable securities or they may acquire and dispose of government securities in the open market. The maturity structure of the securities held by the revolving funds reflects cash flow projections and anticipated interest rate behavior.

**Trust Funds.** The PBGC operates two commingled trusts, one for single employer plans and the other for multiemployer plans. These are maintained for plans for which PBGC is trustee. All the assets of terminated plans under the administration of the PBGC are regarded, for accounting and fiduciary purposes, to be a part of the financial resources of the Corporation.

Through periodic transfers to the revolving funds, plan assets held in PBGC trusts will ultimately be used up in payment of benefits and expenses.

**Premiums.** If the PBGC is to be self-supporting, as intended, its premium income, supplemented by investment earnings and employer liability payments, must be sufficient to underwrite the unfunded benefit obligations that it assumes. However, Congress has imposed some rigid constraints on the setting of premium rates for basic benefits.[54]

As a first principle, ERISA states that separate premium schedules must be developed and maintained for single employer and

---

[54]ERISA §4006.

multiemployer plans. This mandate, along with the corollary requirement that the premiums be accumulated and held in separate revolving funds, reflected an acceptance by Congress of the argument by multiemployer plan representatives that multiemployer plans have different risk characteristics than single employer plans and are, in fact, subject to a lower probability of termination.

The second principle is that the Corporation can change premium rates or change the bases on which premiums are computed only with the advance approval of Congress, acting through a joint resolution. This provision reflects the fact that the Corporation, an insurance agency, is not subject to state insurance regulations and should be accountable to some public body. The prior approval requirement parallels that applicable at the state level to various forms of insurance, except that the approving authority at the state level is an administrative agency.

The PBGC has adopted a third principle, not expressly articulated in the law, that premium rates for all types of benefits and coverages should be set at such a level as to produce annual revenue sufficient when augmented by investment earnings and employer contingent liability payments, to meet the unfunded actuarial liabilities associated with plans terminating during the year to which the premiums relate and to amortize over a period of years any unfunded actuarial liabilities associated with plans terminated during prior years. This is in contrast to an approach under which the premium and other revenues would be sufficient only to pay benefits as they become due, the pay-as-you-go principle. This is a fundamental issue concerned with the distribution of the social costs of plan terminations over successive generations of plan sponsors. The PBGC has taken the position that the full cost of each year's plan terminations should be borne by the plans subject to the risk of termination during that year, rather than being spread over a period coterminous with the future lifetimes of the participants and beneficiaries whose benefits were insured under the terminated plans. Implementation of this principle means that the PBGC must collect premiums each year that are expected to equal the actuarial present value of all unfunded benefit payments that it will make in future years in respect of the plans that terminate in that year and to amortize its unfunded liabilities arising in prior years. This will inevitably lead to a substantial accumulation of assets in the guaranty funds. With each request from the PBGC for an increase in the premium rate, this principle comes under growing attack from certain elements of the business community, who question the need for short-term amortization of the cumulative operating deficit of the Corporation, which at the time of this writing is estimated as $3.8 billion, due to claims well in excess of projections. These critics presumably would prefer, or at least tolerate, a system of financing closer to pay-as-you-go than to full funding.

Premium rates for the insurance protection provided by the PBGC should, in theory, reflect the statistical probability of the occurrence of the insured event and the amount of loss that would be sustained if the insured event should occur. The probability of occurrence of an insured event would be importantly related to the risk characteristics of the plan sponsor, such as the size and financial stability of the firm, the nature of the industry in which the firm operates and the firm's competitive standing in the industry, and the future prospects of the firm and the industry.

The amount at risk would be largely represented by the *unfunded* actuarial liability in respect of insured benefits, reduced by recoveries from plan sponsors under ERISA employer liability provisions. This amount is subject to wide fluctuations because of changes in the market value of accumulated plan assets, the value of guaranteed benefits and the amount of the employer's net worth.

In view of the complexities involved in developing a theoretically correct scale of premium rates and the lack of reliable data on the actuarial status of the insured plan universe, Congress decided that the program should start with a very simple, even crude, premium structure; namely a flat per capita levy. The initial premium, set forth in the statute, was $1 per participant per year for single employer plans and $.50 per participant under multiemployer plans. This simple approach was easily understood and administered, had the capability of generating a reasonably predictable flow of premium income, and would not produce gross inequities among plan sponsors if the initial burden of the program proved to be light, as was expected. Congress anticipated that a more sophisticated premium structure would eventually be needed and indicated that the premiums under such a revised structure could be based on (1) the number of plan participants, (2) the present value of insured benefits, or (3) the excess of the present value of insured benefits over the plan assets, or some combination of the three.

The initial per capita levies proved to be inadequate and, with congressional approval, the PBGC raised the premium for single employer plans to $2.60 per participant per year, effective with plan years beginning after 1977, and to $8.50 per participant per year for plan years beginning after 1985.

For plan years beginning after 1987 the premium was increased to $16.00 per participant per year plus an additional amount for plans with unfunded vested benefits. The interest rate used to determine the value of vested benefits for this purpose must be 80 percent of the annual yield for 30-year Treasury bonds for the month preceding the plan year. This additional amount per participant equals $6.00 for each $1,000 (or fraction thereof) of unfunded vested benefits as of the end of the preceding plan year, divided by the number of participants at the end of such prior year. However, this additional premium may not exceed $34.00 per participant. For plan years beginning before 1993, this $34.00 cap is reduced by $3.00 for each of the five plan years preceding the plan year beginning in 1988 during which the employer contributed the maximum deductible contribution.

If, for example, a plan had 10 participants at the end of the preceding plan year and had unfunded vested benefits equal to $1,700, the additional premium per participant would be $1.20 (2 times $6.00 divided by 10), making the total premium $17.20 ($16.00 plus $1.20). This premium rate would be applied to the number of participants at the end of the preceding plan year.

Proponents of this new approach argue that it assesses the costs of the system more equitably among those plans creating the risk of loss. Some opponents argue that it increases administrative costs for both employers and the PBGC, and that it assesses the higher premiums against employers for whom there is no risk of loss since they are not eligible for a distress termination or since they have net worth sufficient to reimburse PBGC for any unfunded guaranteed benefits. Others have expressed concern that the approach will discourage the granting of past service credits and cost-of-living adjustments for retirees under plans where such benefits could reasonably be expected to be amortized without loss to the plan benefits insurance system.

Premiums for the basic benefits component of the plan benefits insurance program can be paid out of plan assets, but in many cases payment is made directly by the employer. The premiums in respect of a particular plan for a plan year must be paid not later than seven months after the beginning of the plan year, but plans with 500 or more participants must pay estimated premiums within two months after the beginning of the plan year.[55] Failure of the plan administrator to make timely payments of the premium does not affect the insurance protection, but it subjects the plan to interest charges and late payment penalties. This late payment penalty may be waived by the PBGC upon a finding of substantial hardship.

For purposes of determining a plan's premium, the plan administrator must count as a "participant" (a) an individual currently accruing benefits or earning or retaining credited service, (b) a retired employee or a terminated vested employee, (c) a deceased participant whose survivors are entitled to benefits, and (d) anyone else defined as a participant under the plan's terms. A former employee with no vested rights who has incurred a break in service of at least one year's duration is not counted as a participant, nor is a retired or terminated vested employee whose guaranteed benefits are fully and irrevocably insured by a life insurance company.

A plan's premium obligation is based on the number of participants in the plan as of the last day of the preceding plan year. If an individual is a participant in more than one single employer plan covered under the insurance program, each plan must include him in its premium computation.

**Recoveries from Plan Sponsors.** Recoveries from firms primarily or secondarily liable for the unfunded insured benefits of terminated pension plans, described earlier, is another source of revenue for the PBGC.

**Borrowing Authority.** The final potential source of funds for the Corporation is borrowing authority. The Corporation is authorized to borrow $100 million from the U.S. Treasury through the issuance to the Secretary of the Treasury of notes or other obligation in such forms and denominations, bearing such maturities, and subject to such terms and conditions as the secretary may prescribe.[56] The obligations are to bear interest at a rate de-

---

[55]Form PBGC–1 must accompany the premiums.
[56]ERISA §4005(c).

termined by the secretary, taking into consideration the current average market yield on outstanding marketable obligations of the United States with comparable maturities during the month preceding the issuance of the obligations. They must, of course, be repaid, since the Corporation is intended to be self-financing.

Initially, the Corporation borrowed $100,000 to finance its organizational expenses, and the loan was repaid out of the first premiums received.

---

## Questions

1. Why are money purchase pension plans and other types of individual account plans not entitled to the protection of the plan benefits insurance program?
2. Contrast a *plan termination* and a *freezing* of a plan from the standpoint of the effect on:
   a. The future obligations of the plan sponsor.
   b. The benefit rights of plan participants.
3. Explain why most knowledgeable observers believe that the *insured event* for the plan benefits insurance program should be *liquidation of the plan sponsor,* rather than *termination of the plan.*
4. Contrast the procedures followed when a pension plan is *voluntarily* terminated by the plan administrator and when it is *involuntarily* terminated by action of the PBGC.
5. Explain the rationale behind the reporting to PBGC of each of the events included in the list of reportable events.
6. Identify and explain the intended effect of the various provisions or features incorporated in Title IV of ERISA for the primary purpose of protecting the plan benefits insurance program against abuse.
7. What type of actuarial cost method is used by the PBGC to value the liabilities of a terminated pension plan?
8. Should the liabilities of a terminated pension plan be valued on the basis of annuity factors developed by the PBGC or on the basis of current market quotations by life insurers?
9. With respect to the contingent liability of the sponsor of a single employer pension plan, explain:
   a. Its basic purpose.
   b. How and on what date it is computed.

    *c.*  The nature of the PBGC lien against the plan sponsor's assets in connection with the liability.

10.  In your judgment, did Congress have a moral and legal right to impose retroactive contingent liability on plan sponsors?

11.  Does an employer's contingent liability under a pension plan pose any threat to the firm's current or future creditors? Answer carefully and with particular reference to *how* and *when* the amount of the liability is computed.

12.  What types or classes of benefits has PBGC defined as "basic"?

13.  Why did Congress see fit to distinguish between "basic" and "nonbasic" benefits? What are some types of "nonbasic" benefits?

14.  Is there any provison for updating the limits on the amount of monthly benefit insured?

15.  *a.*  What is the purpose behind the phase-in of insurance coverage for newly created benefits of single employer plans?

    *b.*  What changes, if any, would you make in the phase-in provision of the single employer plan benefits insurance program?

16.  Identify the priority classes that were established by ERISA for the allocation of assets of a terminated pension plan.

17.  In your opinion, how could the asset allocation formula be simplified and still serve its original purpose? Describe the process by which the PBGC would administer the affairs of a single employer plan that terminates with insufficient assets.

18.  Explain the difference between a standard termination and a distress termination with respect to:

    *a.*  Eligibility to terminate the plan.

    *b.*  The process of plan termination.

19.  What principles have been adopted by Congress and the PBGC for the determination of premiums for plan benefits insurance?

20.  By what reasoning might certain segments of the business community prefer pay-as-you-go financing of the plan benefits insurance program?

21.  If you had the sole authority to determine the premium structure for the plan benefits insurance program, what features would you include? Would you make provision for backup support from general revenues of the federal government?

22.  In what fundamental respect would a *risk-related* premium for the benefits insurance program differ from an *exposure-related* premium?

23.  "The question of how the benefits insurance program should be financed turns largely on whether the PBGC is viewed as an insurer or a trustee administering a master trust for the pension plans cov-

ered by the insurance program, which trust is designed to hold sufficient assets to assure ultimate payment of the vested benefits of
the covered plan."

    *a.*  Do you regard the PBGC as an insurer or as a trustee of a master
trust supported by periodic contributions from the insured plans?
Give reasons for your views.

    *b.*  From the standpoint of financing the benefits insurance program,
what would be the implications of concluding that PBGC is

      (1)  An insurer.

      (2)  A master trustee.

24.  Describe the arrangements for the investment of assets held by the
PBGC in its corporate and fiduciary capacity. In your answer distinguish between the corporate and fiduciary role of the PBGC.

# 25 | Multiemployer Plan Withdrawals and Plan Benefits Insurance

A MULTIEMPLOYER PLAN is a plan maintained pursuant to one or more collective bargaining agreements and to which more than one employer is required to contribute.[1]

## Plans Covered

As originally enacted, ERISA provided that the plan benefits insurance program for multiemployer defined benefit plans would be basically the same as the program for single employer plans, with some exceptions. On the theory that multiemployer plans are less likely to terminate than single employer plans, the law provided for separate trust funds and different premium rates, the rate for the former being just half that of the latter.

The coverage of multiemployer plans became effective on the date of enactment of ERISA for purposes of premium payments, but PBGC was not *required* to insure benefits of multiemployer plans that terminated before July 1, 1978. However, it had authority to insure the benefits of terminated multiemployer plans on a dis-

---

[1]ERISA §§3(37), 4001(a)(3), I.R.C.§414(f).

cretionary basis, subject to certain conditions designed to safeguard the solvency of the multiemployer plans guaranty fund and to avoid premium increases.[2] Benefits were paid to the participants of several terminated plans under this discretionary authority.

As the deadline for mandatory assumption of the unfunded insured obligations of terminated multiemployer pension plans approached, it became apparent to many that it would be impracticable to extend the program in its original form to multiemployer plans. At the heart of the difficulties was the procedure specified in the law for the allocation of the unfunded actuarial liabilities of a multiemployer plan, especially as between those employers who withdraw from the plan before it terminates and those who remain to date of termination. To permit the PBGC staff and others to devise solutions to the perceived problems, Congress extended the deadline for mandatory coverage several times. Finally, on September 26, 1980, the Multiemployer Pension Plan Amendments Act was enacted, making fundamental changes in the insurance program with respect to multiemployer plans.[3]

## Liabilities of a Withdrawing Employer to a Multiemployer Pension Plan

Under the original Title IV provision for multiemployer plans—which, except for a few terminated plans insured by the PBGC under its discretionary authority, was operative for only about two months immediately prior to the enactment of MPPAA—an employer could withdraw from a plan without any further financial obligation if the plan continued for another five years.[4] Upon eventual termination of the plan, all employers still a member of the plan and all those that had withdrawn during the preceding five years had to assume their pro rata share of the plan's then unfunded insured liabilities, the proration being based on required contributions to the plan during the preceding five years. This arrange-

---

[2]ERISA §4402(c)(2).

[3]Public Law 96–364, 29 USC 1001.

[4]This was not true for a "substantial" employer, as defined in the law, which upon withdrawal was required to post a surety bond or place assets in escrow for the full amount of its allocable share of the plan's unfunded liability to discharge its obligation in the event that the plan were to terminate within the next five years.

ment, if permitted to become operative, would have created a powerful incentive for employer members of a financially troubled plan to withdraw before its ultimate collapse and would have discouraged new employer affiliations, both of which would have exacerbated the problems of the plan and hastened its demise.

MPPAA repealed the original provisions in their entirety and substituted an approach under which employers withdrawing from a multiemployer plan must generally assume their allocable share of the plan's unfunded vested liabilities.

### Definition of Withdrawal

For purposes of assessing withdrawal liability the law distinguishes between a *complete* withdrawal from the plan and a *partial* withdrawal. A *complete* withdrawal occurs whenever an employer (1) permanently ceases to have an obligation to contribute to the plan or (2) permanently ceases all covered operations under the plan, including sale of all assets.[5] The first circumstance is generally associated with decertification of the union that cosponsors the plan, with the employer operating thereafter with a nonunion work force or one affiliated with another union. The second circumstance relates to the discontinuance by the employer of those operations that were subject to the collective bargaining agreement under which the plan functions.

Subject to the exception noted below, a partial withdrawal of a signatory employer occurs if *any one* of the following three conditions is present on the last day of a plan year:

1. The employer's contribution base units (e.g., hours worked) during each of the three consecutive plan years ending with the plan year are 30 percent or less of the employer's contribution base units for the "high base year" (defined below); or,

2. The employer permanently ceases to have an obligation to contribute under one or more, but not all, of the collective bargaining agreements under which the employer has been obligated to contribute to the plan, but the employer continues to perform work in the jurisdiction of the collective bargaining

---

[5]ERISA §4203(a).

agreement(s) of the type for which contributions were previously required, or transfers such work to another location; or,

3. The employer permanently ceases to have an obligation to contribute under the plan with respect to work performed at one or more (but fewer than all) of its facilities, but the employer continues to perform work at the facility (or facilities) of the type for which the obligation to contribute ceased.[6]

In the construction industry, a partial withdrawal does not occur unless an employer continues to have an obligation to contribute for only an "insubstantial" portion of its work within the craft and area jurisdiction of the applicable collective bargaining agreement. Presumably, the responsibility of the plan trustees is to define "insubstantial."[7] Plans in the retail food industry may elect to define a partial withdrawal as a 35 percent reduction in contribution base units (as compared to the otherwise applicable 70 percent reduction).[8] There is no liability for partial withdrawal from a plan in the entertainment industry, except under the conditions and to the extent prescribed by PBGC regulations.[9]

The partial withdrawal test couched in terms of the reduction in contribution base units needs further explanation. Contribution base units are the units upon which the employer is required to contribute to the plan, e.g., hours worked, compensation, tons of coal produced.[10] The three-year period during which the decline in contribution base units must occur is designated as the "test period." Contributions during the test period are measured against those for the "high base year," which is defined as the average number of the employer's contribution base units during the *two* plan years for which such units were the highest during the five plan years immediately preceding the beginning of the three-year testing period.[11] For example:

------

[6]ERISA §4205(a).
[7]ERISA §4208(d)(1).
[8]ERISA §4205(c)(1).
[9]ERISA §4208(d)(2).
[10]ERISA §4001(a)(11).
[11]ERISA §4205(b)(1)(B).

| Plan Year | Employer's Contribution Base Units | Plan Year | Employer's Contribution Base Units |
|---|---|---|---|
| 1 | 19,000 | 5 | 17,000 |
| 2 | 20,000 | 6 | 15,000 |
| 3 | 20,000 | 7 | 10,000 |
| 4 | 18,000 | 8 | 5,000 |

During this eight-year period, the employer's contribution base units declined from a high of 20,000 to a low of 5,000—an overall decline of 75 percent. Yet this overall decline is not determinative of whether a partial withdrawal has occurred. To determine whether a partial withdrawal occurred during Year 8 the contribution hours for Plan Years 6, 7, and 8 must be compared with the contribution hours for Plan Years 2 and 3, the two years of highest contributions during the five plan years preceding the three-year test period. Thus:

$$\frac{\text{Plan Year 6 Contribution Hours}}{\text{High Base Year's Hours}} = \frac{15,000}{20,000} = 75 \text{ Percent}$$

$$\frac{\text{Plan Year 7 Contribution Hours}}{\text{High Base Year's Hours}} = \frac{10,000}{20,000} = 50 \text{ Percent}$$

$$\frac{\text{Plan Year 8 Contribution Hours}}{\text{High Base Year's Hours}} = \frac{5,000}{20,000} = 25 \text{ Percent}$$

Inasmuch as the ratio was 30 percent or less for only one of the plan years in the test period, a partial withdrawal has not occurred. The ratio would have had to be 30 percent or less for *each* of the three plan years for a partial termination to occur. Operations at the reduced level would have to continue for another two years before a partial withdrawal becomes a possibility, but then the high base year hours would drop to 19,000—an average for Plan Years 3 and 4.

Except for a sale of assets (discussed later), a withdrawal is not deemed to have occurred merely because of a change in the employer's corporate structure (or a change to an unincorporated form of business enterprise) if the change causes no interruption in the employer's contributions or obligation to contribute under the plan.[12]

---

[12]ERISA §4218.

Nor does a suspension of contributions during a labor dispute constitute a withdrawal.[13] A successor or parent corporation or other entity resulting from a change in business form is considered to be the original employer.

In the building and construction industry (and certain segments of the entertainment industry), there is a complete withdrawal only if the employer remains in the area (or returns within five years and does not renew its obligation to contribute) and performs work (presumably with nonunion labor) that would have been covered by the plan.[14] A trucking employer that withdraws from a plan in the trucking, household goods moving, or public warehousing industries may post a five-year surety bond or escrow assets in an amount equal to 50 percent of its withdrawal liability until the PBGC can determine whether cessation of the employer's obligation to contribute did not result in "substantial damage" to the plan's contribution base.[15] If the PBGC determines that there was not substantial damage to the contribution base, no withdrawal liability is assessed, and the surety bond or escrowed assets are returned to the employer. On the other hand, if the contribution base was substantially damaged, withdrawal liability is assessed, the surety bond or escrowed assets are paid to the plan, and the employer must commence making payments to discharge the remainder of its obligation. These exceptions to the general rule are based on the premise that withdrawal liability can be prudently waived if the withdrawals in the aggregate do not significantly erode the contribution base, which would be the case if the overall employment level in the industry and locality covered by the plan remains reasonably constant, with new signatory employers (e.g., contractors) replacing those that withdraw. Indeed, the PBGC is authorized to prescribe regulations under which plans in industries other than construction and entertainment may provide for special withdrawal liability rules, if the PBGC determines that the industry characteristics make such rules appropriate and that the rules would not pose a significant risk to the PBGC.[16] The term *industry charac-*

---

[13]ERISA §4218.
[14]ERISA §4203(b),(c).
[15]ERISA §4203(d).
[16]ERISA §4203(f).

*teristics* relates primarily to whether the amount of work (contribution base units) in the jurisdiction of the plan is or is not substantially affected by the movement of union employers out of and into the jurisdiction of the plan.

A plan may provide that an employer can become a member for up to six years and then withdraw without any liability for the plan's unfunded vested benefits.[17] This is the "free look" provision of MPPAA that is intended to help overcome an employer's reluctance to become a member of the plan. An employer can take advantage of the provision only one time. This rule applies to an employer only if its contributions are less than 2 percent of the total contributions to the plan during each of the six years. A plan can extend this privilege only at a time when its assets are at least eight times its annual benefit payments. This free look is not permitted for plans in the building and construction industry.

Withdrawal liability and the statutory definitions of withdrawal not only bolster the financial condition of multiemployer plans but also serve as a strong deterrent to signatory employers to discontinue participation in the plan when withdrawal liability would be assessed, especially to "go nonunion." It was presumably not the intent of the legislation to place this roadblock in the path of non-unionization, but it certainly is one of the results.

A critically important component of the definition of a withdrawal pertains to the sale of assets by a signatory employer. Many small employers, especially family operated businesses, eventually sell out to larger firms. If the seller's business is an incorporated entity, it is the corporation that is deemed to be the employer and sale of the stock of the corporation to a new owner will not trigger a withdrawal by the employer. But if an owner of an unincorporated business sells it, or if a corporation sells part or all of its operations (e.g., sells the factory, equipment, and business as a going concern) to a new owner, the seller (who was the employer) has ceased its obligation to contribute to the plan and withdrawal liability would ordinarily be assessed.

The seller's withdrawal liability under a multiemployer plan can be a serious impediment to the transaction. As a form of relief, MPPAA provides that an employer whose obligation to contribute

---

[17]ERISA §4210.

to the plan is terminated through the sale of its assets in a bona fide, arm's length transaction with an unrelated party within the meaning of the I.R.C. shall not be required to make liability payments if the purchaser of the assets becomes obligated to contribute to the plan in respect of the operations for substantially the same number of contribution base units (typically, hours of covered employment) for which the seller was obligated to contribute.[18] However, this relief is available only if the purchaser posts a surety bond or escrows assets equal to the greater of (1) the average annual contribution required to be made by the seller for the three plan years immediately preceding the plan year in which the sale of assets occurs, or (2) the seller's required contribution for the last plan year before the assets were sold; *and* the contract of sale provides that if the purchaser withdraws from the plan with respect to the acquired operations within five years, the seller will be secondarily liable for any withdrawal liability it would have had to the plan (in the absence of this relief provision) if the purchaser fails to meet its liability payments.

If the seller goes out of business during the five-year period, it must escrow assets or post a surety bond in an amount equal to the present value of the withdrawal liability it would have had in the absence of this exception.

### Allocation of Unfunded Liability for Vested Benefits

Conceptually, there are two general approaches to allocating a plan's unfunded liability for vested benefits: (1) pooling the liabilities and allocating them to the participating employers on some equitable bases, and (2) allocating the liabilities to individual participants in the plan and attributing the liabilities to their various employers on the basis of periods of service with those employers. The first approach may be characterized as *pool attribution* and the second as *individual* or *direct* attribution.

MPPAA recognizes both approaches and sets out three acceptable methods of allocating pooled liabilities.[19] It also directed the PBGC to prescribe by regulation a procedure by which a plan may,

---

[18]ERISA §4204(a)(1).
[19]ERISA §4211(b),(c), and (d).

by amendment, adopt some other method for determining an employer's allocable share of unfunded vested benefits, subject to approval by the PBGC based on its determination that adoption of the method by the plan would not significantly increase the risk of loss to the plan participants and beneficiaries or to the PBGC.

**Attribution of Pooled Liabilities.**    The pool attribution methods sanctioned by MPPAA have certain common characteristics, the most important being the use of plan contributions as the basis for liability allocation. In each case, the numerator of the prorating fraction is the *required* contributions of the withdrawing employer and the denominator is the total *actual* contributions to the plan for the period involved, reduced by the contributions of withdrawn employers. The numerator uses *required* contributions in order that the withdrawing employer not be permitted to profit from any delinquency in its contribution obligation. (Contribution delinquency is a perennial problem in most multiemployer plans.) The denominator uses actual contributions because of the difficulty and expense of determining the required contribution for all signatory employers. In each case, the basis of allocation is contributions to the plan for a period of *five* plan years. Finally, the determination of the unfunded portion of the vested benefits takes into account all outstanding claims for withdrawal liability that can reasonably be expected to be collected by the plan.

The principal differences among the methods relate to (*a*) the period or periods for which the unfunded liabilities are pooled, (*b*) the group of employers assumed to be responsible for the allocable liabilities, and (*c*) the rate at which the unfunded vested liabilities are assumed to be amortized.

MPPAA specifies the method to be employed, unless the plan trustees adopt another approved method. The specified procedure is called the *presumptive* method, which, by explicit mandate of MPPAA, must be used by the building and construction industry.[20] The presumptive method distinguishes between the unfunded liabilities for vested benefits (hereafter, *UVB liabilities*) for plan years ending before April 29, 1980, and those arising in plan years ending on or after that date. Responsibility for that first pool of liabilities,

---

[20]ERISA §4211(b).

which includes the unfunded obligations left behind by employers that withdrew over all the years of the plan's existence, is assigned to that group of employers still participating in the plan during the first plan year ending after April 28, 1980. Any employer in that group who withdraws before these unfunded liabilities are fully amortized must assume that proportion of the unamortized amount of these liabilities which its required contributions over the last five plan years (ending prior to April 29, 1980) bears to the total plan contributions for that period by that group. For the purpose of this allocation, it is assumed that 5 percent of the original amount of the UVB liability is funded each year over a 20-year period beginning with the first plan year ending on or after April 29, 1980.

The UVB liabilities arising in plan years ending on or after April 29, 1980, are segregated by the plan year in which they arise and are prorated among the employers having an obligation to contribute to the plan as of the end of that year. For each plan year ending on or after April 29, 1980, the net change in the UVB liability is computed and prorated over the *then* participating employers on the basis of contributions for that year and the four preceding plan years. The net change in the UVB liability for a given plan year is affected by (*a*) experience gains and losses; (*b*) retroactive plan liberalizations, especially benefit increases; (*c*) reallocation of withdrawal liabilities of earlier plan years that could not be collected or were not assessed because of various relief provisions; (*d*) assumed amortization of the prior year's liability; (*e*) any change in the actuarial assumptions; (*f*) the level of employer contributions for the year; and (*g*) the value of new vested benefits created by employees becoming vested and earning another year's benefit accrual.

As with the pre-April 29, 1980, UVB liability pool, each plan year's UVB liability is assumed to be reduced by 5 percent (or the original amount) per year through contributions. Thus, each pool has a life of 20 years. This produces a "rolling" liability attribution with a "piece" of the total potential liability of an employer expiring after the lapse of 20 years. Stated differently, this method provides for 21 distinct UVB liability pools: the pre-1980 pool and one for each of 20 plan years. By the year 2000, the pre-1980 pool will have been completely funded, according to the assumptions, and thereafter as of any given year, there would be only 20 pools.

It is worth emphasizing that, under the presumptive method, employers joining the plan after April 28, 1980, are not liable for any portion of the pre-1980 UVB liabilities. They are required to assume only a pro rata share of the UVB liabilities arising in respect of the plan years in which they participate.

A second method of allocating pooled liabilities is the *modified* presumptive method.[21] The principal modification introduced by this method is the treatment of unfunded liabilities arising in plan years ending on or after April 29, 1980. These liabilities are pooled without reference to the plan years in which they arise, and are allocated among the participating employers on the basis of contributions to the plan over the preceding five years, irrespective of when the employers became signatories to the plan. (Proration by contributions and annual recomputation of the unfunded liability moderate the potential inequity in this broad type of pooling.) Thus, there are only 2 pools of UVB liabilities under this method, as contrasted with the 21 under the presumptive method. The pre-1980 pool of UVB liabilities is assumed to decline in a pattern reflecting 15-year amortization in equal annual installments, beginning with the first plan year ending on or after April 29, 1980. This is, of course, a faster rate of amortization than that implicit in the 5 percent annual reduction assumed under the presumptive method. The UVB liability for all plan years ending on or after April 29, 1980, is recomputed each year, taking into account collectible withdrawal liability payments. A withdrawing employer is assessed its pro rata share of that UVB liability computed as of the end of the plan year preceding the plan year when the withdrawal occurs.

A third method of allocating pooled liabilities is the so-called *rolling five* method.[22] This method makes no distinction between the pre-April 29, 1980, UVB liabilities and those arising thereafter. All UVB liabilities, irrespective of the plan year or years of origin, are pooled and allocated to withdrawing employers on the basis of contributions over the preceding five years. Thus, there is only one pool under this method. The UVB liability is recomputed each year, which takes into account past amortization payments and with-

---

[21] ERISA §4211(c)(2).
[22] ERISA §4211(c)(3).

drawal liability payments. There is no assumed rate of amortization, the computation reflecting actual experience. This is clearly the simplest method to administer, but it may discourage new employers from joining the plan.

**Direct Attribution Method.** The alternative to pooling the UVB liabilities of a multiemployer plan and allocating them on a basis that achieves only rough equity is to identify the source of the actuarial liabilities and attribute them (with matching assets) to the employers in respect to whom they arose. This is called the "direct attribution" method and, as noted above, its use is sanctioned by MPPAA.[23]

In concept, this is the most equitable of all methods of allocating unfunded liabilities. Unfortunately, it is feasible only for plans in industries that enjoy reasonably stable employment relationships. For most multiemployer plans, the method would be completely impracticable. Even when it is possible to associate a given body of unfunded liabilities with a given employer, it is usually more expensive and more cumbersome to attribute liabilities in this manner than to allocate by contributions, the most accessible and verifiable information maintained by a multiemployer plan.

There is some pooling of liabilities in the direct attribution method, as prescribed in MPPAA. A withdrawing employer is assigned, in addition to its own attributable liabilities (and matching assets), its pro rata share of the unattributable liabilities of previously withdrawn employers. The proration may be on the basis of either attributable liabilities or contributions.

**Partial Withdrawal.** An employer's obligation for a partial withdrawal is determined by multiplying the withdrawal liability for a complete withdrawal by the ratio of contribution base units in the year following the withdrawal to the average contribution base units during the five years preceding the withdrawal. In the event that an employer that has a partial withdrawal one year has a complete or partial withdrawal in a subsequent year, an appropriate adjustment is made.[24]

---

[23]ERISA §4211(c)(4).
[24]ERISA §4206.

**Reductions in Withdrawal Liability.** MPPAA contains several provisions to reduce the withdrawal liability determined according to the allocation methods described above.

Under the *de minimis* rule, enacted for the relief of small employers, especially those wishing to sell their assets or go out of business, an allocable withdrawal liability of $50,000 or less (or 0.75 percent of the plan's UVB liabilities, if less) is waived.[25] The first $50,000 of any assessment of $100,000 or less is waived for any employer, but $1 of the waiver is forfeited for each $1 by which the assessment exceeds $100,000. There is no relief for assessments of $150,000 or more. The law permits the plan trustees to amend the plan to waive instead the first $100,000 of assessments (or 0.75 percent of the UVB liabilities, if less), with the offset beginning at $150,000. The *de minimis* rule is not applicable when all employers withdraw from the plan within a three-year period (a mass withdrawal).

In the case of a bona fide sale of all or substantially all of the assets of any employer other than an employer undergoing *reorganization* under Title 11 of the Bankruptcy Code or state bankruptcy laws, the unfunded vested benefits otherwise allocable to the employer are limited to the greater of two amounts, the unfunded vested benefits attributable to employees of the employer or a proportion of the liquidation or dissolution value of the employer.[26] The alternative related to benefits attributable to the employer applies regardless of whether the plan otherwise uses the direct attribution method, but presumably does not apply if it is not feasible to calculate the unfunded vested benefits according to that method. If the liquidation or dissolution value of the employer is $2 million or less, the proportion used as the limit is 30 percent, increasing to 80 percent of liquidation value in excess of $10 million. For a liquidation value of $10 million, the proportion is 43.5 percent, while for a value of $20 million the proportion is 61.75 percent. As the liquidation value goes up, the proportion asymptotically approaches 80 percent.

In the case of an insolvent employer undergoing *liquidation* or *dissolution,* the amount of unfunded vested benefits otherwise al-

---

[25]ERISA §4209.
[26]ERISA §4225(a).

locable to the employer is limited to the greater of 50 percent of the amount or the liquidation or dissolution value of the employer. For this purpose an employer is deemed to be insolvent if its liabilities, including its withdrawal liability before this adjustment, exceeds its assets.[27]

If, after a complete withdrawal, the employer resumes covered operations or renews its obligation to contribute, its withdrawal liability originally assessed may be adjusted or waived.[28]

### Withdrawal Liability Payments

A withdrawing employer discharges its allocable share of the plan's UVB liabilities through annual level installment payments to the plan. The amount of the installment payment is determined by reference to the contribution *base* and the contribution *rate*.

The contribution base is unique to the withdrawing employer. As stipulated in MPPAA,[29] the base is the *average* annual number of contribution base units for the 3 consecutive plan years for which the employer's contributions were the *highest* during a period of 10 consecutive plan years ending before the plan year when the withdrawal occurs. For most plans, a contribution base unit is an hour of covered employment. This rather stringent definition of the contribution base was intended to discourage employers from deliberately winding down operations before withdrawal to minimize their UVB liability payments. It may work a hardship on an employer that has suffered a genuine, unavoidable decline in operations during the last few years before withdrawal, a not unlikely circumstance. The formula would cause the employer to have to make larger withdrawal payments than the contributions it was making to the plan during its last few years of membership, at a time when it may be experiencing general financial difficulties.

The contribution rate of a multiemployer plan is negotiated by the collective bargaining representatives. The contribution rate has usually been increased with each new labor contract. The rate to be used in calculating an employer's withdrawal liability payment

---

[27]ERISA §4225(b),(d).
[28]ERISA §4207.
[29]ERISA §4219(c)(1)(C)(i).

is the *highest* rate at which the employer was obligated to contribute during the 10-year period *ending with the plan year* in which the withdrawal occurs. The plan year of withdrawal was included in the 10-year period since, under recent experience, the highest contribution rate is likely to be found in that year.

The employer's annual withdrawal liability payment is arrived at by multiplying the contribution rate times the contribution base, both components being derived in the manner described above. The employer is obligated to make a payment of this amount each year until its withdrawal liability is fully amortized but, in no event, for a period of more than 20 years, even though the liability is not fully amortized.[30] Because the higher contribution rate of the final year is often multiplied by a higher number of contribution base units for an earlier period, the required amortization payments may be substantially greater than the level of the employer's contributions had ever been. Partly for this reason, the withdrawal liability will frequently be amortized over a shorter period than 20 years. This has led to criticism that the 20-year cap on installment payments is a meaningless limit.

Payments by an employer to amortize its withdrawal liability are generally deductible for federal income tax purposes when paid.[31]

## Assessment and Collection of Withdrawal Liability

Having been notified or having determined that a partial or complete withdrawal has occurred, the trustees of a multiemployer plan ascertain the amount of the withdrawing employer's liability (in accordance with the principles and rules outlined above), inform the employer of the amount of its liability, and demand payment.[32] Determination of the withdrawal liability is a complex matter, involving, *inter alia,* an actuarial valuation of the plan's vested liabilities and assets, and is carried out by the plan's enrolled actuary under the direction of the plan trustees. The actuary must use actuarial assumptions that, in the aggregate, are reasonable and

---

[30]The law specifies that each annual payment shall be payable in equal *quarterly* installments unless the plan states otherwise. ERISA §4219(c).

[31]I.R.C. §404(g).

[32]ERISA §4219(b)(1).

represent the actuary's best estimate of future experience, and he must use actuarial techniques or methods that are appropriate to the task.[33]

The employer has 90 days after receipt of the notice of assessment in which to contest the amount of the liability or the schedule of payments.[34] However, within 60 days the employer must make its first quarterly payment, even though the amount or legitimacy of the payment is in dispute.[35] If the employer questions the amount of the assessment, the schedule of installment payments, or the legitimacy of any assessment, and if the differences cannot be resolved by the two parties, the disputed matters must go to arbitration.[36]

The arbitration must be conducted in accordance with procedures prescribed in PBGC regulations, unless the parties agree to use alternative procedures that have been approved by the PBGC.[37] An arbitrator is selected in accordance with the procedures, usually from a list prepared by the American Arbitration Association.

For the purpose of the arbitration proceeding, MPPAA states that the plan's determination of the amount of withdrawal liability and the schedule of payments is presumed to be correct unless the employer shows "by a preponderance of evidence that the determination was unreasonable or clearly erroneous."

The Third Circuit ruled that the presumption of correctness accorded the plan trustees' determination of withdrawal liability was unconstitutional in violating the withdrawing employer's right to a fair hearing. Courts in other jurisdictions have held to the contrary. By an evenly divided four to four vote the Supreme Court upheld the Third Circuit.[38] The effect of this evenly divided vote is that the decision is not binding outside the Third Circuit. Further litigation of this issue is expected.

---

[33]ERISA §4213.

[34]ERISA §4219(b)(2).

[35]ERISA §4219(c)(2).

[36]ERISA §4221(a)(1).

[37]29 CFR §2641.

[38]*United Retail and Wholesale Employees Teamsters Union Local No. 115 Pension Plan* v. *Yahn & McDonnell, Inc.*, 787 F.2d 128 (3rd Cir. 1986), aff'd by an equally divided court, 107 S. Ct. 2171 (1987).

Determination of the installment payments does not involve actuarial judgments (other than an interest discount rate) and, hence, these payments are not likely to be in dispute. Thus, it is usually the *amount* of the assessment that is in dispute and that may involve nonactuarial matters such as the determination of the employer's required contributions. If the dispute involves actuarial considerations, to have the liability assessment itself set aside or modified the employer must prove that the actuarial assumptions and methods employed in the determination of the liability were unreasonable or that the plan's actuary made a significant error in applying the actuarial assumptions or methods.

The arbitrator's decision may be appealed to the federal courts by either party within 30 days.[39] In the appeal process, the arbitrator's *findings of fact* are given a rebuttable presumption of correctness.

As indicated earlier, withdrawal liability payments are made quarterly, unless the plan specifies a different pattern. The employer may prepay the outstanding amount of unpaid liability at any time. If a payment is not made when due, interest at the prime rate (as published by PBGC) can be charged from the due date to the date of payment.[40] In the event of default, the plan after 60 days notice may require immediate payment of the outstanding amount of liability (a penalty known as "acceleration").[41]

## Reimbursement for Uncollectible Withdrawal Liability

MPPAA directed the PBGC to establish a supplemental insurance program by May 1, 1982, that would reimburse the multiemployer plan for withdrawal liability payments that proved to be uncollectible because of the employer's bankruptcy or other reasons considered appropriate by the PBGC.[42] Participation in the program was to be voluntary, with an additional premium being charged for the coverage. Because of budgetary limitations, the PBGC has not established such a program and has recommended that the statutory mandate be repealed.

---

[39]ERISA §4221(b).
[40]29 CFR §2644.3.
[41]ERISA §4219(c)(5).
[42]ERISA §4222(a).

The law also authorized the sponsors of multiemployer plans acting in concert to establish a *withdrawal liability payment fund*, dubbed by some as a "super trust fund," that would reimburse a signatory plan for that portion of a withdrawn employer's liability that is unattributable to any given employer, is waived, or is proven to be uncollectible.[43] It could also, at the option of the sponsors of the fund, provide for payment of an employer's attributable liability if the fund provides for the payment of both the attributable and unattributable liability of the employer in a single sum and the fund is subrogated to all rights of the plan against the employer.

No such super trust funds have been established as yet. However, some private insurers are now offering reimbursement for uncollectible or waived liability payments. Moreover, at least one organization, Lloyd's of London, offers an insurance contract designed to protect an employer that is forced to withdraw from a multiemployer pension plan for reasons beyond its control. The contract, subject to a deductible and coinsurance, will reimburse an insured employer for up to $1 million of withdrawal liability and, for an additional premium, will provide additional payments to help defray legal and actuarial expenses involved in evaluating withdrawal liability claims and possible arbitration and lawsuit expenses. The policy insures employers against withdrawals caused by the discontinuance of a major product line, a change in collective bargaining representative pursuant to an election conducted by the NLRB, a physical destruction of an employer's business, a mass withdrawal of all employers in a multiemployer plan, or other unintentional events.

## Reorganization

If a multiemployer plan is financially troubled, as defined by MPPAA, it is in a status known as "reorganization." If a plan is in reorganization, it is subject to more stringent minimum funding requirements than those applicable to plans not in that condition[44] and is also subject to certain notification requirements.[45] Such a plan may

---

[43]ERISA §4223.
[44]ERISA §§4243, 4244, I.R.C. §§418B, 418C.
[45]ERISA §4242, I.R.C. §418A.

be amended to reduce certain nonguaranteed accrued benefits, irrespective of the usual requirement forbidding amendments that reduce accrued benefits.[46] In addition, if a plan is in reorganization, all benefits must be paid in the form of an annuity, except that lump-sum distributions of less than $3,500 are permitted.[47]

To determine whether a multiemployer plan is in reorganization for a plan year, the *vested benefits charge* and the *net charge to the funding standard account* must be determined and compared.[48]

The *vested benefits charge* is the annual amount required to amortize a plan's unfunded vested benefits as of the end of the *base plan year* over certain specified periods. The base plan year is the plan year preceding the plan year for which the vested benefits charge is to be determined or, under specified circumstances, an earlier year.

The value of vested benefits must be determined separately for persons in pay status and for other participants. Next the amount of unfunded vested benefits is determined for each group by subtracting the applicable plan assets from the value of vested benefits for each of these two groups, allocating plan assets first to the value of vested benefits for participants in pay status and, if assets are more than sufficient for that purpose, allocating the remainder of plan assets to the remaining participants. The amount of unfunded vested benefits is subject to adjustment under some circumstances. Next the *vested benefits charge* for the year is determined as the amount required to amortize the unfunded vested benefits for persons in pay status over 10 years and to amortize the unfunded vested benefits for other participants over 25 years.

The *net charge to the funding standard account* for the plan year is the sum of all charges to the funding standard account for the year under the regular minimum funding requirements reduced by all amortization credits to the funding standard account for the year. This net charge is generally equal to what the regular required minimum funding requirement for the year would be if the funding standard account had no credit balance resulting from having received more contributions than required by the funding requirements in prior years.

---

[46]ERISA §4244A, I.R.C. §418D.

[47]IRC §418(c).

[48]ERISA §4241.

The *reorganization index* is determined as the excess, if any, of the vested benefits charge over the net charge to the funding standard account. If the reorganization index is greater than 0, that is, if the vested benefits charge exceeds the net charge to the funding standard account for the year, the plan is in reorganization.

## Plan Benefits Insurance

### Insured Event

Under ERISA's original provisions the insured event that triggers PBGC's guarantee of benefits under a multiemployer plan was plan termination. MPPAA changed the insured event from plan termination to insolvency of the plan. The insured event occurs when it is determined that the plan assets will not be sufficient to pay the plan benefits expected to become payable over the next three years. Under the amended law, a withdrawn employer must continue to make its withdrawal liability payments until its obligation is fully discharged. The procedure by which the resources of the PBGC are made available to a multiemployer plan is complex.

### Liability of a Plan Sponsor to PBGC

Under the original provisions of ERISA the sponsor of a terminated *single* employer plan and the employers signatory to a multiemployer plan were required to reimburse the PBGC for any loss that it incurs in meeting the benefit obligations of the terminated plan, up to 30 percent of the employer's net worth. Amendments to ERISA have removed the 30 percent limit for both single employer plans and multiemployer plans—in effect imposing liability up to the full amount of the employer's net worth.

### Benefits Insured

The definition of the type of benefits insured is basically the same for multiemployer plans as for single employer plans, that is, basic benefits.

**Limitations on Amount of Monthly Benefits.** ERISA imposes a limit on the amount of basic benefit that can be insured by the

PBGC. The limit for multiemployer plans, promulgated by MPPAA, is the sum of 100 percent of the first $5 of monthly benefit per year of credited service and 75 percent of the next $15 of monthly benefit.[49] The benefit to which the ceiling applies is a single life annuity (popularly known as a "straight-life annuity") commencing at the designated normal retirement age. If the benefit is payable at a lower age than the normal retirement age, or in any annuity form other than the straight-life annuity, the limit is actuarially reduced.

**Phase-In of Insurance Coverage.**   For multiemployer plans there is no guarantee until the plan (or amendment) has been in effect for five full years. In other words, there is no phase-in of the coverage for benefits of multiemployer plans.[50]

## Implementation of the Guaranty

The process by which the resources of the PBGC are made available for the payment of benefits of multiemployer plans is more complex than that applicable to single employer plans. The added complexity is attributable to the nature of the multiemployer plan.

A plan need not terminate to qualify for financial assistance from the PBGC. The latter's assistance depends on the plan's inability to meet its basic benefit obligations, whether it is ongoing or terminated.

Actually, the plan must be *insolvent* under the MPPAA definition before the PBGC comes to its rescue. A plan is insolvent when its available resources are not sufficient to pay the plan benefits for the plan year in question, or when the plan sponsor of a plan in reorganization reasonably determines, taking into account the plan's recent and anticipated financial experience, that the plan's available resources will not be sufficient to pay benefits that come due in the next plan year.[51] The term *available resources* means the plan's cash, marketable assets, contributions, withdrawal liability payments, and investment earnings, less reasonable administrative ex-

---

[49]For plans becoming insolvent before the year 2000, the 75 percent is reduced to 65 percent for some plans. ERISA §4022A(c).

[50]ERISA §4022A(b)(1).

[51]ERISA §4245(b)(1),(3).

penses and any amounts owed to the PBGC for the plan year by reason of financial assistance previously provided.

Another concept involved in this process is the *resource benefit level*.[52] This is the estimated level of benefits that can be paid in a given plan (insolvency) year based on the plan sponsor's reasonable projection of the plan's available resources and the benefits payable under the plan. If the resource benefit level is below the level of the basic benefits guaranteed by the PBGC, payment of all benefits other than basic benefits must be suspended for the year, the reduction in benefits to be accomplished equitably in accordance with IRS regulations.[53] If it appears that available resources will not support the payment of all basic (i.e., insured) benefits, the PBGC will provide the additional resources needed *as a loan*.[54] If, by the end of an insolvency year, the plan sponsor determines that the plan's available resources could have supported benefit payments above the resource benefit level for that year, the plan sponsor must distribute the excess resources to plan participants and beneficiaries receiving benefits in that year.

At least three months in advance of each "insolvency year," the plan sponsor of a plan in reorganization must determine the resource benefit level for that insolvency year and inform all interested parties.[55] The PBGC may provide loans to the plan year after year. In the event that the plan recovers from its insolvency status, it must begin repaying the "loans" on reasonable terms in accordance with regulations.

A plan administrator or the PBGC may petition a U.S. court to appoint PBGC trustee of a multiemployer plan to protect the interests of plan participants. The court must agree to PBGC's appointment if the plan is in reorganization or if all employers have withdrawn and the appointment is in the interest of participants. As trustee, PBGC would take over the plan and attempt to recover all amounts owed to the plan. If the available resources of the plan are insufficient to pay all insured benefits, the PBGC would provide financial assistance.

---

[52]ERISA §4245(b)(2).
[53]ERISA §4245(c).
[54]ERISA §§4245(f), 4261.
[55]ERISA §4245(d)(3).

### Premiums

The initial premium, set forth in ERISA, was 50 cents per participant per year for multiemployer pension plans and $1 per participant per year for single employer plans. MPPAA raised the premium for multiemployer plans in stages to $2.60 per participant. The full amount of the increase is not to take effect until 1989, unless the board of directors of the PBGC determines that it is necessary to accelerate the scheduled increases to meet benefit payments.[56]

## Plan Termination

A multiemployer plan terminates when it is amended to stop the accrual of further benefits or credit of any kind under the plan or to convert it to an individual account plan. It is also terminated when all member employers withdraw from the plan or no longer have an obligation to contribute to the plan.[57] In addition, the PBGC may initiate an involuntary termination if the plan fails to satisfy the minimum funding requirements or is unable to pay benefits when due, if there has been a "reportable event," or if the corporation determines that continuation of the plan may reasonably be expected to increase its losses.[58]

The procedures to be followed in order to implement the termination of a multiemployer plan and the requirements that apply to operation of the plan after its termination are specified in ERISA.[59]

## Questions

1.  What special problems were created for multiemployer plans by defining the insured event as plan termination?
2.  When does a complete withdrawal occur? A partial withdrawal?

---

[56]ERISA §4006(a)(3)(A)(iii).
[57]ERISA §4041A(a).
[58]ERISA §4042.
[59]ERISA §§4041A, 4042.

3. With respect to the liability of an employer that withdraws from a multiemployer plan, explain:
   *a.* The various bases for determining the portion of the unfunded vested liability to be allocated to the withdrawn employer.
   *b.* The various reasons for reducing the amount of withdrawal liability initially allocated to an employer.
   *c.* The basis for determining the withdrawn employer's installment payments toward the liquidation of its withdrawal liability.
4. May an employer take a tax deduction for a contribution to a multiemployer plan in discharge of its withdrawal liability?
5. It apparently was the intent of the drafters of MPPAA that an employer withdrawing from a multiemployer pension plan would be able to amortize its withdrawal liability over a 20-year period. Critics of the withdrawal liability provisions, however, allege that in many cases the withdrawn employer must discharge the liability over a much shorter period, sometimes less than five years. What is there about the formulas for allocating the unfunded vested liability of a multiemployer pension plan and determining the liability payments of a withdrawn employer that might cause this result?
6. Some observers of multiemployer pension plans believe that the withdrawal liability provisions of MPPAA greatly bolster the hold of organized labor over management, especially in the construction industry, and thus strengthen joint trust pension plans; but others have concluded that the provisions sound the death knell of collectively bargained multiemployer plans. What is the basis for these diametrically opposed views of MPPAA's impact?
7. Would it be permissible for a management trustee of a joint trust pension plan to oppose a retroactive benefit liberalization on the grounds that it would increase the unfunded vested benefits of the plan, enlarging the exposure of participating employers to withdrawal liability assessment and possibly necessitating an upward adjustment in the rate of contributions to the plan?
8. *a.* In general, how would you characterize plans that are in reorganization?
   *b.* How is it determined that a plan is in reorganization?
   *c.* What are the effects of a plan being in reorganization?
9. Contrast the amount of insurance coverage for single employer and multiemployer pension plans. Why is there a difference in the amount of benefit coverage between the two types of plans?
10. Explain the significance of the fact that the benefit insurance limits are expressed in terms of a single life annuity payable at the designated normal retirement age.

11. Why is there no phase-in of insurance coverage for newly created benefits of a multiemployer pension plan?

12. What role does the *resource benefit level* play in the application of the benefits insurance program to multiemployer pension plans?

# Other Qualified Asset Accumulation Plans Including Federal Tax Treatment of Qualified Plans

# Part Five

# 26 | Profit Sharing, Stock Bonus, and Employee Stock Ownership Plans

An arrangement with many similarities to a qualified pension plan that may be utilized by an employer to provide retirement income to his employees is a *deferred* profit sharing plan. A *deferred* profit sharing plan is to be contrasted with a *cash* profit sharing plan, under which the employer makes periodic distributions, usually annually, of a portion of his profits, as defined, to his employees in cash or in stock in the firm. Cash profit sharing is a form of current compensation, designed to provide a direct incentive to productivity, and will not be dealt with further in this text. Deferred profit sharing, on the other hand, falls into that classification of employer-sponsored financial arrangements known as *asset or capital accumulation* employee benefit plans and shares many characteristics with them. Other plans of this genre include pension plans of all types and deferred compensation arrangements, qualified and nonqualified.

## Profit Sharing Plans

Profit sharing plans are one of the three basic types of qualified plans under the Internal Revenue Code, along with pension plans and stock bonus plans. Profit sharing plans, like stock bonus plans and money purchase pension plans, are a type of defined contribution plan. The characteristics that all defined contributions share in common were described in Chapter 5. Two special types of profit sharing plans which differ from the conventional pattern, thrift plans, and cash or deferred arrangements, will be described in the next chapter.

Profit sharing plans are common among both large and small employers. They have found favor among smaller employers, who felt that they could not afford a pension plan or wanted to avoid the financial commitment and actuarial complexities associated with a defined benefit pension plan. While many large employers operate a profit sharing plan as a supplement to their pension plan, deferred profit sharing, as the dominant source of employee old-age security, is primarily the province of small- and medium-sized employers.

## Plan Design

Deferred profit sharing plans can have the same fundamental objective as pension plans and, historically, have been subject to regulation under the Internal Revenue Code and IRS in much the same manner as pension plans, with any differences being attributable to the peculiar characteristics of the two types of arrangements. As in the case of defined benefit pension plans, many of the pertinent provisions of ERISA apply to profit sharing plans to the extent that they seek to obtain and maintain a qualified status. Indeed, many of the provisions of ERISA will be applicable to such plans regardless of whether they seek tax-qualified status.

Qualification under the Internal Revenue Code and IRS regulations bestows the same tax treatment on profit sharing plans and their distributions as on pension plans. Consequently, profit sharing plans that seek a qualified status must meet most of the general qualification requirements that apply to qualified pension plans, the most significant exception being the requirement that benefits of a pension plan be definitely determinable. Since contributions to a profit sharing plan may depend upon the profits of the plan sponsor, neither the contributions nor the benefits under the plan are definitely determinable. This is the principal distinction between a profit sharing plan and a pension plan. In addition, forfeitures can be, and usually are, allocated to participant accounts, and investment earnings and losses similarly have a direct bearing upon the amount distributed to plan participants. If there are large accumulations, adequate retirement income benefits can be provided. If such accumulations sharply decline, because of investment experience or otherwise, the amount of retirement income may be relatively small. In short, the amount of retirement income is not determinable.

A qualified profit sharing plan must be established and operated for the exclusive benefit of the employees and their beneficiaries. Moreover, it must not discriminate in favor of stockholders, officers, and highly compensated employees as to coverage, benefits, contributions, or otherwise. This pervasive nondiscrimination requirement and the myriad regulations that implement and embellish the requirement exert a strong influence on the design of profit sharing plans, just as they do on pension plans.

**Coverage.**    Both the minimum-age and service requirements for participation and the coverage requirements are the same for a conventional profit sharing plan as for a qualified pension plan.[1] The eligibility requirements for participation tend to be less restrictive than those permitted under ERISA and less restrictive than those typically employed under pension plans. Most profit sharing plans exclude seasonal and part-time employees through a minimum-hours-of-employment requirement and require one year of service of all employees who satisfy the minimum employment test (e.g., 1,000 hours per year). However, these plans seldom impose a minimum-age requirement (although age 21 is sometimes found). Many profit sharing plans allow immediate participation.

There are at least three reasons why the eligibility conditions of a conventional profit sharing plan tend to be less restrictive than those of a pension plan. In the first, profit sharing is believed to provide a direct incentive to productivity, and it behooves the employer to expose as many of his employees to the concept as possible. Second, profit sharing is a simpler mechanism to administer, having no actuarial underpinnings in respect of active employees. Finally, as will be noted later, the nonvested accumulation of terminating employees can be reallocated among the remaining participants. Thus, despite very liberal participation provisions, the monies set aside under the plan are likely to find their way into the

---

[1]See Chapter 4.

accounts of the longer-service employees (depending upon the vesting provisions), whom the employer may prefer to favor.

Most profit sharing plans are not integrated with Social Security.

**Contributions.**   All required contributions to a conventional profit sharing plan are made by the employer; but it is no longer a condition of qualification that the contributions in some tangible way be related to the firm's accumulated or current profits, as to both the *amount* and the *source*. If employee contributions are required as a condition of employer contributions, the plan is technically a profit sharing *thrift* plan. Pure profit sharing plans and thrift plans sometimes permit voluntary employee contributions.

*A. Contribution Commitment.*   The Internal Revenue Code does not require, as a condition for qualification, that a profit sharing plan contain a definite predetermined contribution formula. However, IRS regulations require that contributions to a qualified profit sharing plan be "recurring and substantial."[2] The requirement that the contributions be recurring and substantial is designed to give evidence that the plan was set up in good faith and was intended to be permanent.[3]

To be currently deductible by the employer, the contribution in respect of a particular fiscal year may be made at any time up to the due date for filing the employer's tax return for that taxable year (including extensions), provided the contribution is designated as being on account of that taxable year.[4] The same liberality applies to contributions made by both accrual and cash basis taxpayers.

The obvious advantage to the employer of the discretionary approach to determining his contribution to the profit sharing plan is flexibility. The amount of the contribution can be set in the light of the firm's profit for the year and its working capital needs and can be adjusted from year to year to reflect changing circumstances. Indeed, the employer can select, in a *loss* year, to make a substantial contribution. The degree of flexibility is constrained somewhat, however, by the IRS requirement that the contributions be substantial and recurring.

---

[2]Treas. Reg. 1.401–1(b)(2).

[3]The court rejected this concept in *Lincoln Electric Co. Employees' Profit-Sharing Trust* (CA–6 1951, rev'g and rem'g TC) 51–2 USTC 9371, 190 F.2d 326.

[4]I.R.C. §404(a)(6).

There are certain disadvantages to the discretionary formula approach. It may undermine the participants' confidence in the plan and in the employer, especially if the contributions are below the expectations of the participants. Under the best of circumstances and with the best of intentions on the part of the employer, the discretionary approach has an adverse effect on the financial planning of the participants. Moreover, in an apparent effort to promote the use of a predetermined formula, the Wage-Hour Division of the Department of Labor has ruled that contributions to a profit sharing plan under a discretionary formula must be added to regular pay rates in computing overtime pay, except under certain circumstances.[5] If employer contributions are allocated to participants on a basis that recognizes overtime pay or the plan provides for full and immediate vesting, discretionary contributions are not taken into account in calculating overtime pay rates. Since many employers have the objective of providing the equivalent of one month's salary (or about 8 percent of regular compensation) through the profit sharing plan, recognition or nonrecognition of profit sharing contributions in overtime pay rates is not an inconsequential matter.

These disadvantages of the discretionary approach have caused most large sponsors to include a definite, predetermined formula in their plans. Most small employers, however, keenly concerned with financial flexibility and believing that they can retain the confidence of their work force without a binding, advance contribution commitment, have elected to follow the discretionary approach or a hybrid approach, whereby the plan will provide for both a minimum fixed contribution from profits and a discretionary additional contribution.

***B. Contribution Formulas.***    A plan sponsor who makes no advance contribution commitment may determine his annual contributions in any manner. He may apply a formula of some type, or he may determine the amount to be contributed in a completely arbitrary manner, taking into account all relevant financial and personnel considerations. On the other hand, the plan sponsor who decides to make an advance contribution commitment and incorporate it in the plan document must state clearly and precisely how

---

[5] 29 CFR 549.1(e). Opinion Letter No. 404 of Wage-Hour Administrator, May 23, 1966.

each annual contribution is to be determined. This statement or description is referred to as the *contribution formula*.

While there are many variations, there are only three *basic* or *conceptual* ways of expressing an advance contribution commitment: (1) as a percentage of profits, (2) as a percentage of covered compensation, and (3) as a percentage of employee contributions. Employer contributions as a percentage of employee contributions are a feature of thrift or savings plans, to be discussed separately in the next chapter.

A contribution formula that expresses the commitment in terms of profits must carefully define the term to avoid ambiguity, disputes, and distrust. The definition must obviously be consistent with the accounting system and the terminology used by the employer firm. The definition should lend itself to an objective determination of profits, by technically proficient outsiders, if necessary. A dispute between management and the covered employees may arise as to the amount of "profits" in a particular year, or over a time period, and it should be possible for an arbitrator, court-appointed expert, or other impartial person to make a reasonably accurate determination of what the profit sharing contribution should have been.

The plan document must specify whether contributions are to be based on profits before deduction of federal and state income taxes or on after-tax profits. In theory, after-tax profits are the better measure of the funds available for sharing with the employee group. However, inasmuch as employer contributions to a profit sharing plan are deductible for income tax purposes, after-tax profits cannot be determined until the contribution for the fiscal year is ascertained. If the contribution itself is expressed in terms of the after-tax profit, it will be necessary to apply an algebraic formula to determine the amount of the contribution. This adds a bit of unnecessary complexity to the contribution formula, since the same result can be achieved by applying an appropriately reduced percentage to the before-tax profit. To avoid these problems, many plans express the contribution formula in terms of after-tax profits determined without regard to the contribution to the plan. In addition, profits are sometimes defined to exclude nonrecurring items, such as sales of property.

The contribution formula may call for a flat percentage of profits, however defined, across the board, or the percentage may apply to only that portion of profits in excess of an amount deemed to be a reasonable return on invested capital. For example, a plan might provide that there would be sharing of only that portion of profits in excess of an amount equal to 10 percent of the net worth of the firm. The breakpoint may be stated in terms of a specified dollar amount of profit or a specified dollar amount of dividends. Such a provision assures that the profit sharing plan will not operate to reduce earnings to a point below that needed to attract new capital or to meet the ongoing financial needs of the firm. The formula may call for an increasing percentage of profits to be paid to the plan as profits rise. A few plans decrease the contribution percentage as profits expand. The precise formula adopted will reflect the sponsor's long-range goal for the plan, as well as his perception of the impact of the plan and its contribution formula on employee morale and productivity. As noted above, many employers adopt a contribution formula that is designed to produce plan contributions in normal years equal to one month's covered compensation.

The formula may call for contributions equal to a specified percentage of the compensation of covered employees. The compensation base would have to be defined, as under a pension plan, with particular attention being given to overtime, vacations, sick leave, and so forth. For plan years beginning after 1988, compensation in excess of $200,000 (indexed) may not be recognized.[6] The plan may state that the compensation-based contributions will be made only to the extent that they can be financed out of current profits (or accumulated profits, if the plan sponsor is so minded), or the contribution percentage may be linked to the level of current profits. For example, the contribution schedule might be as follows:

| Profits | Contribution as a Percent of Covered Compensation |
|---|---|
| Less than $100,000 | None |
| $100,000–$199,999 | 5% |
| $200,000–$299,999 | 6 |
| $300,000–$399,999 | 7 |
| $400,000–$499,999 | 8 |
| $500,000–$599,999 | 9 |
| $600,000 or over | 10 |

---

[6]I.R.C. §401(a)(17).

Whether the contribution is expressed as a percentage of profits
or a percentage of covered compensation, there is generally an
overriding provision that the employer's contribution for a given
year will not exceed the amount that can be deducted in that year
for income tax purposes. This limit is 15 percent of covered compensation for such year.[7] There is a limit on the amount of employer
and employee contributions and reallocated forfeitures that can be
added to the account of an individual employee in any year,[8] and
that limitation can reduce the contribution that the employer would
otherwise make.

The plan sponsor reserves the right to change the contributing
formula at any time. This would involve a plan amendment, and,
if the change involved a reduction in contributions, employee morale would probably be adversely affected. Nevertheless, employers have from time to time curtailed their contribution commitment
to adapt to changing business circumstances. If such amendment
is a clear curtailment of benefits, which is viewed by the Internal
Revenue Service as a partial termination of the plan, full vesting
may need to be provided. The entire plan may be abandoned; but
if this occurs within a few years after inception, there may be
adverse tax consequences. (Plan termination is discussed later.)

*C. Limits on Deductibility of Employer Contributions.*   Section
404(a)(3) of the Internal Revenue Code imposes certain limits on
the deductibility of employer contributions to a qualified profit sharing plan. This section of the Code permits an employer to make
tax-deductible contributions to a qualified profit sharing plan equal
to 15 percent of the aggregate compensation of employees covered
by the plan. Stated negatively, tax-deductible contributions are
limited to 15 percent of covered compensation in the aggregate.

For taxable years beginning before 1987 a *credit carry-over* was
created whenever the contribution in a particular year was less
than the maximum allowable deduction; namely, 15 percent of covered compensation for such year. This unused credit is carried
forward and may be applied in any subsequent year in which contributions exceed 15 percent of the aggregate compensation of the
plan participants in that year. Therefore, deductions for contributions made in a given year can exceed 15 percent of a covered

[7]I.R.C. §404(a)(3).
[8]I.R.C. §§415,416. See Chapter 5.

compensation for that year if a credit carry-over is available. There is no limit on the amount of credit carry-over that can be accumulated, but the most that can be used or applied in a given tax year is stated to be 15 percent of covered compensation for that year. There is also a limit on the overall deduction that may be taken when a credit carry-over is used, that limit being 25 percent of covered compensation for the year in which the credit is utilized. With an overall limit of 25 percent of compensation, the effective limit on the use of an accumulated credit carry-over is 10 percent per year, not 15 percent. While such credits may not be created after 1986, many plans have large credits from prior years which may still be used.

A *contribution* carry-over arises whenever the contribution for a given year exceeds the maximum allowable deduction. The maximum allowable deduction in a succeeding year for a contribution carry-over is 15 percent of covered compensation less the amount of contribution made for the succeeding year. The 25 percent limit may not be applied to the contribution carry-over. Contribution carry-overs can be accumulated without limit as to time or amount and deducted in any subsequent year or years in which contribution payments are less than the maximum allowable deduction.

If the employer maintains both a qualified defined benefit pension plan and a qualified defined contribution plan covering the same group of employees, the maximum allowable deduction in any one year for the two plans combined is 25 percent of covered compensation.[9] Under these circumstances, the separate limit on deductibility of employer contributions to each of the two plans still applies, as well as the 25 percent combined limit. A carry-over provision for combined contributions in excess of 25 percent applies, similar to the carry-over provision applicable to the profit sharing plan itself. That is, if the contribution to the pension plan is only 5 percent of covered compensation, the permissible deduction for the contribution to the profit sharing plan is 15 percent of covered compensation, not 20 percent. Furthermore, if the minimum funding provisions of the Internal Revenue Code require a contribution to the pension plan equal to more than 25 percent of covered compensation, the entire required contribution to the pension plan would

---

[9] I.R.C. §404(a)(7).

be deductible, but there would be no deductible contribution to the profit sharing plan.

The Internal Revenue Code imposes a 10 percent excise tax on all nondeductible contributions made for a year.[10] To the extent that any nondeductible contribution is neither withdrawn nor deducted during the following year, the 10 percent tax is applied again, and this continues each year until no nondeductible contribution remains in the plan. However, the employer may not be allowed to withdraw the nondeductible contribution unless it was made by mistake of fact or was originally conditioned on its deductibility.[11] The excise tax on nondeductible contributions also applies to tax-exempt employers, with respect to any contributions exceeding the amounts which would have been deductible if the employer had not been tax-exempt.

**Allocations.**    Employer contributions to a profit sharing plan may be made in bulk, and without reference to the individual participants, especially when the contribution formula is expressed in terms of net profits. Moreover, the accumulated plan assets are usually commingled for investment purposes, and the trust is credited with the investment earnings. Since the plan is operated for the exclusive benefit of the participants and their beneficiaries, there must be a mechanism for establishing the interests of the individual participants in the commingled pool of assets. This function is accomplished through establishing and maintaining a set of individual accounts, one for each participant in the plan. Each account is credited with a share of the plan assets in accordance with the *allocation* provisions of the plan.

The plan must make provision for allocating employer contributions, investment earnings, and the account balances forfeited by employees who leave the plan before their interests are fully vested.[12] Each of these matters will be considered in turn.

*A. Employer Contributions.*    Employer contributions are the most significant source of income to a conventional profit sharing trust, and they must be allocated to plan participants in a manner

---

[10]I.R.C. §4972.

[11]ERISA §403(c)(2)(A),(C); I.R.C. §401(a)(2).

[12]Although employee accounts are maintained, employees usually do not have any specific interest in particular plan assets.

that does not discriminate in favor of highly compensated employees if the plan is to meet the qualification standards of the IRS.[13] While, as noted earlier, the Internal Revenue Code does not require a profit sharing plan to include a fixed formula for determining contributions to the plan, it does require the plan to set forth the basis on which the contributions will be allocated to individual participants. This description is generally referred to as the *allocation formula,* even though it may apply only to contributions.

The most common basis for allocating employer contributions is the compensation of the employees. Under this basis, each covered participant receives that proportion of the employer contribution that his or her annual compensation bears to the total annual compensation of all participants. For this purpose, compensation may include only base earnings, or it may be defined to include base earnings, overtime pay, bonuses, and other forms of cash emolument. If total taxable compensation is not used, the definition used must be shown not to discriminate in favor of highly compensated employees.[14] If the plan does not contain a definite, predetermined *contribution* formula, it must, for federal labor law purposes, include overtime earnings in the compensation base for *allocating* contributions if the allocations themselves are not to be added to base pay rates for purposes of computing overtime pay.[15]

Allocations are usually made only to those employees who were in the plan on the last day of the plan year, which is usually the employer's fiscal year. Some plans credit terminated employees with a pro rata share of the annual allocation. In other words, an employee who was in the plan for three months during a plan year and then terminated would receive one fourth of the share of contributions that he or she would have received had he or she remained in the plan for the entire year at the same earnings level. This is especially true where the employee's termination is by reason of retirement, death, or disability. Pro rata allocation of contributions has sometimes become an issue under collectively bargained plans when a collective bargaining unit withdraws from the plan at any time other than at the end of the plan year.

---

[13]I.R.C. §401(a)(4).

[14]I.R.C. §414(s).

[15]See footnote 5 in this chapter.

Allocation of employer contributions on the basis of current compensation, while equitable in terms of current service, gives no weight to length of service. Some employers believe that the allocation formula should recognize and reward length of service. If length of service is not recognized in some appropriate way, and the employer does not operate a pension plan in tandem with the profit sharing plan, employees with many years of service and in middle age or beyond when the plan is established will not accumulate a sufficient balance in their accounts to provide adequate retirement income. Whatever the motivation, some plan sponsors adopt an allocation formula that recognizes service rendered prior to inception of the plan.

The most common approach to recognizing length of service is the "unit" system. Under this approach, units of participation in employer contributions are credited to the employees according to both compensation and length of service. The weights assigned to these two components can be varied to suit the preference of the plan sponsor, so long as the results do not discriminate in favor of highly compensated employees. For example, the plan may provide that one unit of participation will be credited for each $300 of annual compensation and another unit for each year of service with the employer, whether rendered prior or subsequent to the inception of the plan. Under such a formula, an employee who had 10 years of service with the employer on the date the plan was established and earned $15,000 in the first year of the plan's operation would be credited with 11 units of participation in the first round of allocations for service and another 50 units for compensation. A plan sponsor who wants to give more weight to service, for example, might assign two units to each year of service or, conversely, require $600 of compensation for each unit based on earnings. At the end of each plan year, the number of units credited to the various employee accounts is tabulated and the sum total is divided into the employer's contributions to determine the value of each unit.

The major advantage of the unit system is its flexibility. The plan sponsor has available innumerable combinations of years of service and compensation in setting the basis for participation in the profit sharing contribution. Its major disadvantage is that the relationship between service and compensation is distorted as compensation levels increase in response to inflationary pressures, or for any reason. If a combination of one unit of participation for each year of service and one unit for each $300 of annual compensation is appropriate when average annual compensation is $15,000, it will clearly not produce the same results if average compensation rises to $20,000, $25,000, or $30,000. The original relationship can be restored by plan amendment, but this would involve certain legal or other costs and could prove unsettling to the employee group as they see their respective shares in the profit sharing "melon" changing. Another approach is to index the unit of participation based on earnings, with the amount of annual compensation required for a unit linked to changes in average earnings, or to some other value.

Length of service may be recognized without resort to the unit system simply by determining an employee's share of employer contributions in accordance with a schedule that varies the percentage of compensation to be received by years of service. Under such an approach, an employee with 5 years of service might receive an allocation equal to 5 percent of compensation, while one with 10 years of service might receive 10 percent of compensation. There is also great potential flexibility in this approach through the choice of gradations in the schedule of percentages. Needless to say, the overall level of the percentages is controlled by the amount of the employer contributions to be allocated.

Any allocation formula that recognizes years of service will receive special scrutiny by the Internal Revenue Service to determine whether it discriminates in favor of highly compensated employees. Since highly compensated employees will generally have the longest period of service when the plan is established (and each year thereafter), weighting of service in the allocation formula could cause the IRS to view the formula as discriminatory and, hence, not acceptable. In fact, in most situations, the IRS will not approve the unit system because of its potentially discriminatory effect.[16]

Under some older profit sharing plans, the same dollar amount is allocated to all employee accounts. This is quite logically called the *per capita* basis of allocation. It is appropriate only when the earnings of the various plan participants vary within a very narrow range. This allocation basis is rarely used in newer plans.

---

[16]Rev. Ruls. 68–652, 68–653, 68–654.

The annual addition, including employer contributions, forfeitures, and employee contributions, if any (see below), that can be allocated to an employee's account in a given year is subject to the limitations of Sections 415 and 416 of the Internal Revenue Code, described in Chapter 5.

**B. Investment Earnings.** Title to the assets of a profit sharing plan is held by the trustee but, for accounting purposes, shares in the composite pool of assets are allocated to the individual accounts of the plan participants. These assets generate investment earnings, which, in turn, must be allocated to the participants. The only logical approach to allocating investment earnings is in terms of the individual account balances. Presumably, the assets theoretically assigned to each account contribute on a pro rata basis to the total flow of investment earnings and should participate on a pro rata basis in those earnings.

The investment earnings of a profit sharing plan are measured on a total return basis. Under this concept, the return includes dividends, interest, realized capital gains and losses, and unrealized capital appreciation and depreciation. In other words, the total return recognizes actual investment income plus or minus changes in the market value of the underlying assets during the measurement period. This means that the assets of the plan must be valued from time to time on a market value basis.[17]

The Internal Revenue Service requires that the assets of a profit sharing plan be valued at least once a year.[18] To provide more flexibility in plan administration and more equitable treatment of plan participants, many plans provide for more frequent valuation,[19] some having monthly or daily valuations. Allocations to individual employee accounts are made on total investment earnings for the accounting period, including changes in market value of the assets, that the balance in the account bears to the sum of the balances in all accounts.

---

[17]An exception exists when all the assets of the plan are vested in a contract backed by the general asset account of a life insurance company. Transactions with plan participants under such a contractual arrangement take place on a book value basis and interest is credited to individual accounts in accordance with the accounting procedures of the life insurer.

[18]Rev. Rul. 80–155.

[19]Ibid.

The more frequent the asset valuations and the associated allocations of investment earnings, the less troublesome is the accounting for transactions with the plan that occur between valuation dates. The normal transactions of this type would be total withdrawals by employees terminating membership in the plan and partial withdrawals by continuing members under the terms of the plan. The policy question is whether these accounts should be credited with investment earnings and increases and decreases in market values for the interim between the last valuation date and the date of withdrawal. If annual valuations are prescribed, the gain or loss could be substantial if interim allocations are not authorized. Alternatively, some plans provide for annual valuations and delay all or a portion of the distribution until the annual valuation date. This is especially true if the employee is entitled to a pro rata share of the employer's contribution for the last fiscal year of employment.

Some profit sharing plans permit employees to direct the investment of part or all of their accounts among two or more investment options, such as a common stock fund and a fixed income fund. In this case each subaccount of an employee shares in the investment experience of the particular fund in which it is invested.

*C. Forfeitures.* A participant who terminates from a profit sharing plan before the balance in his or her account is fully vested forfeits the nonvested portion of the account. Under some plans, amounts forfeited by terminating employees are credited against the employer's required contribution, as under a pension plan; but the prevailing practice is to reallocate the forfeitures among the remaining participants. The basic policy question involved here is whether the forfeitures should be reallocated on the basis of compensation or account balances, keeping in mind the IRS stricture against any plan provision that will tend to discriminate in favor of highly compensated employees.

For many years, plans frequently specified that forfeitures were to be reallocated among remaining participants on the basis of account balances, with forfeitures and investment earnings being treated in the same manner. Over time, the IRS concluded that this basis of reallocation tends to favor the highly compensated employees, since their account balances will have been accumulated over a longer period of years (because of lower turnover) than those of other employees and, hence, will be entitled to a disproportionately large share of the forfeitures. The IRS does not flatly prohibit the reallocation of forfeitures on the basis of account balances but, if it concludes that the plan in practice is favoring the highly compensated employees, the plan may lose its qualified status.

Accordingly, the great majority of plans reallocate forfeitures on the basis of employee compensation. The IRS regards allocation on the basis of compensation to be generally nondiscriminatory.

**Distributions.**    The primary purpose of many, if not most, profit sharing plans is to accumulate funds for the enhancement of the old-age economic security of the employee participants. The plan may be the sole mechanism maintained by the employer for this socially desirable objective, or it may be a supplement to a pension plan sponsored and supported by the employer. In either event, it might be assumed that the funds credited to the individual accounts of the employees could not be withdrawn prior to the employee's retirement or death prior to retirement. Such is not the case. As conceived under IRS regulations and reflected in the provisions of most plans, a deferred profit sharing plan is a much more flexible asset accumulation instrument than a pension plan, and distributions are permitted under a greater variety of circumstances.

**A.  Circumstances.**    Regulations[20] permit distributions from a qualified plan "after a fixed number of years, the attainment of a stated age, or upon the prior occurrence of some event such as layoff, illness, disability, retirement, death, or severance of employment." If there is to be any meaningful distinction between a *cash* or *current* profit sharing plan and a *deferred* profit sharing plan, employer contributions to the latter must be held by the trust for some period after they are made. By indirection, the controlling regulation requires that the monies be held for a "fixed number of years," unless one of the other designated events occurs in the meantime. The IRS has given the expression "fixed number of years" a very literal interpretation in ruling that the minimum holding period is two years.[21] This requirement applies to each individual account. That portion of an employer's contribution allocated to a particular employee's account must remain in the account, along with the investment earnings associated with it, for at least

---

[20]Treas. Reg. 1.401–1(b)(1)(ii).
[21]Rev. Rul. 71–295.

two years. If the plan calls for annual contributions by the employer, no distribution could be made from a particular account until the third allocation is made, and at that time an amount equal to the first allocation plus investment earnings could be withdrawn. After the fourth allocation is made, the second allocation could be withdrawn, and so on. If allocations are made monthly, the first distribution from an individual account could be made two years from the date of the first allocation. However, after an employee has participated in the plan for five years he may, if the plan permits, withdraw all employer contributions, including those made within the preceding two years.[22]

The plan is under no obligation to make distributions under all the circumstances mentioned. The only affirmative requirement of the regulation in this respect is that the monies credited to an employee's account be made available to him or her at retirement. Between the two extremes of sequestering the allocations for a minimum of two years and making them available in some form at retirement, the plan sponsor is free, if collective bargaining is not involved, to determine the conditions under which distributions will be made.

The distribution provisions are vitally affected by the concept of vesting and the vesting requirements set forth in ERISA and IRS rulings. Profit sharing plans are subject to the same vesting standards that apply to qualified pension plans under ERISA.[23] Vesting pertains to the retention of certain rights under the plan upon termination of employment, other than by death or disability. Stated differently, vesting protects benefits accrued under a pension or profit sharing plan against loss or forfeiture through termination of employment prior to receipt of the vested benefit. But a benefit derived from employer contributions is not treated as forfeitable solely because it is forfeited upon the participant's death, with the narrow exception of the qualified preretirement survivor annuity.[24]

In practice, profit sharing plans vest account balances on a much more liberal basis than that required by law. This is partially due to the attitude of the IRS, which has traditionally required faster

---

[22]Rev. Rul. 68–24.

[23]See Chapter 7.

[24]ERISA §203(a)(3)(A), I.R.C. §411(a)(3)(A).

vesting for profit sharing plans. Under most plans, account balances are fully vested upon death, total disability, and normal retirement age, the latter being required by law. Moreover, the account balance is distributed to the participant or his beneficiary upon the occurrence of these events. Upon termination of employment, other than by death, disability, and retirement, immediate distribution is often made of the *vested* portion of the account, although participants must consent to any immediate distribution,[25] and although plans may preclude any immediate distribution before some stipulated age.

The proportion of the account vested will depend, of course, upon the vesting provisions of the plan and the amount of service of the terminating employee. Graded vesting is much more common under profit sharing plans than under pension plans. It is not uncommon for a plan to vest 20 percent of employer contributions (and the associated investment earnings) for each full year of service, the account balance being fully vested after five years of service. Relatively few plans defer full vesting beyond five years. Because forfeited account balances are typically reallocated among the remaining participants, the IRS is more concerned (as noted above) with the vesting provisions of a profit sharing plan than a pension plan.

There are four general occasions for the distribution of the account balance of a participant in a qualified profit sharing plan: death, total disability, retirement, and other severance of employment. The first three events may result in distribution of the entire account balance, whereas severance of employment produces distribution of the vested portion of the account balance.

One of the most difficult policy questions in plan design is whether a participant should be permitted to withdraw all or a portion of his or her vested account balance while still in the active service of the employer. This issue goes to the fundamental objective of the plan. If it is designed to serve as a long-term savings medium, perhaps for old-age economic support, withdrawals during active service to meet current needs should not be permitted. On the other hand, if the plan is viewed as a general savings program, utilizing the deferred compensation concept and capable of meeting either current or long-term

---

[25]I.R.C. §401(a)(11).

capital needs, then periodic withdrawals during active employment are entirely appropriate and consistent with the aim of the program. Some plans allow withdrawals only for unusual hardships or certain specific purposes, such as home purchase.

A participant is subject to tax only upon the amount actually distributed from the plan.[26] Prior to 1982, participants were also subject to tax on amounts "made available," under the constructive receipt concept. Many profit sharing plans still contain restrictions or penalties upon withdrawal that were originally designed to prevent application by the IRS of the constructive receipt doctrine. Perhaps the most common such penalty is depriving the employee of membership rights for a specified period, such as six months. Another approach to avoiding the constructive receipt problem was to require approval of all withdrawal requests by a duly constituted committee, using some ascertainable standard. Usually, under this approach, withdrawals are permitted only for emergencies, such as illness or layoff, or to meet such commendable objectives as home ownership or education of the children.

The taxation of distributions is discussed in Chapter 29.

**B. Form.**   Distributions from a qualified profit sharing plan may take several forms. Distributions to employees in active employment or to those terminating employment through voluntary or involuntary withdrawal generally take the form of lump-sum payments. Distributions at retirement may take the form of lump-sum payments, installment payments, or a life annuity, possibly with a survivor income feature. If a profit sharing plan permits a life annuity form of payment, then it must satisfy the rules of ERISA relating to joint and survivor annuities. Some plans permit the participants to elect the form of distribution, within prescribed limits, the choices sometimes including a variable annuity. Distributions upon death or disability may be in a lump sum or in installments, subject to the survivor annuity requirements described in Chapter 8. Participants may be permitted to elect a life income option or other installment settlement of their account to be payable to a designated beneficiary or beneficiaries upon their death during service. If a life annuity is provided, this is almost always done by purchase of an annuity from a life insurance company.

---

[26]I.R.C. §402(a)(1).

If a participant has been given the opportunity to allocate a portion of his account for the purchase of individual life insurance, a distribution of his account at retirement or earlier separation from service would include the life insurance policy or its cash value. At death, the distribution would encompass the proceeds of the life insurance contract, payable in a lump sum or in installments, at the option and direction of the participant.

Under many profit sharing plans, some or all of the assets are invested in the common stock or other securities of the plan sponsor. Under those plans, a distribution may include securities of the employer. If a total distribution of the employee's account is made under conditions qualifying for favorable tax treatment, the value of the securities of the employer for the purpose of determining the employee's gain is the cost to the trust and not the fair market value of the securities at the time of the distribution.[27] In other words, the employee is not taxed at the time of the distribution on the unrealized appreciation. The cost to the trust becomes the employee's cost basis should the securities be sold at a later date. The same treatment of employer securities is accorded under qualified pension plans.

*C. Loans.* Many profit sharing plans provide that a participant may borrow part or all of his vested account balance. All loans are subject to ERISA's fiduciary requirements.[28] Loans to participants are exempt from the restriction against alienation and assignment and from the restriction concerning prohibited transactions if they are adequately secured, bear a reasonable rate of interest, are available to all participants and beneficiaries on a reasonably equivalent basis, and meet certain other requirements.[29]

A participant enters into a loan agreement with the plan, usually agreeing to make periodic payments of interest at an agreed-upon rate and to make payments to amortize the principal of the loan. Payments of interest and principal amortization are often made through payroll deduction.

A loan to a participant is usually secured solely by the participant's vested account balance. If the participant terminates em-

---

[27]I.R.C. §402(e)(4)(J).

[28]ERISA §404.

[29]ERISA §206(d)(2), 407(b)(1); I.R.C. §401(a)(13), 4975(d)(1); Treas. Reg. 1.401(a)–13(d)(2).

ployment or otherwise makes a withdrawal, the outstanding balance of this loan is subtracted from the amount otherwise available to him.

If the loan is considered to be part of the total unsegregated assets of the plan, the plan will account for the loan in the same manner as it accounts for purchase of a bond or a mortgage or for a loan to a disinterested person. Under this approach, the unsegregated plan assets include the outstanding balance of the loan. Interest payments on the loan are included in investment income. Repayments of principal are treated as such and reduce the outstanding balance of the loan. Interest on the loan, together with all other investment income of the plan, is allocated among the accounts of all participants. The account balance of the borrowing participant is treated in the same manner as if he had received no loan. If the participant terminates his employment or otherwise withdraws his account balance, the payment to him is reduced by the outstanding balance of the loan. From the viewpoint of the plan's accounting, this withdrawal is treated as if the entire account balance were paid to the participant and he immediately repaid the loan. Since the individual's account balance under this approach fluctuates with the market value of the plan's assets, it would be imprudent for the plan to lend the participant an amount equal to his entire account balance, lest the fluctuating account balance fall below the outstanding balance of the loan and provide inadequate security for the loan. Depending upon the volatility of plan assets, the plan may restrict loans to one half or two thirds of the individual's vested account balance.

Under the alternative approach, the loan is not treated as part of the unsegregated assets of the plan. Rather, it is treated as a separate investment of a portion of the assets attributable to the borrowing participant's account. In effect, the participant directs the plan to invest part of his account in a loan to himself. After the loan, his account is divided into two parts, one consisting of the outstanding balance of his loan and the other part consisting of his share of the remaining unsegregated assets of the plan. If the participant makes a $60 payment of interest, it is interest income attributable to his own account and increases his own account balance by $60. This $60 interest payment is added to the unsegregated assets of the plan available for reinvestment, and the individual participant's share of the unsegregated assets is increased by $60; his loan account balance is unaffected. If the participant makes a $100 payment to reduce the balance of his loan, the $100 is added to the unsegregated assets of the fund and his share of the unsegregated assets is increased by $100. In the latter case, however, the outstanding balance of his loan is reduced by $100 and the portion of his account balance represented by the loan is reduced accordingly.

Assuming a loan of $6,000 from a $10,000 account balance with interest of 1 percent per month, and ignoring other transactions and investment income on the unsegregated assets, the loan and first month's payment are illustrated as shown in Table 15.

Under this method, the loan asset always exactly equals the outstanding balance of the loan. Therefore, the plan can safely lend 100 percent of the participant's vested account balance. Every payment of principal or interest increases the participant's own net amount available for distribution.

A loan has an effect similar to a distribution, in that it makes money currently available for use by the participant. But unlike a distribution, a loan is not taxable income to the participant if certain conditions and restrictions are satisfied.[30] The loan terms must provide for repayment by level installments (quarterly or more frequently) within five years, or within a "reasonable" time in the case of loans to acquire the principal residence of the participant. When a loan is made, the amount of the loan, plus the outstanding balance of any other loans from the plan, may not exceed the greater of $10,000 or one half of the participant's vested account balance. However, the limit is never more than $50,000, less any principal repayments made during the preceding 12 months. Loans in excess of these amounts, or loans which do not satisfy the repayment requirement, are treated as distributions and are included in the participant's gross income for tax purposes.

The Tax Reform Act eliminated the deduction of interest paid for all loans, whether from a qualified plan or any other lender, with only three generally available exceptions:[31]

---

[30]I.R.C. §72(p).
[31]I.R.C. §163(d).

**TABLE 15**
**Accounting for a Loan to a Participant**

| | Participant's Account Balance | | | Outstanding Balance of Loan | Net Amount Available for Distribution |
|---|---|---|---|---|---|
| | Unsegregated Assets | Loan Assets | Total | | |
| Before loan | $10,000 | $    0 | $10,000 | $    0 | $10,000 |
| Loan | −6,000 | +6,000 | 0 | +6,000 | −6,000 |
| After loan | $ 4,000 | $6,000 | $10,000 | $6,000 | $ 4,000 |
| Interest payment | +60 | 0 | +60 | 0 | +60 |
| After payment | $ 4,060 | $6,000 | $10,060 | $6,000 | $ 4,060 |
| Principal payment | +100 | −100 | 0 | −100 | +100 |
| After payment | $4,160 | $5,900 | $10,060 | $5,900 | $ 4,160 |

1.  The four-year phase-in of the interest disallowance, which temporarily preserves part of the deduction during the years 1987 through 1990.
2.  Deduction of certain mortgage interest.
3.  Deduction of certain investment interest incurred to purchase or carry investments.

In addition to these restrictions which apply to interest deductions generally, new rules further restrict the deduction of interest on loans from qualified plans.[32] No deduction is allowed for interest under any loan made after 1986 to a "key employee" (as defined under top-heavy plan requirements). Nor is any deduction to be allowed for interest on any loan made after 1986 that is secured by an employee's elective contributions under a 401(k) plan or a 403(b) plan. To alleviate this problem some 401(k) plans provide that plan loans will not be secured by accounts attributable to elective contributions unless the loan balance exceeds the balance of the participant's vested accounts that are not attributable to elective contributions.

Even if a participant may not deduct the interest paid on a plan loan, the interest paid does not increase the participant's tax basis in his account.

There are several advantages to a loan provision. It makes money available to meet current needs of employees, perhaps on more favorable terms than the employee could borrow the money elsewhere, and under more favorable tax treatment than a distribution from the plan. In addition, all of the interest paid by the employee benefits himself.

There are also potential disadvantages to such a provision. If the purpose of the plan is to provide for retirement needs, loans that are not repaid can defeat the purpose, just as distributions can. For this reason, some plans limit loans to hardship situations. The administrative work and expense is a disadvantage. Some employees may object to paying interest on their "own money." And if loans are made from the unsegregated assets, there may be dilution of the investment earnings of the trust if the loan interest rate is less than the rate of return on other trust assets.

---

[32]I.R.C. §72(p)(3).

## Purchase of Life Insurance

**On Participants.** A qualified profit sharing plan may provide the participants with the option of having a portion of their account balances applied to the purchase and maintenance of either term or permanent life insurance, purchased under a group contract or individual policies. This is accomplished by including in the profit sharing trust agreement a provision that grants each participant the right to direct the trustee to purchase life insurance, and sometimes other specific investments, for his or her account. If the trust agreement authorizes the trustee to purchase investments earmarked for the accounts of the various participants (and all participants have the right to so direct the trustee), then any participant can instruct the trustee to purchase life insurance on his or her life without disqualifying the plan.

An insurance contract purchased on the life of a plan participant is owned by the trust. The premiums for the insurance are charged directly to the account of the individual. That portion of the periodic premium allocable to the pure insurance or protection component of the contract (i.e., the face amount less the cash value) is viewed as a current distribution from the trust and is, therefore, taxable to the employee as ordinary income in the taxable year in which it is paid.[33] The amount of reportable income is calculated by multiplying the pure protection component of the contract by the one-year term insurance premium rate for the participant's attained age.[34] That portion of the periodic premium allocable to the cash value component of the contract is considered to be an investment of the trust and is not currently taxable as a distribution from the trust. Upon the death of the participant, the insurance proceeds, depending upon the terms of the plan, are either credited in full to the account of the deceased employee or paid directly to the beneficiary designated by the employee. The latter is the more common procedure.

Upon the employee's retirement, the trustee may surrender the contract and pay the cash value to the participant; he may distribute the contract to the participant; or he may permit the participant to exchange the cash value of the contract for a single sum life annuity.

---

[33]Rev. Rul. 56–634.
[34]Rev. Rul. 55–747, Rev. Rul. 66–110.

If the insurance contract is turned over to the participant, he or she may keep the contract in force by continuing to pay the premiums required under the contract.

The disposition of the contract upon severance of employment before retirement depends upon the vesting provisions of the plan. If the participant's vested interest in his account balance exceeds the cash value of the contract, the trustee will normally release the contract to the participant, who may keep the contract in force by continuing the required premium payments. If the vested value of the account is less than the cash value of the insurance contract, the participant can acquire the contract by paying the trustee the nonvested portion of the cash value; the trustee can take out a policy loan in an amount equal to the nonvested portion of the cash value and assign the contract subject to the loan to the participant; or the trustee can surrender the contract for its cash value and pay the participant's vested interest in cash.

If a life insurance contract is part of a distribution from a profit sharing plan, its cash value, less the employee's cost basis, will be considered as taxable income in the year in which the employee receives the contract, even though the contract is not then surrendered for its cash value.[35] Like any other distribution, the distribution will qualify for favorable tax treatment as a lump-sum distribution or as a tax-free rollover to an individual retirement account or to an individual retirement annuity, if all the necessary conditions are met.[36] The employee may also avoid any current tax liability by making an irrevocable election, within 60 days of the distribution, to convert the contract to a nontransferable annuity containing no element of life insurance.[37] If current tax liability is avoided by such an election, the employee will not incur any tax liability until such time as payments are made from the annuity contract. At that time, the payments will be taxable in full as ordinary income.

---

[35]Treas. Reg. 1.402(a)–1(a)(2).

[36]See Chapter 29.

[37]It is worthy of note that, if an employee is entitled to a distribution in cash but has the option under the plan of electing, within 60 days, to receive a nontransferable annuity in lieu of the cash payment, he or she may avoid current tax liability through a timely exercise of this option.

When premium payments for life insurance on plan participants are made by the trustee from funds that have been accumulated for more than two years, the cost of insurance is treated as an allowable distribution and, thus, restrictions or "incidental" death benefits do not apply.[38] Irrespective of the period of fund accumulation, if the insurance is provided through single premium endowment or retirement income contracts, the "incidental" restrictions are satisfied.[39] However, if premiums are to be paid out of monies that have accumulated in the participant's account for less than two years *and* the insurance is to be in the form of whole life insurance (ordinary life and limited-payment life), there are limitations in IRS regulations on the portion of the employee's account balance that can be allocated to premium payments. These limitations are designed to assure that the death benefits under the profit sharing plan are "incidental" to the primary purpose of the plan. The concept of limiting death benefits to amounts deemed "incidental" to the primary purpose of the plan is also applicable to qualified pension plans, as was noted earlier.

The basic premise of the IRS is that no more than 25 percent of the contributions and forfeitures allocated to the employee's account should be used to maintain pure life insurance on a participant in the plan. On the arbitrary but simplifying assumption that over time about one half the gross premium for whole life insurance is applied to the protection component of the contract and the other half is used to build up the reserve, the IRS has ruled that aggregate premiums for whole life insurance for any particular employee must be less than one half of the total contributions and forfeitures that have been allocated to his or her account.[40] In practice, the sum set aside as premiums on whole life insurance generally does not exceed 25 to 33⅓ percent of anticipated average annual contributions to the employee's account. A margin is often provided to avoid violation of the legal limit if contributions were to fall off in future years. For the same reason, some plans do not permit insurance to be purchased until the employee has been a member of

---

[38]Rev. Rul. 60–83.

[39]Ibid.

[40]Rev. Rul. 54–51, Rev. Rul. 57–213, Rev. Rul. 66–143.

the plan for several years. The accumulation in the employee's account provides a cushion in the event that contributions decline in future years.[41] Separate rules apply to the purchase of health insurance.[42]

For whole life insurance on a participant to be incidental to the main purpose of the profit sharing plan, the premium must not only fall within the limit described above but the plan must require the trustee to convert the entire cash value of the life insurance contract at or before retirement into cash, or to distribute the contract to the participant, or to so provide periodic income that no portion of the cash value may be used to continue life insurance protection beyond retirement.

There are several reasons why it may be advantageous to plan participants to allocate a portion of their account to the purchase of life insurance. During the early years of participation in a profit sharing plan, the accumulations tend to be rather modest. The sum of the accumulations, plus any group insurance and Social Security, may not be sufficient to meet the need for death benefits for a young participant with heavy family responsibilities. Over a long time, however, the balance in the employee's profit sharing account may reach a substantial sum and is, of course, distributable upon the employee's death. Thus, life insurance makes it possible to provide substantial death benefits at all stages of an employee's participation in the plan. Moreover, automatic payment of premiums by the trustee from the employee's profit sharing account is a convenient and relatively painless way of maintaining life insurance protection.

**On Key Personnel.**   A profit sharing trust has an insurable interest in the lives of officers, stockholder employees, and key em-

---

[41]Another approach to avoiding violation of the 50 percent limit when profits decline or disappear, presumably for a temporary period, is to surrender the contract for paid-up insurance and then reinstate it when subsequent employer contributions permit.

[42]Rev. Rul. 61–164. No more than 25 percent of the contributions and forfeitures allocated to the employee's account can be used to pay premiums on this type of insurance. If both whole life and accident and health insurance contracts are purchased, the amount spent for accident and health insurance premiums plus *one half* (presumably the half allocable to pure insurance protection) of the amount applied to whole life insurance premiums may not, together, exceed 25 percent of the unseasoned funds allocated to the employee's account. This means that no more than 25 percent of the employee's account can be used to provide a current protection type of insurance coverage.

ployees of the corporation. Contributions to the plan are dependent on the continued profitability of the firm. The future profitability of a business firm, especially a small- or medium-sized one, may well depend on the performance of a few key employees. Therefore, the plan sponsor may regard it to be in the best interests of the plan participants to protect the trust, through the purchase of life insurance, against reductions in future levels of contributions arising out of the death of such key employees. If this is to be done, it is advisable that the plan document and the trust agreement specifically authorize the trustee to purchase the insurance.

The purchase of insurance on key personnel of the plan sponsor is an investment of the trust for the benefit of all participants. The trustee applies for the insurance, owns the contracts, and is designated as the beneficiary under the contracts. The premiums for the insurance are paid by the trustee out of plan assets and, in effect, are charged ratably to the accounts of the individual participants. Upon the death of an insured individual, the insurance proceeds are paid to the trust and are allocated among the participants on the basis of their account balances. If the plan so provides, the account of the deceased key employee will be credited with its proportionate share of the proceeds.

The purchase of insurance on key employees creates no current tax liability for the participants. Likewise, the tests regarding the incidental nature of the insurance are not applicable. Since the purchase is for the benefit of the trust and, thus, the premium payments are not distributions, the limitations on the use of monies accumulated in the trust for less than two years do not apply. As a practical matter, of course, the trust is not likely to invest the bulk of contributions in such insurance contracts. Under ERISA, the trustee will be under a fiduciary obligation to demonstrate that the purchase of insurance on key employees of the plan sponsor is prudent and in the best interests of the participants as a group, and that the diversification requirement is satisfied.

## Termination or Amendment of Plan

The sponsor of a profit sharing plan may reserve the right to alter, amend, or terminate the plan at any time for any reason. If the plan is terminated for other reasons than "business necessity" within a few years from its inception (10 years by an informal IRS interpretation), the action will be construed by the IRS as evidence that the plan, from its inception, was not a bona fide program for the exclusive benefit of employees in general. The plan may be disqualified by the IRS, with employer deductions for all open tax years being retroactively denied. If the employer can demonstrate that the termination was motivated by business necessity, there will be no adverse tax consequences. However, it will generally be more difficult to prove business necessity in connection with a profit sharing plan than with a pension plan (to which the same obligation attaches), since contributions to a profit sharing plan are not required during periods of financial difficulties when no profits exist.

## Stock Bonus Plans

Section 401(a) of the Internal Revenue Code recognizes three types of qualified plans: pension plans, profit sharing plans, and stock bonus plans. Treasury Regulation 1.401–1(b)(1)(iii) defines a stock bonus plan as "a plan established and maintained by an employer to provide benefits similar to those of a profit sharing plan, except that . . . the benefits are distributed in stock of the employer company." Under a stock bonus plan a participant must generally have the right to have his benefits distributed in the form of employer securities.[43] A choice of cash may also be offered. But if the employer's charter or bylaws restrict the ownership of substantially all of the outstanding employer securities to either employees or a qualified plan trust, the plan may provide that distributions will be in cash instead of employer securities.

If the employer securities distributed are not readily tradeable on an established market, the participant must have the right to sell the securities to the employer at a fair price (the "put option").[44] Without this requirement, a distribution of stock might have little value to an employee.

Unless the participant elects otherwise, distribution of his benefits must begin within one year following the plan year of his

---

[43]I.R.C. §409(h).
[44]I.R.C. §409(h)(1)(B),(2).

retirement at normal retirement age or later, disability or death, or within six years of any other separation from service.[45]

Unless the participant elects otherwise, the distribution of his benefits must be in substantially equal periodic payments over a period of five years or less (longer if the account balance exceeds $500,000).[46]

Illustrative contribution formulas under a stock bonus plan are those that express the contribution commitment as a flat percentage of covered payroll or those that require the employer to contribute $X$ percent of profits but not less than $Y$ dollars a year. The latter type of formula can also be used under a profit sharing plan that retains its identity so long as distributions do not have to be made in employer stock.

## Employee Stock Ownership Plan (ESOP)

The term *employee stock ownership plan* (ESOP) has been used to describe a wide variety of defined contribution plans which invest in employer stock. In addition to providing a benefit plan with stock ownership for employees, ESOPs have been used to meet a wide variety of financial and other objectives of the employer.

The laws governing ESOPs have been the subject of frequent amendments, significantly changing the nature of ESOPs and their uses.

### Requirements to Be an ESOP

To be a qualified ESOP a defined contribution plan must meet a number of requirements.[47] First, it must be a qualified stock bonus plan, or a combination of a qualified stock bonus plan and a qualified money purchase pension plan.[48] An ESOP is therefore subject to all of the requirements that apply to stock bonus plans and, if applicable, money purchase pension plans. An ESOP may be a designated portion of another plan.[49]

---

[45]I.R.C. §409(o)(1).

[46]I.R.C. §409(o)(1)(C).

[47]I.R.C. §4975(e)(7), I.R.C. §409 and Treas. Reg. 54.4975–7,11.

[48]I.R.C. §4975(b)(7).

[49]Treas. Reg. 54.4975–11(a)(5).

Second, an ESOP must be designed to invest primarily in qualifying employer securities.[50] "Primarily" means at least half. Employer securities must be common stock or preferred stock of the employer or of a corporation in the same controlled group, and must meet certain statutory requirements.[51] Common stock is almost always used, and most ESOPs are invested solely in employer securities except for temporary cash positions.

Third, an ESOP must be specifically designated as such in the plan document.[52]

In addition, an ESOP must satisfy the following four requirements for stock bonus plans, regardless of whether the ESOP is a stock bonus plan or the combination of a stock bonus plan and a money purchase pension plan.

First, under an ESOP a participant must generally have the right to have his benefits distributed in the form of employer securities.[53] A choice of cash may also be offered. But if the employer's charter or bylaws restrict the ownership of substantially all of the outstanding employer securities to either employees or a qualified plan trust, the plan may provide that distributions will be in cash instead of employer securities.

Second, if the employer securities distributed are not readily tradeable on an established market, the participant must have the right to sell the securities to the employer at a fair price (the "put option").[54]

Third, unless the participant elects otherwise, distribution of his benefits must begin within one year following the plan year of his retirement at normal retirement age or later, disability or death, or within six years of any other separation from service.[55]

Fourth, unless the participant elects otherwise, the distribution of his benefits must be in substantially equal periodic payments over a period of five years or less (longer if the account balance exceeds $500,000).[56]

---

[50]I.R.C. §4975(e)(7); Treas. Reg. 54.4975–11(b).

[51]I.R.C. §409(1).

[52]Treas. Reg. 54.4975–11(a)(2).

[53]I.R.C. §409(h).

[54]I.R.C. §409(h)(1)(B),(2).

[55]I.R.C. §409(o)(1).

[56]I.R.C. §409(o)(1)(C).

A *leveraged ESOP* is an ESOP that borrows money with which to purchase employer securities. Additional requirements apply to leveraged ESOPs. Additional requirements also apply to any ESOP if the employer has a registration-type class of securities.

A *tax credit ESOP* or *TRASOP* was an ESOP for which an employer formerly received a tax credit, rather than a deduction, for its contributions. Such tax credits were eliminated by the Tax Reform Act of 1986.

### Operation of a Simple ESOP

A simple ESOP (not leveraged) functions very much like a profit sharing plan. The amount of contributions may be based on a formula or be determined at the employer's discretion. A formula may be based on profits or the compensation of participants. The contribution commitment is often expressed as a flat percentage of covered compensation. Some employers use an ESOP for the employer matching contributions under a 401(k) plan or a thrift plan.

Contributions to an ESOP may be made in cash or in employer securities. If contributions are made in cash, part or all of the cash is used to purchase stock, either from the employer or in the market. Stock and any contributions not applied to purchase stock are allocated to employee accounts. Any dividends on the stock may be paid in cash to participants or may be used as additional contributions to buy more shares to be added to employee accounts.

Distributions can be made at the same times as under a profit-sharing plan. Distributions may be in cash or stock, in accordance with the requirements summarized above. Distributions of employer securities receive favorable tax treatment, as described in Chapter 29.

Code Section 415(c) limits the amount of contributions and forfeitures that may be allocated to an individual under a defined contribution plan. The dollar limits are increased for a qualified ESOP if not more than one third of the employer contributions are allocated to highly compensated employees. This special rule increases the $30,000 limit on allocations to $60,000, but not to more than the amount of stock allocated to the participant under the ESOP.

### Operation of a Leveraged ESOP

Except as noted below, a leveraged ESOP functions in the same manner as an unleveraged ESOP described above.

Under a leveraged ESOP, the trustee of the trust created under the plan arranges for a loan from a lending institution and uses the loan to purchase employer stock. The employer stock acquired is held by the trustee and gradually allocated to participants as cash contributions are made on their behalf under the plan. The stock is pledged as collateral for the loan, which is customarily also guaranteed by the employer or other party. Since the trust cannot generate income on its own, other than dividends on the stock, the employer corporation or other outside party is usually required to guarantee the loan.

The loan, including interest, is repaid by the trustee from the cash contributions of the employer; and the plan requires the employer to contribute an amount sufficient to repay the loan. As loan payments reduce the principal of the loan, part of the stock is released as collateral for the loan. The plan may provide for allocation of the stock to employees only as the stock is released as collateral, or stock may be allocated to employee accounts at an earlier time.

Distributions to employees are made as under an unleveraged ESOP. However, if a participant becomes entitled to a distribution before all of the stock allocated to his account has been released as collateral, he will receive only those shares that have been released from the collateral assignment, with the remaining number of vested shares being distributed at a later date as they are released from assignment.

### Uses of ESOPs

ESOPs may be viewed as a variation of profit sharing plans. As such they are an employee benefit that may be adopted for all of the reasons that a profit sharing plan would be adopted. Many believe that ESOPs are especially useful in raising employee morale, giving employees a sense of involvement, and motivating employees to make the business more profitable. But if the value of the stock falls, the effect on morale may be negative.

ESOPs are also adopted to meet a wide range of financial and other objectives of the employer. By purchasing outstanding shares, an ESOP can be used to convert a publicly owned company into one owned by the trust and a few major stockholders ("going private"). It may be used to put stock into friendly hands to avoid a corporate takeover. A leveraged ESOP can be used to sell a division of a corporation to the division's management or others. (The selling corporation would organize a new corporation that would establish a leveraged ESOP for the purpose of raising capital used in purchasing the division.) An ESOP can provide liquidity to a major stockholder by agreeing to purchase his shares at death. An ESOP can be used to buy out the interest of a deceased or retiring stockholder in a closely held corporation. Newly issued stock can be sold to an ESOP with less expense and complexity than through a public offering.

## Estate Tax Deduction for Sale to an ESOP

Under certain conditions, if an estate sells employer stock to an ESOP, 50 percent of the proceeds of the sale are excluded from the gross estate for estate tax purposes. For estates subject to estate tax, this deduction can result in very substantial tax savings. The ESOP can bargain with the estate to share the tax savings, and thus get a very favorable purchase price. In some situations the bargain sale by the estate, in combination with the other advantages of an ESOP, may be a reason for establishing an ESOP where none now exists, particularly in connection with the acquisition of the interest of a deceased major stockholder of a closely held corporation.

## Deduction for Dividends on ESOP Stock

A corporation ordinarily receives no deduction for dividends paid to stockholders. But an exception allows an employer a deduction for dividends paid on the stock owned by an ESOP. This exception applies whether the dividends are paid to participants or are applied by a leveraged ESOP to repay ESOP loans.[57] Thus the dividends on stock held by the ESOP that has been allocated to participants can be paid to the participants and the dividends on unallocated stock can be used to repay the loan, with all of the dividends being deductible.

---

[57] I.R.C. §404(k).

### Interest Earned on ESOP Loans

The Code allows banks, insurance companies, and certain other lending institutions to deduct half of the interest received on a loan used by an ESOP for acquisition of securities.[58] This often makes lending institutions willing to make loans at lower interest rates to the ESOP than it would to the employer. The ESOP transfers the money received to the employer in exchange for company stock. This may in effect allow the employer to raise capital at lower cost than it would have had otherwise. The employer has had the cost of providing the employee benefit, a cost incurred indirectly by having more stock outstanding, which tends to lower earnings per share. But the ESOP may be a substitute for a pension or profit sharing plan for which the employer would have had both expense and cash outlay.

### Diversification of Investments

The Code requires that each ESOP participant have the right to diversify his investments during the five-year period following the first plan year that he has both attained age 55 and completed 10 years of participation.[59] Except as noted below, the plan must offer three investment alternatives other than employer securities. During each of the five years the employee must be allowed to make transfers from employer securities to the investment alternatives to whatever extent necessary to raise the alternative investments to 25 percent of the participant's total account. In the fifth year 50 percent replaces 25 percent.

An employer will be deemed to satisfy the requirement if it makes a cash disbursement of the amount that could have been diversified under an election.

### Fiduciary Requirements and Prohibited Transactions

An ESOP is generally exempt from the 10 percent limitation on holding employer securities.[60] But ESOPs are not exempt from the

---

[58]I.R.C. §133.
[59]I.R.C. §401(a)(28)(B).
[60]ERISA §407(d)(3).

general fiduciary requirements of ERISA. If, for example, stock were purchased for more than its fair market value, fiduciaries may be liable.

The loan transactions into which leveraged ESOPs enter would ordinarily be classed as prohibited transactions under both ERISA and the Internal Revenue Code,[61] if there were no applicable exemption. To solve this problem, Congress provided an exemption for ESOPs that satisfy a statutory definition of employee stock ownership plan as well as other statutory requirements. For this purpose, an employee stock ownership plan is a plan that is either a stock bonus plan or a combination of a stock bonus plan and a money purchase pension plan, which is designed to invest primarily in qualifying employer securities and which satisfies detailed regulatory requirements.[62] For purposes of the Code's definition, additional requirements apply. A loan to such an ESOP is exempt from the prohibited transaction rules if the loan is primarily for the benefit of participants and beneficiaries, if the interest rate is reasonable, and if any collateral given by the plan consists only of qualifying employer securities.[63]

## Independent Appraiser

Fair market value of the employer stock plays a critical role in the operation of an ESOP. If participants receive their distributions in cash, the amount must equal the fair market value of the stock allocated to their accounts. By the same token, the ESOP may not pay more than fair market value for any stock that it purchases.

If the stock is regularly traded on an established securities market, fair market value is readily ascertainable. If the stock of the corporation is closely held or not publicly traded, the Code requires valuation by an independent appraiser.[64]

## Advantages and Disadvantages

As indicated above, an ESOP offers several potential advantages to an employer, in addition to its value as an employee benefit.

---

[61] ERISA §406, I.R.C. §4975.
[62] ERISA §407(d)(6), I.R.C. §4975(e)(7), Treas. Reg. 54.4975–11.
[63] ERISA §408(b)(3), I.R.C. §4975(d)(3).
[64] I.R.C. §401(a)(28)(C).

ESOPs also have disadvantages. They often involve more administrative expense than other qualified plans. They may have to be registered under securities laws. There may be great employee dissatisfaction if stock values decline sharply.

There may be additional disadvantages with a leveraged ESOP. In the first place, no portion of the stock purchased with borrowed funds and held in the unallocated trust account can revert to the employer if the trust is terminated prematurely. Second, there is a greater risk that the plan will at some point be disqualified by the IRS on the grounds that it is oriented more strongly toward employer objectives than to the "exclusive benefit" requirement of the law. Finally, if the employer stock held in trust appreciates in value, the employer forgoes a tax deduction that he could have otherwise taken by contributing the appreciated stock to the trust, rather than cash to repay the loan. Simply stated, the employees (through the trust) enjoy the benefits of future appreciation in the value of the pledged stock, rather than the employer.

The participants in an ESOP enjoy the advantage of employer contributions and all benefits associated with stock ownership. The primary disadvantage of the arrangement from their standpoint is that their financial security may be too closely linked with the fortunes of the employer. Thus, as noted above, a base pension plan may be desirable in connection with such an arrangement.

## Other Stock Ownership Plans

In addition to stock bonus plans and ESOPs there is a wide variety of plans involving stock ownership. Many profit sharing plans include substantial investment in employer securities. Two other tax-favored forms of stock ownership are qualified employee stock purchase plans[65] and incentive stock options (ISOs).[66] There are also many types of nonqualified stock option plans and stock purchase plans. Qualified employee stock purchase plans must be made broadly available to employees, but ISOs and nonqualified plans are usually designed for the exclusive benefit of management employees.

---

[65]I.R.C. §423.

[66]I.R.C. §422A.

## Questions

1. Identify those features of a qualified deferred profit sharing plan that must meet the same statutory and regulatory requirements as a qualified pension plan.

2. Why do the eligibility provisions of a profit sharing plan tend to be less restrictive than those of a pension plan?

3. In what specific respects does a qualified profit sharing plan differ from a money purchase pension plan?

4. Indicate, with respect to employer contributions to a qualified profit sharing plan:
   a. Whether the basis for contributions must be set forth in the plan document.
   b. The basic ways of expressing a contribution commitment.
   c. The limits on deductibility of employer contributions.

5. Identify the various types or sources of funds that must be allocated to participants under a deferred profit sharing plan and with respect to each source indicate the permissible bases for allocation.

6. Explain the ways in which length of service may be recognized in allocating employer contributions among profit sharing participants.

7. Explain the procedures followed by the administrator of a profit sharing plan in allocating investment earnings on a total return or market value basis. Under what circumstances would the allocations be made on a book value basis?

8. In what respects do qualified profit sharing plans tend to embody more liberal vesting provisions than those required by ERISA?

9. Explain the impact exerted by applicable tax law on the distribution provisions of qualified profit sharing plans.

10. Describe the *forms* in which distributions from a profit sharing plan may be made.

11. A loan from a profit sharing plan may be treated either as a loan from the total unsegregated assets of the plan or as a loan from a separate investment account within the account balance of the borrowing participant. Contrast the consequences of these two approaches from the standpoint of (a) the borrowing participant and (b) the other plan participants.

12. Is a loan from a profit sharing plan similar in its effect on the various parties involved to a loan made against the cash value of a life insurance policy? Answer in terms of alternative loan provisions that may be found in profit sharing plans and life insurance contracts.

13. Why might a participant in a profit sharing plan prefer a loan interest rate in the upper range of "reasonableness," rather than one in the lower range?

14. For what reasons might the sponsor of a profit sharing plan prefer not to include a loan provision?

15. Explain the restrictions imposed by applicable tax law on the purchase of life insurance by a profit sharing trust on the lives of the plan participants.

16. Does the payment of life insurance premiums from the account of a profit sharing plan participant create any income tax liability for the participant? Why or why not?

17. What are the basic characteristics of an employee stock ownership plan (ESOP)? Is it possible to qualify it as either a profit sharing plan, a stock bonus plan, or a money purchase pension plan?

18. How does a leveraged ESOP differ from a conventional ESOP?

19. Evaluate the ESOP as an asset accumulation type of employee benefit plan from the standpoint of:
    a. The plan sponsor.
    b. The plan participants.

20. Does the use of an ESOP to achieve financial objectives of the employer conflict with its use to provide benefits for employees?

# 27 | Thrift Plans and Cash or Deferred Arrangements

## Thrift and Savings Plans

AN ARRANGEMENT under which a nondiscriminatory grouping of employees of a common employer make voluntary contributions to a defined contribution plan is generically an employee *savings* plan or a *thrift* plan, the two terms being used interchangeably.

If the employer makes no contributions to the plan, the arrangement is commonly referred to as a *pure* thrift plan. Such a plan provides the employees with a convenient mechanism for indulging their instincts for capital accumulation with certain tax advantages and other attractive features discussed below. In a pure thrift plan, the employer usually absorbs all relevant administrative expenses, thus providing an additional incentive for the employee to save. Most thrift plans provide for employer matching contributions as a specified percentage of employee contributions.

The Internal Revenue Code has no separate provisions for thrift plans. To obtain favorable tax treatment under the Code, a thrift plan must qualify as either a pension plan, a profit sharing plan, or a stock bonus plan.

There are important differences between thrift plans that qualify as profit sharing plans and those that qualify as pension plans, reflecting the differences in the Code's requirements for the two types of plans. Under a pension plan, employer contributions must be definitely determinable, whereas a profit sharing plan can provide flexibility in determining contributions. A profit sharing plan may make distributions to active employees, while a pension plan generally may not. A pension plan must make distributions *available* in the form of an annuity ( a life annuity or an annuity certain), while a profit sharing plan is not required to provide annuities at all. Finally, a profit sharing plan can be used as a cash or deferred arrangement (CODA or 401(k) plan), whereas this treatment is not allowed for a pension plan. The great majority of thrift plans are qualified as profit sharing plans.

Stock bonus plans are generally subject to the same requirements as profit sharing plans, except as described in the preceding chapter.

All of the rules and considerations that apply to any money purchase pension plan, profit sharing plan, or stock bonus plan also apply to a thrift plan of that genre. This section is primarily concerned with considerations that are unique to thrift plans. Many thrift plans are cash or deferred arrangements. Some were originally designed as 401(k) plans and others were modified to become 401(k) plans. Such plans are discussed under a separate section of this chapter.

### Advantages of a Thrift Plan

All of the objectives sought by the employer in establishing and maintaining a profit sharing plan can be achieved through a thrift plan. An all-encompassing objective is to attract and retain a competent, productive, and loyal work force. The motivating power of a thrift plan depends upon its features, the dominant ones being the basis of employer contributions to the plan and the vesting provisions. Whatever the reason, some employers have found that they can match the motivating power of a conventional deferred profit sharing plan by a thrift plan that costs less as a percentage of payroll. This has something to do with the fact that the participants appreciate the definiteness of the employer contribution commitment under a thrift plan, in contrast to a profit sharing commitment that produces variable contributions from year to year and, in some years, may yield no contribution at all. Also, it seems that employees have a special attraction to a plan that (in the absence of capital losses) assures an initial rate of return on their contributions (but not on reinvested earnings) at least equal to the employer matching percentage, which is generally not less than 25 percent of the amount contributed by the employees. Plans with employee contributions tend to provide more withdrawal flexibility, at least with respect to the employee's own contributions, and this is a popular feature with the participants. All in all, thrift plans tend to be a very popular form of employee benefit plan, resulting in capital accumulations for retirement and materially enhancing employee morale.

A thrift plan offers a number of advantages to the employees. First of all is the convenience and discipline of saving through payroll deduction. If an employee elects to participate in the plan, the amount that he wishes to set aside can be automatically deducted from his salary each pay period without any further action on his part. This is a great spur to systematic saving. Second, the monies set aside receive the benefit of professional investment management, often at no cost to the employee because they are absorbed by the employer. There are several subadvantages associated with this feature of a thrift plan. The small periodic savings of the individual participants are combined into one or more large pools of assets that are invested in a diversified group of equity and fixed-income securities. The participants thus enjoy a high degree of diversification and have access to a wide range of investment opportunities, similar to a mutual fund. Unless one or more of the investment alternatives happens to be a "load" mutual fund or insurance or annuity contracts, there is no front-end load, the entire amount of the savings going into the investment pool. Furthermore, some employers pay the investment management fee out of corporate assets, giving the employees the benefit of the full investment return. Thus, the employees' savings are given the benefit of professional asset management without any charge for participation and frequently without any charge for the investment services provided.

The third major advantage is related to the second. If the plan meets the qualification requirements of the IRS, the investment income credited to the individual accounts of the employees is not currently taxable to them. It will be taxable as ordinary income when withdrawn, unless it is withdrawn under circumstances that entitle it to favorable tax treatment as a lump-sum distribution, as applicable to profit sharing distributions in general. If the employee views the thrift plan as a long-term savings mechanism and, in fact, lets his investment earnings accumulate to his death, retirement, or earlier separation from service, the earnings will enjoy a net tax advantage, including deferral of tax on the appreciation of employer securities forming a part of the distribution. This, coupled with the payroll deduction feature and professional management of the accumulated assets, makes the thrift plan a very attractive savings medium, entirely apart from any employer contributions.

In practice, virtually all thrift plans involve employer contributions, which form the foundation of the fourth and undoubtedly the most appealing advantage of the thrift plan from the standpoint of the employees. The employer typically contributes at least 50 cents for each dollar set aside by the employee, subject to certain limits, and this practically assures a handsome return on the employee's "investment" in the plan. Even 25 percent matching by the employer, which is at the lower end of the contribution scale, starts the employee's deposit off with a significant increment. The employer can deduct his contributions to a qualified thrift plan, and the contributions are not currently taxable to the employees even when fully vested. When withdrawn, they and their associated investment earnings are taxable as ordinary income, unless the withdrawal satisfies the conditions for favorable tax treatment discussed later. The employee is not taxed on a return of his own contributions.

This is an impressive array of favorable features and employees have responded in predictable fashion. A well-constructed thrift plan can be one of the most popular employee benefit plans offered by an employer, the appeal being disproportionate to the employer's investment in the arrangement, which is commonly 3 percent of payroll or less.

## Plan Design[1]

A qualified thrift plan must meet the general requirements laid down in the Internal Revenue Code and ERISA. Thus, the plan must be

---

[1]Most of the statements about plan design are based on the *1977 Study of Employee Savings and Thrift Plans* published by Bankers Trust of New York City. This is the fifth such study carried out by Bankers Trust. This series of studies is a rich source of information concerning the design and functioning of thrift plans for large employers, being especially valuable in pointing up trends. Plans of smaller employers may have different characteristics.

designed with an eye toward these statutory and regulatory constraints.

**Coverage.**    The majority of thrift plans cover all or substantially all employees of the sponsoring firm. If all employees are not covered, the excluded group is usually the hourly and part-time (less than 1,000 hours of service) employees. Employees who are members of a collective bargaining unit are usually covered only if the bargaining unit accepts the plan. Some plans limit membership to those employees who participate in the employer's pension plan (contributory or noncontributory) or group life insurance program.

**A. Eligibility for Participation.**    The rules governing eligibility for participation in thrift plans have traditionally been very liberal, reflecting the employer's desire to attract new employees and to retain and motivate present employees. The eligibility provisions of the great majority of plans are more generous than those required by ERISA. Most plans have only a service requirement, typically one year or less. Those plans that combine a service and age requirement generally use age 21. Some plans have no age or service requirement, the newly hired employee being immediately eligible for participation. There is no upper age limit on participation, since this would not be permissible under ERISA.

**B. Actual Participation.**    Participation in a thrift plan is always voluntary on the part of the eligible employees. Nevertheless, a remarkably high percentage of eligible employees generally elect to participate. Half of the plans included in the most recent survey of the Bankers Trust Company have an enrollment of over 70 percent of eligible employees. Thirteen percent of the plans had enrollment rates of more than 90 percent.

Employee response to the opportunity of participating in a thrift plan is strongly influenced by the formula for employer matching contributions, the vesting provision, and the availability of investment options. The level of employer contributions is the most influential factor. For example, among plans in the Bankers Trust 1977 survey having an enrollment rate of more than 90 percent, the median employer matching contribution is 100 percent, whereas among plans with an enrollment of less than 50 percent, the median employer match is 30 percent. Among all plans, general economic conditions have an effect on participation that extends beyond plan design.

Thrift plans must satisfy the coverage requirements applicable
to all qualified plans, described in Chapter 4. Low levels of participation could cause a plan to fail to meet these requirements.

**Contributions.  *A. Employee Contributions.*** It is customary
for a thrift plan to set forth a permissible range of contributions,
with the employee choosing the rate at which he or she will contribute. This, in turn, determines the amount that the employer will
contribute on behalf of the employee. The employer may base his
contribution on the total employee contribution or only on a portion
of it. The proportion on which the employer match is based is the
*employee basic contribution,* while the remainder, if any, is the
*employee additional voluntary contribution.*

Among the plans surveyed by Bankers Trust in its 1977 study
the permissible range of employee basic contributions is 1 1/2 percent to 10 percent of compensation, as defined, with 6 percent being
both the median and the most common rate. There is a definite
trend away from basic contribution rates higher than 6 percent of
compensation, because of an IRS rule that an employer permitting
them has to prove to the IRS that such a provision will not be
discriminatory.[2]

In some plans, the maximum basic contribution rate is related
to the employee's service or age, or both, with the older or longer-
service employee being permitted to contribute at a higher rate.
Such a provision is designed to permit the employee at midpoint
(or beyond) in his career to accumulate greater balances in his
account during the shorter-than-average period to retirement. There
is a trend away from this type of provision, also, because of the
necessity of demonstrating to the IRS that it does not discriminate
in favor of highly paid employees.

Some plans impose a maximum dollar limitation on employee
basic contributions, in addition to the maximum percentage limitation. Such a limitation may take one of two forms: (1) a specified
flat dollar ceiling on basic contributions, such as $2,000 per year,
applicable to all employees irrespective of compensation level or
rate of contribution; or (2) a specified level of recognized annual
compensation, up to which the elected rate of contribution is ap-

[2]Rev. Rul. 72–58.

plied. While the limitations in a few plans effectively restrict basic contributions of almost all employees, most dollar limitations are designed to restrict the contributions that may be made—and have to be matched—by higher-paid employees. Such restrictions are clearly permissible under IRS regulations. For plan years beginning after 1988, plans may not recognize annual compensation in excess of $200,000 for any purpose.[3]

More than half the plans surveyed by Bankers Trust permit additional voluntary contributions that are not matched by employer contributions. There is an inducement for an employee to make additional contributions, if he can afford them, because of the attractive investment features (described earlier) and the advantageous tax treatment of the investment income. The IRS imposes a limit of 10 percent of compensation on additional voluntary contributions to which employer contributions or benefits are not geared.[4] Thus, in a plan providing for employee basic contributions of 2 to 6 percent of compensation, the total employee contribution would be limited to 16 percent of compensation, the maximum basic contribution of 6 percent plus a maximum of 10 percent of additional contribution. Where the employer maintains more than one qualified plan to which the employee is eligible to contribute, the maximum aggregate annual voluntary contribution to the plans remains 10 percent of the employee's compensation.[5]

As with basic contributions, the employee chooses his rate of additional contributions from a range specified in the plan. The *maximum* additional contribution rates range from 2 to 10 percent, the median maximum being 6 percent. Some plans permit "makeup" voluntary contributions (i.e., if the employee does not contribute the maximum of 10 percent in any one year he can contribute the "shortfall" plus 10 percent in the following year).[6] Such makeup contributions are subject to the limitations of Section 415 of the Internal Revenue Code. The maximum limits on allocations under a defined contribution plan include not only employer contributions and forfeitures but also employee contributions. An employee's contribution in a given year becomes a part of the maximum annual

---

[3]I.R.C. §401(a)(17).
[4]Rev. Rul. 59–185; Rev. Rul. 70–658; I.R.S. Publication 778, Part 4(h).
[5]Rev. Rul. 69–627.
[6]Rev. Rul. 69–217.

addition that may be made to the individual account of an employee under ERISA.[7]

Because of difficulty in satisfying the new nondiscrimination tests applicable to employee contributions and employer matching contributions, described later in this chapter, many employers no longer allow voluntary employee contributions.

To provide even greater flexibility, a thrift plan generally permits a participant to change his rate of contribution from time to time, as his circumstances change. By the same token, the participant is usually granted the privilege of suspending contributions to the plan for a period, usually of a year's duration, without losing his membership in the plan. The participant continues to accrue plan membership for vesting and other purposes during the period of the suspension, but the employer makes no contributions on his behalf. The right to change contribution rates or to suspend contributions may usually be exercised, after reasonable notice, at various times during the plan year, and in some plans may be exercised at *any* time. Some plans restrict the exercise of this right to the beginning of each quarter; others permit change at the beginning of any pay period following the required notice. To minimize administrative expense and complexity, most plans impose some type of limitation on the number of times changes may be made. For example, the participant may be permitted to change or suspend contributions only once in any 12-month period. Along the same line, most plans stipulate that a suspension of contributions must remain in effect for a minimum period of time, such as six months or a year, the former being more common.

As noted above, some plans allow employees to contribute lump-sum amounts, in excess of the otherwise applicable limits, to make up for prior years during which they did not contribute at the maximum rate permitted. In most plans, the makeup contribution is related to the additional voluntary contribution rate that is not matched by the employer; but in some plans, it is related to the basic contribution rate and is matched by the employer.

Some plans permit the participants to "roll over" their accumulated contributions from other qualified plans into the thrift plan. Also, when a contributory defined benefit pension plan is converted

---

[7]I.R.C. §415(c)(2).

into a noncontributory plan, the employer may refund the accumulated employee contributions by transferring them to the employees' thrift plan accounts. There may be special restrictions on the withdrawal of such one-time contributions. Needless to say, the employer does not match this special employee contribution.

   **B. Employer Contributions.**   The contribution that an employer makes on behalf of a particular employee is typically determined by the amount that the employee contributes. The general approach is to match the employee's basic contribution at a rate specified in the plan. The employer match is usually a single uniform percentage of each employee's contribution. In some plans, however, a range is set forth and the match varies with additional factors, such as the employee's length of service or plan membership, or the level of corporate profits. A small minority of plans use a different approach and contribute an aggregate amount computed in accordance with a prescribed profit sharing formula. This amount is then allocated among the participants in proportion to their own contributions, their compensation, or a combination of their contributions and their compensation.

   For plans that base the employer's contribution on the employee's basic contributions, the typical matching contribution is 50 percent of the employee's basic contribution rate. The range is 20 percent (or less) to 500 percent. While the range is shockingly wide, relatively few plans call for employer contributions in excess of 100 percent of the employee's basic rate or less than 25 percent. As was noted earlier, there is a strong positive correlation between the employer matching contribution rate and the rate of employee participation. In the most recent Bankers Trust study, those plans that match the employee's contribution at a rate of 100 percent or higher have a median employee participation rate of 86 percent, whereas those that match at a rate of 25 percent or lower have a median participation rate of only 52 percent. The median participation rate for firms matching 50 percent of the employee contribution is 73 percent.

   A substantial proportion of plans provide for additional employer contributions (over and above his basic matching contributions) based on corporate profits. In these plans, the employee is assured of a minimum employer contribution, and the amount (and timing) of the additional contribution may be mandatory and specified in a formula related to the level of profits, or it may be optional and occur only on action of the board of directors. There is a strong tendency for plans that match employee contributions at less than 50 percent to provide for additional contributions. This approach is attractive to both the employee, who can receive a larger contribution when the firm had a good year, and the employer firm, which can achieve some cost flexibility.

A not insignificant number of plans have a *graduated* employer contribution formula. In those plans the employer's matching contribution, as a percentage of the employee's contribution, varies with the employer's profits, the employee's length of service, his years of membership, his investment choice, his own contribution rate, or the size of his unwithdrawn employer contribution account. In some of these plans, the employer contribution rate is related to a combination of the employee's service and contribution rate.

The cost of a thrift plan to the employer, as a percentage of payroll is a function of (1) the proportion of eligible employees who elect to participate, (2) the rate at which the participants elect to contribute, (3) the rate at which the employer matches the employees' basic contributions, and (4) the amount of forfeitures applied to reduce employer contributions. If is is assumed that all participants contribute at the maximum permissible rate that will be matched by the employer and that there are no additional employer contributions, the before-tax cost to the employer of a typical thrift plan is approximately 2 percent of payroll. Despite this relatively small cost, such plans have had wide appeal to employees.

**Contribution Percentage Requirement.**     The contribution percentage requirement, described in Chapter 9, limits the average percentage of employee contributions and employer matching contributions for highly compensated employees. If a plan has a high level of participation by employees who are not highly compensated, the requirement may have no actual effect upon a plan. But if there is a low level of participation by lower-paid employees, the contributions of highly compensated employees may be severely restricted. In order to encourage greater participation by lower-paid employees, an employer may decide to increase the matching percentage, provide earlier vesting, add more attractive investment alternatives, or improve communication of the plan.

**Investment of Contributions.** The contributions that a participant makes to a thrift plan, along with those made on his behalf by the employer, are credited to an individual account maintained in his name by the plan administrator. Legal title to the contributions, however, is vested in the plan trustee, who must invest them in accordance with the instructions contained in the trust agreement and any applicable plan provisions. ERISA requires separate accounting for the employee's contributions and the earnings thereon, which must be 100 percent vested at all times.

*A. Investment Media.* Early thrift plans by and large directed the plan trustee to invest both employee and employer contributions in securities, typically common stock, of the sponsoring firm. This was in accordance with the generally held view that the participants would feel greater allegiance to the company, and would be more productive, if they acquired an ownership interest in the company. Such plans required registration with the Securities and Exchange Commission (SEC). Under some plans, only employer contributions had to be invested in employer securities, alternative investment avenues being available for employee contributions. Even today many thrift plans require that some portion of the individual account balances attributable to employer contributions be invested in common stock of the employer, with many of the plans still requiring that all such contributions be invested in that manner. Investment in employer stock is not feasible for small companies with no established market for their stock. Of course, proprietorships and partnerships have no stock.

In recent years, there has been a growing sentiment that the plan participants should be given a voice in the investment of their account balances, especially that portion attributable to their own contributions. It is believed that the participants will have a keener interest in, and greater appreciation of, the plan if they participate in the investment process. Employers are partially motivated by the desire to have the employees share the responsibility for the investment decisions. In the face of rising interest rates, employees in general have developed an interest in investment performance and have become more critical of unsatisfactory results. Thus, it seems wise to many employers to let the plan participants make their own investment decisions. To the extent that the account balances are vested, the employee is, in effect, investing his or her own money.

In the evolution of investment policy for thrift plans, some employers have questioned the wisdom of requiring or even permitting investment in the securities of the employer. The crucial question is whether an employee should be dependent on the same firm for both job security and financial security. The same economic forces that produce layoffs may reduce or even seriously undermine the value of the employee's stockholdings in the company. There is also concern about possible fiduciary liability under ERISA should the value of the employer's stock decline. Also, ERISA's emphasis on the diversification of plan investments has probably influenced some employers' attitude toward investing the plan assets in their own securities. Finally, if a participant has the option of investing any portion of his or her account in employer securities, it may be necessary to register the plan with the Securities and Exchange Commission and issue a prospectus to the employees.[8] Despite these concerns and questions, many plans provide the participants with the opportunity to invest in employer securities on an elective basis. A small but increasing percentage of plans prohibit investment in securities of the employer, despite the fact that ERISA permits such plans to provide for unlimited investment in such securities *if it is prudent to do so.*

The typical thrift plan today provides the participants with a number of investment alternatives, at least with respect to their own contributions. A solid majority of the plans included in the Bankers Trust 1977 survey still mandates investment of *employer* contributions in company securities. As a minimum, a plan is likely to offer participants the opportunity of investing in a commingled pool of fixed-income securities and a commingled pool of equity securities, with each participant having the right to designate the proportion of his individual account balance to be allocated to each pool. There is no obligation to allocate to both pools; the participant may direct the trustee to invest his entire account balance in one or the other of the two funds. This permits each participant to determine the mix of fixed-income and equity securities to be held in his individual account. There may be the constraint, noted above,

---

[8]If the amount of money involved is small, it may be possible, upon application, to receive an exemption from registration with the SEC, pursuant to Regulation A.

that the portion of the participant's account balance attributable to employer contributions be invested in company stock.

Some plan sponsors offer a balanced fund, composed of designated percentages of fixed-income and equity investments. This approach avoids the complexities associated with operating two separate investment funds, but it restricts the participants' freedom of choice between the two broad classes of investments. Some plans sponsor two or more equity funds, each with its own investment objectives and risk parameters. If prudent, a plan may offer a pooled fund invested exclusively in obligations of the federal government or government agencies. To provide almost complete investment latitude, some plans permit the participants to allocate their account balances to one or more mutual funds whose shares are available in the open market. Plans of this type permitting unlimited investment selection were popular for a short time, but they involved increased administrative expense, and employees often had difficulty (as everyone does) in selecting the best investment vehicle.

If a participant allocates a share (or all) of his account balance to an investment fund operated exclusively for the plan, he acquires units of participation in the fund. These units are valued at market, and the participant bears the risk of adverse investment experience (and, conversely, enjoys the benefits of favorable investment experience). To avoid these investment risks, particularly those associated with market value fluctuations of a fixed-income fund from changes in prevailing interest rates, many plans in recent years have offered participants the opportunity of placing monies under a guaranteed income contract (GIC) of a life insurance company. Under this type of contract, developed primarily for profit sharing in a thrift plan, the life insurer guarantees an annual rate of return for a specified period of years. Implicit in a guaranteed rate of return is a guarantee of principal, placing the whole transaction on a book value basis. These contracts have proved to be extremely attractive to plan participants, due in part to the volatility of common stock prices.

Some plans, instead of making guaranteed income contracts of life insurers available, guarantee a minimum rate of return on contributions invested in a fixed-income portfolio. The employer makes good on any deficiency in the actual rate of return as an additional contribution.

Other plans guarantee the participants that they will receive, as a minimum, a sum equal to all or a specified portion of their own contributions. In effect, this is a guarantee of principal of monies contributed by the employees. In most such plans, this guarantee is something of a delusion, since any capital losses that must be made good by the employer may be charged to the employees' nonvested employer contribution accounts. Thus, what an employee gains in one account he loses in another. However, this guarantee has gained popularity because it is possible that where the employee's contribution and the 25 percent matching employer contribution (or lower percentage) are invested in equities the amount returned to the employee can be less (because of market fluctuations) than his own contributions. Any such loss defeats the concept of capital accumulation and is bitterly resented by employees. In many plans, this guarantee, such as it is, is limited to certain circumstances and to specified amounts.

**B. Changes in Investment Instructions.** An important aspect of the investment latitude provided plan participants is the right to change investment instructions to the plan trustee. It is routine for plans that give the participant investment direction over his own or employer contributions, or both, to change his instructions about *future contributions* at least once a year. Some plans permit a change every six months, and some permit even more frequent change. In the past, however, there has been a general reluctance to permit participants to change their investment instructions as to *accumulated contributions* for fear that they might attempt to "play the market" or simply display poor or unfortunate judgment in the *timing* of their switch. More and more plans, however, are permitting participants to transfer past accumulations from one fund to another, irrespective of the investment risk involved. This is part of a general trend toward giving the participants more control over the investment of their account balances, with the concomitant responsibility for the investment outcomes. The change in attitude also represents a growing recognition that employees have different needs, aspirations, and financial sophistication. For example, as an employee approaches retirement he may wish his "nest egg" to be invested in fixed-income securities, rather than chancing the timing vagaries of the equity market. Another factor is that computer systems have become sophisticated enough to overcome the administrative problem attendant upon changes in investment instructions and transfers of accumulated funds.

Most plans limit transfers from one investment fund to another to once a year. A few permit them more often than once a year, while others impose a limit per career, such as three transfers. Some plans require the consent of the administrative committee, a heavy responsibility for that group of individuals. A sizable percentage of plans permit a transfer of accumulated contributions only as the participant approaches retirement or has been in service for a substantial time.

**Vesting.** As might be surmised, a participant's own contributions to a thrift plan and the associated investment earnings are fully and immediately vested in him for all purposes. Furthermore, the employer's contributions on his behalf, and their associated investment earnings, are fully vested upon the participant's death, disability, or retirement.[9] Thus, the conventional vesting provision is concerned with the participant's entitlement to the employer's contributions and their earnings upon termination of employment for reasons other than death, disability, and retirement, or upon exercise of his withdrawal privileges while still in the service of the employer.

The vesting provisions of thrift plans contemplate one or the other of two types of vesting: *membership* vesting and *class system* vesting. Membership vesting is the type found in pension plans and is attained by meeting requirements couched in terms of plan participation or service with the employer. Once the participant has satisfied this participation or service requirement, he is fully vested (except for graduated vesting) in all accumulated employer contributions and all employer contributions made thereafter. Membership vesting must occur within the period of membership service permitted under the minimum vesting standards prescribed by ERISA. In practice, the membership vesting provisions of thrift plans tend to be more liberal than ERISA minimum standards to encourage employee participation. The most common period required

---

[9] Governing tax law requires vesting of employer contributions upon the participant's normal retirement age but not upon death or disability. ERISA §203(a), I.R.C. §411(a).

for full vesting is five years of service; a large number of plans provide for full and immediate vesting.

Class system vesting is unique to defined contribution plans. Under this system, the required period of membership service applies separately to each class of contributions. Employer contributions made in a single month, quarter, one-half year, or year (periods of formation of a class) constitute a class and vest at a designated time following the close of the class formation period. Plans that utilize class system vesting generally vest employer contributions in full in three years or less after they are made. Under this system, a participant would never be *fully* vested except for death, disability, and retirement, and should his employment terminate for any other reason, he would forfeit some portion of the employer contributions credited to his account.

Class system vesting is much more difficult to administer and communicate than conventional membership service. Nevertheless, it has been widely used. Some employers adopted the approach in the belief that it is a deterrent to employee turnover, since some forfeiture is involved in every voluntary separation from service. A plan year is by far the most common period for class formation. In other words, plans using class system vesting typically treat the contributions of a given plan year as a class.

For plan years beginning after 1988, the vesting of all plans must satisfy one of two requirements, either 100 percent vesting after five years of service or 20 percent vesting after three years of service graded up to 100 percent vesting after seven years of service.[10] For top-heavy plans more rapid vesting is required. Years in which an employee declines to contribute while eligible to do so need not be counted. A plan under which vesting is based solely upon the class year method will not satisfy these requirements. Therefore such plans must be amended, either by replacing the class year vesting with a vesting schedule based solely upon service or membership or by superimposing such a vesting schedule in addition to the class year vesting schedule. Thus, for example, it would be possible to retain three-year class year vesting if the plan also provided that every participant with at least five years of service would nevertheless be 100 percent vested in all of his accounts. In an effort to avoid the additional complexity of admin-

---

[10]ERISA §203(a)(2), I.R.C. §411(a)(2).

istration and communication of such an arrangement, most employers are expected to completely replace the class year vesting with vesting based upon years of service or membership, with a grandfather clause to protect existing classes which might otherwise have more rapid vesting.

A majority of the plans using the membership vesting approach provides for full vesting to be achieved in steps, this being known as *graduated* or *graded* vesting and being represented in one of the two minimum vesting standards of ERISA. A simple example of graduated vesting would be a schedule calling for 20 percent vesting after one year of service and 20 percent increments for each of the next four years. Many plans vest one third of the accumulated employer contributions for each year of plan membership. A more liberal schedule found among many plans is 50 percent vesting after one year of membership and 25 percent incremental vesting for each of the next two years of plan membership. Graduated vesting is used by plans with class vesting systems, although less frequently than by plans using membership vesting. Graduated vesting is slightly more complex to administer than the type of vesting, sometimes called "cliff" vesting, that provides for full vesting at a particular time and none before that time.

Regardless of the vesting system utilized, some plans provide for full and immediate vesting of employer contributions in the event of certain specified contingencies (in addition to death, disability, and retirement), such as plant shutdown, layoff, involuntary termination of employment without cause, and military service.

**Allocation of Forfeitures.** Termination of employment, other than that occurring in a specified manner (death, disability, retirement, layoff, and so on), may produce a forfeiture unless the plan provides immediate vesting. Thus, the plan must provide for the disposition of any forfeitures.

The most common disposition by far is to apply the forfeitures to the reduction of the employer's contributions to the plan, thus lowering his costs. Another approach, much less common, is to apply the forfeitures as additional employer contributions, the allocation being made on the same basis as the employer's matching contributions. These additional allocations are subject to the same vesting provisions as regular employer contributions. Some plans allocate forfeitures in proportion to account balances, a procedure normally discouraged by the IRS in the belief that it tends to favor the highly paid and other favored employees. Various other bases for allocating forfeitures may be found, including allocation in equal shares.

**Distributions.** Upon the death, disability, or retirement of a thrift plan participant, his entire account balance is distributed in a lump sum or in some other form elected by the participant, or if applicable, his beneficiary, whether or not the account had previously been fully vested. The full amount in the account may be distributable under certain other circumstances, such as layoff or involuntary termination without cause, irrespective of the normal vesting provisions. Upon termination of employment, regardless of the circumstances, the participant ordinarily is entitled to receive immediately the vested portion of his account. This will include his own contributions, with accumulated investment earnings, and that portion of the employer contributions plus investment earnings that has vested under the normal vesting provisions of the plan and any special vesting provisions that might be applicable.

Virtually all plans also provide for distributions from the individual employee accounts while the participants are still in the active service of the employer. Such distributions are subject to the statutory mandate, discussed in the preceding chapter, that the contributions made by the employer on behalf of a particular employee be accumulated and held for a "fixed number of years."[11] The IRS has interpreted this requirement to mean that employer contributions must be held for a minimum time. As discussed above, withdrawal provisions for defined contribution plans qualified as pension plans are stringent, with the result that most thrift plans are qualified as profit sharing plans.

Provisions of thrift plans relating to distributions to individuals still in active service vary widely, reflecting the desires, biases, and objectives of the plan sponsor, tempered by relevant collective bargaining considerations. These provisions may be broadly classified as to whether they relate to normal (or periodic) distributions or to voluntary withdrawals.

*A. Normal Distributions.* Normal distributions are periodic disbursements to plan participants of a portion of their accounts on

---

[11]Treas. Reg. 1.401–1(b)(ii).

a regularly scheduled basis and without penalty. Plans that have such a provision generally have used a class system of vesting and usually have linked normal distributions to the time period required for each year's contribution to "mature," or vest fully. At some point prior to the time a particular class was to mature, each participant was given the opportunity to indicate whether all or a portion of his share of the class should be distributed at the end of the period or be withheld for later distribution. This allows the participant, at his option, to increase his current income or to accumulate funds for his retirement years or for other purposes. The funds that he elects to accumulate can be withdrawn subsequently in accordance with the plan provisions relating to voluntary withdrawals.

Only about a fourth of the plans surveyed in the 1977 study of Bankers Trust made provision for normal distributions. Of these, about three fourths let the participant decide the disposition of his entire share of the contribution class, including employer contributions on his behalf. Some of the remaining plans automatically distributed or deferred part of each contribution class and extended an election to the participant only over the balance. Other plans gave the participants no choice—some or all of the contribution class was automatically distributed and the balance, if any, was automatically deferred.

**B. Voluntary Withdrawals.** As its name suggests, a voluntary withdrawal is one that takes place on the initiative of the participant in accordance with general rules or conditions laid down in the plan document. A voluntary withdrawal differs from a normal periodic distribution in three ways: (1) it may be made at any time during the year, rather than on a class maturity date; (2) it is not limited to the contributions of any one year, but may involve the entire vested account balance; and (3) it often invokes a penalty of some type.

Most plans permit a voluntary withdrawal only on a plan asset *valuation* date, since a withdrawal typically involves a redemption of units of participation in a commingled asset account valued at market. The great majority of large plans are valued at least as often as quarterly and many are valued monthly. To provide more flexibility, some plans permit partial withdrawals at any time, subject to minimum notice, such as 10 days, the funds made available to the participant being taken from monies in process of being paid over to the plan by the employer. The market value of the employee's account is adjusted on the next valuation date.

The majority of plans permit voluntary withdrawal of all employee contributions and all vested employer contributions, along with the associated investment earnings. Some plans allow withdrawal of only a portion of the vested employer contributions. A few make no provision for voluntary withdrawals.

Some plans provide more liberal withdrawal terms when the withdrawal is occasioned by *hardship*. For example, a plan that permits withdrawal of only employee contributions under normal circumstances may permit withdrawal of vested employer contributions as well under hardship conditions. In some cases no penalty is assessed if withdrawal is due to hardship, provided such hardship is established to the satisfaction of the administrator of the plan. Some plans provide withdrawal privileges only in hardship cases.

Withdrawal provisions of some plans are linked to length of membership, the longer service employees being accorded the most liberal treatment. The treatment may differ as to the dollar amount that can be withdrawn, the availability of partial withdrawals, and the severity of the penalty for a withdrawal.

In the past, withdrawal of employer contributions and investment earnings on employee and employer contributions had to be subject to a meaningful penalty to avoid assessment of federal income tax liability on the participant in the year in which the amounts are credited to his account, on grounds of constructive receipt, and many plans still have such penalties. The types of penalties that may be assessed, listed in order of *increasing* severity, are: (1) a *suspension of membership* in the plan, whereby the employee loses his right to contribute to the plan for a specified time and thereby loses his right to the matching employer contribution for that period; (2) a *termination of membership* in the plan, whereby the employee not only ceases participation in the plan for a time but also loses credit for past years of membership accrued to date for purposes of higher level of employer matching contributions, membership requirements for voluntary withdrawals, or other provisions related to length of membership; and (3) forfeiture of all or a portion of the nonvested employer contributions. The third type of penalty is subject to an ERISA prohibition against the imposition of a forfeiture penalty if, at the time of withdrawal, the participant is 50 percent or more vested in his employer contribution account.

Some plans impose no penalty if the withdrawal is a result of a hardship. In general, the determination of whether a hardship exists is left to the discretion of the employer committee that administers the plan. The committee must apply the hardship provision in a uniform, nondiscriminatory manner.

Although there is no longer a constructive receipt tax problem, an employer may assess a penalty upon withdrawal to discourage withdrawals and encourage long-term thrift.

**C. Forms of Distribution.** Distributions from thrift plans have traditionally taken the form of lump-sum payments and, where applicable, employer securities. As a matter of fact, until recent years profit sharing thrift plans usually made no provision for any other type of distribution. In recent years there has been a growing interest in, and emphasis on, the use of thrift plan accumulations to help meet the financial needs of employees during their retirement years. This had led a significant number of newly established and amended plans to provide alternative forms of distribution, at the election of the employee or his beneficiary.

The most common alternative forms are installment payments over a specified period of years, a life annuity contract purchased from a life insurance company (again, if annuity options are provided, the plan must comply with the rules of ERISA relating to joint and survivorship annuity), and the purchase of an additional monthly retirement benefit through the employer's pension plan. The latter is accomplished through a lump-sum transfer of the employee's thrift plan accumulation to the pension plan at the time of the employee's retirement. In this type of transfer, employer contributions and associated investment earnings lose their identity for federal estate and gift tax purposes. Any life annuity benefits offered in respect of a married employee through either a separate annuity contract or the pension trust must, pursuant to ERISA, be payable in the form of a qualified joint and survivor annuity unless the employee elects otherwise.

**D. Tax Treatment.** Distributions from thrift plans are taxed on precisely the same basis as distributions from other qualified plans, a topic discussed at some length in Chapter 29. The participant's tax liability under a thrift plan, however, is different from his liability under a noncontributory plan because of his own contributions to the plan. This gives him a cost basis that is lacking in a noncontributory plan.

## Cash or Deferred Arrangement (401(k) Plan)

In any sizable employee group, there are some individuals who would prefer a cash profit sharing plan and others who would prefer a deferred profit sharing plan. Younger employees with more limited income and heavier family responsibilities tend to prefer a profit sharing plan that makes annual cash distributions (in the nature of a bonus or salary supplement), whereas the older and higher-paid employees, with the financial pressures of a growing family behind them and conscious of the need to accumulate a fund for old-age maintenance, tend to favor a deferred distribution plan. The needs and preferences of both groups can be met by a profit sharing plan that permits the employees the option of taking cash or having their share of the employer's contribution accumulated in a deferred account. Such a plan is called a "cash or deferred arrangement" (CODA) or "401(k) plan" (for the Internal Revenue Code subsection that regulates them). The earliest 401(k) plans operated in precisely the same manner as a conventional deferred profit sharing plan, except for the participants' option as to the mode of the allocation.

Because direct compensation is currently taxable, while there is no current taxation under a profit sharing plan on either the employer contributions or the investment income they earn, deferral is very attractive, particularly to employees in the higher tax brackets. While the earliest CODA's were established out of employer contributions that were in addition to regular compensation, it was soon recognized that the underlying concept could be applied to the regular compensation itself. Motivated by the potential tax savings, employees could enter into an agreement with their employer to reduce their regular compensation and to make an *employer* contribution to the profit sharing plan in the amount of the reduction. To the extent allowed, this is far more favorable than withholding salary to make *employee* contributions. Withholding for *employee* contributions does not reduce taxable income; the employee contributes after-tax dollars. In contrast, under a salary reduction arrangement, the employee's taxable income is reduced and the *employer* makes a contribution of before-tax dollars on behalf of the employee.

The most common type of 401(k) plan allows salary reductions by employees and some amount of matching contributions by the employer. For example, the plan may allow employees to make elective contributions not exceeding 10 percent of compensation, and may provide for employer contributions equal to half of all elective contributions that do not exceed 6 percent of compensation.

## Special Qualification Requirements

Some were concerned that only the higher-paid employees, who can afford to defer their salary or their share of the employer's profit sharing contribution and who stand to gain the most from the tax-deferral feature of a qualified profit sharing plan, would elect to defer their allocations. To minimize the potential "abuse" of the elective feature of the CODA, Congress added Code Section 401(k) to ensure that lower-paid employees participate to a significant extent.

A CODA must satisfy the requirements of Section 401(k) in order for the plan to be qualified and for the elective contributions to be treated as employer contributions and, thus, be excluded from taxable income. Section 401(k) in effect allows a plan which otherwise would be a qualified profit sharing plan or stock bonus plan to be treated as a qualified plan even if it discriminates somewhat in favor of the highly paid, provided it meets the requirements of a "qualified cash or deferred arrangement."

A qualified cash or deferred arrangement is a *type* of profit sharing plan or stock bonus plan. It is a plan under which an employee can elect to receive employer payments in cash or to have them paid as elective contributions to the plan.

An employee's right to his accrued benefit derived from these elective contributions must be nonforfeitable (i.e., it must be fully and immediately vested). Unlike an ordinary profit sharing plan, however, a 401(k) plan may not make a distribution of any accrued benefit derived from the elective contributions while the participant is still an active employee, except after attaining age 59 1/2 or upon a showing of financial hardship.[12] Hardship distributions are re-

---

[12]Financial hardship has not yet been defined by the IRS at the time of this writing. Proponents of 401(k) arrangements are urging that the purchase of a home and payment of college expenses for dependents be explicitly recognized as a source of financial hardship.

stricted to elective deferrals, excluding income allocable to the elective deferrals.

A 401(k) plan may not require more than one year of service for eligibility for participation, even if it has full and immediate vesting.

In determining whether the *coverage* of a 401(k) plan satisfies the Internal Revenue Code, it is only necessary to consider the employees *eligible* to participate, not the employees who *actually* elect to participate in the deferred arrangement. The employees eligible to participate must be a group that satisfies the coverage requirements of the Code. The minimum period of service required for participation may not exceed one year.

### Actual Deferral Percentage (ADP) Tests

To determine whether *elective contributions* under a 401(k) plan for a plan year are discriminatory, the "actual deferral percentage" must first be calculated for each employee eligible to participate. An employee's actual deferral percentage is a fraction whose numerator is the actual elective contributions paid to the trust on his behalf and whose denominator is the individual's compensation for the plan year. If no elective contribution is made for an employee, his actual deferral percentage is zero percent.

The elective contributions are not discriminatory if the 401(k) plan passes either one of two tests. For purposes of both tests, all eligible employees are divided between the "highly compensated employees"[13] and the remainder. The average of the individual actual deferral percentages is calculated for each of these two groups and the two averages are compared.

The first of the two tests is passed if the average deferral percentage for the high-paid is not more than 1.25 times the average deferral percentage for the low-paid. For example, if the average deferral percentage for the low-paid is 10 percent and that for the high-paid is not over 12.5 percent (1.25 times 10 percent), the first test is passed.

The alternative test is met if the average deferral percentage for the high-paid is not more than 2 times the average deferral percentage for the low-paid and the difference between the two per-

---

[13]Highly compensated employees are defined in I.R.C. §414(q), which is discussed in Chapter 4 herein.

centages is not more than 2 percent. For example, if the average deferral percentage for the low-paid employee is 2 percent and the average deferral percentage for the high-paid is 4 percent, the test would be passed, since 4 percent is 2 times 2 percent and the difference (4 percent less 2 percent) does not exceed 2 percent.

The same rules apply whether the elective contributions are extra employer payments in addition to regular compensation or are salary reduction contributions.

A 401(k) plan may include both elective and nonelective contributions.[14] If it does, it may satisfy the 401(k) nondiscrimination requirement by subjecting the combined contributions to the 401(k) plan requirements (percentage tests, nonforfeitability, and restrictions on distributions), provided the nonelective contributions also satisfy the general nondiscrimination rules. Alternatively, such a combination plan may satisfy the requirement if the elective contributions satisfy the 401(k) plan percentage tests, while the nonelective contributions satisfy the general rules for nondiscrimination, or if the combined contributions satisfy the general rules for nondiscrimination. Employer matching contributions are subject to the separate but similar "contribution percentage requirement" described in Chapter 9.[15]

Most plans that include employer matching contributions have been able to attract a high percentage of participation among lower-paid employees, thus satisfying the tests. Increasing the percentage of employer match and providing immediate or very early vesting generally increases employee participation, making it easier to pass the percentage tests.

For a plan financed solely by employer profit sharing contributions, an employer might decide to make contributions of 4 percent of pay for all employees, including 2 percent of pay as nonelective contributions paid automatically to the trust for all eligible employees and 2 percent of pay as elective contributions, which the employee could either receive in cash or direct into the trust. Under this approach, even if all low-paid employees elect cash and thus have a 2 percent average deferral percentage, while all high-paid employees elect deferral and, thus, have a 4 percent average de-

---

[14]In a proposed regulation, the IRS refers to this arrangement as a "combination plan."
[15]I.R.C. §401(m).

ferral percentage, the percentage test would be satisfied. But if this employer, instead, allowed elections for the entire 4 percent, it is possible that the average deferral percentages for the low-paid and the high-paid would be 0 percent and 4 percent respectively, and the plan would fail the test.

Determining in advance whether the percentage tests will be passed can be a problem under 401(k) plans. Prior experience with the same plan or similar plans may provide reasonable assurance, but for a new plan there may be uncertainty. The employer can almost always assume that at least some low-paid employees will elect deferral, and some high-paid will elect cash. An employer that allows all eligible employees to make elective contributions of up to 6 percent of pay and makes matching employer contributions equal to 50 percent of the elective contributions with one third immediately vested and the remainder becoming vested during the following two years could ordinarily expect that the average elective contributions by nonhighly compensated employees would exceed 4 percent, so that the test would be satisfied even if all highly compensated employees contribute 6 percent. Some employers find that the tests can still be satisfied if all eligible employees are allowed to contribute as much as 10 percent.

Another type of safeguard is to reserve the right to reduce the deferral percentage for the high-paid employee and to observe the experience during the year. In the previous example, if the employer observed halfway through the year that its expectations for elective contributions for the low-paid were overly optimistic, it could then reduce the allowable elective contributions for the high-paid for the remainder of the year in order to pass the test.

It is possible to treat only part of a plan as a 401(k) plan. For example, if a thrift plan allows employees to make basic contributions of 6 percent of pay to be matched by employer contributions and to make additional unmatched contributions of 4 percent of pay, it might treat the basic 6 percent employee contributions as elective contributions under a 401(k) plan (and, hence, excludable from taxable income), while treating the 4 percent unmatched contributions as non-401(k) contributions (and, thus, includible in taxable income), along with the matching employer contributions. Only the 401(k) portion would be subject to the 401(k) rules. This strategy might be followed if the combined plan could not satisfy 401(k) rules.

## Correction of Excess Contributions and Penalties

A plan may pay out to highly compensated employees any "excess contributions," i.e., any elective contributions higher than the maximum amount that would satisfy the ADP tests, together with income allocable to the excess contributions.[16] Such excess contributions may be paid out without any restriction or penalty. Instead of paying out the excess contributions, a plan may correct them by treating them as if they had been paid to the employee and then recontributed to the plan by the employee as after-tax contributions. The employer must pay a 10 percent tax on any excess contribution not paid out (or treated as paid out) within two and one-half months after the end of the plan year.[17] The excess contributions and income paid out are included in the participant's income for the year of deferral. If excess contributions are not corrected by the end of the plan year following their deferral, the plan may be disqualified.

## Limit on Elective Contributions—$7,000

The amount of an individual's elective deferrals is limited to $7,000 per year.[18] This limit includes all elective deferrals of an individual during a year under all 401(k) plans, tax-sheltered annuities (Sec. 403(b)) and simplified employee plans (SEPs). To the extent that any elective deferrals are contributed under a tax-sheltered annuity, the $7,000 limit is increased to $9,500. The $7,000 limit is indexed beginning in 1988, but the $9,500 is not indexed, so eventually the difference between these two limits will disappear.

If an individual exceeds his limit during his tax year (the calendar year for almost all individuals), the excess deferral, together with any income allocable to it, may be paid out to the individual with no penalty or restriction not later than the following April 15, and it will generally be treated as though it had never been made. In such case the income allocable to the excess deferral will be taxable income in the year the excess deferral was originally made. If the

---

[16]I.R.C. §401(k)(8).

[17]I.R.C. §4979.

[18]I.R.C. §402(g).

individual had made deferrals under more than one program, he can decide which one the excess applies to.

If any excess deferral is not paid out to the individual by April 15, the excess deferral will be included in the individual's taxable income in the year it was deferred and again in the year it is eventually paid from the plan.

### Social Security Taxes

Compensation deferred under a Section 401(k) arrangement is subject to Social Security payroll taxes and is so recognized, for Social Security benefit computation purposes, to the extent that the sum deferred in combination with the individual's cash compensation falls within the Social Security tax base. If the individual's cash compensation equals or exceeds the Social Security tax base, the deferred compensation would not be recognized for Social Security purposes. Also, a qualified defined benefit plan may, but is not required to, recognize as compensation amounts set aside under 401(k) arrangements in determining benefit accruals.[19] However, sums deferred are not recognized for unemployment insurance and workers' compensation purposes.

---

## Questions

1.  Why must a thrift plan be qualified with the Internal Revenue Service as a *pension* plan, a *profit-sharing* plan, or a *stock bonus* plan?
2.  If the fundamental differences between a pension plan and a profit sharing plan were fully reflected in the plan design, what distinctions would you expect to find among the provisions of a thrift *pension plan* and those of a thrift *profit sharing* plan?
3.  Explain the various advantages to *the plan participant* of a qualified thrift plan.
4.  Identify and explain those features of a qualified thrift plan that seem to exert the greatest impact on the degree of employee participation in the plan.

---

[19]Rev. Rul. 83–89.

5.  In view of the fact that participation in a thrift plan is voluntary, why is the IRS concerned with the extent and diversity of participation in the plan?

6.  Under what circumstances might the IRS find a thrift plan discriminatory in favor of the highly compensated employees, even if every employee of the firm elected to participate and the matching formula was the same for all participants?

7.  Describe the limitations that may be set out in a qualified thrift plan on the amount of contributions that a participant may make to the plan. Indicate which of the limitations are imposed by the IRS.

8.  Describe the various options that may be made available to participants in a qualified thrift plan on the amount that they will contribute to the plan, including any options to change the contribution rate or to make special contributions.

9.  Explain the various bases that may be used to determine the employer's contribution to a thrift plan.

10. Discuss the arguments *for* and *against* investing some or all of a thrift plan's assets in securities of the plan sponsor.

11. Describe the options that may be made available to participants in a qualified thrift plan as to the manner in which their account balances are invested. Include in your answer observations on the rights of plan participants to change their investment instructions to the plan sponsor.

12. Are the employee accounts under a thrift plan maintained on a *market* value or *book* value basis?

13. To what extent may the participants in a thrift plan be protected against adverse investment outcomes? Explain.

14. Distinguish between *membership* and *class system* vesting.

15. Describe the typical vesting provisions of a thrift plan.

16. Indicate the ways in which forfeitures under a thrift plan may be treated.

17. Identify the bases that may be used by a thrift plan to allocate to individual employee accounts:
    a.  Employer contributions.
    b.  Investment earnings.
    c.  Forfeitures.

18. What provisions may a thrift plan make for the distribution of sums in an employee's account balance while the participant is still in the service of the plan's sponsor?

19. In what forms may distributions from thrift plans be made?

20. Describe the latitude available under existing law for permitting participants in a profit sharing plan to choose between a current cash distribution of the employer's contribution to the plan and deferral of such contribution for later distribution.

21. The nonhighly compensated employees in a qualified 401(k) plan have an *average deferral percentage* of 3 percent of compensation. How large can the average deferral percentage for the highly compensated employees be without violating the IRC tests for discrimination? What would your answer be if the average deferral percentage for the nonhighly compensated employees were 1 percent of compensation?

22. Describe the strategies that an employer may adopt to assure that the contribution discrimination tests for a qualified 401(k) plan are met.

# 28 | Individual Retirement Plans and Voluntary Employee Contributions

## Individual Retirement Plans[1]

TO ENCOURAGE PERSONAL THRIFT and to provide an opportunity to persons not participating in tax-favored retirement programs to make their own individual arrangements for retirement income on a tax-favored basis, ERISA authorized the establishment of *individual retirement plans* with limited tax-deductible contributions. Under the original legislation, the privilege of establishing individual retirement plans was confined to persons not already participating in an employer-sponsored qualified plan or other tax-favored arrangement. Thus, it could be said that the primary purpose of the legislation was to narrow or even to close the existing gap in coverage of the private sector work force by tax-favored retirement programs.

The Economic Recovery Tax Act (ERTA) of 1981 broadened the eligibility provisions to permit employees and self-employed individuals already covered by other retirement programs to establish individual retirement plans, and increased the maximum annual

---

[1]IRS Publication 590 "Individual Retirement Arrangements" describes individual retirement plans.

**715**

tax-deductible contribution for one person from $1,500 to $2,000. The impetus behind the ERTA amendments was the desire to emphasize nongovernmental arrangements for old-age economic needs and to stimulate capital formation through personal savings.

The Tax Reform Act of 1986 retreated somewhat from ERTA. All employees and self-employed individuals are still permitted to contribute to an individual retirement plan, but those who are participants in a qualified plan and have incomes above certain levels may not claim a deduction for their contributions. This cutback in deductions was part of the effort to keep the Tax Reform Act from resulting in a net loss of revenue while reducing tax rates. Tax deductible saving for individuals who were already covered by qualified plans and who did not have low incomes was not considered a high priority item.

### General Features

Any employee, sole proprietor, or self-employed person can establish an individual retirement plan and make contributions to it. This privilege is available to persons participating in staff retirement plans of the federal government and of state and local governments, as well as those in the private sector. The contributions may be accumulated in a trust or custodial account managed by a bank, trust company, or other eligible financial institution or deposited with a life insurer under a flexible premium individual retirement annuity.

**Contributions.** If penalty excise taxes are to be avoided, contributions to the plan must be limited to the maximum permissible amount. The maximum annual contribution for one person is the lesser of $2,000 or 100 percent of the individual's compensation.[2] Compensation includes earned income of self-employed individuals.[3] No contribution is allowed for the tax year in which the individual reaches the age of 70½.[4]

---

[2]I.R.C. §219(b)(1), 408(o).
[3]I.R.C. §219(f).
[4]I.R.C. §219(d)(1).

A married person whose spouse has no compensation or elects to be treated as having no compensation is allowed to contribute to a separate plan for his spouse if the couple files a joint return.[5] The combined contribution for a worker and spouse may not exceed the *lesser* of $2,250 or 100 percent of the working spouse's compensation. The total contribution can be divided between the two plans in any proportions, so long as not more than $2,000 is attributed to either one.

Although all employees and self-employed persons may contribute the amounts described above to an individual retirement plan, not all may claim a deduction for the amounts contributed. A deduction for contributions not exceeding the above limits is allowed unless (1) the individual (or the individual's spouse in the case of a married couple filing jointly) was a participant in a qualified plan at any time during the plan year ending within the individual's tax year and (2) the adjusted gross income (AGI) of the individual for the tax year (or of the individual and spouse if filing jointly) exceeds the "applicable dollar amount." The applicable dollar amount is $40,000 for married couples filing jointly, $0 for married individuals filing separately, and $25,000 for unmarried individuals. If the excess of the adjusted gross income over the applicable dollar amount is less than $10,000, individuals (or couples filing jointly) may still claim a deduction of a fraction of the allowable contribution. For example, a single person with adjusted gross income of $28,000 ($3,000 over the $25,000 applicable amount) could still deduct up to $1,400 (70 percent of his $2,000 limit). Thus no deduction is allowed for plan participants if the adjusted gross income exceeds $50,000 in the case of married couples filing jointly, $10,000 in the case of married individuals filing separately, or $35,000 in the case of unmarried individuals.

An individual can claim a tax deduction for a particular tax year if his contribution is made by the due date (including extensions) for his tax return for that year, whether or not the plan was established before the end of the year.

Certain amounts distributed from qualified pension and profit sharing plans (or other individual retirement plans) may be con-

---

[5]I.R.C. §219(c).

tributed (rolled over) to an individual retirement plan.[6] Such rollover contributions are not limited to $2,000.[7] Nor do they reduce or eliminate the allowable deduction for a regular contribution to the plan for the year of the rollover. No deduction is allowed for a rollover contribution since it is a tax-free transfer.[8]

An employer may contribute to an individual retirement plan for an employee, in which event the amount paid is treated as compensation of the employee. The employee, however, may take a deduction as if he had contributed the amount directly.[9]

If an individual's contribution (other than a rollover contribution) to an individual retirement plan exceeds the allowable amount, a nondeductible excise tax of 6 percent is imposed on the excess contribution.[10] The excise tax is not imposed, however, if the excess contribution, together with the net income attributable to it, is returned to the individual by the funding agency before his tax-filing date (including extensions), and only the net income paid is taxable income.[11] The excise tax on an excess contribution is levied for each year that it remains in the plan. To avoid continuing excise taxes, the individual must either withdraw the excess contribution or offset it against contributions that could otherwise be made in future years.

**Investment Earnings:** The investment earnings of an individual retirement plan, except for unrelated business income, are fully exempt from federal income taxation while held in the plan.[12] The earnings are taxed as ordinary income without benefit of the special five-year forward averaging rule upon distribution to the individual, unless they are a part of a tax-free rollover to another plan.

**Timing of Distributions.** Since Congress intended that individual retirement plans be used to provide old-age income support, it

---

[6]See Chapter 29 for information on rollovers from qualified plans.

[7]I.R.C. §408(a)(1).

[8]I.R.C. §219(d)(2).

[9]I.R.C. §219(f)(5). Deductions for employer payments to SEPs are dealt with in a later section of this chapter.

[10]I.R.C. §4973.

[11]I.R.C. §408(d)(4).

[12]I.R.C. §408(e).

provided for tax penalties for distributions, except for death or disability, made outside a corridor bounded at the lower end by age 59½ and at the upper end by age 70½. A distribution prior to age 59½, except in the case of death or disability, is termed an *early distribution* and is subject to a nondeductible excise tax of 10 percent.[13] On the other hand, under minimum distribution requirements distributions from the plan must not be delayed beyond the April 1 following the calendar year in which the individual reaches age 70½. Early distributions and the minimum distribution requirements are discussed further in Chapter 29.

If the individual (or his surviving spouse) dies before receiving his entire interest in the plan, the remaining interest must be distributed to his (or his surviving spouse's) beneficiaries within five years after death.[14] However, if benefit payments are payable to a designated beneficiary, payments may be made over the lifetime or the life expectancy of the designated beneficiary.

## Types of Plans

Characterized in terms of the funding instruments that may be used, individual retirement plans are of two types: individual retirement account and individual retirement annuity. An individual retirement plan is commonly called an IRA, regardless of which of the two approaches to funding is used. The Code[15] describes with some specificity the characteristics that must be associated with each major type of funding instrument, if it is to qualify as a receptacle for IRA contributions. These requirements are intended to implement the broad purposes of the program and effectuate the various restrictions outlined above. It should be noted, in particular, that the sponsor of each type of instrument is put on notice not to accept any contribution that is not permissible under the applicable rules.

**Individual Retirement Account.** An individual retirement account is a domestic trust or custodial account created by a written instrument for the exclusive benefit of an individual or his bene-

---

[13]I.R.C. §72(p).

[14]I.R.C. §401(a)(9).

[15]I.R.C. §7701(a)(37).

ficiaries. Only banks and other financial institutions falling within the scope of applicable regulations are permitted to offer and operate such an account.[16] In practice, commercial banks, trust companies, mutual savings banks, federally insured credit unions, savings and loan associations, broker-dealers, mutual funds, and life insurance companies sponsor and vigorously promote IRAs. Many of these institutions have developed one or more prototype IRAs, and have obtained IRS approval of the documents employed in the establishment and operation of the prototype accounts.

To meet the requirements of existing law and regulations, the legal instrument creating an IRA trust or custodial account must stipulate that:

- Except for rollover contributions and SEPs, only cash contributions will be accepted and no more than $2,000 will be accepted on behalf of any one individual in any given tax year of the individual.
- The assets of the account will not be commingled with other property, except in an approved common trust fund or common investment fund.
- None of the account assets will be invested in life insurance contracts.
- An individual's interest in his account balance is nonforfeitable.
- Distributions must begin by April 1 following the year the individual attains age 70½ and must satisfy the minimum distribution requirements.

An individual retirement account may generally be invested in any type of asset. However, any investment in collectibles (art works, stamps, rugs, antiques, certain coins, and other types of tangible property) is treated as a taxable distribution and, thus, is prevented for all intents and purposes.[17] The fiduciary statutes of some states may constrain investments. Individual retirement plans are subject to the same rules and penalties for prohibited transactions as those that apply to qualified pension plans. These are designed to prevent self-dealing by "disqualified persons" who exercise control over the individual retirement plan. The trustee

---

[16]Treas. Reg. §1.408–2(b)(2)(ii).
[17]I.R.C. §408(m).

cannot make a loan from the IRA to the individual for whose benefit it is maintained. If in violation of this prohibition an individual should borrow money from his account, it will cease to be an IRA from the first day of the taxable year in which the loan was made. Disqualification of the account triggers a *constructive* distribution to the individual equal to the fair market value of all the assets of the account as of the first day of such taxable year. This amount is taxed as ordinary income. The prohibited transactions excise tax will not be imposed, but a 10 percent penalty tax will be assessed on the constructive distribution if the individual is not disabled or 59½ on the first day of such taxable year.

If an IRA is part of any type of employer-sponsored pension plan, it is subject to ERISA's fiduciary standards.

Despite the general absence of restrictions on the investment of IRA assets, as a practical matter the small size of most IRAs militates against certain types of investments. Most IRA assets are invested in certificates of deposit or in passbook savings accounts of commercial banks, mutual savings banks, and savings and loan associations. A considerable sum is invested in mutual fund shares, including those of growth stock funds, income stock funds, balanced funds, and money market funds. Some individuals establish custodial accounts and direct the investment of their own accounts within the usual range of marketable securities.

**Individual Retirement Annuity.**    The second instrument that can be used to fund an individual retirement plan is an individual retirement annuity. Such an annuity is purchased directly from a life insurance company and does not involve a trust or custodial account.

The following restrictions apply to an annuity used for this purpose:[18]

- The contract must not be transferable by the owner.
- The premiums must be flexible, not fixed.
- Dividends must be applied to pay future premiums or to purchase additional benefits, rather than being distributed in cash.
- The entire interest of the owner must be nonforfeitable.
- The insurer must not accept more than $2,000 in annual premiums, except for SEP-IRAs.

---

[18]I.R.C. §408(b).

- Distributions must be made within the same period as for an individual retirement account.

The owner's interest in the annuity may be distributed in the form of a lump-sum payment, installments over a period of years, a single life annuity on the life of the owner or a joint and survivor annuity on the lives of the owner and his spouse. The owner cannot borrow on the annuity or use it as collateral for a loan. These would be prohibited transactions that would cause the fair market value of the contract to be taxed to the individual as ordinary income on the first day of the year in which the transaction occurred. There would also be a penalty tax of 10 percent on the constructive distribution if the individual was not disabled or age 59½ or older.

### Rollover Contributions

Amounts distributed from qualified pension and profit sharing plans are ordinarily taxable when distributed.[19] But if an individual receives a "qualified total distribution" or a "partial distribution" from a qualified plan and if he transfers part or all of the amount to an IRA within 60 days of receipt, the amount rolled over is excluded from his gross income.[20] Requirements for such rollovers are described in Chapter 29.

IRA-to-IRA tax-free rollovers are also allowed, if the entire amount received from an IRA is rolled over into another IRA within 60 days.[21] Such a tax-free rollover, however, may be made only once in any 365-day period.

Except as noted, any amount distributed from an IRA is taxable as ordinary income to the payee.[22] The amount received in excess of the individual's tax basis is included in gross income. A lump-sum distribution from an IRA is not entitled to the special five-year forward averaging rule.

If an IRA consists entirely of contributions that were rollover contributions from a qualified plan, and if the entire amount is distributed from the IRA and rolled over into another qualified plan within 60 days, the amount rolled over is excluded from gross

---

[19]I.R.C. §§402(a)(1), 403(a)(1).
[20]I.R.C. §§402(a)(5), 403(a)(4).
[21]I.R.C. §408(d)(3).
[22]I.R.C. §408(d).

income. Rollovers from and to tax-deferred annuities receive the same treatment.

The transfer of an individual's interest in an IRA to his former spouse, incident to a divorce, is not a taxable transfer. The former spouse will pay no tax until she receives a distribution from the IRA.[23]

### Payroll Deduction IRAs

In 1982, IRAs first became available to employees who are participants in qualified plans. A number of employers decided to offer a payroll deduction facility for employees to contribute to IRAs, both as a service to employees and to encourage thrift. Some employers who provide payroll deductions for IRAs allow the employee to designate any bank, insurance company, mutual fund, or other entity sponsoring an IRA to receive the withheld sums. Other employers limit the choice to a single funding medium or to a very limited number.

Allowing the choice of any funding medium gives the employee the ultimate flexibility to choose an IRA to fit his own desires and needs. It does not, of course, guarantee a good choice. Allowing complete freedom increases the amount of administrative work. Limiting the choice to a single funding medium, or to a few that the employer has carefully selected, does not necessarily result in favorable investment experience. If the experience is unfavorable, the employee may blame the employer.

By the time many employers considered the question, most employees who were interested in IRAs had already made their own arrangements. In any event, all employees are free to arrange for their own IRAs without the assistance of the employer. For these reasons, and because of the administrative expense and the disadvantages of each of the two possible approaches, most employers have not offered payroll deduction for IRAs.

### Simplified Employee Pensions (SEPs)

Many small employers have been discouraged from establishing a qualified plan because of the expense and administrative burden

---

[23]I.R.C. §408(d)(6).

involved in developing plan documents, obtaining IRS approval, and preparing summary plan descriptions, annual reports for regulatory agencies, and summary annual reports for participants. To encourage small employers to establish pension plans for their employees and reduce the gap in coverage of the private sector labor force, Congress made provision for a simplified form of employer-sponsored pension plan, called logically enough, *simplified employee pensions,* or *SEP.* Since a SEP is essentially an arrangement under which an employer can establish and finance an IRA for each of his eligible employees, this approach is often referred to as a SEP-IRA. Not only does a SEP avoid the expense and complexity of a qualified plan, but it permits the owner of a small business to set aside more money for himself on a tax-deferred basis than he could under a regular IRA. Since in the absence of restrictions the arrangement would lend itself to discrimination in favor of the owner and a few favored employees, a SEP must meet certain requirements designed to prevent such discrimination.

**Participation.**    If an employer contributes to a SEP for himself or any one employee in a given year, he must contribute on behalf of every employee who has attained age 21 and has worked for the employer during at least three of the preceding five years.[24] However, no contributions are required for employees covered under a collective bargaining agreement, if good faith bargaining occurred over retirement benefits.

The employer may choose the funding instrument and agency for the individual IRAs or may permit each employee to choose his or her own IRA or type of IRA. If the employer selects, recommends, or otherwise influences his employees to choose a particular IRA or type of IRA, and that IRA imposes any restrictions on withdrawals (e.g., a penalty for early withdrawal other than the penalty assessed by the IRS), the plan administrator must provide each employee once a year with a clear explanation of the restrictions and a statement that other IRAs may not have such restrictions.

**Contributions.**    The employer's contributions to a SEP are based on the participants' compensation. He need not commit himself to

---

[24]I.R.C. §408(k)(2).

contribute to the plan every year, nor must he commit himself in advance to contribute a specified percentage of compensation. The governing document for the SEP must contain a formula for allocating the aggregate employer contributions to the various employee accounts.[25] The maximum amount that an employer can contribute to a SEP for an employee in any one tax year is the lesser of $30,000 or 15 percent of covered compensation.[26] The deduction for contributions to SEPs reduces the employer's maximum deduction for other tax-qualified plans.[27]

Employer contributions to a SEP are viewed as contributions to a defined contribution plan, and are aggregated with employer contributions made on behalf of an employee to any other defined contribution plan in computing the amount that can be added annually to his account (lesser of 25 percent of compensation or $30,000).[28]

Employer contributions to a SEP are not subject to Social Security (FICA) taxes and unemployment (FUTA) taxes if the employer has reason to believe that the employee will be entitled to deduct the employer contributions under the SEP rules.[29] Similarly, no federal income tax need be withheld by the employer for payments to an employee's SEP.[30]

Employer contributions generally will be deemed discriminatory unless they bear a uniform relationship to the first $200,000 of each individual's compensation.[31] However, a SEP may be integrated with Social Security if the employer does not maintain another integrated tax-qualified plan. Integration of a SEP with Social Security is subject to the same integration rules as apply to qualified defined contribution plans.

SEP contributions on behalf of any one individual may not exceed $30,000. This limit will be subject to upward adjustment on the same basis as for qualified defined contribution plans. This limit, the same as for qualified defined contribution plans, may make

---

[25]I.R.C. §408(k)(5).

[26]I.R.C. §402(h).

[27]I.R.C. §404(h).

[28]I.R.C. §415(e)(5).

[29]I.R.C. §§3121(a)(5), §3306(b)(5).

[30]I.R.C. §3401(a)(12), Treas. Reg. §31.3401(a)(12)–1(d).

[31]I.R.C. §408(k)(3).

SEPs more attractive to a small employer than a qualified plan. Employer contributions to a SEP are included in the employee's taxable compensation but are deductible in full by the employee.[32] The maximum employer contribution allowed as a deduction by an employee is the lesser of $30,000 or 15 percent of compensation.[33] This limit is in addition to the $2,000 deduction that an employee may take for an IRA maintained outside the SEP arrangement. There is no deduction for employer contributions on behalf of an employee's spouse.

**Elective Contributions.** A SEP may allow elective salary reduction contributions by employees, similar to elective contributions under a 401(k) plan.[34] Employees may elect to have the employer reduce their compensation otherwise payable and contribute the amount to a SEP. These elective deferrals are excluded from the employees' taxable income. They are subject to the same $7,000 limit as elective deferrals under a 401(k) plan. In addition, the elective deferrals plus any other employer contributions under a SEP are subject to the regular SEP limitation of the lesser of $30,000 or 15 percent of compensation.

Elective deferrals are not permissible under a SEP unless the employer has 25 or fewer employees throughout the preceding year and unless at least 50 percent of the employees of the employer elect to make salary deferrals. The elective deferral percentage of each highly compensated employee cannot exceed 125 percent of the average deferral percentage of all nonhighly compensated employees.

Elective deferrals are not permitted for employees of governmental employers or of tax-exempt organizations.

**Withdrawals.** Like a regular IRA, an individual's SEP account is fully vested from the beginning. The employer cannot impose any restrictions on withdrawals from the account at any time. The funding agency (i.e., the financial institution sponsoring the IRAs purchased under the plan) may, however, impose penalties for early

---

[32] I.R.C. §219(f)(5).

[33] I.R.C. §219(b)(2).

[34] I.R.C. §408(k)(6).

withdrawal. Moreover, withdrawals from an employee's account before he has reached age 59½ are subject to a nondeductible federal excise tax, unless the withdrawal was a consequence of the employee's death or disability or unless rolled over to another IRA. As with a conventional IRA, there is also a penalty tax for failure to commence distributions by April 1 following the year of attaining age 70½ and for insufficient distributions thereafter.

**IRS Form 5305–SEP.**   In an effort to help employers establish a SEP with minimum expense and trouble, the Internal Revenue Service has developed a form, designated Form 5305–SEP and called the "Simplified Employee Pension—Individual Retirement Accounts Contribution Agreement." By using this form, an employer has assurance that the form of his contribution agreement is in compliance with IRS requirements. All eligible employees must participate in the SEP established by that form. That form may not be used if the employer presently maintains any other qualified plan. Form 5305–SEP is not submitted to the IRS. The IRS will not issue an advance determination of compliance on the basis of Form 5305–SEP, but none is needed. Form 5305A–SEP is a comparable form for use when the plan has a salary reduction feature. At the time of this writing neither form could be used if employer contributions are to be integrated with Social Security.

A request can be filed with the IRS by sponsoring banks, federally insured credit unions, insurance companies, regulated investment companies, or trade or professional societies or associations wanting to obtain an opinion letter that a proposed prototype SEP agreement, which is to be used by more than one employer, is acceptable in form.

An employer may, of course, develop and obtain IRS approval of its own SEP agreement.

**Reporting.**   Simplified reporting requirements apply to employers using model Form 5305–SEP.[35] At the time an employee becomes eligible to participate, the administrator (generally the employer) must provide a copy of the completed and unmodified Form 5305–SEP. At the end of each calendar year, the administrator

---

[35] 29 CFR §2520.104–48.

must provide each participant a written notice of the amount of employer contributions allocated to his account. If an employer does not use model Form 5305–SEP, the reporting requirements are much more rigorous.[36]

## Voluntary Employee Contributions

Employee contributions to qualified plans may be classified as *mandatory* or *voluntary*. The Internal Revenue Service considers contributions to be mandatory if they are required as a condition of employment, as a condition of participation in the plan, or as a condition for obtaining benefits attributable to employer contributions.[37] All other employee contributions are classified as voluntary. Elective contributions under cash or deferred arrangements, even if they result from salary reduction, are treated as *employer* contributions, rather than as *employee* contributions under the Code.

Many defined contribution plans make provision for voluntary employee contributions. This includes contributory plans that allow voluntary contributions in addition to mandatory contributions, as well as "noncontributory" plans that allow only voluntary contributions. Some defined benefit plans also allow voluntary employee contributions.

The Internal Revenue Service does not permit voluntary employee contributions in excess of 10 percent of pay.[38] This 10 percent limit may be applied cumulatively to the aggregate basic compensation for all years of participation.[39]

If voluntary employee contributions are included in a defined benefit plan, the voluntary employee contributions are treated as if they were made to a defined contribution plan.[40] For purposes of determining account balances, the assets must be valued at least annually on a market value basis. This adds a type of record-keeping not otherwise present in a defined benefit plan, and is one

---

[36]29 CFR §2520.104–49.
[37]Treas. Reg. §1.411(c)–1(c)(4).
[38]Rev. Rul. 59–185, Rev. Rul. 69–627.
[39]Rev. Rul. 69–217.
[40]ERISA §204(c)(4), I.R.C. §411(d)(5).

reason for not allowing voluntary employee contributions in a defined benefit plan.

Voluntary employee contributions receive the same tax treatment as mandatory employee contributions. Such contributions are made with after-tax dollars and are not tax deductible. Even though voluntary employee contributions receive no tax benefit at the time of contribution, they enable the participant to invest on a tax-deferred basis, having no taxable income until he receives a distribution. Upon distribution, the investment return earned may be subject to favorable taxation as part of a lump-sum distribution, or may be eligible for a tax-free rollover to an IRA.

In most plans that have allowed voluntary employee contributions, few participants have used them. One current reason for the low usage of voluntary employee contributions is the competition for savings dollars from tax-deductible IRAs and tax-excludable elective contributions under 401(k) plans, as well as from non-qualified investments, some of which have attractive tax advantages.

For plan years beginning after 1986 voluntary employee contributions under both defined benefit plans and defined contribution plans are subject to contribution percentage requirements under the nondiscrimination tests for employer matching contributions and employee contributions. These requirements were described in the previous chapter. Because highly compensated employees tend to make much higher voluntary contributions than other employees, these tests are difficult to satisfy if voluntary contributions are allowed under the plan.

The problems posed by the percentage tests, the work and expense of administration and communication of voluntary employee contributions, the low rate of utilization by employees, and the availability of investment alternatives have led many employers to conclude that they should not allow traditional voluntary employee contributions.

## Other Forms of Retirement Savings

There are a number of other employer-sponsored programs that may serve as a form of retirement savings. For the most part, they fall outside the focus of this book and are not discussed herein. In order that the reader may know of their existence, these programs are set forth below, with the Internal Revenue Code reference, where applicable.

1. Tax-deferred annuities for teachers and employees of certain nonprofit organizations (Code §403(b)).
2. Deferred compensation plans with respect to service for state and local governments and tax-exempt employers (Code §457).
3. Incentive stock options (Code §422A).
4. Employee stock purchase plans (Code §423).
5. Nonqualified stock options.
6. Nonqualified stock purchase agreements.
7. Excess benefit plans to provide benefits in excess of those allowed under Code section 415 (ERISA §3(36)).
8. Shadow stock plans.
9. Other nonqualified plans and deferred compensation agreements.

---

## Questions

1. An unmarried individual is considering the establishment of an individual retirement plan. He has a number of questions concerning contributions to the plan. Specifically, he would like to know:
   a. The maximum amount that he may contribute in any one tax year, apart from rollover contributions.
   b. The maximum amount that he may deduct for income tax purposes.
   c. Whether there is any penalty for contributing more in any one year than the law permits.
   d. Whether his contribution, to be tax-deductible, must be made from current personal earnings.
   How would you answer the foregoing questions?
2. May a married person make a tax-deductible contribution to an individual retirement plan on behalf of his or her spouse? Explain.
3. Apart from the imposition of a nondeductible excise tax, how does the IRS attempt to prevent contributions to an IRA in excess of the permissible amount?
4. What is a rollover contribution to an IRA? Does such a contribution reduce the tax deduction available to an individual for a regular contribution to the IRA in the same year?

5. Explain the difference between the following types of distributions from an individual retirement plan:
   a. A regular or normal distribution.
   b. An early distribution.
   c. An insufficient distribution under minimum distribution requirements.

6. Describe the two financial instruments that have been approved by Congress for the funding of individual retirement plans.

7. How are distributions from individual retirement plans taxed?

8. May an individual borrow against his or her account balance under an individual retirement plan?

9. Are there any exceptions to the general requirement that an individual retirement account be funded through a trust or custodial account?

10. What is the essential difference between (*a*) *a payroll deduction* IRA and (*b*) a SEP?

11. What is the logic, if any, behind permitting an individual employee to set aside only $2,000 per year on a tax-deferred basis under an IRA while permitting up to $30,000 to be set aside on a tax-deferred basis for the same individual under a SEP?

12. Under what circumstances may an employee make elective salary deferrals under a SEP? How much may the employee elect to defer?

13. Describe the federal income tax treatment of voluntary employee contributions to a qualified employee benefit plan.

14. For what reasons might the sponsor of a qualified plan not permit the plan participants to make voluntary contributions to the plans?

# 29 | Tax Treatment

FOR DECADES employment-based asset accumulation plans, principally pension and profit-sharing plans, have been accorded favorable treatment under federal tax laws. This favorable treatment has been extended to employers, participants, beneficiaries, and the trust fund or life insurer account holding the plan assets.

This favorable tax treatment is intended to encourage the use of private sector arrangements to meet old-age economic needs, at least, in part. This approach provides maximum flexibility in retirement planning, creates savings for capital formation, and minimizes federal government intrusion into private sector decision making.

Offsetting these advantages is the loss of tax revenues of the federal government. In practical effect, the private sector is being permitted to allocate for business and personal goals monies that would otherwise have flowed into the federal treasury to be spent in ways determined by Congress. This effect is so real that fiscal authorities characterize these tax concessions as "tax expenditures," a concept objectionable to some. In any event, when considering the nature and extent of a particular tax benefit, Congress weighs in a general way the value of the benefit against the amount of lost revenue. This process has led, for example, to restricting the annual amount of tax-favored pensions under defined benefit pension plans to $90,000, a limit that some think should be further reduced, while others think the limit should be increased or eliminated entirely.

The tax provisions have in part reflected social and philosophical concepts. The difference between the taxation of monthly pensions and lump sum distributions, for example, reflects in part consideration of the relative desirability of encouraging these two forms of payment. Tax provisions also reflect the effectiveness of lobbying of particular groups that have particular goals.

This chapter describes the federal tax laws, but state tax laws are also important. State tax treatment is often quite similar to federal tax treatment, but at times it is very different.

## Taxation of Participants before Benefits Are Received

Most qualified plans are funded entirely by employer contributions. If employees contribute to the plan, their contributions generally are not tax deductible. But the elective contributions of employees under a cash or deferred arrangement (401(k) plan) are excludable from their taxable income, as described in Chapter 27.

Participants and beneficiaries under a qualified plan generally have no taxable income until benefits are actually received.[1] The doctrine of constructive receipt, applicable in most other situations, does not apply. It is immaterial whether the employee could have elected to receive a benefit, so long as he does not actually receive it.

### Life Insurance Protection

If a plan purchases life insurance upon the life of a participant, and if the proceeds of the policy are not payable to the trust, the cost of the insurance protection is currently includible in the participant's taxable income. For this purpose the amount of protection provided equals the excess of the amount of benefit payable upon death over any cash value of the policy. To determine the cost of

---

[1] I.R.C. §402(a)(1).

this protection one multiplies this amount of protection, technically the "net amount at risk," by cost factors published by the IRS.[2] These costs are often referred to as "P.S. 58 costs," reflecting the IRS publication in which they were originally promulgated.

If a plan is contributory and specifies that costs of insurance are to be paid first from the employee's own contributions, the employee has no current taxable income unless the cost of insurance exceeds his own contributions.

A participant has no current taxable income with respect to uninsured death benefit protection provided under a plan.

## Loans to Participants

Many defined contribution plans allow loans to participants, usually from their own account balances, as described in Chapter 26. A few defined benefit plans allow mortgage loans or other secured loans to participants when fiduciary and party-in-interest requirements are satisfied. Fiduciary requirements are discussed in Chapter 2, while some specific requirements of the Internal Revenue Code for loans are described in Chapter 26.

Prior to the Tax Reform Act of 1986, one of the attractive features of plan loans was the deduction of interest paid on the loan, which some considered a deduction for paying interest to oneself. The Tax Reform Act eliminated the deduction of interest for all loans, whether from a qualified plan or any other lender, subject to a four-year phase out and two generally available exceptions.[3]

There are special rules that further restrict the deduction of interest on loans from qualified plans.[4] No deduction will be allowed for interest under any loan made or amended after 1986 to a "key employee" (as defined under top-heavy plan requirements). Nor will any deduction be allowed for interest on any loan made after 1986 which is secured by an employee's elective contributions under a 401(k) plan or a 403(b) plan.

---

[2]I.R.C. §72(m)(3), Treas. Reg. 1.72–16(b), Rev. Rul. 55–747.
[3]I.R.C. §163(d),(h).
[4]I.R.C. §72(p)(3).

## Nonqualified Plans

Contributions to an employees' trust that is not part of a qualified plan are included in each participant's taxable income in the first year that the amounts are transferable by him or that they are not subject to a substantial risk of forfeiture.[5] This generally applies to all vested benefits to the extent that they are funded. Regulations stipulate how the extent of funding of each participant's benefits is to be determined for this purpose under a defined benefit plan.[6]

If a qualified plan loses its qualified status, all participants may have immediate taxable income equal to the value of their funded vested benefits.

## Taxation of Participants Receiving Benefits

Any benefits paid to a participant or beneficiary generally are includible in his taxable income in the year they are received, to the extent that they have not previously been included in taxable income.[7]

## Return of Employee Contributions and Other Basis

A participant generally recovers tax-free the amounts that have previously been includible in his income. A beneficiary generally recovers tax-free the amounts that have previously been includible in the taxable income of either the participant or beneficiary. These tax-free amounts are called "basis," and generally consist of the employee's after-tax contributions and certain costs of insurance previously included in taxable income. Elective contributions under a 401(k) plan are considered to be employer contributions and thus are not included in basis. If the recipient has no basis, all payments are taxable in the year they are received.

If in a single tax year a payee receives a total distribution of all amounts to which he is entitled under a plan, he subtracts the basis

---

[5] I.R.C. §§402(b)(1), 83.

[6] Treas. Reg. 1.402(b)–1(a), 1.403(b)–1(d)(4).

[7] IRS Publication 575 "Pension and Annuity Income" is an explanation of this subject for lay people.

from the total distribution and the remainder is includible in taxable income. But if he receives only part of the amounts to which he is entitled, as in the case of annuity payments expected to continue over several years or a lump-sum payment of only part of his account, it must be determined how much of the distribution is a return of basis and how much is includible in taxable income.

Every distribution that is not received in the form of an annuity and is received prior to the participant's annuity starting date, is generally allocated pro rata between recovery of basis and taxable income.[8] However, there are two important exceptions to this rule. First, a plan may provide that part or all of employee contributions under a defined contribution plan, together with the earnings allocable to them, are treated as though they were in a separate plan, provided the plan separately accounts for the employee contributions and credits them with their share of the trust's investment earnings.[9] Thus, a contributory defined contribution plan is treated as if it were two plans, one consisting of all accumulated employee contributions with the earnings thereon and the other consisting of the remainder of the participants' account balances. Under a defined benefit plan that allows *voluntary* employee contributions which are credited with their share of the trust's investment earnings, the accumulated voluntary employee contributions are treated as a defined contribution plan. In order to obtain this separate treatment for employee contributions, the plan must either designate which of the two portions of the plan any distributions are deemed to come from or delegate this designation to the participant. Allowing election by the participant increases administrative work for the plan, which must report the taxable and nontaxable portions of the distribution on Form 1099-R.

The second important exception to allocating every distribution pro rata between recovery of basis and taxable income is a grandfather clause that preserves the treatment of prior law for the basis derived from employee contributions made before 1987 and pre-1987 costs of insurance. This grandfather clause applies only if, on May 5, 1986, the plan permitted withdrawal of employee contributions prior to separation from service.[10] Under this rule all dis-

---

[8] I.R.C. §72(e)(8).
[9] I.R.C. §72(e)(9), IRS Notice 87–13.
[10] I.R.C. §72(e)(8)(D).

tributions are deemed to be paid tax-free from the pre-1987 basis until the pre-1987 basis is exhausted.

In order to obtain the maximum possible tax deferral, some contributory defined contribution plans that are eligible for this grandfather clause provide that employee contributions made after 1986 and earnings thereon will be treated as a separate plan and that any distributions will be deemed to come first from pre-1987 basis to the extent that it is sufficient, then from post-1986 employee contributions and earnings thereon, and finally from the remaining balance. For example, assume that a participant has a total account balance of $10,000, that this includes $2,000 of basis derived from pre-1987 contributions (without earnings) and costs of insurance, that the $10,000 also includes $800 of employee contributions made after 1986 and $200 of earnings thereon, and that the participant receives a distribution of $2,500. The first $2,000 of the distribution is deemed to come from the $2,000 of pre-1987 basis, and thus to be excludable from taxable income. The remaining $500 of the $2,500 distribution is deemed to come from the $1,000 of accumulated post-1986 contributions and earnings thereon. Since 80 percent of the $1,000 consists of the employee's own contributions, 80 percent of the $500 distribution, or $400, is excluded from taxable income and only the remaining $100 is taxable.

When annuity payments commence, an exclusion ratio is established to determine what proportion of each payment represents the return of the employee's basis. This exclusion ratio is the ratio of the employee's basis to the present value of his expected future benefit payments, determined in accordance with regulations.[11] After the annuity commences, the portion of each payment excluded from taxable income never changes until the amount recovered tax-free exceeds the basis, after which all amounts received are taxable. If the participant and any joint or contingent annuitant die before recovering all of the basis, the remaining unrecovered basis is allowed as a deduction to any beneficiary entitled to a benefit that is in the nature of a refund of employee contributions or a refund of the cost of the annuity, and if there is no such beneficiary, the deduction is allowed to the deceased annuitant in the last year of the deceased.[12] Thus, in the end the total of the amounts excluded

---

[11]I.R.C. §72, Treas. Reg. 1.72.

[12]I.R.C. §72(b)(3).

or deductible exactly equals the participant's basis. Different rules apply to annuities that commenced before 1987.

## Lump-Sum Distributions

Amounts includible in taxable income may be taxed more favorably if they constitute part or all of a lump-sum distribution.

A lump-sum distribution is a distribution from a plan within one taxable year of the recipient of the total balance to the credit of the employee which becomes payable on account of the employee's death or separation from service or which becomes payable after the employee attains age 59½. With respect to self-employed individuals, disability is substituted for the separation from service requirement. However, a distribution will not be treated as a lump-sum distribution unless the employee has been a participant in the plan for at least five taxable years before the year of the distribution. For the purpose of determining whether there has been a total distribution, all qualified pension plans of an employer are treated as a single plan, all qualified profit sharing plans are treated as one plan and all qualified stock bonus plans are treated as one plan.

One time during his lifetime a taxpayer may elect to have all lump-sum distributions received during that year (but only distributions received after age 59½) taxed under a rule referred to as "five-year averaging."

Under this method, one first determines the *total taxable amount,* which is the amount of the distribution that is includible in income, excluding the net unrealized appreciation on any employer securities included in the distribution. If the total taxable amount is less than $70,000, the total taxable amount is first reduced by a *minimum distribution allowance.* The minimum distribution allowance is equal to the lesser of $10,000 or 50 percent of the total taxable amount, reduced by 20 percent of the amount by which the total taxable amount exceeds $20,000. The practical effect of this provision of the law is that half of the total taxable amount not exceeding $20,000 may be excluded from the tax computation, the allowance diminishing in dollar amount for total taxable amounts in excess of $20,000 and disappearing altogether for amounts of $70,000 or more.

Next one computes the income tax on one fifth of this adjusted total taxable amount, determined as though the taxpayer were an individual, not head of a household, with no other income, no

**29 / Tax Treatment**

**739**

personal exemptions and no deductions. The income tax is five times this amount. The intent and effect of this procedure are to tax the distribution in lower tax brackets than those that would apply if the *total* distribution were added to all other income of the employee in the year of receipt.

A provision under prior law to apply capital gains tax treatment to any portion of a lump-sum distribution that is attributable to participation before 1974 is subject to a five-year phase-out rule.[13] Except in unusual situations this phase-out rule will not preserve any lump-sum distribution treatment after 1987, since the tax rates applicable to capital gains and ordinary income will be the same after 1987.

A grandfather provision protects part of prior law provisions for any participant who attained age 50 before 1986. Such participants may make one election, regardless of whether under or over age 59½, to have either the prior 10-year averaging rule apply in combination with 1986 tax rates or the new 5-year averaging rule apply with the new lower tax rates.[14] The 10-year averaging rule was essentially the same as the current 5-year averaging rule except that 10 years was used instead of 5. Either alternative may produce lower taxes in a particular case, depending on the amount of the distribution.

Participants who attained age 50 before 1986 may also elect to continue to have capital gains treatment apply to any portion of their lump sum distribution attributable to pre-1974 participation.[15] For those electing this capital gains treatment, a 20 percent tax rate applies to the capital gains portion. In some cases participants will do better by rejecting this capital gains treatment and having the entire lump sum taxed under the 5-year or 10-year averaging rule.

## Rollover Amounts

Several provisions of the law are designed to encourage the preservation for retirement purposes of the amounts set aside under qualified plans. One of these is the allowance of the tax-free rollover of distributions from plans.

---

[13]TRA Sec. 1122(h)(4)
[14]TRA Sec. 1122(h)(5)
[15]TRA Sec. 1122(h)(3)

Under certain circumstances, if a participant receives a distribution from a qualified plan, he may transfer part or all of the amount received to an individual retirement account or to another qualified plan and exclude it from his current taxable income.[16] The ability to roll over the amount to another qualified plan depends upon the other plan's willingness to accept the rollover distribution. Only a small percentage of plans accept rollover amounts.

To be eligible for rollover, a distribution from a plan must be either a "qualified total distribution" or a "partial distribution." All lump sum distributions are qualified total distributions. Any other amount is a qualified total distribution if it would have been a lump-sum distribution except for the requirement of five years of participation or except for the requirement that the participant elect to treat it as a lump-sum distribution. An employee who receives such a distribution and rolls it over, whether over or under age 59½, will still be able to make his one-time election to treat a subsequent distribution from the plan as a lump-sum distribution. Qualified total distributions also include the distribution of a participant's interest from a terminated plan or from a profit sharing or stock bonus plan under which there has been a complete discontinuance of contributions.

A "partial distribution" is a distribution received upon death, disability, or separation from service that would meet the requirements to be a lump-sum distribution, except that a partial distribution need consist of no more than 50 percent of the balance to the credit of the employee and except that, whether the participant is over or under age 59½, it is not subject to the one-time election. In the case of a partial distribution, rollover is allowed only to an IRA and not to another qualified plan. If a participant rolls over a partial distribution from a plan, he may not elect to treat any future distribution from that plan as a lump-sum distribution.

To be treated as a tax-free rollover the amount received must be transferred to an IRA or another plan within 60 days of receipt. The amount transferred may not exceed the amount which would otherwise be included in taxable income; thus it may not include the recovery of the employee's own contributions or other tax basis. If only part of the taxable amount received in a lump-sum

---

[16]I.R.C. §402(a)(5).

distribution is rolled over, the remainder is not eligible to be taxed as a lump-sum distribution.

When a qualified plan makes a distribution that is eligible for rollover, the plan administrator is required to provide the recipient with a written explanation of the rollover requirements. The IRS has published a standard notice that may be used for this purpose.[17]

## Distribution of Insurance and Annuity Contracts

If a distribution from a qualified plan includes an annuity contract that can be surrendered for a cash value or is otherwise transferable, the value of the contract is includible in taxable income at the time of distribution. But if the contract is nontransferable, generally no amounts are includible in taxable income until actually received.

If a distribution from a qualified plan includes a life insurance policy, the entire cash value of the policy is taxable when the policy is distributed, regardless of whether the policy is nontransferable, unless the recipient converts it into a nontransferable annuity contract within 60 days.

## Distribution of Employer Securities

If a lump-sum distribution includes employer securities, the net unrealized appreciation of the securities is excludable from taxable income.[18] For this purpose "net unrealized appreciation" means any excess of the market value of the securities at the time of distribution over the cost or other basis of the securities when the trust acquired them. When the recipient eventually sells the securities, the excess of the sales price over the original cost or other basis to the trust is includible in the recipient's taxable income.

## Minimum Distribution Requirements

Minimum distribution requirements relate to when benefit payments must begin, the minimum amount that must be distributed each year, and the penalties for failure to comply.

---

[17]I.R.C. §402(f), Treas. Reg. 1.402(f)–1T(b), IRS Announcement 87–2.
[18]I.R.C. §402(a)(1),(e)(4)(J).

For years after 1988 distributions under all qualified plans must begin no later than April 1 of the calendar year following the calendar year in which the participant attains age 70½, regardless of whether he has retired.[19]

The minimum amount required to be distributed annually is to be determined in accordance with regulations. The minimum is determined as though the entire interest of the participant is to be paid as a level annual amount over the life of the employee, or the lives of the employee and a designated beneficiary, or is to be paid in installments over the life expectancy of such person or persons.

An individual who receives less than his minimum distribution requirement in a year will be assessed an excise tax equal to 50 percent of the difference between the required payments and the actual payments during the year.[20] But the IRS may waive the tax if the failure was due to a reasonable error and if reasonable steps are taken to correct the error.

### Early Distributions

An additional income tax of 10 percent applies to any distribution before age 59½ unless it meets one of several exceptions.[21] The exceptions include the following:

1.  Amounts paid as part of a series of substantially equal periodic payments over the life (or life expectancy) of the employee or the combined lives (or combined life expectancies) of the employee and the employee's beneficiary.
2.  Amounts paid on or after a separation from service that takes place during any calendar year in which the participant has attained at least age 55.
3.  Amounts that are used to pay medical expenses that are deductible under Code Section 213, regardless of whether the employee itemizes deductions.
4.  Distributions upon disability or death.
5.  Payments under a qualified domestic relations order.

If a participant escapes the tax by beginning to receive his payments in substantially equal payments but then changes the distribution

---

[19]I.R.C. §401(a)(9), I.R.C. §4974.
[20]I.R.C. §4974.
[21]I.R.C. §72(t).

method before age 59½ or within 5 years, the 10 percent tax will be assessed on all amounts received before age 59½.

No withholding is required with respect to the 10 percent additional tax.

## Excess Distributions

A 15 percent excise tax applies to individuals who receive *excess distributions* from one or more plans in a year.

The tax generally applies to the excess of the total distributions paid in a year with respect to an individual over $112,500 (indexed upwards with the $90,000 limit under Section 415 beginning in 1988).[22] However, except in the case of individuals making the grandfather election described below, the $112,500 (indexed) is replaced by $150,000 (not indexed), if larger. This tax is generally based upon the total of all distributions that the individual receives under all qualified plans of any of his employers, tax-sheltered annuities and IRAs, and which are includible in his taxable income.

The following amounts are not subject to the limitation:

- Distributions after death (which are subject to a separate tax).
- Distributions paid to another person under a qualified domestic relations order.
- Amounts attributable to the employee's own after-tax contributions or other tax basis.
- Amounts not includible in taxable income because they are subsequently rolled over to an IRA or other plan.

Lump-sum distributions are not aggregated with other payments for this purpose, but are instead subject to a separate 15 percent tax on the excess of the distribution over 5 times the limit that otherwise applies. Thus, lump sums in excess of $562,500 (5 times $112,500, with indexation) may be subject to the tax. A larger limit of $750,000 (5 × $150,000, not indexed) will apply to those who do not make the grandfather election.

The grandfather election applies only to individuals having accrued benefits with a value over $562,500 as of August 1, 1986. These individuals may make an election filed with their tax returns for years before 1989 to have the portion of all future distributions

---

[22]I.R.C. §4981.

attributable to the value of their accrued benefits as of August 1, 1986, not subject to the tax.

> Example: On August 1, 1986, John Doe has accrued benefits with a value of $800,000, and he makes a grandfather election. In 1987, when his accrued benefits have a value of $1,000,000, he receives a distribution of $500,000, which is only half of his accrued benefits. Of that amount, 80 percent ($800,000 divided by $1,000,000) of his distribution, or $400,000 (80 percent of his $500,000 distribution), is not subject to the tax. Thus, $100,000 is subject to the tax, since his $112,500 tax-free amount is included in the $400,000 exclusion. The additional tax would be 15 percent of $100,000, or $15,000.

It is not always advantageous to make the election, since one must forego the higher $150,000 annual limit.

Upon death a similar tax on excess benefits is included in the estate tax. The tax equals 15 percent of the excess of the value of the individual's accrued benefits at the date of death over the value of an annuity for an annual amount equal to the applicable annual limit of $112,500 (indexed) or $150,000 (unindexed).

Neither the unified credit nor the marital deduction, which are normally available under estate tax, serve to reduce this new 15 percent estate tax. Thus, this tax will be payable by estates which would otherwise be completely exempt from estate tax.

## Taxation of Benefits Paid upon Death

Benefits payable to a deceased participant's beneficiary or estate are generally subject to federal and state income tax. In addition, they may be subject to federal estate tax and to state inheritance or estate tax. Only federal taxes are described in this text.

### Income Tax on Death Benefits

Payments to a beneficiary or estate are generally subject to income tax in the same manner as payments to the participant. The beneficiary or estate is entitled to recover tax-free any remaining unrecovered basis of the participant at the time of death. A $5,000 death benefit exclusion also applies to certain payments.[23] If the

---

[23]I.R.C. §101(b).

exclusion applies, the $5,000 is added to the employee's unrecovered basis, resulting in exclusion from income.

The $5,000 exclusion applies to nonqualified as well as qualified plans, and to both funded and unfunded arrangements. The exclusion always applies in the case of lump-sum distributions paid from qualified plans. Otherwise the exclusion does not apply to any amount to which the employee had a nonforfeitable right to receive while living, including any amount to which he would have had a nonforfeitable right if he had retired or terminated his employment before death. The $5,000 exclusion does not apply to payments under a joint and survivor annuity under which payments to the participant had begun or could have begun, nor to a qualified preretirement survivor annuity based upon the vested benefit that could have been received by the participant if he had lived. But if a plan provides survivor income benefits that exceed the benefits to which the employee had a nonforfeitable right to receive if he had lived, the exclusion applies to the excess.

If the participant dies after periodic payments have commenced and payments are being continued under a joint and survivor form, the exclusion ratio established when the payments to the participant commenced would continue to apply to the beneficiary. But if payments are being continued to a beneficiary under a period-certain life annuity or under a refund annuity and the basis had not been recovered by the retired employee at the time of his death, the beneficiary can exclude all payments from gross income until the sum of the basis recovered by the deceased employee and the payments received by the beneficiary equal the employee's basis; thereafter all payments are taxable income to the beneficiary.

If a death benefit payable under a qualified plan is paid from a life insurance policy, the pure insurance component of the proceeds, which is the excess of the policy proceeds over any cash value of the policy, is treated as the proceeds of a life insurance policy and is thus excluded from taxable income, while the portion equal to the policy cash value is treated as a distribution from the plan and is subject to the income tax rules.[24] For example, assume that under a noncontributory pension plan a death benefit of $100,000 is paid from a policy with a cash value of $30,000, and under which

---

[24]I.R.C. §72(m)(3)(C), Treas. Reg. 1.72–16(c).

the employee had previously had $2,000 of taxable income for pure insurance cost. The taxable income equals the $30,000 of cash value, reduced by the $2,000 of basis for the previous cost of insurance, and reduced by the $5,000 death benefit exclusion (provided the exclusion is not applied to other employee death benefits), or a net of $23,000 of taxable income. If the $100,000 of policy proceeds were applied under the policy to provide the beneficiary an annuity, the $77,000 that is not taxable ($100,000 less the $23,000 taxable amount) would serve as the beneficiary's basis to determine the exclusion ratio applicable to the future monthly payments.

A lump-sum distribution paid to the employee's beneficiary is entitled to the same favorable treatment as that afforded to lump-sum distributions paid to a participant.

### Estate Tax on Death Benefits

The gross estate subject to estate tax includes the value of all payments or annuities receivable by any beneficiary to which the participant had a nonforfeitable right while living.[25] This generally includes the employee's vested account balance under a defined contribution plan. It includes the value of payments to a joint or contingent annuitant or beneficiary under a joint and survivor annuity, certain and continuous annuity or refund annuity under which payments to the participant began, or could have begun, prior to death.

It should be noted, however, that any amount payable to the surviving spouse of the deceased is subject to the unlimited marital deduction and thus is not subject to estate tax.[26] In addition, the application of the unified credit under estate tax law eliminates any estate tax unless the taxable estate, after subtracting the marital deduction and other applicable deductions, exceeds $600,000.

As noted earlier, there is also a 15 percent excise tax on excess distributions, which is not subject to relief from either the marital deduction or the unified credit.

---

[25]I.R.C. §2039.
[26]I.R.C. §2056.

## Withholding Taxes on Distributions

Benefits paid from qualified plans are subject to income tax withholding similar to the income tax withholding on wages.[27] The plan administrator is responsible for the withholding unless the administrator directs the payor in writing to withhold the tax and provides the payor the necessary information.

For periodic payments the withholding is based upon the assumption that the recipient is married with three personal exemptions unless the recipient provides a withholding certificate (Form W-4P) directing otherwise. For nonperiodic payments a uniform withholding rate of 10 percent applies. But in either case the recipient may elect not to have any tax withheld, and in practice most recipients make such an election.

The payor is required to notify the recipients concerning the withholding and election rules. Regulations include a sample notice which may be used.

## Taxation of the Trust

The trust of a qualified plan is generally exempt from tax on its income.[28] But if the trust engages in an unrelated trade or business, it is subject to tax on its unrelated business taxable income.[29]

## Taxation of Employers

Within prescribed limits employers may deduct their contributions to qualified plans. The limits for pension plans are discussed in Chapter 17, while those for profit sharing and stock bonus plans are discussed in Chapter 26.

### Reversions to the Employer

The opposite of an employer contribution is an employer withdrawal of assets from a plan. Except as noted below, withdrawals

---

[27]I.R.C. §3405, Treas. Reg. 35.3405–1.
[28]I.R.C. 501(a).
[29]I.R.C. §§501(b), 511–514.

are permitted only upon termination, after all liabilities under the plan have been satisfied.

Any reversion of assets to the employer upon plan termination is includible in the employer's taxable income. In addition a 10 percent excise tax applies to any reversion of assets to the employer in connection with a plan termination.[30] But if the excess assets are transferred to an ESOP upon plan termination before 1989, the amount is not includible in the employer's taxable income and the 10 percent excise tax does not apply.

## Excess Contributions

A 401(k) plan is subject to actual deferral percentage (ADP) tests, limiting the amount of elective contributions on behalf of highly compensated employees, as described in Chapter 27.[31] Other plans are subject to similar tests with respect to certain employee contributions and to employer matching contributions, as described in chapter 5.[32] Contributions that cause a plan to fail these tests are referred to as excess contributions and excess aggregate contributions, and may be withdrawn from the plan within two and one half months after the end of the plan year. The employer is assessed a 10 percent tax on any such contributions not withdrawn within this period.[33]

## Excise Tax on Nondeductible Contributions

A 10 percent excise tax is imposed on all employer contributions made for a year that exceed the amount which may be deducted.[34] To the extent that any nondeductible contribution is not either withdrawn or deducted during the following year, the 10 percent tax is applied again, and this continues each year until no nondeductible contribution remains in the plan. However the employer may not be allowed to withdraw the nondeductible contribution unless it was made by mistake of fact or was originally conditioned

---

[30] I.R.C. §4980.
[31] I.R.C. §401(k)(3),(8).
[32] I.R.C. §401(m).
[33] I.R.C. §4979.
[34] I.R.C. §4972.

on its deductibility,[35] and if the full funding requirement has been reached it may be impossible to deduct the amount for many years, if ever. Perhaps regulatory guidance will solve this dilemma without forcing the termination of the plan.

This excise tax on nondeductible contributions also applies to tax-exempt employers, with respect to the amounts that would have been deductible if the employer had not been tax-exempt.

### Penalty on Overstatement of Pension Liability

Upon audit the IRS may determine that an employer's deduction exceeded the deductible limit because of an error in the actuarial computations or because the actuarial assumptions were too conservative. In such a case it may redetermine the deductible limit and disallow any contribution in excess of the revised deductible limit. In such a case the employer must pay the additional tax due with interest, plus the 10 percent excise tax on nondeductible contributions described above. But an additional tax applies when the nondeductible contributions are attributable to the overstatement of pension liabilities.[36] If the resulting underpayment of taxes exceeds $1,000, the employer must pay an additional tax equal to a percentage of the underpayment of taxes. The percentage ranges from 15 percent to 30 percent of the additional taxes due, the percentage depending upon the ratio of the deduction claimed to the properly determined deduction.

## Questions

1. Describe the federal income tax treatment of life insurance premiums and proceeds under a qualified pension or profit sharing plan.
2. Under what conditions is a participant not allowed to deduct the interest paid on a loan from a qualified plan?
3. Is it possible for a participant to make a cash withdrawal from his account under a contributory qualified profit sharing or thrift plan

[35]ERISA §403(c)(2)(A),(C); I.R.C. §401(a)(2).
[36]I.R.C. §6659A.

while still in the active service of the employer without incurring any federal income tax liability? Explain.

4. Describe the tax treatment of an annuity benefit under a contributory qualified plan and explain its rationale.

5. Lump-sum distributions from a qualified pension or profit sharing plan receive favorable income tax treatment, but certain conditions must be met before a distribution qualifies for such treatment. State the conditions that must be met before a distribution is construed to a be a lump-sum distribution and describe the special bases on which such a distribution may be taxed. Should lump-sum distributions be taxed at higher or lower rates than monthly pensions? Why?

6. If an individual is a participant in both a pension plan and a profit sharing plan, would a lump-sum distribution from one of the plans qualify for special income tax treatment if the individual's account in the other plan is not closed out? Would your answer be the same if both plans were of the same type (i.e., both pension plans or both profit sharing plans)?

7. Describe the rules pertaining to the rollover of distributions to an individual retirement account (IRA).

8. In what way does the Internal Revenue Code encourage the holding and eventual distribution of employer securities by a qualified pension or profit sharing plan?

9. When must benefits commence under the minimum distribution requirement? What penalty is imposed upon the participant if the requirement is not satisfied? What arguments may be made for and against having such a requirement?

10. Why is it necessary or, at least, deemed highly desirable, to impose penalties on the early withdrawal of funds by participants in qualified plans? What is the penalty? Under what circumstances is it imposed?

11. What is an excess distribution? How is it taxed?

12. Under what circumstances is the special $5,000 death benefit exclusion available to the beneficiary of a plan participant?

13. Upon the death of a participant what benefits are subject to income tax? Estate tax?

14. Under what circumstances is income-tax withholding required for distributions from qualified plans?

15. Under what circumstances may the investment income of a pension or profit sharing trust be taxable currently to the trust?

16. What tax is imposed upon the reversion of residual assets to the employer following a plan termination?

17. An employer claims a tax deduction for its contributions to a qualified defined benefit plan, but the IRS determines that no contribution was deductible because of an overstatement of pension liability. What are the consequences to the employer?

# Appendix A

## Basic Actuarial Functions and Values for Derivation of Pension Plan Costs and Liabilities

**TABLE A–1**
**Mortality, Disability, and Termination Rates and Related Probabilities of Surviving in Service to Age 65**

| Age | Mortality Rate | Disability Rate | Termination Rate | Probability of Surviving in Service to Age 65 |
|-----|-----------|------------|-------------|---------------------|
| 20 | .0005 | .0004 | .2760 | .0180 |
| 21 | .0005 | .0004 | .2550 | .0249 |
| 22 | .0005 | .0004 | .2200 | .0334 |
| 23 | .0006 | .0004 | .1900 | .0429 |
| 24 | .0006 | .0004 | .1750 | .0530 |
| 25 | .0006 | .0004 | .1624 | .0643 |
| 26 | .0006 | .0004 | .1533 | .0769 |
| 27 | .0007 | .0004 | .1446 | .0909 |
| 28 | .0007 | .0004 | .1362 | .1064 |
| 29 | .0008 | .0004 | .1282 | .1233 |
| 30 | .0008 | .0004 | .1206 | .1416 |
| 31 | .0009 | .0004 | .1134 | .1612 |
| 32 | .0009 | .0004 | .1065 | .1820 |
| 33 | .0010 | .0004 | .1001 | .2040 |
| 34 | .0010 | .0004 | .0942 | .2270 |
| 35 | .0011 | .0004 | .0886 | .2509 |
| 36 | .0012 | .0005 | .0834 | .2758 |
| 37 | .0013 | .0006 | .0785 | .3014 |
| 38 | .0014 | .0007 | .0740 | .3276 |
| 39 | .0015 | .0008 | .0669 | .3546 |
| 40 | .0016 | .0009 | .0663 | .3809 |
| 41 | .0018 | .0010 | .0627 | .4090 |

**752**

## TABLE A–1
(*concluded*)

| Age | Mortality Rate | Disability Rate | Termination Rate | Probability of Surviving in Service to Age 65 |
|---|---|---|---|---|
| 42 | .0020 | .0012 | .0590 | .4375 |
| 43 | .0023 | .0014 | .0553 | .4665 |
| 44 | .0026 | .0016 | .0517 | .4956 |
| 45 | .0029 | .0018 | .0480 | .5248 |
| 46 | .0033 | .0020 | .0443 | .5538 |
| 47 | .0038 | .0022 | .0405 | .5826 |
| 48 | .0042 | .0025 | .0365 | .6108 |
| 49 | .0047 | .0028 | .0324 | .6383 |
| 50 | .0053 | .0032 | .0279 | .6646 |
| 51 | .0059 | .0035 | .0231 | .6896 |
| 52 | .0065 | .0039 | .0231 | .7125 |
| 53 | .0071 | .0043 | .0231 | .7370 |
| 54 | .0078 | .0047 | .0231 | .7631 |
| 55 | .0085 | .0051 | .0000 | .7910 |
| 56 | .0093 | .0055 | .0000 | .8019 |
| 57 | .0100 | .0061 | .0000 | .8139 |
| 58 | .0109 | .0069 | .0000 | .8272 |
| 59 | .0119 | .0081 | .0000 | .8421 |
| 60 | .0131 | .0097 | .0000 | .8592 |
| 61 | .0144 | .0117 | .0000 | .8792 |
| 62 | .0159 | .0132 | .0000 | .9026 |
| 63 | .0174 | .0162 | .0000 | .9294 |
| 64 | .0192 | .0197 | .0000 | .9615 |
| 65 | .0213 | .0200 | .0000 | 1.000 |

## TABLE A–2
**Immediate Annuity Values for Single Male
Life Annuity of $1 per Year Payable Monthly**

| Age | Values |
|---|---|
| 55 | $11.777 |
| 56 | 11.554 |
| 57 | 11.324 |
| 58 | 11.086 |
| 59 | 10.842 |
| 60 | 10.592 |
| 61 | 10.337 |
| 62 | 10.076 |
| 63 | 9.811 |
| 64 | 9.542 |
| 65 | 9.268 |
| 66 | 8.993 |
| 67 | 8.717 |
| 68 | 8.442 |
| 69 | 8.167 |
| 70 | 7.896 |

Basis: 1971 Group Annuity Mortality Table (Male) and 6 Percent Interest.

**TABLE A–3**
**Temporary Life Annuity Values to Age 65 at 6 Percent Compound Interest and Survival Probabilities from Table A–1**

| Age | Temporary Employment Based Life Annuity of $1 per Year to Age 65 | Temporary Employment Based Life Annuity of $1 per year Increasing Annually at Total Salary Scale to Age 65 |
|---|---|---|
| 20 | 3.982 | 6.474 |
| 21 | 4.370 | 7.241 |
| 22 | 4.800 | 8.063 |
| 23 | 5.169 | 8.755 |
| 24 | 5.461 | 9.293 |
| 25 | 5.737 | 9.791 |
| 26 | 6.001 | 10.255 |
| 27 | 6.267 | 10.710 |
| 28 | 6.534 | 11.152 |
| 29 | 6.799 | 11.573 |
| 30 | 7.059 | 11.969 |
| 31 | 7.312 | 12.334 |
| 32 | 7.556 | 12.665 |
| 33 | 7.788 | 12.956 |
| 34 | 8.007 | 13.207 |
| 35 | 8.212 | 13.418 |
| 36 | 8.400 | 13.584 |
| 37 | 8.572 | 13.709 |
| 38 | 8.727 | 13.791 |
| 39 | 8.864 | 13.831 |
| 40 | 8.954 | 13.787 |
| 41 | 9.053 | 13.748 |
| 42 | 9.132 | 13.671 |
| 43 | 9.190 | 13.554 |
| 44 | 9.224 | 13.393 |
| 45 | 9.231 | 13.191 |
| 46 | 9.208 | 12.943 |
| 47 | 9.152 | 12.648 |
| 48 | 9.060 | 12.305 |
| 49 | 8.927 | 11.911 |
| 50 | 8.750 | 11.464 |
| 51 | 8.523 | 10.963 |
| 52 | 8.240 | 10.403 |
| 53 | 7.938 | 9.835 |
| 54 | 7.615 | 9.256 |
| 55 | 7.269 | 8.666 |
| 56 | 6.736 | 7.873 |
| 57 | 6.171 | 7.072 |
| 58 | 5.571 | 6.260 |
| 59 | 4.933 | 5.436 |
| 60 | 4.253 | 4.597 |
| 61 | 3.529 | 3.740 |
| 62 | 2.752 | 2.861 |
| 63 | 1.912 | 1.950 |
| 64 | 1.000 | 1.000 |
| 65 | .000 | .000 |

## TABLE A–4
## Present Value of Sums Payable in Future Years at 6 Percent
## Compound Interest

| | Present Value of $1 | | |
|---|---|---|---|
| Years | Payable n Years Hence | Per Annum Payable for n Years | Per Annum Increasing 4 Percent per Year Payable for n Years |
| 1 | .9434 | 1.000 | 1.000 |
| 2 | .8900 | 1.943 | 1.981 |
| 3 | .8396 | 2.833 | 2.944 |
| 4 | .7921 | 3.673 | 3.888 |
| 5 | .7473 | 4.465 | 4.815 |
| 6 | .7050 | 5.212 | 5.724 |
| 7 | .6651 | 5.917 | 6.616 |
| 8 | .6274 | 6.582 | 7.491 |
| 9 | .5919 | 7.210 | 8.350 |
| 10 | .5584 | 7.802 | 9.192 |
| 11 | .5268 | 8.360 | 10.019 |
| 12 | .4970 | 8.887 | 10.830 |
| 13 | .4688 | 9.384 | 11.625 |
| 14 | .4423 | 9.853 | 12.406 |
| 15 | .4173 | 10.295 | 13.172 |
| 16 | .3936 | 10.712 | 13.924 |
| 17 | .3714 | 11.106 | 14.661 |
| 18 | .3503 | 11.477 | 15.384 |
| 19 | .3305 | 11.828 | 16.094 |
| 20 | .3118 | 12.158 | 16.790 |
| 21 | .2942 | 12.470 | 17.473 |
| 22 | .2775 | 12.764 | 18.144 |
| 23 | .2618 | 13.042 | 18.801 |
| 24 | .2470 | 13.303 | 19.447 |
| 25 | .2330 | 13.550 | 20.080 |
| 26 | .2198 | 13.783 | 20.701 |
| 27 | .2074 | 14.003 | 21.310 |
| 28 | .1956 | 14.211 | 21.908 |
| 29 | .1846 | 14.406 | 22.495 |
| 30 | .1741 | 14.591 | 23.070 |
| 31 | .1643 | 14.765 | 23.635 |
| 32 | .1550 | 14.929 | 24.189 |
| 33 | .1462 | 15.084 | 24.733 |
| 34 | .1379 | 15.230 | 25.266 |
| 35 | .1301 | 15.368 | 25.789 |
| 36 | .1227 | 15.498 | 26.303 |
| 37 | .1158 | 15.621 | 26.807 |
| 38 | .1092 | 15.737 | 27.301 |
| 39 | .1031 | 15.846 | 27.786 |
| 40 | .0972 | 15.949 | 28.261 |

**TABLE A-5**
**Total Salary Scale—Merit Scale Plus 3.5 Percent Annual Inflation and 0.5 Percent Productivity Increase**

| Age | Annual Salary Increase | | | | Ratio of Salary at Attained Age to Salary at Age 20 |
| | Inflation | Productivity | Merit | Total | |
|-----|-----------|--------------|-------|-------|------|
| 20 | .0350 | .0050 | .0680 | .1080 | 1.000 |
| 21 | .0350 | .0050 | .0620 | .1020 | 1.108 |
| 22 | .0350 | .0050 | .0575 | .0975 | 1.221 |
| 23 | .0350 | .0050 | .0533 | .0933 | 1.340 |
| 24 | .0350 | .0050 | .0494 | .0894 | 1.465 |
| 25 | .0350 | .0050 | .0458 | .0858 | 1.596 |
| 26 | .0350 | .0050 | .0431 | .0831 | 1.733 |
| 27 | .0350 | .0050 | .0399 | .0799 | 1.877 |
| 28 | .0350 | .0050 | .0375 | .0775 | 2.027 |
| 29 | .0350 | .0050 | .0355 | .0755 | 2.184 |
| 30 | .0350 | .0050 | .0332 | .0732 | 2.349 |
| 31 | .0350 | .0050 | .0314 | .0714 | 2.521 |
| 32 | .0350 | .0050 | .0296 | .0696 | 2.701 |
| 33 | .0350 | .0050 | .0275 | .0675 | 2.889 |
| 34 | .0350 | .0050 | .0265 | .0665 | 3.084 |
| 35 | .0350 | .0050 | .0248 | .0648 | 3.289 |
| 36 | .0350 | .0050 | .0234 | .0634 | 3.502 |
| 37 | .0350 | .0050 | .0220 | .0620 | 3.724 |
| 38 | .0350 | .0050 | .0207 | .0607 | 3.955 |
| 39 | .0350 | .0050 | .0198 | .0598 | 4.195 |
| 40 | .0350 | .0050 | .0185 | .0585 | 4.446 |
| 41 | .0350 | .0050 | .0176 | .0576 | 4.706 |
| 42 | .0350 | .0050 | .0165 | .0565 | 4.977 |
| 43 | .0350 | .0050 | .0155 | .0555 | 5.258 |
| 44 | .0350 | .0050 | .0146 | .0546 | 5.550 |
| 45 | .0350 | .0050 | .0138 | .0538 | 5.853 |
| 46 | .0350 | .0050 | .0129 | .0529 | 6.168 |
| 47 | .0350 | .0050 | .0120 | .0520 | 6.494 |
| 48 | .0350 | .0050 | .0112 | .0512 | 6.832 |
| 49 | .0350 | .0050 | .0104 | .0504 | 7.182 |
| 50 | .0350 | .0050 | .0098 | .0498 | 7.544 |
| 51 | .0350 | .0050 | .0089 | .0489 | 7.920 |
| 52 | .0350 | .0050 | .0084 | .0484 | 8.307 |
| 53 | .0350 | .0050 | .0075 | .0475 | 8.709 |
| 54 | .0350 | .0050 | .0069 | .0469 | 9.123 |
| 55 | .0350 | .0050 | .0062 | .0462 | 9.551 |
| 56 | .0350 | .0050 | .0056 | .0456 | 9.992 |
| 57 | .0350 | .0050 | .0049 | .0449 | 10.448 |
| 58 | .0350 | .0050 | .0042 | .0442 | 10.917 |
| 59 | .0350 | .0050 | .0037 | .0437 | 11.400 |
| 60 | .0350 | .0050 | .0030 | .0430 | 11.898 |
| 61 | .0350 | .0050 | .0025 | .0425 | 12.410 |
| 62 | .0350 | .0050 | .0018 | .0418 | 12.937 |
| 63 | .0350 | .0050 | .0012 | .0412 | 13.478 |
| 64 | .0350 | .0050 | .0006 | .0406 | 14.033 |
| 65 | | | | | 14.603 |

# Appendix

# B | List of Case Citations

# Appendix

## C | List of Statutes, Rules, and Regulations

## Employee Retirement Income Security Act of 1974 (ERISA)

**758**

## *Internal Revenue Code of 1986*

## Tax Reform Act of 1986 (TRA)

## Other Statutes

## Code of Federal Regulations

## Treasury Regulations

# Proposed Treasury Regulation

# Revenue Rulings

## Revenue Procedures

## IRS Forms

## IRS Publications

## Other Federal Publications

# INDEX

*See also* Appendix B: List of Case Citations *and*
Appendix C: List of Statutes, Rules and Regulations

## A

Accountant, responsibilities under
ERISA, 65–66
Accounting
accumulated benefit obligation, 420
annuity contracts, 421
APB *Opinion 8,* 413–15
asset valuation, 420–21
assumptions, 421–23
balance sheet recognition, 427–28
benefit obligation, 419–20
curtailments, 430–31
defined contribution plans, 429
disclosures, 428
discount rate, 422
by employers, 409 ff.
ERISA requirements, 403–4
*FASB Statement 35,* 406–9
*FASB Statement 36,* 415–16
*FASB Statement 87,* 416–29
*FASB Statement 88,* 430–31
generally accepted accounting
principles, 402–3, 406–9
expected long-term rate of return,
422–23

Accounting—*Cont.*
multiemployer plans, 429
net periodic pension cost, 423–24
for the plan, 403–6
plan terminations, 430–31
projected benefit obligation, 420
service cost, 420
settlements, 430–31
two or more plans, 429
vested benefit obligation, 420
Accrued benefit, 110–11, 157 ff.
anti-cutback rule, 187
backloading, 110, 157–59, 277
employee derived portion, 148–49,
181, 183–84
fractional rule, 159
133⅓ percent rule, 158–59
3 percent rule, 158
Accrued benefit cost method
actuarial gains and losses, 270–71
actuarial liability, 283–85
characteristics, 276–77
as a funding guide, 394–96
group deferred annuity contract,
395–96
normal cost, 277–83

**769**